A MARMAC GUIDE TO DALLAS

A MARMAC GUIDE TO DALLAS

By Yves Gerem

PELICAN PUBLISHING COMPANY
Gretna 2004

ISSN: 07368119
ISBN: 1-58980-199-7

To Larisa, Michael, and Etienne

The Marmac Guidebook series was created by Marge McDonald of Atlanta, Georgia. As owner of a convention and sightseeing service in Atlanta for fourteen years, she learned from visitors and those relocating to Atlanta what information was important to them. She also served as president and CEO of the Georgia Hospitality and Travel Association for four years and in 1978 was named Woman of the Year in Travel by the Travel Industry Association of America.

Manufactured in Canada
Published by Pelican Publishing Company, Inc.
1000 Burmaster Street, Gretna, Louisiana 70053

CONTENTS

MAPS

KEY TO LETTER CODE

I . . . . Inexpensive
M . . . . Moderate
E . . . . Expensive
CH . . . . Charge
NCH . . . . No Charge

PREFACE

No fee or product was ever sought, offered or accepted to include or name any establishment in this guide. Every effort has been made not to be influenced in any way by anyone mentioned herein. Unless the author felt that it would better serve readers' interests, most inquiries were conducted anonymously in a manner you would do when seeking such information.

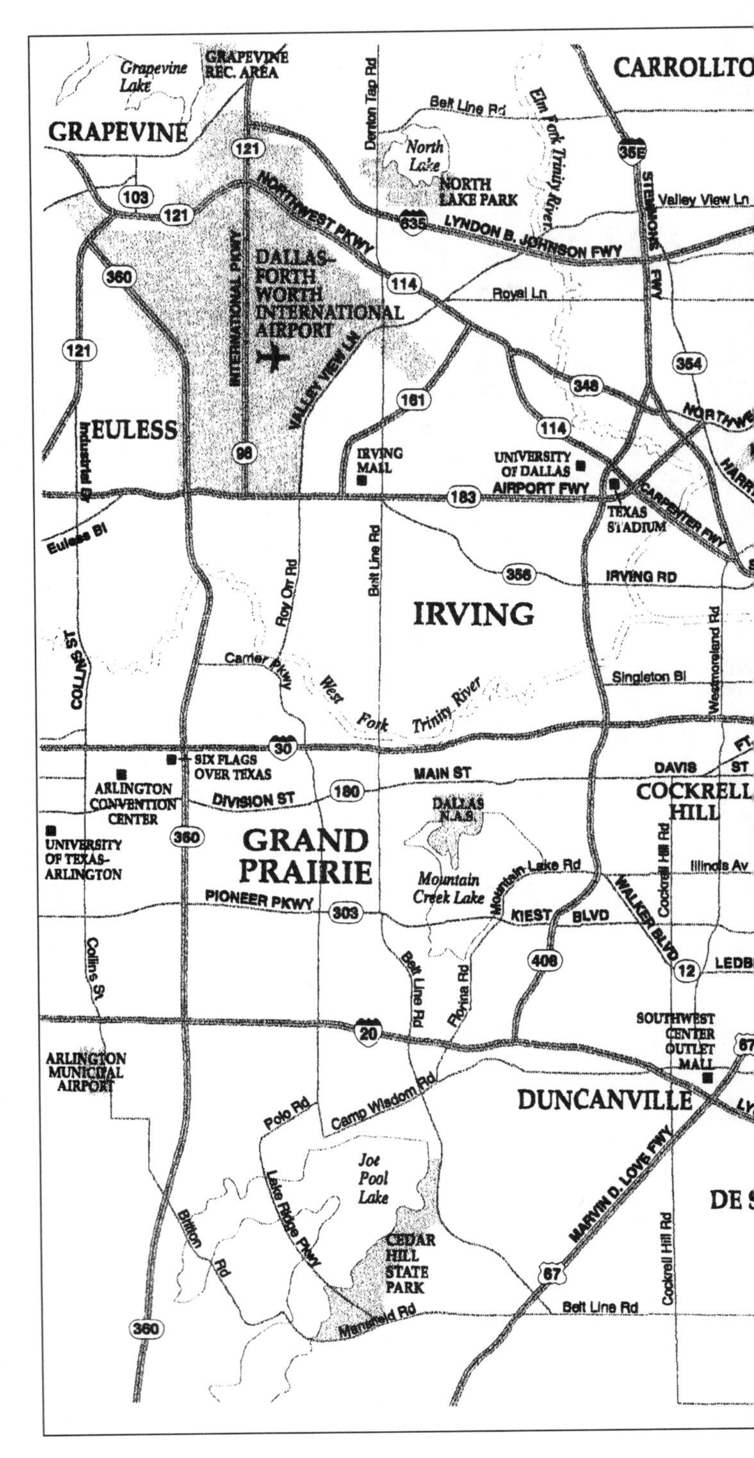

Grapevine Lake
GRAPEVINE REC. AREA
GRAPEVINE
CARROLLTO
Denton Tap Rd
Belt Line Rd
Elm Fork Trinity River
North Lake
NORTH LAKE PARK
NORTHWEST PKWY
LYNDON B. JOHNSON FWY
STEMMONS FWY
Valley View Ln
DALLAS-FORTH WORTH INTERNATIONAL AIRPORT
INTERNATIONAL PKWY
VALLEY VIEW LN
Royal Ln
EULESS
Industrial Dr
IRVING MALL
UNIVERSITY OF DALLAS
AIRPORT FWY
TEXAS STADIUM
CARPENTER FWY
Euless Bl
Roy Orr Rd
Belt Line Rd
IRVING RD
IRVING
Westmoreland Rd
COLLINS ST
Carrier Pkwy
West Fork Trinity River
Singleton Bl
SIX FLAGS OVER TEXAS
ARLINGTON CONVENTION CENTER
MAIN ST
DAVIS ST
DIVISION ST
COCKRELL HILL
DALLAS N.A.S.
UNIVERSITY OF TEXAS-ARLINGTON
GRAND PRAIRIE
Mountain Lake Rd
Illinois Av
Mountain Creek Lake
Cockrell Hill Rd
WALKER BLVD
PIONEER PKWY
KIEST BLVD
Collins St
Belt Line Rd
Florina Rd
LEDB
SOUTHWEST CENTER OUTLET MALL
ARLINGTON MUNICIPAL AIRPORT
Camp Wisdom Rd
Polo Rd
DUNCANVILLE
Joe Pool Lake
Lake Ridge Pkwy
MARVIN D. LOVE FWY
DE S
Britton Rd
CEDAR HILL STATE PARK
Cockrell Hill Rd
Mansfield Rd
Belt Line Rd
121
103
360
635
114
161
348
354
35E
98
183
356
30
180
303
408
12
20
67

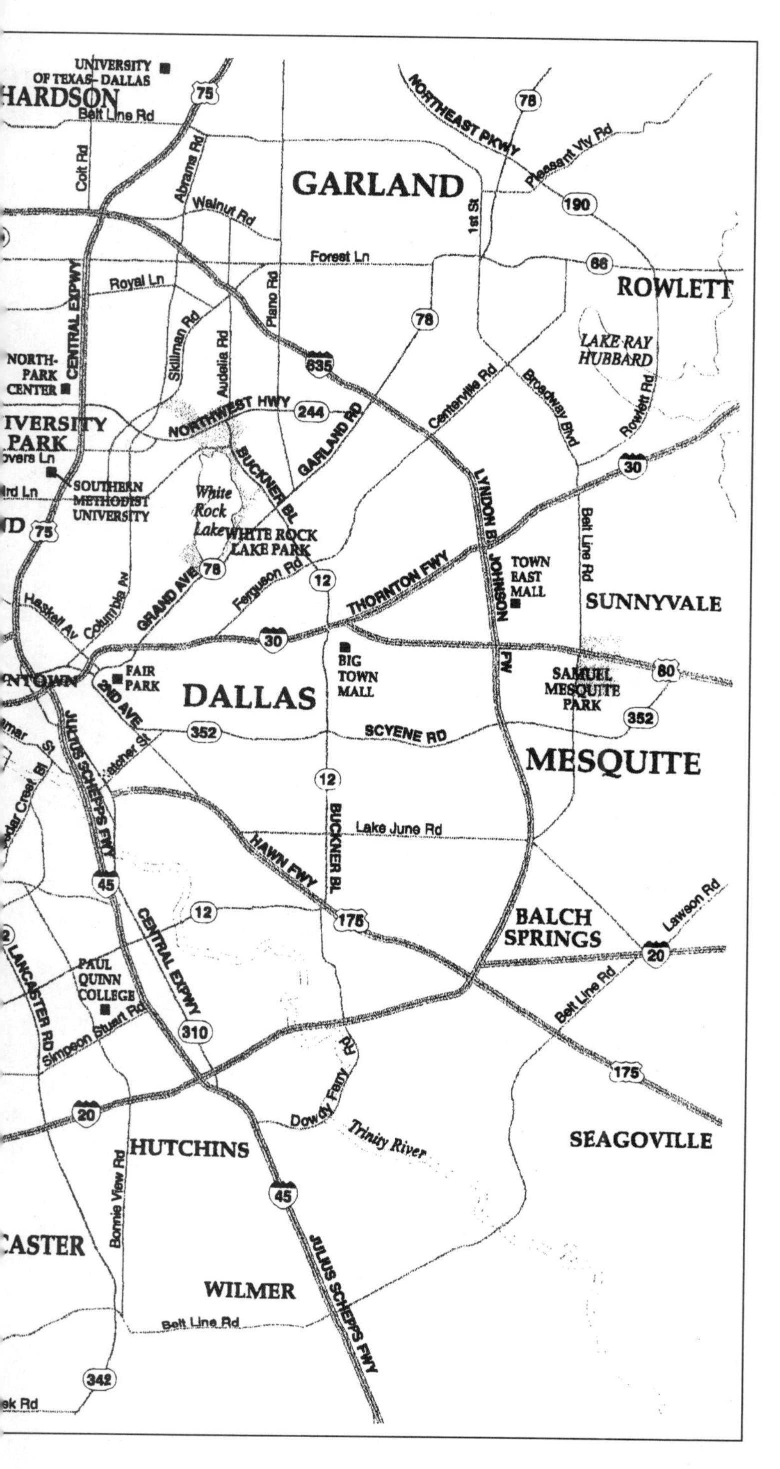
UNIVERSITY OF TEXAS–DALLAS
HARDSON
Belt Line Rd
Colt Rd
Abrams Rd
GARLAND
NORTHEAST PKWY
Pleasant Vly Rd
1st St
Walnut Rd
Forest Ln
ROWLETT
Royal Ln
CENTRAL EXPWY
Skillman Rd
Audelia Rd
Plano Rd
LAKE RAY HUBBARD
NORTH-PARK CENTER
Centerville Rd
Broadway Blvd
Rowlett Rd
NORTHWEST HWY
GARLAND RD
IVERSITY PARK
BUCKNER BL
SOUTHERN METHODIST UNIVERSITY
White Rock Lake
WHITE ROCK LAKE PARK
LYNDON B. JOHNSON FWY
Belt Line Rd
THORNTON FWY
TOWN EAST MALL
Ferguson Rd
GRAND AVE
Haskell Av
Columbia Av
SUNNYVALE
BIG TOWN MALL
FAIR PARK
DALLAS
SAMUEL MESQUITE PARK
2ND AVE
SCYENE RD
JULIUS SCHEPPS FWY
MESQUITE
Lake June Rd
HAWN FWY
BUCKNER BL
BALCH SPRINGS
Lawson Rd
LANCASTER RD
PAUL QUINN COLLEGE
CENTRAL EXPWY
Belt Line Rd
Simpson Stuart Rd
Dowdy Ferry Rd
Trinity River
SEAGOVILLE
HUTCHINS
Bonnie View Rd
ASTER
WILMER
JULIUS SCHEPPS FWY
Belt Line Rd
75
78
190
66
635
244
30
12
80
352
45
175
20
310
342

DALLAS PAST

The Congress of the Republic of Texas was eager for settlers after winning its independence in 1836, the same year that James Madison, the fourth president of the United States, died. The Congress actually offered to newcomers free land and to companies inducements to bring settlers to the new republic.

In 1840, **William Smalling Peters** (1779-1853) of Louisville, Kentucky, organized the Peters Colony, later known as the Texas Emigration & Land Co., to speculate in Texas lands. Peters was an Englishman from Devonshire who arrived in the United States with his wife and six children when 48 years old, but never became an American citizen.

"Peters located the original 20 investors, who petitioned the Fifth Congress of the Republic of Texas to pass the law of February 4, 1841, that authorized the president of the Republic of Texas to enter into an impresario contract with Peters and his associates," notes the Texas State Historical Association, adding that he tried unsuccessfully to interest the English socialist Robert Owen in his project, but did manage to convince the Frenchman Etienne Cabet that the Icarian colony be established in north Texas. Half of the investors were Americans, the other half English. The colony headquarters was in Louisville, Kentucky, where Peter's son operated a music store.

The Peters Colony agreed to bring at least 300 families into the territory within three years, although Peters himself never came to Texas. Each family that came received up to 640 acres (or 259 hectares) of land free and each unmarried man was entitled to 320 acres (or 129 hectares), but they had to cultivate at least 15 acres (six hectares) for three years. As payment for services rendered, the impresarios could retain up to one-half of a colonist's grant as payment for their services. The company sought settlers as far away as England, where it had its agents.

It was tough going and, according to the company's own agent, there were only 197 families and 184 single men in the colony by July 1844. The colony that helped settle north Texas brought little if any profit to the investors and much disagreement among settlers.

One of the first persons attracted by advertisements of the Peters

John Neely Bryan Cabin on the Dallas County Historic Plaza. Behind it, left to right, are George Allen County Courthouse, "Old Red" Courthouse, and Dallas County Records Building. The top of the Reunion Tower can be seen behind the "Old Red." (Photo by Yves Gerem)

Company was **John Neely Bryan** (1810-1877), a young lawyer of Scottish descent from Fayetteville, Tennessee. "He was a complex, often contradictory, and always mysterious, uncommunicative man," says William McDonald in his 1978 photographic chronicle of Dallas. After leaving Tennessee at the age of 17, Bryan lived for some time in Arkansas, where he traded with the Indians and learned their customs and language. He is said to have laid out the town of Van Buren, Arkansas.

During the summer of 1839, he made his first exploring trip through north Texas, looking for a good place for a new trading post serving Indians and settlers. He chose a high bluff and shallow ford on the Trinity River, just steps from where 165 years later President John F. Kennedy was assassinated. He returned to settle his affairs, but while Bryan was gone, a treaty was signed, removing Indians from north Texas. He returned in November 1841, only to find the Indians mostly gone.

He made a camp at the foot of today's Main Street, on the east bank of the Trinity River. The oldest business section of Dallas, around the courthouse downtown, stands on the land of John Neely Bryan, who received his title through the Peters Company. Just a few other settlers were scattered in the area at that time, but he persuaded several families that had settled at Bird's Fort to join him.

A few months earlier, on April 21, 1841, General **Edward H. Tarrant** (1796-1858) headed a company of 70 Republic of Texas soldiers, who expelled the last large group of Caddo Indians living in what is today known as the Metroplex. Tarrant's raid and burning of some 225 dwellings took place on Village Creek, which is now part of the city of Arlington.

Some believe that several months before Bryan set up his hut in what is now downtown Dallas, early in 1841, a fort might have been built by the Republic of Texas soldiers in Cedar Springs, a few miles north of today's downtown. If it indeed was built there, that would make the fort the first structure built by men of European descent in today's Metroplex. Soldiers were dispatched from Austin to chart a military road to the Red River and visited the area known as Cedar Springs in 1840.

Cedar Springs, which was founded in 1843, was once a thriving community, healthy enough to challenge Dallas in an election for the county seat in 1850. The fort might have been constructed in what is now the northeast corner of Cedar Springs and Kings Roads. Preston Trail, farther east and now known as Preston Road, was Cedar Springs' main thoroughfare. In May 1843, Dr. John Cole and his family arrived at Cedar Springs and established a community. By late 1800s, most of Cedar Springs became part of the Oak Lawn development and was annexed by the city of Dallas in early 1900s.

Bryan was not well equipped for farming. His only plow was a forked tree branch, his harness for his Indian pony was made of strips of buffalo hide. Life was difficult then, but food was plentiful. The nearest town was Nacogdoches, more than 150 miles (or 241 kilometers) southeast, but there were no roads leading to Dallas.

On February 26, 1843, two years before Texas was admitted into the Union, Bryan married **Margaret Beeman** (1825-1919), the daughter of his nearest neighbors, John and Emily Hunnicutt Beeman, who came from Illinois. Bryan and Margaret rode on horse to Fort Inglish, near today's Bonham, a journey of more than 100 miles (or 161 kilometers). The bride was 17, the groom 32.

"This was the first marriage of white people within bounds of what is now Dallas County," claimed the *Dallas News* in 1902. For a time the couple lived in a shelter of rough boards, protected from Indians by the river bluff which had been Bryan's first camp. Later the groom felled some cedar trees and built their first home. Around this house of logs—which first stood on Main Street—the city of Dallas was born. The couple had five children.

Here was also held the first court in Dallas County. In it was the first post office, when Bryan was appointed postmaster by the Republic of Texas. In it, too, was born his first son. While living here, Bryan laid off the town of Dallas and donated to the county the public square where the old courthouse now stands.

Here he chose the name for the county and for the town in honor of, the speculation goes, **George Mifflin Dallas** (1792-1864), a Philadelphia lawyer who was then the vice president of the United States under James K. Polk, or his brother, Commodore Alexander J. Dallas.

Some maintain, however, that Bryan could not have known the Pennsylvania politician before his nomination for vice president in 1845. Perhaps it was named after one Walter Dallas, who fought in San Jacinto, or his brother Alexander James, a former Texas Ranger. Another speculation has it named after one Joseph Dallas, who came to Cedar Springs in 1843 from Arkansas, where the two men could have met.

Indians often prowled about this lonely home. Late one night, a large band of them surrounded the house and held a council of war, proposing to kill Bryan and his terrified wife. But Bryan knew their language, so he opened the door and spoke to the chief, then invited him in. The chief told his warriors to disperse because, "This is too brave a man for us to kill."

In 1846, the settlement of Dallas had four families and two bachelors. There was one store and the Dallas Tavern, both in tiny log houses, and the first hotel was still a year away. A trading post was established in 1845 at Cedar Springs, about three miles (or almost five kilometers) north of Dallas. The site was first settled by troops working on the Military Road, an early thoroughfare and the first great Southwest cattle trail, named the Shawnee Trail.

All store goods came by ox wagons, mostly by primitive roadways from Jefferson, east of Dallas, and from Houston. The wagons carried up to 4,000 pounds (or 1,814 kilograms) each and were pulled by twelve oxen.

Jefferson (pop. 2,200), incidentally, a steamboat port on the Red River, 20 miles (or 32 kilometers) from Louisiana, was a "grand" city that died a hundred years ago. It was a leading city of northeastern Texas by 1870 and the sixth largest in the state. In 1873, Jefferson made a fatal mistake of refusing to donate land to the railroad baron Jay Gould who wanted to build Texas & Pacific Railway tracks from Texarkana to San Antonio. As he left the town's Excelsior Hotel, a displeased Gould wrote in the guest book that Jefferson had just committed suicide.

The railroad ran through Dallas instead, although it was several hundred miles out of the way. Gould's private rail car still sits across the street from the 1850 Excelsior.

Also in 1846, Dallas County was created from portions of Robertson and Nacogdoches counties, and Bryan was ordered to organize it to be exactly 30 miles (or 48 kilometers) square with the village of Dallas at its center. That was believed to be the right size to ride on horseback from the farthest edge of the county to town in time for court. It was planned on the county system as devised in rural England more than 300 years earlier.

"There were 45 slaves in Dallas County by 1846," writes an African-American historian. "Most of these lived in the Cedar Springs-Farmer's Branch sector of the county."

When John Neely Bryan's third child was but a few months old, in 1849 (also the year when Fort Worth was established), his father left the family to join the Gold Rush to California, which became a state the following year. He was followed by many other Dallas men. Bryan returned home broke and began to drink heavily.

1850s

In 1852, when Dallas counted about 160 residents—including seven lawyers, three doctors, five carpenters, two tailors, a cabinetmaker, and a stonemason—the French-born **Maxime Guillot** (1824-1889) opened the town's first wagon and carriage factory at Elm and Houston Streets. By then, Bryan was deeply in debt and sold practically all he owned, including his real estate and the cabin where his family had lived, for $7,000. The county's first post office was established in Cedar Hill.

The man who purchased his property was the illiterate native **Alexander Cockrell** (1820-1858), who replaced Bryan's ferryboat with a wooden toll bridge over the Trinity River. After it was destroyed in the flood of 1858, the same year that her husband was killed by a town marshal only three days on his job, his wife Sarah erected an iron bridge, following the Civil War, in 1872.

Born in Kentucky, Cockrell left his parents at age 14 and made his home with the Cherokees, learning their culture and language. He came to Dallas in 1845 and hauled freight with ox teams from Houston and Jefferson, Texas, and Shreveport, Louisiana. Cockrell married **Sarah Horton Horton** in 1847 and established a claim on 640 (or 259 hectares) acres in the Peters colony, about ten miles (or 16 kilometers) west of Dallas.

Her husband operated a sawmill, lumberyard, and gristmill in Dallas. The year before Cockrell was killed, he began building the St. Nicholas, the first luxury hotel in Dallas and the first three-story building. After it burned down in 1860, she opened the Dallas Hotel, which was later renamed the St. Charles. Also in 1860, she was chartered by the Texas Legislature to build an iron suspension bridge across the

Trinity that connected Dallas with all primary roads west and south.

Mrs. Cockrell ordered the bridge from St. Louis, had it shipped down the Mississippi River through the Gulf of Mexico to Galveston. From there, it was transported by railroad to Corsicana and then by ox team to Dallas. Completed in 1972, it not only provided service, it also made a profit.

When she died in 1892, Mrs. Cockrell owned almost one-quarter of downtown Dallas, in addition to properties in Houston. She was the town's wealthiest citizen. Because of its length, her will was printed in a pamphlet form.

On May 27, 1853, Jane Elkins, a slave convicted of murder, became the first woman legally executed in Texas by being hanged in Dallas, according to *Texas Monthly*.

When Henry David Thoreau (1817-1862) published his masterpiece *Walden*, in 1854, the year also that his wife bore his fifth child, Bryan shot a man over a supposed affront to her, fled Dallas, and did not return until his oldest two children were already teenagers.

During his absence, more than 200 French, Swiss, and Belgian immigrants—poets, musicians, lithographers, artisans, dressmakers, and watchmakers—settled on the 1,200 acres (or 485 hectares) of land, three miles (or almost five kilometers) west of Dallas, in a Utopian colony of **La Reunion** that began failing in 1856, even before Bryan returned home. These Europeans did bring a glimmer of culture to the town that has ever since fought the redneck label.

When Bryan did come back in 1861—Abraham Lincoln (1809-1865) was already the president of the United States—he was worn out and haggard, but enlisted in the Confederate Army, when the Civil War broke out in April.

President-to-be, **Woodrow Wilson**, was born in 1856, when the town of Dallas was legislated and claimed a population of about 350 farmers. The city limits were a half-mile square fronting on the river. At the first city elections in 1857, 97 votes were cast and **Dr. Sam Pryor** was chosen as the first mayor. His brother, physician Charles R. Pryor (b. 1832), was responsible for "reports of an alleged abolitionist conspiracy that led to the slave insurrection panic of 1860," which is now known as the Texas Troubles (see below).

"Dallas County had not had enough plantation-sized farms to make slave-holding feasible," writes Texas historian A. C. Greene, "and most Dallas slaves had been house servants."

By the time the steamroller was invented, in 1859, Dallas, which had withstood droughts and floods the year before, had a white population of 678 and 97 black slaves, as well as a French tailor, a photographer, and an insurance salesman. On Independence Day, March 2, 1859, the first circus, with a live elephant, came to town.

That same year the first county fair was held in the oak grove, where Baylor Hospital complex now stands, and 2,000 people attended it.

1860s

During the Civil War a fair corporation was chartered, in 1862, securing 80 acres (or 32.3 hectares) of land, but Dallas was too preoccupied with the war to hold another county fair.

In the hot afternoon of July 8, 1860, when temperature supposedly reached 110 degrees Fahrenheit (or 43 degrees Celsius), a fire so all-consuming started at two o'clock that the village of Dallas was nearly wiped out. On the square only the courthouse and one other house were left standing. In the ensuing hysteria, Charles Pryor, the young editor of the *Dallas Herald* and the mayor's brother, spread suspicion that responsibility for the burning rested with three black slaves, based on confessions extracted from other blacks. Two weeks later they were hanged at the Trinity River bank, about where Commerce Street runs now. Two Iowa preachers, alleged abolitionists, were whipped and run out of town.

Later, the fire was attributed by some to men smoking, by others to the new and volatile phosphorus matches. "At least 30 blacks and whites died by the hands of the secretive vigilantes," during the Texas Troubles, notes the Texas State Historical Association, adding, "Many Texans who formerly had been moderate on the issue of the Union now embraced secession."

When Lincoln was elected president in 1860, the Dallasites were in favor of secession from the Union by 741 to 237, in part as a result of the Texas Troubles. Dallas citizens gave loyally for the cause of the Confederacy and against freeing the slaves, but the Yankee troops never even came near the city.

After the slaves were officially freed by Lincoln's Emancipation Proclamation of January 1, 1863, they had no place to go and most remained with their former masters. About 300 of them formed a Freedmen's Town, near the Greenwood Cemetery at Hall Street and today's North Central Expressway. Several other communities sprang up all over the city and included Deep Ellum, which was nearly destroyed by the construction of the Expressway in the early 1950s.

1870s

In the summer of 1872, when the town boasted a population of about 3,000, the first wood-burning locomotive by the Houston & Texas Central Railway steamed into Dallas, after a 15-hour voyage from Houston. The first train stopped at a spot located where Pacific Avenue crosses under Central Expressway today. The railroad brought employment to hundreds of African-Americans, who in that year numbered about a thousand.

More than 5,000 persons, including John Neely Bryan, attended a barbecue feast on the picnic grounds where Baylor Hospital complex is now located, celebrating the coming of the railroad. After the Texas & Pacific line extended to Dallas, the following year, Dallas' population zoomed to 7,000.

The rail line was to have been built eight miles (or nearly 13 kilometers) east of Dallas' courthouse, but **William Henry Gaston** (1841-1927), a banker and major landowner, offered the railroad right of way, along with $5,000 in cash, and swayed the rail men. A former Confederate captain, Gaston co-founded Dallas' first permanent bank in 1868, and was the charter member of the State Fair association. He gave 80 acres (or 32.3 hectares) of what is now Fair Park. His plantation became the town of East Dallas.

The Texas & Pacific Railroad followed the following February, after it, too, extorted a similar amount in cash. Trains were overflowing with emigrants from other states.

Eighteen seventy-two, the last year in the life of Samuel F. B. Morse, inventor of the telegraph and Morse code, was also the year when telegraph was extended to Dallas. (Morse, incidentally, offered officials of the Republic of Texas his invention in 1838, but was ignored.)

In 1873, when buffalo were still shot in the countryside nearby, a mule-drawn streetcar, carrying up to 14 people, began operation. To amuse themselves, Dallas men maintained more than one red-light district, as well as several dance and beer halls. They held boxing matches and distracted themselves with cockfighting.

William Lewis Cabell (1827-1911), a Confederate general born in Virginia, who had moved his family to Dallas in 1872, was elected Dallas mayor in 1877, and again in 1883. His son **Ben E. Cabell** (1858-1931) also served as Dallas mayor, from 1900 to 1904, as did his younger son **Earle Cabell** (1906-1975), from 1961 to 1964. Ben Cabell's son **Charles** (1903-1971), who attended Oak Cliff High School, was an Air Force general and later deputy director of the CIA.

Earle Cabell was Dallas' first full-time mayor, who resigned to run for U.S. Congress, serving four terms, from 1965 to 1973. He and his brother founded Cabell's Dairy and Cabell's Minit Market, which were later sold to 7-Eleven (see listing). The main federal building downtown is named after Earle Cabell, who graduated from Southern Methodist University, died at age 68, and is buried at Restland Memorial Park. Many of the Cabells are buried at Greenwood Cemetery in Uptown.

John Neely Bryan's wife admitted her husband to the State Lunatic Asylum (later the Austin State Hospital) in Austin, Texas, on February 20, 1877. Six months and 25 days later he died there. Margaret Bryan lived for another 42 years and died on September 6, 1919, 23 days before her 94th birthday, when Dallas had a population of 150,000, according to one estimate.

The Bryans had five children, one of whom was John Neely Bryan Jr., who died of food poisoning at the State Fair of Texas in 1926. He had a son named Robert E. Lee Bryan, who died of cancer in 1936. Robert Bryan had two children: a daughter, Maxine, and a son, John Neely Bryan III.

Bryan III, the great-grandson and namesake of the Dallas founder, moved from Texas to Kansas in 1948 and died in March 2001 in Emporia, Kansas, at age 83. He had a cattle farm in Emporia and worked as a meat inspector for the U.S. Agriculture Department for 26 years, then retired in 1983. He was buried in Alpine Cemetery in Osage County on the eastern edge of Kansas. Bryan III was survived by his wife of almost 60 years, Ada Wynona Bryan, a daughter, two sons, six grandchildren, and one great-grandchild.

1880s

Dallas' population grew to more than ten thousand by 1880, Fort Worth had 6,666, while New York City surpassed one million. By 1882, when billiard parlors, tennis, electricity, and trolley cars were introduced, the city's population almost quadrupled and made Dallas the largest city in Texas.

Around 1890, Dallas' population increased to about 38,000, and in another decade approached 43,000, with the city already numbering 600 streets. Traffic congestion only increased with the invention of the automobile. Streetcars were segregated, and African-Americans were required to give their seats to whites when the cars were full. Conductors carried guns and could shoot a black passenger without much pretense.

William McKinley (1843-1901) was the president at the turn of the century, when a seven-room cottage in Dallas could be bought for about $2,200, or a six-room house with bath and stable on McKinney Avenue for $3,500. A fine man's suit could be had for under $20, a hat for $1.50, the same as some of the best shirts. Cigars cost five cents each.

A woman's suit cost up to $15, or she could buy four or five yards of cloth, at up to 25 cents a yard, and sew her own. A woman would pay $2.50 for a good pair of shoes and less than $1 for a pair of gloves. "Honest men" were offered a salary of $780 a year plus expenses at one company. There was no federal income tax yet.

1900s

On June 10, 1902, Coca-Cola opened a bottling plant at 2628 Elm Street in Dallas' Deep Ellum district. The plant started with three employees, who sold 37 cases on the first day, and a one-horse wagon. Dr Pepper, which was invented in nearby Waco, had, of course, already been around for years.

Theodore Roosevelt was the first U.S. president to visit Dallas in 1905, followed by **William H. Taft** four years later. In 1907, the same year that the pricey Highland Park residential community opened, Neiman Marcus, for many years the most prestigious luxury store in Texas, opened in downtown Dallas.

But all their wealth could not help Dallasites when it came to taming the Trinity River, which most of the time is but a sluggish trickle. The north Texas terrain is so flat and filled with water-resistant clay that when violent spring weather comes, the Trinity is a beast, killing people and causing millions of dollars of damage.

The first great flood of the Trinity took place in 1844, when the water rose 51 feet (or 15.5 meters) high. Twenty-two years later, in 1866, came another, and this time the river rose 56 feet, causing Dallas, which then occupied the western half of today's central business district, to be cut off from the outside world, except for the road to McKinney.

In 1989, the rain-swollen Trinity River caused tens of millions of dollars in damage and killed 17 people. While the city council in 1997 finally approved enlarging and extending the Trinity's levees and developing new wetlands, the project might not be finished for years, if ever. Although the Trinity has three major forks, the West, the East, and the Elm, it received its name in the late 17th century from the Spaniards who named it Rio de la Santisima Trinidad, or River of the Most Holy Trinity.

In 1908, a disastrous flood struck Dallas, ruining homes, carrying away bridges, and separating Oak Cliff from Dallas for several days. On the Oak Cliff side, Zang Boulevard was covered by 12 feet (or 3.65 meters) of water, while on the Dallas side, McKinney Avenue was under six to ten feet (or 1.82 to three meters). The water flooded the lobby of the Adolphus Hotel (see entry) downtown, killed eleven people, forced 4,000 out of their homes, and caused $5 million in damage. The city broke the record for the heaviest 24-hour rainfall, 15 inches.

1910s

To deal with such calamities, a 5,106-foot-long (or 1,556-meter) reinforced concrete bridge, today known as the Houston Street viaduct, was built in 1912. It was the longest concrete bridge in the world at the time and the first to connect Dallas with Oak Cliff. (Ten years later the 13-year-old Clyde Barrow took up residence below this bridge.) It eventually also led to moving the main channel of the Trinity River to the west and a ten-lane freeway, which now runs up the old riverbed.

By then Dallas already had four daily newspapers, 200 saloons, 300 lawyers, and 400 prostitutes who worked in a red-light district, east of Lamar Street and just north of downtown. There were 14 Methodist, 14 Baptist, and 12 Presbyterian churches in the city.

On a muggy March day in 1910, Dallasites hanged Allen Brooks, a 68-year-old African-American accused of molesting a three-year-old white girl. "At the Dallas County Courthouse—Old Red on Main Street—a mob rushed into a second-floor courtroom, looped a rope around his neck and hurled him out a window," according to the *Dallas Morning News*. The crowd was estimated at more than 2,000 at a time when Dallas numbered about 92,000 residents. "The mob dragged Mr. Brooks to the corner of Main and Akard and hanged him from a telephone pole there."

The facts in the case are unknown because county records were lost in a 1950s flood so it cannot be determined whether the accused was guilty of the charge. At least 175 "novelty" postcards are known to document such lynchings in the South, including in Dallas. The U.S. Post Office banned their mailing in 1908.

Towering over the telephone pole where Brooks was hanged, near today's Jeroboam French brasserie (see entry), a three-story steel Elks Arch, constructed at $50,000, loomed from 1908 until 1910, when it was "disassembled in disgrace" over the lynching and moved in pieces to Fair Park. Featuring flowing fountains at each corner, it was erected to welcome the delegates of the 1908 Elks Grand Lodge Convention.

Herbert Marcus leased for 99 years a site in 1913 for the new Neiman Marcus store downtown, where it still stands today, after the original store perished in a fire just a few blocks away. Dirt was flying at Southern Methodist University in University Park to meet the deadline of admitting the first class of students in 1915.

The first flight made from Dallas Love Field Airport took place in 1917, the same year that John Fitzgerald Kennedy was born. It was established to train Army fliers for the coming war. Some 8,000 Dallasites served in World War I, from April 1917 until November 1918.

1920s

The Ku Klux Klan was an embarrassment to Dallas in the 1920s. The original organization was believed to have been founded in Tennessee in 1866 by six young Confederate veterans. The Klan, which numbered 13,000 men here, some among them unsuspecting dupes, included citizens as illustrious as **Robert Lee Thornton** (1880-1964), the civic booster after whom Interstate Highways 30 and 35 East are named. To be against the Klan was often considered as being against America, the Bible, and morality.

The Klan showed its claws on April 1, 1921, when 800 robed Klansmen paraded through the city streets. They dragged African-American bellhop Alex Johnson from the Adolphus Hotel downtown and branded letters KKK on his forehead with acid. Although the Klan was publicly denounced, no one was charged.

In 1922, a dentist and imperial wizard of the KKK, Dr. Hiram Wesley Evans, was enthusiastically greeted by 75,000 Klan sympathizers at the special day for KKK at the Texas State Fair. The son of an Alabama judge, he arrived in Dallas at the turn of the century and had a downtown dental practice on Main Street, across from Neiman Marcus.

Dallas grew to a city of 160,000 by 1920 and surpassed 200,000 by 1927, when aviator **Charles Lindbergh** (1902-1974) came to Love Field to dedicate it as a municipal airport and was honored with a parade that claimed 10,000 spectators, until then the largest crowd in Dallas' history.

"Other than being where John Neely Bryan parked his covered wagon on the east bank of the Trinity River in 1841, there was no logical reason for a city to develop there," notes Kenneth Ragsdale in his 1987 history of the Texas Centennial Exposition, quoting Dallas merchant to the monied, Stanley Marcus, who once reflected on Dallas' geographical deficiency thus:

"The Lord must have created Dallas on Sunday when he was resting because there's no mountains, no lakes, no water, just a flat piece of land with no reason for being." Yet, Dallas grew and prospered, says Ragsdale. As far as the Trinity River was concerned, it did help a lot that from the year that most Americans remember for its gut-wrenching stock market crash, until 1931, four more viaducts across the Trinity were constructed.

The New York-born writer Warren Leslie, who had spent 17 years in Dallas, agrees: "The truth is, there really isn't any reason for Dallas. It sits in the middle of nowhere and nothing."

1930s

During the Great Depression as many as 18,000 were unemployed, although Dallas did not suffer as much as many other cities because of the discovery of oil. A 70-year-old, Shakespeare-quoting wildcatter **Columbus Marion "Dad" Joiner** (b. 1860) struck oil 100 miles (or 161 kilometers) east of Dallas in 1930, and the city greatly benefited from it.

Banks made loans to develop the oil fields, and Dallas became a financial center. By 1935, with a population of 270,000, Dallas ranked second only to Houston, according to the census, and transformed its economic base from cotton to petroleum. This transformation also cushioned the severity of the Great Depression so keenly felt by most of the rest of the country.

When the Texas Legislature in 1934 authorized creation of a commission to select a site for a centennial fair, no one knew where the exposition might end until candy salesman Robert L. Thornton gathered other influential businessmen and brought it to Dallas, even though the city had nothing like San Antonio's Alamo or the battlefield at San Jacinto, near Houston. In fact, Dallas did not even exist a hundred years earlier.

Thornton must have caught the bug in 1888, when his father brought him for the first time to visit the Texas State Fair and he spent a whopping fifty cents. During his one-hour presentation, the gravel-voiced Thornton, "a big rangy fellow with quick, shrewd eyes" assured the 21 commission officials that a centennial fair will be held, "whether the State of Texas or the government of the U.S. contribute one cent" or none.

By September 1935, says Ragsdale, Dallas embarked on one of the largest peacetime construction programs in the state's history. In approximately ten months a 185-acre (or 75-hectare) site, encompassing the State Fair of Texas complex, was transformed into a $25-million world's fair. More than 6.3 million people attended the Centennial Exposition, which prompted merchant Marcus to conclude, "I have frequently said that modern Texas history started with the celebration of the Texas Centennial, because it was in 1936 . . . that the rest of America discovered Texas."

When San Antonio, where the Alamo is located, lost the world's fair to Dallas, one of its representatives exclaimed: "If we want to perpetuate Texas history, for God's sake, let's don't go to Oklahoma to do it!"

Bonnie & Clyde

Starting in 1932, bank robbers Clyde Chesnut Barrow and Bonnie Parker began plaguing the country in a two-and-a-half-year crime spree across Depression-era America. "Bonnie Parker was generous, sensitive, adventurous, compulsive, and doggedly loyal, a small flower of a girl with reddish-gold hair and profoundly blue eyes, vulnerable and fragile and yet tough as nails and willful to the extreme," according to *Texas Monthly*, which describes Clyde as "a scrawny little psychopath with jug ears and the sense of humor of a persimmon, cruel, egotistical, obsessive, vindictive, and so devoid of compassion that he appeared to care more for his machine gun and his saxophone than he did for the women in his life."

Clyde (b. 1909) was the son of an illiterate Texas tenant farmer who had eight children and lived in a makeshift camp under the Houston Street viaduct when arriving in Dallas in 1922. First arrested in 1926, he was eventually sentenced to a 14-year term at hard labor in the state penitentiary, but was not willing to endure the work and "had another convict chop two toes off his right foot with an axe." Unexpectedly, he was given a general parole and released in 1932, after which his worst crimes were yet to be committed. Clyde's remains lie next to those of his older brother Buck at Western Heights Cemetery, up the hill at 1617 Fort Worth Avenue in Dallas. A marker says, Gone But Not Forgotten.

Bonnie (b. 1910), who had met Clyde in January 1930 in west Dallas, came from a divorced family. After making her way to Dallas in 1914 with her mother and two sisters, she lived off Lamar Street. She was a struggling waitress in a downtown café near the Dallas County Courthouse and was married to a small-time hood named Roy Thornton. The couple lived in the Devil's Back Porch, where not many houses had running water and only two of the streets were paved.

She supposedly did not like guns and is said to have fired one only once when she accidentally shot herself in the foot. FBI director J. Edgar Hoover called her "that dirty, filthy, diseased woman." When killed she was five months short of her 25th birthday. She is buried at Crownhill Memorial Park Cemetery, at 9700 Webb Chapel Road, north of Love Field Airport, and a few miles from Clyde.

The pair went through a series of violent holdups in the Southwest and Midwest, killing 13 people along the way, usually just a step ahead of the law. There were 50,000 other robberies in the United States in 1933. Our bandits were mowed down from ambush by Texas Rangers led by the legendary Frank Hamer as they rode down a deserted Louisiana country road in a stolen tan four-door V-8 model Ford in 1934.

They were killed in a barrage of some 170 bullets near Gibsland, a town of 1,200 between Shreveport and Monroe, on May 23rd, just after 9 AM. A graffiti-stained, chipped-away lump of granite now stands on the spot, about six miles (or 9.6 kilometers) east of Gibsland, on State Highway 154. To cash in on the town's notoriety, Gibsland's City Hall doubles as a Bonnie and Clyde souvenir store, offering coffee cups, bumper stickers, and T-shirts.

More than 40,000 nosy Dallasites could not resist the temptation of seeing their bullet-ridden bodies that were brought to the A. H. Belo Mansion (see entry) downtown in 1933. Sixty-four years later, the Barrow's bullet-thorn blue shirt with pearl buttons sold at auction in San Francisco for $75,000.

The Dallas Historical Society's 2001 Bonnie and Clyde exhibit at the State Fair of Texas "recorded 104,000 more visitors than an exhibit the following year that was devoted to the memory of President John F. Kennedy," observes the *News*.

An epidemic followed in 1939, when 82 people were stricken with smallpox in Dallas County, and two died.

1940s

After the Pearl Harbor attack in 1941, many Japanese nationals were arrested in Dallas and Japanese-made goods were removed from the stores. By the war's end the city had grown to 90 square miles (or 233 square kilometers), by 1960 to 283 square miles (or 732 square kilometers), and to 400 (or 1,036 square kilometers) today.

Ten years after the Adolphus became one of the nation's first fully air-conditioned hotels in 1940, the city numbered 435,000. Dallas began war rationing in 1943, and some 376,000 ration books were distributed. Three years later, a Dr Pepper soda plant opened at Mockingbird Lane and Central Expressway, where the Phoenix apartment complex and Kroger supermarket are located today.

Starting in 1949, Dallas was run by a 36-year-old University of Virginia and Harvard Law School graduate, **Wallace Savage** (1913-2000), a progressive mayor who "took on the injustices against blacks at a time when segregation was the norm and violence kept many minorities in constant fear," according to the *Dallas Morning News*.

He did away with the city's segregated ambulance service, which forced African-Americans to ride in different ambulances, where they often received substandard medical treatment, and made city parks accessible to them. Wallace cut the ribbon to open the North Central Expressway, also known as U.S. Highway 75.

1950s

A devastating drought fell upon Dallas, starting in 1951, and lasted for five years. Perhaps in part because of the drought, the city felt it needed a strong leader, and in 1953 the citizens elected decisively that icon of the business establishment, Robert Lee Thornton, already known to many as "Uncle Bob" and soon to earn the sobriquet "Mr. Dallas." Although Thornton, who had "enormous charm and humor and a gift of phrase," claimed he was not a politician and did not want to be one, he was reelected three more times and ruled the city hall until 1961.

During the 1957 election day, on April 2, a tornado touched down and wrought a 16-mile-long (or 25.7-kilometer) path of destruction from west to northwest of downtown Dallas killing ten persons, injuring 170, and destroying 800 homes and businesses. Winds were estimated to have reached 212 miles (or 341 kilometers) per hour.

Between 1950 and 1996 some 75 tornadoes killed 33 residents of Dallas County. A tornado of a different kind arrived on April 16, 1955, when the barely known, then-country-music-singer Elvis Presley appeared for the first time at the Dallas Sportatorium, a dump on South Industrial Boulevard near Corinth Street, south of downtown, that opened in the 1930s and was demolished in 2003.

He came back in May, in June, and in July, and again in September of that year, when his fame took off so the singer seldom played this kind of venues in the future. When Elvis returned the following April, 26,000 fans greeted him at the Cotton Bowl in Fair Park.

The Dallas Opera was founded in 1957 with the arrival of the temperamental Greek-American soprano Maria Callas, and two years later Frank Lloyd Wright's Dallas Theater Center opened on a wooded site along Turtle Creek Boulevard. During the 1950s and 1960s, Dallas became the nation's third-largest technology center, according to Texas State Historical Association, with the growth of such companies as Ling-Tempco-Vought (LTV Corporation) and Texas Instruments.

By 1959, when the city numbered almost 670,000, the 75-year-old Thornton felt being a three-term mayor was enough, but was convinced to run one more time. This time he ran against Earle Cabell (d. 1975), whose father and grandfather had both served as Dallas mayors. Cabell won the mayor's seat in 1961 during a time when many Dallas restaurants and stores would serve white customers only. The first African-American elementary schoolchildren were admitted to previously all-white schools in the fall of 1961.

Such racial differences spurred the Dallas-born author **John Howard Griffin** (1920-1980), a white man disguised as an African-American to experience the segregated South in the late 1950s. His account was published by Houghton Mifflin in a book titled *Black Like Me*, translated into 13 languages, and caused a furor on its publication.

"In his hometown of Mansfield [southwest of Dallas], he was hanged in effigy from a light pole on Main Street," notes the *Fort Worth Star-Telegram*, after being written about by *Time* magazine and interviewed by CBS broadcaster Mike Wallace.

1960s

(For details about John F. Kennedy's assassination on November 22, 1963—the most traumatic single event in the history of Dallas—please see the Sixth Floor Museum entry in the VISUAL ARTS chapter.)

"In the process of reinvention, Dallas became a city struggling for an identity and frightened by the anxieties accompanying rapid growth and the complexities of a changing world," writes Dallas cultural historian Ronald L. Davis. "Emotionally much of its citizenry remained rooted in a vanished frontier, ill-prepared to cope with the uncertainties of a fractured metropolis in an age of global involvements."

In 1964, the wealthy industrialist **Erik Jonsson** (1901-1995) was picked as the next mayor. Just three years later, Texas Instruments, his high-technology company, which was founded in the 1930s, manufactured the first electronic hand-held computer using integrated circuits that were invented in 1958. Forty-two years after he invented the fingernail-size circuit, Dallas engineer **Jack St. Clair Kilby** received the Nobel Prize in physics in Stockholm, Sweden, at age 77. The integrated circuit market is now a $177-billion business worldwide.

The 6-foot-6 (or 1.98-meter) "humble giant" from Great Bend, Kansas, and a Dallas resident since 1958, a solitary widower whose wife Barbara died in 1982, shared the prize with the Russian and German scientists. Kilby, who once failed the entrance exam at the Massachusetts Institute of Technology, received about $455,000 of the $915,000 award. He claims he holds a master of science degree in electrical engineering from the University of Wisconsin.

Eight Texans have been honored with Nobel Prizes so far, including James Cronin, a graduate of the Highland Park school system and Southern Methodist University. He won the prize in physics in 1980 for research on subatomic articles called neutral kaons. Cronin now teaches at the University of Chicago. Four other Nobel prize-winners work at the University of Texas Southwestern Medical Center at Dallas (see entry for more details).

Jack Kilby does not own a cell phone and has never bought anything on the Web. He has an old Dell personal computer at home that uses a 368-megahertz processor to run the now-outdated DOS operating system, according to the *Fort Worth Star-Telegram*. Kilby, who has worked for TI for 12 years, holds more than 50 patents on various electronic products, including the pocket calculator, which debuted in 1965. He maintains that Intel founder Robert Noyce (d. 1990), who developed the production method for how chips today are built on silicon wafers, would probably share in the Nobel prize were he still alive. He arrived in Stockholm aboard a Texas Instruments corporate jet and later met President Bill Cinton in the White House. Friends say Kilby still enjoys half a pack of cigarettes a day and an occasional shot of Jack Daniels bourbon.

On Friday, September 18, 1964, the Beatles took Dallas by storm and gave one performance at the Dallas Memorial Auditorium, which in 1957 was the first among the buildings that now comprise the Dallas Convention Center. Tickets started at $2.50 each.

In mid-August of 1969, shocking news came from Los Angeles: Dallas native Charles "Tex" Watson, with the help of three accomplices, shot and stabbed a 26-year-old fellow Dallas native, actress Sharon Tate, married to film director Roman Polanski (b. 1933) and eight months pregnant. Her husband was in London. The mastermind behind this brutal murder was the deranged fanatic Charles Manson. Seven other persons were slaughtered. The intended victim was the son of actress Doris Day who supposedly reneged on a promise to help Manson get his songs published.

The oldest of a U.S. Army intelligence officer's three children, Tate graduated from Vicenza American High School in Italy in 1961. She appeared in the films *The Americanization of Emily* in 1964 and *The Sandpiper* the following year. She landed a part in the film *Eye of the Devil,* along with David Niven and Deborah Kerr, in London, where she met Polanski. They were married in January 1968.

A year after the murders, Watson was extradited from McKinney, Texas, where family members with political clout had delayed his return to California. Sentenced to death in 1971, Watson (b. 1946) and his accomplices have so far served 30 years of their life sentence because California abolished the death penalty the following year.

Mayor Jonsson, a native of Brooklyn, New York, served until 1971, when Dallas had a population of about 850,000. He was instrumental in building the Dallas/Fort Worth International Airport, which was three times the size of Kennedy Airport in New York. Dallas and Fort Worth, "a mismatched couple trapped in a rocky marriage," according to the *Houston Chronicle*, squabbled for 20 years over which city would build the region's airport, until Jonsson received a telegram from the Civil Aeronautics Board, informing him in 1964:

"You have six months to select a site for a joint airport with Fort Worth. If you don't select it, we will." Jonsson was also instrumental in erecting the Dallas City Hall.

1970s

By the time the D/FW Airport was inaugurated in 1973 and touted as the world's largest, Dallas already had another mayor—one of the few upsets in the establishment-run city—a photogenic former sportscaster, **Wes Wise,** who also witnessed the groundbreaking ceremonies for the new city hall.

The year 1973 is also a sad reminder of the death of a 12-year-old Hispanic boy, **Santos Rodriguez,** who died in the hands of Dallas police. A Dallas native, whose alien father was deported to Mexico and mother sentenced in 1971 to five years in prison for murder, Santos was placed in the care of his elderly foster grandparents.

On July 24, at about 2 AM, a patrolman spotted three boys fleeing from a service station where a soda machine had just been burglarized. He and another patrolman thought they recognized two of the Rodriguez brothers, who had been in trouble before. The brothers were handcuffed and taken to a lot behind the gas station for questioning. The boys denied being involved in the burglary. A patrolman pointed his revolver at the back of Santos's head urging him to tell the truth. They boys denied their involvement. The gun clicked but did not fire.

The policeman spun the cylinder and squeezed the trigger again. This time the gun fired and killed the youth instantly.

Later that month, violence erupted downtown resulting in widespread property damage. The policeman was convicted of murder with malice and sentenced to five years in prison, while Santos was buried in Oakland Cemetery in south Dallas, the resting place of such venerable past residents as the Caruths, the Sangers, and the Harrises; A. H. Belo, son of the *Dallas Morning News* founder; Highland Park developer John Armstrong; the Ervays, the Thorntons, and the Akards.

While the economy boomed, race relations continued to wobble. The school desegregation was a sore spot for most African-American children still attending the predominantly black schools. The suburbs were exploding with the fleeing white parents who sought a more accommodating racial climate. The Dallas/Fort Worth Metroplex, a term coined by an advertising copywriter in 1971, was about to be born.

Wise served three terms but resigned in 1976 to run for Congress and was replaced by **Robert Folsom,** another developer and a former captain of the Southern Methodist University football team. When **Adlene Harrison** became interim mayor of Dallas that year, she was the first Jewish woman to be mayor of a metropolitan city in the United States.

On January 22, 1973, the U.S. Supreme Court ruled 7-2 in *Roe v. Wade* that Norma McCorvey (or Jane Roe as she was known until the 1980s, when she disclosed her identity) could have an abortion. The 21-year-old, pregnant Dallas waitress, with the legal help of Dallas attorneys Sarah Weddington (b. 1946) and Linda Coffee, in 1969 sued Henry M. Wade (b. 1914), Dallas County district attorney for the right to have an abortion.

It was Wade's job to enforce Texas abortion laws, which prohibited abortion other than to save a mother's life. Her case was rejected, and McCorvey (b. 1948), a ninth-grade dropout, was forced to give birth. Her lawyers filed an appeal with the Supreme Court. Weddington, a law school classmate of U.S. Senator Kay Bailey Hutchison, was elected to the House of Representatives in 1972.

In 1995, McCorvey was baptized in a Dallas swimming pool as a born-again Christian. She changed her allegiance in the abortion-rights cause and became a staunch anti-abortion activist. Wade was the one who also prosecuted Jack Ruby, the man who shot Lee Harvey Oswald on national television.

Weddington, now practicing in Austin, Texas, discovered in 2001 that she had breast cancer. The next day, she departed for a vacation in France, "and had a great time. I really resented having to take those nasty little cells to Paris," she told the *Houston Chronicle*. Coffee (b. 1943) went on to represent debtors in Dallas bankruptcy cases. Texas now has nearly 19 abortions for every 1,000 women ages 15 to 44, compared with more than 32 for California.

The Metroplex economy raged on and, after its premiere in 1978, so did the televised fantasy about Dallas, where a mythical television ***Dallas*** family ruled amid cheating, backstabbing, and adultery. A record 80 million Americans tuned in to see who shot J. R. Ewing, the fictional Dallas businessman and a fraud, in an episode televised in 1980. (For more details, please see the Southfork Ranch entry in the SIGHTS & ATTRACTIONS chapter.)

The soap opera ended 13 years later as the second longest-running television fluff ever, and the Dallas economy, too, was in deep trouble well before the series expired in 1991.

In the fall of 1979, when the Dallas population stood at about 900,000, the price of silver was around six dollars. As the winter approached, Dallas billionaires Nelson Bunker Hunt (b. 1926) and William Herbert Hunt (b. 1929) attempted an astonishing feat—to corner the global silver market by buying up to 200 million ounces, more than half the world's deliverable silver.

1980s

In January 1980, the price of silver shot to an unimaginably high price of $50 an ounce. It then dropped as precipitously. The Hunt brothers covered their losses by mortgaging their oil properties. They lost $2 billion when the price of oil crashed in the 1980s. They declared corporate bankruptcy in 1986 and a personal one two years later. Bunker had to sell 580 thoroughbreds for $46,900,000. In 1994, the pair forked over some $150 million in overdue taxes to the Internal Revenue Service.

But don't feel sorry for the Hunts, they still had the money from their personal trusts set up by their father in 1935 to tide them over in an emergency. By the mid-1990s, that amounted to some $170 million for each man. The trusts hold the oil companies that the brothers run.

Bunker's Hunt Exploration & Mining is engaged in Australia, Nicaragua, Pakistan, and the Philippines, while Herbert's Petro-Hunt provides exploration in East Texas and the Gulf Coast and is largely run by his three sons. In 1999, Bunker attended a sale of two-year-old horses at Lone Star Park (see entry) in Grand Prairie and, after an 11-year absence, bought his first 13 horses for $360,000.

Bunker and Herbert, both living in Dallas, are two among the 14 children of Texas' most famous oilman and for years one of the world's richest, Haroldson Lafayette Hunt (1889-1974). (You will find the mention of some of his offspring under the descriptions of the Mansion on Turtle Creek and Hyatt Regency hotels, as well as the Reunion

Tower and Reunion sports arena.) "They tend, like Bunker and Herbert, to be driven, extremely successful prominent workaholics who have refused to coast on their fabulous wealth," observes the *Texas Monthly*.

Bunker and Herbert Hunt both got their start in the oil business in the 1940s. Bunker acquired the rights to an extraordinarily rich oil field in Libya in 1961 and was once worth more than $16 billion. He lost most of that wealth 12 years later, when Col. Muammar Qaddafi nationalized Libya's oil fields.

"The awesome development and construction boom in the Dallas area in the late 70s and early 80s was fueled at first by profits from skyrocketing oil prices, always handy for Texans," says historian Darwin Payne, "and then carried further after deregulatory policies of the Reagan administration permitted savings and loan institutions to build up their deposits overnight by offering extra-high dividends."

Instead of financing homes, the banks and thrifts, whose deposits were insured by the government, financed some of the most outrageous schemes. Exorbitant loans were approved on inflated appraisals, but when the economy cooled down, millions of dollars worth of loans ended in default.

A savings and loan collapse, centered in Dallas, took place "at a cost to taxpayers estimated as much as $300 billion for the thrifts alone," says Payne. "By 1993, in the Northern District of Texas alone, more than 700 individuals had been convicted of some form of bank fraud," notes *D Magazine*, observing that ten of "the most heinous S&L guys" caused losses estimated from bank failures totaling some $8.8 billion. When the son of one of these scoundrels married, his father "hired the entire Oklahoma City Symphony Orchestra to play for the wedding."

FirstRepublic, consisting of the once-respected First National Bank and RepublicBank, was sold in 1988 to what is today the Bank of America/NationsBank at a cost to taxpayers of $3.6 billion, until then the most expensive bank failure in the nation's history.

Even the election of **Annette Strauss** (1924-1998), a graduate of Columbia University and the first woman as Dallas' mayor in 1987, and her reelection two years later, could not boost the city's deflated ego. She was nevertheless one of the first mayoral candidates to defeat a business-anointed candidate and "tried to persuade Dallas to look honestly at its racial divisions in the 1980s."

She rests at Sparkman Hillcrest Memorial Park, together with former U.S. Senator John Tower (1925-1991), former Dallas mayor J. Erik Jonsson (1901-1995), and Sarah Hughes (1896-1985), U.S. District Court judge, who swore in Lyndon B. Johnson as the new U.S. president following Kennedy's assassination. Before the decade was out, Dallas became Big D, surpassing the one-million population mark.

1990s

In 1991, when Strauss left the mayor's office, about a third of all available space downtown was vacant, including R. L. Thornton's Mercantile National Bank building across from Neiman Marcus. The Merc was still vacant 11 years later. The city soon led with the highest office vacancy rate in the nation. Downtown Dallas became a ghost town, overtaken by the homeless when the office workers left for the day.

The city has never completely recuperated. The demand for office space surged again in 1999, but by the fall of 2002, 50 million square feet (or 4.64 million square meters) of the Dallas-Fort Worth office space sat empty—out of the 236 million square feet in the entire Metroplex—again the highest vacancy rate in the country. That is more than the amount of office space that is located in the entire downtown Dallas.

Steve Bartlett (b. 1947), also a former congressman, ruled Dallas from 1991 to 1995, when the city evolved to single-member council districts.

With almost 21 million people in the 2000 census, Texas surpassed New York as the nation's second most populous state after California. Dallas, in contrast, has nearly 1.19 million inhabitants, making it the ninth largest city in the United States.

But even though Dallas grew bigger, it was not necessarily wiser.

In 2002, the Dallas County district attorney had to dismiss more than 80 police narcotics cases against 53 defendants, many of them Hispanics, after laboratory tests showed that the seized substances often contained no illicit drugs. The finely ground substance turned out to be mostly gypsum, the material often found in Sheetrock.

"Because the Dallas County district attorney's office had a policy that no drugs would be analyzed by its forensic lab unless the case was going to trial," notes the *Dallas Observer*, "any defendant unwilling to risk a jury verdict and long sentence would never know if the drugs he had just pleaded guilty to selling were, in fact, drugs."

Police records showed that one informant in these cases received more than 60 payments in excess of $200,000 "for the seizure of nearly 1,000 pounds [or 453 kilograms] of cocaine and amphetamines, all of which turned out to be bogus."

The mostly poor Hispanics who nearly had their lives destroyed by illegal arrests were soon to learn the flip side of the American legal system. Said one defense attorney: "They're going to get rich. But after all, isn't that the American way?" Television station WFAA-TV (Channel 8) won the Alfred I. DuPont Columbia-University award, broadcast journalism's Pulitzer Prize, for investigating this story.

The late 1990s were the age of telecommunications and .com entrepreneurs who made huge fortunes left and right, practically blindfolded. At Kirby's steakhouse in Southlake, patrons, clad in Ermenegildo Zegna and Rolex watches, spent a minimum of $50 a person, while strategizing under a wall-sized portrait of James Dean as Jett Rink in the film *Giant*. At Reunion Arena downtown, some Mavericks fan paid up to $2,000 for one ticket to one game. At Marty's Wine Bar in Oak Lawn, customers bought $750 bottles of wine without checking their price.

"To be sure, conspicuous consumption has always played a sociological role in North Texas," observed the *Dallas Morning News*. "In the birthplace of Neiman Marcus, the region's tourist brochures tout malls as must-see destinations right alongside Dealey Plaza, near the site where John F. Kennedy was assassinated."

Well over 100 million-dollar homes sold in the Dallas area in the late 1990s, with a few selling for $10 million or more. Boyd Levinson furniture store sold dining tables for up to $30,000 each and chairs for more than one-tenth that price. At Dominic Shoes boutique on West Lovers Lane, customers snapped up $700 stiletto-heeled peacock boots as fast as they could be made, prompting the proprietor to exclaim: "Now, that's prosperity."

"When the music stopped playing in Richardson's Telecom Corridor, thousands of workers and a host of businesses found themselves tossed from one of the liveliest parties they had ever attended," reported the *News* in 2001, informing its readers that more than 7,000 jobs were lost in the area that year alone. Alcatel of France (which in 1998 paid $3.5 billion for Dallas' DSC Communications), Nokia Oyj of Finland, and Texas Instruments cut at least 30,000 full- and part-time jobs nationwide, more than a third of them in north Texas.

By the end of 2002, about a third of all office space in the Telecom Corridor was vacant, and 15,000 telecommunications jobs disappeared in and around Richardson. San Antonio, Texas-based SBC Communications—the second-biggest employer in the Metroplex—alone cut 5,000 jobs in north Texas. Ericsson now employs one-half the number it did in the late 1990s in north Texas.

An investor who was rebuffed when trying to purchase Ericsson's ten-story former U.S. headquarters building and 12 surrounding acres (or 4.85 hectares) for $33 million in 2001, bought the same property for $16 million the following year. By then, the office vacancy rates had risen to more than five million square feet (or 464,500 square meters) or 25 percent of the available Telecom Corridor office space.

Among the two probably most stinging defeats to the boundless optimism of Dallasites in recent memory were losing the Olympic bid to Houston and losing the Boeing Co. headquarters relocation to Chicago.

The conviction that the 2012 Summer Olympic Games could be held in Big D ran amok. Declared the mayor: "I believe even the Russian judges would give Dallas a 10." The region spent about $5 million of private money in the process.

Dallas Councilwoman Laura Miller, who strongly opposed the Olympic bid, said: "I think the reason we didn't make it is the same reason we didn't get Boeing: because we don't have the basic infrastructure to be an attractive place for an Olympic city."

Dallasites should have taken notice as early as the summer of 2000, when the Olympic Games were held in Sydney, Australia, and a *Dallas Morning News* correspondent, comparing the two Olympic contenders, declared:

"Dallas-Fort Worth can't be Sydney. Not in 12 years, not in a million years." If the Olympics were held in Dallas, said the correspondent elsewhere, NBC-TV "would probably wind up showing you actual footage of competitions because there wouldn't be any breathtaking panoramas to show with all that sappy music."

But as America has irrevocably changed since September 11, 2001, so has Dallas. Although 1,600 miles (or 2,575 kilometers) away, the 3,000 that perished in the terrorist bombing in New York and Washington, D.C., have affected travel and daily life in north Texas. Texans were almost as affected by these acts of savagery as New Yorkers were by the death of John F. Kennedy in 1963.

DALLAS TODAY

Texas is a state of mind. Everything here is bigger and better, or so the Dallasites would have you believe. Come visit and you, too, might write back home something like what writer Warren Leslie did in 1964:

> Everything in Dallas is bigger and better; the parties are plusher, the buildings are more air-conditioned, the women better dressed and the girls more fetching. It is one of the cleanest, best policed, best managed cities in the country. Dallas doesn't owe a thing to accident, nature or inevitability. It is what it is—even to the girls—because the men of Dallas damn well planned it that way.

Texans love being larger than life, and sometimes they almost are. They even nicknamed their third-largest city Big D. Texas is still one of the friendliest states anywhere—even if it found it necessary to execute more than 300 hardcore criminals since the death penalty was resumed in 1982—and the people in Dallas are no exception. It is one of the few remaining large American cities where complete strangers might still greet you warmly on the street, while you can just feel the frost in the air upon landing in Philadelphia or New York. Texans, although clannish, will go out of their way to make you feel welcome, whether you are visiting from England, California, or Canada.

Funny, native Dallasites are harder to find these days than $20 gold Eagles. At least one out of 12 Dallasites is foreign-born, and 100 languages are said to be spoken in the Metroplex. Almost one-third of all residents have lived in the city less than ten years.

What writer and businessman Warren Leslie wrote in 1964, still goes:

> The men get up early, go to work early, lunch early and return home late in Dallas. Despite popular legend, it is not a town of ease, luxury and a slow pace. It is a working town and its Establishment men, between attention to their business and civic work, will go step for step with any of the New Yorkers with whom I grew up. Still, Dallas gives the impression of a slower pace because its people seem friendly and, on the surface, hospitable. Men always stop for a word or two on the streets, and people seem genuinely glad to see other people. It is a first-name city, more than are the older, eastern cities.

Almost 13 million visitors, domestic and foreign, supposedly come to Dallas annually and spend up to $8.5 billion dollars. About 10 percent of them are from Europe, Canada, Japan, and Mexico. Only New York, Florida, and California have more international visitors than Texas, claims the Dallas convention bureau. More than 3.3 million out-of-town visitors attend 3,000 Dallas conventions, although the figures are disputed by outsiders.

If Dallas gained notoriety because of the Kennedy assassination, the debut of the television soap opera, titled *Dallas*, in 1978, began a worldwide infatuation with a city that only exists in imagination. A mythical, greedy, devious, rich Texas oil baron and rancher still fascinates viewers from Austria to Russia. Tourists flocked to Dallas like never before, only to discover that the real Dallas is much less glamorous. But by the time the last episode aired in 1991, Dallas was a household word the world over.

The Dallasites often refer to their metropolitan area as the Metroplex—a term coined by an advertising copywriter in 1971—which includes the cities of Forth Worth, Arlington, Plano, and Garland, as well as a dozen smaller but fast-growing cities that surround them both from all sides. This Metroplex spans 100 miles (or 160 kilometers), going as far north as Denton, which is less than 40 miles (or 64 kilometers) from the Oklahoma border, and has a population of more than five million. Dallas alone accounts for more than one-quarter of that and has the eighth largest Latino population in the nation, behind San Antonio, but ahead of San Diego.

The Metroplex is one among the least expensive large metro areas in the country, just behind Houston, Baltimore, and Tampa, Florida. The Dallas-Fort Worth area is half as expensive as San Francisco or New York City, according to the American Chamber of Commerce.

Texas' largest metropolitan area now has more residents than 31 U.S. states. The entire state of Arizona, for example, has fewer people than the Dallas-Fort Worth Metroplex. The 13 counties that make up the consolidated metropolitan area added nearly 1.2 million new residents between 1990 and 2000, a population increase that is the size of Dallas.

Come to Dallas before the area explodes into a metropolis of untold millions, where life will become a purgatory on the model of Mexico City, Bombay, or Sao Paulo. Already, Dallas is a jumble of races and nationalities.

Big D is one of the least densely populated major metropolitan areas in the world. It covers a geographic area almost as large as Moscow, which has nearly ten million inhabitants, so it is practically impossible to get around with the help of its spotty public transportation. Only having a car will do if you want to go places in the Metroplex and have fun. Even then the areas of interest to visitors are scattered over many miles.

After the bust of the late 1980s, the city was booming again in the late 1990s, and construction once more bloomed all over Dallas and in the suburbs. But downtown, entire blocks were still shuttered for lack of tenants at the turn of the 21st century. More than eight million square feet (or 743,200 square meters) of office space stood empty downtown throughout 2001, while more than 34 million square feet (or 3,158,600 square meters) "went begging in Big D," according to the *Dallas Morning News*.

One real estate developer, who has bought and renovated several buildings downtown, was quoted by the *News* as saying that "parts of downtown are still an embarrassment to the city."

"D-FW is a place of social inequities and economic polarities; increasingly complex environmental and ecological problems; and unhealed physical scars from poorly designed infrastructures," writes the Italian-born city planner Antonio di Mambro, with a master's degree from the Massachusetts Institute of Technology and a consulting firm in Boston. "D-FW has become a place that displays stark contrasts of opulence and poverty, expansion and obsolescence, community and individualism, connectivity and isolation."

A British visitor, a reporter for London's *Financial Times*, had this to say: "Dallas exceeded all my expectations and overturned many of my preconceptions; the heat was more intense, the terrain flatter and more arid than I had imagined; the size of the trucks, the freeways and the airport were overwhelming. Everywhere ruggedness was set alongside politesse."

If Dallas-Fort Worth were a country, opines the *Dallas Business Journal*, its economy would be the 24th largest in the world. And with only about $839 million in unpaid general obligation debt, Dallas holds Standard & Poor's prized AAA bond rating. Only four other cities, with populations greater than 500,000, boast AAA rating: Charlotte, North Carolina; Columbus, Ohio; Indianapolis, Indiana; and Seattle, Washington.

Climate & Dress

It is so hot in Dallas in July and August that your hair will melt—well, almost. (Just a little Texas exaggeration, you understand.) But seriously, out-of-towners sometimes underestimate Texas temperatures and end up being treated for heat exhaustion. If you love the heat, come in the summer, but don't forget comfortable cotton clothing, a hat, and a sun blocker, or you could fry alive. The sun here is so intense you risk skin cancer if exposed to it for a prolonged period of time and your skin is not conditioned for it.

There have only been two years since 1898, when records began to be kept, when Dallas did not reach a 100-degree Fahrenheit (or 38-degree Celsius) day, in 1906 and 1973. The first 100-degree day can come as early as March or as late as October.

A word about air-conditioning. Dallas spends more for it than the entire state budgets of some African countries. Air-conditioning is a badge of the Texas lifestyle. You may live in a decrepit little hut in a back alley, but nobody will deprive you of your air-conditioning. It is so cold in some offices at the height of the summer that some workers are blue in the face and have to turn on their portable heaters and bundle up, while others strut around in utter bliss. A breakdown in one's air-conditioning is tantamount to a national crisis. It is just as unthinkable to be without air-conditioning today as it is asking for drinking water without ice in a restaurant.

Between June 23 and August 3, 1980, Dallas endured 42 consecutive days when the temperatures reached 100 degrees Fahrenheit or higher, surely an aberration that does not appear but every 50 years, if that frequently. Since 1898, the city has had 12 summers when temperatures shot to between 108 and 113 degrees Fahrenheit (or 42 and 45 Celsius).

January is usually the coldest month, and May is the rainiest.

Here are Dallas' *average* precipitation and temperatures:

	Inches of Rainfall	**Fahrenheit Temperatures**	**Celsius Temperatures**
January	1.31	56-35	13-2
February	1.97	59-38	15-3
March	2.34	68-46	20-8
April	**3.88**	**75-55**	**24-13**
May	**4.63**	**83-63**	**28-17**
June	**2.91**	**91-71**	**33-23**
July	2.23	95-74	35-24
August	2.23	95-74	35-24
September	2.94	88-67	31-19
October	**3.00**	**79-57**	**26-14**
November	**2.20**	**67-46**	**19-8**
December	**1.92**	**58-37**	**14-3**

The coldest day on record in Dallas is February 12, 1899, when temperature fell to ten degrees Fahrenheit below zero (or -12 Celsius). Streetcars did not run for two days. Winters can be downright hot in Dallas: on February 25, 1918, the thermometer climbed from 60 degrees Fahrenheit (or 15 degrees Celsius) at 7 AM to 93 degrees (or 34 Celsius) by 2 PM.

From 1950 to 1994, Texas had 5,490 tornadoes that claimed 475 lives, with both numbers being far ahead of any other state. The tornado season is the time between March and June.

Perhaps the most important piece of advice about clothing for visitors to Dallas would be: make it comfortable, which often means casual. Unless you go to a formal business gathering, to an expensive restaurant for dinner, or to a cultural event, like the opera or symphony, stay comfortable.

At the height of summer, shorts are worn by all but some real oldtimers. In 2001, even the Dallas police officers began wearing shorts, the most drastic change in apparel since the early 1970s, when they cast off their ties and hats.

FINDING YOUR WAY AROUND DALLAS

Dallas covers an area of 400 square miles (or 1,036 square kilometers), not a small feat to overcome whether you want to check out your next restaurant or find an interesting sight. New York City, by contrast, encompasses just over 300 square miles, but has nearly seven times the population.

"Most of its growth has resulted from the annexation and consolidation of small towns and villages, both incorporated and unincorporated," notes *Legacies*, a Dallas historical journal. "From the acquisition of East Dallas at the end of 1889 up through the smaller strip annexations of the 1990s, there have been more than 600 separate annexations of land."

Metropolitan Dallas is a city of suburbs, and this Metroplex could take hours to circle, even if you included only Collin, Dallas, Denton, and Tarrant counties that are always understood to be the Metroplex. Here is a brief description of major area cities and neighborhoods.

DOWNTOWN DALLAS—WEST END—DEEP ELLUM—FAIR PARK

Downtown is bounded by Interstate Highway 30, Central Expressway (also known as U.S. Highway 75), Interstate Highway 35 East (or Stemmons Freeway), and the east-west Woodall Rodgers Freeway, which runs along the northern edge of downtown.

Downtown Dallas, like such areas of so many other American cities, is no longer a traditional downtown, no matter how hard the city is trying to reverse the flight to the suburbs. There is only one department store, if you can call it that, Neiman Marcus, left here. A ten-screen cinema in the West End historic district, the first theater to open in more than 20 years, closed in 2000. There has been no full-size bookstore downtown for ten years.

"After office hours, the central city offers more creepiness than charm," opines *D Magazine*. In "the car-centric downtown, only

Neiman Marcus' flagship survives among the empty, burglar-barred storefronts and the facade of long-gone banks," declares the *Dallas Observer*. "We're a poster child of a bad downtown," observes the Central Dallas Association.

In 1990, the U.S. census listed only 478 housing units within a one-mile (or 1.6 kilometer) radius of downtown. Ten years later it placed that number at 10,000, while several thousand additional units were still to be built. Compared with most of the world's cities of comparable size, that is still an amazingly small number of downtown residents.

The unfortunates living downtown must drive to McKinney and Lemmon Avenues uptown, where an Albertson's supermarket is the only major grocery store near downtown. But don't worry, you will still be able to spend to your heart's desire. There are supposedly more shopping centers per capita in Dallas than in any other American city. It is just that they have all gone to the suburbs.

"Downtown Dallas remains a stark, abstract place, far more appealing from a distance than up close," notes the *Dallas Morning News*. "In its fascination with big fixes it has neglected the small, everyday ones that make downtowns livable: parks, trees, walkable streets, places to buy a good baguette or a $3 shine."

Adds the *Dallas Observer*: "Downtown is being developed entirely for rich people. The yuppie loft thing in the old buildings, which assumes downtown will be vibrant once it had been taken over entirely by infertile cappuccino-heads, was launched on the back of a $25 million subsidy with money hijacked from poor neighborhoods." The weekly claims that "downtown owes poor people money."

Downtown Dallas has some 2,500 businesses, including some of the largest Metroplex banks and accounting firms. It also has much more office space that it knows what to do with it. About 125,000 people work in downtown Dallas, and no fewer than 6 percent of them live in Fort Worth. Twenty percent of downtown workers earn more than $100,000 a year. More than a half of all downtown workers are Caucasians, almost a third are African-Americans, and 10 percent are Hispanic.

Things have hardly changed since 1964, when a former *Dallas Morning News* reporter wrote about downtown in a book on the Kennedy assassination:

"Almost no one lives there. By day it is a hustling salesman city of several hundred thousand. They stream in from the north, the west, the east and the south, between eight and nine in the morning, and they stream out again between five and six in the evening. By six o'clock in the evening the downtown area changes its character completely. The clubs and restaurants which were bustling at noon are almost empty."

Thirty-five years later, city planner Antonio di Mambro goes a step further: "The center of Dallas suffers from arrested development, empty

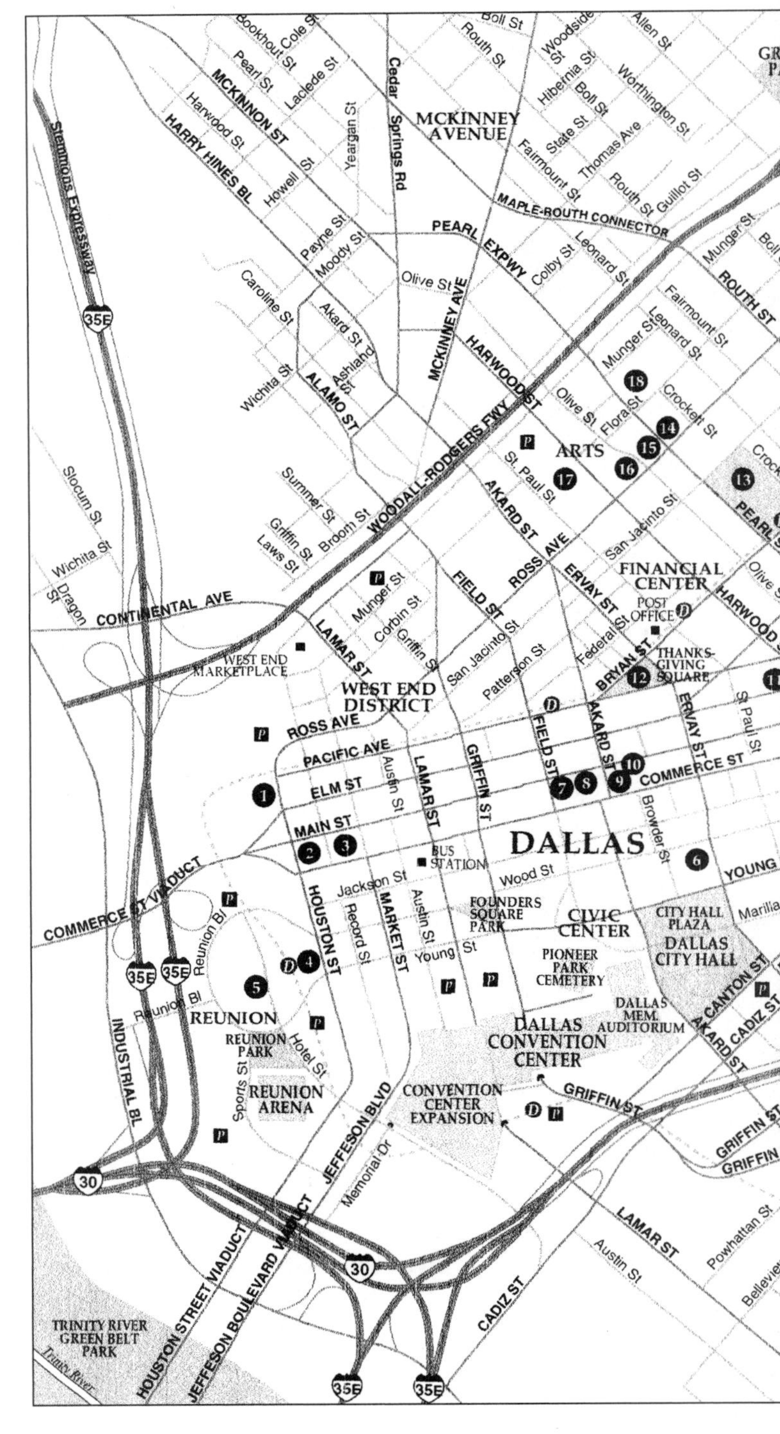

DALLAS
MCKINNEY AVENUE
ARTS
FINANCIAL CENTER
WEST END DISTRICT
WEST END MARKETPLACE
POST OFFICE
THANKS-GIVING SQUARE
BUS STATION
FOUNDERS SQUARE PARK
CIVIC CENTER
CITY HALL PLAZA
DALLAS CITY HALL
PIONEER PARK CEMETERY
DALLAS MEM. AUDITORIUM
DALLAS CONVENTION CENTER
CONVENTION CENTER EXPANSION
REUNION
REUNION PARK
REUNION ARENA
TRINITY RIVER GREEN BELT PARK
Trinity River
Stemmons Expressway
HARRY HINES BL
MCKINNON ST
Cedar Springs Rd
PEARL EXPWY
MAPLE-ROUTH CONNECTOR
MCKINNEY AVE
HARWOOD ST
WOODALL-RODGERS FWY
CONTINENTAL AVE
ROSS AVE
PACIFIC AVE
ELM ST
MAIN ST
COMMERCE ST
COMMERCE ST VIADUCT
YOUNG ST
HOUSTON ST
MARKET ST
LAMAR ST
GRIFFIN ST
FIELD ST
AKARD ST
ERVAY ST
BRYAN ST
ROUTH ST
PEARL ST
CANTON ST
CADIZ ST
INDUSTRIAL BL
JEFFERSON BLVD
HOUSTON STREET VIADUCT
JEFFERSON BOULEVARD VIADUCT
Memorial Dr
Reunion Bl
Hotel St
Sports St
Record St
Austin St
Jackson St
Wood St
Marilla St
Browder St
Federal St
Patterson St
San Jacinto St
St. Paul St
Olive St
Flora St
Crockett St
Munger St
Leonard St
Fairmount St
Colby St
Boll St
Allen St
Woodside St
Hibernia St
State St
Thomas Ave
Worthington St
Guillot St
Routh St
Cole St
Bookhout St
Pearl St
Laclede St
Harwood St
Howell St
Yeargan St
Payne St
Moody St
Caroline St
Akard St
Ashland St
Alamo St
Wichita St
Slocum St
Dragon St
Summer St
Griffin St
Laws St
Broom St
Corbin St
Powhattan St
Belleview
35E
30

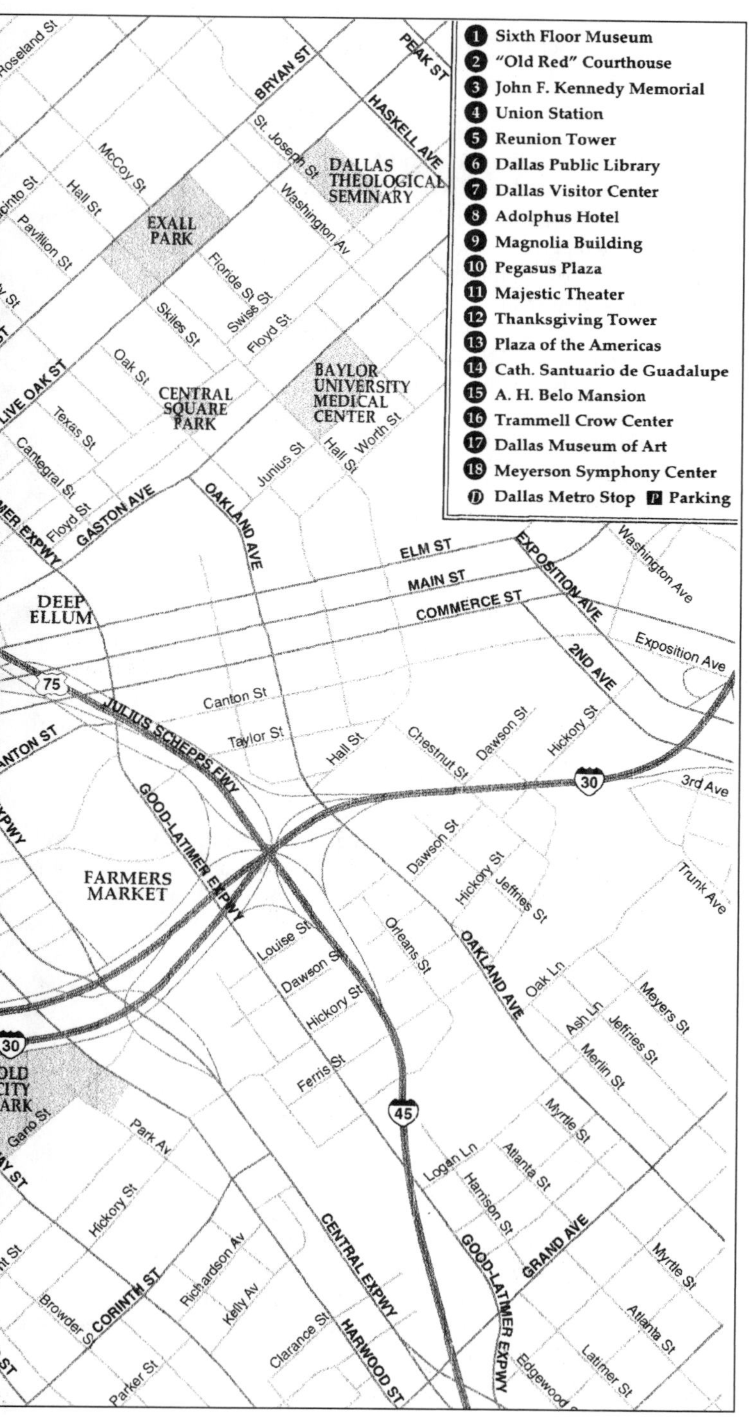

1 Sixth Floor Museum
2 "Old Red" Courthouse
3 John F. Kennedy Memorial
4 Union Station
5 Reunion Tower
6 Dallas Public Library
7 Dallas Visitor Center
8 Adolphus Hotel
9 Magnolia Building
10 Pegasus Plaza
11 Majestic Theater
12 Thanksgiving Tower
13 Plaza of the Americas
14 Cath. Santuario de Guadalupe
15 A. H. Belo Mansion
16 Trammell Crow Center
17 Dallas Museum of Art
18 Meyerson Symphony Center
D Dallas Metro Stop
P Parking
Roseland St
BRYAN ST
PEAK ST
HASKELL AVE
St. Joseph St
DALLAS THEOLOGICAL SEMINARY
McCoy St
Jacinto St
Hall St
Washington Av
EXALL PARK
Pavillion St
Floride St
Swiss St
Skiles St
Floyd St
Oak St
LIVE OAK ST
BAYLOR UNIVERSITY MEDICAL CENTER
CENTRAL SQUARE PARK
Texas St
Worth St
Hall St
Junius St
Cantegral St
Floyd St
GASTON AVE
OAKLAND AVE
ELM ST
EXPOSITION AVE
Washington Ave
MAIN ST
DEEP ELLUM
COMMERCE ST
Exposition Ave
2ND AVE
75
Canton St
JULIUS SCHEPPS FWY
CANTON ST
Taylor St
Hall St
Chestnut St
Dawson St
Hickory St
30
3rd Ave
GOOD-LATIMER EXPWY
EXPWY
FARMERS MARKET
Dawson St
Hickory St
Jeffries St
Trunk Ave
Orleans St
Louise St
OAKLAND AVE
Dawson St
Oak Ln
Meyers St
Hickory St
Ash Ln
Jeffries St
30
Merlin St
Ferris St
OLD CITY PARK
Gano St
45
Myrtle St
Park Av
Logan Ln
Atlanta St
Harrison St
Hickory St
CENTRAL EXPWY
GRAND AVE
GOOD-LATIMER EXPWY
Myrtle St
Richardson Av
CORINTH ST
Browder St
Kelly Av
Atlanta St
Clarance St
HARWOOD ST
Edgewood
Latimer St
Parker St

streets, an overwhelming number of parking lots, and blight and poverty in many of its surrounding neighborhoods to the east and south. The city was thrown out of balance when its freeway loop was built so close to its center, a process that added massive barriers and scars to an urban fabric that already faced economic obsolescence." He also points to "an increasing number of homeless people" on the downtown streets. "Their numbers range from 3,000 to 6,000, depending on whose estimate is used," observes the *Dallas Morning News*.

Observes *D Magazine*: "We need to spend a billion dollars on downtown alone, another half-billion on parks, and probably as much on our roadways. We need trees by the thousands, parks by the scores."

The Arts District, decades in planning, is a 17-block area covering 61.7 acres (or 25 hectares) and bounded by Woodall Rodgers Freeway, St. Paul Street, Ross Avenue, and Routh Street. It includes the Dallas Museum of Art, the Meyerson Symphony Center, and the Nasher Sculpture Garden. (See individual entries for more details.)

Also part of the Arts District is Annette Strauss Artist Square, the city-owned, open-air, special-event facility named for a former Dallas mayor. And so are the Belo Mansion, Cathedral Santuario de Guadalupe, Crow Collection of Asian Art, Trammell Crow Center with its sculpture garden, and Booker T. Washington High School for the Performing & Visual Arts, where arts are taken seriously. (All are described in more detail elsewhere.)

Still in the planning stage here is the Dallas Center for the Performing Arts, which is to include a 2,400-seat Winspear Opera House, or lyric theater as it is also being called, a separate 800-seat multiform theater, and possibly one other space for smaller music and dance groups. The opera house, which would also host ballets and musicals, might be located on the corner of Routh Street and Ross Avenue. At $250 million, the performing arts center would be the largest cultural monument built in the city for decades.

Adding to the haphazard planning of the district is the Dallas Museum of Natural History that wants to build a $100-million museum designed by architect Frank Gehry, who also drafted the Guggenheim Museum in Bilbao, Spain, prompting one local critic to ask through *D Magazine*:

"When will someone figure out that buildings are supposed to interact, that human beings are supposed to walk from one to another, and that in an arts district, encouraging people to wander around is more important than encouraging some famous architect to express himself?"

West End Historic District (Internet www.dallaswestend.org), lies on the northwestern edge of downtown, within walking distance of Dealey Plaza, where President Kennedy was assassinated. Deep Ellum is eastward and at the opposite end of downtown, and Fair Park still farther east.

Formerly a warehouse area dating back to 1846, the 55-acre West End Historic District, which encompasses some 36 blocks, is now primarily an entertainment area that boasts more than 40 restaurants and clubs. (Photo by Yves Gerem)

All three are accessible by bus. West End consists of restored red-brick warehouses, the site of an 1841 settlement, where some 80 stores and 50 restaurants are located.

In the 1870s, this was a red-light district known as Frogtown, named after thousands of croaking bullfrogs that came out of the Trinity River at night about the time that prostitutes began catering to the working men. By World War I, Frogtown was transformed from a residential area to a warehouse and commercial district. When the automobile replaced the railroad, the West End declined, as did similar areas nationwide in the 1950s and 1960s.

The indoor MarketPlace, at 603 Munger Ave., also a former warehouse, is now an arcade with numerous gift shops and food establishments.

Deep Ellum (a corruption of the word Elm, after Elm Street), located east of downtown, is bounded by Elm Street on the north and Canton Street on the south. A railroad hub with a depot in the 1860s, it was settled by African-Americans after the Civil War, and became a hotbed of blues music in the 1920s. Such blues greats as Blind Lemon Jefferson and his sidekick Huddie "Leadbelly" Ledbetter, as well as Sam "Lightnin'" Hopkins, performed here for small change.

"In the 1870s, soon after the railroads came, the future Deep Ellum was a ragtag collection of pastures, cornfields, cattle and hog pens, restaurants, lodging houses and saloons," write A. B. Govenar and J. F. Brakefield in their 1998 book, titled *Deep Ellum and Central Track*. "Cowboys whooped and fired their pistols as they rode up and down the unpaved streets—sometimes right into the saloons." Nearby, a Freedmantown was founded by freed slaves.

Robert S. Munger (1854-1923), the Texas-born inventor of a new cotton gin, built his first factory to manufacture that new gin in Deep Ellum in 1884. One of Henry Ford's regional assembly plants to supplement the manufacture of Model-Ts was erected here. More than 94,000 Jeeps were made at the plant during the Second World War.

By the thirties, the area accommodated small businesses, light industry, and dry-goods stores. Almost two dozen nightclubs, cafes, and domino parlors operated here at one time, but the district declined in the late 1940s and 1950s. The new elevation of Central Expressway bisected Deep Ellum in 1969 and eliminated the 2400 block of Elm Street, which once was central to the community.

The former warehouse area evolved in the early 1980s into the host of a variety of lively avant-garde nightclubs, restaurants, galleries, and shops that are concentrated in a 20-block area. (For more details, visit the Web site www.ondaweb.com/deep_ellum, or www.deepellumtx.com.) Watch for panhandling by the homeless, which was outlawed in 2003, and car break-ins.

"But Deep Ellum is not like [Fort Worth's] Sundance Square, or many entertainment districts in Dallas such as the West End, the West Village or even Greenville Avenue," observes the *News*. "It has always had more of an 'edge' that attracts young people."

Local artists will also be found here, although only an Alamo City-born writer for the *San Antonio Express-News* would call Deep Ellum "Dallas' equivalent of New Orleans' French Quarter."

In downtown Dallas you can get around by DART's trolley buses #706, which run Mon-Fri, 6 AM-7:55 PM, as well as DART Light Rail. (For details, please see the TRANSPORTATION chapter.)

Fair Park, a 277-acre (or 112-hectare) Art Deco cultural and entertainment complex, two miles (or 3.2 kilometers) east of downtown, near the Interstate Highway 30, is the largest historical landmark in Texas. It is now home to museums of science, history, and technology. During the three weeks in September and October, it also hosts the popular yearly State Fair of Texas (see entry), attended by more than three million visitors from all over the world.

Oak Cliff, southwest of downtown, with more than 100 square miles (259 square kilometers) of territory, is Dallas' largest neighborhood. Oak Cliff, as originally chartered, is confined to a 14-square-mile (or 36.2-square-kilometer) area within what is now known as Old Oak Cliff, or North Oak Cliff.

The first settlers to what is now Oak Cliff—Judge William Henry Hord (d. 1901), his family, and his three slaves—arrived three years after Dallas founder John Neely Bryan. Hord's wife, the former Mary Jane Crockett, was the sister of John Crockett (1816-1887), who became the second mayor of Dallas.

In an 1850 referendum, which also included Dallas and Cedar Springs, Oak Cliff missed becoming the seat of the newly created Dallas County by 28 votes. Three years after settling in today's Oak Cliff in 1855 and struggling with meager crops and mismanagement, members of the French, Swiss, and Belgian utopian colony of La Reunion also gave up on it.

In 1880, the railroad came through Hord's Ridge, as the area was initially known. The modern history of Oak Cliff started in 1887, when real estate developers Thomas L. Marsalis and Highland Park founder John S. Armstrong bought 2,000 acres (or 809 hectares) of rocky cliffs and fields in the area, including Hord's Ridge, on the south bank of the Trinity River, and renamed it after the stately oak trees. The city of Oak Cliff was formed in 1891.

They developed the land into an elite residential area and sold more than $60,000 worth of lots during the first two days. Marsalis held some of the remaining lots off the market, hoping for even higher prices. Armstrong disagreed with the practice, dissolved the partnership at once, and relinquished control over the development to Marsalis who added a railway to connect it with downtown Dallas.

Marsalis (b. 1852) was born near New Orleans of Dutch Quakers who had immigrated to Pennsylvania in the 1840s. He came to Dallas in 1872 and opened a wholesale grocery house that did $750,000 worth of business by 1877. Marsalis organized Dallas' first fire company and paved a city street here, using bois d'arc blocks, in 1881. He built waterworks and an electric light plan for his development and set aside 150 acres (or 60.7 hectares) for a park now known as the Dallas Zoo.

Marsalis had invested nearly $1 million in the Oak Cliff venture and went bankrupt during the depression of 1893. He left for New York the following year to get a new start, but died penniless a few years later, although no one seems to know exactly when.

Oak Cliff was incorporated in 1890, when it had a population of 2,470, was annexed by Dallas in 1903 by 18 votes, and has felt like a stepchild ever since.

Until she planned to move to Preston Hollow in 2003, Dallas mayor Laura Miller was perhaps the most identifiable Oak Cliff resident in recent years.

South of the Interstate Highway 20, also known as Lyndon B. Johnson Freeway, **Duncanville** (pop. 36,000), **DeSoto** (pop. 38,000), **Lancaster** (pop. 26,000), and **Seagoville** (pop. 11,000) form a ring around Dallas' southern edge.

The land on which Duncanville lies originally belonged to the Peters Colony. The settlement began when Crawford Tres arrived from Illinois in 1845 and purchased several thousand acres (404 hectares) in the area. Duncanville incorporated a 225-acre (or 91-hectare) city in 1947 and is now 57 percent white and 25 percent African-American.

DeSoto, founded in the 1840s and incorporated in 1949, is located 12 miles (or 19 kilometers) south of Dallas on Interstate 35. The city's population is 45 percent white and 45 percent African-American.

Located 14 miles (or 22.5 kilometers) south of Dallas, Lancaster was named after one of the founder's birthplace in Kentucky, and incorporated in 1887. A Confederate gun factory was located on West Main Street in Lancaster during the Civil War and torn down in 1906. Colonel John M. Crockett, Dallas mayor in 1857 and Texas lieutenant governor in 1861, was the plant superintendent.

On April 25, 1994, a powerful tornado skipped across north Texas and left behind a "six-mile [or 9.7-kilometer] stretch of utter destruction" in the heart of old Lancaster. It flattened more than 200 homes and 30 businesses. Three people died and at least 20 were injured. Lancaster's population was 30 percent African-American in 1990 and is now 53 percent black, according to the U.S. Census Bureau.

Seagoville, which measures 16.2 square miles (or 42 square kilometers) and was incorporated in 1926, is located 15 miles (or 24 kilometers) southeast of downtown Dallas. It was founded by settler T. K. Seago, who built a general store there.

West of DeSoto and south of Duncanville lies the town of **Cedar Hill** whose population almost doubled between 1990 and 2000, to 32,000, 51 percent Caucasian and 12 percent African-American. The black population increased by 280 percent.

DALLAS: MARKET CENTER—LOVE FIELD AIRPORT—OAK LAWN—UPTOWN & MCKINNEY AVENUE—NEAR-EAST DALLAS & GREENVILLE AVENUE

Dallas Market Center, a complex of buildings developed between 1957 and 1999, is the world's largest wholesale trade mart, conducting 50 markets annually for 200,000 professional buyers. Covering more than 100 acres (or 40 hectares), it is located just north of downtown Dallas on Interstate Highway 35 East, locally also known as Stemmons

Freeway. The Center includes the Market Hall, World Trade Center, Trade Mart, and International Floral Design Center. The International Apparel Mart closed in 2004.

Dallas Market Center stands on the land developed by the father-and-son team of Leslie and John Stemmons who had moved the Trinity River about a mile (or 1.6 kilometers) to the west and transformed the nearly worthless 10,000 acres (or 4,047 hectares) north and west of downtown, subject to devastating floods, into the business corridor with a ten-lane freeway that today provides 23 percent of the city's tax revenue.

Infomart, located on the other side of Stemmons Freeway, is an office automation center.

Dallas Love Field Airport was the city's first commercial air facility. This 1,300-acre (or 526-hectare) airfield opened in 1914 as a U.S. Army aviation training center and was purchased by the city in 1928. With 12,000 employees, and once one of the largest airlines in the world, the Dallas-based Braniff Airlines moved its administrative headquarters from Oklahoma to Love Field in 1942.

Serving more than seven million passengers a year, Love Field is one of the 50 largest airports in the United States and is located within the city limits.

Oak Lawn, just northwest from downtown, stretches roughly east of Harry Hines Boulevard, west of Central Expressway, and south of Highland Park. Oak Lawn now claims more than 55,000 residents, about 40 percent of them Hispanics.

"The original Oak Lawn was carved out of the 1,000 acres [or 404 hectares] of farmland homesteaded by Obadiah W. Knight during the days of the Republic of Texas," wrote the Dallas-born historian Sam Acheson. It was so named in the early 1870s after the tree that predominated here and located one and a half miles (or 2.4 kilometers) north of the city limits.

Businessman and legislator Oliver P. Bowser (1842-1915) and Capt. William Hughes Lemmon (1840-1893) acquired 1,500 acres (or 607 hectares) of farmland here and developed parts of Oak Lawn.

Born in Polk County, Missouri, Lemmon was a schoolteacher and helped organize a Confederate Army company. After the war, he teamed with Bowser to open a hardware and farm implements business in Dallas. In 1887, the partners sold the business and bought the land for two residential subdivisions.

Before 1885, this area had a handful of settlements, mostly located around natural springs. One such habitat was Cedar Springs, which barely numbered 100 people, if that many, most of whom were related to Dr. John Cole (1795-1850) and his family who arrived here from Arkansas in 1843.

Cole was a Peters Colony settler who constructed a general store and established what is believed to have been the first medical practice in Dallas. His property was about three miles (or almost five kilometers) north of John Neely Bryan's trading post on the Trinity River.

Oak Lawn was one of the city's first suburbs along the old Cedar Springs Road. In the 1890s, it boasted some of Dallas' most elegant homes, but only until the 1920s, when Turtle Creek remained the sole address of distinction.

To the consternation of some of the area's longtime residents, Oak Lawn as they knew it even in the 1990s is disappearing, overwhelmed by developers who only seem to care about the profits on still another condominium. Even lifelong residents of the area might not recognize entire blocks in Oak Lawn.

Once a peaceful suburb with a few restaurants and bars, it has over the years transformed into rows of inexpensive apartments and a meeting place of choice for Dallas homosexuals, with some establishments on Cedar Springs Road, near Oak Lawn Avenue, catering almost exclusively to clientele of such persuasion.

Uptown is a 125-year-old neighborhood bounded by Woodall Rodgers Freeway, Central Expressway, East Lemmon Avenue, and the Katy (Missouri-Kansas-Texas) railroad tracks that run along Turtle Creek Boulevard, resembling perhaps the Upper West Side of New York City. The former MKT railroad tracks are now a three-mile (or five-kilometer) walking, jogging, and bicycling Katy Trail that stretches from Knox Street to Reverchon Park. It will eventually be expanded to run through the Victory development downtown that includes the American Airlines Center (see entry).

Uptown was an area first developed as vineyards and orchards about 150 years ago. Its southeastern edge was known as Freedmantown where many freed slaves settled after emancipation.

In the 1880s this became one of the most affluent areas, until the 1920s, when automobiles allowed the well-to-do families to move away from downtown. Today it again teems with new apartments and town homes, adding a residential flavor to an area already popular for its restaurants, art galleries, and antique shops.

Near-East Dallas occupies a rather large area east of North Central Expressway, practically from Deep Ellum downtown to about East Mockingbird Lane, which once delineated the northern boundary of Dallas.

Many of the almost 1,000 Tudor-style 1920s homes on the so-called M Streets, south of Mockingbird, have doubled in price in less than a decade because their residents could be downtown in a matter of minutes. The M streets, an area whose roads start mostly with the letter M, have recently also become a battleground for those wishing to preserve the older homes.

There is also the **Old East Dallas,** starting north of Deep Ellum and including Swiss Avenue. This was one of Dallas' earliest neighborhoods settled in the 1850s by Europeans who had seen advertisements for free land in the Republic of Texas and wanted to escape from Napoleon. It became an area inhabited by doctors and lawyers whose grandest homes were built on Swiss and Gaston Avenues.

East Dallas was an independent municipality from 1882 to 1889 and at its peak measured 1,429 acres (or 578 hectares), an area that was larger than Dallas. By 1890, when the two merged, East Dallas had about 6,000 inhabitants and its own city hall building that also housed a school, which stood about where today's Baylor Hospital is located.

The State Fair originated in the city of East Dallas. Former Confederate army officer, banker, and major landowner William Henry Gaston and Col. Christopher Columbus Slaughter were perhaps its best-known residents.

An area west of White Rock Lake—a 1911 scenic, man-made water supply reservoir along White Rock Creek—also in east Dallas is known as **Lakewood,** where many wealthy Dallasites live. The Lakewood neighborhood includes the Swiss Avenue historical district, which encompasses eight blocks of mansions built in the early twentieth century.

Greenville Avenue, Upper and Lower, runs north from Ross Avenue, on the northern edge of downtown, through near-east Dallas and northeastward into the city of Richardson. It boasts many restaurants, clubs, and avant-garde shops.

This avenue is named after the original highway from Dallas to the town of Greenville, which is located northeast of Dallas.

Lower Greenville is an old commercial strip, one of the first shopping areas outside of downtown, that stretches up to Mockingbird Lane, where it becomes Upper Greenville. It still has some of the atmosphere of the 1920s. It also has a lot of nightclubs and many residents up in arms over its noise, litter, and parking problems.

Upper Greenville is newer and more expensive, running through Old Town shopping center where East Lovers Lane intersects it. There are restaurants and nightclubs here, too, and singles bars. The Lower Greenville is more laid back and funkier, the Upper sprinkled with more young professionals.

The cities of **Garland** (pop. 220,000) and **Mesquite** (pop. 130,000) are two major suburbs, still farther to the east.

Garland (Internet www.ci.garland.tx.us) is located 17 miles (or 27.3 kilometers) northeast of downtown Dallas. It was named for President Grover Cleveland's attorney general, Augustus Hill Garland (1832-1899), in 1887, although settlers began arriving here in the 1850s.

Garland, once U.S. senator and governor of Arkansas, apparently never set foot in the town that numbered 478 people in 1890.

The original Duck Creek was bypassed by the Santa Fe Railroad in 1886, when a village of Embree grew up near the depot. The post office was moved between the two towns and its new location named Garland. On Mother's Day in 1927, a tornado wrecked several dozen houses and killed 15 people in the town of 1,500.

With its 57.3-square-mile (or 148-square-kilometer) area and a population well beyond 200,000, Garland is a large Dallas suburb, the tenth largest Texas city, and one of the 100 largest in the United States. The town only had 478 residents in 1890. Garland, which incorporated in 1891, has some 875 hotel rooms and two hospitals with more than 300 beds.

Garland's population is 54 percent white, 26 percent Hispanic, and 20 percent foreign born. More than 17 percent of its population does not speak English "very well," according to the U.S. Census Bureau.

With a median household income of $49,156—beating Dallas' by almost $11,500—Garland also has less than half of Big D's percentage of those living in poverty, 8.9 percent compared with 17.8 percent in Dallas.

Garland has 69 public parks with a total of 2,000 acres (or 809 hectares) and 20 miles (or 32 kilometers) of trails. The median age is almost 32 years. An average Garland home sells for more than $115,000, with about 66 percent occupied by owners. With almost 50,000 students in 62 schools, the city has the 14th largest school district in Texas

In **Mesquite** (Internet www.cityofmesquite.com) you can pay traffic tickets and property taxes, report code violations and crimes to police, and search an animal shelter database through this Web site.

The city was established in 1873 by an engineer for the Texas & Pacific Railway between Dallas and Garland. It was probably named after an abundance of mesquite trees. In the mid-1870s, the town had a saloon, a blacksmith shop, the post office, and four homes.

Mesquite had 135 residents in 1890 and 270 in 1900. In the spring of 1878, the train robber Sam Bass held up a Texas & Pacific train here, but took just $152, while overlooking a hidden shipment of $300,000.

Located about 14 miles (or 22.5 kilometers) east of Dallas, it ranked as one of the safer cities in the United States in a survey by *Money* magazine. The median age of residents is 32 years.

The city has more than 1,000 hotel rooms, 60 baseball fields, 1,340 acres (or 542 hectares) of parks, 30 tennis courts, and 320 hospital beds. Town East Mall (see entry), one of the area's largest, is located here.

According to the U.S. Census Bureau, 66 percent of Mesquite's population is white and 16 percent Hispanic. (Read more about its famously popular Mesquite Championship Rodeo in the SIGHTS & ATTRACTIONS chapter.)

East of Mesquite lies the town of **Sunnyvale** (pop. 3,000), which is located about 16 miles (or 25.7 kilometers) east of downtown Dallas and just west of Lake Ray Hubbard.

Almost 90 percent of its residents are Caucasians, with 5 percent of Asian descent, and 4 percent Hispanics. More than three-quarters of its residents are married, and almost 40 percent have children. Sunnyvale's elementary school has a top rating from the Texas Education Agency.

The median age is just shy of 41 years. The average home sells for more than $200,000, and about 94 percent of homes are occupied by owners.

PARK CITIES & SOUTHERN METHODIST UNIVERSITY—HIGHLAND PARK VILLAGE & NORTHPARK SHOPPING CENTERS

Consisting of **Highland Park** (pop. 9,000), directly north of downtown, and **University Park** (pop. 24,000), connected to its northern border, the Park Cities are arguably the most affluent towns in north Texas and Dallas' equivalent of Beverly Hills, California. A median resale home here sold for more than $500,000 in 2002. Both park cities are continuously being listed among the top residential communities in Texas and even the United States.

The per capita income in Highland Park (Internet www.hptx.org) was pegged at $97,247 among the 3,600 households by the 2000 U.S. Census Bureau survey. In University Park, where 8,000 households reside, the per capita income was $63,414.

In contrast, California's Rancho Santa Fe, the wealthiest such community in the United States, claimed a per capita income of $113,132 for its 1,200 households. Dallas, incidentally, claims a per capita income of $22,183 and a median household income of $37,678.

John Armstrong, the founder of Highland Park, was born in Memphis, Tennessee, and was taken to Kentucky as a child during the Civil War. In 1906, he bought 1,326 acres (or 536 hectares) of land north of the Dallas city limits, which his family developed as Highland Park. Today, *Texas Highways* magazine calls it "a tiny incorporated island of opulence."

In 1913, Highland Park wanted to join the city of Dallas, but was rebuffed. The 2.2-square mile (or 5.7-square-kilometer) residential enclave's property was bought in 1889 for about $500,000. One among the many well-known Highland Park residents is the son of the former British Prime Minister Margaret Thatcher.

The 3.7-square-mile (or 9.5-square-kilometer) University Park began as mostly dwellings for professors after Armstrong's widow donated 100 acres (or 40 hectares) on which Southern Methodist University was to be built. William Walter Caruth Sr. also gave a large parcel of land for the university. When both Dallas and Highland Park refused to annex the area, University Park, which incorporated in 1924, became an independent town, now coveted as an exclusive residential address.

In 2003, University Park (Internet www.uptexas.org) was the only debt-free city in Texas with a population of 20,000 to 30,000.

University Park's media age is under 33, in part at least because of the SMU campus, while Highland Park's is 42. More than 94 percent of residents in both are Caucasian. While about 55 percent of University Park residents are married, and 40 percent have minor children, fewer than 35 percent in Highland Park have families with young children.

Highland Park and University Park are five to six miles (or eight to 9.7 kilometers) from downtown. Million-dollar homes are strewn throughout their six-square-mile (or 15.5-square-kilometer) area, where the median household income is $150,000 a year, and the public schools are among the most desirable in the state. Property tax rates in University Park have been reduced for eight straight years to $0.33999 per $100 in 2002, and for three consecutive years in Highland Park to $0.229 per $100.

Crime incidence is relatively low: Highland Park, with 52 police officers, had a total of 294 crimes—including three robberies and four aggravated assaults—in 2002. University Park, which has 21 officers, had a total of 612 crimes, including 14 robberies and seven aggravated assaults.

But do not rely on statistics alone. The author was robbed at shotgunpoint at a University Park condominium carport, across the street from the SMU tennis courts, at 6:15 AM, while cars drove by on Dublin Street nearby. The University Park police department gingerly listed it in a local newspaper as a small-time theft.

The **Highland Park Village** mall, a collection of elegant shops, restaurants, and cinemas—which a local real estate tycoon snapped up for a paltry $5 million in 1975 and now charges among the highest retail rents in the Metroplex—is located in Highland Park.

Designed by architects Marion F. Fooshee (1888-1956) of Weatherford and James B. Cheek (1895-1970) of Hillsboro, both of Texas, the Village was completed in the 1930s and is believed to be the first self-contained shopping center in the nation. It is the closest thing Highland Park has that could be considered a downtown.

The **NorthPark,** an even larger mall, is situated just northeast of University Park.

FAR NORTH DALLAS & GALLERIA SHOPPING CENTER—THE METROCREST

The **Far North Dallas** is a somewhat difficult-to-pin-down large expanse of the city still farther north of West Northwest Highway, from Love Field Airport on the east to the accursed North Central Expressway (so named because of its probability to ensnare you in a traffic accident), up to and beyond Lyndon B. Johnson Freeway (also known as Interstate Highway 635), a three-quarter loop that encircles much of Dallas.

The median price of an existing home in far north Dallas stands at well over $225,000.

The **Galleria,** located at LBJ Freeway and Dallas North Tollway, is perhaps the most spectacular north Texas shopping center. You may have shopped in London or Paris, New York or Sydney, but you probably have not seen many malls like the Galleria.

In 1842, Methodist preacher Isaac B. Webb came from Tennessee and settled down in what is today **Farmers Branch** (pop. 30,000), located roughly between Lyndon B. Johnson Freeway, Interstate Highway 35, and the Dallas North Tollway. Webb Chapel Road is named after him. By the following year, there were already 21 settlers in this area, which is the birthplace of Dallas County.

Today, slightly more than one-quarter of all residents are foreign-born, and the U.S. Census Bureau claims that almost 22 percent of all residents do not speak English "very well." The first county school opened in Farmers Branch. The U.S. Postal Service recognizes addresses in the Farmers Branch city limits as both Farmers Branch and Dallas.

More than 50 of the Fortune 500 companies have offices in Farmers Branch, which in 1946 only had 800 residents. The town, located 14 miles (or 22.5 kilometers) northwest of downtown Dallas, has some 400 first-class and 950 deluxe accommodations.

Nearly 57 percent of its population is white and another 37 percent Hispanic. The chamber of commerce claims there are 2,600 companies in Farmers Branch, but in spite of its name, not one single farmer in its 12.5 square miles (or 32 square kilometers).

A 65,000-square-foot (or 6,038-square-meter) former church of televangelist Robert Tilton, bought by Farmers Branch for $6.1 million has been converted into a convention and conference center, on the northbound service road of Interstate 35 East, south of Valley View Lane, at an additional cost of $6 million. Its auditorium seats about 3,300.

Addison (Internet www.addisontexas.net). In addition to Farmers Branch, **Addison** (pop. 15,000) and **Carrollton** (pop. 115,000) form the rest of what is locally known as the Metrocrest because the three communities sit geographically in the crest of the Dallas metropolitan area. Farmers Branch and Addison are located in the two-million-population Dallas County, Carrollton in Dallas and Denton Counties.

The town of Addison is located about 14 miles (or 22.5 kilometers) north of downtown Dallas and situated on a 4.4-square-mile (or 11-square-kilometer) area that was once part of the Peters Colony. It was settled as early as 1846, but not so named until 1902 because until then it was just a collection of farms. The village, named after Addison Robertson, its first postmaster, was established in the 1880s when the St. Louis Southwestern Railroad arrived.

The town has grown some 44 percent since 1995. The median age of an Addison resident is less than 32 years. An average home here costs about $250,000, but only about 20 percent of them are occupied by their owners. Property taxes are among the highest in the area.

Cavanaugh Flight Museum and WaterTower Theatre (see entries) are located here. Addison boasts what is probably the largest concentration of restaurants in the Metroplex, about 150, from the continental Addison Café to Sambuca jazz club, from Mi Piaci to Chamberlain's steakhouse. Belt Line Road in Addison is referred to as Restaurant Row.

There are 21 hotels in Addison with more than 1,000 first-class and 2,000 deluxe accommodations. The town has eight public parks.

Carrollton (Internet www.cityofcarrollton). Carrollton's beginnings go back to 1843, when the first family arrived, and until 1913 the settlement was called Peters Colony. The city is just minutes away from Lake Lewisville and has more than 1,200 acres (or 485 hectares) of parks and playgrounds.

In 1902, two years after railroads came through the area, there were only 13 houses and six stores in what is today the historic Carrollton Square, between Broadway, Fourth, Elm, and West Main Streets. A spring flowed through the center of the square where the gazebo now stands.

The first Carrollton school was started in 1856, and electricity came in 1913, the year when the town was incorporated. Carrollton is situated 14 miles (or 22.5 kilometers) north of downtown Dallas.

Between 1980 and 1990, Carrollton's population doubled, in part because the city is located just north of Dallas, west of the Dallas North Tollway, and ten miles (or 16 kilometers) northeast of Dallas/Fort Worth Airport. The fast-growing city, whose residents' average age is

33 years, measures 36.6 square miles (or 95 square kilometers).

Carrollton's population is 62 percent white, 20 percent Hispanic, and almost 12 percent Asian, the second largest Asian population in the Metroplex, after Richardson. The city's median household income is $62,406 (compared with less than $38,000 in Dallas), with 5.6 percent of its residents living below the poverty line, according to the U.S. Census Bureau.

(For a few of Carrollton's attractions, please see the SIGHTS & ATTRACTIONS chapter.)

Between Carrollton and D/FW Airport lies **Coppell** (pop. 40,000), which is located about 20 miles (or 32 kilometers) northwest of downtown Dallas by car. The city has grown at an annual rate of 9 percent since 1995.

Coppell residents are among the safest in the Metroplex from violent crime. The city also boasts one of the lowest percentages of high school dropouts among north Texas towns and cities, fewer than 3.5 percent.

More than 80 percent of residents are Caucasian, almost 10 percent Asian, and 7 percent Hispanic. More than three-quarters of locals consist of families with minor children. The median household income is about $90,000. Home prices here range from $200,000 to $1 million.

Troy Aikman, a former Dallas Cowboys quarterback, lives on Brock Street in a 4,134-square-foot (or 384-square-meter) home valued at $520,000.

Richardson (Internet www.cor.net). You can pay water bills or court fines and fees, view property taxes, and post lost animals over this Web site.

Some 14 miles (or 22.5 kilometers) northeast of downtown Dallas lies Richardson (pop. 95,000), a thriving bedroom community and, like the Metrocrest, a magnet for high technology companies. Chartered in 1873 and named after E. H. Richardson, who built the railroad from Dallas to Denison, Richardson is now home to more than 600 such technology firms.

Among the first was Texas Instruments, which located its corporate campus at the intersection of U.S. Highway 75 and LBJ Freeway in 1956. It was followed by Collins Radio, an Iowa electronics company that set up shop in Dallas in 1957. Collins was bought by Rockwell International in 1971, and 20 years later that unit was acquired by Alcatel of France. Ericsson of Sweden, Fujitsu of Japan, and Nortel of Canada came in the 1980s and gave the area its name, the Telecom Corridor, registered as an official trademark in 1992.

There are now more than 500 high-technology companies employing an estimated 70,000 persons in this T-shaped, five-mile-long (or eight-kilometer) stretch of Richardson universally known as the

Telecom Corridor. In 2001 alone, following the dot.com bust, the area's 28 biggest high-tech and telecom companies eliminated 26,000 jobs. Ericsson moved its north Texas headquarters to Plano.

The 28.5-square-mile (or 73.8-square kilometer) Richardson has 840 acres (or 340 hectares) of park land in 26 developed parks. An average home sells for more than $160,000, and 64 percent of such homes are owner-occupied. The median age in the city is almost 36 years.

The city consists of 71 percent white residents, 10 percent Hispanic, and more than 12 percent Asian, the largest percentage of Asians in any Metroplex community. Its population is projected to grow to 125,000 by 20025.

Richardson's median household income is about $62,392, compared with $37,678 in Dallas, with 63 percent of Richardsonians owning homes, and 6.3 percent of them living in poverty, compared with 17.8 percent in Dallas.

Visitors to Richardson, too, struggle to find its downtown. Some believe it is the newly built 500-acre (or 202-hectare) mixed-use Galatyn Park Urban Center; others lean toward Main Street, now an industrial area that is to be revitalized following the arrival of DART's light-rail station in 2002.

Richardson has about 1,800 hotel and motel rooms.

The 159-acre (64-hectare) city of **Buckingham,** Dallas County's smallest municipality, is located entirely within the city limits of Richardson. The town was incorporated in 1958 to avoid being annexed by Richardson. It has about 44 families with just over 100 residents. Convenient for some, Buckingham can sell alcohol in a dry Richardson.

Plano (Internet www.discoverplano.com). You can pay utility bills, register for recreation classes, search the city library and suggest titles, and request garage sale permits and building inspections on the city's Web site (www.planotx.org).

Nineteen miles (or 30.5 kilometers) northeast of downtown Dallas, on Interstate Highway 75 (or North Central Expressway), and north of Richardson lies the city of Plano (pop. 235,000). It is part of the fast-growing Collin County, whose population of 400,000 is 81 percent Caucasian and 7 percent Asian. With a median household income of $70,835, it is also the most affluent county in Texas and one among the top two dozen nationwide.

Plano is one of the ten largest cities in Texas. As recently as 1960, Plano, measuring 71.5 square miles (or 185 square kilometers), had only 3,700 residents and in 1970 still only 17,600. By 2001, Plano had already used up 90 percent of its residential land.

Plano was founded by William Foreman in 1846 and named four years later by Kentucky native Dr. Henry Dye who thought the word was Spanish for "flat." Dye wanted to name it after Foreman, but his prominent neighbor would not hear of it. Plano was once listed as one of the safest cities in the United States in a survey by *Money* magazine.

The city's racial composition, according to the U.S. Census Bureau, is 78 percent white and almost 11 percent Asian, the third largest Asian contingent in the Metroplex. Plano's Asian population has almost quadrupled since 1990 to about 23,000, of which 18,000 were born overseas. There were only 841 in 1980.

Fifteen percent of the students in the school district are of Asian heritage, and they are among the top 10 percent who are honor graduates. Few, if any, other American cities have seven cricket fields, like Russell Creek Park in Plano has, attracting Asians who grew up with the game.

The city has a 86,400-square-foot (or 8,027-square-meter) convention center that accommodates up to 3,000. There are more than 3,500 hotel rooms and more than 50 restaurants in Plano. You will find six golf courses, three of them public, more than 80 tennis courts, and 72 parks sprawled over its 3,395 acres (or 1,374 hectares).

For walkers and bikers, there is the two-mile (or 3.2-kilometer) Arbor Hills Nature Preserve hike-and-bike path, south of The Colony, along West Parker Road, and a few miles west of Dallas North Tollway.

Plano has one of the best school districts in the Metroplex, a geographical area that usually includes at least Collin, Dallas, Denton, and Tarrant counties, at other times also Ellis and Kaufman Counties. Plano also has had a reputation for drug use. More than 20 fatal heroin overdoses have taken place here since 1996.

Should you find yourself at Plano's Collin Creek Mall and want to see an interesting block of the historic Plano, drive up to 15th Street, east of the North Central Expressway. The section of this downtown street between Avenues J and K has several antique and gift stores and other shops, and still looks as it may have 50 or more years ago. A DART light-rail station is two blocks away.

Also located nearby is the renovated Haggard Park, named in the memory of N. Kate Haggard after her husband donated $2,000 in 1925 to establish the park. In the late 1800s, the park was a simple tract of land surrounded by houses along 15th and 16th Streets, the Interurban train station, and a handful of cotton and grain mills. Where the bandstand is situated now there once was a spring.

For those who can afford two-story homes with swimming pools and three-car garages, starting at about $250,000 and going up to $6 or $7 million, the western edge of Plano offers zip code 75093, with the Shops at Willowbend (see entry) mall. Located roughly north of President George Bush Turnpike (or State Highway 190) and east of Dallas North Tollway, the area of zip code 75093 includes mostly corporate executives, managers, highly paid professionals, and consultants whose cars of choice are sport utility vehicles.

Plano has a median household income more than double Dallas's $37,678 and less than one-quarter of its 17.8 percent of residents live in poverty. Almost 68 percent of Plano residents are homeowners, as opposed to 40 percent in Dallas, according to the U.S. Census Bureau.

Plano native Lance Armstrong, who has won the Tour de France bicycle race five consecutive times, is probably one of the best-known Plano individuals, although he now lives in Austin, the capital.

The area is also home to such prominent country clubs as Gleneagles and Prestonwood, whose members regularly take vacations in Europe, while their children want to drive Porsches as soon as they can get behind the wheel.

With a daytime population of more than 40,000, Plano's Legacy corporate campus in northwest Plano is bigger than many Texas towns. The 150-acre (or 60.7-hectare), $500-million Legacy Town Center, located at Dallas North Tollway, includes a 400-room Doubletree hotel, a three-building, mid-rise luxury apartment complex, restaurants, and shops.

The 2,660-acre (or 1,076-hectare) Legacy complex is owned by Electronic Data Systems, which has some 10,000 employees in the area. Started in the early 1980s, Legacy is one of the Southwest's largest and most successful campus-style business parks. Only Las Colinas (see listing) in Irving is larger in the Metroplex.

Murphy (pop.5,000), about 28 miles (or 45 kilometers) northeast of downtown Dallas, is situated east of Plano. Measuring 3.8 square miles (or 9.8 square kilometers), it was just a village until the 1950s. In the 1970s, several one- and two-acre (or 0.4- and 0.8-hectare) subdivisions were developed. Almost one-half of all residents are Caucasian, with another 10 percent each African-American and Asian.

The media age of a Murphy resident is about 34 years. The town, which ranks as one of the top education destinations, has grown 130 percent since 1995. Home prices range from $150,000 to $400,000.

Immediately north of Plano, and 27 miles (or 43 kilometers) north of downtown Dallas, lies **Frisco** (pop. 60,000) (Internet www.ci.frisco.tx.us). A once-sleepy farming community, it is now one of the fastest-growing cities in the region that in 1980 only had 3,499 residents, 6,138 in 1990, and 23,050 in 1998.

Once named Lebanon, Frisco changed its name to commemorate the coming of the St. Louis & San Francisco Railway. Frisco's population is projected to top 75,000 by 2005 and to double again by 2010. The median age is about 31 years.

Measuring 70 square miles (or 181 square kilometers), Frisco is divided between Collin and Denton Counties. It is home to Stonebriar Centre Mall (see entry), one of the largest shopping centers in the area, and Centre at Preston Ridge. There are more than 50 restaurants located in and around the mall. Frisco also has 12 public parks.

(For more about the Texas Sculpture Garden, in the Hall Office Park, please see entry in the Art in Public Places section of the VISUAL ARTS chapter.)

Until now, Frisco lacked the employment base found in Richardson's Telecom Corridor, where 90,000 people worked, or Plano's Legacy business park. The city sold its 16-year-old, 202-acre (or 81-hectare) airport in 2002 and planned to replace it with a business development designed for information technology companies, similar to Plano's Legacy.

In 2003, the four-million-square-foot (or 371,600-square-meter) Frisco Square opened, a $600-million project that includes several city buildings, townhouses, one million square feet (or 92,900 square meters) of office space, and 700,000 square feet (or 65,000 square meters) of retail shops.

Frisco's student population, at about 7,200 students in 2001, is expected to grow to about 54,700 by the 2010-2011 school year. In the fall of 2001 alone, nine elementary schools, two middle schools, and one high school opened. The Frisco school district projects that it will need to build 56 new schools by 2010.

And, yes, in a typically American style, Frisco has its own Bar Association, which numbers 32 members.

West of Frisco, wedged in between two arms of Lewisville Lake, lies **Little Elm** (pop. 8,000), about 37 miles (or nearly 60 kilometers) northwest of downtown Dallas. The town has grown 340 percent since 1995, but to the delight of many it only had one traffic light in 2002. With growth came the first fast-food chain, Sonic on FM 720, also that year.

The average home sells for more than $100,000, and 83 percent of such homes are owner-occupied. The median age of Little Elm residents is 28 years.

Retractable Technologies, one of the 175 largest Metroplex public companies, is located here. The company, which did not exist in 1995 and now employs 170 in Little Elm, makes retractable needles for doctors' offices and hospitals.

West of Plano and east of Lewisville Lake lies **The Colony** (pop. 30,000), located almost 29 miles (or nearly 47 kilometers) north of downtown Dallas. It began as a subdivision of affordable homes and duplexes by Fox & Jacobs in 1973, along a lonely stretch of State Highway 121, in an unincorporated area of Denton County. Now, The Colony, which has grown to 15.7 square miles (or 40.6 square kilometers) is the county's fifth-largest city. The 437-restaurant Pizza Inn has its test kitchen and $12-million headquarters located here.

The median age in The Colony is 31 years. Close to 14 percent of the residents are Hispanics and 6 percent are African-Americans. An average home sells for about $130,000.

About five miles (or eight kilometers) northeast of Plano lies **McKinney** (pop. 65,000) (Internet www.mckinneytexas.org). The city boasts the 280-acre (or 113-hectare) Heard Natural Science Museum & Wildlife Sanctuary (972-562-5566, www.heardmuseum.org), which was established in 1967 by Bessie Heard.

Fewer than 30 percent of McKinney's housing units are rentals, one of the smaller percentages in the nation.

DALLAS/FORT WORTH INTERNATIONAL AIRPORT—GRAPEVINE—IRVING & LAS COLINAS

D/FW International Airport, located in the town of Grapevine, northwest of downtown Dallas, lies halfway between Dallas and Fort Worth. Claiming 18,000 acres (or 7,284 hectares), it is larger than New York's island of Manhattan, and is the nation's third busiest airport with nearly 864,000 takeoffs and landings a year.

Some 2,500 daily flights connect D/FW Airport to 200 markets worldwide. Ranked by the number of passengers, D/FW ranks about fifth.

Grapevine (pop. 45,000) (Internet www.ci.grapevine.tx.us), located on Texas Highway 114 and 22 miles (or 35 kilometers) from downtown Dallas, was established in 1844, a year before Texas became part of the United States.

You can visit three vineyards in Grapevine and participate in an annual GrapeFest festival each September. Delaney Vineyards' French-style chateau is a city landmark. "Texas is the Mediterranean of the U.S.," says the Wine Society of Texas president. "The grapes that do well here are the types of grapes grown in Spain, Italy, and Southern France."

The town has about 2,300 deluxe hotel accommodations, a historic downtown, and Grapevine Mills Mall (see listing), which brings in enough income that Grapevine homeowners have had their property decreased five times since the mall opened in 1997.

More than 82 percent of Grapevine residents are Caucasian, and another 12 percent are Hispanic. The median age of residents is 34 years. Almost 60 percent are married, and more than 42 percent are families with children under the age of 18. The city is located in the Grapevine/Colleyville Independent School District. Homes here sell for $100,000 to $200,000.

(For more about Grapevine, please see also Marmac's Fort Worth & Arlington guide.)

Irving (Internet www.ci.irving.tx.us). You can request code enforcement, bid to do business with the city, check for pets at the animal shelter, and request dead animal pickup on this Web site.

About ten miles (or 16 kilometers) northwest of Dallas, centrally located between Dallas and the Dallas/Fort Worth International Airport, lies Irving (pop. 195,000), which grew during the railroad age at the turn of the century. Having bought 80 acres (or 32 hectares) of the land here in 1902, the following year Julius Otto Schulze and Otis Brown drew the town plat on a wagon cloth that hangs today in Irving City Hall.

Some believe the city came to be named Irving after novelist and historian Washington Irving because Mrs. Brown enjoyed his novels and asked her husband to honor the writer.

The town, which voted 27 to 16 to incorporate in 1914, now measures 67.6 square miles (or 175 square kilometers). Around 1922 Irving had a mere 357 inhabitants. Today it even boasts a billionaire, Albert Lee Ueltschi, a Depression-era dairy-farm boy from Franklin County, Kentucky, who made his fortune through Flight Safety International.

Between 1960 and 1990, its population has doubled to make it close to the 100th largest city in the country. It grew by another 40,000 residents in the 1990s and now claims a population that is almost one-half Caucasian and 31 percent Hispanic. The median age is about 30 years.

Irving, with about 60,000 Hispanics, has the largest Spanish-speaking population among the cities outside Dallas, followed by 55,000 in Garland. As a matter of fact, nearly 27 percent of all Irving residents are foreign-born, mostly Mexican-Americans. More than 20 percent do not speak English "very well," according to the U.S. Census Bureau.

Settled in 1850 by slaves whose white owners lived nearby, the Bear Creek area of Irving is believed to be the oldest African-American settlement in Dallas County. By 1900, nine African-American families owned land in Bear Creek, which was annexed by Irving in 1968.

Thirty years later, the Bear Creek Heritage Center opened on the corner of Gilbert and Jackson Streets, just south of Highway 183 and off Belt Line Road. The black history museum contains two of the earliest homes in the area, that of Irving's first black schoolteacher and of an area farmer.

There are 5,400 acres (or 2,185 hectares) of parks, lakes, nature trails, and bike paths in Irving. The city has some 60 hotels with 10,000 rooms, generating more than $180 million in revenue annually—more than any other city in north Texas, except Dallas—and more than 50 restaurants.

About 70 percent of all travelers to Irving come on business trips and 13 percent come for leisure travel. Dallas, on the other hand, which attracts an estimated 13 million visitors annually, has 40 percent coming for business. One of Irving's best-known events is the Byron Nelson Championship, which draws up to 300,000 golf fans spending some $40 million.

Irving is the site of the municipally owned **Texas Stadium,** home of the Dallas Cowboys football team, and **Las Colinas,** a fast-growing and totally planned, privately funded commercial development. In the Metroplex, only Fort Worth's Alliance business park, with 15,000 acres (or 6,070 hectares) surpasses Las Colinas' total acreage.

In the late 1970s, Texas rancher Ben Carpenter found out that the land near the D/FW Airport and around his 6,000-acre (or 2,428-hectare) ranch was to be developed. He built a town now known as Las Colinas (daytime pop. 100,000), a 12,000-acre (or 4,856-hectare) development with an urban center, office buildings, and a few shopping and recreation facilities. His father Ben Carpenter had established a ranch in the area in 1928. More than 2,000 acres (or 809 hectares) of land are still undeveloped.

With its marble office towers and manicured lawns, Las Colinas is an upscale home to more than 1,000 of Irving's 5,000 businesses, including Citigroup, ExxonMobil, General Motors, Hewlett Packard, Kimberly-Clark, and Microsoft.

More than 25,000 residents live in Las Colinas. There are 3,200 single-family homes, with an average selling price of $350,000, and 10,500 multifamily units. In 2002, a 17-story luxury apartment building, the Grand Treviso, opened in the Urban Center. About 250 apartments, ranging from 733 square feet (or 68 square meters) to 3,600 square feet (or 334 square meters) rent for $1,100 to $7,000 a month.

Las Colinas alone boasts 3,700 hotel rooms, including Four Seasons (see entry), and 80 restaurants, including the recent arrival, Japanese-cuisine Benihana, at Whitehall Street and Walnut Hill Lane. But no matter how many hotels it boasts, Las Colinas is as dead as a doornail after 5 PM and on weekends.

You will also find in Las Colinas four 18-hole championship golf courses, three private country clubs, an equestrian center with two polo fields, and ten miles (or 16 kilometers) of hiking and biking trails.

(For more about Las Colinas, please see also entries Las Colinas and the Movie Studios at Las Colinas in the SIGHTS & ATTRACTIONS chapter, entry The MacArthur Park in the SHOPPING chapter, and entry the *Mustangs of Las Colinas* in the VISUAL ARTS section Art in Public Places.)

South of Irving, between Dallas and Arlington, is located the suburban city of **Grand Prairie** (Internet www.ci.grand-prairie.tx.us), with a population of about 135,000, 33 percent of it Hispanic, and a median household income of $47,000.

In 1865, Alexander Deckman settled here and named his little village after himself, but as the land was developed its residents kept saying they lived on a grand prairie, and the name stuck.

In 1997, horse racing came to Grand Prairie with the opening of the **Lone Star Park**. The city has about 1,600 moderate and 135 first-class accommodations. Its population is 48 percent white and 33 percent Hispanic. The median age in Grand Prairie is almost 31 years. An average home sells for more than $100,000, and 62 percent of all homes are owner-occupied.

The white flight seems to continue to the suburbs, farther north and northwest of Dallas. Some of the nation's fastest-growing cities ring Lewisville Lake. One of them is **Colleyville** (pop. 20,000), founded in 1956. It is located in Tarrant County, west of the D/FW Airport and 25 miles (or 40 kilometers) northwest from downtown Dallas. In its 2000 survey, the U.S. Census Bureau found it to be the 12th wealthiest Texas community, just ahead of nearby Southlake.

More than 90 percent Caucasian and 3 percent Asian-American, Colleyville boasts a median household income of more than $120,000, and a median resident age of about 40 years. Although the average price of a home here is more than $330,000, you will have difficulty finding one under $200,000.

More than 85 percent of residents are married, and 50 percent have minor children. The town has a 3 percent high school dropout rate, one of the lowest in north Texas.

Flower Mound (pop. 55,000), or "the Beverly Hills of Dallas' urban sprawl," situated north of D/FW Airport, has almost quadrupled its population since the 1990 census. Once a sleepy cattle and farming town, Flower Mound is still 88 percent white.

Situated 29 miles (or almost 47 kilometers) northwest of Dallas, the city has grown more than 77 percent since 1995. At rush hour, traffic on a twisty, two-lane FM 3040 can grind at an unrelenting snail's pace.

The city has less than 8 percent of renters, one the lowest percentages among the nation's 660 cities with a population of more than 50,000. The remaining 92 percent are homeowners, perhaps the largest such percentage in the Metroplex. It also has one of the largest median household incomes, $95,416, or close to three times that of Dallas. It then comes as no surprise that only 2.5 percent of Flower Mound residents live in poverty.

The median resident age in Flower Mound is 33 years. An average home sells for well over $200,000. Residential property taxes account for about 90 percent of the local property taxes, an imbalance that residents fear will worsen unless commercial growth increases. The city has the distinction of claiming a high school dropout rate of less than

3 percent, one of the best showings among the north Texas cities.

Like so many new Texas cities and towns, Flower Mound, which incorporated in 1961, does not have an official downtown. A developer tried to create a downtown—a series of old-fashioned buildings designed to resemble a downtown—when he built Parker Square in 1991.

A 39-mile (or nearly 63-kilometer) equestrian trail, starting in Flower Mound and running around Grapevine Lake, is scheduled for completion sometime in 2004. Coordinated by the Cross Timbers Equestrian Trails Association, a regional group of horse enthusiasts, it will also span the communities of Northlake, Roanoke, Trophy Club, and Southlake, among the dozen wealthiest communities in Texas, according to a 2000 census bureau survey.

One distinguished Flower Mound resident is Kathy Whitworth (b. 1940), a native of the West Texas town of Monahans, who turned golf professional at 19 and was the first female golfer to earn $1 million. The gold icon holds the record for the most wins—88—on both the men's and the women's U.S. tours.

North of here lies **Denton** (pop. 87,000), a college town that boasts two Miss Americas, Phyllis George in 1971 and Shirley Cothran in 1975, both born and raised here. The city only had 26,000 residents in 1960.

George, now a resident of Lexington, Kentucky, where she was married to former Gov. John Y. Brown, still returns to Denton a couple of times a year "to lie low, to refuel and recharge and refocus." Cothran Barrett, for 46 years a resident of Denton, where she attended North Texas State University and later received a doctorate in education, now lives on a farm near Weatherford, Texas.

Not quite as pretty is the Denton State School for the mentally retarded, where 420 of the 650 residents function at the intellectual level of toddlers, and 550 have speech that is largely unintelligible. There are more than 5,100 such residents in 13 state-run institutions.

Lewisville (pop. 82,000), located north of the D/FW Airport and 24 miles (or more than 38 kilometers) northwest from downtown Dallas, is 70 percent white and 18 percent Hispanic. An average home here costs more than $150,000, but only about one-half are owner-occupied.

Lewisville's median household income in 2000 was $54,771, with 6 percent of its residents living in poverty (compared with 17.8 percent in Dallas), and more than 50 percent of all residents owning homes.

Bordering Lewisville in the northeast is the residential community of **Highland Village** (pop. 13,000), a 30-mile (or 48-kilometer) commute northwest of downtown Dallas. An affluent bedroom community that measures about 5.5 square miles (or 12 square kilometers), it is almost 95 percent Caucasian, although it once boasted an African-

American mayor.

The median age in Highland Village is about 38 years, and more than half of the households have minor children. Fewer than 3 percent become high school dropouts, one of the best such accomplishments in North Texas. Home prices range from $100,000 to $1 million. Fewer than 4 percent of the residents are renters.

MATTERS OF FACT

Here is a list of telephone numbers, addresses, and Web sites that you can use whether you visit Dallas once, are a new resident, or have lived in the city for years.

(These and other facts of interest to you may also be listed in the chapters INTERNATIONAL TRAVELER, NEW RESIDENTS, TRANSPORTATION, etc.)

0—Telephone operator.

(214/469/972) 555-1212—Telephone directory assistance for individual area codes.

311—Dallas' 24-hour non-emergency citizens' service line to handle requests for services, such as broken water mains, icy or flooded streets, or illegal dumping. It is available to Dallas residents only. From outside the city limits, dial (214) 670-5111.

•377 (or •DPS)—A 24-hour Texas Department of Public Safety wireless phone number for motorists to report non-life-threatening situations on roads and highways, such as stranded cars, hazardous road conditions, or suspicious activity at a rest area. This number is operational only for customers of Alltel, Nextel, Cingular Wireless, and Verizon Wireless companies. It is similar to the DPS Roadside Assistance number, (800) 525-5555, to contact a state trooper.

911—Emergency, medical or otherwise.

AirportShuttle—(888) 294-7433. Vans, limousines, and charter busses to D/FW and Love Field airports. Another transportation provider is **SuperShuttle,** (817) 329-2000 metro.

Airports—Dallas/Fort Worth International, (972) 574-8888; Airport Assistance Center, (972) 574-4420; Ground Transportation, (972) 574-5878; Visitor Information, (972) 574-3694; Lost & Found, (972) 574-4454; Emergency Car Service, (817) 283-2121.
Love Field, (214) 670-6080; Lost & Found, 670-6155; Parking Information, 670-7275.

American Airlines Center—2500 Victory Ave.; event information, (214) 665-4200; box office, 665-4797; Mavericks tickets, (214) 747-MAVS; Stars tickets, (214) GO-STARS; Internet www.americanairlinescenter.com.

American Airlines Departures & Arrivals—(817) 267-7756/2222; radio station 1640 AM.

American Automobile Association—24-Hour Emergency Road Service, (214) 528-7481 or (800) AAA-HELP. To join AAA, call (800) 765-0766.

Central district office, 3001 Knox St., Suites 102 and 200, (214) 526-7911 or 526-7911; open Mon-Fri 9AM -6 PM and Sat 9 AM-1 PM.

Other offices at 5445 Belt Line Rd., (214) 526-7911; 1237 Northwest Hwy., Garland, (972) 926-1513; 7200 Independence Pkwy., Plano, (972) 661-3300.

A similar service is provided by the **Exxon Travel Club** through U.S. Auto Club, (800) 833-9966 or (800) 438-3996.

Or try **Oil @ Work,** an on-site vehicle service, (972) 481-1818, Internet www.oilatwork.com, once highlighted by *D Magazine*.

American Cancer Society—8900 Carpenter Fwy., (214) 819-1200, Internet www.cancer.org. It employs 30 locally and has an annual budget of $6 million.

American Express Travel Service—Stolen cards, (800) 992-3404; Member services, (800) 528-4800; Travelers Checks, (800) 221-7282; Travel agencies, (214) 363-0214 or (972) 233-9291.

American Heart Association—7272 Greenville Ave., (800) 242-8721 or (214) 373-6300.

Ambulance—911 for emergencies; (214) 744-4444 for non-emergency calls.

American Red Cross—4800 Harry Hines Blvd., (214) 678-4800, Internet www.redcrossdallas.org. It employs locally more than 100 and spends $8 million annually.

Amtrak—Union Station, 400 South Houston, (800) 872-7245 or (214) 653-1101.

Appraisals—

Central Appraisal District of Collin County, (972) 562-1404, Internet www.collincad.com.

Dallas Central Appraisal District, (214) 631-0910, Internet www.dallascad.org.

Denton Central Appraisal District, (940) 566-0904, Internet www.dentoncad.com.

Ellis County Appraisal District, (972) 937-3552, Internet www.elliscad.org.

Kaufman County Appraisal District, (972) 932-6081, Internet www.kaufmancad.org.

Rockwall County Central Appraisal District, (972) 771-2034, Internet www.taxnetusa.com/rockwall.

Area Codes—214, 469, or 972. See also Telephone & Telegrams in THE INTERNATIONAL VISITOR chapter for more details on when to dial which prefix.

Arthritis Foundation of North Texas—2824 Swiss Ave., (800) 442-6653 or (214) 826-4361, Internet www.arthritis.org.

Attorney General of Texas—Consumer Protection, (800) 621-0508; Child Support, (800) 846-5789.

Automobile Registration License & Title—Dallas County Tax Assessor's Office, Records Building, 500 Elm St., (214) 653-7621/7811. Same number applies for all Metropolitan offices, as well as for property taxes.

Office locations: **Duncanville,** 100 East Wheatland Rd.; **East Dallas,** 3443 St. Francis Ave.; **Farmers Branch,** 2436 Valley View Ln.; **Garland,** 675 West Walnut; **Grand Prairie,** 525 West Hwy. 303, Suite 591; **Irving,** 530 North O'Connor Rd.; **Mesquite,** 210 West Grubb Dr.; **North Dallas,** 10056 Marsh Ln.; **Oak Cliff,** 408 South Beckley Ave.; **Richardson,** 516 Twilight Trail.

Automobile Inspection—Inspections Only, Parker Rd. at Independence Pkwy., (972) 612-4687. A private company, located roughly between North Central Expressway and Dallas North Tollway, providing car inspections only. Its Lewisville shop is on State Hwy. 121.

Baby-Sitting/Caring Hands Sitters—1824 Tracey Circle, Irving, (877) 824-4453 or (972) 259-1184, Internet www.caringhands.net. Claims to have been in business since 1975, but under another name. Sitters go through a screening process that includes face-to-face interviews. Charges about $7 hourly for one child, for a minimum of four hours. There is also a one-time $50 registration fee.

Babysitters of Dallas—(214) 692-1354. Claims to be the oldest agency in business, operating since 1955, but under new management since its previous owner, the well-known Audrey Schneer Festinger, died in mid-2000. Charges about $8 hourly for one child, for a minimum of four hours, but has no registration fee.

Baylor College of Dentistry—3302 Gaston Ave. at Hall St.; Appointments (214) 828-8440 and 828-8464. Open Mon-Fri 8 AM-5 PM. Located next to Baylor Medical Center hospital.

Better Business Bureau—1600 Pacific Ave., Suite 2800, downtown, (214) 220-2000, Internet www.dallas.bbb.org.

Boy Scouts of America—1325 Walnut Hill Ln., (972) 580-2000, Internet www.bsamuseum.org.

Bus & Light Rail—Schedule & Route Information, (214) 979-1111, Internet www.dart.org; Lost & Found, (214) 748-7471; Information for the Mobility Impaired, (214) 828-6800.

Chambers of Commerce—See the Dallas Facts section of the NEW RESIDENTS chapter.

Children's International Summer Village—(214) 521-9755, Internet www.cisv.org. An international nonprofit volunteer organization that runs camps worldwide, including in the Metroplex, for youths ages 11-25 years. It was founded after World War II by a Maine-born psychologist, Dr. Doris Allen (1901-2002).

Children's Medical Center Hospital—1935 Motor St., (214) 456-7000. See also entry in the health section of the NEW RESIDENTS chapter.

City Hall/Dallas—1500 Marilla St., (214) 744-1000. Call 311 for access to city services 24 hours a day, or (214) 670-5111, Internet www.dallascityhall.com. You can schedule and obtain inspections, request street repairs and other services, and download job applications.

Mayor's Office, (214) 670-4054.

City Council Office, (214) 670-4050; City Manager, (214) 670-3302; Cultural Affairs Office (214) 670-4081; Park & Recreation Department General Information, (214) 670-4100; Special Events at City Hall Plaza, (214) 939-2701.

Climate—See Climate & Dress in DALLAS TODAY chapter.

Colleyville City Hall—5400 Bransford Rd., (817) 577-7575, Internet www.colleyville.com.

Collin County—Internet www.co.collin.tx.us. On this Web site, you can register your vehicle and pay property taxes, both at a fee.

Community Helpline—An information and referral service, (214) 379-HELP (or 4357).

Consumer Product Safety Commission—(800) 638-2772, U.S. Government agency.

Convention & Visitors Bureaus—

Dallas Convention & Visitors Bureau, 1201 Elm St., Suite 2000, (214) 571-1000; Visitor Information Center, (214) 571-1300; 24-Hour Events Hotline, (214) 571-1301 or (800) 232-5527, Fax 571-1008, Internet in English, French, German, Japanese, Portuguese, and Spanish, Internet www.dallasconventioncenter.com.

Garland Convention & Visitors Bureau, (972) 205-2749, Internet www.ci.garland.tx.us.

Irving Convention & Visitors Bureau, (800) 2-IRVING, Internet www.irvingtexas.com.

Plano Convention & Visitors Bureau, (972) 422-0296, Internet www.planocvb.com.

Richardson Convention & Visitors Bureau, (972) 234-4141, Internet www.telecomcorridor.com.

Courtesy Patrol—(800) 525-5555 or (214) 320-4444, beeper 512-2726. State courtesy patrol will change a flat tire, help you with gas, help start your vehicle, or call a tow truck when you are stuck on a major road, such as Interstate 20, 35 East, LBJ Freeway, or Central Expressway.

Crime Stopper's Hotline—(800) 252-8477.

Cultural Affairs Office of Dallas—Majestic Theatre, 1925 Elm Street, (214) 670-4081, Internet www.dallasculture.org.

Dallas Arboretum & Botanical Garden—8525 Garland Rd., (214) 327-8263, Internet www.dallasarboretum.org.

Dallas Area Rapid Transit—See entry DART, below.

Dallas Art Dealers Association—5600 West Lovers Ln., (214) 925-9558, Internet www.dallasartdealers.com.

Dallas Central Public Library—1515 Young St., (214) 670-1700, Internet www.dallaslibrary.org. Open Mon-Thu 9 AM-9 PM, Fri-Sat 9 AM-5 PM, Sun 1 PM-5 PM.

Dallas City Hall Service Desk—(214) 670-3011.

Dallas Convention Center—650 South Griffin St. at Akard, (214) 939-2700/2724, Fax 939-2795, Internet www.dallascc.com.

Dallas Convention & Visitors Bureau Information Center—Dallas County Historical Plaza at Houston St., between Main and Commerce Sts., (214) 571-1000/1300; 24-Hour Events Hotline, (800) 232-5527

Dallas County—Pop. 2,219,000, 45 percent Caucasian, 30 percent Hispanic, 20 percent African-American; (214) 653-7011, Internet www.dallascounty.org.

On this Web site, you can register your vehicle, pay traffic citations, and pay property taxes, each at a 3-percent fee.

Dallas County Historical Commission—411 Elm St., (214) 653-7601, Internet www.dallaschc.org.

Dallas County Sheriff—(214) 749-8641.

Dallas Cowboys—Texas Stadium, (972) 579-5000, Internet www.dallascowboys.com.

Dallas Environmental & Health Services—(214) 670-3696.

Dallas/Fort Worth International Airport—(972) 574-8888, Internet www.dfwairport.com.

Dallas Historical Society—Hall of State, Fair Park, (214) 421-4500.

Dallas Independent School District—Administrative Offices, 3700 Ross Ave., (972) 925-3700.

Dallas Love Field Airport—(214) 670-6073, Fax 670-6051, Internet www.dallascityhall.org.

Dallas Market Center—2100 Stemmons Frwy., (214) 655-6100, Internet www.dallasmarketcenter.com.

Dallas Mavericks—American Airlines Center, (214) 373-8000, Internet www.nba.com/maverics or www.dallasmavericks.com.

Dallas Morning News—Customer Service & Delivery; (214) 745-8383; Friday Guide, 977-8400; Metropolitan desk, 977-8456. See also Press, Radio & TV in the DALLAS FACTS section of the NEW RESIDENTS chapter.

Dallas Museum of Art—1717 North Arwood St. at Ross Ave., (214) 922-1200, Internet www.dm-art.org.

Dallas Nature Center—7171 Mountain Creek Pkwy., (972) 296-1955, Internet www.dallasnaturecenter.org.

Dallas Parks & Recreation Dept.—(214) 670-4100, Internet http://www.ci.dallas.tx.us/html.www.ci.dallas.tx.us/html. For hike and bike information, call (214) 670-4039.

Dallas Peace Center—4301 Bryan St., (214) 823-7793, Internet www.dallaspeacecenter.org. Founded by a local Mennonite Church in 1981 and located in a renovated east Dallas warehouse, the center's goal is to maintain peace and justice. Rep. Lon Burnam, Democrat of Fort Worth, is its director.

Dallas Stars—(214) GO-STARS, Internet www.dallasstars.com.

Dallas Visitor 24-Hour Information—(214) 571-1301.

Dallas World Aquarium—1801 North Griffin, (214) 720-2242, Internet www.dwazoo.com.

Dallas Zoo—650 South R.L. Thornton Fwy., (214) 670-5656, Internet www.dallaszoo.com.

DART (Dallas Area Rapid Transit)—Internet www.dart.org; Schedule and route information, (214) 979-1111; Transit Police, 928-6300; HOV Information office, 749-2819; Lost & Found, 749-3810.

Dentists—See Health Care section in the DALLAS FACTS section of the NEW RESIDENTS chapter.

Denton County—Internet www.dentoncounty.com. On this Web site, you can pay your vehicle registration and pay your property taxes, both at a fee.

Department of Public Safety—Call (800) 525-5555 to report a stranded motorist.

Doctors—Call 911 for emergencies, otherwise see Health Care in the DALLAS FACTS section of the NEW RESIDENTS chapter.

Driver's License—Texas Department of Public Safety, (214) 861-2100 for general information, Internet www.txdps.state.tx.us.

Renewals & duplicates only at 1500 Marilla St., at Ervay and Young, Suite 1-B South, in downtown Dallas, (214) 651-1859. Open Mon-Fri 8 AM-5 PM. All locations closed on state and federal holidays.

Testing locations:

Carrollton, 2625 Old Denton Rd. at Trinity Mills, Suite 310, (972) 245-5800. Open Mon-Thu 7 AM-5 PM, Fri 8 AM-5 PM.

Dallas East, 11411 East Northwest Hwy. at Jupiter Rd., Suite 111, (214) 553-0033. Open Mon-Fri 7 AM-5 PM.

Dallas, 721 Wynewood Village, Illinois Ave. at Zang Blvd., (214) 948-7233. Open Mon-Thu 8 AM-6 PM, Fri 8 AM-5 PM.

Garland, 350 West Interstate Hwy. 30 at Belt Line Rd., on east-bound access road, (214) 861-2125. Open Mon-Fri 7 AM-5 PM, Thu 7 AM-6 PM.

Irving, 1003 West Sixth St. at MacArthur Blvd., (972) 253-4171. Open Mon-Thu 7:30 AM-5:30 PM, Fri 8 AM-5 PM. Located two miles (or 3.2 kilometers) south of State Hwy. 183.

Lewisville, 190 North Valley Pkwy. at Main St., (972) 221-8081. Open Mon-Fri 8 AM-5 PM. Located behind the government center.

Plano, 2109 West Parker Rd. at Custer, Suite 224, (972) 867-4221. Open Mon-Wed 7 AM-5 PM, Thu 7 AM-6 PM, Fri 8 AM-5 PM.

Drug Enforcement Administration—(214) 640-0801, U.S. Government agency.

Earle Cabell Building—1100 Commerce St., between Griffin and Field Sts. downtown.

The one-million-square-foot (or 92,900-square-meter) building, completed in 1970, and the adjoining Santa Fe building house 35 government agencies. Nine district judges, four magistrate judges, and their courts are located in the top four floors of the Cabell building, along with a U.S. marshal's office, pre-trial services, and other agencies that support the civil and criminal courts.

Electricity—TXU Electric, (800) 232-9113 or metro, (972) 791-2888.

Ellis County—Internet www.elliscounty.org.

Emergency/Medical or Otherwise—911

Emergency Counseling—

Brighter Tomorrow/Grand Prairie, (972) 263-0506; Child & Family Guidance Center, (214) 351-3490; Contact Counseling & Crisis Line, (972) 233-2233; Crisis & Suicide Center of Dallas, (214) 828-1000; Dallas County Rape Crisis Center, (214) 590-0430; Dallas Police Department Victim Services, (214) 670-4378/3568; The Family Place, (214) 941-1991; Friends of the Family/Denton, (940) 382-7273 or (800) 572-4031; Genesis Women's Shelter, (214) 942-2998; New Beginning Center/Garland, (972) 276-0057; New Tomorrows Women's Shelter/Irving, (972) 438-6785; Victims Outreach, (214) 358-5173; Texas Council on Problem & Compulsive Gambling, (972) 490-9999 or (800) 742-0443.

Fair Park—Administration, (214) 670-8400; 24-Hour English/Spanish Information, (214) 421-9600, Internet www.fairparkdallas.com.

The Family Place—24-hour crisis assistance and counseling for domestic violence victims, (214) 941-1991; Abuser's hot line, (214) 692-8295, Internet www.familyplace.org.

Federal Bureau of Investigation—(214) 720-2200, Internet www.fbi.gov, U.S. Government agency.

Federal Information Center—(800) 688-9889; TDD Hearing Impaired, (800) 326-2996.

Fire—Call 911 for emergencies, other 311. Non-emergency, (214) 670-4319.

Arson Hotline, (214) 670-4597; Fire Hazards, (214) 670-4319; Fire

Reports, (214) 670-4312; Fire Station Tours, (214) 670-5466.

Food and Drug Administration—(214) 253-5200, Internet www.fda.gov. U.S. Government agency.

Foreign Currency Exchange—See section Foreign Currency Exchange at D/FW Airport in the TRANSPORTATION chapter, and Currency Exchange & International Banking section in the INTERNATIONAL VISITORS chapter.

French-American Chamber of Commerce—2665 Villa Creek Dr., Suite 214, (972) 241-0111, e-mail faccdallas@aol.com.

Garland—

Central Library—625 Austin St., (972) 205-2503.
City Council Information—(972) 205-2404.
Convention & Visitors Bureau—(972) 205-2749.
Driver's License—Interstate 30 at Broadway, (214) 861-2000.
Fire Department—(972) 205-2250.
Parks & Recreation Department—634 West Apollo Rd., (972) 205-2750.
Police Department—(972) 205-2018.
TXU Electric & Gas Service/Oncor Group—(214) 741-3750.
Water Department—(972) 205-2673.

Genesis Women's Shelter—24-hour hot line, (214) 942-2998, Internet www.genesisshelter.org.

Golf & Tennis Courses Information—Call individual facility.

Governor's Office—(800) 843-5789.

Greater Dallas Community of Churches—624 North Good Latimer, (214) 824-8680.

Greater Dallas Council on Alcohol & Drug Abuse—(214) 522-8600, Internet www.prc3.org.

Hospital Emergency Rooms—

Baylor University Medical Center Emergency, (214) 820-2501.
Children's Medical Center Emergency, (214) 456-2100.
Las Colinas Medical Center, (972) 969-2000
Medical City Dallas Hospital Emergency, (972) 566-7200.
Methodist Medical Center Emergency, (214) 947-8100.
Parkland Memorial Hospital Emergency, (214) 590-8000.
Presbyterian Hospital of Dallas Emergency, (214) 345-7886.
St. Paul University Hospital Emergency, (214) 879-2790.

Hospitals—See Health Care in the DALLAS FACTS section of the NEW RESIDENTS chapter.

Humane Society—4830 Village Fair Dr., Dallas, (214) 372-9999, Internet www.hsus.org. Open Wed-Sat 9:30 AM-12:30 PM and 2 PM-5 PM. Promotes the protection of animals.

Immunization Information—(214) 670-0519/0505; state, (800) 252-9152.

Immigration and Naturalization Service—(214) 905-5886; forms, (800) 870-3676; U.S. Government agency.

Internal Revenue Service—1100 Commerce St. downtown, (214) 767-1289; U.S. Government agency. Federal tax forms only, (800) 829-3676; Federal tax questions, (800) 829-1040; 24-hour recorded tax help, (800) 829-4477. Has about 2,800 local employees.

Irving—

Convention & Visitors Bureau—1231 Greenway Dr., Suite 1060, (972) 252-7476

Driver's License—(972) 253-4171.

Fire Department—(972) 721-2514.

Irving Arts Center—3333 North MacArthur Blvd., (972) 252-7558.

Las Colinas Medical Center—6800 North MacArthur Blvd., (972) 969-2000, Internet www.lascolinasmedical.com.

Library—(972) 721-2608.

Mayor's Office—(972) 721-2410.

Parks & Recreation Department—(972) 721-2501.

Police Department—(972) 721-2518.

Property Taxes—(972) 721-2591.

TXU Electric Service/Oncor Group—(972) 791-2888.

Water Utilities—(972) 721-2281/2411.

Lawyer Referral Service—Dallas Bar Association, 2101 Ross Ave., downtown, (214) 220-7444, Mon-Fri 8:30 AM-4:30 PM.

League of Women Voters—2720 North Stemmons Frwy., Suite 510, (214) 688-4126, Internet www.lwvdallas.org.

Legal Aid—Legal Services of North Texas, 1515 Main St., (214) 748-1234.

Library—Central Library, 1515 Young St., (214) 670-1400. See also the DALLAS FACTS section of the NEW RESIDENTS chapter.

License Plates & Title Transfers—Dallas County, (972) 231-1459; Collin County, (972) 881-3010.

Local Laws—You must be at least 21 years old to drink in public places in Texas. Liquor stores are open 10 AM-9 PM, and are closed Sundays and some holidays; no alcoholic beverages can lawfully be sold before noon. If driving while intoxicated, you may be subject to a mandatory jail sentence.

Love Field Airport—(214) 670-6073.

Marriage License—Dallas County, (214) 653-7559; Collin County, (972) 881-3025.

Mexican Trade Commission—2777 North Stemmons Frwy., Suite 1622, (214) 688-4095.

Mexico Trade Center—Pinnacle Park, off Interstate 30, Oak Cliff, (469) 385-5648.

Missing Persons Clearinghouse—(800) 346-3242.

Newspapers—see Press, Radio & TV in the DALLAS FACTS section of the NEW RESIDENTS chapter.

Music Hall at Fair Park—Dallas Summer Musicals, 909 First Ave., (214) 421-5678.

North Texas Poison Center—911 or (800) POISON or (800) 764-7661.

Office of International Affairs—Dallas City Hall, (214) 670-3319. Founded in 1970 and now part of World Affairs Council of Dallas, it promotes international business, meets and greets foreign dignitaries, plans trade missions abroad, and maintains Sister City relationships with Brno, Czech Republic; Dijon, France; Monterrey, Mexico; and Riga, Latvia.

Old City Park—1717 Gano St. at Ervay, (214) 421-5141, Internet www.oldcitypark.org.

Parkland Hospital—5201 Harry Hines Blvd., (214) 590-8000; 24-hour emergencies same number; Administration, 590-8006; Poison Center, (800) 764-7661; Rape Crisis & Sexual Abuse Center, (214) 590-0430, Internet www.pmh.org.

Passports-Information, (214) 653-7691; Passport Office, (214) 653-6774.
North Dallas Passport & Marriage License Office, 10056 Marsh Ln., Suite 137, (214) 904-3031.

Peace Corps—207 South Houston St., Suite 527, downtown, (214) 767-5435; American volunteers serving abroad.

Pets—Animal registration, (214) 821-3400; 8414 Forney Rd. animal shelter, (214) 670-7430.

Pharmacies—Please see listings in the INTERNATIONAL VISITORS chapter.

Physician Referral Services—
Children's Medical Center, (214) 456-2770.
Medical City Hospital, (972) 566-6727.
Methodist Hospital, (214) 947-0000; outside Dallas, (800) 727-6131.
Presbyterian Hospital, (800) 477-3729.
St. Paul University Hospital, (214) 879-3099.

Planned Parenthood of North Texas—(214) 987-3228 or (817) 882-1155, Internet www.plannedparenthood.org. There are 25 clinics in 12 counties serving more than 60,000 patients.

Plano—
Convention & Visitors Bureau—(800) 81-PLANO or (972) 422-0296.
Driver's License—(972) 867-4221.
Fire Department—(972) 424-5678.
Independent School District—(972) 519-8100.

Information—(972) 941-7000.
Parks & Recreation Department—(972) 941-7250.
Police Department—(972) 424-5678.
TXU Electricity Service/Oncor Group—(972) 791-2888.
Water, Sewer & Garbage Collection—(972) 964-4150.

Poison Control—(214) 590-5000 or (800) POISON-1.

Police—Emergency 911 for all; non-emergency for Dallas residents, 311. For suburban police and fire non-emergency departments, see Your Safety section in the INTERNATIONAL VISITOR chapter.

Pollen Count—(972) 255-3749.

Population—1,200,000 city, 5.5 million Metroplex, including Fort Worth.

Post Office—General information, 8 AM-4:30 PM weekdays, (972) 393-6700; locations 24 hours a day, seven days a week, (800) 275-8777.

Preservation Dallas—2922 Swiss Ave., (214) 821-3290, Internet www.preservationdallas.org.

Property Tax Offices—see **Automobile Registration License & Title** heading above.

Radio Stations—see Press, Radio & TV in the DALLAS FACTS section of the NEW RESIDENTS chapter.

Reunion Arena—Box office, (214) 800-3089; Event information, (214) 670-1395, Internet www.reunionarena.org.

Richardson—
Citizens Information Services—(972) 238-4260.
City Manager's Office—(972) 238-4209.
Electricity—(972) 791-2888
Fire Services—(972) 238-3940.
Golf—(972) 234-1416.
Library—(972) 238-4000.
Marriage License—(972) 881-3025.
Medical Center—(972) 234-3198.
Municipal Court—(972) 690-3618.
Parks & Recreation—City Hall, Room 208, (972) 238-4250. Open weekdays 8 AM-5 PM. Recorded 24-hour information line, (972) 238-4251.
Police—(972) 238-3800.
Post Office—(972) 235-8353.
School District—(469) 593-0000.
Tax Office—(214) 653-7811.
Water & Sewer Customer Service—(972) 238-4120.

Roadside Assistance—Call (800) 525-5555 to contact a state trooper when you are stranded, are confronted with hazardous road conditions, or have witnessed a suspicious activity at a rest area.

Runaway Hotline—(800) 392-3352.

The Salvation Army—6500 Harry Hines Blvd., (214) 6000, Internet www.salvationarmydallas.org. It employs 230 and has an annual budget of $16 million.

Shopping in Texas—www.shopacrosstexas.com. A Web site that links travelers with shopping venues and visitors bureaus in 70 Texas cities. You can plan a road trip that hits most of the antique hot spots in north Texas, or the key retail centers in the Hill Country.

Six Flags Over Texas—Interstate 30 at Six Flags Dr., Arlington, (817) 530-6000, Internet www.sixflags.com.

Sixth Floor Museum—411 Elm St. at Houston; (214) 747-6660, Internet www.jfk.org.

Social Security Administration—For information and services, or to schedule an appointment, call 7 AM-7 PM, (800) 772-1213; 24-hour information line, (800) 325-0778, Internet www.ssa.gov.

Social Services—United Way of Metropolitan Dallas, 901 Ross Ave., downtown, (214) 978-9000.

Society for the Prevention of Cruelty to Animals—362 South Industrial Blvd., (214) 651-9611, Internet www.spca.org.

Southern Methodist University—Hillcrest Ave., between Mockingbird Ln. and Daniel, (214) 768-2000; Admissions, same number; Events, (214) SMU-ARTS or 768-2787; Meadows Museum, 768-2516, Internet www.smu.edu.

Southfork Ranch—3700 Hogge Rd., Parker, (972) 442-7800, Internet www.southfork.com.

Southlake City Hall—FM 1709 at Carroll Ave., (817) 481-1653, Internet www.ci.southlake.tx.us.

SPCA of Texas—362 South Industrial Blvd., (214) 651-9611 or (972) 562-7387, Internet www.spca.org. It has shelters in Dallas, The Colony, and McKinney.

State Bar of Texas—Call (800) 633-6630, to report illegal or improper solicitation by a lawyer.

State Board of Medical Examiners—To lodge a complaint against a doctor, (800) 201-9353; for physician profiles, Internet www.tsbme.state.tx.us.

State Fair of Texas—September 27-October 20, Fair Park, (214) 565-9931, Internet www.bigtex.com.

Tarrant County—Internet www.tarrantcounty.com.

Teen CONTACT—(972) 233-8336. A Dallas-based crisis hotline for teenagers.

Telephone Directory Assistance—1411 or (214/469/972) 555-1212.

Telephone Operator—0.

Telephone Service—SBC Communications, (800) 464-7928.

Television Stations—See Press, Radio & TV in the DALLAS FACTS section of the NEW RESIDENTS chapter.

Tennis Reservations—See individual center under SPORTS.

Texas Department of Public Safety—10233 East Northwest Hwy., (214) 553-0033, Internet www.txdps.state.tx.us. The latest version of the Texas Drivers Handbook is available on this Web site.

Texas Department of Transportation—24-Hour Road Conditions, (214) 374-4100.

Texas Health Care Information Council—(512) 482-3312, Internet www.thcic.state.tx.us. Texas online access to information for death rates in 25 medical conditions, such as heart attacks and bypass surgery, at most Texas hospitals.

Texas Highway Patrol—Drivers licenses, (214) 861-2000.

Texas Motor Speedway—Interstate 35 West at Highway 114, Fort Worth, (817) 215-8565.

Texas Parks & Wildlife—(800) 792-1112.

Texas Rangers—The Ballpark in Arlington, (817) 273-5100, Internet www.texasrangers.com.

Texas Rangers Law Enforcement—350 West Interstate Hwy. 30, Garland, (214) 861-2000.

Time & Temperature—(214) 844-4444.

Time Zone—Central Standard Time, on Daylight Savings Time, April-October.

Traffic—(214) 374-4100, Internet www.dfw-traffic.dot.state.tx.us.

Traffic Laws—Seat belts and infant seats are required by law. You may turn right on red. Consuming alcohol while driving is illegal.

Traffic Tickets Information—(214) 670-0109 or 747-3800.

Travel Insurance—

Access America, (800) 284-8300, Internet www.worldaccess.com.

Travelex, (888) 457-4602, Internet www.travelexinsurance.com.

Travel Guard, (800) 826-1300, Internet www.travelguard.com.

Universal Travel Protection, (888) 795-1561, Internet www.utravelpro.com.

Trinity Railway Express—(817) 657-0146, Internet www.trinityrailwayexpress.org.

TXU Electric & Gas/Oncor Group—(800) 460-3030 or (972) 791-2888, 24 hours, seven days a week. Oncor Group maintains the transformers and power lines carrying TXU electricity.

U.S. Customs Service—at D/FW International Airport; (972) 574-2131 at Terminal A; (972) 574-2132 at Terminal B; (972) 574-2010 at Terminal E.

U.S. Marshall Service—(214) 767-0836, U.S. Department of Justice agency.

United Way of Dallas—901 Ross Ave., (214) 978-0009, Internet www.unitedwaydallas.org. It employs 80 locally and has an annual budget of $40 million.

Visitors 24-Hour Hotline, Special Events—(214) 746-6679 or http://cityview.com/dallas.

Water Service—City of Dallas Water Department, (214) 651-1441; open weekdays 8 AM-5 PM.

Weather—National Weather Service forecast, (214) 787-1111; Recreation travelers weather, (214) 787-1701. Local forecasts also available from WFAA-TV, at (214) 977-6588.

West End MarketPlace—603 Munger Ave., (214) 748-4801, Internet www.westendmarketplacedallas.com.

Western Union Telegrams & Money Transfer—(800) 325-6000 or (800) 225-5227, Internet www.westernunion.com.

Wildflower Hotline—Texas Department of Transportation, (800) 452-9292. Open daily 8 AM-6 PM. Receives 5,000 calls a day about wildflowers from March through May.

WRR-FM Classical Radio—Fair Park, (214) 670-8888, Internet www.wrr101.com.

YMCA of Metropolitan Dallas—601 North Akard, (214) 880-9622, Internet www.ymcadallas.org. It employs 2,800 locally and has an annual budget of $51 million.

Zoo—650 South R.L. Thornton Fwy., (214) 670-5656.

TRANSPORTATION

Air

Chances are that you will be coming to Dallas through the Dallas/Fort Worth International Airport, which is located halfway between the two cities. One of the largest and most advanced facilities in the world when it opened in 1974, it was built at a cost of about $750 million, with its tenant airlines investing another $2 billion in improvements since then.

Though the beginnings of D/FW Airport go back to the 1960s, the amassing of that much real estate and technology "would today be beyond the democratic capabilities of even Dallas and Fort Worth," noted historian A. C. Greene in 1984, while writing about the former mayor Erik Jonsson.

"No other man in Dallas history could have demanded, and obtained, support from the cities, the state, and the federal agencies affected. Thus, D/FW Airport is probably the final monument to Dallas' famous (or infamous) oligarchy, because the decision to build it, to operate it in conjunction with Fort Worth and the method of operation through an independent board came only because there was unity in the views of those who made the decisions—and unity in their acceptance of Jonsson as a man every participant trusted. The project was a gamble that could have produced an irreversible regional disaster."

Actually, the Civil Aeronautics Board in 1964 "ordered the two cities to come up, in less than 180 days, with a voluntary agreement on the location of a new regional airport, or the federal government would do it for them," according to the Texas State Historical Association.

Dallas/Fort Worth International Airport, (972) 574-8888; Airport Assistance Center, (972) 574-4420; Ground Transportation, (972) 574-5878; Visitor Information, (972) 574-3694; Lost & Found, (972) 574-4454; Emergency Car Service, (817) 283-2121.

Non-Emergency Police & Fire, (972) 574-4454; TDD for Hearing-Impaired, (972) 574-5555; Parking, (972) 574-PARK; Hyatt Regency D/FW, (972) 453-1234; Ambassador Airport Volunteers, (972) 574-1492 or 574-1493; Western Union, (972) 574-4420; Internet www.dfwairport.com.

Since the September 11, 2001, terrorist bombings in New York and Washington, D.C., D/FW Airport suggests that you check in two hours ahead of your scheduled international flight, and at least one hour if flying inside the United States. You are limited to one carry-on bag, a pocketbook or briefcase, which includes a laptop computer. A list of items now prohibited in aircraft cabins includes everything from dog repellent spray to portable power drills. To discourage would-be trespassers, the airport added barbed wire along its 35-mile (or 56-kilometer) perimeter fence.

Federal agencies serving D/FW Airport: USDA/APHIS, Plant Protection & Quarantine, (972) 574-2166; Veterinary Services, (972) 885-7850; Department of Interior, Fish and Wildlife Service, (972) 574-3254; Drug Enforcement Administration, Airport Narcotic Task Force, (972) 574-2111: Dallas, (214) 767-7151, Fort Worth, (817) 334-3455; Immigration & Naturalization Service, (972) 574-2187; Federal Aviation Administration, (972) 453-4200; U.S. Customs Service, (972) 574-2170; U.S. Postal Service, (972) 574-2687; Express Service, (972) 574-2685.

About half of the airport is located in Grapevine, with smaller portions in Coppell, Euless, and Irving. You can enter the airport from the south on State Highway 183, also known as Airport Freeway. From the north, enter on Highway 114, Highway 121, or Interstate Highway 635, also known as Lyndon B. Johnson Freeway. All exits are to your left.

The airport's main road, International Parkway, runs the length of the airport, from north to south. When departing the airport, the parkway connects directly to major freeways serving the Metroplex.

Downtown Fort Worth and Dallas are about 17.5 miles (or 28 kilometers) from the airport, or one hour's drive, possibly longer, depending on the time of the day.

Like other major airports, D/FW generates revenues without taxpayer support. Co-owned by Dallas and Fort Worth—the only airport in the nation so owned—it earns money through airline leases, landing fees, concessions, parking, and passenger fees. About one-half of the airport's $300-million budget comes from non-airline revenue sources, including concessions, rents, parking, car rentals, and the airport's hotel rooms.

For construction projects, such as the new Terminal D, which is to have 23 gates and house all international flights, the airport relies on the sale of bonds that are guaranteed by airlines instead of taxpayers to generate cash flow.

Covering 28.1 square miles (or almost 73 square kilometers), with seven runways and the eighth under construction, the airport is larger than the island of Manhattan in New York City. Four heavy jets can land simultaneously in good weather, and three heavy jets can land using cockpit instruments in bad weather.

D/FW now is the fourth busiest airport in the nation—and sixth worldwide, after London and Tokyo, but ahead of Frankfurt and Paris—in the total number of passengers.

There are some 2,300 passenger takeoffs and landings daily with 160 destinations worldwide serving 57 million passengers every year. Terminals include 150 aircraft boarding gates.

A *Dallas Morning News* writer claims the airport "is efficiently designed and simple to navigate—but it has all the romance of a bus station. It needs less advertising and more art."

The airport area is also the headquarters for 14 Fortune 500 companies. Some 42,000 people—more than the equivalent of the entire population of the town of Grapevine—work at the airport.

In 2000, D/FW airport began a $2-billion expansion, overhauling the airport's terminals, building new concourses and terminals.

A $170-million, 4.8-mile (or 7.7-kilometer) automated people-moving rail system is to link the terminals and replace the quarter-century-old trams in use until now. When operational in 2005, each of the 64 people-moving cars, costing a total of $846 million, will carry as many as 69 passengers and travel up to 35 miles (or 56 kilometers) an hour. A train headed in either direction should arrive at one of the three stations in each terminal about every two minutes.

All baggage claim areas are located on the arrival level. Ground transportation services, other than taxicabs, depart from the lower level and arrive on the upper roadway. All terminal buildings, parking facilities, rental car lots, and the airport hotels are accessible from International Parkway that runs through the airport.

About 2,500 (or 1,011 hectares) of the airport's 18,000 acres (or 7,284 hectares) have since 1979 been officially designated as a foreign trade zone—as lying outside of the U.S. Customs territory—by the U.S. Commerce Department. The zone allows business activity to occur under the same rules as would apply if the activity were performed outside the United States. (For more details, call (972) 574-3121.) In addition to two at D/FW, there are six other foreign trade zones in the Metroplex.

By 2005, the newly built 1.9-million-square-foot (or 176,510-square-meter) international Terminal D, "a massive, sweeping structure of steel and glass," twice as large as Terminal C, is expected to be completed at a cost $560 million. Some 100,000 square feet (or 9,290 square meters) will be set aside for restaurants and stores.

Terminal D, having 23 gates and tinted, heat-treated glass on much of its exterior, will accommodate up to 14 million international passengers a year. It will be constructed in a way that can withstand a terrorist blast of the kind that destroyed the Oklahoma City federal building on April 19, 1995, when 169 perished.

The $840 million Terminal F, also on the drawing boards, could be completed in 2008. More than 40 cargo carriers also serve the airport.

Airlines Serving the Metroplex

You are within a three-hour flight of any city in the continental United States from here. D/FW Airport is served by two dozen airlines, connecting Fort Worth with more than 150 U.S. cities and 30 international destinations in Canada, Mexico, Central America, Europe, South America, and Asia.

Airline	Terminal & Gate(s)	Reservations/Web site
Aeromexico	Terminal E, Gates 37-38	(800) 237-6639 www.aeromexico.com
Aero California	Terminal A, Gates 21-28	(800) 237-6225 No Web address
Air Canada	Terminal E, Gate 35	(888) 247-2262 www.aircanada.com
AirTran Airways	Terminal E, Gate 2	(800) 247-8726 www.airtran.com
America West Airlines	Terminal B, Gate 16	(800) 235-9292 www.americawest.com
American Airlines	Terminal A, Gates 13-39 Terminal B, Gates 2-13 Terminal C, Gates 2-39	(800) 433-7300 (214) 267-2222 www.aa.com
American Eagle Airlines	Terminal A, Gates 1-12	(800) 433-7300 (214) 267-1151 www.aa.com
American Trans Air	Terminal B, Gate 12	(800) 435-9282 www.ata.com
ASA-Delta Connection	Terminal E, Gates 22-30	(800) 221-1212 www.delta.com
British Airways	Terminal B, Gate 34	(800) 247-9297 www.british-airways.com
China Airlines	Terminal A, Gates 16-39	(800) 227-5118 www.china-airlines.com
Comair-Delta Conection	Terminal E, Gates 23-30	(800) 221-1212 www.delta.com
Continental Airlines	Terminal B, Gates 14-18	(800) 525-0280 (972) 263-0523 www.continental.com
Delta Air Lines	Terminal E, Gates 8-36	Dom. (800) 221-1212

Airline	Terminal & Gate(s)	Reservations/Web site
Delta Air Lines continued		Intl. (800) 241-4141 (214) 630-3200 (817) 336-8341 www.delta.com
Frontier	Terminal B, Gate 15	(800) 432-1359 www.frontierairlines.com
Grupo TACA	Terminal A, Gate 19	(800) 535-8780 www.grupotaca.com
Iberia	Terminal A, Gates 21-28	(800) 772-4642 www.iberia.com
KLM Royal Dutch Air	Terminal E, Gates 4-6	(800) 374-7747 www.klm.nl
Korean Air	Terminal B, Gate 34	(800) 438-5000 www.koreanair.com
LOT Polish	Terminal A, Gates 21-28	(800) 223-0593 www.lot.com
Lufthansa Airlines	Terminal B, Gate 33	(800) 645-3800 www.lufthansa.com
Mesa Airlines	Terminal B, Gate 18	(800) 637-2247 www.mesa-air.com
Midwest Express	Terminal B, Gate 18	(800) 452-2022 www.midwestexpress.com
National Airlines	Terminal B, Gate 34	(888) 757-5387 www.nationalairlines.com
Northwest Airlines	Terminal E, Gates 4-6	(800) 225-2525 www.nwa.com
Quantas Airways	Terminal B, Gate 6	(800) 227-4500 www.quantas.com.au
South African Airways	Terminal E, Gates 17-34	(800) 722-9675 www.saairways.com
Swissair	Terminal A, Gate 7	(800) 221-4750 www.swissair.com
TAM Brazilian	Terminal A, Gates 25-33	(888) 235-9826 www.tam-usa.com
United Airlines	Terminal B, Gates 28-31	(800) 241-6522 www.ual.com
USAirways	Terminal B, Gates 18-21	(800) 428-4322 www.usairways.com

Internet service is available at all four terminals. At the American Airlines AAccess Showroom (Terminal A), you can try the AAccess Interactive Travel Network to rent a car or make hotel reservations. A Laptop Lane business center is near Gate A-38.

Terminal B has a data port in the Airport Assistance Center. Terminal C has three data ports, as has Terminal E. There are fax machines scattered at all four terminals. Wireless Internet service is also available, thanks to almost 100 access points installed in ceilings throughout the airport.

D/FW also offers Internet kiosks operated by Verizon in several of its terminals and a wireless network throughout the airport operated by Wayport Inc., which is based in Austin, Texas, and owns Laptop Lane centers.

Two locations of **mail drops** will be found in each terminal. At least three **ATMs** are located in every terminal. **Duty-free shops** are situated in Terminals A, B, and E. **Barber shops** are located at B-24, C-17, and E-17.

D/FW Airport Parking (Internet www.theparkingspot.com), (972) 774-6772 for recorded parking information, (972) 574-PARK for current parking lot status. The airport has some 29,000 parking spaces bringing in more than $200,000 a day. There are four classes of parking, although some off-airport companies offer rates that are lower than the airport's:

Terminal parking (green signs), located directly in front of each terminal in a covered parking garage, costs up to $16 for up to 24 hours.

Express North & South parking (red signs), designed for the business traveler and providing door-to-gate service to any terminal, is $9 for up to 24 hours at north and south lots.

Remote North & South parking (yellow signs), with scheduled bus service every 15 minutes, from 5:30 AM to 11 PM, and still farther removed from the terminals, costs $5 for up to 24 hours.

A five-story parking garage is also open in Section A of Terminal C, with an additional 1,808 parking spaces. Each terminal garage has designated parking for the disabled. Parking or waiting for passengers along upper and lower level terminal roadways is not permitted.

You can pay for parking at all airport booths with most credit cards.

Until the terrorists killed hundreds at New York's World Trade Center in 2001, there were 200 restaurants and shops located at the airport and doing about $400,000 worth of business daily. They are open roughly between 7 AM and 10:30 PM.

Au Bon Pain restaurant has six locations in three terminals. Chili's is in Terminals B, and C. Dickey's barbecue will be found at three terminals. Harlon's barbecue is at two locations in Terminal B. There are multiple locations of McDonald's, Mr. Gatti's Pizza, and Pizza Hut Express.

One of the more unusual airport stores is La Bodega Winery in Terminal A, where Texas wines from 15 wineries can be sampled and about 30 bottles are open for tasting every day. In 2001, it was the only winery at any U.S. airport. The airport has restricted vendors from charging more than 5 percent above "community rates."

The **U.S. Post Office** is located at 2300 West 32nd Street, off International Parkway, (972) 456-2060. It is open 24 hours a day, 365 days a year, and also provides passport and notary services.

Smoking has been banned in the terminals since 1993, except in the six frequent-flier clubs, so it is not uncommon to see hordes of passengers smoking outside terminal entrances. To alleviate their discomfort, the airport plans to build separately ventilated smoking lounges inside the four terminals.

Foreign Currency Exchange at D/FW Airport—You can exchange up to 30 foreign currencies at these Travelex/Thomas Cook (Internet www.travelex.com) airport locations, which also sell dollar-denominated travelers checks that you can use to pay for lodging, meals, and while shopping:

Terminal A: Gate 26, (972) 574-4686, open daily 7 AM-9 PM.

Terminal B: Gate 33, (972) 574-3878, open daily 9 AM-5 PM.

Terminal E: Gate 13, (972) 574-2814, open daily 9 AM-5 PM.

All three locations are inside the airport's secured area. Outside, there is one at:

Terminal A: Gate 36, (972) 574-2357, open daily 9:30 AM-7 PM.

Dallas Love Field Airport, 8008 Cedar Springs Rd., (214) 670-6073/6080; Airport security, (214) 670-6163; Lost & Found, (214) 904-5598, Internet www.dallas-lovefield.com. Located north of Mockingbird Lane at Cedar Springs Road, about seven miles (or eleven kilometers) northwest of the central business district.

This city-owned airport serves more than seven million passengers annually and is one of the 50 largest in the United States With 32 gates in operation, the airport has almost 300,000 takeoffs and landings a year. Shops and restaurants serve this airport, which underwent a complete reconstruction in the 1990s. There are several hotels within a few minutes of driving distance.

Its terminal was drafted in the mid-1950s by the Oklahoma-born architect Jack Corgan (d. 2000), who also designed Dallas' first drive-in theater in 1941.

In 1917, Love Field served as a 650-acre (or 263-hectare) World War I training base and in 1927 began passenger service. It was named in memory of First Lt. Moss Lee Love—not a Dallasite—a pilot from Fairfax, Virginia, killed in an airplane crash in San Diego, California, in 1913.

Aviator Charles Lindbergh arrived at Love Field in his *Spirit of St. Louis* aircraft on September 25, 1927, just 27 days after the state's first commercial airline passengers were carried from here to Kansas City. After dedicating it as a municipal airport, Lindbergh was the object of adulation by a crowd of 10,000 at a downtown parade.

That same year the city purchased Love Field for $432,500. In 1930, French flyers Coste and Bellonte claimed $25,000 for the first one-stop flight from Paris to New York to Dallas that was offered by philanthropist and aviation enthusiast William Edward Easterwood (1883-1940) who had adopted Dallas as his hometown. He is also credited with bringing the first talking movie to Texas.

On Thursday evening, November 14, 1957, operatic diva Maria Callas flew into Love Field to inaugurate the Dallas Opera, her only American appearance that fall, and was whisked to the Adolphus Hotel downtown.

A daily jet service from Love Field to Europe was inaugurated the year before John F. Kennedy was assassinated. The airport now covers 1,300 acres (or 526 hectares) and has been designated a Texas historical site.

A $59-million, 4,000-car, four-level garage was completed next to the airport in 2003 and includes a climate-controlled glass concourse with moving sidewalks and a sky bridge that takes passengers to the terminal's lobby. Dallas artists Philip Lamb and Susan Magilow provided art works for the new garage.

This brought the total parking capacity to more than 7,000 spaces. (Call (214) 670-PARK for parking information.)

Since Dallas/Fort Worth International Airport was built, Love Field has been served mostly by **Southwest Airlines,** (800) 533-1222 or 214 263-1717, Internet www.iflyswa.com, with flights to 47 cities in 23 states.

When the D/FW opened in 1974, the cities of Dallas and Fort Worth sued Southwest to force it to move with other airlines to the new airport. Southwest won the right to remain at Love Field as long as it was a commercial airport, although the Dallas city council attempted to close Love Field to commercial traffic.

In the minds of many Dallasites, Love Field stands for the highly successful Southwest Airlines that has practically monopolized the airport for many years. Begun as a small air-taxi service called Wild Goose Flying Service, the company was taken over by entrepreneur Rollin King, who charged a young attorney, Herb Kelleher, to transform it into a no-frills airline flying out of Love Field.

"Kelleher thought King was crazy, but after doing some homework, decided that he was just crazy enough to go along with the plan," according to the Texas State Historical Association.

The "talkative, chain-smoking, whiskey-drinking" Kelleher, who had been John B. Connally's Bexar County campaign manager in his 1962 gubernatorial race, lined up investors, such as the future Russian ambassador Robert S. Strauss and future Texas governor Dolph Briscoe.

Air Southwest planned to begin serving Dallas, Houston, and San Antonio, although Braniff and Continental Airlines tried to stop Southwest's intrastate flights.

Southwest prevailed through a Supreme Court decision of December 7, 1970, which is generally considered the beginning of deregulation in the airline industry. Southwest began service with its inaugural flight on June 18, 1971, between Dallas and San Antonio, with $148 in the bank.

To enhance the company's image, Southwest clad its flight attendants in shorts called "hot pants," and the airline has remained profitable every year since 1973. Southwest hit the billion-dollar revenue mark in 1990 and introduced ticketless travel four years later.

Colleen Barrett (b. 1946), Kelleher's former secretary in San Antonio, who had joined Southwest in 1978, is now its chief operating officer.

To the sometimes extreme annoyance of residents around the airport, "Love Field is open for flight operations 24 hours a day, including base operations for numerous helicopters and loud, low-flying prop planes that carry cargo such as canceled checks for the Federal Reserve," in the words of the *Dallas Morning News*.

Addison Airport, 4651 Airport Pkwy., Addison, (972) 392-4850, Internet www.ci.addison.tx.us. Located northwest of downtown Dallas, north of Belt line Rd. and west of Dallas North Tollway.

The municipally owned 366-acre (or 148-hectare) airport began its operations as a dirt strip in 1952, a year before the town of Addison was incorporated. The airport's original owner sold the airfield to Addison in 1976.

Surrounded by residential, retail, and office developments, Addison airport is managed by a real estate company and an engineering firm. It has a single runway that is 7,000 feet (or 2,133 meters) long and 100 feet (or 30.4 meters) wide and accommodates 170,000 takeoffs and landings a year.

Addison Airport is home to the Cavanaugh Museum (see entry), Frito-Lay's corporate aviation facilities, and several flight schools.

The Addison airport toll tunnel, north of Belt Line Road, the first such facility in Texas, links Keller Springs Road on the east side of the airport with its continuation on the west side. The $20 million, two-lane tunnel is 3,660 feet (or 1,115 meters) long.

McKinney Municipal Airport, 1500 West Industrial Blvd.,

McKinney, (972) 562-5555, Internet www.wingspointaviation.com. Established in 1978, it has a runway that is 7,000 feet (or 2,133 meters) long and 100 feet (or 30.4 meters) wide. Home to corporate fleets of Texas Instrument and Fleming Cos.

Denton Municipal Airport, 5000 Airport Rd., (940) 349-7736, Denton, Internet www.dentonairport.com. Established in 1946, it has a runway that is 6,000 feet (or 1,828 meters) long and 150 feet (or 45.7 meters) wide.

Mesquite Metro Airport, 1130 Airport Blvd., Suite 100, Mesquite, (972) 222-8536, Internet www.cityofmesquite.com/airport. Established in 1975, it has a runway that is 6,000 feet (or 1,828 meters) long and 100 feet (or 30.4 meters) wide.

Lancaster Municipal Airport, 730 Ferris Rd., Lancaster, (972) 227-5721, Internet www.airnav.com/airports/inc. Established in 1967, it has a runway that is 5,000 feet (or 1,524 meters) long and 100 feet (or 30.4 meters) wide.

Grand Prairie Municipal Airport, 3116 South Great S.W. Pkwy., Grand Prairie, (972) 237-7591. Established in 1968, it has a runway that is 4,000 feet (or 1,219 meters) long and 75 feet (or 22.8 meters) wide.

Dallas Executive Airport, 5303 Challenger at U.S. Hwy. 67, Dallas, (214) 670-7612, Internet www.dallascityhall.org. Established in 1945, Redbird, as it was known until 2002, has a runway that is 3,800 feet (or 1,158 meters) long and 150 feet (or 45.7 meters) wide.

The city-owned general aviation field that sits on 1,070 acres (or 433 hectares) is slated to have a new terminal, control tower, and entrance plaza with a monument and sculpture. The eccentric billionaire Howard Hughes owned hangars here in the 1950s.

Ground Services to and from Dallas Airports

The D/FW and Love Field airports are serviced by the city-owned bus service, private tour companies, rental car agencies, and some 15 taxi companies.

One of the least expensive ways to go to or from the D/FW Airport is by DART, the city bus service, on route **202 Express,** running as frequently as every 15 minutes during the rush hours and as seldom as every hour at other times, every day of the year.

From downtown, these airport buses run from the West Transfer Center, at Griffin Street and Pacific Avenue, on the edge of the West End entertainment district, and take about 45 minutes. There are only a few stops on the way.

From D/FW Airport, you can catch a bus going downtown at North Shuttle Parking, but you first have to take the airport shuttle to this parking area. The last bus for the airport leaves downtown at 10:30 PM, and the last bus departing from the airport toward downtown does so at 10:45 PM.

If this seems like a lot of bother, keep in mind that the fare is only a couple of dollars each way. (For more details call DART at (214) 979-1111.)

If going to the D/FW Airport or Love Field Airport, you can also call one of several shuttle services, such as Classic Shuttle, (214) 841-1900, or SuperShuttle, (800) 258-3826.

The shuttle cost to or from the international airport to downtown Dallas or Fort Worth is about one-half that of a taxi, but you could spend considerably more time waiting for the shuttle van to make its way through all the stops to where you are waiting for it.

Taxi

Taxi, as you already know, is expensive and only a sensible alternative if you use it sparingly. Dallas has 24-hour taxi service provided by many companies. You will find taxis in front of many better hotels.

It is preferable to call for a taxi on the phone than trying to hail one on the street. Never get inside a taxi that already has more than one person, the driver.

Ask questions beforehand and get an estimate of how much your fare will cost. If you go from the D/FW International Airport to downtown Dallas, or the other way around, the taxi might cost you $30-35, about the same as if you traveled to Fort Worth. The minimum charge from D/FW Airport is $12.

Dallas is saturated with taxis and because of that "taxi service is deplorable," according to a consultant, who found idle drivers taking out their frustrations on passengers. There are 2,200 taxis operated by 15 companies in Dallas. By comparison, Los Angeles is served by fewer than 1,000 cabs.

Allied Taxi Service, 2616 West Mockingbird Ln., Dallas, (214) 819-9999.

Checker Cab Company, Post Office Box 1510, Fort Worth; Dallas phone, (214) 426-6262; Fort Worth phone, (817) 469-1110.

Choice Cabs, Inc., 6218 Cedar Springs Rd., Dallas, (972) 222-2000.

Republic Taxi Company, 6102 Maple Ave., Dallas, (214) 902-7077.

Terminal Taxi Corporation, 6218 Cedar Springs Rd., Dallas, (214) 352-4445.

West End Cab Company, 6102 Maple Ave., Dallas, (214) 902-7000.

Yellow Cab, Post Office Box 1510, Fort Worth; Dallas phone, (214)

426-6262; Fort Worth phone, (817) 428-3786. Nine companies combined under the Yellow Cab name operate more than 1,000 cabs.

For more information about taxi fare regulations or to complain, call the city of Dallas Department of Transportation at (214) 670-3161.

Helicopter

Helicopter service. Sightseeing tours of Dallas, Fort Worth, or any other Metroplex area of your choice can be had from a helicopter.

Sky Helicopter, 2559 South Jupiter Rd. at LBJ Frwy., Garland, (214) 349-7000, Internet www.skyhelicopters.com.

Founded in 1992, Sky provides helicopters for holiday sightseeing tours, aerial photography, and surveys. Thirty-minute tours of White Rock Lake, Fair Park, Deep Ellum, downtown Dallas, Texas Stadium, Love Field, and Park Cities for up to three persons start at $225. One-hour tours that also include South Fork Ranch start at $440.

Zebra Air, 7515 Lemmon Ave., Building J, (214) 358-7200, Internet www.zebraair.com. Prices start at $300 for one-half hour for four passengers.

Established in 1988, Zebra operates six mostly Bell helicopters that accommodate from four to six passengers. It provides helicopters for sightseeing, aerial photography, real estate surveys, promotions, executive charter, fire suppression, pipeline and powerline inspection.

Among the tours available are a 30-minute tour of Dallas, a two-hour South Fork ranch tour, and a 2.5-hour Texas barbecue tour. Claims to have flown more than "21,000 hours with no accidents or violations."

They promise to whisk you out to the Texas Motor Speedway, Texas Ranger and Dallas Cowboys games, and horse racing at Lone Star Park in a matter of minutes.

Surrey

An interesting and romantic way to tour some historic parts of Dallas is to travel by a horse-drawn surrey. Half a dozen local companies operate some 22 carriages. Tours include the West End Historic District, Old City Park, McKinney Avenue, and Turtle Creek Boulevard.

The surreys can accommodate up to six passengers at a time and operate nightly on Market Street in the West End, starting at 6:30 PM. Prices start at $25 for four individuals, with a $5 charge for each additional person. The fee for larger parties is negotiable.

Texas Star Carriage Service, Post Office Box 1670, Mabank, (214) 946-9911, cell phone, (214) 616-1694, Internet www.texasstarcarriage.com.

It offers horse-drawn carriages for sightseeing, birthdays, anniversaries, and weddings. You can be picked up at home or in your hotel.

Automobile

Without an automobile in Dallas today, you might well feel like its founder John Neely Bryan did 150 years ago, except that then only four families and two bachelors lived here, and there was only one general store and one saloon to get to.

The colorful, London-born railroad capitalist Edward Howland Robinson Green (1868-1936) was the first person to bring a gasoline-powered car to Dallas in the fall of 1899.

You are as good as done for without a car in the Metroplex, a geographical area often defined as including at least Collin, Dallas, Denton, and Tarrant counties, at other times also Ellis and Kaufman Counties. Yes, you can travel by public transportation, but the city is so spread out—measuring 400 square miles (or 1,036 square kilometers)—it might take you a year to explore it by public transport.

But seriously, you basically have four choices: walking, buses, light rail, or private automobile.

Walking is fine within the neighborhoods, such as downtown or West End Historic District, if the weather is all right and you do so during the day. In a survey commissioned for the *Dallas Morning News*, "Only 32 percent of those surveyed said they feel safe at night in downtown."

Practically the only sensible way to get through the rest of the city is by car.

Even if it now makes feeble attempts to change its course, Dallas has been catering to car owners for decades and woe be to the hapless traveler who falls for the line that pedestrians can co-exist with car drivers in Big D. Not in this century.

Dallas is also one of the six most congested urban areas in the United States, according to a study by the Texas Transportation Institute, which claims that drivers spend an average of 74 hours a year stuck in traffic, just behind Houston, and waste 120 gallons (or 454 liters) of fuel. The area's congestion also claims $2 billion in lost productivity.

But do not feel sorry for yourself, because it could be a lot worse: "Each morning, 40,000 cars, trucks and buses an hour pour (or trickle) into central London, using roads meant for horses, carriages and pedestrians," reports the *New York Times*. Since 2003, it costs five British pounds "a day for the privilege of driving into central London at peak times."

While more than 65,000 households in Dallas County have no vehicle, more than 310,000, or 40 percent, have two cars, and 110,000, or 14 percent of all households in the county have three or more vehicles.

Of the more than one million workers in Dallas County, nearly 75 percent drive alone in their car, truck, or van. A surprisingly high 18 percent of Dallasites car pool, more than in any large American city. Fewer than 4 percent use public transportation, and fewer than 3 percent work at home.

The city is almost entirely encircled by a three-quarter loop, Interstate Highway 635 (also known as the Lyndon B. Johnson Freeway). It runs from D/FW Airport eastward and around the city until it joins Interstate Highway 20 in the south and then west to Fort Worth.

Among the north-south thoroughfares are Interstate Highway 35, which runs from the Mexican border through San Antonio and Austin, through Dallas and on to Oklahoma. North of downtown it is called Stemmons Freeway and south of downtown R. L. Thornton Freeway.

Interstate Highway 35 East runs through Dallas and I-35 West through Fort Worth. North of here the two meet at Denton, and south near Hillsboro, about 75 miles (or 120 kilometers) from Dallas.

The speed limit in Texas is 70 miles (or 112.6 kilometers) per hour on most rural interstates and 60 miles (or 96.5 kilometers) on freeways, unless otherwise specified. The speed limit on most residential streets is 30 miles (or 48 kilometers) per hour and 20 miles (or 32 kilometers) per hour in marked school zones.

To check on local road conditions, visit the *Dallas Morning News*' Web site at www.dallasnews.com/index/traffic.htm. To check on the condition of Texas interstate highways, U.S. highways, state highways, and other roads, go to the state's Web site, www.texas.gov.

Well over one million cars are registered in Dallas County, an area that covers 908 square miles (or 2,352 square kilometers).

(See also section titled Private Car in this chapter.)

Governor Rick Perry proposed that Texas build a $185-billion, 4,000-mile (or 6,437-kilometer) network of toll roads and rail corridors next to current interstate highways, which would be a major shift in statewide transportation policy. The Trans Texas Corridor, paid for with the money coming from investors who buy government-backed bonds, would bypass the major Texas cities. Once on the corridor, motorists could travel up to 80 miles (or 128 kilometers) an hour and stop only to pay tolls.

Construction of the first segment of the corridor, which would steer traffic around congested Metroplex highways and offer the area residents an autobahn-style alternative to Interstate 35, could begin as early as 2004.

Bus

Dallas Bus Terminal, 205 South Lamar at Commerce Sts., (214) 655-7082. Open 24 hours.

Greyhound Bus Lines terminal. Schedules & information, (800) 231-2222 or (214) 655-7000/7082; Spanish-speaking travelers, (800) 531-5332, Internet www.greyhound.com.

Greyhound suburban bus stations are located in **Carrollton** at 1017 Elm St., (972) 242-3133; **Garland** at 2121 Northwest Hwy., (972) 276-5663; **Irving** at 969 East Irving Blvd., (972) 254-8412; **Lewisville** at 695 Fox Ave., (972) 221-6903; **Mesquite** at 1331 East Hwy. 80, (972) 288-1374; and **Richardson** at 400 North Greenville Ave., (972) 231-1763.

Greyhound Lines, which has 1,600 local employees, is owned by the Canadian Laidlaw Inc., which filed for bankruptcy in 2001. One-quarter of all passengers are Latinos.

Rail

Passenger rail service is available via **Amtrak** at Dallas' Union Station (see entry in the SIGHTS & ATTRACTIONS chapter) downtown, 400 South Houston, (214) 653-1101 or (800) USA-RAIL, Internet www.amtrak.com/texaseagle.html.

You can take an Amtrak train to Fort Worth; Austin; San Antonio; Little Rock, Arkansas; and Chicago, Illinois; daily on the *Texas Eagle.*

Meals are available in the dining car. Some trains feature movies and a children's hour, and have laptop computer outlets. Smoking is allowed in designated areas of the lounge cars.

In San Antonio, there is connecting service available to Los Angeles, California, through the *Sunset Limited.* Sleepers accommodate up to four persons each, with two adult and two child berths, but at a considerable additional cost to the fare

A 15 percent discount is available to students and travelers over age 62, except in first-class accommodations. Children aged 2-15 years ride at half-price when accompanied by a full-fare paying adult.

The round trip coach fare to San Antonio from Dallas is about $65 per person and another $100 for a family bedroom. The train leaves Union Station in Dallas daily at 1:55 PM and arrives in San Antonio just before midnight.

"There's one hitch: The train is usually late," observes the *Dallas Morning News*. You can travel to Fort Worth for about $5 per person.

Going north, you can take an Amtrak train from Dallas to Little Rock, St. Louis, and Chicago. The coach fare to Chicago starts at $120 per person each way, a deluxe bedroom is another $300. The train leaves Dallas at 4:10 PM and arrives in Chicago at 2:20 PM the following day.

Amtrak began service in 1971, when it took over the passenger operations of most remaining railroads at the time. It serves more than 500 stations in 45 states and operates on more than 22,000 miles (or 35,404 kilometers) of tracks. Amtrak serves some 22 million passengers a year, or 61,000 a day. The company operates 2,188 railroad cars, including 173 sleepers, and employs 24,000.

Amtrak has never turned a profit since it was created and has consumed more than $25 billion in federal subsidies since then. The current subsidy is more than $200 per passenger. That will come as no surprise to those who have been subjected to shabby treatment on its trains. When we traveled from San Antonio to Dallas, we found that some supervisors run those trains as their private fiefdoms, and service can be erratic.

The *Crescent Star*, the first direct service from Dallas to New York in more than 40 years, has been proposed by Amtrak, following an agreement between it and the Kansas City Southern Railway. The one-way trek is estimated to take 40 hours and would take place via Shreveport, Birmingham, Atlanta, Charlotte, and Washington, D.C.

That compares with a three-and-a-half-hour flight and a 24-hour trip by automobile. Trains would leave Dallas' Union Station every evening.

AROUND DALLAS

Public Transportation

Until 1996, when light-rail was inaugurated in Dallas, the city had a sorry record for its public transportation. Considering that it measures 400 square miles (or 1,036 square kilometers), Big D still leaves plenty to be desired for those who are forced to or would like to rely on bus and rail transportation to get at least to and from work.

Worn-out buses could be up to half an hour late even on workdays, and when they do come their drivers sometimes behave as though they are doing you a favor by coming at all. It at times seems as though it is hotter inside some of the buses than outside at the height of summer.

The light-rail has relieved the driving slightly, but only for those who are lucky enough to live near one of the stations.

Years after DART's light-rail went into effect, the project still exposes a predictable, deep-seated animosity toward public transportation. One author in the *Dallas Business Journal* wrote, "Fewer people ride DART today than before spending $1 billion on light rail." Not surprisingly, he claims that no city in Texas has made any headway with public transportation.

DART (Dallas Area Rapid Transit)

DART, 140 Pacific Ave., between Akard and Field Sts., at Akard light-rail station; Customer information, (214) 979-1111; Transit police, 928-6300; Complaints, 749-3333; Lost & Found, 749-3810; Handicapped services, 515-7272, Internet www.dart.org.

The transit authority maintains more than 1,000 buses, vans, and trains to transport well over 200,000 passengers each weekday in a 13-city and 700-square-mile (or 1,813-square-kilometer) service area. The transportation agency carries five million passengers a month.

DART has 2,800 employees and an operating budget of $300 million, much of which comes from the 1 percent sales tax charged in its 13 member cities. The agency generates only about 20 percent of its operating revenue from fares. It also receives federal funding.

Get a DART system map at DART headquarters downtown if you plan to travel in this manner. All bus routes are identified by numbers only, while signs on the front of the buses display the route number and the final destination, the same as DART trains do.

There is bus service between downtown Dallas and Love Field Airport, as well as between downtown and D/FW Airport.

Most buses coming to or from downtown stop at either East Transfer Center, at Live Oak and Pearl Streets, across from the Adam's Mark Hotel, or West Transfer Center, at Pacific and Griffin, across from the Doubletree Hotel (see entry). You can then transfer to another bus line or the nearest light-rail station.

DART bus stop signs are color-coded: *purple* for DART rail connections, *green* for express service between transit centers and /or downtown, *blue* for local, crosstown, and limited stop routes, *dark blue* for trolley-bus. Bus schedules are coded in the same manner.

Express routes for suburban riders who travel to or from downtown, usually coming to work in the morning and returning in the evening, are color-coded in green. These express routes connect downtown Dallas with the suburbs like Plano, Richardson, Irving, Carrollton, Farmers Branch, Addison, and Garland.

The route numbers indicate the following type of service:

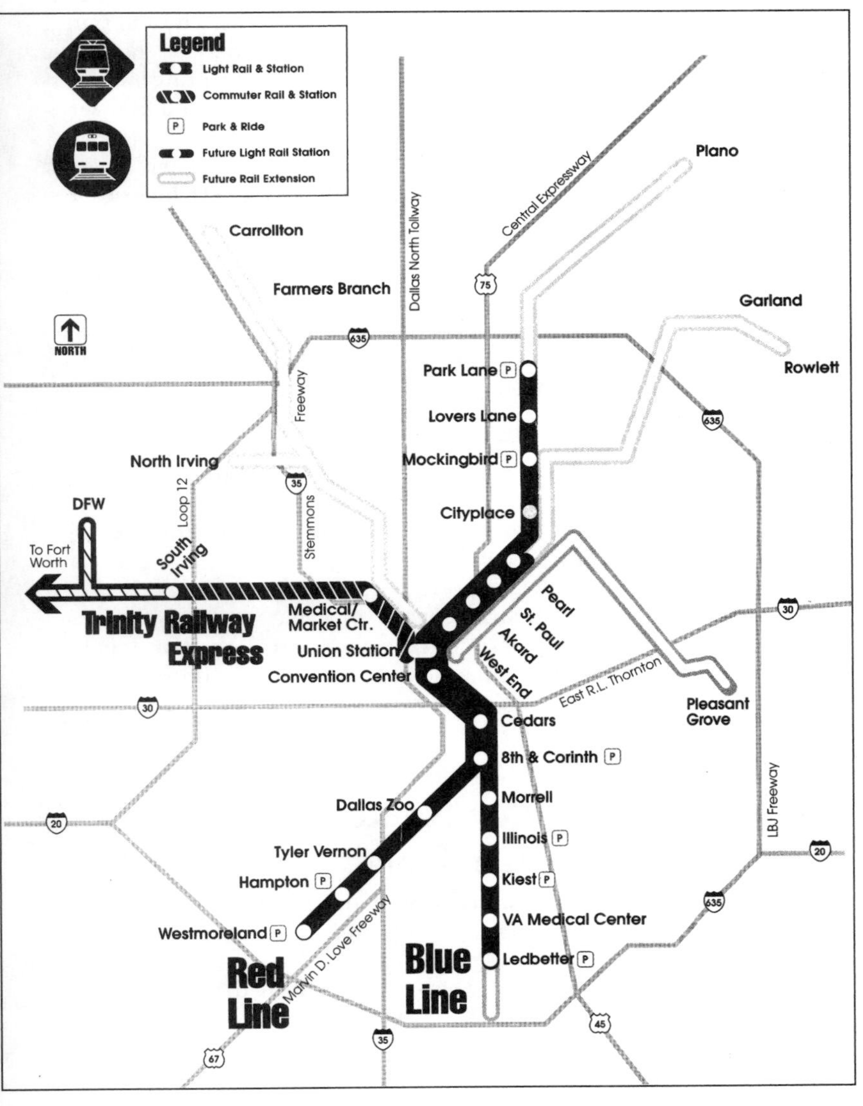

Legend
Light Rail & Station
Commuter Rail & Station
Park & Ride
Future Light Rail Station
Future Rail Extension
NORTH
Plano
Carrollton
Central Expressway
Dallas North Tollway
Farmers Branch
Garland
Rowlett
Freeway
Park Lane
Lovers Lane
Mockingbird
Cityplace
North Irving
Loop 12
Stemmons
DFW
To Fort Worth
South Irving
Trinity Railway Express
Medical/ Market Ctr.
Union Station
Convention Center
Pearl
St. Paul
Akard
West End
East R.L. Thornton
Pleasant Grove
Cedars
8th & Corinth
Morrell
Illinois
Kiest
VA Medical Center
Ledbetter
LBJ Freeway
Dallas Zoo
Tyler Vernon
Hampton
Westmoreland
Marvin D. Love Freeway
Red Line
Blue Line

Numbers lower than 100 indicate a local bus; 100 series routes are limited-stop routes that use highways to serve downtown; 200 series—like the 202 bus route to D/FW Airport described under Ground Services, above—are nonstop express routes to downtown from transit centers; 300 series are local neighborhood buses that do not serve downtown Dallas; 400 series are crosstown buses connecting areas outside downtown Dallas, such as Plano to Las Colinas; and 500 series buses only feed DART rail stations.

You must enter the bus at the front door and pay by putting your paper bills or coins in the farebox or presenting your monthly pass. You should have the correct fare because you will not receive any change, no matter what bill you insert. If you know your stop, about a block before getting there, press once lightly on the yellow or black strip near your window to notify the driver you wish to get off at the next stop.

Transfers are no longer free, but you can buy a day pass for unlimited rides on buses and trains. Persons with certified disabilities can ride mostly free of charge. Monthly passes are available for all services, including Trinity Railway Express (see below).

As in any other large American city, DART buses, which normally are an adequate means of transportation, can be unsafe, particularly at night. The transit police suggest in their pamphlet that, while waiting for a bus or train, you "try to avoid isolated bus stops and train stations. To avoid pickpocketing, secure your wallet, clutch purse, credit cards and cash inside your coat. Carry only what you plan to use for that day." Once on board, "stay alert and be aware of people around you. If someone bothers you, change seats or tell the driver to call the transit police. During off hours, sit as close to the driver as possible." Food, beverages, loud music, and smoking are never permitted on DART buses.

Downtown Trolley Route 712 & McKinney Avenue Trolley

In addition to the regular bus service, described above, DART also maintains a downtown Route 712 for visitors to the greater downtown area.

The buses circulate continuously from 7:30 in the morning until 9:30 in the evening and connect with DART light-rail stations in the West End and on Bryan Street. This service is available about every 15 to 20 minutes, but Monday through Friday only.

There is no charge for Route 712 trolleys, which travel eastward on Main Street (past the Adolphus Hotel and Neiman Marcus department store), turn north on Harwood, and continue to the Arts District on

Olive Street (past the Adam's Mark and Le Meridien Hotels), to within a block of Meyerson Symphony Hall.

From there, they turn southwest at Ross Avenue (passing the Dallas Museum of Art and the Fairmont Hotel) to Lamar and the West End Historic District (near the Sixth Floor Museum), and back to Main Street.

As an extension of this downtown route, you can also ride a trolley by the **McKinney Avenue Trolley Authority** (MATA), 3153 Oak Grove, (214) 855-0006, Internet www.mata.org, e-mail stcar@airmail.net. The service is available every 15-30 minutes, seven days a week, 7 AM-10 PM, Fri-Sat 10 AM-midnight. MATA is a non-profit corporation established in 1989 and initially run by volunteers.

The service, sponsored by the merchants and restaurants on this popular street, runs up and down McKinney Avenue, between Haskell Street uptown and Akard at St. Paul Street in the Arts District downtown. It begins near the Oak Grove trolley barn at McKinney Avenue, passes hotels and restaurants—such as the Crescent Hotel and the Hard Rock Café-offices, and retailers, continuing to the Dallas Museum of Art and back.

The four streetcars provide service on the 2.8-mile (or 4.5-kilometer) route with 21 stops. The rails are the remains from the old Dallas Street Railway.

The electric streetcars used include Car #636, nicknamed Petunia, that was built for the Dallas Consolidated Electric Street Railway in 1920 and was in service until 1947. Car #122, nicknamed Rosie, was built in 1906 by J. G. Brill of Philadelphia and ran in Oporto, Portugal, for 72 years. Car #186, nicknamed Green Dragon, was built for service in Dallas in 1913 and is the only car of its type in daily service today; it was used as a hay barn for 22 years. Car #369, nicknamed Matilda, was built in Australia by the Melbourne Metropolitan Tramway in 1925 and is MATA's largest car. The agency has also purchased ten 1950s-vintage General Motors buses from a storage yard in Sioux Falls, South Dakota.

In 2002, the service was expanded by another mile to the West Village development and Cityplace, DART's light-rail station, where a turntable turns the trolley cars around at the end of the line and sends them in the other direction.

Since it incorporated, MATA has spent more than $13 million to lay tracks and expand its routes, more than $8 million of it from federal taxes.

The rides are free for adults and children, although they cost taxpayers more than $3 per passenger. Bus and light-rail tickets are also honored.

Estimates have it that, excluding charters like the weekend birthday parties for kids, only about 200 riders use the service daily.

The McKinney Avenue Trolley does not go to the West End or Deep Ellum historic districts.

The **SMU Mustang Express,** supposedly serving students living in the apartments east and northeast of Southern Methodist University, operates on a DART subsidy of close to $2 per passenger. The buses run about every 15 minutes during school days and apparently serve fewer than 500 students daily, although other citizens can also ride free of charge.

DART Light-Rail Service

Trains operate every ten minutes or so in peak periods and 20-30 minutes at other times, roughly from 5 AM to midnight. The fleet consists of some 95 four-door cars sitting 76 passengers each, or 200 including standing room. Every car can hold two wheelchairs. The length of Dallas' city blocks limits the number of light-rail train cars to three, the same as in Baltimore, Maryland.

You can buy your ticket at vending machines located at all stations, or get a $30 monthly pass. Do not discard your ticket while on the train because it is the only proof that you paid your fare. Inspections by some 70 police officers assigned to rail patrol and fare enforcement is irregular. The maximum fare-evasion fine is $250. Smoking, drinking, gambling, and eating are not allowed in the cars.

Armed transit police officers no longer are stationed on every train at night. Instead, one officer is responsible for patrolling several light-rail stations and trains.

In the summer of 1996, after years of debates and digging, DART inaugurated the first 20 miles (or 32 kilometers) of a rail system that will eventually crisscross the Metroplex. The initial cost was $860 million. By the following summer, almost 30,000 rode DART's electric trains. That number has now more than doubled on weekdays.

"If there ever seemed an unlikely setting for successful urban rail transit, it probably would have been the Dallas-Fort Worth Metroplex, the mythological birthplace of Suburban-style sport utility vehicles," opined the *San Antonio Express-News* in 2000. "The common wisdom has been that Texans, many of whom have a primal attachment to their cars and pickups, were too independent and too proud to submit to the tyranny of light rail that lets them go only where tracks have been laid."

For long-time residents of Dallas, who are used to bragging that everything is the biggest and the best in Big D, the only surprise are the DART's Osaka-made toy-like rail cars, that appear minuscule compared with a system like the Moscow metro. Two grown men sit next to each other with a bit of discomfort.

The system extends for more than 44 miles (or 70 kilometers) and includes 35 stations, one up to 123 feet (or 37.5 meters) under the North Central Expressway. That is the $20-million, 33,000-square-foot (or 3,066-square-meter) underground station below the landmark 42-story Cityplace Tower (see entry), also called Cityplace. It is situated along a 3.25-mile (or 5.2-kilometer) tunnel that connects downtown with north Dallas. The person responsible for Cityplace station's look is Dallas artist Robert Barsamian, who turned schoolchildren's drawings into etched tiles for the station's walls and mezzanine.

The downtown light-rail stations include Pearl, St. Paul, Akard, West End, Union Station, and the Convention Center.

Two lines are operational: the **Red Line** starts southwest of downtown with the Westmoreland station and runs northeast—bypassing the Dallas Zoo (see listing)—and cuts through downtown Dallas. You can visit the zoo from the rail's West End station downtown in about 15 minutes.

It takes about 42 minutes from Dallas' West End to downtown Plano and another three minutes on foot to have a lunch or dinner at Joerg's Café Vienna, at 1037 East 15th Street, where you can sample Austrian-Hungarian goulash and pork or chicken cutlets from Carinthia.

From downtown, the Red Line runs to the so-far only underground Cityplace station and the popular Mockingbird station (at Mockingbird Lane and North Central Expressway), where parking is available for several hundred cars.

It will take you up to 30 minutes to take the Red Line from downtown to NorthPark shopping center (see listing), at North Central Expressway and Park Lane, almost the same if you drove a car on the congested expressway.

A trolley shuttles between the DART station at Greenville Avenue and Park Lane and the west entrance of the mall. Save your light-rail ticket, and the shuttle ride will be free. If you take a taxi from downtown Dallas to NorthPark, the fare might run as high as $15. The shuttle operates about every 15 minutes Mon-Sat 9 AM-10 PM, Sundays 11 PM-7 PM.

The Red Line continues along Central Expressway through Richardson and into downtown Plano, where the Collin Creek Mall trolley will take you to the shopping center. Counting downtown Dallas, Mockingbird Station, Cityplace and West Village, NorthPark, and Plano's Collin Creek Mall (see individual entries), there are more than 300 stores comfortably at your disposal without having to use a private automobile.

The **Blue Line** starts south of downtown, at Ledbetter station, and runs northward through downtown Dallas, then via Mockingbird Lane station to downtown Garland, northeast of here.

Construction on the $56-million extension of the Blue Line from Mockingbird Lane station to White Rock was completed in 2001. The White Rock station, on Northwest Highway west of White Rock Lake, has 500 parking spaces.

You can park your car free of charge at several stations, such as Mockingbird, if you come early enough, while space is available.

From White Rock, the segment that leads to LBJ/Skillman and Forest/Jupiter stations opened in 2002, the same year that the first trains reached downtown Garland, at Walnut and Fifth Streets, where 700 parking spaces are available. It now takes about 32 minutes to travel from downtown Garland to the West End in downtown Dallas.

Trinity Railway Express

Since 1997, a commuter rail line, known as the Trinity Railway Express (TRE), Internet www.trinityrailwayexpress.org, (214) 979-1111, has utilized diesel trains with upholstered seats and climate control.

The Trinity Express links downtown Dallas' Union Station, which is within walking distance of Dealey Plaza; Medical/Market Center station, within walking distance of some hospitals; South Irving station, where free parking and restrooms are available; West Irving station (off Esters Road), with free parking; CentrePort Dr. station at Statler Blvd. in Irving (south of D/FW Airport); Hurst/Bell station (south of State Highway 10, near the Bell Helicopter plant), with free parking; and the Richland Hills station, at Handley-Ederville Road and Burns St., just south of State Highway 121.

Seventeen years in planning, the Express cost $254 million since north Texas' two largest cities bought the former Rock Island Railroad line in 1983 to connect Dallas with Fort Worth.

The line extended to downtown Fort Worth, at Intermodal Transportation Center, 1001 Jones Street, in 2001 and might do so to Dallas/Fort Worth International Airport by 2005.

Intermodal, a $14-million, 30,000-square-foot (or 2,787-square meter) facility, brings together the Trinity Railway, Amtrak, Greyhound, city bus and taxi service.

CentrePort railway station is linked to all D/FW terminals by Route 30 shuttle buses that depart every 20 minutes during weekday rush hours, and hourly at other times, including Saturdays. The shuttle is free to paying TRE passengers. This service is not available on major federal holidays or Sundays. It takes up to one hour from downtown Dallas to the airport. The one-way fare is $2.

Up to 8,000 passengers ride the 34-mile (or 54-kilometer) rail line between downtown Fort Worth and downtown Dallas each weekday. Trinity Railway is a joint project between DART and the Fort Worth Transit Authority, toll-free (877) 657-0146.

The Trinity Express trains on this line will get you from Irving to Dallas in about 16 minutes. It takes about 70 minutes from downtown Dallas' Union Station to Fort Worth's Texas & Pacific Station. Some 26 trains operate Mon-Fri 5:35 AM-11:05 PM, Sat 8 AM-12:30 AM, mostly on a single track.

"The rail cars are spacious and comfortable, sporting shaded windows, good air conditioning, cushioned seats and tables at which passengers may write, read or listen to music with headphones," observes the *Dallas Morning News*. "The passing landscape is not exactly what one would call prepossessing." About half the trains have restrooms.

Although the cost of running the railway works out to more than $7 per passenger, the fare is just $1 for each of the three zones, and children under five years of age ride free. A local monthly pass allows you to travel within one zone. Fares include free transfers to DART light-rail and both DART and Fort Worth's T bus service. Ticket vending machines are located on all station platforms, as well as at Albertson's, Minyard, and Fiesta Mart stores.

Car Rental

But all this public transport seems just a drop in the bucket when you consider that Dallas alone measures 400 square miles (or 1,036 square kilometers). And visitors are not likely to stand on street corners, often in the broiling summer heat, waiting for a bus that might take them only part of the way to where they want to go.

Dallas residents take comfort in their automobiles. Even though subjected to nerve-wracking traffic tie-ups and scorching sun in the summer, they often refuse to surrender to public transportation. It is a Texas badge of independence and no accident that most cars you see on public byways contain but one passenger. Dallasites love the freedom that goes with having a car, and it will take many years before they change their habits, if ever.

And where does that leave you? At the doorstep of a car rental agency, probably.

If the expense of renting an economy car for about $50 a day is acceptable to you, there is no alternative to having an automobile in the Metroplex, although parking is expensive, time-consuming, and sometimes difficult to find. More than 2,000 parking tickets are issued every week in the downtown area alone.

Upon your arrival at the Dallas/Fort Worth International Airport, the rental company's shuttle bus can pick you up and take you to the 1.4-million-square-foot (or 130,060-square-meter) parking center, where 5,000 cars can be parked. The $150-million rental car facility was finished in 2000 on a 200-acre (or 80.9-hectare) site near the airport's south shuttle parking lot in Tarrant County that houses ten rental car companies under one roof.

You cannot pay cash for your rental car, unless you have made prior arrangements at home. Most rental agencies require that you be at least 21 to 25 years old. Remember that you can never ask too many questions; better take your time and be safe than sorry. Find out, for example, what the charge is for child safety seats if you have kids riding in the car.

Car rentals are subject to a 15 percent sales tax, but if you pick up your vehicle at the D/FW Airport the tax is 18 percent, which includes a levy to pay for the American Airlines Center, a downtown events arena. It may be to your advantage to take a bus, van, or taxi to your destination, then pick up the rental vehicle downtown or in the suburbs.

Among the major car rental companies with branches in the Metroplex, you will find:

Advantage Rent-a-Car	(800) 777-5500, Internet www.arac.com.
Alamo Rent-a-Car	(800) 327-9633, Internet www.goalamo.com.
Avis Rent-a-Car	(800) 331-1212, Internet www.avis.com.
Budget Rent-a-Car	(800) 527-0700, Internet www.rent.drivebudget.com.
Dollar Rent-a-Car	(800) 800-4000, Internet www.dollar.com.
Enterprise Rent-a-Car	(800) 325-8007, Internet www.enterprise.com/car_rental.
Hertz Rent-a-Car	(800) 654-3131, Internet www.hertz.com.
National Rent-a-Car	(800) 227-7368, Internet www.nationalcar.com.
Thrifty Rent-a-Car	(800) 367-2277, Internet www.thrifty.com.

Dallas has more than 1,000 cash-key meters installed downtown, where car owners who do not have change can park their vehicles with the help of a plastic key that works like a debit card. Keys are sold at face value, with $25 to $200 stored on them in $5 increments, between 8 AM and 5 PM weekdays, on the ground floor at City Hall, the same place where violators pay their parking tickets.

Each time a key is used, the meter indicates digitally how much credit remains on it. Lost keys cannot be replaced.

There are some 4,400 parking meters in the city. Metered parking in central downtown area costs about $1 an hour. An expired meter earns a fine of $20, if paid within 15 days, and $35 thereafter. Parking in a no-standing zone will cost you $25, or $45 after 15 days, standing or parking in a fire line $40 and $75 after 15 days.

The fine for illegally parking in a handicapped space is $100; if the ticket is not paid within 15 days, it increases to $195. Dallas police write about 3,000 handicapped-parking citations each year. Anyone with three or more outstanding parking tickets within a year can have the car immobilized by a wheel boot, which costs an additional $60 to remove.

Private Car

A couple of tidbits that will lighten the confusion surrounding the Dallas streets:

Downtown streets are divided by Main Street into north- and south-side streets, with the block numbers progressing northward and southward.

U.S. Highway 75, commonly known as Central Expressway, is the dividing line between east and west Dallas. The roadway becomes North Central Expressway when it passes Interstate Highway 30 downtown.

The north-south Hillcrest Avenue becomes Hillcrest Road once you cross West Northwest Highway going north.

Greenville Avenue is often identified as Lower Greenville up to East Mockingbird Lane; farther north it is known as Upper Greenville.

Highway frontage roads, usually called service roads, and often lined with strip malls, are as Texan as pickup trucks with gun racks. The state began building frontage roads in the 1950s, and their presence has separated Texas from almost every other state.

The Texas Department of Transportation in 2001 scrapped its long-time policy of building service roads along highways. Instead, it plans to funnel freeway traffic directly to key city streets supposedly to improve safety and traffic flow and reduce construction and maintenance costs.

Building two-lane service roads on both sides of a highway costs about $1.5 million per mile (or 1.6 kilometer). The state already spends millions of dollars every year to maintain existing frontage roads.

These are some of the major roadways and byways in the Metroplex:

Airport Freeway—State Highway 183 from State Highway 114 to the south entrance of D/FW Airport.

C. F. Hawn Freeway (or U.S. Highway 175)—Located south of downtown and named after the former state highway commissioner Charles F. Hawn, the oldest among six brothers, who made his fortune in the lumber business in Athens, Texas, but lived in Dallas.

Dallas North Tollway—A 21-mile (or 33.8-kilometer), six-lane, limited-access expressway passing through or along the cities of Dallas, Highland Park, University Park, Addison, Farmer's Branch, and Plano.

It runs from Stemmons Freeway (Interstate Highway 35 East), just north of downtown, going north about four miles (or 6.4 kilometers) beyond I-635 (or LBJ Freeway), to State Highway 121 in Collin County. Its service road is known as the Dallas Parkway.

The idea of buying the Cotton Belt Railroad property and turning it into the tollway was the brainchild of Clarence Albert Tatum (1907-1986), president of Texas Utilities Co. The first section of the tollway, from downtown to the LBJ Freeway, opened in 1968. In 1989, it became one of the first roads in the nation to use high-technology, automatic vehicle identification tags, known as toll tags, which allow motorists to drive through toll booths without stopping. The toll is 30 cents to $1.50, depending on the length of your trip. You can also buy an electronic TollTag pass from which the proper toll is automatically deducted. The TollTag store is located at 12300 Inwood Rd. at Forest Ln., (972) 991-0033; toll-free outside Metroplex, (877) 991-0033, Internet www.ntta.org, e-mail tolltagsupport@ntta.org.

Although becoming increasingly congested, the tollway could still be a welcome alternative to North Central Expressway if you need to get from north to south or the other way around.

Interstate Highway 30 connects Dallas with Fort Worth. Part of it is also known as the East R. L. Thornton Freeway.

A portion of this highway was renamed for Dallas Cowboys coach Tom Landry, who coached the professional football team for 29 seasons and retired in 1989 with 270 victories, 13 division titles, and five trips to the Super Bowl. He died in 2000 from leukemia.

Dallas' downtown mixmaster—the convergence of Interstates 30 and 35 East—is among the nation's worst traffic problems, according to the American Automobile Association. The mixmaster, through which more than 200,000 vehicles travel daily, has been a trouble spot for more than 30 years. The convergence is located on the edge of the southwest downtown area, near the Reunion hotel complex (see entry). Both Interstates 30 and 35 East are being considered for a drastic rebuilding along the downtown's south and west borders. The city might create a tunnel along I-30 and leave room for parks and walkways on top as a way to bridge downtown and the Cedars neighborhood to the south.

Interstate Highway 35 East—Also known as Stemmons Freeway (see entry) north of downtown and R. L. Thornton Freeway (see entry) south of downtown. In Texas alone, it is about 590 miles (or 949 kilometers) long.

"I-35 between Dallas and Austin is the most dangerous interstate in the nation," according to Republican state senator Florence Shapiro of Plano. Almost one-half of North American Free Trade Agreement (NAFTA) traffic that reaches Texas goes through the area via Interstate 35. The 40-plus-year-old Interstate 35 leads from Laredo, Texas, to Duluth, Minnesota. South of the Metroplex, roughly at Hillsboro, it divides into 35 West, which cuts through Fort Worth, and 35 East, which slices through Dallas; then going north, it converges again near Denton.

J. Elmer Weaver Freeway—U.S. Highway 67 from Interstate Highway 635 (or LBJ Freeway) to the south.

John Carpenter Freeway—State Highway 183 and Highway 114 from Interstate Highway 35 East to the north entrance of D/FW Airport.

John William Carpenter (1881-1959) was born on a farm near Corsicana, Texas, and later took courses at what is now the University of North Texas in Denton. Over the years, he managed a dozen utilities, including Dallas Power and Light Co. and Texas Power and Light. He organized the predecessor of Texas Security Life Insurance, which later became Southland Life Insurance Co., one of the nation's largest publicly owned life insurance companies.

(For more about Carpenter's statue downtown, please see under Adam's Mark Hotel in the LODGING chapter.)

Julius Schepps Freeway—Interstate Highway 45 southward from downtown. It is named for a Jewish civic leader, born in St. Louis, Missouri, whose parents emigrated from Russia in 1890. Ten years later, the Scheppses came to Dallas, where they opened a bakery.

Julius (1895-1971) attended Texas A & M on a basketball scholarship in 1914, but had to withdraw after a few weeks, when it came to light that he had no high school diploma. He married in El Paso around 1915 and took over the Dallas bakery when his father died seven years later. In 1928, Schepps sold the bakery and began his insurance business, which he carried on for 43 years. He established a brewing company, began a wholesale liquor business, and had business interests in a Dallas radio station, a baseball club, and several baking companies.

"Schepps believed in the American ideal that anything was possible if you worked hard enough for it," observes the Texas State Historical Association.

Loop 9—Plans are in the works for the route of a new road looping south of Interstate 20 that will run from Mesquite through Seagoville, Wilmer, Lancaster, DeSoto, Cedar Hill, Mansfield, and Crowley. It would then extend into Tarrant County and meet State Highway 360 south of Mansfield.

Envisioned as a six-lane urban parkway, Loop 9 would be part of an outer loop that runs around the Metroplex and is scheduled for construction toward the end of the decade.

Loop 12—A loop that completely encircles the core of Dallas. It includes Northwest Highway on the north, Buckner Boulevard on the east, Ledbetter Drive on the south, and Walton Walker Boulevard on the west. Walton Walker was a lieutenant general killed in the Korean war in 1950.

The next larger ring around metropolitan Dallas is Lyndon B. Johnson Freeway (or Interstate 635), the area's most congested highway, which forms a near-loop with Interstate 20 that leads to Arlington and Fort Worth.

A third and still larger 100-mile (or 161-kilometer) highway loop around Dallas—similar to Loop 1604 in San Antonio—was envisioned here four decades ago, but might not be completed until 2025.

Lyndon B. Johnson Freeway—Interstate Highway 635, begins at the north entrance of D/FW Airport and circles the city from the north, east, and south. It includes I-20 on the south.

In 2002, a $261-million reconstruction of LBJ and Central Expressway Interchange began here and is expected to be finished in 2007. The project, called the Dallas High Five because of a five-level interchange, will replace the current triple-decked structure. When completed, Central Expressway will be four lanes in each direction, and LBJ will be five lanes—plus two high-occupancy-vehicle or HOV lanes—each way.

The interchange, which is considered one of the most heavily traveled in the state, handles about 400,000 vehicles each day and is clogged with bumper-to-bumper traffic. (For more details, go on the Web at www.dallashighfive.org.)

Marvin D. Love Freeway—U.S. Highway 67 from Interstate Highway 35 East to Interstate 635 south of downtown.

Named for Marvin D. Love (d. 1964), who served in the Navy during World War I, moved to Dallas, was manager for the Dallas Power and Light Co., and became Dallas County Commissioner.

North Central Expressway—U.S. Highway 75, northward from downtown, where it runs through Richardson and Plano. Southward from downtown it is called South Central Expressway. It is more bearable since its $500-million expansion that was completed in 2000.

For decades the favorite traffic scapegoat in Dallas. Initially suggested as Central Avenue in 1911, the mayor made it his priority project for the city in 1927. Evolving from the path of the old Houston-Texas Central Railroad, its construction began in 1947, and the expressway opened two years later. It was elevated in 1969.

Originally designed to carry 75,000 vehicles, it counted up to 200,000 a day by 1997, and now has a capacity of 230,000 cars a day. DART's light-rail line is presumed to have lessened the traffic by another 50,000 vehicles a day. The pessimists claim that even with the reconstruction it is already outdated.

Once the most damnable roads in north Texas, it perhaps personifies the worst of Dallas and the fallacy that the automobile gives one freedom. After years of reconstruction, its northern part has gained a lane in each direction, but it seems just as dangerous as ever. It is still an accident magnet, so stay away from it if you can, rush hour or not.

"Ten miles [or 16 kilometers] long and ten years in construction, the new North Central fulfills its role as primary traffic artery, and now with beauty and grace," claims the Dallas branch of the American Institute of Architects.

A four-mile (or 6.4-kilometer) stretch of South Central Expressway, between Interstate 45 and Loop 12, is known as the S. M. Wright Freeway. It is named for Rev. Wright, a city civil-rights leader and pastor of Peoples Baptist Church for 37 years. He is said to have helped prevent race riots that hit other major cities during the 1960s.

President George Bush Turnpike—Also known in part as State Highway 190. Named after the 41st president of the United States and George W. Bush's father, the highway was begun in 1998 and was slated to be completed in 2005.

The 30.5-mile (or 49-kilometer) road stretches from State Highway 78 in Garland to Interstate 635 East in Irving, passing through seven cities and three counties. Interstate 35 East, the Dallas North Tollway, and North Central Expressway all connect to the turnpike, which has grown as north Texas' northern suburbs have.

More than 200,000 vehicles pass through the turnpike each day. The toll from Garland to Carrollton is about $3. Toll tags are available by registration at the North Texas Tollway Authority Web site, www.ntta.org, e-mail tolltagsupport@ntta.org.

R. L. Thornton Freeway—It begins as Interstate Highway 35 East and U.S. Highway 77 south of Dallas at the Interstate 635 interchange, passes south of downtown, and continues east as Interstate Highway 30.

Robert Lee Thornton (1880-1964), banker and Dallas mayor, was born on a farm near Hico, Texas. Having lost their farm because of a title flaw, the family moved several times. Barely finishing eight grade, he took a business course at the Metropolitan Business College in Dallas and in 1904 became a traveling candy salesman.

Borrowing $18,000 from his relatives, Thornton organized a private bank, which eventually became the powerful Mercantile National Bank. He was the first Dallas banker to make car loans. Although a successful businessman, Thornton's civic involvement earned him the title Mr. Dallas. Thornton was a four-term Dallas mayor who served in that capacity from 1953 to 1961. It was largely through his efforts that Dallas hosted the 1936 Texas Centennial Exposition in Fair Park (see entry) to celebrate Texas' independence from Mexico, although the city did not even exist a hundred years earlier.

Stemmons Freeway—Interstate Highway 35 East northward from downtown opened in 1959.

"The Dallas that exists today is largely the product of a few citizens' drive to reshape the Trinity corridor," observes the *Dallas Morning News*. "Before developer Leslie Stemmons advocated moving the river a mile [or 1.6 kilometer] to the west and confining it between levees more than 75 years ago, the area north and west of downtown was largely worthless, subject to devastating floods."

Taming the river in stages, from the 1930s to the 1950s, created more than 10,000 acres (or 4,047 hectares) of usable land and made the Stemmons family one of the most powerful in Dallas.

Walton Walker Boulevard (or Loop 12) gets its name from the World War II general and commander of the 36th Texas Infantry Division, who was killed in the Korean war in 1950.

Woodall Rodgers Freeway—Spur 366, a short freeway (with no numerical designation) north of downtown that connects Interstate Highway 35 East with U.S. Highway 75 (Central Expressway) and Interstate Highway 45.

An eight-lane extension of the Woodall Rodgers Freeway is planned over the Trinity River to connect it with Singleton Boulevard at Beckley Avenue on the river's west side. (Please see entry Calatrava's Suspension Bridge across the Trinity River in the SIGHTS & ATTRACTIONS chapter for more details.)

James Woodall Rodgers (1890-1961), after whom the freeway is named, was born in Alabama and did his graduate work at Columbia University. His law career began in Dallas in 1916, and nine years later he founded a law firm that specialized in gas and oil law and for many years represented Standard Oil Company of Indiana. Rodgers was the mayor of Dallas from 1939 to 1947 and was instrumental in building the Central Expressway.

(For more details about Dallas streets, please see also heading Dallas Streets & How They Were Named in the SIGHTS & ATTRACTIONS chapter.)

High Occupancy Vehicle (HOV) System—The system's first HOV lane, which opened in 1991, was 5.2 miles (or 8.4 kilometers) of reversible lane on the east R. L. Thornton Freeway (or Interstate 30) from downtown east to Jim Miller Road. It is open for inbound traffic in the morning and outbound traffic in the evening.

Another HOV lane on Interstate 635 (or Lyndon B. Johnson Freeway) runs from Interstate 35 to the North Central Expressway (or U.S. Highway 75).

You can be stopped and ticketed if found alone on an HOV lane in your vehicle. To use any Dallas HOV lane, you must have at least one other passenger, even if only a child, in the car. The annual HOV ridership has jumped to 33 million.

Tours

Some two dozen companies provide a variety of tours, either scheduled or tailored to your interests, among them:

Executive Star Tours, 2077 North Collins Blvd., Suite 101-B, Richardson, (972) 208-1500, or out-of-town toll-free, (888) 972-1500, Internet www.aaacablimo.com, is a family-owned business. Brothers Gary and Alex came to Dallas from Russia in 1992 with $400 between them and started this company five years later.

Among the half a dozen tours offered is a three-hour tour of the Sixth Floor Museum (see entry), which includes the admission. A Dallas art tour that includes the Dallas Museum of Art (see entry) and the Meyerson Symphony Center (see entry) is offered.

Also available, for a minimum of ten persons, is a five-hour tour, titled Shop 'til You Drop, to the Grapevine Mills mall (see entry), and a three-hour tour of Southfork Ranch (see entry), the home of the imaginary Ewing clan from the television soap opera *Dallas*.

Texas Trails Tours, 3621 Works Ave., Dallas, (972) 222-5838, provides a daily five-hour tour, titled All About Dallas, which includes most of the usual sights, including Dealey Plaza, where John F. Kennedy was assassinated, at a cost of $35, half-price for children up to age 12. Pick-ups are available from half a dozen major Dallas hotels. Southfork Ranch and tours to Fort Worth are available for groups of at least 20.

D-Tours, (972) 241-7729, will tailor a tour to your requirements, but for no fewer than 20 people. **Longhorn Tours,** (972) 228-4571, handles tours with groups of at least ten persons.

(Please see the section Tours in THE INTERNATIONAL VISITOR chapter for additional details.)

For more information, call also the Dallas Convention & Visitors Bureau, 1201 Elm St., Suite 2000, (214) 571-1000; Visitor Information Center, (214) 571-1300; 24-Hour Events Hotline, (800) 232-5527, Fax 571-1008, Internet in English, French, German, Japanese, Portuguese, and Spanish at www.dallasconventioncenter.com.

Walking

Walking is a fine alternative in a few neighborhoods, provided the weather is all right and you do so during the day.

But first this observation: When Dallasites brag about theirs as a "world-class" city, one would think a basic prerequisite for such a boast would be civilized sidewalks. Dallas has hundreds of miles of roads where sidewalks are harder to find than a Swahili-speaking scholar.

Drive up Preston Road, one of Dallas' oldest roadways, and you will find no sidewalks while passing through the tony Highland Park. O.K., you say, those rich elitists just want to keep nosy busybodies out.

Keep going northward, and you will find that mile after mile, from the Northwest Highway to the Lyndon B. Johnson Freeway, for example, there are few sidewalks along Preston Road, except where it leads through shopping areas. Drive up and down Hillcrest and many another street, and you will get nowhere on foot, unless you want to walk over grass, gravel, mud, or on the street, none of which we recommend.

It is safe to say that it will take at least a generation before Dallas becomes walker-friendly, if ever. At every step, outside of downtown, you have to be prepared for confrontations by motorists or barriers that make walking in this city unpleasant, even dangerous.

While the *Texas Drivers Handbook* states that at crosswalks without stop signs or signals, "if the pedestrian has entered the crosswalk, you should give him the right-of-way," do not count on it. "Most drivers I know," writes the transportation reporter for the *Dallas Morning News*, "use them as target practice. The unwritten rule, as I have seen it, is: 'If pedestrians enter a crosswalk, creep up on them as they walk in front of you and make them uncomfortable for slowing you down.'" The writer claims to be "astonished" at the level of courtesy motorists provide pedestrians in Maine and towns around Boston.

Downtown is fine if you feel like walking from your hotel to a few downtown sights or to go shopping at Neiman Marcus. We do not recommend walking downtown before 6 AM or after 6 PM, unless you are with a group. You had better not engage in conversation with the homeless and the beggars, because you never know the outcome.

"Not only have overzealous panhandlers become a danger to themselves and motorists, they have staked out so many intersections that a Dallas visitor might assume the whole city is homeless," observes in part a *Dallas Morning News* editorial. In 2003, the city council finally banned panhandling.

West End warehouse district is a fine choice for walking, lunching, trinket or T-shirt shopping during the day. Be cautious if walking around here in the early evening, and alert at night.

Deep Ellum is a reasonably good choice to walk in during the day and enjoy provocative alternative entertainment in the evenings. But, please, be careful at night, and stay away from dark alleys.

Fair Park is interesting to walk in during the annual State Fair, but even then we recommend caution, particularly after dark, for the area has a relatively high crime rate.

Oak Lawn is all right for leisurely walking, lunching, and dining, but because it is the area of choice for homosexuals, harassment at night is not unheard of for persons of such persuasion.

Parts of **McKinney Avenue** might be of interest for sampling a large selection of restaurants, but will be even more rewarding for walkers if they want to explore Uptown and its many art and antique galleries.

East Dallas' **Greenville Avenue,** Upper and Lower, also have many restaurants and bars, but Lower Greenville is a better choice for walking, preferably during the day. We suggest that women refrain from walking alone on any part of Greenville Avenue at night.

Park Cities (University Park and Highland Park) are of particular interest for walking around the Southern Methodist University campus, Snider Plaza shops, Highland Park Village mall, and a few well-cared-for parks. Safety here is probably the best, but robberies are not unheard of early in the morning or late at night. The Southern Methodist University campus also has to deal now and again with rapes.

(See also section Underground Walkways in the SIGHTS & ATTRACTIONS chapter. A downtown walking tour is included under SELF-GUIDED TOURS, but is recommended during the day only.)

LODGING

Dallas claims more than 44,000 lodging rooms, about 10,000 more than Houston, the state's largest city. Eighty-five percent of all rooms are booked by convention guests or individual business travelers; leisure travelers make up only 10 percent of Dallas' hotel occupants.

Hotels below are arranged according to one of the neighborhoods explained in the introduction, then grouped into one of these approximate price categories:

I *Inexpensive*, up to $50 for a single room
M *Moderate*, $50-100 for a single room
E *Expensive*, more than $100 for a single room

Classifications are based on the regular daily rates, although many hotels offer special weekend and holiday deals. Ask also whether you qualify for a business, government, or another discount rate. Practically all hotels accept major credit cards, but few will take foreign currencies as payment. Some of the luxury ones will assist you, however, with information on where to exchange the money. Many hotels offer complimentary breakfast. Check-in time is usually between noon and 3 PM, check-out time between 11 AM and 1 PM.

To pay for a new sports arena downtown, the American Airlines Center (see entry), the hotel-room tax went up from 13 to 15 percent in 1998. In 2003, the city had the third-highest hotel tax rate in the nation.

Toll-free 800 and other telephone numbers are included, where available, so you can call these hotels free of charge from anywhere in the United States to make reservations. When you dial area codes 214, 469, or 972 from another area code, it is a long-distance call.

Some Dallas hotels will let you make local telephone calls, meaning inside these three area codes, free of charge, while others may charge for them. Ask, if the expense is of concern to you. You will always pay for long-distance calls—such as from Dallas to Fort Worth or Arlington and the other way around—and sometimes you pay whatever the traffic will bear.

You may be asked for a credit card number when you reserve your hotel room. Ask about the penalties before you book your room.

If you cannot make up your mind as to how much to tip your hotel maid, this might help: the *Washington Post* reports that "hotel maids get paid about 17 cents per room per day for their labors."

Standard amenities available are noted with these abbreviations:

AC—alarm clock and/or **radio** in rooms.

ATM—automatic teller machine on premises.

BC—business center on premises, although there is usually a charge for copying, faxing, and printing.

C—concierge available.

CB—complimentary breakfast served, although food selection may be limited.

CF—no charge for children who occupy the same room as the adult who accompanies them; the minimum age limit varies.

CM—cable television and/or **movies** in rooms.

COF—complimentary in-room **coffee** and/or **tea**.

CP—complimentary parking.

DCL—dry cleaning and/or **laundry** service.

EX—express check-in and/or **check-out** available.

FLC—free local telephone **calls**; in Dallas area that is within area codes 214 and 972.

FT—free shuttle to and from the airport, or complimentary **transportation** within a few miles, such as to the nearest shopping center, or both.

GS—gift shop on premises.

HC—health club facilities available, although there may be a charge.

HR—handicapped-accessible rooms.

IH—iron/ironing board and/or **hair dryer** available in most rooms.

MF—meeting facilities, although there is usually a charge for them.

PA—pets allowed, depending on their size.

PT—near public transportation, such as city bus route, trolley, or light rail.

RS—room service available, sometimes only until midnight.

SDB—safe deposit boxes available at front desk or elsewhere on premises.

VMD—voice mail and/or **data port connections** in many rooms.

WN—complimentary **weekday newspaper,** such as *USA Today*, provided.

Such amenities as air conditioning, television, or telephone are not listed because all hotels listed here have them. Most hotels now also provide rooms for non-smokers.

The Dallas City Council voted in 2003 to ban smoking in all hotel and motel guest rooms not designated for smoking, restaurants, and private clubs with eating establishments. Smokers are allowed to light up on restaurant patios, as long as they are not enclosed. The smoking ban was also extended to all Dallas museums, cinemas, shopping malls, department and grocery stores.

The only exceptions to the ban are specifically designated areas of stand-alone bars and pool halls, tobacco shops and cigar bars, and outdoor patios. Fines range from $25 to $500.

DOWNTOWN DALLAS HOTELS

There are no hotels in Deep Ellum, Fair Park, or Oak Cliff that meet the criteria for inclusion.

ADAM'S MARK, 400 North Olive St. at Live Oak, (800) 444-ADAM or (214) 922-8000, Fax 969-7650, Internet www.adamsmark.com/dallas, e-mail adamsmark.dallas@cwixmail.com. *E*. It has 1,844 rooms and suites, many for the handicapped and non-smokers.

Located in the northeast part of downtown in the three-building former Southland Center skyscraper complex that was originally designed by Welton Becket & Associates of Los Angeles. Plaza of the Americas complex, with its year-round skating rink and shopping center, is only one block north. Situated between St. Paul and Pearl light-rail stations.

Amenities: Children ages 17 and younger stay free with parents. Restaurant & sports bar. Safe deposit boxes. Large work desk in many rooms. Fourth-floor fitness center with stair climbers, treadmills, bicycles, locker rooms, & showers. Outdoor swimming pool & sauna. Business center open Mon-Fri. It has 230,000 square feet (or 21,367 square meters) of meeting space, with the largest room measuring 40,800 square feet (or 3,790 square meters). Flower shop. Game room with video arcade and pinball machines for kids. Also AC, C, CM, COF, DCL, EX, FT, GS, HR, IH, MF, PA, PT, RS, VMD.

Concierge level rooms with breakfast & other amenities available at additional cost. Pets are not allowed.

Formerly a Sheraton Hotel inaugurated in 1958, and then the redecorated Harvey, which became an Adam's Mark luxury convention hotel in 1997, it is housed in a 29-story Skyway Tower with 500 "eclectically decorated" rooms and suites. The adjacent 42-story Southland Life Building, which was one of the first modern offices when it opened in 1959, and another 32-story building, also became part of Adam's Mark in 1998 and were converted into an additional 1,230 rooms and suites at a cost of $150 million.

This makes Adam's Mark the largest Metroplex hotel, and one of the largest in Texas, with meeting facilities for almost 5,000. Check out that 1998 18-foot (or 5.48-meter) bronze of a man riding a horse, titled *Slicker Shy*, by the Colorado sculptor Herb Mignery in the main lobby.

In a survey of 41,000 *Consumer Reports* readers, Adam's Mark was rated the worst among the "upscale" hotel chains nationwide, such as Embassy Suites, Marriott, Hilton, Crowne Plaza, Wyndham, Omni, and Doubletree.

For more about the **Chaparral** restaurant, located on the 38th floor of the hotel, please see the DINING chapter. Pearl Street Café and Atrium Brasserie serve breakfast, lunch and dinner, while Bagels on Bryan offers bagels, sandwiches, pastry, and beverages. Up to 100 cooks and 200 waiters prepare and serve the food.

Silhouettes and Tiffany Rose nightclubs will entertain you into the wee hours, while Players Sports Bar will let you enjoy televised sports. Silhouettes, one of the better dance spots downtown, features live music Tuesday through Saturday.

A former Southland's president was businessman and civic leader **John William Carpenter** (1881-1959) after whom State Highway 114 was named as John W. Carpenter Freeway. You can see his larger than life-size bronze about a block southeast, at Carpenter Plaza, 400 North Pearl at Crockett Streets. It was installed by sculptor Robert Berks (b. 1922) in 1980.

Carpenter was born on a farm near Corsicana, Texas, and in 1905 joined the General Electric Co. in Schenectady, New York. He came to Dallas in 1918 as the general manager of Dallas Power & Light Co. Carpenter organized two dozen major companies in the Southwest and was awarded an honorary doctorate of engineering by Southern Methodist University.

THE ADOLPHUS,1321 Commerce St. at Akard, (800) 221-9083 or (214) 742-8200, Fax 651-3563, Internet www.hoteladolphus.com or www.noblehousehotels.com, e-mail concierge@adolphus.com. *E*. Has 435 rooms and suites, some for the handicapped and non-smokers, some with private patios. The Adolphus has about 400 employees.

Centrally located, two blocks west of Neiman Marcus luxury department store, a bit farther from the City Hall, and four blocks west of Dealey Plaza, where John F. Kennedy was assassinated. Bell Plaza and the Telephone Pioneer Museum are across the street. (Please see individual entries for more details.)

Jack Ruby, who in 1963 shot President Kennedy's alleged assassin Lee Harvey Oswald, had his club Carousel at 1312 1/2 Commerce St., where the SBC Communications building now stands, across the street from the Adolphus.

Amenities: Limousine service can be arranged for airport pick-up. Foreign language capabilities. Children 11 or under stay free with parents. Safety deposit boxes. The Skylight Suites have floor-to-ceiling windows, wet bars, & refrigerators. Three telephones & work area with desk in most rooms. Kitchenettes with refrigerators in suites & marble baths.

Fifteenth-floor fitness club has stair steppers, exercise bicycles, rowing machines, & treadmills. Business center is open Mon-Fri 7:30 AM-4:30 PM & includes computer workstation, laser printer, fax machine, photocopier, & Internet access. Free transportation downtown daily 7 AM-7 PM.

It has 23 meeting rooms on two levels, including a 5,200-square-foot (or 483-square-meter) ballroom. Airline desk. Barber & beauty shop. Valet parking at 500-car adjacent garage. Shoeshine, bathrobe, & bath scale. Also AC, C, CF, CM, DCL, EX, FT, GS, HC, IH, HR, PT, RS, VMD, WN. One of the few hotels where you will still find cloth towelettes, instead of paper in the bathrooms.

The 22-story Beaux Arts-styled Adolphus was built in 1912 at a cost of $2.5 million, amid an outbreak of meningitis, by the beer magnate Adolphus Busch, who died one year and eight days later in his native Germany. Styled after New York's Plaza Hotel, it has been declared a historical landmark for its original architecture.

Several additions followed, including one in 1926 by Sir Alfred Bossom, an "eccentric" British architect, who also designed the building housing today's Magnolia Hotel (see entry) across Akard Street.

In 1940, when the population of Dallas was just shy of 300,000, it became the first hotel to be fully air-conditioned. The Adolphus was known nationwide for its fine dining, dancing, and entertainment. Its shows were featured in the now-defunct Century Room, now converted into the parking drive, which at one time operated a retractable ice rink for skating shows.

Many a personage has stayed at the Adolphus, from poet William Butler to Queen Elizabeth II in 1991, from chanteuse Edith Piaf to aviatrix Amelia Earhart. Bandleader Glenn Miller played here during the second year of the Texas Centennial, while Tommy Dorsey performed at the Baker Hotel across the street, and Benny Goodman swung at the fair grounds.

The previous building at this site housed the third City Hall (see entry), which was constructed in 1889 on a design by architect A. B. Bristol.

The number of rooms, now averaging 550 square feet (or 51 square meters), had been halved and soundproofed in 1980; many are furnished in Queen Anne and Chippendale styles. The Adolphus Busch penthouse measures 2,500 square feet (or 232 square meters). The hotel is owned by Noble House Hotels & Resorts of Kirkland, Washington.

(For details about the **French Room** restaurant, serving "traditional

French cuisine adapted to contemporary American tastes," please see the DINING chapter.)

For more casual and undistinguished fare, there is the Bistro, next door and open daily 6:30 AM-10 PM, and serving huevos rancheros (eggs), grilled trout, or boneless pork loin. At Walt Garrison's Rodeo Bar & Grill on the ground floor, you can sample Western fare, such as Bubba's pasta or brisket sandwich, in a Texas-style honky tonk.

In the English tradition, afternoon tea is served to the accompaniment of a piano in the glass-roof lobby, Thu-Sat 3 PM-4:45 PM, September through June. Another tearoom to consider nearby would be Lady Primrose, 500 Crescent Court, in Uptown.

Adolphus guests also have access to the Texas Club (see entry), a private health club located a couple of blocks west of here.

AMERISUITES WEST END, 1907 North Lamar at Corbin Sts., (800) 833-1516 or (214) 999-0500, Fax 999-0501, Internet www.amerisuites.com. M. Has 74 regular and 75 business suites with desks.

A downtown all-suite hotel on the edge of the West End historic and entertainment district, located within a few blocks of the Sixth Floor Museum, John F. Kennedy Memorial, Dallas World Aquarium (see individual entries), and the Arts District. DART light-rail station is two blocks away. There are no eating facilities on the premises, but you will find West End restaurants galore the moment you step out of the hotel.

Amenities: Sleeper sofas in some units. Oversized desk with light. Refrigerator, microwave, & wet bar in some suites. Outdoor swimming pool. Two meeting rooms measure 610 square feet (or 57 square meters) and can accommodate up to 50 persons. Also BC, CB, CF, CM, COF, DCL, FLC, HC, IH, PT, VMD, WN.

Opened in 1997. "AmeriSuites is a pleasant, low-key background building that fits into its surroundings without trying to make a big statement," says a *Dallas Morning News* architectural review. "The only public spaces with any gumption are the two-story lobby, which has the right scale and the wrong layout, and a small outdoor pool on the second floor that offers spectacular views of the skyline." The building was designed to resemble the neighboring warehouse buildings in the district.

THE ARISTOCRAT, 1933 Main St. at Harwood, (800) 231-4235 or (214) 741-7700, Fax 939-3639. M. Has 172 rooms, 73 of them suites, on 15 floors.

Until 2001 a Holiday Inn hotel, the Aristocrat is located in the eastern part of downtown, diagonally across from C. D. Hill's 1914 Old

City Hall building, in whose basement Lee Harvey Oswald, the alleged Kennedy assassin, was killed on live national television. The Majestic Theatre, which opened in 1921, is located on the next street north. The exclusive Neiman Marcus department store is two blocks west. (Please see individual entries for more details.)

Amenities: Safe deposit box. Restaurant & cocktail lounge. Bar with mini-refrigerator in suites. Big-screen TV in the club room downstairs. Washer/dryer on premises. Parking at a fee. Also C, CF, CM, COF, FT, GS, HC, HR, MF, PT, RS, WN.

This European-style hostelry was built in 1925 by hotelier Conrad Hilton on the grounds originally owned by an undertaker. It was the second hotel in Hilton's original chain, but the first to bear his name. Restored in 1985, the 14-story building is now a registered historical landmark.

For 35 years bearing the name White Plaza and afterwards Clarion, it was later renamed as Aristocrat and is now part of the Wyndham Hotels franchise. The hotel is connected by a skybridge and tunnel system to shops, restaurants, clubs, banks, and a secured, covered self-park Elm Street Garage.

The restaurant is open daily 6:30 AM-10:30 PM and the bar 4 PM-2 AM.

THE FAIRMONT, 1717 North Akard St. at Ross Ave., (800) 527-4727 or (214) 720-2020, Fax 720-5269, Internet www.fairmont.com, e-mail dallas@fairmont.com. *E*. It has 551 rooms and suites in two towers, some for the disabled and non-smokers.

Located in the northern part of downtown, on the edge of the Arts District, two blocks from the Dallas Museum of Art, and a few blocks southwest of the Meyerson Symphony Center. The First Baptist Church, the largest such congregation in the United States, is two blocks southeast, and the Catholic Cathedral Santuario de Guadalupe is a few blocks northwest. (Please see individual entries for more details.)

Amenities: Safety deposit boxes. Three restaurants & three cocktail lounges. Work desk in most rooms. Business center with fax, copy, computer, print, and secretarial services is open Mon-Fri 7 AM-7 PM, Sat 10 AM-2 PM. Has 24 meeting rooms with a total of 77,000 square feet (or 7,153 square meters) of space & in-house audio-visual services.

Olympic-sized outdoor terrace swimming pool on the third level. Same-day laundry & valet service. Overnight shoeshine & 24-hour pressing service. Shopping arcade on ground floor, with gift shop, florist, clothing and jewelry stores. Beauty salon. Children's video games on television.

Also AC, ATM, C, CF, CM, HC, HR, PA, PT, RS, VMD. The hotel does not offer complimentary transportation downtown, but bus and trolley transportation is available across the street. Overnight valet parking is $18. A limousine service is located in the lobby.

Just for signing up for the President's Club, you can make free local calls, receive a 15 percent discount at Fairmont's boutiques, complimentary health club privileges, overnight shoeshine, daily newspaper, and two complimentary room upgrade certificates each year. To upgrade to the club's gold benefits and receive a complimentary third night, when staying three consecutive nights, you must have stayed at least 25 nights or spent $5,000 in any calendar year.

This Fairmont opened in 1969 as "Texas' first luxury hotel" and one of the city's tallest buildings, according to the management. It consists of two 25-story towers connected by a block-long building that houses restaurants, ballrooms, and meeting facilities.

The American Automobile Association gives it four of the possible five diamonds, and the *Mobil Guide* four stars. Renovated in 1998, it could use more of the same, particularly its creaky elevators.

The Fairmont was designed by the Virginia-born architect George Foster Harrell (1906-1980), who maintained a private practice in Dallas. Parisian architect Jean Nouvel, one of the finalists to design the Dallas Opera building downtown, labeled the structure derisively as "this crap place," according to the *Dallas Morning News*.

The Fairmont boasts well-decorated, spacious, and comfortable rooms. This has long been a hotel for wealthy Texans and businessmen. Its quest for perfection is reflected in details, such as down pillows, extra-long custom-made mattresses, and bath scales in suites.

Across the street is the YMCA Metropolitan Fitness Center, a large spa, which includes 19 indoor handball and racquetball courts, four squash courts, five volleyball courts, three basketball courts, steam rooms, saunas, whirlpools, three jogging tracks, and three gymnasiums. There is a small daily fee to use these facilities.

For more about the **Pyramid,** please see the DINING chapter. It was here that the Italian tenor Luciano Pavarotti had a "grand dinner" following his second Dallas appearance in 2002. The casual dining takes place in the café. Sunday brunch is available in the Venetian Room, which in the past has featured such headliners as Sammy Davis Jr., Jerry Lewis, and The Platters. There is also a lobby lounge with live piano music.

Situated across the street is the **YMCA of Metropolitan Dallas,** 601 North Akard St., (214) 954-0500. Open Mon-Fri 5:45 AM-9 PM, Sat 7:30 AM-5:30 PM, Sun 12:30 PM-5:30 PM. It has four floors of facilities that include aerobics and other fitness exercises, three basketball courts, and 20 racquetball and volleyball courts. A full-size swimming pool, two indoor tracks with another on the roof, a steam room, and a sauna can be found here.

"But the best thing about the YMCA gym," notes the *Dallas Observer*, which named it the best place in Dallas to work out, "is that there are not a bunch of dudes lifting a dumbbell every five minutes and spending the rest of their time hanging onto exercise equipment talking to each other and trying to hit on the women."

DOUBLETREE/HAMPTON INN, 1015 Elm St. at Griffin, (214) 742-5678, Fax 744-6167. M. Has 311 rooms on 23 floors, some for the disabled and non-smokers. A West End light-rail commuter station is a block away, and the Greyhound bus station is two blocks away.

Located in the western part of downtown, just a couple of blocks from the West End Historic District with its many restaurants, and across the street from the Bank of America building, the tallest in Dallas.

Amenities: 160-seat Italian restaurant. Rooftop swimming pool. Work desk with lamp. Valet service. The reconstructed full-service Doubletree has 8,000 square feet (or 743 square meters) of meeting space. Also CM, COF, FLC, HC, IH, PT, VMD, WN.

After a multimillion-dollar renovation of the former Holiday Inn hotel at this location, a large Hampton Inn, a Hilton property, opened here in 1996. In 2003, after a $6-million reconstruction, it was transformed into a Doubletree hotel. The top floor was converted into a concierge level, where four rooms were consolidated into two luxury suites.

THE HOTEL LAWRENCE, 302 South Houston St. at Jackson, (877) 396-0334 or (214) 761-9090, Fax 761-9334, Internet www.hotellawrencedallas.com. M. It has 118 rooms and suites on ten floors, some for the disabled and non-smokers.

Centrally located just one block southeast of Dealey Plaza, where President Kennedy was assassinated, and one block northeast of Union Station, a 1916 railroad station housing the Dallas Amtrak depot. You will find the John F. Kennedy Memorial one block north of here, and the replica of Dallas founder John Neely Bryan's cabin, another block beyond. (Please see individual entries for more details)

Amenities: Restaurant and bar. It has a business center and a workout room. Free transportation within five miles (or eight kilometers) 6 AM-10 PM. Some rooms have two-line phones and CD players. Cookies and milk served nightly in the lobby. Also CB, COF, IH, MF, PA, PT, VMD.

The 76-year-old hotel, which opened as the Hotel Scott, served primarily Union Station rail passengers. It was named the Paramount from 1995 on, and before that the Bradford. The Lawrence has undergone a $4-million renovation by the building's new owners, Big D Hotel

Associates of Annapolis, Maryland. The "intimate, European-style boutique hotel" is managed by the Magna Hospitality Group, Internet www.magnahospitality.com.

The Lawrence claims it is competing with hotels like the Aristocrat downtown and the Melrose and Stoneleigh (see individual entries) in Oak Lawn.

A gargantuan royal chair, for years on display in the Paramount's lobby, was just the gimmick to have people talking. On second thought, it fit just right in the city, where egos are often Texas-sized.

Located on the ground floor of the hotel is a well-thought-of Houston Street restaurant. You can see the Sixth Floor Museum and the "Old Red" Courthouse (see entries) from here.

HYATT REGENCY, 300 Reunion Blvd., (800) 233-1234 or (214) 651-1234, Fax 651-0018/742-8126, Internet www.hyatt.com. *E*. It has 1,122 rooms—including 42 suites with parlors—on 28 floors, some for the disabled and non-smokers. Singles start at $175, doubles at $220, suites go for $500-3,000 a night. Hyatt has more than 600 employees.

Located on the southwestern edge of downtown Dallas and just southwest of Dealey Plaza, where President Kennedy was assassinated in 1963. The Sixth Floor Museum, shedding some light on that tragedy, is within walking distance. The West End entertainment district starts at the museum. The municipally owned Reunion Arena indoor stadium is just south of the hotel and the companion 52-story Reunion Tower.

Conveniently situated at Interstate Highway 35 East (also known as Stemmons Freeway) for those having business at the Dallas Market Center (see individual entries). A DART light-rail station—located at Union Station depot, which is connected to the hotel by a tunnel—makes it possible to travel to NorthPark shopping center to the north and the Dallas Zoo on the south.

Amenities: Safe deposit boxes at front desk. Presidential suite has three bedrooms, a parlor to hold up to 50 persons, and measures 2,335 square feet (or 217 square meters). Dry sauna & Jacuzzi. Outdoor swimming pool & whirlpool on third floor is open 8 AM-10 PM.

A two-thousand-square-foot (or 186-square-meter) health club, open daily 6 AM-10 PM, has recumbent and upright bikes, treadmills, stair-steppers, full-body & elliptical cross-trainers, free weights, & a rowing machine.

The restricted-access 17th-floor Regency Club serves complimentary breakfast, has a lounge, data port work station with fax machine, copier & printer, complimentary coffee, and reading materials—but at additional charge. The Business Plan rooms include a desk, fax machine, and free local telephone calls, again at an additional daily charge.

The business center on the lower level contains printers and copiers and is open Mon-Fri 7 AM-8 PM, Sat 7 AM-2 PM. Meeting facilities include 55 meeting rooms and three ballrooms with 160,000 square feet (or 14,864 square meters) of space. There are also 41 hospitality suites.

Self- or valet parking is available at a cost for the hotel and its restaurants. There is a billiards room with pool and shuffleboard tables. Also AC, C, CF, CM, DCL, EX, FT, GS, HR, IH, RS, SDB, VMD.

Parrino's Oven, a casual Italian bistro on the second floor atrium level, is open for dinner only Mon-Sat 5 PM-11 PM and seats about 60. It serves pizzas, pastas, and entrées, such as fire-grilled filet mignons, chicken, and red snapper filets.

Centennial Cafe, an open-air Southwestern-style restaurant, serves breakfast, lunch, and dinner between 6 AM and midnight and can accommodate up to 190. Monduel's lounge, open daily until 1:30 AM, on the second floor atrium level, is a sports bar seating about 100. Coffee's Post specialty coffee store serves coffees and snacks to up to 50 persons at a time until 2 AM.

Ray Lee Hunt (b. 1943), Dallas real estate developer and chairman of Hunt Oil Company, initiated the Reunion complex in 1978. He is now worth more than $2 billion. Hunt is the eldest child of Texas oil magnate and bigamist Haroldson Lafayette Hunt. The complex consists of the Hyatt Regency Hotel and the Reunion Tower, with an observatory on the 50th floor. The Reunion Arena, which was inaugurated in 1980, was the home of the Dallas Mavericks basketball team until 2002.

The hotel, the fourth largest in the city, displays a 28-story, blue-tinted glass facade that reflects the downtown skyline. It completed a $72-million expansion in 1998 and was renovated in 2000. Hunt's sister, Caroline Rose Hunt, controls what are two among the costliest hotels in the city, as well as the Mansion on Turtle Creek restaurant that attracts attention seekers like honey attracts flies.

In a survey by *Consumer Reports* magazine readers, the Hyatt chain was judged to be the worst value among the luxury hotels, such as Four Seasons, Ritz-Carlton, Renaissance, and Westin.

At the turn of the century, the site of today's Hyatt was the bed of the Trinity River, before its course was altered by the construction of the levee system in the 1930s. Hunt chose the name Reunion to honor the French and Swiss colonists who came to Dallas in the 1850s to settle less than three miles (or 4.8 kilometers) west of here.

(For more about the restaurant **Antares,** revolving atop the Reunion Tower, please see the DINING chapter.) The revolving Dome Lounge (located above the Antares) serves hors d'oeuvres and has dancing nightly. It can accommodate more than 200. After 6 PM, business casual dress is preferred. It is open daily 2 PM-1:30 AM.

LE MERIDIEN, 650 North Pearl St. at San Jacinto, (800) 225-5843 or (214) 979-9000, Fax 953-1931. *E.* It has 400 rooms and suites, some for the disabled and non-smokers.

Located in the northeastern part of downtown, in an office, shopping, and restaurant complex known as the Plaza of the Americas, which has a large 15-story atrium with glass elevators overlooking a skating rink. There are two dozen shops and eating places on two levels. The DART light-rail Pearl station, leading to the West End historic and entertainment district one way, and the NorthPark shopping center (see entry) in north Dallas the other, is on the same block.

Le Meridien is situated two blocks southeast of the Meyerson Symphony Center and one block from the Belo Mansion historical building. The Dallas Museum of Art is three blocks west, and the Trammell Crow Center, with its 22 sculptures by Auguste Rodin, Aristide Mailol, and Emile Bourdelle, is at Ross Avenue and Olive Street nearby. (Please see individual entries for more details.)

Opened in 1980, the hotel was remodeled in 1998.

Amenities: Up to two children age 17 or younger may share parents' room free of charge if no extra bed is required. Restaurant & bar. French-, Spanish-, & English-speaking staff. Fax machine & in-room entertainment system. Complimentary transportation downtown. Secretarial services available. Shoeshine. Also AC, BC, C, CM, DCL, FT, GS, HC, HR, IH, MF, PA, PT, RS, VMD. The concierge level rooms with continental breakfast, snack basket, bathrobe, scale, and slippers are available at additional cost. Cribs can be requested.

The rooms are large, luxuriously appointed, and have elegant decor; they overlook the atrium or offer a view of Dallas' skyline. The Presidential Suite goes for upward of $2,200 a night.

The new-American cuisine 650 North, open for breakfast, lunch, and dinner, seats up to 100 and is the most formal restaurant inside the Americas complex. The food is well prepared, and the service is what you would expect in a brasserie of this caliber. Yellow fin tuna steak, marinated filet of venison, and crusted filet of beef tenderloin are available. There is also a 24-ounce (or 680-gram) T-bone steak, and a 12-ounce (or 340-gram) roasted prime rib of beef, each one more than $32.

THE MAGNOLIA, 1401 Commerce St. at Akard, (888) 915-1110 or (214) 915-6500, Fax 253-0053, Internet www.themagnoliahotel.com, e-mail reservations@themagnoliahotel.com. *E.* It has 330 rooms, including 130 suites with kitchens & refrigerators, some for handicapped and non-smokers. Room rates include a "lavish" breakfast buffet. Parking is extra.

Located downtown, four blocks southwest of the Dallas Convention Center, one block from the Neiman Marcus luxury department store, and across the street from the Telephone Pioneer Museum of Texas (see individual entries). The Adolphus Hotel with the French Room (see individual entries), one of the best restaurants in the city, is situated across Akard Street. Across Main Street, you will find a much newer French bistro Jeroboam (see entry) in the renovated Kirby Building.

(For more about the history of the 27-story Magnolia building and the Pegasus neon sign atop it, please see entry Magnolia Building & Pegasus Plaza in the SIGHTS & ATTRACTIONS chapter.)

Amentities: Safe deposit box. Informal bar on second floor. Business desk in every room. Suites include living room with sofa bed, two telephones & CD player, refrigerator & microwave oven. Has a library with a fireplace on the second floor. Free transportation within a three-mile (or 4.8-kilometer) radius of the hotel, including West End & Deep Ellum historic and entertainment districts.

Complimentary cocktails & hors d'oeuvres each evening. Health club with cardio & strength training equipment, steam room, & rooftop whirlpool. Has five meeting rooms with 8,000 square feet (or 743 square meters) of space for up to 100. Nintendo games on television for kids. Also AC, C, CM, COF, IH, PT, RS, VMD, WN.

The lobby is a "totally chinz-free zone," declares *Texas Monthly*. "You could call the style Prairie Zen deco, a sort of Restoration Hardware meets Tokyo via Radio City Music Hall: dark-wood accents, frosted glass, curvaceous seating." Original elevators still bear the Pegasus logo. Some suites "boast a living area large enough for cartwheels, a life-size kitchen, a huge bathroom with a tub for two, and a corner bedroom with a view east to Deep Ellum."

"The hotel rooms themselves are spacious and well appointed: blond wood furniture, soft leather armchairs, fine linens, and everything cast in calming shades of taupe, gray-green, and powdery brown," notes *Texas Highways*, which rarely criticizes anything in Texas.

The Magnolia Building, formerly the headquarters of the parent of Mobil Oil, was turned into a hotel at a cost of $42 million by a Colorado developer, Stevens Holtze, who also owns a hotel in Denver, Internet www.holtzedenver.com.

MARKET CENTER/LOVE FIELD AIRPORT/OAK LAWN/NEAR-EAST DALLAS HOTELS

Hotels listed here are located from Elm Fork River, Bachman Lake, and Love Field Airport on the west, and all the way to White Rock

Lake on the east, but only up to Northwest Highway in the north. North Central Expressway divides east and west Dallas. Market Center is located less than three miles (or 4.8 kilometers) northwest of downtown.

THE BRADFORD AT LINCOLN CENTER, 8221 North Central Expwy. at Caruth Haven, (888) 486-STAY or (214) 696-1555, Fax 696-1550, Internet www.bradfordsuites.com, e-mail bradlp@swbell.net. *E*. It has 150 suites, some for the disabled and non-smokers. Discounts are available for weeklong stays.

Located northeast of downtown Dallas and University Park, in the southwest corner of North Central (or U.S. Hwy. 75) and West Northwest Hwy., behind Lincoln Park mall and the Caruth rental apartment community. NorthPark mall (see entry), with its 160 shops and restaurants, is located on the north side of Northwest Highway. Doubletree Hotel at Campbell Centre (see entry) is situated across the expressway.

Amenities: Three floor plans with separate living, bedroom, and kitchen, including refrigerator, electric range, dishwasher, microwave, glassware, and cutlery. Has sofa, ottoman, and work area with desk. Video cassette player is available. Some units overlook an outdoor swimming pool. Weekly housekeeping & laundry facility. Has a grocery store. Free local phone calls. Also AC, BC, CM, CP, HC, IH, MF, VMD. No pets accepted. Breakfast at additional charge.

Opened in 2000 and was spotlessly clean when revisited in 2002. The four-story $15-million facility features a parking structure that allows guests to park on the same level as their room.

The Bradford Homesuites, its sister brand, is located at 2914 Harry Hines Blvd. at Wolf St. downtown, next door to KERA 90.1 FM studios, the non-commercial National Public Radio station, (888) 486-7829 or (214) 965-9990.

CRESCENT COURT HOTEL, 400 Crescent Court, Cedar Springs Rd. at Pearl St., (800) 654-6541 or (888) 767-3966 or (214) 871-3200, Fax 871-3272. *E*. It has 177 rooms and 41 suites, some for handicapped and non-smokers, most with king-size beds. Guest rooms average more than 400 square feet (or 37 square meters), while suites range from 700 to 3,000 square feet (or 65 to 279 square meters).

Located in Uptown, on the northern edge of the downtown business and arts districts, within walking distance of restaurants, galleries, and antique shops on nearby streets. The 146-room ZaZa boutique hotel, with its "over-the-top" suites, is a couple of blocks west of here.

Amenities: Safe deposit boxes. Foreign language capabilities. Some suites are on two levels and have wood-burning fireplaces. All rooms exhibit works of art and feature fresh flowers. Stereo system, fax machine, safe, & mini-bar in suites. Most rooms have a sitting area and open to small balconies. Twice-daily maid service.

It has 13 meeting rooms, with the ballroom seating 250, and 13,630 square feet (or 1,266 square meters) of space. Year-round heated outdoor swimming pool. Laundry & valet services. Complimentary transportation is available within a five-mile (or eight-kilometer) radius, including to downtown. The complex has an underground garage that holds 4,000 cars. Also AC, C, CM, HC, HR, IH, MF, PA, PT, RS, WN.

The 10.5-acre (or 4.25-hectare), seven-story "gray stone fortress" was designed by architect Philip Johnson (b. 1906), who also created the John F. Kennedy Memorial downtown, together with his sidekick John Burgee, with whom he formed a partnership in 1967. "Visually, it's ridiculous," claimed a critic in the now defunct weekly the *Met*. "It's ostentatious and over-the-top, an attitude Dallasites adore."

The lobby contains Louis XV furnishings, handwoven carpets, Louis XIV tapestries, a second-century figure of the Roman god Aesculapius, and 18th-century paintings.

"A typical centerpiece in the hotel might be ten dozen long-stemmed chocolate roses, each weighing more than a pound and requiring two hours to make," observes American Express' *Travel & Leisure* magazine, adding that the hostelry is "slick and polished to a fare-thee-well, with crackling service."

The Crescent Court development includes, in addition to the hotel, three 18-story office towers and several shops. The *Mobil Guide* gives it four stars. Owned by Rosewood Hotels, which has properties in New York, London, Tokyo, Panama, and Riyadh, Saudi Arabia, the seven-story hotel was inaugurated on New Year's Eve 1985. It was inspired by the Royal Crescent in Bath, England.

Rosewood is controlled by Caroline Rose Hunt (b. 1923), the youngest of the five children from the "first family" of oil billionaire Haroldson Lafayette Hunt (1889-1974) and also owns the Mansion on Turtle Creek (see entry), a few blocks north of here. Educated at Mary Baldwin College and the University of Texas, she has been named one of the 100 most influential women in the United States.

"The Ultimate in Romance" package costs an unromantic $1,100 and gets you a suite, a bottle of champagne, a box of truffles, a fresh floral arrangement, and a dinner at Beau Nash restaurant. Taxes and gratuities are extra. If you want to stay an additional night, that will be $850 more, please. Crescent Spa, which *Smart Money* magazine singles out as "just plain goofy" the $95 "barbecue wrap," is located on the lower level. Oh, and did I mention "a luxurious flower petal bath?" For brides, the spa has the Ultimate Bridal Package for $1,745.

Beau Nash dinery has live jazz on weekends, while Gumbo's serves

Creole-Cajun cuisine, with shrimp "the size of Lyndon Johnson's ears," claims *D Magazine*.

Afternoon tea is served in the 45-seat Lady Primrose, (214) 871-8333, a European antique gallery nearby, where prawns and spinach salad will cost you about $15. It is open Mon-Sat for lunch 11:30 AM-2 PM and for tea 3 PM-5 PM. The 5,000-square-foot (or 464-square-meter) shop downstairs is "jammed with over-the-top collectibles, ranging from antler chandeliers to a $6,000 music box."

Other tearooms in the city include:

• **The Adolphus Hotel** (see listing), 1321 Commerce Street, (214) 742-8200. Afternoon tea is served to the accompaniment of a piano in the lobby, Wed-Sat 3 PM-4:45 PM.

• **Lavendou Bistro,** 19009 Preston Rd., (972) 248-1911. Mon-Fri 3 PM-5:30 PM. (For more details, please see listing for Chez Gerard restaurant.)

CROWNE PLAZA MARKET CENTER, 7050 North Stemmons Fwy. at West Mockingbird Ln., (800) HOL-IDAY or (214) 630-8500, Fax 630-9486, Internet www.crownplaza.com. *E*. It has 354 rooms and suites on 22 floors, some for the disabled and non-smokers.

Located northwest of downtown, three miles (or 4.8 kilometers) south of Love Field Airport, west of the University of Texas Southwestern Medical Center (see entry), on the freeway also known as Interstate 35 East, the highway which opened in 1959, when it was named after developer Leslie Stemmons.

Amenities: Restaurant & cocktail lounge. Safety deposit box. Large work desk with lamp. Indoor swimming pool & sauna. Complimentary transportation within a five-mile (or eight-kilometer) radius of the hotel, including the downtown business district, Market Center area, & Love Field Airport. Business center with copy, fax, computer, and printing services. Has 12 meeting rooms with 11,000 square feet (or 1,022 square meters) of space with on-site audio & video. Fitness room, whirlpool, & sauna. On-site washer & dryer. Nintendo games on television for kids. Also AC, C, CM, COF, CP, GS, HC, IH, PA, RS, VMD, WN.

First named a Holiday Inn, it was later known as Harvey Brookhollow Hotel, and became a Crowne Plaza in 1997.

Whether staying at Crowne Plaza or Sheraton nearby, you will not miss the **Stemmons Plaza Tower,** a 16-story office building next to Crowne Plaza, at 7200 Stemmons Freeway. Although designed by the noted New York architect Paul Rudolph (d. 1997), this ghastly tower built out of prefabricated concrete panels is considered by some one of the ugliest architectural sights in the city. Rudolph was chairman of the

Department of Architecture at Yale University and worked on commissions all over the world. Some even compared him with Le Corbusier.

Opened in 1969 and occupied until 1989 by Mobil Oil, the tower stood vacant because it contained toxic asbestos. Unlike most skyscrapers, the Stemmons tower is made of precast, modular panels. Texas Industries Inc. built the concrete panels miles away and trucked them to the site. Cranes hoisted the panels onto the structure, floor by floor, and locked them together. It was the tallest precast structure in the world at the time. Low ceilings and unconventional floor plans made it hard to utilize the space.

In 2002, an investor bought the tower to convert it into 156 one- and two-bedroom luxury rental units, averaging 1,250 square feet (or 116 square meters), for the elderly. An indoor swimming pool and cinema are also to be added.

DOUBLETREE AT CAMPBELL CENTRE, 8250 North Central Expwy. at East Northwest Hwy., (800) 222-TREE or (214) 691-8700, Fax 706-0186, Internet www.doubletreehotels.com. M. Has 302 rooms, 12 of them suites, and many for non-smokers.

Located on the southeast corner of Central Expressway, which until recently was "the most horrendous traffic relic pestering the city," and Northwest Highway. Love Field Airport is six miles (or 9.7 kilometers) southwest of here.

Amenities: Two complementary two-ounce chocolate chip cookies when checking in. Children 12 and younger stay free. Restaurant & lounge. Work desk with lamp. Health club (open 6 AM-1 AM) with exercise equipment, four whirlpool spas, shuffleboard, & putting green. Laundry & valet service.

Complimentary transportation within a five-mile (or eight-kilometer) radius, including Love Field Airport, is available 7 AM-10 PM. Jacuzzi, wet bar, and refrigerator are featured in suites. Children's video games are featured on television. Also AC, C, CF, CM, COF, CP, HR, IH, MF, PT, RS, VMD, WN. Tennis courts & jogging track are a mile (or 1.6 kilometer) away.

The 21-story Doubletree tower, a property, has one-way, floor-to-ceiling glass windows with lots of natural light in each room. It is flanked by the twin towers of Campbell Center, made famous by the opening sequence of the popular television soap opera *Dallas*.

The hotel's Princeton Grill restaurant is a full-service restaurant serving breakfast, lunch, and dinner, as well as Sunday brunch. An 18-ounce, bone-in, ribeye steak with baked potato will cost you about $30.

The "monstrously popular" Cheesecake Factory restaurant with its enormous platters is on the other side of Central Expressway. The food is a shade above average, but the crowds after 6 PM are as thick as those at a rock concert.

NorthPark Center, with 160 shops and restaurants, is located diagonally from the hotel. Upper Greenville Avenue, with its many restaurants and nightclubs, is behind the hotel.

The Bradford at Lincoln Park all-suites hotel (see listing) is located across the expressway.

HOLIDAY INN SELECT LOVE FIELD, 3300 West Mockingbird Ln. at Cedar Springs Rd., (214) 357-8500, Fax 366-2670, Internet www.showhotel.com/holiday/7523501, e-mail hislove@mindspring.com. M. It has 244 rooms and suites on eight floors, some for the disabled and non-smokers.

Located five miles (or eight kilometers) northwest of the downtown business district, west of the wealthy Park Cities, and across from the south entrance to Love Field Airport. Love Field Antique Mall (see entry) is within a walking distance, at 6500 Cedar Springs and Mockingbird.

There is not much else to do in this immediate area, except watch the planes take off and land. We do not recommend that you walk around here alone at night, but you will be conveniently located to much of Dallas.

Amenities: Safe deposit box. Restaurant & cocktail lounge. Business center with computer, printer, and fax machine. Outdoor swimming pool. On-site washer & dryer. Also AC, CP, GS. This full-service hotel underwent a $20-million remodeling and repainting in 2000.

The first Holiday Inn was opened by a millionaire homebuilder, Kemmons Wilson (1913-2003), in Memphis, Tennessee, in 1952. For the first time, a hotel allowed children to stay free and offered a swimming pool, air-conditioning, and restaurant on each property. By 1975, there were 1,700 Holiday Inns, all named after the 1942 Bing Crosby film, which introduced the song "White Christmas."

In a survey of 41,000 *Consumer Reports* readers, the Holiday Inn chain was judged one of the three worst "values" among the "moderate" hotel chains nationwide, along with Ramada Inn and Howard Johnson.

HOTEL ST. GERMAIN, 2516 Maple Ave. at Mahon St., (800) 683-2516 or (214) 871-2516, Fax 871-0740, Internet www.hotelstgermain.com. *E*. It has seven European-style suites, some for smokers, starting at $300 a night, including a full breakfast. "A seven-day advance notice is required to receive a refund." Open year-round except ten days in August and on Christmas Day.

Located just north of downtown, across the street from the Crescent

Court Hotel (see entry), and southeast from the Dallas Market Center. McKinney Avenue, with its many restaurants, galleries, and antique shops starts on the next block. The Quadrangle shopping center, at 2800 Routh Street, is also within walking distance and beckons with such restaurants as Ruggeri's.

Amenities: French & Spanish are spoken. Restaurant with two dining rooms & Parisian-style champagne bar are open Tue-Sat. Full-time butler is on call. Complimentary breakfast. Video cassette recorder & CD player. On-site laundry & dry cleaning. Jacuzzi or soaking tubs are available. Some units have fireplaces. Terrycloth robes & European toiletries. Valet parking. Also AC, C, CM, IH, RS, VMD. Fitness club is off-premises nearby.

Maple Avenue was just a trail until 1888 and was annexed to Dallas in 1890. This house with 14-foot (or 4.26-meter) ceilings was built in 1906 for John Patrick Murphy, president of a real estate investment company, and twice director of the State Fair of Texas (see entry). It was the first residence on this street and occupied by generations of Murphy's family until the 1950s.

The Dallas chapter of the American Institute of Architects claims that this elegant Victorian mansion "is the best remaining example of Maple Avenue's turn-of-the-century role as the city's silk-stocking district."

St. Germain is outfitted in turn-of-the-century French antiques, including a large Baccarat chandelier and a 17th-century Aubusson tapestry in the dining room. All of the suites, renovated in 2000, are decorated with the turn-of-the-century antiques from France and New Orleans. Each one is distinct, featuring canopied beds, Jacuzzis, and wood-burning fireplaces, and priced accordingly. Some guests particularly like Room No. 7.

"Staying at the Hotel St. Germain is like eating French pastry after a fast-food meal," once noted *Bride's Magazine*. *Town and Country* magazine claimed in 1997 that St. Germain's Suite Six is "the most romantic hotel suite" in Texas. Both the *Mobil Guide* and the American Automobile Association give it either four stars or four diamonds, out of the possible five.

The proprietress has been quoted as saying that her interest is in attracting "the couple wanting to get away for a private interlude. This is a house of indulgence—spiritually, emotionally, and probably in carnal ways, too." Prince Albert of Monaco and crown Prince Henri of Luxembourg stayed here.

Claire Heymann, bought the property in 1990 and opened the hotel the following year. Originally from Louisiana, she spent a year in Paris and graduated with a degree in French.

Its restaurant serves elegant and customized meals in a romantic setting. White-gloved waiters serve your food on 75-year-old Limoges china, and you will sip your wine and champagne from Waterford or Schotts-Zwiesel crystal. Only the $85 fixed-price, seven-course dinner is served Tue-Sat.

The *Dallas Morning News* would give it five out of the possible five stars, but for one technicality: "Executing a fixed menu ordered in advance for no more than a dozen diners a night presents less of a challenge than preparing meals on the spot from multiple menu options. But make no mistake: Hotel St. Germain serves up five-star excellence."

Except for the dining room charm and "excellent service," *D Magazine* would disagree with the *News*: "all else appears to be average performance theatre with expensive seats."

HOTEL ZaZa, 2332 Leonard St. off McKinney Ave., (800) 597-8399 or (214) 468-8399, Internet www.hotelzaza.com, e-mail info@hotelzaza.com. *E*. It has 146 rooms—and 13 "over-the-top" suites, such as the Erotica Suite with the mirrored ceiling—starting at $175 a night.

Located in Uptown, across from the Crescent Court Hotel (see entry). Its wealthier and more staid neighbor, Crescent Court Hotel (see entry), is situated a couple of blocks east of here.

Amenities: In-room safe. Restaurant & bar. Wireless Web access from all public areas, including the pool. "Oversized televisions," two-line portable telephones, and mini bars. "Luxurious bathrooms with rainforest showers," guest robes, and down-filled pillows. Swimming pool with bar, spa, and fitness center. It has 4,000 square feet (or 372 square meters) of meeting facilities for up to 300. Underground parking garage.

What is a hotel? What is not a hotel? If in Dallas, why not design something that the owner thinks resembles a villa in southern France, then paint it rich yellow. *Voilà*, a hotel!

Charles Givens (b. 1949), an Oklahoma developer decided this is what Texans need and came to Dallas to built this French neoclassical architectural-style "boutique" hotel meant for the cutting-edge crowd. The owner promises "oversized and sexy rooms, averaging 420 square feet (or 39 square meters), a totally cool hotel experience. You will need a sense of humor to stay here," he adds. He does most of the week.

"My real dream was to be a Broadway producer," Givens told the *Dallas Morning News*, "but that didn't work out. This is as close as I could get." Zaza opened late in 2002, during the worst slump in the Dallas hospitality industry in almost 20 years.

The $30-million, four-story lodging, which claims a mix of European luxury bed and breakfast experience provided by the Hotel St. Germain (see entry) nearby and the high-end traditional style of the Adolphus (see entry) downtown, is calculated to appeal to the entertainment, arts, fashion, and design crowd with the best beds and the finest linens, as well as "interesting artwork."

Furnishings vary from room to room. "You may have a Ralph Lauren room one time and a Versace room the next," says the owner. The interior design firm of Duncan & Miller, which designed interiors at restaurants Actuelle in Dallas and Bistro Louise in Fort Worth, is responsible for its flair.

Surprisingly, to say the least, *Forbes* magazine's Web site, Forbes.com, proclaimed ZaZa one of the best new business hotels in 2002—one month after its opening.

The owner snagged the superstar chef Stephan Pyles as "consulting concept chef" to develop Dragonfly, (214) 550-9500, a 100-seat Mediterranean and Asian-cuisine restaurant with dining room, wine room, bar, and terrace dining overlooking the pool. The *Fort Worth Star-Telegram* calls it "an intriguing, intoxicating" dining spot. "We found nirvana in a plate of seared foie gras." The *News* gave it four out of the possible five stars.

The developer claims ZaZa means nothing in particular, he just wanted a name people are not going to forget and will go gaga over.

"The mini-bar includes Gummi Bears and what Givens calls an 'intimacy kit,' which includes condoms and lubricant," notes the *Star-Telegram* in another review.

THE MANSION ON TURTLE CREEK, 2821 Turtle Creek Blvd. and Gillespie St., (888) 767-3966 or (214) 559-2100, Fax 528-4187. *E*. It has 126 luxury rooms and 15 suites, some for handicapped and non-smokers, starting at about $350 a night.

Located on a 4.63-acre (or 1.87-hectare) site off Cedar Springs Road, a few blocks from Oak Lawn Avenue and accessible to the restaurants, galleries, antique stores, and shops in Uptown and Oak Lawn.

Amenities: Foreign languages capabilities. Most suites include kitchens, balconies, & mini-bars. Armoires, desks, easy chairs, & ottomans are standard issue. Many rooms have VCRs, CD players, tape decks, fax machines, or in-room safes. The business center has personal computers, a laser printer, Internet access, a copier, and fax machines.

Heated outdoor swimming pool. Fitness studio includes free weights, treadmills, starmasters, massage & sauna rooms. Hair salon. One-day laundry & dry cleaning available, also clothes pressing. Courtesy car is available within a five-mile (or eight-kilometer) radius, including downtown business and arts districts, as well as NorthPark and the

Galleria shopping centers. Also AC, C, CM, FT, HR, IH, MF, PA, RS, VMD, WN.

This is the only Metroplex hotel that was awarded five stars from the *Mobil Guide* and five diamonds from the American Automobile Association. It is controlled by Caroline Rose Hunt through Rosewood Hotels & Resorts, which also claims properties in London and Tokyo. The hostelry was designed by Dallas architect Philip Shepherd, who also worked on the Crescent Court complex nearby. The Mansion provides the ultimate in quality, style, and elegance, but at a price. Hotel claims to have "2-to-1 staff-to-guest ratio."

Formerly named the Sheppard King Mansion, after a cotton baron, this tri-level 1925 Italian Renaissance-style residence was converted into the Mansion restaurant in 1980. The following year, a nine-story tower was inaugurated as a hotel.

The rooms measure 450 square feet (or 42 square meters) each. Suites go up to 1,300 square feet (or 121 square meters), with the largest among them including 900-square-foot (or 84-square-meter) living and dining areas, 400-square-foot (or 37-square-meter) bedrooms, with large baths and separate showers.

"Nothing at the Mansion is designed to scare the horses," observes *Travel & Leisure* magazine, which voted it their number one choice for service. In one instance, the hotel drained its swimming pool to find a dropped engagement ring. You are so important here, you can make that phone call to your underlings even from your bath, which has "more marble than the Vatican."

Only the finest and sometimes custom furnishings and linens are provided, in the most expensive rooms, that is. Presidents Clinton, Bush, Carter, and Ford stayed here, as did Princess Margaret, the King and Queen of Sweden, and King Olaf of Norway. King Juan Carlos I and Queen Sofia of Spain stayed here in 2001, while in Dallas for unveiling of the Meadows Museum (see entry) on the campus of Southern Methodist University.

The readers of *Travel & Leisure*, an American Express monthly, picked the Mansion hotel as having "the world's best service," in 2002, a somewhat dubious award after you read that one "measure of greatness" are "11,000 cars parked each year by valets at the Ritz-Carlton in Naples," Florida, which makes it hotel number five on that same list.

During the years when the television soap opera *Dallas* was actually filmed here, its main protagonist, Larry Hagman, lived at the Mansion in a ninth-floor suite with a large patio.

But not everyone adores the Mansion without qualifications: "The bed wasn't the best, big as Rhode Island, yes, but the pillows were wedges of foam," the *Fort Worth Star-Telegram* travel editor once noted.

Caroline Rose Hunt is the youngest of the five children from oil billionaire Haroldson Lafayette Hunt's (1889-1974) "first family." Caroline Hunt inherited a fortune estimated at $600 million and raised five children before opening the Mansion and a chain of Lady Primrose shops that sell knickknacks and toiletries. All of her children are believed to be on the executive committee of the Rosewood Corporation, the hotel's holding company. While she made the *Forbes* list of the 30 wealthiest Metroplex residents in 1996, by 2000 her name was gone from the list of the 35 such area residents whose worth had to be at least $1.1 billion to be included.

Hunt received a degree in English literature from the University of Texas. In 2001, she published her first novel, *Primrose Past: The 1848 Journal of Young Lady Primrose*, which the *Star-Telegram* diplomatically reviewed as "an honorable attempt, but not the literary equivalent of Hunt's The Mansion on Turtle Creek."

Her brothers William Herbert and Nelson Bunker gained notoriety in 1980, when they bid silver prices to $50 an ounce and lost billions when it crashed to $16 two months later.

(For more about the **Mansion** restaurant, which is housed in the 10,000-square-foot (or 929-square-meter) Sheppard King Mansion, please see the DINING chapter.)

THE MELROSE, 3015 Oak Lawn Ave. at Cedar Springs Rd., (800) THE-MELROSE or (214) 521-5151, Fax 521-9306. *E*. It has 184 spacious rooms and suites, "with no two rooms alike," some for the disabled and non-smokers.

Located north of downtown, in Oak Lawn, one of the oldest Dallas neighborhoods. Within walking distance of many restaurants and clubs on Cedar Springs Road and Oak Lawn Avenue. The Centrum health club is across the street. Dallas Love Field Airport is situated three miles (or 4.8 kilometers) northwest of the hotel.

Amenities: Restaurant & pub. Valet parking. Complimentary Continental breakfast. Free transportation from and to Love Field Airport available 7:30 AM-10:30 PM. Work desk with chair. Also AC, C, CP, FT, HC, HR, IH, MF, PT, RS, VMD.

The Melrose Court Apartments were built on this site in 1924 as a residential hotel at a cost of $2 million. The hotel was refurbished in 1982 and 1999, and became a Dallas historical landmark the following year. In the past it was popular with visiting opera singers and musicians. *Dallas Business Journal* named it the "best" local "hotel for out-of-town guests."

The Melrose Apartments architect, C. D. Hill, also designed Fair Park's Coliseum, as well as the Oak Lawn Methodist Church across the street.

This is a small European-style luxury hotel, with mahogany furnishings, blending Old World comfort with attentiveness to today's demanding traveler. Two private-access concierge floors provide breakfast and afternoon tea.

The *Mobil Guide* rates the 92-seat **Landmark,** (214) 522-1453, on the premises as a four-star restaurant, out of a possible five stars. It is open daily for breakfast, lunch, and dinner. Landmark's American cuisine dishes with Southwestern and Cajun influences make this elegant restaurant a worthwhile dinner choice.

Landmark's specialties include Maryland-style blue crab cakes, peppered breast of chicken, pan-seared duck, Angus cowboy steak, and salmon. Other main courses might be Texas spiced Angus filet, grilled lamb, seared jumbo shrimp atop saffron risotto, and center-cut pork chops.

The wood-paneled, piano Library Bar, where bookshelves line the walls, is an English pub open for lunch. It transforms into a bar with live entertainment at night. "The Library has maintained the sophistication of the original 75-year-old hotel, with enough new cool to entice twenty- and thirtysomething upscale types to sip classic cocktails weekly," claims *D Magazine*.

Where the hotel stands there was once a home and farm owned by Col. George M. Mellersh (1836-1910), a Civil War veteran who was born in Surrey County, England, and came to Dallas in 1873. The very large, brick, two-story Mellersh mansion, built in 1876, was known for its many dances, literary club, and other social events. However, the severe depression of the 1890s forced the family to abandon the house, which fell into disrepair and was eventually used as a sheep barn.

In 1904, the site was purchased and restored by banker Ballard Burgher, who owned it until the original 385-room Melrose was constructed. Conductor Antal Dorati, playwright Arthur Miller, opera singer Luciano Pavarotti, and actress Elizabeth Taylor stayed here.

During a trip to south Texas in December 1877, Mellersh and his fellow stage passengers were held up by the well-known robber Sam Bass near Fort Worth. When the outlaw later learned that Mellersh had hidden his gold ring in his mouth during the robbery, he threatened to kill him the next time they meet. He died the following year, on his 27th birthday.

A block from here, at 3828 Cedar Springs Road, stands Fire Station No. 11, the oldest operating fire station in the city, which goes back to 1909.

RENAISSANCE DALLAS, 2222 North Stemmons Frwy. at Wycliff Ave., (800) 468-3571 or (214) 631-2222, Fax 905-3814, Internet www.renaissancehotels.com. *E*. It has 540 rooms and suites, some for the disabled and non-smokers. The hotel has 300 employees.

Located on North Stemmons (also known as Interstate Highway 35

East), between the former International Apparel Mart building and Market Hall. The Wyndham Anatole Hotel is across the freeway. The tony Highland Park Village shopping center is almost three miles (or 4.8 kilometers) northeast of here. (Please see individual entries for more details.)

Amenities: Restaurant & cocktail lounge. Safe deposit box at front desk. Work desk with lamp in most rooms. Suites have mini-bars. Two concierge floors with 24-hour butler service. Rooftop health club with Nautilus weight room, saunas & lap pools, year-round outdoor heated swimming pool.

Has 12 meeting rooms with 15,000 square feet (or 1,393 square meters) of space. Bathrobe & shoeshine. Also AC, BC, C, CM, COF, CP, EX, FT, GS, HR, IH, MF, PA, PT, RS, WN. Childcare services are available upon request.

The 30-story pink granite elliptically shaped former Stouffer hotel was inaugurated in 1983 as the Wyndham and taken over by the Stouffer chain four years later, when it was completely refurbished. It is now part of Marriott's Renaissance chain. Its chandelier, which extends three floors through a winding marble staircase, is composed of 7,500 Italian crystals. But in spite of all the hoopla, the *Mobil Travel Guide* gives it only three out of the possible five stars.

T-Bones steakhouse serves New American cuisine daily 5 PM-10 PM. The more informal coffee shop is open for three meals a day. Additional restaurants are located inside the Wyndham Anatole Hotel (see entry) across the freeway.

THE STONELEIGH, 2927 Maple Ave. at Wolf St., (800) 255-9299 or (214) 871-7111, Fax 880-0820, Internet www.stoneleighhotel.com. *E*. It has 158 rooms, 35 of them suites, some for the handicapped and non-smokers.

Located just north of downtown and southeast of Reverchon Park, which is named after the French-born professor of botany at Baylor College of Medicine, Julien Reverchon. The Stoneleigh is situated within walking distance of restaurants on McKinney and Quadrangle mall, as well as galleries and antique stores on Routh and Fairmount Streets.

Maple Avenue was annexed to the city of Dallas in 1890. After its developer built his lavish home at the corner of Cedar Springs and Maple, near here, in 1888, it was soon joined by other mansions, making it the predecessor of today's Highland Park.

Amenities: Children age 18 or younger stay free with parents. Safe deposit boxes. Many of the suites have kitchenettes and dining areas. Some rooms have whirlpool, refrigerator, microwave oven, & mini-bar. Courtesy car. Heated outdoor swimming pool at Stoneleigh Terrace

Apartments across the street. Tennis court. Also AC, C, CM, COF, CP, DCL, FT, HC, HR, IH, MF, PA, PT, RS, VMD, WN.

The 11-story Stoneleigh Court Apartment Hotel, built at a cost of $1.1 million in 1923 and completely refurbished in the early 1990s, is a Dallas historic landmark and once modeled itself after European hotels. It was designed by local architect F. J. Woerner.

Elvis Presley spent the night of October 11, 1956, after performing at the Cotton Bowl in Fair Park, and evading his persistent fans. He was followed the following year by the founding general manager of the Dallas Civic Opera, Chicago native Lawrence Vincent Kelly. Dallas theater pioneer Margo Jones lived here in 1955, when she died of uremic poisoning.

Bob Hope and Judy Garland also stayed here, as did the wealthy entrepreneur, Col. William Stewart, who bought it in 1938, then converted the entire 11th floor into his 7,000-square-foot (or 650-square-meter), five-bedroom, five-bathroom penthouse with a view of downtown. Later, Hard Rock Café founder Isaac Tigrett occupied the floor.

"The Stoneleigh has been known as an eccentric place, a sort of funky chic hotel in a great neighborhood that draws artists and bands," says a hospitality insider.

"Our staff anticipates your every need with grace and elan," claims the management. "Room service is, of course, superb." Hold them to their promises.

The Stoneleigh is co-owned by former six-term state legislator Alvin Granoff, who also owned Ecco Italia, a restaurant that went bust in 2003. Late in 2001, impresario Ian Schrager, who also operates popular hotels in New York, San Francisco, and London, took over management of the Stoneleigh.

The only hotel restaurant is Nineteen Twenty-Three, which features American continental cuisine. Such well-known restaurants as Nick & Sam's steakhouse, Lola and Perry's are located within walking distance.

The younger set might prefer Sushi at the Stoneleigh, next door, "the WASPiest sushi bar in town," open for lunch and dinner, or Lion's Den bar, also inside the hotel.

Across the street from the hotel, but not owned by the Stoneleigh, is the popular and somewhat bohemian **Stoneleigh P,** (214) 871-2346, a hamburger and bar hangout, which was fashioned from a World War I-era pharmacy, and opened in 1973.

The beef for its hamburgers comes from the B&R Ranch in the Texas Panhandle and is "100 percent natural." The menu admonishes aggressive males, "Don't hassle the single women." Instead, they can read magazines, shoot pool, or belly up to the old soda fountain for a Bass ale.

WYNDHAM ANATOLE, 2201 North Stemmons Frwy., between Wycliff Ave. and Market Center Blvd., (800) 996-3426 or (214) 748-1200, Fax 761-7520, Internet www.wyndham.com. *E*. It has 1,620 rooms and suites on 27 floors, some for the disabled and non-smokers, starting at about $150 a night, including a complimentary continental breakfast. The Anatole has about 1,500 employees.

Located in the Dallas Market Center (see entry), across Stemmons Freeway (also known as Interstate Highway 35 East), from the Market Hall, Trade Mart, and World Trade Center. Western Warehouse apparel and boot store (see entry) is situated about half a mile (or 0.8 kilometer) away.

Amenities: Children ages 18 or younger stay free with parents. It has 18 restaurants, bars, & cocktail lounges. Foreign currency exchange & ATM. Mini-bar, safe, & telephone in bathroom available in suites. Bookstore; Western shop; children's, men's, & women's stores. Beauty salon. Doctor is on call at the Anatole.

There is a business center. It has 58 meeting rooms, including four ballrooms & six theaters. Free parking for 3,000 cars. Also, AC, C, CM, COF, DCL, HC, HR, IH, PT, RS, VMD, WN. Special-access, concierge-level rooms with further amenities are available at additional charge.

Domestic telephone calls, faxes, photocopying, and Internet access are free for members of the Wyndham By Request program in response to a "severe dissatisfaction about hotel phone fees among travelers," according to the *New York Times*. Wyndham, like most hotels, gets volume discounts, so the more its customers use its phones, the less each minute costs.

Responding to widespread dissatisfaction about sky-high prices for food and drink items in its minibars, Wyndham has lowered the prices, too. Says Wyndham's chairman and chief executive Fred Kleisner. "I just don't think you should have to pay $15 for a can of peanuts."

Both the American Automobile Association and the *Mobil Guide* give the hotel only three diamonds and three stars respectively, out of the possible five.

The Anatole, situated on 45 acres (or 18 hectares) near downtown, is one of the largest convention hotels in the Southwest and the second largest in the Metroplex, practically a village all by itself. "Unfortunately, the project's exterior distinguishes itself with little more than sheer volume," observes the Dallas chapter of the American Institute of Architects.

The Dallas-based hotel's parent, Wyndham International, was founded in 1981 as a vehicle for hotel holdings of the Trammell Crow Co. The Anatole is controlled by the billionaire Crow family, one of the nation's leading real estate developers. Its parent company "has been fighting for its life in recent years, saddled with too much debt from an ill-conceived hotel-buying binge that began in 1997," according to the *Dallas Morning News*. The Dallas-based chain groaned under more than $2 billion in debt in 2003.

The first 900 rooms were completed in 1979 and, after the development of the Dallas Market Center, a 720-room tower was added in 1984. The tower served as President Reagan's headquarters for the 1984 Republican National Convention in Dallas. In the spirit of Texas, everything here is supposedly the biggest and the best, including such dubious achievements as "separate spigots for filtered and unfiltered water."

Anatole has two stadium-sized atrium areas filled with trees and flowers, as well as tapestries, batiks, and sculptures. It is all a bit gaudy, filled to the rafters with conventioneers, and expensive.

The hotel's recreational facilities include a seven-acre (or 2.83-hectare) landscaped park with a pond and the $12-million **Verandah Club,** an 82,000-square-foot (or 7,618-square-meter) fitness center with these amenities: aerobics studio, basketball gymnasium, weight room, indoor and outdoor jogging tracks, indoor seven-lane 25-meter (or 27-yard) lap swimming pool, outdoor swimming pool, eight racquetball courts, six outdoor tennis courts, two croquet courts, boxing gym, whirlpool, sauna, steam & massage rooms.

The Verandah is open weekdays 5:30 AM-9:30 PM, and weekends 7 AM-7 PM. There is a daily fee to use these facilities. For guests seeking a good gym, says *American Health* magazine, "checking out the Verandah Club is like sightseeing in Disneyland." And there is "a grill that makes fabulous low-fat lunches."

The Anatole has six restaurants, among them an atrium Terrace Cafe, the Tex-Mex cuisine La Esquina, the heart-healthy Socio Grill, the 24-hour deli Kiosk, and the basement sports bar Rathskeller, serving American food. There are also four lounges, and nightclubs Crocodile and Nana Bar, both offering dancing.

Restaurant **Nana,** (214) 761-7479, located atop a 27-floor tower, is open daily for lunch and dinner. It has a "spectacular" nighttime view of downtown, and strolling musicians complementing this fine and exceedingly expensive eatery that reopened the week after 0terrorists struck New York's World Trade Center.

The Crows loaned Nana several artworks from their Asian art collection, including a 300-year-old, nearly life-sized statue of Buddha. The 6-by-9-foot (or 1.82-by-2.74-meter) painting of a reclining, Rubenesque temptress Nana in the nude was painted by Russian-Polish artist Gospodin Marcel Gavriel Suchorowky in 1881.

If you can handle $20 appetizers and $44 for veal Rossini, you should have a splendid time. Wild Texas antelope chop goes for $45, while the

American rack of lamb is a bit less. Alaskan king salmon with asparagus and potato salad, spiced roasted duck, tuna and scallops with carrots, and grilled prime filet with truffled potatoes are still other main dishes.

The *Mobil Travel Guide* gives it four out of the possible five stars, while the *Dallas Morning News* confers on it five stars, the highest possible rating. The *Dallas Observer* restaurant reviewer found the Dover sole "virtually inedible and at 39 bucks, hard to digest."

You will find a permanent collection of art on display at the Anatole, from the 18th-century bronze Chinese Fu lions to stained glass by Dane Bjorn Wiinblad, from batik banners by Ena de Silva of Sri Lanka to ten lithographs by the 89-year-old Pablo Picasso that are displayed at Atrium I mezzanine, between Batik A and Cardinal B meeting rooms.

A larger-than-life equestrian statue of humorist Will Rogers (1879-1935), titled *Riding Into the Sunset,* by Electra Waggoner Biggs (b. 1912), keeps watch near the main entrance. A like statue is located at Will Rogers Memorial Center in Fort Worth. It was unveiled in 1947 by Dwight D. Eisenhower, who six years later became the 34th president of the United States.

In 2001, the Anatole started a $10-million expansion and renovation, including improvements to the guest rooms and the Nana restaurant. The hotel added 27,000 feet (or 2,508 square meters) of meeting space, and a 35,000-square-foot (or 3,251-square-meter) **Golden Door Spa**.

The **Medieval Times** dinner theater (see entry), with jousting knights on horses pretending to go back a thousand years, is about four blocks east of here.

PARK CITIES HOTELS

Strictly speaking, there are no hotels in the Park Cities, which consist of Highland Park and University Park.

PARK CITIES HILTON, 5954 Luther Ln. at Douglas Ave., (800) HILTONS or (214) 368-0400, Fax 691-3157, Internet www.hilton.com. *E*. It has 224 "luxuriously appointed" rooms and suites.

Located in Dallas, not Park Cities, between Preston Road and Dallas North Tollway, about four miles (or 6.4 kilometers) northeast of Love Field Airport. Preston Center (see entry) shopping center starts across the street; Macaroni Grill restaurant is situated a couple of blocks north of here, on West Northwest Highway.

NorthPark Center shops are a couple of miles (or 3.2 kilometers) northeast of here, Highland Park Village mall just a bit farther, but southeast of here (see individual entries).

Amenities: Valet parking at a charge. New American cuisine restaurant serving breakfast, lunch, & dinner, bar & coffee bar. Work desk with lamp, two phone lines with speakers and high-speed Internet access, voice mail. Twenty-nine-inch televisions, high-speed Internet access, and video games for kids. Fitness center. Outdoor rooftop swimming pool and whirlpool with a view of Dallas.

Executive floor, with separate registration, includes restricted access, Continental breakfast, evening cocktails, and hors d'oeuvres. Has 8,000 square feet (or 743 square meters) of meeting space, including a 4,000-square-foot (or 372-square-meter) ballroom. Also AC, BC, C, CM, COF, IH, PT, RS, WN.

The *Mobil Travel Guide* gives it three out of the possible five stars, while the American Automobile Association awards it three diamonds.

A handsome Hilton hotel catering to business travelers that opened in the fall of 2000.

Preston Center mall (see entry), with covered complimentary parking, is within walking distance and has more than a hundred stores and restaurants serving the affluent neighborhoods of Highland and University Park around it. (For more about the Tramontana Mediterranean bistro here, please see the restaurant section.)

The hotel's own ground-floor restaurant, Opio, serves dry-aged New York strip steak for $30. Its Sunday breakfast buffet is from 6 AM to 1 PM.

NORTH & FAR-NORTH DALLAS HOTELS

Listed here are far-north Dallas hotels located north of Northwest Highway, which runs roughly from east to west, north of Bachman Lake and Love Field Airport, and touches the northern border of University Park. North Central Expressway (or U.S. Highway 75) divides western Dallas from its eastern part.

More than two dozen hotels are located inside or within about three miles (or 4.8 kilometers) of Dallas/Fort Worth International Airport terminals.

CROWNE PLAZA PARK CENTRAL, 7800 Alpha Rd. at Coit, (972) 233-7600, Fax 701-8618. *E.* It has 295 two-room suites with separate living room on ten floors surrounding a multi-level atrium, some for the disabled and non-smokers.

Located in the Dallas Park Central business district, at the northwest corner of Lyndon B. Johnson Freeway (also known as Interstate Highway 635), and Coit Road. Situated east of Valley View and the Galleria shopping centers (see individual entries).

Amenities: Children 12 & under stay free with parents. Coffee shop & cocktail lounge in atrium lobby. Safety deposit box. All units have sofas, 25-inch television sets, wet bar, microwave, & refrigerator. Heated indoor & outdoor swimming pool. Fitness room with cardiovascular & Nautilus equipment.

Business center with e-mail & Internet service, copier, fax machine, computer, & printer. Complimentary transportation available within five miles (or eight kilometers) of the hotel. Has 11,000 square feet (or 1,021 square meters) of meeting space, including 15 breakout rooms on the ground floor. On-site washer & dryer. Also AC, ATM, C, CB, CM, COF, CP, DCL, FT, GS, HC, HR, IH, MF, PA, PT, RS, VMD, WN.

Crowne Plaza has a huge atrium lobby and a surprisingly plain and small coffee shop. While the hotel is pleasant and its staff friendly, I am compelled to remind you that unless you have your own transportation, you are in the wrong neck of the woods. There is nothing worth seeing within walking distance, and there are just a few fast-food restaurants. The area, which cries out for greenery and landscaping, has a harsh face to it and is often littered with trash blowing from one parking lot to the next.

You must cancel your reservations at least 24 hours before your arrival to avoid a charge.

On the east side of Coit Road, you will find a Wyndham Garden Hotel, and just south from it and across LBJ Freeway, a Doubletree Hotel. On the southwest corner of Coit and LBJ, there are the Westin and Sheraton hotels. (Please see individual entries for more details.)

Also located near here is **Bristol House Suites,** at 7880 Alpha Rd. at Coit, (972) 391-0000. It has 127 rooms and one- and two-bedroom suites on three floors. There is an outdoor swimming pool, exercise room, and free transportation to local businesses and shopping centers.

DOUBLETREE CLUB PARK CENTRAL, 8102 Lyndon B. Johnson Frwy. at Coit Rd., (800) 222-TREE or (972) 960-6555, Fax 960-6553, Internet www.doubletreehotels.com. *E*. It has 204 rooms and suites, some for handicapped guests and non-smokers.

Located 15 miles (or 24 kilometers) north of downtown Dallas, 16 miles (or 25.7 kilometers) east of D/FW Airport, and in the southeast corner of LBJ and Coit. Valley View Mall and the Galleria (see entries) are situated a couple of miles (or 3.2 kilometers) west of here. Medical City Dallas Hospital (see entry), Texas Instruments, Boeing, and Raytheon offices are close by.

Amenities: You receive two complementary two-ounce chocolate chip cookies when checking in. Coffee shop & bar. Free television video games for kids. Complimentary transportation within five-mile (or eight-kilometer) radius, as well as the Galleria, Valley View, and NorthPark shopping centers (see individual entries). Outdoor swimming pool & exercise room. Work desk with lamp & two-line telephone in many rooms.

"You can make copies, send faxes, and print documents free of charge in our 24-hour business center or work in private office space that is equipped with supplies," promises the hotel's Web page. Complimentary conference rooms equipped with phones and data ports. Coin-operated laundry room. Also AC, CM, COF, CP, FT, IH, VMD.

This is a Dallas Park Central business district Hilton property so deserted on several weekends when visited, one might think the hotel has closed. The clean and well-maintained grounds in front of the hotel really promise more than what you get when you step inside the low-ceilinged lobby.

Food and beverages are available in the lounge and the all-day Au Bon Pain Café, where freshly-baked breads, pastries, sandwiches, salads and soups are available—but weekdays only. Benihana, a Japanese steakhouse, is located a couple of blocks west of here, at 7775 Banner Drive, (972) 387-4404.

Several other hotels are located at the intersection of LBJ and Coit.

GUEST LODGE AT COOPER AEROBICS CENTER, 12230 Preston Rd., between Churchill Way and Willow Lane, (800) 444-5187 or (972) 386-0306, Fax 386-2942, Internet www.cooperaerobics.com/hot.htm. *E.* It has 62 rooms, 12 of them suites with private balconies, some for the disabled and non-smokers, starting at $200 a night, including complimentary Continental breakfast.

Located three blocks south of Lyndon B. Johnson Freeway (also known as Interstate Highway 635), named after the former president who was never popular in Dallas. The European-style Dallas International School is on the next block north of here. The exclusive Galleria mall is farther to the northwest, at Dallas North Tollway and past LBJ Freeway.

Amenities: Restaurant. Safe deposit box. Eight meeting rooms that can accommodate up to 250. Cooper fitness center privileges. Six-lane outdoor heated swimming pool. Tennis courts & jogging tracks.

Suites have separate sitting areas with wet bar and refrigerator. Conference & meeting facilities for up to 250. Also AC, CM, CP, HC, HR, IH, PT, WN. Childcare available on request.

A small colonial-style hotel nestled on the 30-acre (or 12-hectare)

Cooper Aerobics Center estate, named after Dr. Kenneth Cooper, author of 17 fitness books that have sold 30 million copies in 41 languages. Born in Oklahoma City and a graduate of Harvard School of Public Health, he is also a Fellow at the American College of Sports Medicine.

After 13 years in the U.S. Air Force, where he served as a flight surgeon and director of the Aerospace Medical Laboratory in San Antonio, Dr. Cooper founded his first center at the Preston Center shopping plaza in 1970. During the early days of the NASA space program, he shocked many by suggesting that astronauts' physical fitness should be tested.

When during his early years in Dallas, he gave patients treadmill stress tests, other doctors were so horrified that he was called before the local medical board for an explanation. "Soon after the hearing the head of the board became the second physician in Dallas to start doing treadmill stress tests on patients," he says.

Dr. Cooper (b. 1932) has been George W. Bush's personal physician since 1989. Years before being named as U.S. surgeon general, Cooper proposed that Americans get a $250 tax break for each of the four important health targets: keeping their body mass index (a crude measure of obesity) below 25, blood pressure under 140/90, total cholesterol under 200, and not smoking. A taxpayer would be able to reduce his taxable obligations by $1,000 by complying with all four.

"Successful by any measure, Cooper gives the impression of a man who is used to expressing his opinions and having them thoughtfully considered once they're spoken," observes the *San Antonio Express-News*, quoting Cooper as saying: "What's killing us isn't AIDS or cars or guns. We've got to change physical America's habits."

In 1982, the *London Times* named him one of "the greatest" among 75 people in the world in the previous 20 years and noted: "The drop in deaths from heart disease in America by 14 percent in the 1970's is commonly credited to Dr. Cooper, as is the jogging boom which put more than 25 million Americans on the road by the end of that decade." In Brazil running is called "coopering." Near Tokyo, Japan, a 750-acre (or 303-hectare) model of the Dallas aerobics center was constructed with his counsel.

The internationally recognized **Cooper Clinic,** (800) 444-5764 or (972) 560-2667, provides preventive medicine expertise and has19 physicians on the staff specializing in preventive and internal medicine, cardiology, radiology, nuclear medicine, cholesterol management, and women's health. A typical exam, says a clinic's handout, lasts six to eight hours and starts at $1,800.

Cooper's success rests on scientific studies put out by the **Cooper Institute,** (972) 341-3200, Internet www.cooperinst.org, the center's nonprofit research arm that gets its funding from the National Institute of Health.

"What has made us successful is our credibility," Dr. Cooper tells the *Dallas Morning News*, adding it is the reason why he never franchised. "I could have made a fortune by franchising, but I wouldn't have kept my credibility." He has nevertheless been criticized for his financial stake in a line of nutrition supplements dubbed Cooper Complete.

Guests at the lodge have complimentary use of the 40,000-square-foot (or 2,716-square-meter) Cooper Fitness Center next door, which promotes a "heart-healthy lifestyle." For a fee, you can consult one of the clinic's 19 doctors who give comprehensive physical exams to more than 7,000 men and women annually. You can reduce stress by attending a Tai Chi or Pilates class. Boasting a $36-million budget, the center claims two outdoor swimming pools and tennis courts.

Cooper Fitness Center, (888) 964-8875 or (972) 233-4832, Internet www.cooperfitness.com. Open Mon-Fri 5 AM-9:30 PM, Sat 5:30 AM-8:30 PM, Sun noon-7 PM.

Established in 1971, this is one of about a dozen of the largest fitness centers in the Metroplex. It has a 40,000-square-foot (or 3,716-square-meter) facility with a gym, and about 3,700 members. Initiation fees for individuals start at $1,175.

Monthly fees for singles start at $130, families at $205 for a couple. The guest passes sell for $20 a day, but are limited to three visits a month. The second Thursday of each month is a complimentary guest day.

Cooper Center provides strength training, cardiovascular, Pilates, tai chi, and yoga. Sauna, whirlpool, and massage are available, as is wellness education. It has indoor and outdoor tracks; two heated, 25-yard (or 27-meter), six-lane swimming pools; a basketball and a volleyball court; four lighted tennis courts; and dance classes. Childcare is available, and a coffee shop with lots of greasy chips is on the premises.

The Spa, (888) 964-8875 or (972) 392-7729, at the Cooper Aerobics Center opened its 3,200-square-foot (or 297-square-meter) facility in 1998. The day spa offers therapeutic massage and a full range of body treatments and salon services, including aromatherapy massage, deep cleansing facials, manicures, and pedicures. The Spa hours are Mon-Fri 9 AM-8 PM, Sat 8 AM-8 PM, Sun noon-6 PM.

The lodge's Colonnade restaurant serves "heart-healthy" cuisine and is open Mon-Fri for lunch and dinner. A more casual eatery is located in the Cooper Fitness Center.

To tour the campus, call (972) 716-7093.

HILTON HOTEL, 5410 Lyndon B. Johnson Frwy. at Dallas North Tollway; (800) 222-TREE or (972) 934-8400, Fax 701-5244, Internet www.hilton.com. *E*. It has 502 rooms, including 16 suites, some for handicapped and non-smokers.

Located on the southeast corner of LBJ Freeway (also known as Interstate Highway 635) and Dallas North Tollway, across the highway from the Galleria and a short distance from Valley View shopping centers (see individual entries). D/FW Airport is west of here.

Amenities: Safe deposit box. Children 17 and younger stay free with parents. Two restaurants & cocktail lounge. Work area with desk in some rooms. Has 27 meeting rooms with 25,000 square feet (or 2,322 square meters) of space.

Fitness center, outdoor swimming pool, & whirlpool. Pool table. Complimentary transportation within three-mile (or 4.8-kilometer) radius 9 AM-10 PM. Has four restricted floors with a business center and a lounge. Also AC, ATM, BC, C, CM, COF, EX, FT, GS, HC, HR, IH, RS, VMD, WN.

A luxury Hilton hotel located in Lincoln Centre, a 32-acre (or 12.9-hectare) resort and business complex on an artificial lake. There is a small fee for parking and to use the facilities at Lincoln City Club. It opened as Lincoln Hotel in 1982, became Doubletree at Lincoln Centre five years later, and a Hilton in 2003. The American Automobile Association gave it four diamonds for seven years in a row.

A seven-foot (or 2.1-meter) bronze statue cast in Italy and titled *Reclining Muse*, by Charles Umlauf, is located at the water fountain in front of the hotel.

Restaurants include the formal and rather expensive Crockett's Grill, serving dinner nightly 5 PM-10 PM. The three bronzes you will see about you are by the sculptor of the West, Frederic Remington. The restaurant's Sunday brunch is popular with regulars.

A more casual Center Cafe is open daily for breakfast and lunch, as is delicatessen and bakery L'Express. There is also a wine, scotch, and cigar bar, Basie's Lounge, and a sports bar.

The Galleria mall, with its 200 shops, like Macy's, Saks Fifth Avenue, and Gucci, also a skating rink, is located across LBJ, but you cannot walk over to it. Just a couple of blocks east is Valley View, another mall that boasts almost as many stores and restaurants.

HYATT REGENCY D/FW, International Pkwy., D/FW Airport, (800) 233-1234 or (972) 453-1234, Fax 615-6825/456-8668, Internet www.hyatt.com. *E*. It has 1,369 soundproofed rooms and suites, some non-smoking or for disabled guests, starting at $150 a night. This Hyatt has 850 employees.

Located in two 12-floor towers inside the D/FW International Airport.

Amenities: Free parking & business center. Foreign languages capabilities & currency exchange. Heated outdoor swimming pool. Has 81 meeting rooms with 130,000 square feet (or 12,077 square meters) of space. Also AC, C, CM, COF, DCL, FT, GS, HC, HR, IH, RS, SDB, VMD.

Claims to be the nation's largest airport hotel. Hyatt Regency D/FW consists of two separate towers that have the third largest number of hotel rooms in the Metroplex, after Adam's Mark and Wyndham Anatole hotels:

The **East Tower,** having 815 rooms, was built in 1980. It houses three restaurants: Papaya's, serving Southwestern and Tex-Mex cuisine for lunch and dinner, is also popular for its weekend seafood buffet. There is also Mr. G's, serving steaks and seafood Mon-Fri 6 PM-10 PM. Il Nonos, an Italian-cuisine restaurant, is open Mon-Sat, also 6 PM-10 PM.

The **West Tower,** once containing 550 rooms, was constructed in 1972. To make space for the international Terminal D and an 8,100 car garage at D/FW Airport, both part of a $2.6-billion reconstruction that is to be completed in 2005, the 12-story west tower was imploded in 2001.

The midnight explosion was originally to kick off United Way annual drive in Dallas and Tarrant Counties to raise $55 million for the activities of 110 nonprofit organizations in the area, but it was canceled after the gruesome terrorist destruction of New York's World Trade Center, where 2,800 perished on September 11. United Way is Dallas' largest source of non-governmental financing for social services. Hyatt was paid more than $30 million for the 83 years remaining on its 99-year lease.

To replace the West Tower, a 300-room, $56-million Grand Hyatt Hotel will be built atop the new two-million-square-foot (or 185,800-square-meter) Terminal D that will serve 37,000 passengers a day.

Hyatt's two 18-hole golf courses, seven tennis courts, and ten racquetball facilities are located in the southwest section of D/FW Airport, at Bear Creek, off State Highway 360 and Mid-Cities Boulevard, about five miles (or eight kilometers) from the airport. Opened in 1980, the golf facility with a traditional layout, abundant trees, and rolling hills, still ranks as a favorite.

TERRA COTTA INN, 6101 Lyndon B. Johnson Frwy. at Preston Rd., (800) 533-3591 or (972) 387-2525, Fax 387-3784, Internet www.terracottainn.com. M. It has 90 rooms and suites, some for the disabled and non-smokers, and includes a "lavish" complimentary breakfast.

You will be charged for one full night should you fail to inform the inn by 6 PM on the scheduled day of arrival that you are not coming.

Located in a low-rise strip shopping center on the north side of LBJ

Freeway (also known as Interstate Highway 635) and several blocks west of Hillcrest Road. Valley View Mall is situated across the street, and the Galleria shopping center a few more blocks to the west.

Wild West Outfitters, with a large selection of Western wear and boots, is adjacent to the inn. Cavender's Boot City, another Western apparel store, is situated farther to the west.

Amenities: Outdoor swimming pool. Complimentary local phone calls. Fax and copy service. Meeting facilities for 45 people. Also AC, CM, CP, IH, RS, VMD, WN. No pets accepted.

A small three-story motel in hacienda-style design, with red-tile roof, run by a Southern Methodist University advertising and marketing major and her mother, who have spent a decade transforming a rundown flophouse into hospitable lodgings.

The mother took possession of the former Valley View Inn in 1989 as part of a divorce settlement that also included the Denny's 24-hour restaurant in front of the inn. The two women sank $3 million into improvements.

"The Terra Cotta Inn is a paradox in an age of cookie-cutter sameness," observes the *Dallas Morning News*. "There is nothing ordinary about this place." *Texas Highways* magazine claims the inn "offers charm and quiet that belie its surroundings."

THE WESTIN GALLERIA, 13340 Dallas Pkwy., (800) 228-3000 or (972) 934-9494, Fax 450-2979. *E*. Has 432 rooms, including 13 suites, some for handicapped and non-smokers, starting at $200 a night. The hotel has some 400 employees.

Located inside the Galleria shopping center in far north Dallas, at Dallas North Tollway and Lyndon B. Johnson Freeway, also known as Interstate Highway 635.

The Sixth Floor Museum and Dallas World Aquarium (see entries) downtown are about a half-mile (or 0.8 kilometer) south of here. Kittrell/Riffkind Art Glass gallery is within two miles (or 3.2 kilometers).

Amenities: Foreign languages capabilities. Safe deposit boxes & in-room safes. Foreign currency exchange. Restaurant & two lounges. Complimentary self-parking, or valet parking at a charge. Outdoor heated swimming pool. It has an executive floor with limited access rooms, private wet bar, in-room printer/fax/copier at additional charge.

Twenty-two meeting rooms totaling 28,000 square feet (or 2,601 square meters) include a 2,138-square-foot (or 199-square-meter) ballroom. Also C, CM, COF, DCL, FT, GS, HC, HR, IH, MF, PT, RS, VMD, WN. Babysitters are available upon request. Health club & fitness center is located nearby.

The American Automobile Association awards it four out of the possible five diamonds.

A luxury hotel inside a luxury shopping mall with 200 stores and two dozen restaurants, but also with nerve-wracking traffic tie-ups. Some of the most desirable and fashionable shops, such as Macy's, Nordstrom, and Saks Fifth Avenue, are located here. There is a multi-screen cinema and an indoor ice rink.

A survey of 41,000 *Consumer Reports* readers judged the Westin chain nationwide as the least desirable among the luxury hotels, such as the Four Seasons, Ritz-Carlton, Renaissance, and Hyatt.

Westin once boasted a highly regarded and equally expensive Huntington's restaurant, which was replaced by Oceanaire Seafood Room, serving lunch and dinner. Oceanaire, with retro 1930s supper club decor and serving 30 kinds of seafood and steaks, opened in 2002. It also has Options restaurant and bar.

Outside the hotel, on the third level of the mall, you will find Nicola's Ristorante, where "recipes are simple but honest and good." Bennigan's, La Madeleine French Bakery & Café, and Corner Bakery are in the mall.

THE WESTIN PARK CENTRAL, 12720 Merit Dr. at Lyndon B. Johnson Frwy. (or Interstate Hwy. 635), (888) 625-5144 or (972) 385-3000, Fax 991-4557, Internet www.westin.com. *E*. It has 545 rooms, including 22 suites, some for handicapped and non-smokers.

Located north of downtown Dallas, in the southwest corner of LBJ and Coit, southeast of the Galleria and Valley View Mall, and next to the 438-room Sheraton Park Central Hotel, which closed following the 2001 terrorist attacks in New York and Washington, D.C.

Benihana, a Japanese steakhouse, is situated across the street.

The Galleria and Valley View shopping centers are farther west, north of LBJ Freeway, between Preston Road and Dallas North Tollway.

Amenities: Two restaurants & three lounges. Safe deposit boxes in some rooms. CDs & VCRs in most suites. Free transportation within a five-mile (or eight-kilometer) radius of the hotel, or limousine at a fee. Complimentary on-site fitness center or nearby Landmark Club at a small fee. Landmark Club also features a well-regarded rooftop restaurant. Outdoor swimming pool & exercise room on third level. Beauty salon & barbershop.

Executive floor at an additional charge includes complimentary breakfast and evening hors d'oeuvres. Twenty-three meeting rooms with 28,519 square feet (or 2,649 square meters) of space, with the largest measuring 15,050 square feet (or 1,398 square meters). Parking at a daily fee. Also AC, BC, CM, COF, EX, GS, IH, PA, RS, VMD.

An informal Cafe in the Park serves breakfast, lunch and dinner. Next door is McNelly's Pub.

A handsome hotel with an airy and bright multilevel atrium lobby.

There is not much to do in the immediate vicinity if you are on foot, except perhaps walk to Benihana Japanese steakhouse across the street, at 7775 Banner Drive, (972) 387-4404, where one of the costlier entrées is the $36 hibachi chateaubriand steak and lobster tail.

The independently owned **Landmark Club,** (972) 392-1500, health facility next door is open Mon-Thu 6 AM-10 PM, Fri until 8 PM, Sat-Sun 9 AM-6 PM. Coming from any hotel, there is a small charge for a 24-hour pass, which entitles you to use all equipment.

AN ADDISON HOTEL

HOTEL INTER-CONTINENTAL DALLAS, 15201 Dallas Pkwy., Addison, (800) 426-3135 or (972) 386-6000, Fax 991-6937, e-mail ihcdallas@interconti.com, Internet www.interconti.com. *E*. It has 528 soundproofed rooms, including 31 suites, some for the disabled and non-smokers, starting at $150 a night. The hotel employs about 400.

Located on the west side of Dallas North Tollway, between Belt Line and Arapaho Roads, less than a mile (or 1.6 kilometers) northwest of the Village on the Parkway shopping center.

The Galleria shopping center, with its 200 stores and restaurants, is about two miles (or 3.2 kilometers) south of here, Valley View Mall farther east of there. Cavanaugh Flight Museum and WaterTower Theatre are also nearby. (Please see individual entries for more details.)

Amenities: Multi-lingual staff. In-room safe. Valet indoor parking at charge or complimentary outdoor parking. Two restaurants, lounge, bar, & nightclub. Outdoor swimming pool. Fitness center & spa on lower level features treadmills, stepper, free weights, life cycles. Beauty salon & barber. Gift & flower shop.

Twenty-six individual meeting rooms, including a 25,000-square-foot (or 2,322-square-meter) ballroom, with a total of 100,000 square feet (or 9,290 square meters) of space. Business center with computer, printer, fax machine, & secretarial services. Four lighted rooftop tennis courts & two indoor racquetball courts. Sauna & steam bath, Jacuzzi & massage. Jogging track on the premises, golf course nearby. Also AC, C, CM, COF, CF, DCL, EX, HR, PT, RS, VMD.

Opened in 1983 and first called the Registry, the 14-story Grand Kempinski, as it was known until 1997, is a luxury hotel with a bit of European flair, although it is also the largest Addison hotel. Two private concierge floors are available to the handicapped and non-smokers, where hors d'oeuvres and Continental breakfast are served at an additional charge.

In 2001, Registry Dallas Associates, its owners, initiated a three-phase, $10-million renovation that is to include the conversion of the hotel's indoor swimming pool into 3,000 square feet (or 278 square meters) of meeting space.

The highly-rated Monte Carlo restaurant, where the service and atmosphere are better than the food, features southern French and northern Italian cuisine and is open daily 6 PM-10:30 PM. The more casual Le Cafe serves breakfast and lunch.

KEMPI's nightclub on the premises is open Tue-Fri 5:30 PM-2 AM, Sat 8 PM-2 AM; closed Sun-Mon. The Malachite Room features, according to the *Dallas Morning News*, one of the best Sunday brunches, but the dress code is strictly enforced.

If you wish to sample a restaurant outside the hotel, try Mirabelle, which is situated at 17610 Midway Road at Trinity Mills, (972) 733-0202, in a strip shopping center about three miles (or 4.8 kilometers) north of here. A four-star, 55-seat new-American and Latin cuisine seafood restaurant, where lobsters, blue prawns, and sea bass are available, Mirabelle is open for lunch Mon-Fri 11 AM-2 PM and serves dinner daily 5 PM-11 PM. There is live music Thu-Sat.

A FRISCO HOTEL

THE WESTIN STONEBRIAR RESORT, 1549 Legacy Dr., between Town & Country Blvd. and State Hwy. 121, Frisco, (888) 625-5144 or (972) 668-8000, Fax 668-8100, Internet www.westin.com. *E*. It has 301 rooms, including 20 suites, some for handicapped and non-smokers, starting at $200 a night.

Located north of downtown Dallas, about one-half mile (or 0.8 kilometer) south of Stonebriar Centre Mall, featuring Foley's, Macy's, and Nordstrom's department stores.

Amenities: Restaurant & lounge. Safe deposit boxes. Complimentary self-parking or valet parking at a charge. Large work desk in most suites. Has 6,400-square-foot (or 595-square-meter) health club & fitness center open daily 6 AM-10 PM. Outdoor swimming pool, spa, & whirlpool.

Complimentary transportation to Stonebriar Mall and Legacy business park. Limousine service available to other points. Thirteen meeting rooms totaling 24,000 square feet, (or 2,230 square meters), with the largest measuring 6,265 square feet (or 582 square meters).

An 18-hole, par-72 Tom Fazio golf course next door is shared with Stonebriar Country Club. Also AC, BC, C, CM, COF, DCL, GS, IH, RS, VMD, WN.

Opened in 2000, this Westin markets itself as an urban resort that competes with the Four Seasons Resort & Club.

"We're luxury hoteliers," sniffs the Four Season's general manager, "while the Westin Stonebriar is 'full-service.' It's the difference between flying first class and business class. No mere hotel, the Four Seasons is a series of experiences."

The Westin's management, however, insists that accommodations have "all the elegance of a world-class resort and all the amenities of a leading business hotel." One- and two-bedroom suites feature balconies overlooking the golf course.

IRVING HOTELS

FOUR SEASONS RESORT & CLUB, 4150 North MacArthur Blvd. at Mills Lane, Irving, (972) 717-0700, Fax 717-2550, Internet www.fourseasons.com/dallas. *E*. It has 357 luxury rooms and suites on nine floors, some for the disabled and non-smokers, starting at $250 a night. The rates include the use of the spa and sports club. Special packages, including golf, tennis, and the spa, are also available. The resort employs almost 1,000.

Located at Las Colinas in Irving, between State Highways 183 and 114, on 400 acres (or 161 hectares) of rolling hills. Dallas/Fort Worth International Airport is about eight miles (or 12.8 kilometers) away, the downtown Dallas business district 13 miles (or 21 kilometers).

Southwestern cuisine restaurant Via Real is situated across the street. The *Mustangs of Las Colinas* bronze sculptural ensemble on William Square and the Movie Studios at Las Colinas (see individual entries) are located about four miles (or 6.4 kilometers) north of here.

Amenities: Three restaurants & two bars. Complimentary transportation is available within a ten-minute radius of the property, "on a first-come, first-served basis." One-hour pressing, overnight laundry & dry cleaning.

A 176,000-square-foot (or 16,350-square-meter) sports club with 12 tennis courts and racquetball. There is one indoor & three outdoor swimming pools, with the largest measuring 5,500 square feet (or 511 square meters). Jacuzzi, sauna, & massage.

Eight outdoor & four indoor tennis courts with professional instructors. Also indoor & outdoor jogging tracks. Jay Morrish designed the 1986 Tournament Players Course, par 70, 6,960 yards, where the Byron Nelson Golf Classic has been played since then. There are nine holes on each side of MacArthur Boulevard. A lake was added in 1993.

"The TPC is the best course money can buy," claims the *Dallas Business Journal*. The conference center, which includes 28 multi-purpose rooms, totals 32,000 square feet (or 2,973 square meters). It has a 24-hour business center with fax & photocopy machine. Cellular telephone rentals.

Twice-daily housekeeping service. Valet parking. Down pillows, wool blankets, & terry bathrobes. Children under 18 years stay free with their parents, can have special meals, video games, even bedtime milk & cookies. Children's activities are available daily 9 AM-8 PM.

Also AC, C, CM, CP, EX, FT, GS, HR, IH, RS, VMD, WN. Babysitting services are available on request.

Four Seasons opened as a sports club in 1982, and in 1986 a luxury hotel was added to the 400-acre (or 161-hectare) resort. The hotel is known for "its high-level and often secret corporate meetings—whether it's the signing of a major athlete, a merger agreement or high-pressure union negotiations," claims the *Dallas Morning News*. "Some guests get their room keys and check-in information delivered to their limousine, eliminating the front desk."

Most rooms have private balconies overlooking the fairways. Fifty rooms are grouped in private villas. To keep the guests cool, the Four Seasons pays an electric bill that would keep an entire village comfortable. Leisure travelers comprise about 15 percent of the hotel's business. The property is owned by the San Antonio-based United Services Automobile Association and managed by Four Seasons Hotels of Toronto.

Consumer Reports magazine readers rated the Four Seasons their top hotel chain nationwide in the luxury category, where Ritz-Carlton, Renaissance, Hyatt, and Westin were also considered.

The club has two 18-hole golf courses, one the site of the Professional Golf Association Tour's annual **Byron Nelson Golf Classic,** named after the well-known Texas golfer, which takes place each May. The Byron Nelson Golf School can accommodate groups of eight to 24 on the 88,000-square-foot (or 8,175-square-meter) practice facility.

That nine-and-one-half-foot (or 2.89-meter) bronze statue of the smiling Byron Nelson leaning on his golf club, was created in 1992 by Robert Summers (b. 1941), who also sculpted the 39 steers and three cowboys on the Pioneer Plaza (see entry) in front of the Dallas Convention Center downtown. A tabletop replica of this statue will be found in the lobby overlooking the outdoor swimming pool.

One outdoor tennis court has a stadium seating for 2,500 spectators. Four Season's spa, open daily 9 AM-9 PM, provides massage, facial, manicure, sauna, steam bath, whirlpool, and cold plunge. Other treatments include Swedish massage, herbal wrap, parafango body wrap, and detoxifying seaweed body mask. Salon provides haircuts, manicure, and pedicure and is open daily 9 AM-7 PM.

Cafe on the Green is a contemporary Asian-cuisine restaurant open for breakfast, lunch, and dinner 6:30 AM-11 PM and seats 184. Jackets are not required for men. Sunday brunch is held 11 AM-2 PM. The restaurant was named one of the top ten in 2001 by the *Dallas Morning News*. It provides babysitting services for children of local dinner guests.

Byron's at the Sports Club serves lunch weekdays only 11:30 AM-2 PM. Racquets serves sandwiches and snacks in the Sports Club 8 AM-8 PM. Three lounges are also on the premises, including a pub with billiards, shuffleboard, pinball games, and television.

The 600-seat Trail Dust Steak House, at 10841 Composite Dr., (214) 357-3862, and the Old San Francisco Steakhouse, at 10965 Composite Dr., (214) 357-0484, with 550 seats—both roughly at Stemmons Freeway North (or Interstate 35 East) and Walnut Hill Lane—are located about six miles (or 9.7 kilometers) northeast of the Four Seasons. The 500-seat Pappas Brothers Steakhouse, at 10477 Lombardy Lane, (214) 366-2000, and the 360-seat Pappadeaux Seafood Kitchen nearby, are also in that direction.

MARRIOTT D/FW AIRPORT NORTH, 8440 Freeport Pkwy., Irving, (800) 228-9290 or (972) 929-8800, Fax 929-6501, Internet www.marriotthotels.com. M. It has 491 rooms and suites on 20 floors, some for the disabled and non-smokers.

Located at the crossroads of John W. Carpenter Freeway West (also known as State Highway 114) and Freeport Parkway, less than one mile (or 1.6 kilometers) east of D/FW Airport.

Situated near the north entrance of the airport and close to the Las Colinas Urban Center. It is one of about two dozen hotels located within three miles (or 4.8 kilometers) of the airport.

Amenities: Restaurant & cocktail lounge. Safe deposit boxes. Work desk with lamp in many rooms. Provides 24-hour complimentary airport shuttle & free transportation to Grapevine Mills Mall (see entry). Indoor & outdoor swimming pools. Valet & laundry services. Self-serve laundry facilities. Shoeshine.

The business center—open Mon-Thu 7 AM-6 PM, Fri 7 AM-3 PM—provides faxing, photocopying, and desktop publishing services. Has 24 meeting rooms with 17,500 square feet (or 1,626 square meters) of space. Also AC, C, CM, COF, CP, EX, GS, HC, HR, IH, PA, RS, VMD, WN.

The second largest Irving hotel, it underwent a renovation in 2000. Claims to be "specifically designed for the business traveler," but the *Mobil Travel Guide* gives it only three out of the possible five stars.

JW's Steakhouse, open Mon-Sat 6 PM-10:30 PM, serves dinner in luxurious surroundings. The Marriott Cafe is a more casual setting for breakfast, lunch, and dinner. Pitcher's Tavern is a sports bar with games and satellite television. There is also a coffee house.

Grapevine Mills Mall, with a Bass Pro Shop, is about three miles (or 4.8 kilometers) away, the 150-store Irving Mall 5.5 miles (or 8.8 kilometers). Golf and tennis facilities are available nearby.

OMNI MANDALAY AT LAS COLINAS, 221 East Las Colinas Blvd., Irving, (800) THE-OMNI or (972) 556-0800, Fax 556-0729, Internet www.omnihotels.com. *E*. It has 410 rooms, about a quarter of them suites, some for handicapped and non-smokers. Many rooms overlook Lake Carolyn or downtown Dallas. Has about 400 employees.

Located on 5.5 acres (or 2.22 hectares) in the Las Colinas Urban Center, near North O'Connor Boulevard and east of John Carpenter Freeway. Williams Square, with its large equestrian ensemble, *Mustangs of Las Colinas* (see Art in Public Places for more details), is located nearby.

Dallas Cowboys' Texas Stadium is three miles (or 4.8 kilometers) away. D/FW Airport is eight miles (or 12.8 kilometers) west from here.

Amenities: Two restaurants & lobby lounge. Heated lakeside swimming pool, whirlpool & sauna. Full-service fitness center with stationary bikes, treadmills, free weights, Stairmaster & Nautilus equipment. Business center.

Has 14 function rooms, including a 10,000-square-foot (or 929-square-meter) ballroom, with 31,200 square feet (or 2,898 square meters) of meeting & banquet space. Children's playground on the back courtyard. Also AC, C, CM, COF, CP, DCL, FT, HC, HR, IH, MF, PA, RS, VMD.

A 28-story hotel located on the Mandalay Canal in the heart of Las Colinas, which in Spanish means the Hills. Management promises "sophisticated elegance, fine attention to detail, and Texas-size hospitality." This Omni ranks as one of the 50 best U.S. mainland resorts.

In 1928, this land was a Texas cattle ranch. In 1973, a master plan for the 12,000-acre (or 4,856-hectare) Las Colinas community was unveiled. Cobblestone walkways wind along the Mandalay Canal near the hotel and lead to a few boutiques and cafes that once had a potential to remind one of Europe. Venetian-style water taxis are available to transport you through the Urban Center with prior reservations.

A casual upscale Italian restaurant is located on the canal level of the hotel and features a patio with a view of the 126-acre (or 51-hectare) Lake Carolyn. Sunday brunch also has a waterside view.

Championship golf courses and tennis courts are available at a nearby equestrian center. Walking, jogging, and biking paths are located around the hotel.

Also nearby is a spotless if lifeless **Marriott Las Colinas,** 223 West Las Colinas Blvd. and John W. Carpenter Fwy., (800) 228-9290 or (972) 831-0000, with 361 rooms and three suites on 15 floors. Located in Las Colinas Center, behind William Square with the *Mustangs of Las Colinas* bronze ensemble (see entry). It has an American-cuisine restaurant and lounge.

DINING

There are almost 7,000 restaurants in the Dallas area, according to the *Official Visitors Guide*, which also claims for the city a higher per capita number of restaurants than for New York City.

Dallasites are said to spend more than $4 billion a year in restaurants, and it is estimated that almost half of their food budget is spent dining out. Close to 60 percent of all restaurant visits in the Metroplex are to fast-food restaurants, and McDonald's leads with an almost 10 percent share of that market.

While here, you can treat yourself not only to the usual fare you will find in other cities at home and abroad, but also to excellent barbecue, chili, Mexican food, and superb steaks, all foods that Texas is famous for. "With its moneyed population and Eastern orientation (it feels and look more like Atlanta than Houston or San Antonio), Dallas can surprise the unsuspecting with the quality of its food," reflects the *New York Times*.

Medieval Times Dinner & Tournament (see listing in the SIGHTS & ATTRACTIONS chapter) is the largest Metroplex dining facility, with a seating capacity of 1,000. It is followed by **III Forks** steakhouse, and **Maggiano's Little Italy** (Internet www.maggianos.com), at NorthPark mall, which seats 750.

Reviews of the 50-plus restaurants below are often a composite of impressions by more than one diner. Restaurant food being so subjective, I have also included brief press quotes.

As the *Dallas Observer* noted, paraphrasing a provocative article on the state of food in *Reason* magazine: "No longer just a necessity to keep the belly rumbles at bay, food has become a mark of sophistication, a form of expression, an entertainment, a topic of conversation as passionate as the babble over sports or politics." That is Dallas today.

None of the establishments knew when the reviewers visited. No food, gratuity, or service was ever given or offered to influence any review. These reviews should not be considered as an endorsement of any establishment and are meant to serve mainly as an introduction to your selection process. Most restaurants' menus are changing continuously, so dishes named are meant to give you merely an idea of the scope of a restaurant's repertoire.

For more details on these and other restaurants, see also the *Dallas Morning News Friday's Guide* and *Fort Worth Star-Telegram Friday's Startime*, weekly *Dallas Observer*, monthly *D Magazine* and *Texas Monthly*, and Zagat's consumer surveys, which are published in a booklet form.

All restaurants are grouped into one of these three price categories:

I *Inexpensive* (up to $10 per person)
M *Moderate* ($10-25 per person)
E *Expensive* (more than $25 per person)

While meals in the moderate and expensive categories could include an appetizer, an entrée, a dessert, or a non-alcoholic beverage, the prices do not factor in alcohol or gratuities. Prices, where shown, were quoted early in 2003 and are likely to change by the time you read this.

A word about Texas wines: Texans overwhelmingly favor French wines over Texas wines. Test subjects at Texas A&M University were poured two glasses of wine in a blind test and told that one was from Texas and the other French. Even after the participants found out after the test that both samples were produced in the Lone Star State, most still insisted they prefer French wines.

Credit cards are so widely accepted that I single out only a few establishments that do not take any of them. Dallasites usually tip 10-20 percent, depending on the level of service, but almost never less than $1.

Smoking

The Dallas City Council voted in 2003 to ban smoking in all restaurants, hotel and motel guest rooms not designated for smoking, and private clubs with eating establishments. Smokers are allowed to light up on restaurant patios, as long as they are not enclosed. Dallas thus became the first large city in north Texas to go smoke free. With that in mind, I have eliminated most references to smoking in Dallas restaurants.

The smoking ban was also extended to all Dallas museums, cinemas, libraries, shopping malls, department and grocery stores. Neither is smoking allowed in Dallas hospitals and nursing homes, hair salons, bowling alleys, Laundromats, bingo parlors, city facilities, and, of course, schools.

The only exceptions to the ban are specifically designated areas of stand-alone bars and pool halls, tobacco shops and cigar bars, and outdoor patios. Drinking establishments must derive 75 percent or more of their gross revenue each quarter from the sale of alcoholic beverages to allow smoking, and even they must provide no-smoking sections. Fines range from $25 to $500.

Carrollton also bans smoking in restaurants; it requires separate rooms for smokers and additional filtration. In Plano, smoking is banned unless the smoking section has separate ventilation. Highland Park, University Park, and Addison have no such rules against smoking.

RESTAURANTS BY AREA

West End and Deep Ellum restaurants are listed under downtown location. (For a better understanding of these areas, please refer to the chapter FINDING YOUR WAY AROUND DALLAS.)

Addison

Blue Mesa, Southwestern
Chamberlain's Steak & Chop House, Steaks
Ferrari's Villa, Italian
The Londoner, English

Downtown

Antares, New American
Chaparral Club, New American
El Fenix, Mexican
The French Room, French
Jeroboam, French Brasserie
Monica's Aca y Alla, Tex-Mex
Morton's of Chicago, Steaks
The Palm, Steaks
The Pyramid, New American
Sambuca Jazz Cafe, Mediterranean
Tolbert's Texas Chili Parlor, Chili

East Dallas

Dickey's, Barbecue
The Grape, New American
The Tipperary Inn, Irish

North Dallas

Del Frisco's Double Eagle Steakhouse, Steaks
Gershwin's, New American
Luby's Cafeterias, Home Cooking

Oak Lawn

Al Biernat's, Steaks
Bob's Steak & Chop House, Steaks
The Mansion on Turtle Creek, New American
Ruth's Chris Steak House, Steaks
Sonny Bryan's Smokehouse, Barbecue
Steel, Japanese/Indochinese

Park Cities

Adelmo's, Mediterranean
L'Ancestral, French
Cafe Pacific, Seafood
Chez Gerard, French
City Café, New American
Il Sole, Italian
La Madeleine Bakery & Cafe, French
Tramontana, American
Ziziki's, Greek

Uptown

Abacus, New American
Arcodoro & Pomodoro, Italian
The Old Warsaw, Continental
Watel's, French

RESTAURANTS BY CUISINE

Barbecue

Dickey's Barbecue, 4610 North Central Expwy. at North Henderson Ave., (214) 823-0240. *I.* Open daily from 11 AM to 8 PM. Located north of downtown Dallas, across the expressway from Highland Park and bordering on an area with several antique shops.

Alfredo and Libre restaurants are within the next couple of blocks farther east. The Old Monk nearby serves more than 60 beers, including those from Belgium, England, Germany, and Ireland.

Perhaps one of the ugliest food joints in North America, but with the "mouth waterin', lip smackin', finger lickin', rib ticklin', knee slappin', foot stompin', great tastin'" barbecue that you will enjoy for sure if extra calories are of no concern. "Sometimes it's great to dine where it's socially acceptable to be messy," observes the *Dallas Morning News*. "It's nothing fancy, but it gets the job done."

Established at this location in 1941, Dickey's now has more than 45 restaurants throughout Texas and as far away as Colorado, including at the Dallas/Fort Worth International Airport. Dinners are mostly under $10 and can include beef, sausage, chicken breast, ham, turkey, and hot link, as well as two vegetables. You can also buy meats by the pound.

Roland Dickey, who has worked at family restaurants since he was 12 years old, and his brother T. D. supervise the expanding business now that their parents are gone. Their mother, who "only had a sixth-grade education," handled the money for the company until she was in her 80s, a "brilliant lady, but a terrible cook."

A popular freebie at Dickey's, since cheese was taken out for health reasons, is free, self-service ice cream. "Ya know," Dickey told the *News*, "Ross Perot Sr. eats at the store on Forest Lane all the time, and he never misses his free ice cream."

There is a **Dickey's** downtown, at 726 North Harwood St., (214) 740-1661.

Roland Dickey's favorite Dallas restaurants, by the way, are Adelmo's and Bob's Steak and Chop House (see individual listings).

Sonny Bryan's Smokehouse, 2202 Inwood Rd., (214) 357-7120, Internet www.sonnybryansbbq.com. *I*. Open Mon-Fri 10 AM-4 PM, Sat 10 AM-3 PM, and Sun 11 AM-2 PM. It has a bar.

Located between Harry Hines Boulevard and Forest Park Road, near Parkland and St. Paul Hospitals, and next door to a Salvation Army thrift store. Situated here since 1958, Bryan's is a must-stop for locals, celebrities, and tourists from home and abroad.

Elias Bryan brought his family to Texas from Tennessee and opened the first Bryan's Barbecue in 1910. His son William Jennings Bryan, known as Red because of the color of his hair, followed with his own restaurant in Oak Cliff in 1935.

His grandson, called Sonny, left Red in 1957 and opened his own place the following year on February 13th, the same day on which his father and grandfather opened their establishments. Sonny Bryan started looking for a buyer in 1989, after he was diagnosed with cancer and because his two sons were not interested in running the business.

The chain was bought by Waco-born Walker Harman, who had graduated from Baylor University and earned his MBA from the University of Oklahoma. There are now some 20 Sonny Bryan's restaurants throughout the Metroplex, and the chain is the official barbecue caterer at the Mesquite Rodeo (see listing).

"Except for maybe the Mansion on Turtle Creek, no Dallas restaurant is as well known as Sonny Bryan's Smokehouse," claims the *Dallas Morning News*.

Many meals are priced under $10. The exceptions would be two- and three-meat combo plates, and the Pitmaster and Ribman platters, which cost less than $20. There are smoked chicken sandwiches, hickory smoked barbecue plates, and rib combo plates, the last two served with two vegetables or onion rings. There is a child's menu. Cobbler and pecan pie are two among the desserts. Meats and vegetables are also sold in bulk.

The Inwood Road location was one of only three Metroplex barbecue joints that made the list of 50 best such places in Texas. Five staffers from *Texas Monthly* magazine ate at 245 establishments in 1997 and judged the top three to be located in Lockhart, Taylor, and Llano.

"The raison d'eat here is hickory-smoked brisket sandwiches, pork ribs, and thick, crunchy onion rings," says the *Texas Monthly* review of this Sonny's. "The pork-and-beef sausage and ham are forgettable, the potato salad and slaw pedestrian, the beans not helped by pit time."

In 2000, Sonny Bryan's was one of eight regional restaurants honored at the annual James Beard foundation awards for culinary excellence and achievement. On the other hand, the *News*' food reviewer opines that "going corporate with multiple locations has exacted a small, but measurable, toll on the quality of barbecue at the Inwood Road drive-in."

Bryan's in the basement of the 50-story and 36-story Republic Towers, 325 North St. Paul St. downtown, (214) 979-0102, is open Mon-Fri 10:30 AM-2:30 PM only. Another Bryan's is at 302 North Market St., downtown, (214) 744-1610, next to Landry's Seafood House in the West End Historic District. You will also find one at Macy's, on the third floor of the Galleria mall (see entry) in north Dallas.

Chili

Tolbert's Texas Chili Parlor, One Dallas Centre, 350 North St. Paul at Bryan Streets, (214) 953-1353. *I*. Open Mon-Fri 11 AM-7 PM. Wheelchair accessible. Located diagonally across the street from the 1929 U.S. Post Office & Courthouse building (see listing).

Buried beneath one of five I.M. Pei and Partners skyrises, the 30-story One Dallas Centre, designed by Henry Cobb, is the last remaining Tolbert's chili parlor made famous by *Dallas Morning News* columnist Frank X. Tolbert who died in 1984. This restaurant opened in the mid-1960s.

He became celebrated for his book, titled *A Bowl of Chili*, supposedly the definitive book on Texas chili. Although you might come here to sample the original "five-alarm" beanless chili, you will also find a Tex-Mex menu with several other local dishes. If you are from out of town, watch what you say about Texas chili or you might get a mouthful from a local bubba.

The "original" Texas red, five-alarm chili runs from $5 for a cup to $10 for "Texas size (really big bowl of chili)." Quesadillas, hot wings, nachos, and jalapeno peppers stuffed with cheese and chicken are some among the appetizers.

There are homemade tortilla and baked potato soups on the menu as are half a dozen salads. Tolbert's serves ten varieties of hamburgers that weigh half a pound (or 23 grams). Texas cheese steak, fried chicken, and fried catfish are just three among the sandwiches available.

The costliest meal at Tolbert's is the eight-ounce (or 311-gram) sirloin steak, followed by the charbroiled cowboy strip steak. Chicken sour cream enchiladas, chicken burritos, and soft beef or chicken tacos are the Tex-Mex selections. You can top your meal with Tolbert's fudge pie, warm apple or pecan pie, or chocolate sundae.

Each fall, an outbreak of chili madness occurs in Terlingua, in the Big Bend region, 80 miles (or 129 kilometers) from Alpine, where hundreds of chiliheads and thousands of tipsy males and barely-clad females journey for an annual Frank X. Tolbert chili championship. The event takes place on the first weekend in November, when two competing chili cook-offs take place simultaneously on either side of Terlingua, a former home of the miners who once dug mercury ore from the surrounding hills.

The first chili cook-off, a publicity stunt at the old Terlingua store in 1967, was a ploy by a Dallas public relations man who hoped it would draw attention to land available for sale.

Tolbert's son, also Frank X. Tolbert (b. 1945), is an artist in his own right and has been married for more than 20 years to art photographer Ann Stautenberg (b. 1954).

Continental

The Old Warsaw, 2610 Maple Ave., (214) 528-0032, Internet www.theoldwarsaw.com. *E*. Open daily for dinner only 5:30 PM-10:30 PM. There is nightly piano and strolling violinist entertainment. Four private rooms seat up to 70 diners. It has a bar. Wheelchair accessible. Reservations are recommended. Limousine service and valet parking are available.

Located in the Uptown neighborhood just north of downtown Dallas, between Cedar Springs Road and McKinney Avenue. Maple Avenue was annexed to the city of Dallas in 1890. After its developer built his lavish $20,000 home at the northwest corner of Cedar Springs and Maple, near here, in 1888, it was soon joined by other mansions, making it the "social and architectural successor of Ross Avenue and the predecessor of Highland Park."

Opened by a former Polish diplomat, Stanley Slovak, in 1948, La Vieille Varsovie, as it was initially known, was originally located on the corner of Oak Lawn Avenue and Cedar Springs and claims to be Dallas' first haute cuisine French restaurant. Slovak sold it in 1970. Around 1956, the Old Warsaw was perhaps the first Dallas restaurant to serve wine with meals. It moved to its current location 14 years later.

The candlelit restaurant sports crystal chandeliers, dark floral walls, and paintings in gilded frames. Some find the large saltwater tanks with two barracudas inappropriate.

The Old Warsaw was bought in 1985 by Al Heidari , whose younger brother Mohsen owns Arthur's steakhouse in Addison, as well as St. Martin's Wine Bistro, and San Francisco Rose bar, both on Lower Greenville Avenue.

The restaurant has been the recipient of many awards and recommendations over the years, including from the *New York Times*, which named it one of the best eateries in the United States in 1951. More adventurous diners, however, consider it a bit behind the times, and some say the quality of food and service has dropped over the years as well.

The restaurant "is an imposing figure that leans heavily on accolades long ago earned and bronzed into perpetuity by virtue of its staying power," notes the *Dallas Observer*. "The Old Warsaw is near comatose, hooked up to a respirator of its past laurels."

Female diners get a menu without prices, and for a good reason, they are among the highest in the city. Meals here are an affair that can last up to three hours, so you just might feel you got your money's worth. The Old Warsaw serves well-known French and California wines, mostly by the bottle.

Cold hors d'oeuvres, such as the beluga caviar with vodka, which cost $45 in the 1999 edition of this guide, were $55 in 2003. Try a half-portion of French foie gras. Lobster crepes and baked oysters are but two hot hors d'oeuvres.

Among the fish dishes you might enjoy fresh Dover sole or sautéed sea bass. Fresh lobster's price is determined daily. Fresh braised salmon is also available. If game is what you desire, the Old Warsaw can oblige with braised pheasant, roasted quail, breast of chicken, or roasted duckling.

The most expensive meat entrée is roast rack of lamb for two, followed by veal chop garnished with crabmeat, filet of beef sauté with fresh goose liver, center-cut tenderloin, and New York sirloin strip.

The Old Warsaw is well known for its classic Caesar's salad. "The ceremony begins when a tuxedo-clad waiter arrives at your table with a rolling cart bearing a wooden salad bowl, chilled romaine, small silver dishes filled with Parmesan cheese, a lemon half, an egg, croutons, garlic, and anchovies, plus Worcestershire sauce and black pepper," explains *Texas Monthly*.

He mashes the anchovies and garlic, cracks the egg, and squeezes the lemon into the bowl. "Then, amid much clacking of wooden spoons, he performs various feats of prestidigitation with the lettuce and remaining ingredients and ceremoniously places in front of you and your companion chilled white plates of honest-to-god Caesar salad." The cost is about $12 for two.

D Magazine noted once: "Like an aging heavyweight champ hoping to win close fights on the basis of reputation rather than performance, the Old Warsaw might well be the old warhorse of Dallas, a disappointing reminder that in this town, it's tough at the top."

By 2002, either the chef at the Old Warsaw or the food editor at *D Magazine* must have changed, for the monthly later had this to say: "Chateaubriand pour deux and Dover sole sautéed with lemon butter were timeless and perfect. The concept may be old but there isn't a wrinkle in the food, service, or ambience."

The *Dallas Morning News*, which once gave it four out of the possible five stars, claimed that excluding the wine by-the-glass selection, "Nearly everything else is close to perfection, though. But from the old school." In mid-2002, the daily downgraded it to three and a half stars, although it praised a more extensive wine by-the-glass selection.

Next door to the restaurant is located the Maple Manor Victorian Hotel (Internet www.maplemanorhotel.com), a six-suite bed & breakfast located in an 1898 building that was inaugurated one hundred years later.

English

The Londoner, 14930 Midway Rd. at Beltway Dr., Addison, (972) 458-2444. *I*. Open for lunch Mon-Fri 11 AM-3 PM, and dinner daily until 2 AM. Only small plates are available after 10 PM. It has a bar. Live pop music on Saturday night starts at about 9:30 PM. Saturday brunch is held 11 AM-3 PM. Wheelchair accessible.

Located south of Belt Line Road and west of Dallas North Tollway. Blue Goose restaurant is across from the Londoner. The Addison Airport is north of here.

An unassuming British establishment serving generous portions that most expatriates will enjoy. It relocated in 2000 and now includes a balcony overlooking a courtyard. There are more than 20 beers on tap and soccer on the telly.

The small plates might range from chicken tenderloins to quesadillas, from London wings to Scotch eggs. There will always be at least one soup and tortilla wrap.

The big plates, too, are generous in size and moderately priced. There is steak and mushroom pie with mashed potatoes and baked beans, chicken curry, and chicken tikka masala, voted by the British to be their number one dish. Old Compton Street pasta with mushrooms and blackened chicken is named after a street in London's Soho.

Smaller appetites might consider one among several sandwiches or Covent Garden salad with chicken, or London Caesar's, which has "nothing to do with London, but who cares," proclaims the menu. An "extremely" sticky toffee pudding made with dates and eggs would be a typical dessert.

The *Dallas Morning News* raves about an "extremely fresh and flaky cod, wrapped in a light beer batter that seemed so lightly fried that we wonder how the fish got cooked." *D Magazine* opines that "The Londoner is an impressively authentic British pub."

Yes, just as you would expect, there are plenty of drafts and darts, too.

For aficionados, there are also several area locations of **Fox and Hound English Pub and Grille,** where multiple television screens will usually be found, and the food is edible, too.

An English-style pub owned by a Dallasite who has only been to England a couple of times is **British Rose,** 8989 Forest Ln. at LBJ Fwy., (972) 690-8340. Live music Fri-Sat.

Those who yearn for authentic English cakes and ale, cheddar cheese and Devon cream, beer, bangers, and biscuits, will find a quick fix at **World Service UK,** an unassuming shop at 1923 Lower Greenville Ave., (214) 827-8886, Internet www.worldservice-uk.com.

For authentic Irish fare, go to the **Tipperary Inn** (see listing) nearby, also in near-east Dallas.

French

L'Ancestral, 4514 Travis St. at Knox St., (214) 528-1081, no Internet address. *E*. Open for lunch Mon-Sat 11:30 AM-2 PM, for dinner Mon-Thu 6 PM-10 PM, Fri-Sat 6 PM-11 PM. It has a bar. Wheelchair accessible. Reservations are recommended.

Located on Travis Walk at Armstrong Avenue, two blocks east of the southern edge of Highland Park. Samba Room nightclub and Il

Sole restaurant (see listing) are nearby. Across the street is Café Madrid, the city's original tapas bar and "a hot spot for young professionals with a shared heritage," and the club Sipango (see listing).

A superb country French dinery, plain to some, elegant to others, but Gallic to all. L'Ancestral, established in 1982, is one of the oldest restaurants in this area serving mostly older and well-heeled patrons.

The menu is usually laden with hors d'oeuvres, such as homemade pâté, hard-boiled eggs filled with crabmeat, avocado with shrimps, snails sautéed in garlic and cognac, grilled artichoke hearts marinated in olive oil, and leeks with homemade vinaigrette.

The fish dishes include sea scallops with capers, sautéed trout with grilled almonds, shrimp sautéed in white wine, grilled salmon with fresh basil, and grilled orange roughy with lime. The costliest meat entrées are the filet mignon flamed with cognac, and Steak Tartare, but all main courses are served with fresh vegetables, fries, or rice.

Grilled breast of chicken, pork medallions with Dijon mustard sauce, grilled lamb chops, and lamb tenderloin sautéed with mint and flamed with cognac might also be available, along with wines that will complement your meal.

Cheese plate, vanilla ice cream with liqueur, French custard, and chocolate truffled cake could be the featured desserts when you visit. Cappuccino and espresso are always available.

The *Dallas Morning News*, which gives it four out of the five possible stars, observes that "For all the virtues of the rest of the menu, it's the desserts that really send you off happy."

Chez Gerard, 4444 McKinney Ave. at Armstrong, (214) 522-6865, Internet www.chezgerardrestaurant.com. *E*. Open for lunch Mon-Fri 11:30 AM-2:30 PM, for dinner Mon-Sat 6 PM-10:30 PM. Has no bar. Seats up to 60. Smoking on the patio only. Wheelchair accessible. Dress code is relaxed, but reservations are suggested for dinner.

Located uptown and on the southwestern edge of Highland Park, a block west from Central Expressway, and across McKinney from **Abacus** (see listing) restaurant. Chuy's, which looks like a Stalingrad bomb shelter, but offers decent Tex-Mex fare, is a block north of here, on the corner with Knox Street.

The legendary chef Guy Calluaud opened this country restaurant in 1984. It was later bought by Pascal Cayet, whose chef and much of the other staff members have stayed on for years. A small, romantic country French restaurant in a "crotchety old cottage" with a wooden floor and a covered patio, some would call it a provincial bistro, with the flowery wallpaper and coziness of your grandmother's parlor. But few grandmothers cook like this.

The signature dish at Chez Gerard is beef tenderloin served with cognac cream sauce and mushrooms. The costliest entrée is Dover sole, followed by fish dishes, such as mixed seafood served with tagliatelle pasta, fresh water shrimp with asparagus, sautéed trout with mushrooms, and grilled snapper with sardine caviar.

Other meats include rack of lamb with mushrooms, tenderloin with cognac, veal medallions, sautéed ribeye with artichokes, pork medallions sautéed with snails, grilled spring chicken, sautéed rabbit with rice, sautéed veal sweetbreads with garlic, and veal liver with raisins.

Hors d'oeuvres range from terrine du chef to Scottish smoked salmon, and snails in garlic butter, steamed mussels in white wine, sea scallops in red wine, and sauteéed frog legs in between. Daily specials might include roasted duck with raspberry sauce, halibut with pistachios, or grilled salmon with langoustinos. Warm apple tart, tarte brûlée with raspberry sauce, and chocolate mousse are just three among the desserts. Wines range from the $20 Reserve St. Martin Chardonnay to the $500 Chateau Cheval Blanc, St. Emilion, 1989.

Gourmet magazine readers once rated it one of the best Dallas restaurants, while the *Dallas Morning News* gives it four out of the possible five stars. *D Magazine* named it one of the 25 best restaurants in the Metroplex.

Pascal Cayet also owns **Lavendou Bistro,** a southern France bistro Provencal, established in 1996 and located in a strip center north of Frankford Rd., at 19009 Preston Rd. at Lloyd Dr., (972) 248-1911, Internet www.lavendou.com. It has a full-service bar and a patio that seats 40. A few doors away is a Middle Eastern-cuisine Ali Baba Café.

The *Dallas Morning News*, which again gives it four stars, raves about its dishes and desserts. "Though Lavendou doesn't have the quaint charm of Chez Gerard," notes the *Dallas Observer*, "somehow the food comes across as more impressive and consistent." *Texas Monthly* reviewers "were in heaven just nibbling on the fantastic bread with olive oil."

The French Room, Adolphus Hotel, 1321 Commerce at Akard Streets, (214) 742-8200. *E*. Open for dinner Mon-Sat 6 PM-10 PM only; closed Sundays. A bar next door, open daily 6 PM-10 PM, features a musical ensemble Fridays and Saturdays. Wheelchair accessible. Reservations are recommended, and jackets are suggested for men.

Located downtown in a splendid baroque dining room decorated with lofty murals, arched 18-foot (or 5.5-meter) ceilings, hand-blown crystal chandeliers, and antique furniture inside the venerable Adolphus. A bit pretentious and very expensive, but the food and service are superb.

The French Room, which opened in 1981, serves classic French cuisine "adapted to contemporary American tastes." China is Bernardaud, flatware Reed & Barton silver plate, glassware courtesy of Masterpiece Crystal in Jane Lew, West Virginia—with the red wineglasses made exclusively for the French Room.

If you like chilled appetizers, you can start with thyme-encrusted ahi tuna with a fried tomato, jumbo lump crab salad with smoked salmon and trout, or Maine lobster served with white asparagus. Should you prefer warm starters, sample soy-marinated breast of quail, seared Massachusetts scallop with spinach and spice potato cake, or roasted Maine lobster tail with morel mushrooms. There is always a soup on the menu.

Entrées might include pan-seared snapper served with oven-fried tomato, sweet white miso marinated East Coast halibut, pan-seared filet of Chilean sea bass wrapped with potato, filet of Dover sole served with scallion whipped potatoes, and Long Island duck. There could also be Maverick Creek Ranch venison chops with pumpkin bread pudding, oven-roasted Colorado rack of lamb, and pan-seared prime tenderloin of beef.

For dessert, tempt yourself with a roasted apple tart, caramelized cheesecake, or chocolate Bavarian bombe with raspberry compote.

You might enjoy the $95-to-$135 fixed-price six-course chef's menu or à la carte selections, where you pay by the number of courses, up to $100 per person.

If you have not declared bankruptcy by then, the French Room has a list of classic wines that include Chateau Mouton d'Armailhac and Chateau Haut Brio, both from 1928 and each at $3,000 a bottle. The restaurant stocks 340 selections of wines from the Bordeaux region, California, and Texas.

Arguably the finest restaurant in the Metroplex, but definitely one of the top three or four, the *Mobil Travel Guide* gives it four stars, the same as its competitor, the Mansion on Turtle Creek (see entry). *Gourmet* magazine named it the best Metroplex restaurant in the past, while *Condé Nast* believes it to be one of the "top 20" restaurants in America.

The *New York Times* describes it as "indisputably the most striking and sumptuous restaurant in Dallas." *D Magazine* expected "perfect food that matches the fairy-tale room," but was "disappointed by reality. Sea bass in red wine sauce was fishy," it claims. The French Room is one of a handful Dallas restaurants that get the maximum five stars from the *Dallas Morning News*, which proclaims its staff "suave, unobtrusive and unflappable."

For more casual lunch or dinner, try the less expensive Bistro, open daily 6:30 AM-10 PM, located a few steps away. Tea, finger sandwiches, and fruit tarts are served Wed-Sat 3 PM-4:45 PM in the lobby to the accompaniment of a piano.

Walt Garrison's Rodeo Bar & Grill, featuring Texas Western fare, such as the filet of beef tenderloin, is located on the ground floor and overlooking Commerce Street.

Jeroboam, Kirby Building, 1501 Main St. at Akard St., (214) 748-7226, Internet www.jeroboam-ub.com, e-mail jeroboam@theec.com. *E*. Open for lunch and dinner Mon-Fri 11 AM-11 PM, Sat-Sun 5:30 PM-midnight. It has a full-service bar and cocktail lounge. Happy hour Mon-Fri 4 PM-7 PM.

Located downtown on the ground floor of the renovated Kirby Building, across the street from the Adolphus and Magnolia hotels (see entries).

"Will people come downtown at night?" asks *Texas Monthly*, a question that has been on the lips of Dallasites avoiding downtown like the plague for decades. "Evidently they will if you offer them an encyclopedic wine list, crisp fried oysters, steak au poivre, and perfect Dover sole in a theatrically stylish atmosphere."

Texas Monthly was referring to the JeroboAM urban brasserie, which became an instant success.

The 6,500-square-foot (or 604-square-meter), high-ceilinged restaurant, which takes its name from an oversized three-liter wine bottle and seats up to 150, was, in 2000, the first white-tablecloth restaurant to open downtown in several years. It includes an 18-seat communal table with a special menu.

The *Fort Worth Star-Telegram* finds the setting "extremely tasteful in an old-fashioned way—not in the least bit overdone in the typical Dallas way." But the restaurant "only dazzles here and there," if the *Dallas Observer* is to be believed.

Appetizers include escargots with country sausage, horseradish-fried East Coast oysters, and cassoulet de Toulouse. Caviar is sold by the ounce. Seafood includes pickled rock shrimp, blue crab claws, and whole Maine lobster.

"Perfect for the hungry, meat-eating Texan was the butcher's plate, a large dish filled with grilled, smoked Texas sausage and wurst, sensationally tender veal shank and exquisite duck leg," observes the *Star-Telegram*.

The costliest entrée is probably the lobster cooked in the Breton style, followed by beef tenderloin Madagascar, basil-marinated yellowfin tuna, braised lamb shank, roasted pork loin à la Alsacienne, grilled duck breast, and trout with almonds, which the *Dallas Observer* reviewer judged "about as perfect as food gets." For dessert, enjoy a plate of French cheese. The wine selection encompasses some 250 French wines from nearly every region, starting as low as $25 a bottle.

The thirtysomething brothers Brandt and Brady Wood of New

Orleans had so much success with this restaurant that they opened a bar, Umlaut, on the south side of Main Street, four doors down from the Neiman Marcus department store (see entry).

La Madeleine French Bakery & Cafe, 3072 Mockingbird Ln. at North Central Expwy., (214) 696-0800, Internet www.lamadeleine.com. M. Open for breakfast, lunch, and diner daily 6:30 AM-11 PM. The café is a popular meeting place for singles of all ages. Located across the street from the Southern Methodist University football stadium in University Park.

La Madeleine founder Patrick Esquerre arrived in Dallas in 1982 from France and opened his first bakery on the edge of the Southern Methodist University campus the following spring. He credits the late merchant Stanley Marcus with helping him launch the restaurant. Three thousand employees now operate more than 60 La Madeleine cafés in seven markets.

But the Tours, France-born founder, who once said, "Food is not just something you feed your body with. It's a way of life," sold out in 1998, and his American pupils took over what they claimed was a nearly bankrupt chain. Esquerre opened the Café Patrique concept in 2002, but with the recession at his heels, the restaurant closed within a year.

The Dallas-based La Madeleine now has sales exceeding $120 million and is one of the 60 largest local companies.

In 2001, the chain was sold to a private group of European and American investors. The following year, the high-powered restaurant executive Wallace Doolin was named La Madeleine's chief executive. He made some patrons ill at ease with his remarks in *Forbes* magazine, where he implied that wait staff at dinner could turn tables a little faster, as is supposedly done at TGI Friday, his previous employer.

"The gathering aspect is nice, but then the [patrons] control when they leave," Doolin told *Forbes*, revealing his ignorance of the European-style cafés, where patrons often linger over an additional cup of coffee and some can go through an entire newspaper after their meal.

Since Esquerre left, La Madeleine's food has been more streamlined and Americanized, and its quality has suffered noticeably. Some of the dishes have lost their adventurous spark, but there is still a cafeteria-style self-service to keep the steadily rising prices somewhat in check. La Madeleine once had a good reputation with the Caesar salads, pastas, and soups that were almost as tasty as those you would find in France. Grilled chicken and chicken pesto pastas have gone from creamy to watery, at least at this location. Children's pizza is downright awful. These days the Caesar's could be either too dry or overwhelmed by the dressing.

Caffeine addicts still can have unlimited cups of several varieties of coffee and tea, although the coffees are weaker. At the bakery counter, you can buy baguettes, croissants, and a shrinking variety of breads, most of which are now baked elsewhere and brought in daily. Gone are the days when the still-hot baguettes came out of the oven on these premises twice a day.

Managers at some locations change faster than the seasons. And freshly cut flowers, which once graced tables, disappeared soon after the Americans took over.

Other Dallas locations include:

• 2121 San Jacinto St. at Pearl, between Plaza of the Americas and the Arts District, (214) 220-3911. This downtown location is open Mon-Fri 7 AM-3 PM only.

• 3906 Lemmon Ave. at Oak Lawn Ave., (214) 521-0183.

• NorthPark Shopping Mall, 628 NorthPark Center, across from Dillard's, at North Central Expressway and West Northwest Hwy., (214) 696-2398.

• 11930 Preston Rd. at Forest Ln., (972) 233-6446.

Watel's, 2719 McKinney Ave. at Worthington St., (214) 720-0323, Internet www.watels.com. *E*. Open for lunch Sun, Tue-Fri 11:30 AM-1:30 PM; no lunch on Saturday or Monday. Open for dinner Tue-Sun 6 PM-9 PM, Fri-Sat 6 PM-9:30 PM. Sunday lunch and brunch is held 11:30 AM-1:30 PM. Wheelchair accessible. Dress code is dressy casual. Reservations are suggested.

Located just north of downtown, west of North Central Expressway (or U.S. Hwy. 75), two blocks north of the Hard Rock Café and east from the Quadrangle mall (see listings). The 15-year-old Avanti Ristorante is across McKinney, and S & D Oyster Company restaurant is just south of here. Watel's moved from lower McKinney Avenue to its current location in 1997, although it has been in business since 1987.

An informal but superb little French bistro with likeable service, although the minimum food charge is $20 per person at night, the amount that will buy you all but the half-dozen costliest entrées. It is owned by chef Rene Peeters, who was born in the former Belgian Congo to a Belgian father and French mother. He spent his youth in Africa and southern France, but has also lived in Laos and Greece.

Raw tuna with jicama mango relish, crabmeat cocktail, escargots in Chardonnay, lobster and shrimp chowder, polenta cake with warm mozzarella, dill-cured salmon with cucumber, and smoked sea scallops are some among the appetizers. Salads could include sliced duck breast with couscous, spinach with mushrooms and bacon, or Caesar's.

The most expensive main courses are aged prime sirloin strip steak, Lobster Napoleon with spinach and mushrooms, and tuna with corn tomatillo relish. Other entrées might include grilled shrimp with coconut curry, grilled salmon with arrugula pesto, seafood stew, and spinach ravioli with Chardonnay and walnuts.

There is also crabmeat lasagna, peppered duck breast with Cognac sauce, veal escalopes with dried tomatoes, chicken breast with Dijon mustard and mushrooms, cassoulet (white bean stew with duck, sausage, bacon, and ham). You can even feast on such hard-to-find organ meats as grilled veal kidneys with mustard sauce, and calf brains with capers and lemon butter.

Pear poached in spiced port, tiramisu, warm chocolate bread pudding, and fresh fruit tartelette are some among the desserts. Wines are available by the glass or by the bottle. Cooking classes are offered at the restaurant.

The *Dallas Morning News*, which gives Watel's four and a half out of the possible five stars, notes that "this airy, casually elegant dining room serves some of Dallas' best French fare at affordable prices." *D Magazine*—whose reviewer claims its fruit tart is "simple, sweet, and unpretentious, just like Watel's"—named it one of the Metroplex's best restaurants. "We always feel civilized when we dine here," says *Texas Monthly*.

Greek

Ziziki's, 4514 Travis Walk at Armstrong Ave., (214) 521-2233, Internet www.zizikis.com. M. Open for lunch Mon-Sat 11 AM-2 PM, and for dinner Sun-Thu 4 PM-11 PM, Fri-Sat 4 PM-midnight. The Sunday brunch is served 11 AM-3 PM. It has a bar.

Ziziki's main room seats up to 50, a private dining room 35. It also has a patio. Wheelchair accessible. Valet parking is available. Dress is casual.

Located north of downtown Dallas, on the southern edge of Highland Park, three blocks west of North Central Expressway, and just south of Knox Street.

Costa Arabatzis opened this comfortable and handsome neo-Greek bistro with an exhibition kitchen and a patio in 1994. The name comes from the Greek sauce made with yogurt and cucumbers that is used on many of the menu items, but without the letter *t* in front of it. The cherry-wood mahogany bar was a gift from the owner's father, who for several years himself operated a Greek bistro in Maui, Hawaii.

Born of a Greek father and an Italian mother, Arabatzis began as an "assistant dishwasher" in his father's California restaurant and helped him open the bistro in Hawaii in 1986. He came to Dallas in 1990 and first opened a bistro on Lower Greenville.

There are Greek and Mediterranean salads, as well as grilled chicken and lamb. The most expensive entrée is the marinated grilled rack of lamb with Grecian herbs, followed by grilled filet mignon served with mashed potatoes. Other entrées include sliced marinated leg of lamb, chicken or lamb souvlaki on homemade pita bread, Greek island chicken marinated with Greek spices, and mousaka, which is "a tasty mess" of grilled eggplant blended with chopped leg of lamb and served with mashed potatoes.

Lunch menu dishes include the Greek lasagna, which consists of chopped lamb baked with tomatoes and blended with macaroni pasta. For dessert, try baklava ice cream cake.

Ziziki serves more than 100 varieties of Greek, Italian, and California wines, including some by the glass.

"Odysseus would never have sailed off if he had had home cooking like this Greek place offers," declares *Texas Monthly*, while the *Dallas Morning News* claims, "You will not eat like this in Greece. Not on Sunday, not ever." The entire menu is available for takeout, except for Fri-Sat between 6 PM-10 PM, but the restaurant does not deliver.

In 1999, Arabatzis and his wife Mary opened another **Ziziki's** in the Shops of Spanish Village, at the northwest corner of Coit and Arapaho Roads, (972) 991-4433.

Home Cooking

Luby's Cafeteria, 10425 North Central Expwy. at Meadow Road, (214) 361-9024. M. Open daily for lunch and dinner 11 AM-9 PM. No alcohol is served. Wheelchair accessible.

Located north of downtown Dallas, in a small shopping center, next door to Denny's and Grandy's fast-food restaurants. Residence Inn Marriott is situated on the next block.

Cafeterias were for many years a Southern as well as a Texas institution, particularly for those eligible for an AARP membership card. But they are disliked by affluent singles. "I'd rather have my feet cut off than eat in a cafeteria," one professional in his 30s was quoted by the local press.

While cafeterias had a 5 percent market share in Texas in 1987, it has since dwindled to just over 2 percent. Luby's, as a result, defaulted on millions of dollars of bank debt.

There are some 130 Luby's cafeterias in the United States and about 20 of them in the Metroplex. Their premises are clean and attractive, the food is reasonably fresh and usually decent of taste, and the personnel friendly. Servers and the cleaning staff, however, often look as though they just came from a halfway house. Patrons over 40 years of age seem to predominate.

There are daily specials and several other entrées, from fish to chicken to beef. "Luby's Cafeteria has everything a good cafeteria should," says the *Fort Worth Star-Telegram*, "a great selection, fresh food, large servings and, of course, dessert."

Desserts are passable, but the coffee is barely drinkable, particularly the decaffeinated variety. If you eat here, consider having your dessert at La Madeleine French Bakery & Café.

Other Luby's cafeterias in Dallas include:

• 3802 Cedar Springs Rd. at Oak Lawn Ave., (214) 520-6505.

• 6221 East Mockingbird Ln., near Skillman St., (214) 826-4400.

• 4940 Highway 121 at Preston Rd., west of Stonebriar Mall, Plano, (972) 668-6828. This is a prototype for a new generation of Luby's cafeterias.

Irish

The Tipperary Inn, 5815 Live Oak St. at Skillman St., (214) 823-7167, Internet www.tippinn.com. M. Open Mon-Fri 4 PM-2 AM, Sat-Sun noon-2 AM. It has a full bar. There is occasional live music. Happy hour is Mon-Thu 4:30 PM-6:30 PM, Irish hour Mon-Fri 11 PM-midnight. Wheelchair accessible. Parking is not easy to find.

Located in the Lakewood area east of Lower Greenville Avenue and near La Vista Drive. The Gold Rush Café, where good breakfasts and hamburgers are served, is nearby.

Run by a couple from Tipperary, Ireland, this is one of the few authentic Irish pubs in Dallas, with relaxed atmosphere and live Celtic music. It was remodeled in 2000, with everything from the hardwood floors and bar to the booths, even exterior facades, constructed in Dublin, Ireland. But the food has undergone an equally welcome improvement.

The menu headings are written in Gaelic. Appetizers include chips and green chili tomato salsa, pretzels with horseradish mustard sauce, Guinness queso and chips, potato skins with cheese and bacon, ploughman's lunch with three cheeses, baked potato soup, and Irish smoked salmon with soda bread. The Tipperary Breakfast, served any time, "is the ultimate feel-good meal," claims the *Dallas Morning News*.

The most expensive entrée is the grilled ribeye steak with Gaelic sauce. Other choices include soup and Caesar's salad, loaded baked potato, shepherd's pie, corned beef and cabbage, Guinness beef stew, mixed grill with pork chop, Irish bacon, and Irish sausage.

Among the desserts, you might enjoy the gooey bread pudding. And try a pint of the Tipp's Guiness or Harp. That's what the well-known Irish step-dancer Michael Flatly of the stage show *Riverdance* does when coming to Dallas.

The *News*'s reviewer, who says, "The Irish feel is so intense that I wondered whether I was dreaming or had been whisked across the pond," gives it no fewer than four out of the possible five stars.

"The Tipp is rich, classic, warm, cuddly, romantic, sophisticated, quaint," gushes the *Dallas Observer*. You can just imagine the crowds around here on St. Patrick's Day.

Other Irish hangouts, all located east of North Central Expressway, south from Mockingbird Lane, include:

• **The Blarney Stone,** 2116 Lower Greenville Ave. at Richmond, (214) 821-7099.

• **Cock & Bull,** 6330 Gaston Ave. at La Vista Court, (214) 841-9111.

• **The Dubliner** (see listing in the NIGHTLIFE chapter), 2818 Lower Greenville Ave. at Goodwin St., (214) 818-0911.

• **Trinity Hall Pub & Restaurant,** 5321 East Mockingbird Ln. at North Central Expwy., (214) 887-3647. (See also the SHOPPING chapter, under Mockingbird Station.)

For British fare, go to the **Londoner** (see listing), located in Addison.

Italian

Arcodoro & Pomodoro, 2708 Routh St. at Mahon St., (214) 871-1924, e-mail pomodoro@arcodoro.com. *E*. Open for dinner only Thu-Sat 6 PM-midnight, Sun-Wed 6 PM-11 PM. There is a full bar and patio. Seats about 160 on two levels. Wheelchair accessible. Valet parking is available.

Located uptown, just north of downtown Dallas, a block northwest from Hard Rock Café (see entry) and from the Paris Bistrot on McKinney Avenue.

This was once the location of Baby Routh, a popular restaurant that Texas chef Stephan Pyles, a co-founder of Southwestern cuisine, grew up with.

Once two adjoining restaurants, opened in the late 1980s by Sardinian chef Efisio Farris and previously located a block and a half away, on Cedar Springs Road, they are now combined under one roof that covers the 7,000-square-foot (or 650-square-meter) building.

The larger Arcodoro, with red-clay tiles on the roof over the bar, has a woodburning pizza oven in the back. Pomodoro is the more formal and secluded part of the restaurant. There is a little cove at the entrance to Pomodoro with wine racks, which serves as a private room for a dozen diners, but it is hardly private. When the restaurant is even half full, you may not hear a single note of arias playing on the sound system.

Antipasti include a traditional Sardinian clam soup, polenta topped with baby calamari, sea scallops tossed in a balsamic vinaigrette, and buffalo mozzarella with sautéed wild mushrooms. There are salads, homemade bruschetta, and focaccia breads.

Pastas and risotti could include Sardinian teardrop pasta, ribbon pasta with Italian sausage, handmade potato gnocchi, squid ink risotto with grilled prawns, artichoke-filled ravioli, whole-wheat fettucini, spinach linguine, and arborium rice with asparagus tips.

Try Raviolo Arcodoro—stuffed with shrimp, scallops, herbs, pecorino, and ricotta—for which owner Efisio Farris and his brother Francesco received first place in the Italian Ultimate Ravioli contest. The dish made front-page headlines in their native Sardinia and can now be bought in Italian grocery stores.

The costliest entrée is the aged prime ribeye steak grilled in the woodburning oven and served with homemade mashed potatoes and arugola salad.. It is followed, price-wise, by split veal shank with risotto milanese, broiled lobster tail served with raviolone vegetale and Sardinian caviar, broiled chops of lamb with Sardinian bread, grilled jumbo scallops and shrimp with fried leeks, and poached Norwegian salmon. Wines come from the Italian regions of Sardinia, Abruzzi, Apulia, and Tuscany.

Pizzas are served in the Arcodoro part of the restaurant only. They include vegetable, eggplant and goat cheese, Napoletana, homemade Italian sausage, and marinated shrimp and mushroom pizza.

A *Dallas Observer* reviewer, who once named Pomodoro the best Italian restaurant in Dallas, later noted that "the desserts were tight as a rusted screw. Tiramisu [was] by far the best version I've sampled in Dallas." The *Dallas Morning News* gives it four out of the possible five stars

Ferrari's Italian Villa, 14831 Midway Rd., Addison, (972) 980-9898, Internet www.ferrarisrestaurant.com. *E*. Open for lunch Mon-Fri 11:30 AM-2 PM, for dinner Sun-Thu 5 PM-10 PM, Fri-Sat 5 PM-10:30 PM. It has a bar and a private dining room that accommodates up to 30. Wheelchair accessible. Seats up to 150. Reservations are suggested.

Located west of the Dallas North Tollway, between Belt Line and Spring Valley Roads, and next to Morton's of Chicago steakhouse (see listing). Harvey Hotel and Courtyard by Marriott are also nearby.

Owned by Sardinian-born Francesco Secchi and his wife Jane, this is a popular meeting place for singles. The main dining room surrounds the restaurant's open kitchen that boasts a woodburning oven. One of their three sons, Stefano, a graduate of the Culinary Institute of America, will be found in the kitchen during dinnertime. The elder Secchi, who speaks several languages, opened his first Dallas restaurant, Ferrari's Oven, in 1983.

In addition to hot focaccia bread, the starters include fried calamari, fresh mixed seafood, and pasta soup. You will find here some ten pastas, from mushroom risotto to fettuccine Alfredo and smoked salmon in between.

The house fish specialties could include halibut with sun-dried tomatoes, and jumbo shrimps. Several varieties of veal and chicken dishes are available. The costliest dinner is the linguine entrée topped with jumbo shrimps. The 21-day aged filet mignon, Dover sole, and grilled veal chops stuffed with Parma ham or mozzarella are priced upon your arrival.

Homemade pastries, ice cream, cappuccino and espresso could top off your meal. Ferrari's has a good selection of wines, including by the glass.

The *Dallas Morning News* rated it the best new restaurant in 1994 and gave it four out of the possible five stars in 2002. Its reviewers tasted what "may be the best carpaccio we've had in Dallas," but said that their crème brûlée dessert "didn't live up to the stellar dishes that preceded it."

Il Sole, 4514 Travis St. at Armstrong, Second Floor, (214) 559-3888, Internet www.ilsole-dallas.com. *E*. Open for dinner Sun-Thu 5 PM-10 PM, Fri-Sat 5 PM-midnight. Main dining room seats 80, terrace 50, bistro 40, wine room 25. It has a bar and patio. Personal checks are not accepted. Wheelchair accessible. Reservations are suggested.

Located on the southern edge of Highland Park, three blocks west of North Central Expressway (or U.S. Hwy. 75). Next door is the bar Samba Room, across the street club Sipango (see individual listings).

Another Dallas hangout that claims all those, oh, so bored beautiful people. But at least you can keep your breath fresh with the help of all that mouthwash in the bathroom. Start with a spinach or Caesar's salad, Tuscan white bean soup, or a cheese board.

The Black Angus center-cut filet with wild mushroom ragout is perhaps the costliest entrée, followed by tamarind-glazed Chilean sea bass with lemon basil risotto, and seared scallops that come with sweet potato polenta.

Other main dishes could include pasta with spicy tomato sauce, smoked chicken linguine, housemade tortelloni stuffed with jumbo lump crab, pan-roasted breast of chicken stuffed with lemon ricotta cheese, veal picata with zucchini pasta, Niman Ranch "gorgeously white and full of subtle, bacony flavor" pork chop with whipped potatoes, and sautéed Atlantic salmon served with sun-dried tomato risotto.

Il Sole's desserts might consist of chocolate tart, maple crème brûlée, white chocolate tiramisu, or an assortment of housemade cookies.

There are two dozen wines that can be had by the glass or half-glass, but they can be expensive. The restaurant offers more than 170 wine selections, particularly from Italy and California, and has an inventory of 2,200 bottles.

The *Dallas Morning News*, which gives Il Sole four out of the possible five stars, notes the restaurant has "great pairings of money and beauty, as well as lots of well-dressed, attractive thirtysomethings whose glossy prosperity makes you wonder where they get all their cash."

Highland Park Pharmacy, half a block north of here, serves breakfast and lunch only. It has been owned by pharmacist Thell Bowlin for a quarter-century and beloved by local residents as a bargain throwback to the 1950s. "One of the last authentic drugstore fountains anywhere," the *Dallas Morning News* calls it. Customers swear the pharmacy's pimento cheese sandwiches, homemade chicken, tuna, and ham salads are among the best.

Japanese/Indochinese

Steel, Centrum Building, 3102 Oak Lawn Ave. on the corner of Hall and Wellborn, (214) 219-9908, Internet www.steelrestaurantlounge.com. *E*. Open for lunch daily 11:30 AM-3 PM, for dinner Tue-Wed 5:30 AM-11 PM, Thu-Sat 5:30 PM-1 am. It has sushi and sake bars. Wheelchair accessible. Valet parking is available. Reservations are recommended.

Located in the Oak Lawn neighborhood north of downtown Dallas, near the Melrose Hotel.

Heavy iron doors bar your way to Steel, while the decor inside is Asian contemporary with a polished steel column and drapes separating the sushi bar and main dining rooms from the sake bar in the back. The walls and floors are embellished in mahogany and Brazilian cherry wood. If a celebrity, you will probably be whisked to the secluded Wasabi Booth by the bar in the back, behind sheer white curtains.

Two dozen top chefs terrorize delighted Steel's patrons with some of the most revolutionary Japanese dishes that draw on flavors from China, Korea, and Southeast Asia.

Steel's prices are the size of mortgage payments, even before you consider the market-priced whole lobster sautéed in sea salt or Vietnamese prawns: chef Jimmy's Vietnamese dish, which requires a 20-minute notice, cost a whopping $65 in 2003.

Indochinese appetizers range from the house spring rolls filled with shredded chicken breast to the soft-shell crab. Grilled sea bass marinated with miso and sake is one of a half-dozen Japanese starters.

Steamed filet of red snapper, sautéed shrimp, sliced beef marinated in lemon grass, Korean beef, Vietnamese-style pork chops, and crispy duck breast are others among the dinner dishes, usually served with steamed rice. Beef, chicken, and shrimp tempura, grilled salmon steak with vegetables, and filet mignon with steamed asparagus and mashed potatoes are some among the Japanese entrées.

Banana tempura with strawberries and a variety of ice creams are some of the desserts. Steel's wine list serves wines from Australia, California, France, Germany, and New Zealand. There are numerous varieties of sake served warm.

"Steel is a rarity: a hip, urban hangout where substance wins over style," declared *D Magazine* in 2001. "Steel is easily the most attractive new restaurant of the year." The *Dallas Morning News* reviewer named it one of the top ten new restaurants in 2001, but gave it only three and a half out of the possible five stars, declaring: "Steel is very good and, I predict, will get even better."

The *Dallas Observer* reviewer claims that the Vietnamese carpaccio, "This delicate and astounding dish, flush with fragrance and alive with refreshing piquancy, is possibly the best carpaccio you'll ever have in Dallas." The *Fort Worth Star-Telegram* calls Steel "astoundingly stylish."

The owner of Steel is the Saigon-born Khanh Dao, who, on the final day of America's involvement in the Vietnam War in 1975, escaped at age five with her father, mother, and brother aboard one of the last available ferries. They were plucked from the sea by a U.S. Navy ship and taken to Guam. Dao was sent to Pennsylvania and Indiana, and, at age six, landed in Fort Worth, where she graduated from Southwest High School.

She entered Texas Christian University intent on becoming an architect, but never graduated. Exceedingly generous to friends, acquaintances, and employees, she is held in high regard by most of those who come in contact with her. She was a managing partner at the former Voltaire restaurant, later resurrected as Bamboo Bamboo, and lived with its owner for two years. Her father, from whom she says she inherited her sense of generosity, died of cancer in 1997. In 2003, Dao opened Dralion (half dragon, half lion in translation) Kobe steakhouse, also in the Centrum.

Also located in this complex was Star Canyon, a "cowboy heaven" from 1994 to 2003, according to its Web page, "a creative corral where the young and the beautiful rub elbows with local stars and captains of industry." You had to book reservations up to two months ahead.

Stephan Pyles was its original owner, but later sold out. Among his main courses at Star Canyon you could have had bone-in cowboy ribeye steak with pinto-wild mushroom ragout, spit-roasted natural chicken with goat cheese, orange- and tamarind-glazed grilled pork chop with apple grits, braised lamb shank with chipotle chiles, or barbecue-glazed sea bass with sweet corn.

Pyles (b. 1952) started by helping out in his family's truck-stop café on Interstate 20 in Big Spring, Texas, when growing up, busing tables on weekends and cooking tamales, tacos, and barbecue. He later cooked for presidents Mikhail Gorbachev and Jimmy Carter.

Pyles told *D Magazine* that the worst summer job he ever had was working for Kentucky Fried Chicken, where he was fired for confusing the breading with gravy and burning a whole batch of chicken. His first kitchen job of note, after he moved to Dallas, was at the Bronx in Oak Lawn, a restaurant where he was made the executive chef.

Pyles, a co-founder of Southwestern cuisine (along with Dan Fearing of the Mansion on Turtle Creek), now lives in a 5,000-plus-square-foot (or 464-plus-square-meter) Turtle Creek house valued at $2.2 million, much of the excitement about his mastery gone.

"Star Canyon Dallas is the most famous restaurant in Texas," once claimed *Texas Monthly* magazine, which in its heyday awarded it two of the possible three stars. "I'm not saying it's the best, though I would put it in the top five or so."

Mediterranean

Adelmo's Ristorante, 4537 Cole Ave. at Knox St., (214) 559-0325, Internet www.adelmos.com. *E*. Open for lunch Mon-Fri 11:30 AM-2 PM, for dinner Mon-Sat 6 PM-10 PM; closed Sundays. It has a bar. Wheelchair accessible. Reservations may be in order.

Located in a two-story building diagonally across the street from On the Border Mexican restaurant and around the corner from Weir's Furniture store on Knox Street.

A cozy bistro whose owner, Adelmo Banchetti, opened it in 1989. Many consider it one of the city's most romantic restaurants. Blackboard specials change daily.

Start with an appetizer, like crab cakes, escargot Provencal, lobster ravioli, smoked Norwegian salmon, Caesar's salad, or one of the soups. Adelmo's specialties include ravioli Florentine stuffed with spinach and ricotto, salmon-laced fettuccine Romano with artichokes and mushrooms, marinated and grilled shrimp, fresh salmon, and veal scallopini.

The most expensive entrée is the 16-ounce (or 453-gram) bone-in veal chop, followed by grilled rack of lamb served with couscous, tenderloin of beef, 16-ounce prime ribeye steak, and roasted duck with strawberry sauce, all served with vegetables and house salad.

"Best bets for dessert are chocolate mousse or creme brulee," claims *Texas Monthly*. There are also chocolate cake with walnuts and tiramisu cake. Most lunch dishes are more reasonably priced. Several wines go up to and beyond $300 a bottle.

"This is the place to go in Dallas and eavesdrop to stay on the cutting edge of wine," observes the *Dallas Morning News*. "Most of the world's great winemakers and winery owners lunch there when in town."

D Magazine once named it one of the Metroplex's best restaurants. The *News*, which previously gave it four out of the possible five stars, reduced its rating to three and a half stars in 2002.

Sambuca Jazz Cafe, 2618 Elm St. at Good-Latimer Expwy., (214) 744-0820, Internet www.sambucajazzcafe.com. *E*. Open for lunch Mon-Fri 11 AM-2:30 PM, and for dinner Sun-Wed 6 PM-11 PM, Thu 6 PM-midnight, and Fri-Sat 6 PM-1 AM. It has a bar with happy hour Mon-Fri 4:30 PM-7 PM. Live music is featured seven nights a week, starting at about 8:15 PM.

Located between Crowdus Street and Good-Latimer Expressway in the Deep Ellum entertainment district of noisy clubs, east of downtown Dallas. Trees rock club is across the street.

Opening in 1991, the supper club features decor with exposed brick walls and leopard-skin booths in a Chicago speakeasy style. It is owned by former professional tennis player Kim Forsythe and her sister.

Mediterranean dishes are served, and live mostly mainstream jazz can be heard, everything from pianist Cedar Walton to saxophonist Marchel Ivery. The *Dallas Observer* voted it the "best jazz restaurant" from 1993 to 1998. *Texas Monthly* calls it a "sophisticated restaurant cum cocktail lounge." Specialties from France, Greece, Italy, and North Africa will be found on its menu.

Appetizers could include escargot Provencal, tiger shrimp, crab cake, and salmon carpaccio. The most expensive entrée is the eight-ounce (or 226-gram) lobster stuffed filet mignon, followed by the grilled New York strip steak with mashed potatoes, and braised veal shank. Seafood and pastas go from cappelini with shrimp to Chilean sea bass.

A larger **Sambuca,** with similar menu and live jazz, is located at 15207 Addison Rd. at Belt Line, (972) 385-8455, west of North Dallas Tollway, in Addison, a town bordering on north Dallas. Reviewing the food, *D Magazine* claims, "It's not bad, just average."

Mexican

El Fenix, 1601 McKinney Ave. at Fields St., (214) 747-1121 or 747-6643, Internet www.elfenixtexmex.com. *I*. Open daily 11 AM-8:30 PM, Fri-Sat until 10 PM. Located downtown, just north of Woodall Rodgers Freeway, and close to the American Airlines Center (see listing).

One of 15 such restaurants in the Metroplex that were started by

Miguel Martinez (1890-1956), a penniless immigrant from Mexico. As a seven-year-old youth, he worked for two cents a day as a silver-mine mule-train driver to help his widowed mother, who scraped out a living as a maid.

Following the Mexican Revolution, Martinez left his native Nuevo Leon for Dallas, where he worked as a laborer with the Dallas Railway & Terminal Company and as a dishwasher at the luxury Oriental Hotel downtown. In Dallas he met Faustina Porras (1900-1990), the daughter of a rural Mexican physician from Chihuahua state. She worked as a field hand and married Martinez in 1915.

The couple saved just enough money to open the Martinez Café, a one-room Mexican restaurant at Griffin and McKinney three years later. El Fenix operated at that location until 1966, when the construction of Woodall Rodgers Freeway forced it to move across the street to its present location.

In 1922, assisted by his wife, Martinez enlarged the restaurant, renamed it El Fenix, and changed its menu to Mexican food exclusively. Martinez pioneered the "Mexican combination plate," including beans, a tamale, an enchilada, and rice, supposedly to free him from dishwashing. When the Martinezes turned the business over to their eight children, they were prosperous and well known. Faustina Martinez outlived her husband by 34 years.

"Despite being one of the city's earliest Hispanic business success stories, the family had to overcome opposition when they purchased a home on Cole Avenue and moved into a previously non-integrated neighborhood," notes the Texas State Historical Association. Today, it is one of the largest Hispanic businesses in the Metroplex.

You can have an entire meal for a little over $10 per person. A more expensive entrée is tenderloin of beef prepared Mexican style and served with cheese enchilada. Two other similarly priced meals would be the charbroiled beef entrée served with Spanish rice and cheese nachos, and marinated beef or chicken served with flour or corn tortillas and refried beans.

Beef or chicken rancheras with beans, boneless breast of chicken with beans and Spanish rice, chicken or beef flautas, Poblano pepper stuffed with cheeses and dipped in egg batter, traditional fajitas, and large flour tortillas filled with beef or seasoned chicken are some among other El Fenix specialties.

You will also find some 20 combination dinners. Children's plates are available. American dishes, such as chicken fried steak and hamburger are also on the menu. You can sample margaritas, beer, tequila, wines, cocktails, and several varieties of coffee.

Other El Fenix restaurants, open daily 11 AM- 9 PM, include these locations:

- 6811 West Northwest Hwy. at Hillcrest Rd., (214) 363-5279.
- 120 East Colorado Blvd. at Beckley Ave., (214) 941-4050.
- 5622 Lemmon Ave. at Inwood Rd., (214) 521-5166.
- 810 North Central Expwy. at Plano Pkwy., Plano, (972) 578-1020.

New American

Abacus, 4511 McKinney Ave. at Knox St., (214) 559-3111, Internet www.abacus-restaurant.com. *E*. Open for dinner Mon-Thu 6 PM-10 PM, Fri-Sat 6 PM-11 PM. Bar opens at 5 PM Mon-Sat. Wheelchair accessible. It seats up to 140. Complimentary valet parking is available. Reservations are recommended.

Located in Uptown, a block south of the Knox Street shopping area, across McKinney from Chez Gerard country French restaurant (see listing) and the tony Forty-Five Ten clothing, jewelry, and accessories shop.

On the next block north of here stands the well-regarded Latin-cuisine La Duni cafe, created by Espartaco Borga. *Esquire* magazine and the *Dallas Morning News* rated La Duni one of the year's ten best restaurants.

Abacus claims for itself "contemporary global cuisine" featuring Southwestern, Creole, Mediterranean, and Pacific hues in a contemporary setting that will take you aback on your first visit. The decor "is modern, goofy, clownish, with vaguely Japanese feel," observes the *New York Times*.

Executive chef Kent "Rathbun has created a menu that borders on precious but is restrained at the level of whimsical and tongue-in-cheek," declares the *Dallas Morning News*, which gives it the maximum five stars and once named it one of the ten best new restaurants.

Salt-crusted calamari with barbecue sauce, wood-roasted shrimp on chanterelle risotto, ahi tuna tartare with purée, and soy-glazed duck spring rolls with red chile are the so-called small plates, or appetizers. Lobster "shooters" are chunks of roasted lobster served in a shot glass of lobster bisque flavored with red chile and sake.

Entrées range from grilled vegetable enchiladas on red bean-roasted corn ranchero stew, or grilled prawns on lemon pepper linguine, to prime "cowboy" ribeye steak with leek potato cake, lamb T-bone steak with blue cheese-roasted corn grits, or prime tenderloin filet with grilled Portobelo whipped potatoes.

There might also be cedar-smoked salmon, macadamia-crusted sea scallops with shrimp fried rice, roast Peking duck with Napa cabbage, and barbecued pork tenderloin with twice-baked Yukon potatoes.

"Designed" sushi, roled sushi, sashimi, and nigiri cost up to $18, but if you would like to taste a little of everything, that will cost you $30. Even breads, ranging from crispy papadum Indian flat bread to crusty sourdough, will make you sit up.

"Desserts stole the show," observes the *New York Times* reviewer. "Exactly what high-end desserts should be, they were fun, delicious and unpretentious." You can be one of the ten diners who sit at the chef's table, "set at the bow of Dallas' first-ever European-style kitchen, which is a theater of culinary arts," according to the management. Dinner for two with wine will run at least $150.

The *News*'s other five-star restaurants—The French Room inside Adolphus Hotel, The Mansion on Turtle Creek in the hotel of the same name, Nana in the Anatole Hotel, and the Riviera—are more formal. "Mr. Rathbun's Abacus achieves superlatives in food, service and atmosphere in a hip, at-ease setting," claims the daily.

The Abacus' wine list was singled out by *Wine Spectator,* and *Food and Wine Magazine*. It claims some 450 wine selections, many from California, from an inventory of 3,000 bottles. Abacus is one among a handful of Dallas restaurants that claim four out of the possible five stars from the *Mobil Travel Guide*.

Chef Rathbun catered two balls, one at the Lincoln Memorial in Washington, D.C., during George W. Bush's 2001 inaugural festivities. He helped prepare hors d'oeuvres for thousands of guests at the Blue Ball for the Texas and Wyoming delegations, then cooked for another 5,000 at the Red Ball, which was organized for major donors, both at the Washington Convention Center.

Cooking classes are available Sunday afternoons at Abacus for $350 per person, and you get to eat your own creations at 5 PM, along with your invited guest.

Owner Robert Hoffman claims to have spent $6 million to transform what was previously the location of Big Shots sports café with decor that included the $1,000 lamps imported from Italy and the billiard parlor with 16 tables costing $3,000 each.

Antares, Hyatt Regency Hotel, 300 Reunion Blvd., (214) 712-7145, Internet www.dallas.hyatt.com. *E*. Open for lunch Mon-Sat 11:30 AM-2 PM, and for dinner daily 6 PM-11 PM. Sunday brunch is held 10:30 AM-2:30 PM. It seats about 250. Wheelchair accessible. Jackets are suggested for men during dinner. Valet or self-parking is available.

Located on the southwestern edge of downtown Dallas, southwest of Dealey Plaza, where John Kennedy was assassinated in 1963.

Antares is situated just below the observation deck atop the Hyatt's 52-story, 837-step Reunion Tower. Antares and the Dome Lounge atop it are located on a rotating platform that will enable you to see the entire Dallas scene every hour or so, something akin to the Ostankino Tower restaurant in Moscow, Russia.

Named after the brightest star in the Scorpio constellation. Because it is so popular with out-of-town tourists, Antares has taken a drubbing with the locals; some consider it a glorified and overpriced tourist trap.

Main courses could feature stuffed chicken, garlic chili-rubbed prime rib, soy-marinated glazed salmon, grilled pork chops, cilantro-marinated shrimp, lamb T-bone, seafood fricassee, marinated filet of beef, aged New York sirloin steaks, and Yukon sea bass.

Desserts include raspberry sorbet, cappuccino cheesecake, and deep-dish pecan pie. Enjoy a cognac, port, or espresso. Its California wine list is also respectable.

The *Dallas Morning News* food reviewer once liked its sirloin steak: "It was a bodacious little steak—high and proud and red and tender; delicious, too." He called the service "pleasant and perfunctory" at another time.

The Chaparral Club, Adam's Mark Hotel, 400 North Olive St. at Pearl St., (214) 922-8000. *E*. Open for dinner Tue-Thu 6:30 PM-10 PM, Fri-Sat 6:30 PM-11 PM. Closed Sunday and Monday nights. Live entertainment Mon-Sat. Sunday brunch is served 11 AM-4 PM. Wheelchair accessible. Valet parking is available. Reservations are recommended.

Located on the 38th floor of the largest Dallas hotel and featuring "what has to be Dallas' most stunning restaurant view," according to the *Dallas Morning News*.

During the 1960s and 1970s it was one of the city's toniest private clubs with a four-star restaurant and lounge where oil deals were made. The restaurant building was originally part of the Southland Center built in 1958 and the tallest skyscraper west of the Mississippi when it opened the following year.

The Chaparral reopened in 1998 as part of the Adam's Mark hotel (see entry). It serves classic European dishes with American and Asian influences. Some might consider it a Dallas equivalent to New York's Rainbow Room.

Appetizers could include cognac-flamed lobster bisque, herb-crusted tuna carpaccio, applewood smoked quail, or marinated Chaparral salmon. Texas center-cut venison chop with poblano-spiked sweet potato is one of the costliest entrées, followed by lavender honey duck breast, and Hawaiian sugar cane-cured pork.

You might also find lobster spring rolls with sweet chili sauce, grilled tequila shrimp, tortilla-crusted lamb chops, and duck leg confit strudel with chambord glaze. You could also be served mustard-marinated quail with spinach or vine-ripe tomato salad with feta cheese.

The restaurant features more than 500 wines, mostly from California. You should have no difficulty spending $100 a person.

The Chaparral was selected by *D magazine* as one of the "best new restaurants" of 1999.

City Café, 5757 West Lovers Ln. at Dallas North Tollway, (214) 351-2233. M. Open for lunch Mon-Sat 11:30 AM-2:30 PM, for dinner daily 5:30 PM-10 PM. Reservations are suggested for "one of the most popular [Sunday] brunches in the area." Seats up to 210. It has a full bar. Wheelchair accessible. Valet parking is available. Reservations are suggested.

City Café to Go, (214) 351-3366, next door, is open for pick-up Mon-Sat 10 AM-8 PM. You can take home garlic herb-rubbed beef tenderloin by one-half pound (or 22 grams).

Located on the northwestern edge of University Park, in a shopping strip known as the Miracle Mile, and across the street from a McDonald's fast-food restaurant.

A relaxed, white-tablecloth neighborhood bistro that impressed even Julia Child, the doyenne of American chefs. The menu changes monthly, but it retains the New American-California character that has been the restaurant's trademark since 1986.

The most expensive meat entrées might be the red wine-cured beef tenderloin with roasted carrots, followed by shellfish bouillabaisse with roasted fennel, seared sea scallops with cauliflower, and pan-seared Atlantic salmon sweet onion oyster stew.

Other dishes could include gemeli pasta with ham and English peas, maple-glazed pork chops with scalloped potatoes, and red peppercorn-crusted calves liver over tomato grits.

"You're making a huge mistake if you eat here and don't have a slice of the Blum's cake," advises *D Magazine*. This is the place where now and then you could bump into someone like U.S. Sen. Kay Bailey Hutchison and her family.

City Café also has an exemplary wine list that claims 250 wine selections mostly from California and an inventory of 3,000 bottles.

"It's one of the most civilized and convivial locations you could find for a sophisticated, yet comfortable, business lunch," gushes the *Dallas Business Journal,* while the *Dallas Morning News* claims, "It's an inviting, cozy spot that encourages lingering."

Diagonally across the street from City Café is Goff's Charcoal Hamburgers, where its owner, Harvey Gough, has gained notoriety by insulting his patrons and made a statement with a concrete statue of Lenin that he had shipped a decade ago from Odessa after the fall of the Soviet Union.

Actually collecting the statues and busts of communist tyrants is the millionaire Harlan Crow, who claims Nicolae Ceausescu, Vladimir Lenin, theoretician Karl Marx, Joseph Stalin, Marshall Tito, and Mao Tse Tung.

Gershwin's, 8442 Walnut Hill Ln. at Upper Greenville Ave., (214) 373-7171, Internet www.gershwinsrestaurant.com. *E*. Open for lunch Mon-Fri 11:30 AM-3 PM, dinner Mon-Thu 3 PM-10 PM, Fri 3 PM-11 PM, Sat 5 PM-11 PM; closed Sundays. Seats 225. Live piano entertainment nightly. Happy hour Mon-Fri 4 PM-7 PM. Wheelchair accessible. Valet parking.

Located northeast of downtown Dallas and University Park, across Greenville from the Presbyterian Hospital (see listing).

It opened in 1984 and was taken over by new owners in 2000. It is named after George Gershwin and styled after the era in which the composer of the opera *Porgy and Bess* lived. A trendy yuppie outpost that also has a reputation for good food and atmosphere.

Appetizers range from glazed shrimps to grilled quail, to Gershwin's crabcake with pickled melon. You can treat yourself to prosciutto and goat cheese or Caesar chicken pizza. Among the pastas you might enjoy fettuccine with braised veal shank.

The costliest entrée could be the herb-roasted prime beef tenderloin with grilled jumbo prawns. Next in price would be prime beef tenderloin with lobster rissotto, followed by grilled New York sirloin steak or grilled ribeye. There is mushroom-crusted loin of venison, herb-crusted lamb loin with Yukon scallion potatoes, oven-roasted Chilean sea bass with sweet corn custard, red snapper baked with crabmeat, veal medallions with onion marmalade, and halibut with Portobelo mushroom vinaigrette.

Desserts could include fresh banana cake and Gershwin's signature dessert, the self-proclaimed "sublime" chocolate sac, filled with white cake, white chocolate mousse, strawberries, kiwi, and whipped cream.

There are all the yuppie coffee drinks, dessert wines, liqueurs, and cordials. Wines by the glass range from the French Merlot to the California Cabernet. Try one of the 50 varieties of Scotch whiskey. Gershwin's, to the surprise of some, gets four out of the possible five stars from the *Dallas Morning News*.

Enclave, a supper club located in the Woodhill Medical Park, where some 150 physicians practice, less than two blocks northwest from here, is situated at 8325 Walnut Hill Lane and across Walnut Hill from the Presbyterian hospital. It has the same owners as Gershwin's.

The Grape, 2808 Lower Greenville Ave., (214) 828-1981. *E*. Open for lunch Mon-Fri 11:30 AM-2:30 PM, for dinner Sun-Thu 5:30 PM-11 PM, Fri-Sat 5:30 PM-midnight. It has a bar. Smoking is permitted on the patio only. Wheelchair accessible. Valet parking is available. Reservations are suggested.

Located in east Dallas, about one mile (or 1.6 kilometers) south of Mockingbird Lane, between Goodwin Avenue and Vickery Boulevard, across the street from Greenville Bar & Grill (see entry).

The Grape, which seats about 45, is often voted one of Dallas' most romantic restaurants, "seemingly only because it makes generous use of low-wattage lightbulbs," according to the *Dallas Observer*. To some, the noise detracts from the romance. As the city's oldest wine bistro, it has a large following among the east Dallas intellectuals.

The daily blackboard selections always hold a surprise or two and may include crabcake, baked Brie, smoked trout salad, chili fried calamari, or Thai shrimp broth in the way of appetizers. Although the menu changes regularly, the mushroom soup has been a signature dish since 1972, when the restaurant opened and charged 35 cents for a bowl of it; today it is more than $5.

The costliest dinner dish could be the twin tournedos of beef with mashed potatoes and fresh asparagus, followed by classic coq au vin. Some among the entrées, such as seared beef snapper, roast pork tenderloin, or tournedos of beef, can be ordered in two sizes at corresponding prices, depending on your appetite.

Other platters only come in one size and could include lamb tenderloin, pistachio crusted salmon, seared scallops, and cinnamon venison leg. Vanilla-bean crème brûlée and the much too rich chocolate pudding are two among the desserts. The Grape has a solid wine list.

The *Dallas Morning News* gives the Grape four out of the possible five stars. *Glamour* magazine once named it one of the top kissing spots in the nation.

The Mansion on Turtle Creek, 2821 Turtle Creek Blvd. at Gillespie St., (800) 527-5432 or (214) 559-2100 or 526-2121, Internet www.mansiononturtlecreec.com. *E.* Open for lunch Mon-Sat 11:30 am-2 PM; for dinner Sun-Wed 6 PM-10:30 PM, Thu-Sat 6 PM-10:30 PM. Sunday brunch is held from 11:30 AM until 2:30 PM.

It has a bar with live music on weekends. The Promenade is a garden-style breakfast room. Half a dozen private dining rooms are available. A three-course Sunday brunch is $40 and served 11 AM-2:30 PM.

"Coat required, tie recommended for men. No tennis shoes, jeans or shorts," advises the Mansion's Web site, although the tie requirement has quietly been dropped.

Located in the historic Oak Lawn neighborhood, on the scenic Turtle Creek, almost halfway between Reverchon Park and the Dallas Theater Center (see entry). The Uptown art galleries, antique shops, and restaurants are almost within a walking distance were it not for Dallas' aversion to sidewalks.

Nestled into four oak-studded acres (or 1.61 hectares), the 1925-era

10,000-square-foot (or 929-square-meter) Mansion, once the home of a cotton baron and now a favorite with the rich and publicity-hungry, retains much of its original splendor. The dining room was designed by the French architect M. Jacques Carre.

It features a hand-carved wood ceiling, composed of 2,400 pieces that took six carpenters eight weeks to install, fireplaces at each end of the dining room that are in the British style, and fine art and antiques scattered throughout. China is Bauscher porcelain made in Germany, flatware Savoia silver plate from Italian Eme Posaterie, glassware consists of Judel and Riedel, linens are 100 percent cotton.

The hotel and restaurant are controlled by Caroline Rose Hunt, whose brothers William Herbert and Nelson Bunker bid silver prices to $50 an ounce (or 28 grams) in 1980 and lost billions when it crashed to $16 two months later.

One of the best and the most expensive half a dozen restaurants in the Metroplex, although some guests think that prices are inflated, to put it mildly. The Mansion and the French Room in the Adolphus Hotel (see entry) downtown are usually neck to neck in culinary superlatives in the Metroplex.

"What the Mansion does, it does it better than any restaurant in town; it enjoys a much-coveted reputation and mystique, both as a restaurant and a favorite spot for both local and national celebrities and power brokers," said a 1987 review, and it could still be said today.

Unless you are well known locally, nationally, or internationally, chances are you will be banished to the Garden Room, considered Siberia at the Mansion restaurant.

The *Dallas Morning News*, which until mid-2002 gave it the maximum five stars, calls it "one of Dallas' most glamorous spots. Former hotel manager Jeffrey Trigger addressed the Mansion's reputation for snotty attitude as well as the rumored necessity for big tips before service."

The kitchen alone employs 40 cooks, which may explain why the entrées run up to and beyond $50 each, and Sunday brunch for two is $100. Actually, if you need to know the prices, you probably cannot afford to eat here and may just as well go to EatZi's takeout nearby (see entry). Its chef is the Kentucky-born Dean Fearing (b. 1955), who claims to be the Father of Southwestern cuisine, and has previously cooked at the Fairmont Hotel's Pyramid Room. "A Mozart of the cooking world," Fearing has been in the Mansion's kitchen for 15 of its more than 20 years in business.

His "signature" dishes include warm lobster taco with yellow tomato salsa, tortilla soup, red jalapeno Caesar salad, and crème brûlée with raspberry sauce. Other entrées could be grilled swordfish, potato enchilada, sautéed chicken breast, shrimp in lemon, and barbecued venison fajitas. Also grilled ribeye steak, goat cheese quesadillas, pork in sweet soy sauce, beef tenderloin marinated in molasses, shrimp enchilada, chicken Provencal, pan-seared ostrich filet, or roasted rack of lamb.

"Alas, though Fearing's cooking may have once been zingy and incisive, my meal looked and tasted a muddle," writes a *Travel & Leisure* critic.

The Mansion also wants to be seen as a top wine destination. The restaurant stocks more than 10,000 bottles of California and Bordeaux wines with some 600 selections. Wines by the glass are also available. At a gala dinner in 1985, the restaurant uncorked an 1870 Mouton Rothschild, which was then priced at $38,000.

"And we firmly believe the Mansion's banana cream tart is a culinary treasure," once opined the food reviewer for the *Texas Monthly* magazine.

For a mere $1,600 per person, you can be "chef for a day" at the Mansion, and "you will receive your very own monogrammed chef's coat," for demonstration-style classes that last two to three hours.

But if coming here once a year is not enough, you can always look up the Mansion's recipes on the Web or purchase "signature" sauces, salsas, and dressings that the hotel is also pushing on-line. For the status-conscious, the Mansion peddles $25 chef's aprons and $55 chef's jackets.

Perhaps it was these distractions that cost chef Fearing a star in the prestigious *Mobil Travel Guide* in 2002. While the hotel retained its five-star rating, the loss of the fifth star in the restaurant impoverished the entire state, which now has no five-star Mobil dining establishment. There were only 14 Mobil five-star restaurants nationwide in 2003.

The previous summer, the Mansion was also downgraded from its top three-star rating by *Texas Monthly* magazine down to a single star. The magazine's restaurant guide editor noted it was "one of the hardest things I've ever had to do." Chef Fearing told the *Dallas Morning News* he was "devastated" by the downgrade.

There are those who stand behind the Mansion. "It's my contention that the Mansion doesn't deserve to lose any stars, because it's exactly as good as it's always been," counters *D Magazine*'s restaurant critic, acknowledging that, "Yes, it's a little snooty, and, yes, the menu is a little wild." She added elsewhere that her vegetarian plate of potato enchiladas was "ridiculously overpriced at $26."

And, bordering on the absurd, more than two dozen Mansion servers wear, as part of their uniform, handmade, custom-fitted Lucchese kangaroo leather boots with a Mansion logo. The Mansion's restaurant captains and the maitre d' wear custom ostrich boots "for a more formal look." The Mansion has spent up to $1,000 on each of the more than three dozen pairs of boots.

The Pyramid Grill, Hotel Fairmont, 1717 North Akard St. at Ross Ave., (214) 720-5249. *E*. Open for lunch daily 11:30 AM-3 PM, for dinner daily 6 PM-10 PM. Live music Fri-Sat. Sunday jazz brunch is served 11:30 AM-2:30 PM. Wheelchair accessible. Valet parking is available. Dinner reservations are suggested.

Located in the northern part of downtown, two blocks west from the Dallas Museum of Art and next to I. M. Pei's Fountain Place building (see individual entries).

For many years, especially during the 1970s, the standard bearer among the luxury downtown restaurants, the Pyramid has lost much of its exclusivity. However, the restaurant will not disappoint if you expect high prices.

An eight-ounce (or 226-gram) dry-aged center-cut filet mignon will set you back handsomely; the *Fort Worth Star-Telegram* tells its readers that "no amount of the accompanying bearnaise sauce could rescue its parched skin." Other meat entrées could include roasted prime rib, double lamb chop, Dover sole, 16-ounce (or 453-gram) prime T-bone steak, 12-ounce (or 340-gram) grilled ribeye steak, grilled tuna, and roasted Cornish game hen.

Lobster supreme, Maryland crabcake, and smoked salmon from Scotland are just three among the appetizers. Chocolate or Grand Marnier soufflé might be the costliest dessert, followed by Cointreau ice soufflé, and warm melting chocolate cake.

The fixed-price four-course dinner is more than $50 without wine. You can spend hundreds of dollars on a bottle of wine, or $10 a glass. The costliest lunch entrée is about $20 and—gasp!—there are sandwiches on the menu.

The *Dallas Morning News*, which gives the Pyramid four out of the possible five stars, informs that "the best dish on the menu," a two-pound (or 90-gram) grilled lobster, is also the most expensive.

"Pyramid Grill has everything except pizzazz, charisma, and a reason to visit—other than a competent menu stocked with items you can find at virtually any run-of-the mill Dallas steakhouse," claims the *Dallas Observer* weekly, which had previously labeled it the "best fancy restaurant."

Tramontana, 8220-B Westchester Dr. at Luther Lane, (214) 368-4188, Internet www.mybistro.net. *E*. Open for lunch Tue-Fri 11 AM-2 PM, and for dinner Tues-Thu begining at 5:30 PM. Closed Sun-Mon. It has a bar. Wheelchair accessible.

Located on the northwestern edge of University Park, in the Preston Shopping Center, south of West Northwest Highway, a couple of blocks south from Preston Center Pavilion, and across the street from 24-Hour Fitness.

Tramontana, which originally opened in 1995, has been owned by James and Lisa Neel since 1999. It is named after the tramontana cold northern winds blowing off the Mediterranean Sea through the mountains between Spain and France. Decor at the New American-cuisine Tramontana, with French and Italian accents, consists mostly of a Montmartre-style mural that could have been done by a Henri de Toulouse-Lautrec student.

Appetizers might range from baked goat cheese with grilled Portobello mushrooms to duck confit with wild mushroom risotto, from sautéed crabcakes with mustard to potato-crusted calamari. Soups and salad include wild mushroom bisque, lobster gazpacho with fresh avocado, seafood salad with lobster and crab, warm goat cheese with tomato vinaigrette, and grilled pears with buttered walnuts and apple-smoked bacon.

The costliest dinner entrées are the apple bacon wrapped beef tenderloin with double cheese whipped potatoes and crispy onions, red wine-braised veal Osso Bucco with saffron risotto, and rack of Colorado lamb with walnuts and whole grain mustard-rosemary

Other main dishes might include peppered New York strip steak with pork tenderloin and goat cheese chicken, Maui snapper with caramelized salmon and pan-roasted sea bass, pecan-crusted salmon with horseradish cream, Pernod-grilled snapper with prawn and shrimp, Maui snapper with macadamia nuts, shrimp-stuffed chicken breast, and horseradish-crusted pork tenderloin.

There are desserts, like Grand Marnier crème brûlée, warm apple tartelette with ice cream, and warm sourdough chocolate cake. There are a dozen white and red wines available by the glass.

The *Dallas Morning News*, which gave it four out of the possible five stars, noted that "there are few places in Dallas that deliver as much quality for as little, pricewise." In a follow-up, it reduced that rating to three and a half stars.

Around the corner from Tramontana is Neel's **Bistro Latino,** 6112 Luther Lane, which offers Latin American and Caribbean cuisine, and also earned four stars from the *News*.

Salvadoran

Gloria's, 4140 Lemmon Ave. at Douglas Ave., (214) 521-7576, Internet www.gloriasrestaurants.com, e-mail info@gloriasrestaurants.com. M. Open Sun-Thu 11 AM-10 PM, Fri-Sat 11 AM-11 PM. Happy hour is Mon-Tue & Wed-Fri 3 PM-7 PM, when prices are one-half off. Wheelchair accessible.

Located north of downtown Dallas, in the Oak Lawn neighborhood between Douglas Avenue and Knight Street.

Small and plain, this Gloria's location is a popular lunchtime spot. Salvadoran, Salvadoran Tex-Mex, and Mexican dishes are served. Shrimp nachos, beef or chicken fajita nachos, shrimp cocktail, and chili con queso could be some among the appetizers.

The $13 seasoned or sautéed jumbo shrimp with guacamole salad is among the costlier entrées on the Salvadoran menu, followed by mesquite grilled quail, grilled shrimp and chicken salad, and mariscada, a broth-base soup made with shrimp and scallops.

Grilled pork tenderloin, grilled flank steak, marinated chicken breast, Poblano pepper stuffed with Wisconsin Monterey Jack cheese and served with a beef or chicken enchilada, all with black beans and rice are the SalvaTex combinations. Try such Central American delicacies as pupusas, or handmade corn tortillas stuffed with cheese or pork, or deep-fried yucca.

Mexican dishes include a variety of eggs, beef and chicken fajitas, and three grilled chicken breast tacos, and are all served with black beans, rice, and guacamole. There is also a great variety of enchiladas and quesadillas.

Desserts include tres leches, milk flan, and chocolate flan. Margaritas are big business at Gloria's, but beers and wines by the glass are also available. Children's plates for those under 12 years of age are available.

Other **Gloria's** restaurants will be found at:

• 3715 Lower Greenville Ave. at Matalee Ave., (214) 874-0088. Opens daily at 11 AM. A warmly painted eatery abuzz with activity.

• 600 West Davis St. at North Llewellyn Ave., Oak Cliff, (214) 948-3672. Open daily 11 AM-10 PM. The original restaurant opened by El Salvador natives Gloria and Jose Fuentes in 1986.

• 5100 Belt Line Rd. at Dallas North Tollway, Addison, (972) 387-8847. There is live music and salsa dancing Saturdays 10:30 PM-2 AM.

All Gloria's locations are well known for fresh tortillas made by hand throughout the day.

Seafood

Café Pacific, 24 Highland Park Village, (214) 526-1170. *E*. Open for lunch Mon-Fri 11:30 AM-2 PM, and for dinner Mon-Wed 5:30 PM-10 PM, Thu 5:30 PM-10:30 PM, Fri-Sat 5:30 PM-11 PM. Saturday brunch is held 11:30 AM-2:30 PM. Closed Sundays.

It has a bar. Personal checks are not accepted. Wheelchair accessible. Valet parking is available on weekends. Reservations are suggested for dinner.

Located in the tony Highland Park Village shopping center (see listing), at the crossroads of Mockingbird Lane and Preston Road. Across the street is its sister restaurant, **Patrizio,** a pizza and pasta trattoria, where you can keep track of those entering the tony Hermes of Paris accessories shop and where you can also display your vanity feathers to the maximum effect.

Open since 1980, it boasts such regulars as Andrew Litton, the music director of the Dallas Symphony Orchestra. This is a good place to impress your date or partner, but you'll have to spend to occupy its real estate. The menu says you are expected to order at least one entrée, and they include the grilled vegetable plate and the lamb chops.

In between, you will find specialties, such as a pricey oven-roasted rack of Colorado lamb with whipped potatoes, prime New York strip with french fries and green beans, lobster tail with white truffle risotto, pepper-crusted filet mignon with matchstick potatoes, onion-crusted sea bass with sweet corn risotto, and marinated pork tenderloin over blue cheese polenta cake.

Grilled dishes include plump seared Atlantic scallops, salmon, jumbo shrimp, and red snapper, all served with potatoes and vegetables. The lunch is cheaper.

There is a decent variety of appetizers, soups, salads, and desserts. Café Pacific's wines by the glass include Chardonnays, Pinot Noirs, Merlots, and Cabernet Sauvignons. More than 100 selections, many from California, from an inventory of 2,800 bottles are available.

The *Dallas Morning News,* which gives it four out of the possible five stars, notes: "Service sparkles like the fancy, black-and-white marble tile flooring in a dining room that is small and tightly packed with white linen café tables—so close you're bound to hear your neighbor's conversation."

Notes the *Fort Worth Star-Telegram*: "Wonderfully unobtrusive and attentive with none of the 'Hello, I'm Gavin and I'll be your struggling-actor for the night' superficial pleasantries." In the opinion of *Gourmet* magazine, this is one of the best seafood restaurants in the city.

Also located in the shopping center is a Tex-Mex restaurant Mi Cocina, whose owner had never been to Mexico until he opened his first Mi Cocina eatery.

Southwestern

Blue Mesa Grill, Village on the Parkway, 5100 Belt Line Rd., Addison, (972) 934-0165, Internet www.bluemesagrill.com. M. Open for lunch and dinner Mon-Thu 11 AM-10 PM, Fri-Sat 11 AM-10:30 PM, Sun 10 AM-9:30 PM. Sunday brunch is held 10 AM-2:30 PM. Wheelchair accessible.

Located in the southeast corner of Belt Line and Dallas North Tollway, behind the Bed, Bath & Beyond store.

This is Santa Fe-inspired cuisine made well known by its owners, former clinical psychologist Jim Baron and his wife Liz, who has a fine arts degree in design from New York's Pratt Institute.

You could start with appetizers, such as skewers of marinated steak and chicken, blue corn nachos, spice-rubbed shrimp, or flaky pastry stuffed with smoked chicken. Quesadillas made with Mesa panna bread and steak, portabella mushrooms, or roasted chicken could also be had. There is a tortilla soup, southwestern chicken Caesar, and Navajo chicken salad.

Grill specialties include the smoky Texas ribeye with corn and crispy potato cake, followed, according to prices, by skewers of cold smoked ribeye steak with beef tenderloin and jumbo shrimp, grain-fed beef tenderloin with cheese chile relleno, grilled salmon with black bean adobe pie, Latin barbecued chicken with roasted vegetables, pan-seared fresh salmon filet, and Baja shrimp wrapped in crisp bacon.

Among the Southwestern specialties, you might want to try grilled chicken or steak tacos, roasted vegetables enchiladas, red chile salmon tacos, Southwestern steak or chicken fajitas, or smoked chicken enchiladas. There are sampler plates for the indecisive.

Almond cookie taco stuffed with chocolate mousse, creamy caramel custard with raspberry sauce, and lemon tart brûlée with fresh berries are some among the desserts. "The blue margarita is the signature drink," informs the *Dallas Morning News*, "but the real treat is the top-shelf margarita." The *Dallas Observer* once claimed that Blue Mesa has the "best Sunday brunch," and the best tortilla soup.

Another **Blue Mesa Grill** is located in Lincoln Park across the street from NorthPark mall, at 7700 West Northwest Hwy. at North Central Exwy., 2nd floor, (214) 378-8686.

There is a Blue Mesa also at Granite Park, 8200 Dallas Pkwy., the southeast corner of the Dallas Tollway at Hwy. 121 in Plano, (972) 387-4407. Both of these have architecture and interior design that "dazzle with unexpected little flourishes," to borrow the words from the *Observer*, adding that the Plano restaurant's architecture "is more fascinating than the food—though it's pretty good, too."

Steakhouses

Steak is the food of choice in the Dallas area. Nearly 70 steakhouses are located here, and more are on the way all the time. Far-north Dallas, especially along Dallas North Tollway, is particularly abundant in steakhouses.

Al Biernat's, 4217 Oak Lawn Ave. at Herschel Ave., (214) 219-2201, Internet www.albiernats.com. Open for lunch Mon-Fri 11:30 AM-2:30 PM, for dinner Mon-Fri 5:30 PM-10 PM, Sat 5:30 PM-11 PM, Sun 5:30 PM-9 PM. Seats up to 200.

A private dining room accommodates up to 35 guests. It has a full-service bar with a fireplace. Wheelchair accessible. Valet parking is available. Reservations are suggested.

Located in Dallas' Oak Lawn neighborhood on the southern edge of the tony Highland Park, about ten blocks south of the Highland Park Village mall (see entry). The entrance to the restaurant, which serves about 300 diners on a good day, is on Herschel.

In 1998, Biernat bought the lease from what was then Joey's restaurant and converted an outdoor patio into a garden room. San Antonio artist Larry Brooks painted a Majorcan mural on a dome over the bar area. The Spanish Mediterranean-style dinery opened that same year.

You would be hard pressed to find more than three local restaurants that greet more celebrities than Al Biernat's. One of the reasons is that its proprietor spent 14 years managing the Palm steakhouse (see listing) and 22 years in all with the Dallas restaurant. Another reason is that he serves good food and makes you feel at home, even if you are a nobody. The noted New York food critic John Mariani raves about the eatery at every opportunity, while peddling his cookbooks on the premises.

"Everyone dresses to kill, and getting a table on weekends is like getting season tickets to the Cowboys" football game, notes Mariani in *Esquire*, concluding, "Everything here is just a bit over-the-top, which, in Texas, is just about right."

Mariani describes Mobil's stars for excellence of food as "outdated" and AAA's diamonds as "fuddy-duddy awards." To get five stars, "be French, be very expensive, and pretend to be difficult to get into," he suggests in his Internet newsletter.

Dallas Cowboys quarterback Troy Aikman and his bride held their wedding rehearsal dinner here. Dallas Mayor Laura Miller sought refuge at Al's the night the votes were counted, and she was declared the winner. The former New York City mayor turned down Al's steaks for pastrami sandwiches and chicken salad.

A 19-year-old Biernat started out as a busboy at the Palm in Los Angeles, then continued with the same restaurant chain in Houston and Dallas. His is now one of the highest-grossing restaurants in the city.

Appetizers alone cost more than an entire meal at many chain restaurants and might include potato-crusted calamari, baked goat cheese on semolina toast, smoked North Atlantic salmon, shrimp cocktail, sautéed lump crab cakes, and tempura battered shrimp. Russian beluga caviar is priced on the day of your purchase, as are East Coast jumbo lobsters and Australian lobster tails.

One of the costliest among the house specialties is the $40 Biernat's signature Chicago prime porterhouse, followed by aged prime New York strip, filet mignon, prime rib, Colorado lamb chops, "cowboy cut" ribeye, and pepper-crusted yellowfish tuna.

Other entrées could range from swordfish, fresh salmon, grilled shrimp pasta with roasted corn, chicken Parmesan, and steamed vegetable plate with baked potato. Vegetables are sold à la carte and include creamed spinach, green beans, baked potato, or onion rings.

Al Biernat's desserts include warm chocolate cake with Amaretto crème anglaise, warm apple cobbler, Grand Marnier crème brûlée, and Texas pecan pie.

Expect to spend $100 per person even if you drink one of the lower priced from the collection of 600 wines, many from California, which go for up to $1,700 a bottle. The restaurant claims an inventory of 9,500 bottles.

You can also opt for Biernat's two-course fixed-price lunch special, which includes soup or salad and a choice of grilled fish, pasta, or chicken.

"Best at Biernat's—maybe the best salad in Dallas—is undoubtedly Al's Salad, a lovely melding of hearts of palm, avocado, crab and shrimp," opines the *Dallas Morning News*, which gives it four out of the possible five stars, adding that "you eat there more for reliability and comfort than for menu innovation."

Bob's Steak & Chop House, 4300 Lemmon Ave. at Wycliff Ave., (214) 528-9446, Internet www.bobs-steakandchop.com, e-mail bobsteak@swbell.net. *E*. Open for dinner Mon-Thu 5 PM-10 PM, Fri-Sat 5 PM-11 PM; closed Sundays. It seats up to 250. Attire is business casual, jackets are preferred but not required. Wheelchair accessible. Reservations are recommended.

Located south of Highland Park and north of Oak Lawn Avenue. Gloria's (see entry), one of several such Salvadoran-cuisine restaurants in Dallas, is located a couple of blocks away, at 4140 Lemmon.

Bob's opened in 1993 in the original location of Del Frisco's steakery (see listing), which now does business in far-north Dallas. Initially co-owned by restaurateur Dale Wamstad of the Del Frisco fame, it almost went belly up the following year, but now feeds up to 600 diners on a busy Saturday. Former New York Mayor Rudy Giuliani is just one celebrity who dined here.

Clad in dark mahogany woods and clubby, it has three dining rooms. Prime meat comes from the animals that are less than 30 months old, and only 2 percent is graded prime by the Agriculture Department.

Bob's steak prices are far from reticent: the most expensive cut is the 28-ounce (or 793-gram) prime porterhouse steak that goes for $50, although it probably contains enough meat to feed a small family since all entrées also include a vegetable and a choice of a potato, "the size of T-Rex eggs, and they are moist and hearty," according to the *Dallas Observer*.

It might be followed by a bone-in veal chop and a prime filet mignon. A 20-ounce (or 567-gram) New York strip is for hungry men, but there are smaller versions for lesser appetites.

Sample a prime T-bone steak, côte de boeuf, or rack of lamb. Other entrées include the pork chops, while broiled shrimp scampi, fried jumbo shrimp, and 12-ounce (or 340-gram) prime ribeye. The ribeye that the *Dallas Observer*'s reviewer tasted, "knocked our socks off. This is the best ribeye we've had, bar none."

Unless you are independently wealthy, you can afford coldwater Southern Australian lobster tails only if you have recently won a lottery; the price is quoted on the day of your purchase. There is no chicken on the menu. Side dishes are plentiful. The desserts include lime pie and crème brûlée.

"I'd rank the bone-in ribeye here, featuring an earthy mineral tang and a particularly toothsome outer crust, second only to [Brooklyn's] Peter Luger's porterhouse," claims a *Money* magazine reviewer. The *Dallas Morning News* gives Bob's three and a half out of the possible five stars.

Many reviewers think highly of the "downright obstinate and obsessively driven" Bob Sambol (b. 1954), who grew up in New York and now owns the restaurant. "His steakhouse is the best in Dallas," claims *D Magazine*. "Hand's down, Bob's is our top choice for great steak, ambience and personality." The service, unfortunately, can be abrupt, unless you are a free-spending regular.

Another Bob's steakhouse opened at the Shops at Legacy (see entry), near the Dallas North Tollway, in Plano in 2002.

Chamberlain's Steak & Chop House, 5330 Belt Line Rd. at Montfort Dr., Addison, (972) 934-2467, Internet www.chamberlainsrestaurant.com. *E*. Open for dinner Mon-Fri 5 PM-10 PM, Sat 5 PM-10:30 PM, Sun 5 PM-9 PM. Seats 250. It has a full bar. Reservations are suggested. Wheelchair accessible. Complimentary valet parking is available.

Located between Montfort Drive and Preston Road, next to Houston's restaurant. Ruggeri's Italian-cuisine restaurant is behind Chamberlain's.

A traditional wood-clad steakhouse with the 1930s lithographs, named after the chef and proprietor Richard Chamberlain. His cooking features the original New American touches. Chamberlain's serves prime beef that is wet-aged for 21 days and cooked in an upright broiler at 1,000 degrees and served with a stock-based juice.

The costliest steak might be a 24-ounce (or 680-gram) porterhouse, followed by a 22-ounce (or 623-gram) bone-in New York strip, veal chop, and lamb chops, all served with mashed potatoes or an à la carte vegetable of your choice, such as grilled asparagus. Other meat entrées include filet mignon, peppercorn steak, and ribeye.

Among the Chamberlain's specialties, consider also the mixed game grill, which consists of prime beef, elk, and pheasant sausage brochette, pork chops served with honey mustard glaze, and grilled chicken breast. Grilled mountain trout, salmon, and Gulf shrimp sauté could be some among the seafood selections.

Crab cakes and seared ahi tuna are two appetizers, followed by Caesar's, pepper, and spinach salads. There are wines galore, including by the glass. One hundred and fifty selections in all, largely from California, are available in an inventory of 1,400 bottles. And there is the Havana Cigar Room.

The national *Bon Appétit* magazine voted it one of the best new restaurants after it opened in 1993, and the readers of *Gourmet* magazine also like it. The *Dallas Morning News*, which gives it four out of the possible five stars, claims the reviewer's prime beef "was thick, juicy, tender cut with hearty flavor and just a hint of smoke," but the "veal chop fell short."

D Magazine rated it one of the top two Dallas steakhouses, just behind Bob's Steak & Chop House. "Our smoky flavored 12-ounce (or 340-gram) cut of prime rib equaled any we've eaten, and the giant shrimp are the best we've had in ages," declares *Texas Monthly*.

Just down the street from his beef emporium, the proprietor opened **Chamberlain's Fish Market Grill,** 4525 Belt Line Rd., (972) 503-3474, also in Addison.

Del Frisco's Double Eagle Steakhouse, 5251 Spring Valley Rd. at Dallas North Tollway, Addison, (972) 490-9000, Fax 934-0867. *E*. Open for dinner Mon-Thu 5-10 PM, Fri-Sat 5-11 PM. It has a hand-carved bar and cigar lounge with private cigar lockers. Live entertainment Thu-Sat nights. Dress code is business casual. Reservations are suggested. Valet parking is available.

Located less than a block east of Dallas North Tollway, north of the Galleria mall. Valley View Shopping Center is also nearby (see individual entries).

Like Chamberlain's (see listing), Del Frisco's also opened in 1993. A businessman's place to dine, it is one of the favorite Metroplex steakhouses, with the dining room and bar filled to capacity on many days. On busy nights more than 800 meals are served in the 450-seat restaurant, which is also one of the largest in the city.

There are five dining rooms, including a wine cellar that seats ten, and the restaurant has a huge selection of wines. The restaurant screams "money" and feels like a private club.

This is one of the top steakhouses in the Metroplex, according to a *Gourmet* magazine readers' poll. Del Frisco's serves prime beef that is first wet-aged and then dry-aged for a total of 21 days and cooked in an upright broiler at 1,800 degrees.

Be prepared to spend up to $100 per person for a meal that could include a 24-ounce (or 680-gram) prime porterhouse, or just a bit less expensive 12-ounce (or 340-gram) filet mignon. Also on the menu are the prime strip, Santa Fe peppercorn steak, and ribeye. Lobster, which is priced upon your arrival, and several varieties of veal are also served.

Vegetables are served à la carte. With those Texas-sized portions, who has space for appetizers? If you do, choose from among shrimp cocktail, marinated shrimp, or fried oysters. Desserts include the cheesecake.

Del Frisco boasts a wine inventory of some 10,000 bottles with 800 selections, particularly from California and the Bordeaux region.

"The prime strip is the best in town," observes *D Magazine*. "This is *the* steakhouse that guys bring their wives and girlfriends to." If you hope to meet the dot.com billionaire Mark Cuban, who owns the Dallas Mavericks basketball team, this is a place where you could bump into him.

Morton's of Chicago, 501 Elm at Houston Sts., (214) 741-2277, Internet www.mortons.com. *E*. Open for dinner Mon-Sat 5:30 PM-11 PM, Sun 5 PM-10 PM. Seats up to 120. Bar opens at 5 PM. Wheelchair accessible. Complimentary valet parking.

Located in the northwestern part of downtown, known as the West End entertainment district, across the street from the John F. Kennedy Sixth Floor Museum and diagonally across from Dealey Plaza (see individual entries).

This "tres elegant beef palace," according to the *Fort Worth Star-Telegram*, opened in 1986 and is situated in the basement of an office building with a wood-clad atrium-style lobby. Morton's and the Palm (see listing) are among the oldest steakhouses in downtown Dallas.

To experience a good American steak, to see how it should look, smell, and taste, come to Morton's, a steak chain, which has some 40 units nationwide. The most tender steaks come from the short loin, which, when cut into steaks with the bone left in, produces the porterhouse, the T-bone, and club steaks. Morton's "divine" prime beef is aged three weeks and grilled over a fire.

To insure uniform quality in all of its restaurants, Morton's beef is shipped fresh from Chicago, smoked salmon from Seattle, lobster from Boston, and its cheesecake from New York.

The costliest dinner entrées might be double filet mignon, porterhouse steak, and New York strip sirloin. They are followed in price by rib lamb chops, ribeye steak, Cajun ribeye steak, Sicilian veal chop, and broiled center-cut swordfish steak.

Whole baked Maine lobster is priced on the day of your purchase. The least expensive are the chicken dishes. Vegetables are priced à la carte, potatoes come baked or mashed. They weigh a pound (or 45 grams) apiece.

Unless your appetite is extraordinary, you may have to forgo appetizers, such as sautéed wild mushrooms, lobster bisque, oysters on the half shelf, shrimp cocktail, smoked Pacific salmon, or broiled sea scallops.

Each Morton's shares a similar clubby, dark-wood decor and table setting in a windowless environment to create "a timeless place of refuge." It includes large booths, bars-and-glass room dividers, and brick wine bins. There is a good selection of spirits, wines, and cigars.

Readers of *Gourmet* magazine once rated Morton's as one of the best steakhouses in the city. The *Dallas Observer* weekly claims it serves the best lobster. "Gargantuan, top-quality steaks, good side dishes and service fine despite corny show-and-tell menu presentation," notes the *Dallas Morning News*, which rates it lower than Al Biernat's, Bob's Steak & Chop House, Chamberlain's, and The Palm.

Another Morton's is located in the town of Addison, north of downtown Dallas, at 14831 Midway Rd., (972) 233-5858, less than two blocks south of Belt Line Road.

Nick & Sam's, 3008 Maple Ave. at Wolf St., (214) 871-7444, Internet www.nick-sams.com. *E*. Open Sun-Wed 5 PM-11 PM, Thu-Sat 5 PM-11 PM. The bar opens at 4 PM. Seats up to 300. It has a bar and two private dining rooms. Wheelchair accessible. Reservations are suggested. Dress code is business casual, but no jeans and no shorts are allowed. Valet parking is available.

Located just north of downtown Dallas, across the street from the Stoneleigh Hotel (see listing) and Stoneleigh Terrace Apartments. Previously, this was the location of Lawry's steakhouse.

Cold appetizers include the "exquisite" Scottish smoked salmon, shrimp cocktail, oysters, and caviar. Pan-roasted quail, fried calamari, grilled Portobelo mushrooms, and the daily soup are hot starters. There are several salads on the menu, including Caesar's.

The sky is the limit when it comes to steak prices, even if you exclude the $150, 12-ounce (or 340-gram) New York cut Kobe beef sirloin. Bone-in 22-ounce (or 623-gram) prime aged sirloin and the prime aged porterhouse are still other choices.

They are followed closely by veal chop Milanese, filet mignons, 22-

ounce Cowboy steak, Colorado lamb chop. It will take some searching to find an entrée under $20, most likely chicken.

Lobster tail is priced on the day of your arrival. Chilean sea bass, grilled swordfish, broiled lemon sole, grilled tuna, and grilled salmon are some among the fish dishes. For those who never outgrew their Kraft macaroni and cheese craving, there is Sam's version.

You can top it all off with a dessert like crème brûlée, tiramisu, chocolate molten soufflé, or warm pineapple cake. The wines, some rather costly, are available by the glass. The prices of wines over $400 are "negotiable." You will probably feel you got your money's worth at Nick & Sam's, but you may have to declare bankruptcy in the process.

The Chef's Table, located in the kitchen, seats up to ten diners.

Nick & Sam's was co-founded in 1999 by the New York-born restaurateur Philip Romano, whose other creations include Fuddruckers, Romano's Macaroni Grill, and EatZi's (see listing). There are more than 150 Fuddruckers and 120 Macaroni Grills nationwide.

The *Dallas Morning News*, which gives Nick & Sam's four out of the possible five stars, observes that it is "a hybrid, mostly a steak house, but with enough haute cuisine to keep discriminating diners interested: entertainment for big shots with manners." *D Magazine* named it the "best new restaurant" in 1999.

The Palm, 701 Ross Ave. at Market St., (214) 698-0470, Internet www.thepalm.com. *E*. Open Mon-Thu 11:30 AM-10 PM, Fri 11:30 AM-10:30 PM, Sat 5 PM-10:30 PM, and Sun 5:30 PM-9:30 PM. It has a full bar. Wheelchair accessible. Provides valet parking. Reservations may be in order.

Located across Ross Avenue from the Tony Roma restaurant in the downtown's historic West End district. Next door to the Palm there once stood the old city jail.

The original Palm was started in New York City at 837 Second Avenue in 1926, and the 23-restaurant chain is now run by the grandsons of both founding partners.

The name Palm supposedly originates from the owners' native home of Parma, Italy, that was mispronounced in their Italian accent and translated into Palm. "Steaks and seafood were not part of the original concept of the Palm, but began out of an effort to cater to its clientele of artists and writers," informs the company's Web site.

The casual Dallas restaurant has been in the West End since 1983. With caricatures of notable entertainers, businessmen, and customers on the walls, it is usually busy and noisy. For high-power deals there is a private near-secret back room.

The tradition with the hundreds of caricatures you will see inside started with the lack of money by the original owners to promptly decorate a restaurant in a traditional way. King Features artist Jolly Bill Steinke supposedly spent so much of his free time at the Palm that he was often asked by other regulars to draw their caricatures.

You could start with clams, shrimp, or soup appetizer. The costliest steak is the prime aged porterhouse, followed by steak à la stone, filet mignon, prime aged New York strip, and prime rib of beef. There are lamb, pork, and veal chops, as well as chicken. The 26-ounce (or 737-gram) double New York strip for two costs $60 and is a house specialty.

Seafood entrées include broiled scallops and filet of sole. Pastas and veal dishes are also available. Vegetables are served à la carte. The Palm has an inventory of 3,000 bottles of wine, encompassing 150 selections of Cabernet Sauvignon, Chardonnay, Meritage, and Merlot.

The *Dallas Morning News*, which gives it four out of the possible five stars, notes that the Palm is "known for outstanding steaks, behemoth lobsters and good people-watching."

Ruth's Chris Steak House, 5922 Cedar Sprigs Rd. at Inwood Rd., (214) 902-8080, Internet www.ruthschris.com, e-mail rgwsizzlin@att.net. *E*. Open for dinner Sun-Thu 5 PM-10 PM, Fri-Sat 5 PM-11 PM. It has three private dining rooms accommodating up to 245. There is a cigar-friendly bar. Wheelchair accessible. Dress code is business casual. Reservations are suggested.

Located near the Love Field Airport, a couple of blocks southeast of Mockingbird Lane, and across the street from Weichsel Park.

Ruth's is an 80-plus restaurant chain based in Metairie, Louisiana, with annual sales of more than $300 million. The name stems from Ruth Fertel, a struggling single mother of two boys who in 1965 purchased Chris Steak House in New Orleans with the $18,000 she borrowed by mortgaging her house.

Ruth Udstad was born in New Orleans and at 19 earned a degree in chemistry from Louisiana State University, taught college briefly, and married. Fourteen years later, and by then divorced, she reentered the work force as a laboratory technician, but feared she would not be able to send her boys to college.

Fertel bought Chris Steak House in New Orleans through a classified advertisement, although having no business experience. She granted her first franchise in 1977 in Baton Rouge, Louisiana's capital. Her first Dallas restaurant opened in 1981.

Ruth's steaks are cooked in a high-temperature broiler at 1,800 degrees. "You can actually hear your steak coming from across the room," says Ruth's menu, and it sizzles with butter.

Unless your appetite is extraordinary, go straight for the steaks, which are so large you will not likely finish any one of them but with an effort. The most expensive cut is the T-bone U.S. prime beefsteak.

(Only 2 percent of all beef produced in the United States receives the prime designation, and it costs 20 to 30 percent more than choice, the next highest grade.) The porterhouse is a bit less.

They are followed by lamb chops, broiled filet mignon, New York strip steak, and broiled veal chop. Other entrées include the ribeye steak, lamb and veal chops, marinated chicken, fresh lobster, barbecued shrimp, salmon filet, and king crab legs.

Fresh lobster and king crab legs are priced upon your arrival, but you can order poached salmon filet and barbecued shrimp at set prices.

After all this, who has space for appetizers, some of which cost as much as, or more than, practically the entire meal at a chain restaurant. If you do, treat yourself to a dessert, such as the creamy homemade cheesecake served with fresh berries. By the time you have a bottle of wine uncorked, you might be thinking Chapter 13 bankruptcy. And Ruth's claims more than 100 wine selections, many from California, and an inventory of 1,500 bottles.

Gourmet magazine readers voted Ruth's one of the best Metroplex steakhouses.

Ruth Fertel was inducted into the exhibit, titled "How I Did It," at the **Women's Museum** (see entry) in Fair Park. For years a heavy smoker, she was found to have lung cancer in 2000 and died the following year at age 75. According to the Associated Press, "in 1999 she gave a lavish party to unveil the mausoleum she and a friend had bought for $500,000 in Lake Lawn Metairie Cemetery."

"She was a very classy example of the American dream," said former Louisiana governor Edwin Edwards, a frequent diner at Fertel's restaurants. She "catered to the good-old-boy network that flourishes in Louisiana, and from the beginning her restaurant attracted local politicians, as well as athletes, businessmen and reporters," notes the *New York Times*.

Another Ruth's Chris is located in far-north Dallas, at 17840 Dallas Pkwy., between Trinity Mills and Frankford, (972) 250-2244.

Tex-Mex

Monica's Aca y Alla, 2914 Main St. at Malcolm X Blvd., (214) 748-7140. M. Open for lunch daily 11 AM-2 PM, for dinner Mon-Thu 5 PM-10 PM, Fri-Sat 5 PM-midnight. Sat-Sun brunch is held 10 AM-3 PM. It has a bar. Wheelchair accessible. Live Latin jazz music Thu-Sat, salsa Sun nights. Located in Deep Ellum, just east of downtown Dallas.

"Depending on whom you ask, the best of this (Tex-Mex) cuisine is to be found at either Monica's Aca Y Alla or Sol's Taco Lounge," observes the *New York Times*. (Sol's Taco Lounge is located at 2626 Commerce St.) "Monica's is more upscale, Sol's is funkier."

Adds *D Magazine*: "The good news is that Monica's is also one of the best spots in Dallas for Mexican food, so make a night of it."

Monica's caters to a stylish crowd and features dishes as creative as spinach jalapeno fettuccine with chicken, roasted corn, and whole black beans. Most dishes on the menu are around $10 at lunch, Tuesday through Friday. There are good margaritas to be had here.

"The room can be insanely loud—especially Friday and Saturday nights, when it's downright deafening—but the high energy here is contagious," opines the *Dallas Morning News*. "Sit in the dining room at the peak of the evening and you can't help but feel like you're part of something happening."

The Mexico City-born owner, Monica Greene, who was Eduardo before a sex-change operation, greets guests when she is not standing watch at her newer restaurant, **Ciudad D.F.,** located at 3888 Oak Lawn Ave. and Irving Ave., (214) 219-3141, in the Oak Lawn neighborhood north of downtown. The popular four-star Ciudad serves dishes based on Mexico-City-style cuisine.

Children-Friendly Restaurants

With the exception of a handful of eateries that discourage very young children, few area establishments will turn them down. How many restaurants are children-friendly is, of course, open for discussion. The one name that comes to mind is **Luby's Cafeteria** (see listing).

We always thought of **Benihana** Japanese restaurants as meant mostly for adults, but magazine writers just cannot resist touting them as showplaces for kids. You decide whether they will entertain or bore yours. One Benihana is located in north Dallas, just south of the LBJ Freeway, at 7775 Banner Dr., (972) 387-4404.

If lots of noise and running around is more important than food to your 3-7-year-old, try one of the half-dozen locations of **Chuck E. Cheese,** Internet www.chuckecheese.com. But take your earplugs. CEC Entertainment, its parent, claims that more than two million children each year celebrate their birthday parties at one of its 400 entertainment spots nationwide.

CiCi's Pizza, Internet www.cicis.com, has locations all around town and comes perhaps the closest to being inexpensive and fun at the same time.

A restaurant name that writers local and national keep passing on as a godsend is **Dream Café,** 2800 Routh St. at Laclede, (214) 954-0486, Internet www.thedreamcafe.com. *Dallas Child* calls it "This trendy spot with family-friendly decor." Trendy for kids or their middle-class parents? I call it average.

While some, perhaps childless adults, rave about a patch of grass with a few plastic diversions, I call it scary because the area is entirely open, and a kid could run straight under a car or even disappear if the parents, lounging on plastic chairs, turned their backs on the offspring at the wrong time.

The *Fort Worth Star-Telegram* gushes about the Dream Café's "cloud-like, crepelike pancakes" and "tofu stir-fry and steamed vegetables."

Another Dream Café opened in the Village on the Parkway in Addison, at Belt Line and Dallas Parkway, and at least has an iron fence on the patio.

Magic Time Machine, 5003 Belt Line Rd., west of Dallas North Tollway, Addison, (972) 980-1903. Open Mon-Thu 5:30 PM-10 PM, Fri 4:30 PM-10:30 PM, Sat 11 AM-10:30 PM, Sun 11 AM-9 PM.

Servers are dressed in costumes, the tables are disguised as teepees or school buses, kids are encouraged to wander around. The Magic Time potions in various colors always seem a hit.

Dallas Child monthly magazine claims that **Purple Cow** restaurants have the "best kids' menu." In Dallas, there is one at 110 Preston Royal Shopping Center, at Preston Rd. and Royal Ln., (214) 373- 0037. It is open Sun-Thu 11 AM-9 PM, Fri-Sat 11 AM-10 PM.

Just as noisy is **Slider & Blues,** 8517 Hillcrest Rd. at West Northwest Hwy., (214) 696-8632, where the food is barely edible and the service equally passable. Adjoining the restaurant is a room full of video games, pinball machines, and an air-hockey table for children.

Next door to it is **Holy Smokes Barbecue,** 8611 Hillcrest, (214) 691-RIBS, not catering specifically to children, but a good option if Slider & Blues drives you to distraction. The *Dallas Morning News* and *D Magazine* both named it one of the ten best new restaurants of the year. "The margarita pie is a dandy," chimes in *Texas Monthly*.

A Comedy Venue

Addison Improv Comedy Theater & Restaurant, 4980 Belt Line Rd. at Quorum, Suite 250, Addison, (972) 404-8501, Internet www.improvclubs.com. *CH*. Restaurant opens two hours before the first performance. Wed-Thu shows start at 8:30 PM, Friday at 7 PM, Saturday at 8:30 PM and 11 PM, Sun 8:30 PM. You must be 21 to drink here.

Located west of Dallas North Tollway, between Hotel Inter-Continental Dallas and Marriott Quorum Dallas. Diagonally across Belt Line from here is Truluck's Steak & Stone Crab restaurant.

Addison Improv is part of a nationwide franchise and was started in 1988. You must be 21 years of age or older to be admitted.

The seating is on a first-come, first-served basis for all 8:30 PM shows. The seating for the 10:30 PM shows Fridays and Saturdays is pre-assigned in the order the tickets were purchased. There is a two-item minimum in any combination of food or beverages.

Among the performers here has been Rick Rockwell, who scandalized traditionalists as the title character in Fox's 2000 television program *Who Wants to Marry a Multi-Millionaire?* on which he married Darva Conger from among 50 women.

If you wish to eat inexpensively, but before 8:30 PM, consider Gilbert's New York Delicatessen, at 4930 Belt Line Rd., or behind the Addison Improv. The Gilberts, who once operated a restaurant on Long Island, New York, before moving to Dallas in 1987, will dazzle you with sandwiches that are "stacked insanely high with meat."

To sample Gilbert's "extraordinary" breakfasts, as judged by the *Dallas Morning News*, you will have to show up between 7 AM and 8:30 AM.

PERFORMING ARTS

Not many visitors come to Dallas for its cultural offerings, although you could do worse elsewhere. There is the symphony with a handsome downtown hall, the Fair Park opera house that Maria Callas put on the map, a dozen theaters scattered from Deep Ellum to Southern Methodist University, the summer Shakespeare festival, a couple of dance ensembles, and two ballet companies the city shares with Fort Worth.

Then there is the quadrennial Van Cliburn international piano competition in nearby Cowtown (as Fort Worth is often called) for those who like to speculate about who the next Horowitz might be.

Dallas's Office of Cultural Affairs is budgeted at around $12 million a year, about half of which goes to running and maintaining its facilities, from the Meyerson Symphony Center to the Music Hall in Fair Park. The OCA can be reached at (214) 670-3687, Internet www.dallasculture.org.

At a recent city council public hearing, "hundreds of arts purveyors and supporters turned out to denounce the proposed cuts" of up to $600,000 because of a multi-million-dollar shortfall in sales-tax revenues. The commotion surprised few who have lived in Dallas over the decades. As far back as 1942, the year when composer Sergey Rachmaninov gave a piano recital here, John Rosenfield, the *Dallas Morning News* amusement editor for 40 years, declared:

"The arts are to the human spirit what food is to the body. Dallas is one of the few important centers in which the fine arts are financed by persons who really don't care for them."

Your best bet to find out which events take place where and when is the "Guide," a tabloid-sized pullout section in the Friday *Dallas Morning News*. The *Dallas Observer* weekly also has a decent overview of the arts, and *D Magazine* carries articles monthly.

DANCE

If dance was once the Metroplex's weakest cultural link, things are looking up again since the birth of the Bruce Wood Dance Company.

As early as February 7, 1911, a large Dallas audience welcomed the famed ballerina Anna Pavlovna with the Imperial Russian Ballet. Since the Dallas Ballet was dissolved in 1988, and Ballet Dallas went out of business early in 1996, several ensembles worth mentioning were born.

One of the first local dance groups was the Dallas Civic Ballet, which was founded in 1957 with amateurs and students. It became the Dallas Ballet when the group turned professional in 1975. When the Dallas Ballet accumulated $1.8 million in debt over the next 12 years, the company went bankrupt. The following year, the Fort Worth Ballet began filling the Metroplex cultural void.

"In spite of small successes here and there and a modicum of critical acclaim, Dallas dance companies suffer half-full houses, skimpy seasons, and fickle audiences who would rather visit Texas Stadium every Sunday than watch ballet, tap, or modern dance on any day of the week," notes the *Dallas Observer*.

The Southern Methodist University Dance division, directed by Jeremy Blanton, a former principal dancer with the National Ballet of Canada, claims graduates who have joined the Dance Theatre of Harlem, Parsons Dance Company, Paul Taylor, and the talented Bruce Woods Dance Company in Fort Worth.

Ballet Arlington, 500 West Abram St., between Davis Dr. and Fielder Rd., Arlington, (817) 465-4644; ballet school, (817) 275-1000, Internet www.balletarlington.org.

A company formed in 1997 by Russian dancer Svetlana Stanova and her husband Nikolay Semikov, a former principal dancer with Moscow's Bolshoy Ballet. Ballet Arlington's repertoire ranges from 19th-century Russian classics to new works by a variety of choreographers. It is quickly becoming a premier Metroplex ballet company which "has captured the imagination of its community," claims the *Fort Worth Weekly*.

"I think Arlington is ready for a classical ballet company," former artistic director Stanova once told the *Dallas Morning News*. Her husband stood out at the Fort Worth Dallas Ballet, now renamed the Texas Ballet Theater (see entry), for his immensely authoritative interpretation of prince roles, a testament to the years of intensive schooling in style and character that Russians are noted for, observed the *News*.

Since then, the company has grown to nine full-time dancers, many of them Russians, such as Aleksandr Vetrov (b. 1960), a long-time dancer with the Bolshoy and since 2000 a principal dancer with Ballet Arlington. Vetrov, a decorated People's Artist of Russia, and his wife, Yelena Borisova, also a Bolshoy dancer, receive no insurance benefits in any of their multiple jobs they keep to survive and provide for their young son. Vetrov, who in 1985 was awarded the gold medal at the Fifth International Ballet Competition in Moscow, has toured in more than 50 countries.

Two former principal dancers of the San Francisco Ballet, the world-renowned San Sebastian, Spain-born ballerina Lucia Lacarra and Frenchman Cyril Pierre, a husband-and-wife team, joined the company in 2002. Lacarra won the biannual Nijinsky Award 2002 for best female dancer, which was established by Princess Caroline of Monaco and presented by Prince Albert. The ballerina is also a member of the Bayerisches Staatsballet in Munich, Germany. She and her husband performed at La Scala in Milan, Italy, and the World Ballet Festival in Japan.

The company, which employs 13 dancers on a 32-week contract annually, has a budget of less than $1 million and a season that lasts from September through June. Ballet Arlington, "an oasis of first-class dancing," in the words of the weekly *Dallas Observer,* can sell out performances at Fort Worth's Bass Performance Hall. In 1998, the Lima, Peru-born Paul Mejia (b. 1948), a former artistic director of the Fort Worth Dallas Ballet (see entry) joined the company as artistic adviser and was hired as executive director and the group's first full-time paid staffer two years later. Mejia and Vetrov were named as co-artistic directors in 2002.

Texas Chamber Orchestra of Carrollton, (817) 461-0318, e-mail info@texaschamberorchestra.org, is the official orchestra for Ballet Arlington.

The Bruce Wood Dance Company, Box 111, Fort Worth, 76101, (817) 926-9151, Internet www.brucedance.org, performs in Fort Worth and Dallas. Its studio occupies a former 4,200-square-foot (or 390-square-meter) grocery store in Fort Worth's Fairmount neighborhood south of downtown.

Founded in Austin in 1996, the company moved to Fort Worth the following year and has a budget of about $1 million a year. The troupe consists of nine dancers, including some from the Texas Ballet Theater (see entry) and focuses mostly on works by its founder. "It took the company about 15 minutes to leave all rivals in the dust," says the *Dallas Morning News*. "Mr. Wood has money and taste, evident in spare but striking stage designs and enormously assured choreography."

Its founder, Bruce Wood (b. 1961), the son of a Haltom City, Texas, high school football coach and an English teacher, graduated from Richland High School in Fort Worth. He began dancing at 15 and performed classical, jazz, and modern dance as a soloist with the San Francisco Ballet, principal dancer with Le Ballet Jazz de Montreal, and the Twyla Tharp Dance Company. By age 30, he was burned out and returned to Texas to raise horses in Wise County. He worked in Fort Worth for a pharmaceutical company and as a free-lance art director in Austin. Wood tried his hand at choreography and soon warmed up to the idea of having his own company.

In 1998 and 1999, the company won over the Metroplex critics, but had no financial backing until its "guardian angel" Rosalyn Rosenthal "wrote the check that saved the company." Among the company's recent performances was Maurice Ravel's *Bolero*, although Wood's version "plays on alienation more than sexual satisfaction," according to the *Fort Worth Star-Telegram*. "Never afraid to take risks, Mr. Wood threw caution to the wind with *Bolero*, a work that begs for trouble," observes the *News*. "Somehow he got it right—the intensity that builds, the sexual overtones, the frenzy."

"Just when you thought you'd had it up to here with Ravel's bouncy war horse, Bolero, choreographer Bruce Wood comes along and blows preconceived notions and calloused cliches out of the water," says the *Los Angeles Times* admiringly, adding, "Wood needn't worry—he's welcome in this town anytime."

Dallas Black Dance Theatre, 2627 Flora St., (214) 871-2376; tickets, 871-2390 or Preston Center box office, 691-7200, Internet www.dbdt.com. Performances are given at the Majestic Theatre located in downtown Dallas.

Founded in 1976 by its artistic director Ann M. Williams—who modeled her company on the internationally acclaimed Alvin Ailey Dance Theater—this is the area's oldest continuously operating professional dance company.

Ailey (b. 1931), born in Rogers, Texas, was a talented African-American dancer who grew up in rural Texas. He formed the Alvin Ailey American Dance Theatre in 1958 and exploded on the New York stage with his inventive choreography. When Williams met Ailey in 1968 at Bishop College, where she founded the dance program, he suggested that she never have more than 16 dancers so they could travel.

On a hot summer night in 1986, Williams (b. 1937) was hit in her car by a drunken driver on North Central Expressway and suffered severe injuries to her legs. After two months in the hospital and three operations, she moved from a wheelchair to crutches. By December of that year, Williams appeared in public again, on crutches, at the premiere of the new ballet, *Deep Ellum Blues*. She requires her dancers to have a college education.

Her ensemble is a contemporary company of professional dancers with a mixed repertory of modern, jazz, ethnic, and spiritual works. It consists of a dozen African-American, Hispanic, Anglo-American, and Italian-American dancers. The troupe, "it seems, has built a bridge between populism and elitism," opines the *Dallas Observer*. "It maintains all the trappings of a professional dance company while still giving its audiences an approachable art form set to popular music."

The Dallas Black Dance Company performed at the 1996 Olympic

Games in Atlanta, Georgia, the first and only Texas arts group to participate in the history of modern games. In 2000, it participated at the Harare International Festival of the Arts in Zimbabwe. Two years later, the company performed at the U.S. ambassador to Ireland Independence Day gala. The troupe, which operates on an annual budget of almost $1 million, has also toured Austria, Mexico, Great Britain, South Africa, Spain, Italy, Peru, and Ireland. "A lot of my dancers feel we get better support outside the city of Dallas than we do inside the city," the founder was once quoted as saying.

When, in 1996, the famed Martha Graham Dance Company performed in El Paso, Texas, within a week of the Dallas Black Dance Theatre's performance, the *El Paso Times* dance critic opined that "this performance was better. The [Dallas Black Dance Theatre] company has more depth and soul than most and rates up there with the best of companies in terms of dance mastery and expertise."

The Dallas Black Dance Company bought the old Moorland YMCA building on Flora Street, a turn-of-the-century structure downtown, for $1.4 million. The renovation of its new home, with the help of a city bond issue, is expected to be completed in 2004.

Texas Ballet Theater/Fort Worth Dallas Ballet, 6845 Green Oaks Rd., Fort Worth, (817) 763-0207. Situated in Fort Worth, but claiming the entire Metroplex as its home. Dallas performances are usually given at the Majestic Theatre (see entry) and the Music Hall in Fair Park. In Fort Worth, the ballet's stage is the Bass Performance Hall.

The Fort Worth Ballet was founded in 1961 as a civic troupe and reorganized as a professional ballet organization in 1985. It added Dallas to its name in 1995. The company has performed throughout Texas, as well as in Chicago, New York, Washington, D.C., Japan, and Taiwan.

In part as a result of the September 11, 2001, terrorist bombings, the company's budget was reduced to less than $5 million and the number of dancers to 30, several of them married to each other. Their pay is miserable for 30 weeks of performing, although they do get health insurance and long-term disability insurance.

The troupe includes Enrica Guana Tseng, the Italian-born principal female dancer who has won critical raves since arriving in Fort Worth in 1998. She is the wife of the Taiwanese-born Tseng Chung-Lin, who began his dancing career as a figure skater in Taiwan. They met while both were dancing in the Universal Ballet Company in Seoul, South Korea.

After the demise of Ballet Dallas in 1996, both Dallas and Fort Worth claimed the company as their own, naming it Fort Worth Dallas Ballet until 2003. The troupe performs to music that ranges from Albinoni to Stravinsky.

In 2002, before a group of private donors gave it $1.3 million, the company faced a $700,000 deficit. Also that year, the company hired the Portsmouth, England-born Ben Stevenson, then artistic director of the Houston Ballet. He was once the principal dancer with the London Festival Ballet. His ballets have been staged by the English National Ballet, the Paris Opera Ballet, the National Ballet of Canada, and La Scala in Milan. In 1999, Queen Elizabeth II named Stevenson an officer of the Order of the British Empire in recognition of his achievements in dance.

In his 27 years in Houston, Stevenson (b. 1936) "transformed a small company into a national powerhouse, staging imaginative productions and nurturing talents," according to the *Dallas Morning News*. "We can count our blessings that a figure of his stature is willing to come in," noted the *Fort Worth Star-Telegram*.

MUSIC

Dallas is a regular stop for many of the world's finest classical and jazz musicians, singers, and chamber groups.

While the Dallas Symphony Orchestra does not command the respect of a first-tier American orchestra, you will find its concerts an enjoyable experience and its program varied enough to satisfy your thirst for the classics.

In 1960, when the Dallas metropolitan area had a population of 1.1 million, the Dallas area had only the Dallas Symphony Orchestra, four decades later, with a population approaching four times the previous number, there are at least ten other orchestras and several other, smaller musical groups.

Morton H. Meyerson Symphony Center, 2301 Flora St. at North Pearl, (214) 871-4000, Internet www.dallassymphony.com. For tickets call the box office, (214) 692-0203, or go to the lower level of the symphony center Mon-Sat 10 AM-6 PM. Tickets are also available on-line, but must be requested at least 24 hours in advance. The Symphony performs from August through May, Thu-Sat starting at about 8 PM, Sunday matinees at 2:30 PM.

Located in the Arts District downtown, across the street from Cathedral Santuario de Guadalupe and two blocks from the Dallas Museum of Art (see individual listings). The Arts District came about in 1979, when the citizens voted to set aside 60 acres (or 24 hectares) in downtown Dallas for the arts and culture. The Dallas Museum of Art emerged at one end of the district, while the Dallas Theater Center (see listing) began operating the Arts District Theater. Meanwhile, the

Dallas Symphony Association began the site selection for its future home, which at that time was still in Fair Park.

Conceived when the Dallas economy was booming, it was completed when Texas real estate went to the dogs. Violin virtuoso Isaac Stern inaugurated the new symphony center on September 6, 1989. More than 100 architectural proposals from all over the world, including Philip Johnson's, were considered, but the well-regarded I. M. Pei received the commission. This was Pei's first concert hall. Dallas billionaire and a two-time presidential candidate, Ross Perot Sr., contributed $12 million to the $80 million already spent to insure that the new hall met international standards. His gift made possible the limestone cladding, travertine marble floors, and mahogany paneling inside the hall. Perot earned the honor of naming the facility after his business colleague, Morton H. Meyerson, who headed the concert hall planning committee, although he could have named it after his own family.

The concert hall also houses a $2-million, 4,535-pipe organ donated by the Lay family and built by the Gloucester, Massachusetts, firm of C. B. Fisk. It is "one of the finest organs in the world, rich-toned and amazingly versatile," according to the *Dallas Morning News*.

"A decade after its opening, it remains the only modern orchestra hall, at least in North America, to replicate the acoustical sumptuousness of such 19th century gems as Musikvereinssaal in Vienna and the Concertgebouw in Amsterdam," notes the *News*.

"While other cities are passing the hat to rescue their symphonies, Dallas is dining on musical caviar," once gushed a writer in the *San Antonio Express-News*. "If the acoustically perfect Morton H. Meyerson Symphony Center says anything, it is that Dallas demands the best."

"Unfortunately," observes *D magazine*, "Pei's boxlike Meyerson and Barnes' cool, low-set Museum of Art [see entry] do not lend a welcoming presence to the neighborhood." The monthly quotes an out-of-town architect as saying, "The overall impression that's communicated is that these are temples, and the laity is not welcome to enter."

"It doesn't help the DSO that, for all its architectural and sonic qualities, the Meyerson isn't the most welcoming facility," observes a *News* classical music reviewer, continuing, "walled off from busy Pearl Street, secluded among cypress trees, it can seem unfriendly, a place of secret rites." There is no sign outside the hall telling you what the program is on any day.

The history of the **Dallas Symphony Orchestra** (DSO) goes back to May 22, 1900, when Dallas' population was about 43,000 and a 40-member ensemble performed for the first time under the direction of the German-born conductor Hans Kreissig (1856-1929) at Turner Hall, at Harwood and Young Streets.

The orchestra was a bunch of amateurs, officially known as the Dallas Symphony Club, which played music by Haydn, Rossini, and Wagner. A German-born pianist and conductor, Kreissig came to Dallas with a touring London opera company in 1883 and started teaching piano here the following year. In 1886, he was offered $30 a month and guaranteed a dozen private students should he remain as conductor.

Kreissig led these amateurs for five seasons until he could form the first Dallas Symphony Orchestra in 1900. At one time, he "trod the streets of Dallas, going from merchant to merchant and soliciting funds" for his musical projects, according to the Texas State Historical Association.

"Most of the musicians were competent, some were even excellent," he claimed. "But we just couldn't make Dallas take us seriously."

Kreissig was succeeded by two other Germans, Walter J. Fried and Cologne, Germany-born Carl Venth. Fried came from Milwaukee, where he was a violin teacher, in 1905, and conducted a series of concerts in the City Hall auditorium.

In 1925, Dr. Paul van Katwijk, for 30 years the dean of music at Southern Methodist University, assumed the directorship and took the orchestra to the Dallas Music Hall in Fair Park. However, by 1936, rehearsals had been trimmed as a result of growing financial problems of the Great Depression. "For nearly two years the Dallas Symphony Orchestra was not heard, except for the three concerts in the Fair Park bandshell," notes Dallas cultural historian Ronald L. Davis.

The Austrian-born Jacques Singer succeeded van Katwijk in 1938. In 1945, the Dallas Symphony Orchestra came under the direction of the well-known Budapest-born conductor Antal Dorati, while the principal cellist was the renowned Janos Starker. Dorati "was appalled by the dilapidated state of Fair Park Auditorium and insisted on some retouching before the orchestra's opening performance." He enlarged the symphony's season from 16 to 22 weeks. Under him, the orchestra reached the heights some believe it has never since surpassed. Maestro Dorati stayed for three years, then moved on to lead the Minneapolis Symphony Orchestra for eleven years, replacing Dimitri Mitropoulos.

From the 1930s until 1989, the Dallas Symphony performed in the "cramped and airless" McFarlin Auditorium at Southern Methodist University and at the Fair Park Music Hall, which became its home in 1973.

Dorati was followed by not-yet-33-years-old Walter Hendl, an assistant conductor of the New York Philharmonic for four years. An accomplished musician and a concert pianist, he led the orchestra from 1949 to 1958, then left to head the Eastman School of Music in Rochester, New York.

In the autumn of 1951, the Dallas Symphony left the State Fair Auditorium for McFarlin Auditorium on the campus of Southern Methodist University and stayed for five years. In 1952, Van Cliburn, an 18-year-old Texas pianist who six years later would win the Tchaikovsky International Competition in Moscow, performed MacDowell's Second Piano Concerto at McFarlin.

The Polish-born maestro Paul Kletzki (1900-1973), who gained his Swiss citizenship through marriage, came in 1958 and stayed for about three years. His "audiences frequently were moved to cheers and standing ovations by the depth of his interpretations of Beethoven, Brahms, Schumann, and Mendelssohn."

In 1977, Mexican-born Eduardo Mata (b. 1942) was appointed music director and conductor of the orchestra for the next 17 years. Mata founded the University of Mexico orchestra, conducted the Guadalajara Symphony Orchestra, and led the Phoenix orchestra from 1975 until his Dallas appointment.

Under him, the Dallas Symphony made its first European tour, to London, Paris, Berlin, Stuttgart, Frankfurt, Madrid, and Barcelona and released several recordings. When Mata retired in 1993, he had the longest tenure as music director in the orchestra's history. He died in 1995, while piloting his private airplane in Mexico.

In 1994, the New York native Andrew Litton (b. 1959) succeeded Mata. He trained in piano and conducting at the Juilliard School, where the notoriously intense violinist Nadja Salerno-Sonnenberg occasionally threw her bow at Litton who played piano in a trio that included her.

Litton studied conducting at the Salzburg Mozarteum and served one season as assistant conductor at Milan's Teatro alla Scala, then joined the Washington, D.C., National Symphony Orchestra as assistant conductor to music director Mstislav Rostropovich. He became principal conductor of the Bournemouth Symphony Orchestra in 1988 and led it until coming to Dallas. His contract runs through the 2005-2006 concert season. Litton's British-born wife, Jayne, was a violinist with the Bournemouth Symphony.

Beginning in the fall of 2003, Litton also became principal conductor and artistic adviser of the 230-plus-year-old Bergen Philharmonic Orchestra in Norway. The Bergen orchestra is one of Europe's oldest, going back to 1765, and counts among its conductors the composer Edvard Grieg. Litton is the first American to head the Norwegian orchestra.

"Mr. Litton presides over an orchestra that has probably never sounded so good," claimed in 2001 the *Dallas Morning News*, whose classical music critic could not resist inflating the players's mastery to "world-class." His hearing "the DSO in close proximity to legendary counterparts in Philadelphia and Cleveland suggested that Dallas suffers only a little in comparison. Philadelphia has a more sumptuous string sound, Cleveland a more silken sheen, and both perhaps a little more expressive subtlety."

The Pulitzer Prize-winning critic Martin Bernheimer observes that "His [Litton's] interpretations are usually notable for clarity and energy, not for profundity of sensitivity." Adds the *News*: "Mr. Litton's DSO is a trophy bride, flashily coiffed and dressed but well behaved. She isn't going to ask us any hard questions or take us anywhere we haven't been before."

The orchestra, which numbers some 95 players and is the eighth oldest in the United States, has had several Carnegie Hall appearances under Litton. Observed the *New York Times* about its 1999 Carnegie concert: "Mr. Litton drove its players into frenzies of sound. My eardrums have not buzzed so much since the time I forgot to take my sound-filtering earplugs to a Sting concert," then adds, "But it was undeniably exciting."

The DSO made its third, 19-day, $1.4-million tour of four European countries in 2000, flying practically free courtesy of American Airlines. In Stockholm's half-filled 1,800-seat Konserthuset, "the clapping seemed more polite than genuinely exultant" following Aaron Copland's Third Symphony. At the end of the orchestra's performance of Shostakovich's Tenth Symphony in the London suburb of Basingstoke, two days later, "the explosion of applause came as a communal catharsis, and it went on and on," reported the *News*' critic who had traveled with the orchestra.

"I have not heard a more honest or moving account," of Shostakovich "at this year's Proms," wrote the *London Times* critic following DSO's performance at the Royal Albert Hall the following day, while the daily *Independent* called it "one of the low points of the season. Shopping-mall Shostakovich."

It was followed by a performance of Dvorak's Cello Concerto in Birmingham, England, where the DSO and cellist Lynn Harrell were again greeted by "the house [that] was only half full," according to the *News*. Then it was on to Lucerne, Switzerland, where the orchestra played at the Culture and Congress Centre Concert Hall. In Germany, they gave concerts in Nurenberg, Munich, Bremen, and Frankfurt.

In 2003, DSO undertook a $1.3-million, 17-day tour of Berlin, Frankfurt, Munich, Innsbruck, Vienna, London, Birmingham, and Edinburgh. American Airlines, then on the verge of bankruptcy, was flying 143 players and their support staff with nearly five tons of equipment, back and forth across the Atlantic, again for free.

In Berlin the orchestra played in the 2,400-seat Philharmonie, the hall of the Berlin Philharmonic, "only about half full," but "there were bravos and whistles aplenty, and applause went on and on," according to the *News*. [In Firebird Suite] "Stravinsky's weightless fairytale style became a greasy Kentucky Fried Chicken," opined daily *Der Taggesspiegel* of Berlin.

"We don't want to endanger the tender seedlings of German-American friendship yet again, but these Texans really are full of themselves sometimes," noted the *Frankfurter Rundschau* about the DSO's Frankfurt concert, adding that the orchestra was "making a striking, marvelous noise" in the Alter Oper hall "without really saying very much at all."

While the Rachmaninoff and Tchaikovsky "got warm applause and a healthy chorus of bravos" in the "drab early 1970s convention center" in Innsbruck, Austria, "the DSO has yet to get a standing ovation," reported the *News* correspondent, while the *Tiroler Tageszeitung* daily observed that "the Dallas ensemble proved itself to be a homogeneous, sensitive and very thoughtful body of musicians that does not rush away unchecked when playing the Russian composers."

In Vienna's Great Hall of the Musikverein, where Brahms, Mahler, and Strauss had conducted, the DSO "got an enthusiastic response from one of the toughest audiences anywhere —curtain call after curtain call and plenty of bravos," noted the *News*. During rehearsal, "Andrew Litton had tears in his eyes as soon as he conducted his first measures in the hall," so overcome was he by the acoustics.

The orchestra received "enthusiastic reception" at Royal Festival Hall in London, but "filled barely a fourth of the 2,000-seat hall" in Edinburgh, Scotland. The *London Times* critic said about a London concert, "The night's finale was a powerful reading of Stravinsky's Firebird Suite, and the excitement continued."

The DSO has a dozen CDs recorded with Litton, most of them with the Hollywood-based Delos label. The orchestra has a budget of more than $22 million, in budgetary terms one of the top-ten American orchestras.

In 2002, Dr. Fred Bronstein took over as president of the Dallas Symphony Association. His predecessor, Detroit-born Eugene Bonelli (1934), who had served for five years as dean of the Meadows School of the Arts at Southern Methodist University, held the job since 1993. A Boston native, Dr. Bronstein (b. 1957) holds a doctor of musical arts degree in piano from the State University of New York at Stony Brook.

Dallas Bach Society, 6202 East Mockingbird Ln., (214) 320-8700, Internet www.dallasbach.org.

The society specializes in baroque and classical period music. Through it, American and foreign musicians bring public performances of Handel, Bach, Vivaldi, and Mozart to the following venues in the

Metroplex: Church of the Incarnation on McKinney Avenue in Uptown, Meyerson Symphony Center downtown, Church of the Transfiguration on Hillcrest Road in north Dallas, Mesquite Arts Center in Plano, and Perkins Chapel on the Southern Methodist University campus.

James Richman, a graduate of the Juilliard School and Curtis Institute of Music, is the society's artistic director and harpsichordist. A prizewinner in four international competitions for harpsichord and fortepiano, he was knighted by the French government in the Ordre des Arts et des Lettres for his contributions in music. Richman has appeared at Spoleto USA, the Boston Early Music Festival, and the Mostly Mozart Festival in New York's Lincoln Center.

Dallas Chamber Orchestra, Sammons Center for the Arts, 3630 Harry Hines Blvd., (214) 321-1411, Internet www.dallaschamberorchestra.org. Located east of Infomart, at Harry Hines Boulevard and Oak Lawn Avenue, in a historic landmark building that sat idle for 50 years as the site of the former Turtle Creek Pump Station, which operated from 1910 to the 1930s.

The DCO was founded in 1977 and is still led by its founding director and violinist, Ronald Neal. Initially, the group performed as the resident orchestra of the Highland Park Presbyterian Church and was known as the Highland Park Chamber Orchestra. As it became more widely known and attracted patrons outside Highland Park, it changed its name to the Dallas Chamber Orchestra. Among its alumni is John Sharp, principal cellist of the Chicago Symphony.

The DCO is in part funded by the city of Dallas. It usually gives eleven concerts from September through May at various locations, including Southern Methodist University. The repertoire includes Bach, Handel, Corelli, and Mozart.

"For quarter of a century the Dallas Chamber Orchestra has been playing music that the bigger Dallas Symphony Orchestra largely ignores," observes the *Dallas Morning News*. "The difference is scale, not quality, for the composers are often the same."

"An ensemble of notable refinement and artistry," *High Fidelity Musical America* calls it.

Dallas Chamber Music Society, 6140 Dilbeck Ln. at Preston Rd., (972) 392-3267 or (214) 526-7301, Internet www.dcms.us. Located north of downtown Dallas and east of Valley View Mall (see listing).

The Chamber Music Society is, following the Dallas Symphony Orchestra, the second oldest continuing civic music organization in Dallas. It presents five concerts each season. They are usually held on Monday nights in Caruth Auditorium, at Southern Methodist

University, where you can also hear the school's all-student Meadows Symphony Orchestra. Established in 1947, it has hosted some of the most prestigious chamber ensembles, including the Beaux Arts trios, the Amadeus, Bartok, Budapest, Borodin, Emerson, Guarneri, Julliard, and Shostakovich quartets, and the octet of the Berlin Philharmonic.

Dallas Classic Guitar Society, Post Office Box 190823, Dallas 75219, (214) 528-3733. The society grew out of the efforts of students and professionals interested in classical guitar music in the 1960s and was formalized in 1977.

The society presents its concerts at Caruth Auditorium on the campus of Southern Methodist University and at the Meyerson Symphony Center downtown. Some of the world's greatest classical guitarists—such as Andres Segovia—have performed here through the society. The season runs from September through April.

Eisemann Center for Performing Arts, 2351 Performance Dr., Richardson, (972) 744-4600, Internet www.eisemanncenter.com. Located northeast of downtown Dallas, in Galatyn Park Urban Center, north of Campbell Road and east of Central Expressway, along Richardson's Telecom Corridor. A DART light-rail station opened here in 2002.

The $42-million, 53,500-square-foot (or 4,970-square-meter) center, funded mostly through hotel taxes, is owned by the city of Richardson. Among the tenants in the Eisemann Center is the Richardson Symphony Orchestra, which gives concerts at the 1,550-seat, 14,600-square-foot (or 1,356-square-meter) two-level, Margaret & Al Hill Performance Hall, whose family donated land that was valued at more than $1 million. The farthest seat in the Hill Hall is a mere 90 feet (or 27.4 meters) from the stage. The center was designed by architect Eurico Francisco of RTKL Associates in Dallas and inaugurated in 2002. "It is bold, contemporary and every bit the civic showpiece that city officials have been hoping for," opines the architecture critic of the *Dallas Morning News*.

Richardson Symphony, "the grandmother of Dallas-area suburban orchestras," founded in 1961, gives about half a dozen concerts annually under the baton of Anshel Brusilow, the former musical director of the Dallas Symphony Orchestra. He also teaches conducting at the University of North Texas in Denton.

Margaret Hunt Hill (b. 1916) is the oldest child of oilman Haroldson Lafayette Hunt and a Dallas philanthropist. She and her husband, developer Albert Galatyn Hill, were married for 50 years until he died in 1988. Albert Galatyn's family developed a portion of the Telecom Corridor and donated land for major roadways. His family traces its roots back to Albert Gallatin, the longest-serving Secretary of the Treasury (1801-1814), who was appointed by Thomas Jefferson. Gallatin helped negotiate the Treaty of Ghent, which ended the War of 1812, and was the founder of New York University.

The performance hall is one of three sections of the Eisemann Center complex. The other two include a smaller 5,960-square-foot (or 554-square-meter), shoe-box-shaped, 350-seat facility for theater and dance, and a 3,150-square-foot (or 293-square-meter) meeting hall. Backstage support areas include more than a dozen dressing, performers', and wardrobe rooms. The center was named for a Richardson banker, Charles W. Eisemann, and his wife who have lived here since 1971 and who donated $2 million for the naming rights. Born in 1940 in San Antonio, Eisemann grew up in the Alamo City and earned a master's degree in business administration from the University of Texas.

In addition to the Eisemann Center and the light-rail station, the Galatyn urban center includes a 15-story, 335-room, full-service Marriott Renaissance Hotel, a two-acre (or 0.8-hectare) public plaza, and a 12-acre (or 4.85-hectare) mixed-use development site. The 500-acre (or 202-hectare) center was developed in a partnership with Hunt Petroleum, Dallas Area Rapid Transit (DART), and the city of Richardson. Galatyn Park, is already the third largest office park in the Metroplex, after Las Colinas in Irving and Park in Plano.

Latino Cultural Center, 2600 Live Oak St. at Good-Latimer Expwy., (214) 670-3320, Internet www.dallasculture.com/latinocc. Located in northeastern downtown Dallas, across the street from the Live Oak Lofts. Completed in 2003, the $9.8-million center is a focal point for Hispanic heritage and culture, showcasing plays, musical performances, dance, and art that had been scattered across the city.

The city-owned 27,000-square-foot (or 2,508-square-meter) center includes an art gallery, a 400-seat performance hall, classrooms, and a 75-foot (or 22.8-meter) landmark tower. A cylindrical 25-foot (or 7.6-meter) mural printed on flexible plastic, created by the El Paso-born Latino artists Celia Alvarez Munoz (b. 1937) and her daughter, is on display inside.

Built on the 3.5 acres (or 1.41 hectares) of land donated by the Meadows Foundation, the center was drafted by the noted Mexican architect Ricardo Legorreta (b. 1931), who had also designed the enchilada-red San Antonio Public Library. He first gained recognition for a resort hotel that he designed for the Camino Real chain in Mexico in 1968, where "guests must often walk 15 minutes through a labyrinth to reach their" rooms.

"When Tom Monaghan, owner of the Domino Pizza company, first saw the newly built cathedral in the Nicaraguan capital of Managua, which he had helped to fund, he wept," claims the *London Financial Times* about the effect that the 1993 Legorreta structure could have on those seeing it for the first time.

"A committed modernist, Mr. Legorreta is never doctrinaire or humorless," observes the *Dallas Morning News* architectural critic. The American Institute of Architects honored Legorreta with its 2000 Gold Medal, a top annual architectural award, for "connecting the past to the future using his own inventive and innovative approach." He was the first Mexican and only the 11th architect from outside the United States to receive the award.

In 1995, Dallas voters approved $3.5 million for the center as part of a bond package, with the remaining funds coming from private sources. When the latter were not forthcoming, Guinness United Distillers offered the city $1 million for the right to name its 300-seat theater as the Jose Cuervo Performance Hall. Some council members were not happy with associating Latino culture with tequila and talked the Oak Farms Dairy into coughing up the needed million dollars. Oak Farms is part of Dallas-based Dean Foods, the nation's largest processor of dairy products.

Patty Granville Arts Center, 300 North Fifth St. at Austin St., Garland, (972) 205-2785. Located in downtown Garland, one block from the city hall and a bit farther from the Plaza Theatre (see entry). A DART light-rail station is nearby.

The original 30,000-square-foot (or 2,787-square-meter) center opened in 1982. It was renamed in 2003 for Patty Granville Holcomb, director of the arts center since its opening. She was one of the founders of the Garland Summer Musicals. A $6.2-million expansion added the Atrium at the Arts Center and a banquet hall that seats 500 in 2003. It also enlarged the former Performing Arts Center with spacious lobbies and new box office areas.

Plaza Theatre, 521 West State St. at Sixth, Garland, (972) 205-2782, box office 205-2790. Auditorium seats about 345. Located in downtown Garland, northeast of downtown Dallas.

The original art deco building on the town square dates back to 1918, when it opened as a dry-goods store. It was inaugurated as a theater on April 4, 1941, with the premiere of the film *Western Union* that starred Robert Young and Randolph Scott. During the 1970s, the Plaza became a country-music dance hall known as the Texas Opera House. Its current facade was designed by Dallas architect Jack Grogan in 1950. The theater operated as a first-run cinema until the 1970s, then declined with the changing times. After the owner's death, the trustee of the estate donated the one-story Plaza Theatre to the city in 1991.

The Plaza underwent a $1.2-million restoration and reopened in 2001. It augments the Performing Arts Center's 200- and 700-seat theaters nearby.

Sammons Center for the Arts, 3630 Harry Hines Blvd., (214) 520-3121/7788, Internet www.sammonscenter.org. Located east of Infomart, between Harry Hines and Dallas North Tollway, in a historic landmark building that sat idle for 50 years as the site of the former Turtle Creek Pump Station, the oldest public building in Dallas.

The original 1909 building, designed by C. A. Gill, served as the city water department's primary pump station that handled more than 15 million gallons of water each day. The station was the sole source of water for the city of Dallas from 1909 to 1930, and the pump station building was retired from active service in 1954. In 1981, when it became an official historic landmark, the city-owned building was reconstructed into a multipurpose arts facility that opened in 1988.

The nonprofit center is home to a dozen Dallas nonprofit arts organizations, such as the Dallas Chamber Orchestra, Fine Arts Chamber Players, Dallas Jazz Orchestra, Turtle Creek Chorale, and Shakespeare Festival of Dallas (see entry). More than twice as many organizations also use the center for rehearsals, auditions, and performances. Sammons Center also hosts an annual jazz festival.

The neoclassical building, which features 19,000 square feet (or 1,765 square meters) of office, rehearsal, and performing space, is named in honor of the late millionaire Charles A. Sammons (d. 1988), the principal benefactor of the center. Orphaned at 11, Sammons made his fortune in insurance and cable television, and was one of the 400 wealthiest Americans in the late 1980s. The nuclear medicine center at Baylor Medical Center also bears his name.

Symphony Park, located between Preston Rd. & Ohio Dr., north of Spring Creek Pkwy., Plano.

A 27-acre (or 10.9-hectare) development, eight acres (or 3.23 hectares) of which are occupied by a performing arts center, which includes the Plano Repertory Theatre (see listing), Plano Symphony, and other arts groups, it is scheduled to be completed in 2005. Until then, the Plano Symphony has moved its concerts to Richardson's Eisemann Center for Performing Arts (see entry).

The Repertory Theatre was established in 1975. The symphony orchestra, which is led by Hector Guzman, who is also in charge of the Irving Symphony, goes back to 1962, numbers some 35 musicians, and gives nine concerts a year. Fresnillo, Mexico-born Guzman (b. 1956) has been a student of two former Dallas Symphony Orchestra music directors, Anshel Brusilow, who now directs the Richardson Symphony

Orchestra, and his late countryman Eduardo Mata, also a close friend. Guzman also studied in Siena, Italy, under Carlo Maria Giulini.

The office and retail development is to include four retail and restaurant buildings and two office buildings.

Turtle Creek Chorale, Morton H. Meyerson Symphony Center, 2301 Flora St. at North Pearl, (214) 526-3214 or (800) 746-4412, Internet www.turtlecreek.org.

A Dallas-based, all-male chorus that was formed in 1980. Today, the singing membership has grown to 225 and a staff of 15. The chorus has toured the United States; sung in Barcelona, Berlin, and Prague; and made two dozen recordings. Dr. Timothy Seelig, who holds a doctorate in music from the University of North Texas, has been its artistic director since 1987. Dr. Seelig is also the artistic director of the Women's Chorus of Dallas, which originated in 1989 and numbers more than 100 singers. The TCC performs an annual four-concert subscription series that includes works such as Carl Orff's *Carmina Burana.*

The eleventh **Van Cliburn International Piano Competition,** which is held every four years, took place in June 2001 at Bass Performance Hall in Fort Worth.

Van Cliburn, actually born in Louisiana, was an unknown pianist from Kilgore, Texas, until he appeared with the Dallas Symphony in 1952. On April 14, 1958, he won, against all odds, the first International Tchaikovsky Piano Competition in Moscow, although Nikita Khrushchev himself had to approve the award going to the young capitalist. Cliburn (b. 1934) was the first classical musician to be honored with a ticker tape parade through downtown New York.

The Van Cliburn competition began in 1962 to honor the pianist for his Moscow success. It is considered one of the "world's great music contests," according to the *Dallas Morning News.* Thirty finalists from an original field of more than 100 compete for the prize valued at more than $250,000, a début recital at Carnegie Hall in New York, and two seasons of tours and recordings.

Olga Kern of Russia and Stanislav Ioudenitch of Uzbekistan both won gold medals in 2001, along with $20,000 each, two years of U.S. and international concert engagements, and recordings on the Harmonia Mundi label. Muscovite Kern (b. 1975) was the first woman to win a Van Cliburn gold medal since 1969, when Brazilian Cristina Ortiz won a similar honor.

"Her bulldozing of the Schumann Piano Quintetin the semifinal round was a disgrace," noted the *News.* "But she's a player of enormous brilliance and passion, and one who whips audiences into frenzies, and her final performance of the Rachmaninoff Third Piano Concerto was stunning." Kern was eliminated after the preliminaries of the tenth competition in 1997.

"Mr. Ioudenitch, by contrast, is a musician of aristocratic elegance and imagination," noted the *News*. Ioudenitch (b. 1972), had to abandon his quest four years earlier, during semifinals, because he burned his hand making tea in the home of his Fort Worth host.

Maksim Philippov of Russia and Antonio Pompa-Baldi of Italy both won silver medals. No bronze medal was awarded.

Media coverage of the 2001 Van Cliburn was shabby even by the already lowered Metroplex standards. Local NBC affiliate, KXAS-TV, Channel 5, which is headquartered in Fort Worth, ran an itsy-bitsy item about the gold medalists as its third news segment—following news about the escape of an elephant from the Denver zoo.

The twelfth competition will be held in 2004. Call (817) 738-6536 or check the Internet site www.cliburn.org. WTCU-FM (88.7), the Texas Christian University radio station, broadcasts most performances.

Cliburn was one of the first 13 recipients of the state-sponsored Texas Medal of the Arts in 2001, when, for once, the arts triumphed over gaudy entertainment pretending to be art. "This is for real artists," noted emcee Dan Rather, a Texas-born national television anchor. "No stubble-bearded, whiskey-breathed, running-around-with-his-shirt-tails-out reporter ought to be thought of in the same way."

That same year, Van Cliburn—along with the Italian singer Luciano Pavarotti, music producer Quincy Jones, and actors Julie Andrews and Jack Nicholson—was also honored by the Kennedy Center in Washington, D.C., for his lifetime contribution to American culture. President and Laura Bush attended the event and hosted a reception for the honorees at the White House.

"If any sour note was sounded over the weekend, it was by the *Washington Post* music critic, who wrote in Sunday's paper that Cliburn had peaked by age 30," noted the *Fort Worth Star-Telegram*.

OPERA

Dallas Opera, Dallas Music Hall at Fair Park, 909 First Ave, (214) 443-1043; tickets, 443-1000, Internet www.dallasopera.org. Individual tickets cost from $20 to $200. Wheelchair accessible and equipped with infra-red listening system.

Located east of downtown, the Dallas Opera has staged its productions in the Music Hall for four decades. The Meridian Room restaurant and bar is situated across the street.

The first opera presented in Dallas was titled *Martha*, by German composer Friedrich Flotow (1812-1883). The performance took place in a poorly ventilated, second-floor room at Field's Opera House on February 12, 1875. It was located on the south side of Main Street, between Austin and Lamar Streets, and across from the Sanger Brothers dry-goods store. With access to the backstage through a window, and lacking a dressing room, it was later renamed the Opera House.

A more appropriate, three-story Dallas Opera House was then built on the southwest corner of Commerce and Austin Streets in 1883 at a cost of $43,000. It could seat 1,200 persons. An orchestra came from New Orleans at the cost of another $6,000 for its grand opening performance. The Chicago Ideal Opera Company inaugurated the facility with Gilbert and Sullivan's *Iolanthe*. Lily Langtry, Edwin Booth, and Sarah Bernhardt also performed at the Dallas Opera House. Today the Greyhound bus station stands on the spot.

The building burned down in 1901 and was replaced by a red-brick building at Main and St. Paul Streets in 1904. It had a capacity of 1,700, although it, too, went up in smoke in 1921. In 1905, the Metropolitan Opera of New York included Dallas in its 16-city nationwide tour with one performance of Wagner's *Parsifal*.

The well-known Russian basso Fyodor Shalyapin (1873-1938) sang in *Boris Godunov* in Dallas in 1929, the same year that Italian tenor Beniamino Gigli sang a recital at Fair Park Auditorium.

Operatic soprano Lenore Cohron (b. 1900), a Dallas native who was later known as Leonora Corona, burst into prominence after she signed a long-term contract with the Metropolitan Opera in 1927 and made her début as Leonora in Verdi's *Il Trovatore*. By then, she had already sung at La Scala in Milan, the Opéra Comique in Paris, and Carnegie Hall. Her eight-season career at the Met concluded in 1935, although she continued to perform professionally. Practically nothing is known about Corona after she appeared at what is today the University of North Texas. Not even the year of her death is known.

But in most residents' minds, the history of the Dallas Civic Opera only begins on November 21, 1957, when Maria Callas, "glowing in a Venetian-gold gown and diamonds at her ears, looking and sounding like the goddess she was," sang five operatic scenas to open the Opera's first season. Observed *Time* magazine: "She raised a commanding hand over her head, then threw her arms wide and sent that last full note straight up through the roof." A 73-minute monophonic recording of a rehearsal at the State Fair Music Hall the day before was issued in 2003 by EMI Classics under the title *Maria Callas in Rehearsal: Dallas 1957*.

Callas returned in October1958 to sing in Verdi's *La Traviata* and Cherubini's *Medea*. And, incredibly, again in 1959, when she flew in at five o'clock in the morning on the day of the final rehearsal. She missed a high E-flat in *Lucia di Lammermoor*—stage craftsman Franco Zeffirelli would recall only "an awful croak"—and launched into a death cry as she collapsed. Even with that flaw, Callas took ten curtain calls and accepted an eight-minute ovation. Back in her dressing room she hit several high E-flats in a row to prove to those present that all those "damn reporters" made her miss the note.

When in Dallas, Callas was usually ministered to by John Ardoin (1935-2001), the music critic of the *Dallas Morning News*, who took her to the doctor, to the movies, and to buy horoscope magazines, "which could be a problem, since she would never tell her age." His long friendship with La Divina ended when the critic wrote a negative review about her in 1974. Ardoin wrote four books about Callas before he retired to Costa Rica and died two years later.

The founder of the Dallas Civic Opera was the "brilliant, energetic" Lawrence Vincent Kelly (1928-1974), a Chicago native, who established himself as an insurance broker and real estate salesman in 1954, when he also co-founded the Lyric Theatre of Chicago, where Callas made her American début.

Only half of the tickets had been sold by the time Callas arrived in 1957, so the socialite Elsa Maxwell volunteered to buy $2,000 worth of tickets to be distributed among college students and music teachers. Neiman-Marcus, Sanger Brothers, and A. Harris employees received free tickets, too. Still, the State Fair Music Hall was one-third empty on the inaugural night.

Nevertheless, "Callas's audience was mesmerized; they had never heard anything like it," writes Ronald L. Davis in *La Scala West*, the name given to the Dallas Opera in its earlier years. By the 1958 season, when Callas appeared in Verdi's *La Traviata*, the Dallas Opera was better known in Greece, Italy, even in New York, than in Dallas. It had a budget of $150,000 for a few weeks of performances. An impulsive Florence, Italy-born designer Franco Zeffirelli (b. 1923), still an unknown at the time, created and staged the production.

Callas's admirers from across the United States, Canada, Mexico, and even Europe wanted to hear La Divina and bought a sizeable number of tickets. While having the reputation as a tempestuous diva, Callas is said to have none of her temper tantrums in Dallas, was first at rehearsals and the last to leave.

Attending the opening performance on October 31, 1958, the *Time* magazine reviewer noted that "Callas held her audience in a kind of hushed trance." Santa Fe Opera founder John Crosby and Spanish mezzo-soprano Teresa Berganza were some among the nearly 4,000 who attended the opening night. Afterwards, Callas and many of her admirers attended a supper dance in the grand ballroom of the Adolphus Hotel downtown.

Callas's *Medea* was her only performance of the Cherubini opera in the United States. A well-known Greek designer created the sets and costumes and another Greek staged the work. Costumes were made in Athens. On the day she sang *Medea*, La Divina found out that her contract with the New York Metropolitan Opera had been canceled because she refused to sing *La Traviata* between two performances of *Macbeth* at the Met. Callas was nevertheless electrifying as Medea and "delivered a breath-taking range of emotions." Canadian tenor Jon Vickers sang the role of Jason, while Berganza was Neris.

"*Medea* was a monumental experience," declared the *Dallas Morning News*, while the *New York Herald Tribune* noted that, "Here, in Dallas, Madame Callas was enabled at last to show American audiences what a very great and total opera artist she is." Declared Callas upon boarding her airplane for Italy: "I love Dallas." Some began calling the Dallas Opera "Callas Civic Opera."

In 1959, Callas was made an honorary citizen of Dallas, but she or the city must have forgotten that fact because in 1968 she received another honorary citizenship. The Dallas Opera had a $35,000 deficit at the end of the 1959 season. As she flew to Paris, Callas promised that she would be in Dallas again soon. But she never returned. The diva was off the stage for almost a year, during which time she developed vocal problems. Although she sang *Medea* at La Scala and at Epidaurus, Greece, the best of her career seemed to have been coming to an end. In Dallas, she has been honored since 1991 with the Maria Callas Debut Artist of the Year award that carries no cash prize, but is considered a significant honor for the promising young artists. Soprano Cecilia Bartoli is one of those winners.

To the continuous amazement of a few Dallasites and many outsiders, Callas was followed in 1960 by an equally talented Joan Sutherland from Australia and Elisabeth Schwartzkopf, both singing in Mozart's *Don Giovanni*, although almost half of the opera house was empty.

The State Fair Music Hall resembled "a made-over aeroplane hangar," Sutherland later recalled in her memoirs. Her fee was only $2,000 a performance. Dallasites tried to make it up to her in other ways: "We were nearly killed by Texas hospitality," the Australian wrote.

One socialite flew from New York to see the performance and left lamenting, "It's really incredible—incredible—the greatest opera in the world in a little town like Dallas." After her American début in Dallas, *Newsweek* called Sutherland "the mistress of bel canto," while the *New York Times* noted that "when she ended the opera [*Alcina*] with a fortissimo, secure, effortless high D, the audience went wild."

The following year, a 19-year-old Spanish tenor, Placido Domingo, made his American début in Dallas, singing a small supporting part in *Lucia de Lammermoor,* and was followed in 1962 by Mario del Monaco, another operatic heavyweight at the time, in *Otello.* American Regina Resnik, Italian Giuseppe di Stefano, Spaniard Montserrat Caballe, and many, many others who later defined the opera, also appeared in Dallas.

"Lavishly supported by a small group of civic-minded business leaders, the Dallas Opera during its early seasons was perhaps as close as the United States has ever come to having court opera, a modern extension of the type found in the palaces of Louis XIV and Catherine the Great," observes Ronald L. Davis in his 2000 narrative, titled *La Scala West.* Davis claims that by 1962, the Dallas Opera was rivaled only by the Metropolitan, the San Francisco Opera, and the Chicago Lyric, perhaps Santa Fe.

Closing the 1963 season was Verdi's *Un Ballo in Maschera,* ready to open on Friday, November 22, 1963, when President Kennedy was assassinated. The budget was so tight that only two operas were staged the following year.

By 1966, the Dallas Opera was operating on a budget of more than $500,000, with each new production costing at least $150,000 and finances kept deteriorating. By the close of the 1970 season, the Dallas Opera was $1.2 million in debt, but was saved with a $750,000 grant from the Ford Foundation.

In 1974, Kelly found out he had cancer of the liver and pancreas. He hid the fact from his staff until July, when he was unable to walk and was forced to enter Baylor Hospital. Later in the year, he was taken to a private plane sent for him by a close friend, who cared for him in Kansas City until his death that September. Jon Vickers sang Handel's *Total Eclipse* for Kelly to the accompaniment of the Dallas Symphony Orchestra.

In 1977, Plato Karayanis became the Opera's general manager. And after 33 years in Dallas, the 73-year-old maestro Nocola Rescigno left the company in 1990, severing the last tie with the original organization. La Scala West was no more. Maestro Rescigno returned to Italy and now lives in retirement near Rome.

The Dallas Opera performs at the 3,400-seat, wedge-of-pie-shaped auditorium in Fair Park Music Hall, where the barnlike "acoustics are dreadful for the unamplified human voice," from November through February. The hall is "just too sprawling for either visual or aural connection with the stage," claims the *Dallas Morning News.*

A new opera house is planned for the downtown Dallas Arts District (for more details, please see listing in the SIGHTS & ATTRACTIONS chapter). In 2002, Margot and William Winspear, Canadian-born Dallas residents, gave $42 million—the largest single contribution by an individual or a family to a public project in Dallas history—

toward a 2,400-seat opera and dance theater that will bear their name.

The Winspears are longtime supporters of the Dallas Opera. Businessman Bill Winspear has served as president and chairman of the opera board. He said he "converted" his wife to opera when they were engaged. He called in to a local radio station with a request that they play the trio that ends the opera *Faust*, later saying,"I proposed to that." The couple was married in 1955.

The Opera's budget is $12 million, about half of what the Houston Grand Opera spends. The orchestra's core group numbers some 55 tenured players. They earn about $20,000 a year for a 19-week contract. The musicians negotiated during most of 2001 for better pay, health insurance, and disability pay at a time when supporters were raising $250 million for a new opera building downtown. The orchestra now has a contract that "barely begins to address the problem," according to the *News*.

Among its recent stagings, the opera company performed Jules Massenet's *Manon*, and Verdi's *Rigoletto*, one of the performances "good enough to dampen the [tear] ducts of the most jaded opera patron," according to the *Fort Worth Star-Telegram*.

In addition to the opera, the Music Hall also hosts the annual **Dallas Summer Musicals,** (214) 691-7200, where Broadway musicals have been performed since 1941, when the event was known as Starlight Operetta.

Since 1994, the Opera's music director has been British-born Graeme Jenkins, whose English teacher once told him, "It is time, dear boy, you experienced opera," and Jenkins replied: "But, sir, I don't want to see those fat people sing!" Since coming to Dallas, he was quoted as saying, "It's been my ambition to move the company away from La Scala West," referring to the years when Maria Callas sang here.

Its general director from 2000 on was British native Anthony Whitworth-Jones (b. 1945), the former chief executive officer of the prestigious Glyndebourne Festival Opera. His wife Camilla is the great-great granddaughter of English naturalist Charles Darwin. Two years after arriving in a scorching Dallas, the couple got so homesick that, after a visit to London, he announced, "Camilla and I need to get back home" and they were gone within a week.

He was replaced by Memphis, Tennessee, native Jonathan Pell (b. 1949), who declared in an interview that he had "no children, no pets, no time." He had previously worked with Luciano Pavarotti, Placido Domingo, Renata Scotto, and Frederica von Stade.

Dallas Wind Symphony, Morton H. Meyerson Symphony Center, 2301 Flora St. at North Pearl, (214) 565-9463; tickets, 528-5576, Internet www.dws.org.

Located in the Arts District downtown, across the street from Cathedral Santuario de Guadalupe and two blocks from the Dallas Museum of Art (see individual listings).

The idea for the Wind Symphony, according to orchestra lore, was born one Saturday morning in the summer of 1985, when a young man stopped in the office of Southern Methodist University music professor Howard Dunn, and told him he would like to start a "reading band of the finest wind and percussion players in the city, and I want you to conduct it," to which the professor supposedly replied, "I have been waiting for you all my life."

Since 1990, it performs at the Morton H. Meyerson Center. Comprised of 50 woodwind, brass, and percussion players, the band performs a blend of musical styles ranging from Bach to Bernstein and from Sousa to Strauss.

The DWS, one of only a handful of professional wind bands in the United States, performed a special concert for Queen Elizabeth II in 1991.

Jerry F. Junkin is the band's artistic director and conductor. Prof.essor Junkin became conductor of the University of Texas Wind Ensemble in 1988. The *Dallas Morning News* calls him "an invigorating leader who can mold a phrase and build a climax . . . a band version of Leonard Bernstein."

"The amazing" Frederick Fennell (b. 1914), "virtually the godfather of wind-band music in America," according to the *News*," is the DWS's principal guest conductor. He was born in Cleveland, Ohio, and received his master's degree from the Eastman School of Music at the University of Rochester in New York.

THEATER

The first dramatic performances in Dallas go back to the Civil War when shows that traveled by wagon provided a somewhat questionable entertainment. During the late 1800s, theaters, to the dismay of the city fathers, often featured crude burlesque shows, and several of them were burned down as they were alleged to harbor "the most depraved characters in the country."

Dallas' first actual theater was the Thompson Variety Theater, at South Jefferson Street, on the site of the old post office, which opened in 1872. A year later, real estate developer Thomas William Field (b. 1847) built the Field Opera House on the south side of Main Street, near Lamar. By 1876, *The Merchant of Venice* and *Oliver Twist* were being performed at Field's. When *Hamlet* was shown on February 24, 1887, the Opera House was sold out, despite an unheard-of price of $15 for each seat. In 1905, the theater magnate, Karl St. John Hoblitzelle, built the Majestic (see entry) vaudeville house on the corner of Commerce and St. Paul Streets; it was relocated to the present theater at 1925 Elm Street in 1921.

The Dallas Little Theater was founded in 1920 and two years later moved to its own 242-seat wooden playhouse at 417 Olive Street, but soon folded. The amateur company took its production of the one-act play *Judge Lynch,* written by *Times Herald* reporter John Williams Rogers, to New York and entered it in the prestigious Belasco tournament. The play, which dealt with the lynching of an innocent black man, won the national competition named after the well-regarded producer and director David Belasco. Some 23,000 saw the play *Judge Lynch* at the Dallas Majestic Theatre (see entry) alone. The troupe won its third Belasco competition in New York in 1926, but in spite of all its critical success, folded its tent in 1973.

The first professional theater opened on June 3, 1947 in the Gulf Oil Building of the Texas State Fair, when Margo Jones directed *Farther Off From Heaven,* by William Inge, a play that later became a Broadway success under another title.

There are about two dozen local theater companies without permanent performance space. "Dallas is a great city, a wealthy city, but it's theater-poor," the executive director of the Fort Worth Dallas Ballet, now Texas Ballet Theater, told the *Fort Worth Star-Telegram.*

Bath House Cultural Center, 521 East Lawther Dr. at Buckner Blvd., (214) 670-8749, Internet www.bathhousecultural.com. Galleries are open Tue-Wed noon-6 PM, Thu-Sat 10 AM-6 PM, or until 10 PM on performance nights.

Located in northeast Dallas, on the eastern shore of the 1,120-acre (or 453-hectare) White Rock Lake, almost two miles (or 3.2 kilometers) north of Dallas Arboretum & Botanical Garden (see entry). Driving in either direction on Buckner Boulevard, turn toward the center on Northcliff Drive.

The city-owned Bath House Cultural Center, originally inaugurated as a public bathhouse on White Rock Lake in 1930, opened as Dallas' first neighborhood cultural arts center in 1981. This was the city's first neighborhood cultural center and one of the earliest art deco buildings in Texas.

For 23 years, the bathhouse provided lockers, changing rooms, and rentable bathing suits to swimmers at White Rock Lake. It closed in 1953 because of drought, polio fears, and racial tensions, and was vacant until 1978.

This is a multi-cultural facility, particularly receptive to Hispanic artists, where visual and performing arts events take place throughout the year. In addition to two galleries, the facility boasts a 120-seat theater. Each July, the Bath House hosts an annual Festival of Independent Theatres for companies with no homes of their own.

In addition to the Bath House, the Latino Cultural Center, and the Morton H. Meyerson Symphony Center (see entries), the city also owns and manages these facilities that you can explore in more detail on the Dallas Cultural Center's Web site, www.dallasculture.org:

- **The Ice House Cultural Center,** 1004 West Page St., (214) 670-7524.
- **The South Dallas Cultural Center,** 3400 South Fitzhugh Ave., (214) 939-2787.
- **Juanita Craft Civil Rights House,** 2618 Warren Ave., (214) 670-8584.

Bob Hope Theatre, Southern Methodist University, Hillcrest Ave. at Granada, (214) 768-3510. Located in the Owen Fine Arts Center, in the town of University Park, north of downtown Dallas. Open during SMU's school year only.

This 390-seat theater is named after the late comedian and film actor Bob Hope. Hope's connection with Southern Methodist University goes back to the 1930s and the actor's interest in the university's football team, the Mustangs. Hope was so popular with students that in the 1950s he was brought to the campus by helicopter one year, and students staged a parade to and from the Love Field Airport in his honor on another.

Constructed in two phases over a five-year period, at a cost of $9.5 million, the Owen Fine Arts Building, which houses the Bob Hope Theatre, was completed in 1968. Bob Hope Theatre stages up to a dozen theatrical events each school year.

Cara Mia Theatre Company, Post Office Box 226144, Dallas, Fax (214) 670-3243, e-mail info@caramiatheatre.org.

A critically praised nonprofit theater company founded in 1996 by Adelina Anthony, who now lives in Los Angeles. The *Dallas Observer* named her this city's best theater director. Aside from Teatro Dallas (see entry), it is the only Latino theater troupe in the city, and, unfortunately, does not have a permanent venue.

Cara Mia's artistic director is Marisela Barrera, with a theater degree from Southern Methodist University. She drew favorable reviews for her performance in a one-woman show called *Virgen Manifestations*, based on the 1531 apparition of a woman whom many Catholics believe to be Mary, the mother of Jesus, outside of today's Mexico City. In 2002, Barrera became the director of theater arts for the Guadalupe Cultural Arts Center in San Antonio, Texas.

Not having a permanent stage, the Cara Mia company presents some shows in the Undermain's (see listing) basement space

Dallas critics have singled out the company's adaptation of Cherrie Moraga's *The Hungry Woman: A Mexican Medea*, "a timeless force that seems to embrace, not revise, the Medea of Euripides," claims the *Dallas Morning News* about the story that takes place in a Balkanized North America, where the races have pulled back behind separate borders.

Contemporary Theatre of Dallas, 5601 Sears St. at Lower Greenville Ave., (214) 828-0094. Located in a former Baptist church built in 1925 in near-East Dallas, northeast of downtown.

Founded in 2003 by several local actresses in their late 30s and 40s who "thought there weren't enough opportunities for them to act on Dallas stages," the company emphasizes opportunities for female artists. Sue Loncar is the artistic director who wants her company's work to be accessible, both "Shakespeare-free" and avoiding anything too avant-garde.

Dallas Children's Theater, Rosewood Center for Family Arts, 6343 Northwest Hwy. at Skillman Rd., (214) 978-0110. Located northeast of downtown, east of Central Expressway (or U.S. Hwy. 75) and NorthPark Mall, and behind Steakley Chevrolet car dealership. So far the surrounding area is somewhat raw, so you do not want to linger around by yourself at night.

Rosewood Corporation, a Dallas developer and supporter of the theater, bought this 54,890-square-foot (or 5,099-square-meter) former bowling alley on DCT's behalf for $3.15 million in 2000. The theater purchased the building from the developer the following year and inaugurated the facility in the fall of 2002. The bowling alley's $8.6-million makeover includes a 360-seat Paul & Kitty Baker Theater auditorium, named for the founder of the Dallas Theater Center and his wife, who are the parents of Robyn Flatt, artistic director of the theater.

Dr. Baker (b. 1911), a Texas native from Herford, developed the theater programs at Baylor and Trinity universities before founding the Dallas Theater Center (see entry) in 1959. He also founded the well-regarded Arts Magnet High School—now known as Booker T. Washington High School for the Performing Arts—in 1975.

Eventually, the facility is to include classrooms, costume and scenery studios, rehearsal space, a gift shop, a concession area, an art gallery, and administrative offices. Also planned is a "black box" theater with 100 seats for use by Dallas' many independent performing-arts groups.

The Children's Theater was founded in 1984 by two professional artists. It is the second largest professional theater in Dallas. Each year, the troupe mounts 11 productions and gives 380 performances with 170 actors and other artists. DCT's annual budget is about $2.5 million. It is one of 160 children's theaters in the nation and one of only two dozen with a budget of more than $1 million.

In 2002, almost 14 years after it settled at Cedar Springs Road and Maple Avenue, across the street from the Crescent Court complex, the company moved to where the former Don Carter's All-Star Lanes bowling alley was once located.

Kathy Burks Theatre of Puppetry Arts, which presents the *Nutcracker,* among its other shows, is also part of this theater.

Among the plays staged by DCT recently was *Deadly Weapons*, an uncharacteristically realistic portrayal of violence among today's teenagers. Much easier to enjoy was the dramatization of Judith Viorst's children's classic, titled *Alexander and the Terrible, Horrible, No Good, Very Bad Day,* which the *Dallas Morning News* labeled as "delightful." The book's author attended the opening-night performance.

Dallas Theater Center, Kalita Humphreys Theater, 3636 Turtle Creek Blvd. at Blackburn St., (214) 526-8210; box office, 522-8499, Internet www.dallastheatercenter.org. Box office is open Mon-Fri 10 AM-8 PM, Sat-Sun noon-8 PM. Tickets are also available on-line. Located north of downtown on a steep slope in the wooded area at Turtle Creek Boulevard, while its downtown location is across the Annette Strauss Artist Square, at 2401 Flora St.

Conceived in 1954, this theater became reality five years later. Its founding father was the "brilliant, stubborn" Paul Baker, former head of the drama department at Baylor University in Waco, Texas. He directed the company for 23 years, until 1982. Dr. Baker (b. 1911), whose daughter Robyn Flatt is artistic director of the Dallas Children's Theater (see entry), has the 360-seat main stage at DCT named after him and his wife.

Richard Hamburger, the theater's fourth artistic director, has guided DTC since 1992 in plays as varied as *A Streetcar Named Desire* and *Angels in America.* Previously, he served as artistic director of the Portland Stage Company, and has directed the Eugene O'Neill Theater Center.

The center's Kalita Humphreys Theater was one of the last buildings that architect Frank Lloyd Wright supervised before he died in 1959. Initiated in 1915, it was originally drafted as a West Coast theater that was never built, then adapted for a Hartford, Connecticut, playhouse for which the money could not be raised.

"Wright arrived in August 1955, when it was scorching hot, walked over the site, seemed delighted with it, and agreed to design the theater," writes Dallas cultural historian Ronald L. Davis. This circular theater is one of only three existing theaters designed by Wright.

The building was named after a South Texas heiress and actress who had died in a 1954 plane crash. Her parents contributed $120,000 to the theater so it could, among other things, purchase 440 seats. Built of reinforced concrete at a cost of $1 million, it uncannily resembles the Guggenheim Museum in New York, which, incidentally, was built at about the same time. Its entrance faces a hill in the back. A larger stage has since been built atop the old one, and the original seating was enlarged after Wright's death. A new lobby was added in 1990. This is one theater where you will see and hear everything, no matter where you sit.

Playwright Preston Jones (1936-1979) was a well-known actor at this theater. Born in Albuquerque, he went to graduate school at Baylor University and was invited to join the Dallas Theater Center company. In the early 1970s, when finding that the plays submitted by local playwrights were unsatisfactory, Jones wrote his own. It was a major success, and Jones's career was underway.

DTC has staged everything from Shakespeare to Arthur Miller, from Schiller to Tennessee Williams, from Aristophanes to Chekhov. Actor Charleton Heston and his wife Lydia performed here in A. R. Gurney's play *Love Letters* in 2000. The following year, the company won six awards for outstanding work in Metroplex theater chosen by the Dallas-Fort Worth Theater Critics Forum.

DTC has a budget of about $5.5 million. It has been struggling with recurring deficits that rose as high as $1.75 million in the late 1990s.

Garland Civic Theatre, Garland Performing Arts Center, 300 North Fifth St. at Austin, Garland, (972) 485-8884. Located northeast of downtown Dallas and near the Garland City Hall.

Among the company's performances was Aaron Sorkin's *A Few Good Men,* the court-martial drama Sorkin wrote in 1989 at age 28. He later created television's mega hit *The West Wing.* Here you could also have seen Ketti Frings' 1958 Pulitzer Prize-winning stage adaptation of Thomas Wolfe's novel *Look Homeward, Angel,* in which the Civic Theatre's director, Susan Sargent, cast 19 roles with three actors and a basket of wigs.

Also located at the Garland Performing Arts Center is the **Garland Symphony,** founded in 1978, having an orchestra of more than 90 musicians and giving half a dozen concerts yearly. It is guided by Robert Carter Austin. The Garland and Las Colinas symphonies are the same entity, except for budget and organizational structure. The Garland Summer Musicals have also been performed for more than 20 years at the center.

Greer Garson Theatre, Southern Methodist University, Meadows School of the Arts, Hillcrest Ave. at Granada, (214) 768-2787. Located inside the Owen Fine Arts Center in the Meadows School of the Arts in University Park, north of downtown.

The Greer Garson Theatre opened in 1992 at a cost of $10 million and was paid for entirely by the late actress Garson. It was designed by Dallas architects, Milton Powell & Partners, and has 386 seats on three levels. The facility was modeled after the Chichester Festival Theatre in England and the Stratford Festival in Ontario, Canada. Film archives and screening rooms are also located in the building.

This 390-seat theater is open during SMU's academic year only and presents classics, such as Federico Garcia Lorca's *As Five Years Pass*. One company staged *Six Characters in Search of an Author* by Luigi Pirandello. It was directed by Mahmood Karimi-Hakak, whose production of Shakespeare's *A Midsummer Night's Dream* was closed in Iran by the Muslim regime. "I wept for terror and joy all through the final half hour of this production," admitted the *Dallas Morning News* theater critic. "I wept walking back to the car; I wept all the way home."

The Meadows School of the Arts professional acting program is one of the few in the country offering full-tuition scholarships and stipends for most of its students. Each spring, third-year students from the university's professional acting program showcase their talents for entertainment industry leaders in Dallas, New York, and Los Angeles.

Greer Garson, the Irish-born actress and philanthropist, died in Dallas in April 1996 at the age of 92. She and her late husband, Dallas oilman Buddy Fogelson, paid for the complex overlooking Hillcrest Avenue.

Irving Arts Center, 3333 North MacArthur Blvd. at Rochelle Blvd., Irving, (972) 252-7558 or 256-4270, Internet www.irvingartscenter.com, e-mail minman@ci.irving.tx.us. Gallery is open Mon-Wed & Fri 9 AM-5 PM, Thu 9 AM-8 PM, Sat 10 AM-5 PM, Sun 1 PM-5 PM. Box office is open Wed-Sat noon-5 pm. Located east of D/FW Airport and about a mile (or 1.6 kilometers) north of State Highway 183 (or Airport Freeway West).

Built by the city in 1980, the center houses three theaters, four galleries, and an outdoor sculpture garden on a six-acre (or 2.42-hectare) site. Some 300 performances are held annually, while the galleries showcase more than 30 exhibitions of mostly local and regional art. Irving's three symphony orchestras utilize the center's 710-seat Carpenter Performance Hall

The 70-member, professional **Irving Symphony Orchestra** was established in 1962. It gives eight concerts each season, and has been directed since 1991 by conductor Hector Guzman, who also conducts the Plano and San Angelo symphony orchestras. A native of Mexico and a 1983 master's graduate of Southern Methodist University,

Maestro Guzman worked with two Dallas Symphony Orchestra music directors, the late Eduardo Mata, and Anshel Brusilow, who now conducts the Richardson Symphony Orchestra. In addition to Mexico, he has also toured the Czech Republic and Japan. This was Irving's first symphony orchestra.

"A series of disagreements resulted in the formation of the New Philharmonic," according to the *Dallas Morning News*.

New Philharmonic Orchestra was founded in 1987, consists of 65 musicians, and presents five concerts each season. This is chronologically the second of the three Irving symphony orchestras. It is a volunteer orchestra. Its music director and conductor is Richard Gianguilo, a trumpet player with the Dallas Symphony Orchestra who received a First Prize from the Paris Conservatory, where he studied with Maurice Andre while on a Fullbright grant.

Las Colinas Symphony Orchestra, established in 1991, presents a season of six subscription concerts annually. The ensemble of 93 musicians is directed by the Tennessee native Robert Carter Austin, who had previously led the Cheyenne Symphony Orchestra in Wyoming. Most of the musicians playing in this orchestra are also members of the Garland Symphony (see entry), but the organizational structure and budgets are different. Aside from a master's degree in music from Stanford University, Austin also has a bachelor of science degree from the Massachusetts Institute of Technology, and a diploma in computer science from Cambridge University in England.

Also based here is the **Lyrick Stage** (see listing below), Irving's theater company devoted to musicals.

The Arts Center sculpture garden was inaugurated in 1999. Its permanent collection consists of Texas art, from architectural to experimental. It includes a monumental granite fountain commission from the city, titled *Fountain Columns*, created by Texas sculptor Jesus Bautista Moroles. The garden's limestone benches are by sculptor Michael Manjarris. On loan to the center could be works by Luis Jimenez; David Iles of Bolivar, Texas; and Dallasite David Hickman, who is on exhibit at the Texas Sculpture Garden (see entry) in Frisco. The Corpus Christi, Texas-born Mexican-American Moroles (b. 1950) has lived in nearby Rockport since 1982. In recent years, he has completed monumental-scale installations of his sculpture for the Egyptian government in Aswan, and in Changchun, China.

Kitchen Dog Theater, the McKinney Avenue Contemporary Art Gallery, 3120 McKinney Ave., (214) 953-1055, Internet www.kitchendogtheater.org. Performs Thu-Sat evenings and Sun matinees. Thursday's pay-what-you-can performances benefit walk-up patrons only. Wheelchair accessible. Located in Uptown at McKinney and

Bowen Street. There are a dozen restaurants and bars located within a few blocks of the theater.

The company's name is derived from a song in Beckett's *Waiting for Godot*, "A dog came in the kitchen and stole a crust of bread; Cook came up with the ladle and beat him 'till he was dead."

Kitchen Dog Theater was founded in 1990 by five graduates of Southern Methodist University. The company's mission is to stage original new and classic plays "where questions of justice, morality and human freedom can be explored." The first show, titled *Mud*, by Maria Irene Fomes, was staged in a room above a Deep Ellum coffeehouse in 1991. Artistic director Dan Day is the only founder who is still a company member.

The McKinney Avenue Contemporary art gallery (MAC), of which KDT is a part, is a brainchild of the wealthy art patron Claude Albritton, who contributes about one-quarter of the MAC's annual $400,000 budget. Its only local equivalent is the Undermain Theatre (see listing), established in 1984, both of which have built a reputation for artistic quality and integrity. The company, which is composed mostly of SMU theater graduates, has received critical praise and numerous awards, as well as a healthy number of grants.

In 2002, KDT won eight awards by the Dallas-Fort Worth Theater Critics Forum. Among its recent plays, the company staged Howard Brenton's *Christie in Love*, which the *Dallas Morning News* labeled as "obscene," and Shakespeare's final great tragedy, *Coriolanus*, which tells the entire story with nine male actors wearing burlap-textured kilts.

"Even if Shakespeare's *Coriolanus* was as familiar and oft staged as, say *A Midsummer Night's Dream*, it would be difficult to find a production of the tragedy that's more fresh than the one being produced by Kitchen Dog Theater," claims the *Fort Worth Star-Telegram*.

Lyric Stage, Irving Arts Center, Dupree Theater, 3333 North McArthur Blvd., between Northgate Dr. and Rochelle Rd., Irving, (972) 252-2787. Located east of D/FW Airport, one mile (or 1.6 kilometers) north of Highway 183, and one mile south of the Four Seasons Resort & Club (see entry).

Built by the city in 1980, the center houses three theaters, four galleries, and an outdoor sculpture garden on a six-acre (or 2.42-hectare) site. More than 300 performances are held annually, while the galleries showcase some 30 exhibitions of mostly local and regional art.

Lyrick Stage, established in 1994, is the Irving theater company devoted to new musicals. The *Fort Worth Star-Telegram* called Lyric Stage "a champion of new and daring musicals" at one time and noted that "all of the performers are stunning, both vocally and in their characterizations" in the world premiere of the musical *Children's Letters to God*. The *Dallas Morning News* notes that "Lyric Stage's cast is terrific."

Among its recent stagings was Texas natives' Tom Jones and Harvey Schmidt's world premiere of *Roadside*, which deals with civilization as it encroaches on the Old West. The authors also wrote the world's longest-running musical, *The Fantastics*, which has had more than 16,500 performances in its 40 years.

Margo Jones Theatre, Southern Methodist University, Hillcrest Ave. at Granada, (214) 768-3510. Located inside the Owen Fine Arts Center on the campus of Southern Methodist University in University Park.

Margo Jones Theatre honors the memory of the late theater pioneer, who presented stage premieres of 58 new plays from 1947 until her death. The theater accommodates up to 125 and presents classics, such as Anton Chekhov's *The Cherry Orchard*.

A native of Livingston, in east Texas, Margaret Jones (b. 1911) grew up in Denton and graduated from Texas Woman's University. She directed theater companies in Pasadena, California, and Houston, Texas. Jones was named one of 12 outstanding directors outside of New York in 1939. In 1942, she met playwright Tennessee Williams with whom she had a personal and professional association. Jones directed his plays in Pasadena and in Cleveland, Ohio, while considering creation of a network of nonprofit theaters.

She coaxed a grant from the Rockefeller Foundation to found the Dallas theater that for 12 years updated its name according to the year of operation. The 198-seat Theatre '47 was located in the Gulf Oil Building, a stucco-and-glass-block building designed by Swiss-born architect William Lescaze, on the grounds of Fair Park. It was the first professional theater-in-the-round in the nation and the first modern nonprofit professional resident theater. There are some 300 such theaters in the United States today. During the early years of Jones' theater, Williams, who nicknamed her the Texas Tornado, spent a great deal of time at the theater.

Almost three-quarters of the plays that Jones produced were world premieres. Actors such as Larry Hagman, Louise Latham, Brenda Vaccaro, and Jack Warden got their start at Margo Jones' theater. The Fair Park facility closed in 1959.

By mid-1950s, Jones was often depressed, drank excessively, and suffered from loneliness. "She never scored the success on Broadway she coveted and had made her biggest accomplishment in regional theater," observes Dallas cultural historian Ronald L. Davis. To overcome her depression, she took up painting, which indirectly led to her death at age 43. She accidentally poisoned herself by carbon tetrachloride, a carpet-cleaning solvent used to remove paint at her Stoneleigh Hotel (see listing) apartment. She was admitted to St. Paul's Hospital semiconscious and died on July 24, 1955 of uremic poisoning.

Following her death, philanthropist Eugene McDermott (1899-1973) and his wife Margaret gave $200,000 toward the founding of the Margo Jones Theatre at SMU. McDermott founded Texas Instruments in 1951 and was the company's chairman until 1958. He also helped found St. Mark's private school (see listing).

In 2002, President Gerald Ford's granddaughter, Tyne Vance, an SMU theater major, directed Don Nigro's play *Anima Mundi* here.

Mesquite Arts Center, 1527 North Galloway Ave., Mesquite, (972) 216-8122 or 216-6444, Internet www.cityofmesquite.com. Located east of downtown Dallas and east of the LBJ Freeway, about a mile (or 1.6 kilometers) south of U.S. Highway 80.

The center was designed for vocal, chamber and orchestral music, drama, and the visual arts, and completed in 1995. Its concert hall seats 492 and contains a canopied stage for music. The center's courtyard is landscaped with Japanese red maples, bald cypress, and live oaks.

About a 1,000 events are held annually, many under the auspices of the Mesquite Arts Council, a nonprofit entity designated to support arts in the city. More than a dozen arts groups belong to the council, including the Black Box Theatre, Mesquite Community Theatre, and Mesquite Symphony Orchestra.

Mesquite Symphony was established in 1986, numbers more than 60 musicians, and gives half a dozen concerts annually under the direction of Roger Gilliam, a free-lance trumpet player.

Theatre Quorum, (972) 216-8131, was founded by director Carl Savering and playwright Angela Wilson, whose work has been performed from Los Angeles to New York. Theatre Quorum performed its adult-oriented plays in various Dallas theaters before becoming the resident company at the Mesquite Arts Center in 1998.

The *Dallas Morning News* noted that "the Quorum's elegant, beautifully acted production" and the American premiere of the 1990 satire of market research in England, titled *No One Sees the Video*, by British playwright Martin Crimp, "confirms the young company's status as one of the most discerning and adventurous in the area."

The local audiences do not always see it that way. Co-founder Wilson told the *News* that the most "painful" part of the Quorum is the audience. "They don't like what we do." Families and senior citizens seem to prefer the Mesquite Community Theatre presentations. "They don't like our shows."

Pegasus Theatre, Stemmons Towers, 6110 East Mockingbird Ln. at Stemmons Frwy., Suite 102, (214) 821-6005. Located northwest of downtown Dallas, southwest of the Love Field Airport, and south of the Brook Hollow Golf Club.

Pegasus Theatre was founded in a converted warehouse in 1985 and was part of the first wave of artistic renaissance that took root in the Deep Ellum area. Over the years, the theater has matured both artistically and financially, but it has remained true to the original purpose for which it was founded, to focus on comedy.

"At Pegasus Theatre, we have a passion for comedy. We exist to communicate this passion to the public in a way that lightens the heart and perhaps offers some insight into the foibles of humanity," says in part a theater flyer.

The company's artistic director since the beginning has been Kurt Kleinmann, the general manager, and his wife Barbara Weinberger. Kleinmann plays a bumbling detective in Pegasus' live black-and-white mystery spoof, titled *Cross Stage Right: Die!*, with costumes, sets, lighting, and makeup that simulate the look of 1930s movies.

The building at 3916 Main Street in Deep Ellum, which Pegasus occupied since 1985, was sold in 2002, when the company had to move to its current address. Like a dozen other local companies, Pegasus now performs on various stages without a permanent facility.

Plano Repertory Theatre, Courtyard Theater, 1517 Avenue H at 15th St., Plano, (972) 422-7460, Internet www.planorep.org. Located in the Haggard Park historic district, adjacent to downtown Plano, and a two-minute walk from the DART light-rail station. Plano Repertory moved from the Plano ArtCentre in 2002. The main parking lot is situated off of Avenue G.

Established in 1975 as the Plano Players, an amateur community theater, the company entertains audiences with classics, musicals, and dramas. In recent years, Plano Repertory has gained a reputation for presenting area premieres, ambitious musicals, and historically significant works. The company's subscriber list has grown to about 2,500, its budget to $750,000 a year.

Among its recent performances, the theater staged a 1938 play, titled *Not About Nightingales*, by Tennessee Williams, which was "entertaining, purely and simply," in the words of the *Fort Worth Star-Telegram*. Also performed here was Oscar Wilde's classic, *The Importance of Being Earnest*, "and to say that the entire cast showcases this wonderfully is praise enough," notes the *Star-Telegram*.

In 2001, Plano Repertory took home eight Dallas Theatre League's Leon Rabin Awards, more than any other Dallas theatrical group.

Its artistic director is Mark Fleisher (b. 1970), who came on board in 1993 and enlarged the company, play by play, into a major area troupe, then left in 2002 to follow his wife to Ann Arbor, Michigan.

Courtyard Theater is a $6-million renovation of a 1938 Works Progress Administration gymnasium that had doubled as an auditorium until being converted to school district offices in the 1950s. Measuring 20,000 square feet (or 1,858 square meters), it includes 325 seats, a lounge, and a movable stage that can accommodate everything from classical drama to small dance recitals.

Plano Repertory uses it for part of the year. Dressing rooms and staff offices are situated in the old locker rooms. The main entrance to the theater is on the side, facing the parking lot, instead of facing the street. The architects preserved the brick shell and vaulted roof of the original building.

Pocket Sandwich Theatre, 5400 East Mockingbird Ln., Suite 119, (214) 821-1860. Located in east Dallas, in a small strip shopping center, across the street from the Mockingbird Station loft, a shopping and entertainment spot, just off North Central Expressway.

Performances, from slapstick to Shakespeare for the Modern Man, are held Thu-Sat at 8 pm, with food service starting at 6:30 pm. The Sunday performance is at 7 pm, with food service starting at 5:30 pm. An occasional detour to a more serious fare, such as *The Elephant Man*, gets critical praise, but little applause, from Pocket's audiences.

Pocket Sandwich Theatre is a tiny facility that dishes out more than just comedy with food and drink. In the words of one playwright, it gets more playwrights started than any other company in Dallas. R-rated shows are not uncommon. This is one of the favorite venues of Broadcast.com billionaire Mark Cuban, who sold his company to Yahoo for $5.7 billion.

There is table seating and the optional menu consists of sandwiches, soups, salads, nachos, baked potatoes, chicken breast, pizza, and desserts. Soda, beer, and wine are also available.

"Pocket Sandwich Theatre is one of those rare companies that can boast a sure-fire formula," notes the *Dallas Morning News*. "The café/theater has a loyal following for its slapstick melodrama, during which patrons get to throw all the popcorn they can grab."

Richardson Theatre Centre, 718 Canyon Creek Square Shopping Center, Custer Pkwy. between West Lookout Dr. and Renner Rd., Richardson, (972) 699-1130, Internet www.richardsontheatercentre.org. Located in a shopping center northeast of downtown Dallas, west of North Central Expressway (or U.S. Hwy. 75) and south of President George Bush Turnpike (or State Hwy. 190). A non-profit community theater. Among its recent plays, the company staged Neil Simon's Pulitzer Prize-winning work, *Lost in Yonkers*, William Inge's *Bus Stop*, and Agatha Christie's *Verdict*.

Shakespeare Festival of Dallas, Sammons Center for the Arts, 3630 Harry Hines Blvd., (214) 559-2778, Internet www.shakespearedallas.org. *NCH*. Offices are located in the former Turtle Creek Pump Station, which operated from 1910 to the 1930s, at Harry Hines and Oak Lawn Avenue. Performances are held at Samuell-Grand Park Ampitheater, 6200 East Grand Blvd., in east Dallas, in Addison and Frisco.

The Shakespeare festival originated in the summer of 1971, when a Dallas theater director produced an evening of readings in Fair Park with Shakespearean actors. Over the subsequent 20 years, the festival has grown into one of the most prolific cultural organizations in Dallas, staging two productions each summer. It is now the leading Shakespeare festival in the state and the second oldest such free festival in the nation.

The festival presents professional productions based on the works of William Shakespeare. Each year, 40,000 Dallasites enjoy these performances free of charge.

Cliff Redd directed the Shakespeare Festival from 1989 to 1997 and again from 1999 to 2001, when he was named director of the ArtCentre of Plano. A Houston native, he founded Theatre Arlington in 1972 and ran it for 18 years. In 2002, the festival's board appointed Raphael Parry, one of the city's theatrical pioneers, as its artistic director. He co-founded the city's "most revered avant-garde company," Undermain Theatre (see listing), and has performed major roles at the Dallas Theater Center (see listing). Parry also acted and directed for Kitchen Dog Theater (see listing).

Teatro Dallas, 1331 Record Crossing Rd., (214) 689-6492. Located northwest of downtown Dallas, off Stemmons Freeway (or Interstate 35 East), and south of Mockingbird Lane.

Teatro Dallas, a Hispanic venue, was co-founded in 1985 by its current artistic director, Mexico City-born and -educated Cora Cordona (b.1951), who came from Austin a year earlier. She "almost instantly became creator of some of the city's bloodiest, sexiest, most sophisticated theater, often commissioning new work or translating existing Latino scripts from Mexico and Spain and Portugal into English world premieres," notes the weekly *Dallas Observer*.

It is a company not afraid to produce a play by a newcomer, and it produces classics as well. Dallas needs Theatro "not only because the city is lacking in quality Hispanic theater in proportion to its exploding Latino population, but because we cannot lose another theater of fervor and risk," adds the *Observer*.

Teatro was located at 2204 Commerce Street at Central Expressway, between downtown Dallas and Deep Ellum, from 1990 until late in 1998, when its rented space "burned to a crisp hollow." The theater's new facility, funded by the city's Office of Cultural Affairs and the Meadows Foundation, houses its business office and a 600-square-foot (or 56-square-meter) rehearsal hall with an 18-foot (or 5.48-meter) ceiling. A 100-seat theater was added in 2002.

Teatro organizes an annual international theater festival at which domestic and foreign Spanish- and Portuguese-language theater companies, singers, puppeteers, and dancers perform.

Theatre Three, 2800 Routh St., between Howell St. and Laclede St., (214) 871-3300/2933, Internet www.theatre3dallas.com. Located uptown next to the Dream Café in an increasingly deserted Quadrangle center. Dream Café, Silver Room, Tin Star, and The Ginger Man are some among the restaurants nearby.

Theatre Three is the oldest and one of the largest professional theaters in Dallas. It was founded in 1961 by Norma Young, who, along with her husband, Jac Alder, served the theater until 1998, when she died after a prolonged illness. For many years she was the artistic director and he the executive producer, so the title Alder (b. 1935) retains to this day. He left a career in architecture to co-found the theater. Before that, he helped start a theater on a U.S. Army base in Metz, France.

The non-profit theater's first home was the various meeting rooms of the former Sheraton Dallas Hotel, now known as the Adam's Mark. To put food on the table, Alder continued practicing architecture with George L. Dahl, the architect who supervised the construction of some 45 buildings for the 1936 Texas Centennial Exposition in Fair Park (see entry). In 1969, the theater moved to the Quadrangle mall and bought the building following an offer from Ken Hughes, who years later developed the Mockingbird Station lofts and shopping (see entry). One year, Theatre Three won six Dallas Theater Critics Forum Awards. It was voted the best theater company by the readers of the city's alternative weekly, the *Dallas Observer*.

The theater's main, in-the-round theater has been quite successful in recent years, while the refurbished downstairs space brings in additional income. Film actress Morgan Fairchild got her start at Theatre Three, which now has a budget of about $1.4 million and even a small surplus. Here you could have seen plays, such as *I Love You, You're Perfect, Now Change*, which was staged simultaneously here and at Fort Worth's Circle Theatre.

Undermain Theatre, 3200 Main St. at Murray St., (214) 747-1424; box office, 747-5515, Internet www.undermain.com, e-mail undermain@aol.com. Located in the concrete Basement Space in Deep Ellum, east of downtown and across Interstate Highway 45, also known as Julius Schepps Freeway.

Undermain Theatre is a company of about 16 artists, established in 1984, with a strong record of producing and commissioning new plays. "Dallas' most daring and accomplished theatrical group," the *Dallas Morning News* calls it.

"We believe in challenging our audiences emotionally, intellectually and philosophically," says the troupe's Web site. Perhaps its only local equivalent is the Kitchen Dog Theater (see listing), both of which have built a reputation for artistic quality and integrity. In recent years, it has won numerous Dallas Theater Critics Forum Awards.

Undermain, which is named for its basement-level performance space under Main Street, was co-founded by its artistic director, Odessa-born Katherine Owens and her husband, Bruce DuBose, the executive producer, who heads its New York operations in the Astoria neighborhood of Queens. The company has staged several off-Broadway productions.

Raphael Parry, who has performed major roles at the Dallas Theater Center (see listing), is an Undermain co-founder. He has directed Shakespeare for the Shakespeare Festival of Dallas (see listing).

"There are many companies vying for attention on the DFW scene, but Undermain is one of the handful we simply can't imagine doing without," notes the *News*, adding that the company "shows the most consistent sensibility and artistic precision of any theater." The San Diego, California, *Union-Tribune* once named it "one of the best small theaters in America."

Among its past productions were Chekhov's *The Seagull*, Shakespeare's *The Comedy of Errors* and *Macbeth*, Faulkner's *The Sound and the Fury*, and Tennessee Williams' *Camino Real*. In 2001, the theater received a UNESCO grant to perform *Judges 19: Black Lungs Exhaling*, a "proletarian operetta," in Belgrade, Yugoslavia. The company presented the play, titled *Sarajevo*, in Macedonia in 1995.

WaterTower Theatre, Addison Conference & Theatre Center, 15650 Addison Rd. at Morris Ave., Addison, (972) 450-6220, Internet www.watertowertheatre.com, e-mail info@watertowertheatre.org. Performances are held Thu-Sun. A three-dollar processing fee is added to all phone orders.

Located north of downtown Dallas, between Dallas North Tollway and Addison Road, just west of Addison Circle and a few blocks north of Belt Line Road. Several fine restaurants are situated in the area. WTT has been the resident theater company of the Addison Center since 1996, when the Addison Center Theatre went belly up financially. The town of Addison subsidizes WaterTower to the tune of $200,000 a year.

"Good actors, good directing, good plays, good time," claims the weekly *Dallas Observer*, which also proclaims Alabama native Terry L.

Martin (b. 1957), who took the reins in 1992, as the "best theater director" in the area.

The "extraordinary" 200-seat theater is designed to be transformed for each production into a new environment as the need be. Entire or partial second and third floors can be added. There is no orchestra pit, since the instrumentalists are sitting under the viewers' seats, watching the actors via closed-circuit television. The *Dallas Morning News* calls it "the most innovative theater building in the country." The concrete, glass, and stone 32,000-square-foot (or 2,973-square-meter) space opened in 1992. Among its recent productions, WaterTower staged *Ravenscroft*, a Gothic whodunit written by Don Nigro, Eugene O'Neill's *Desire Under the Elms*, and Tennessee Williams' *Cat on a Hot Tin Roof*.

"Bold stuff for 1955, bold stuff still," notes the *Dallas Observer* admiringly of *Cat*, adding, "And so beautifully written—and at WaterTower so beautifully acted—it makes you ache to share the characters' physical and emotional pain over confronting their deepest secrets."

In the summer, WaterTower stages the annual Stone Cottage New Works Festival, named after a 75-seat cottage that was built in 1939 as part of the Works Progress Administration and is still a center component.

ART CINEMAS

From Inwood Cinema's three screens as recently as 2000, Dallas is now blessed by no fewer than 18 screens devoted to independent and foreign films, all located just a few miles apart:

Angelika Film Center & Café, 5321 Mockingbird Ln. at North Central Expwy., (214) 841-4700. Tuesday and Wednesday matinees are for parents with young children, and a changing table is provided.

Located in the Mockingbird Station (see entry) mixed development across the expressway from the Park Cities. The newest movie center in the city is the eight-screen Angelika, which opened amid a ten-acre (or four-hectare) collection of restaurants, upscale retailers, and lofts in the summer of 2001. Angelika has a fine café and a full bar. Mockingbird light-rail station offers plenty of free parking within a short walk.

If you enjoy quality films, after Angelika stop at Premiere Video (see entry), across Mockingbird Lane for an equally good feature on tape.

Landmark's Inwood Cinema, 5458 West Lovers Ln. at Inwood Rd., (214) 352-5085, Internet www.landmarktheatres.com. Located in the Inwood Village Shopping Center (see entry) northwest of downtown Dallas and just east of Love Field Airport.

The 50-year-old, three-screen Inwood is the oldest art cinema in Dallas. It is part of the Landmark chain with 52 cinemas and 166 screens, the nation's largest art-house chain. A Bookstop bookstore is situated next door.

The 100-seat Lounge at the Inwood Theater, (214) 350-7834, is open Tue-Sat 5 PM-2 AM, Sun-Mon 5 PM-midnight and has attracted intellectuals for more than 20 years. The lounge, "where people smoke Gitanes and whisper about the foreign films playing next door, is the ultimate in retro chic," claims *D Magazine*, while *In Style* magazine picked it as one of the best such places in the country.

The Magnolia, 3699 McKinney Ave. at Lemmon Ave., (214) 520-0025. Dallas- and Austin-based investors opened this five-screen, stadium-seating and Dolby-sound art cinema in 2002 in the West Village development uptown. It specializes in independent and foreign-language films. A full-service bar and "gourmet" concessions are also on the premises. There are 850 parking spaces inside the development.

"From the latest art film offerings to classic movies to little-seen documentaries, the Magnolia never fails to delight," claims *D Magazine*, which named it the best art cinema in the city.

Regent Highland Park, Mockingbird Ln. at Preston Rd., (214) 526-9668, Internet www.regententertainment.com. Located in the Highland Park Village shopping center, east of North Dallas Tollway. A former four-screen AMC cinema complex that went artsy in 2001, it is owned by Dallas-based Regent Entertainment Corp., an independent producer and distributor of low-budget films. The Highland Park Village Theatre originally opened in 1935.

The USA Film Festival, Internet www.usafilmfestival.com, established in 1970, is the oldest such event in the Metroplex, followed by the **Dallas Video Festival,** Internet www.videofest.org, started in 1986. Other area festivals that sprouted up in recent years include:

- **The Deep Ellum Film Festival,** est. in 1998, which takes place in November, (214) 752-6759, Internet www.def.org.
- **The Fort Worth Film Festival,** est. in 1997, which takes place in October, (817) 390-8711, Internet www.fortworthfilmfestival.com.
- **The Jewish Film Festival,** est. in 1995, which takes place in March, (214) 739-2737, Internet www.jccdallas.org.
- **The Vistas Film Festival,** est. 1998, which takes place in October, (214) 220-3260, Internet www.vistasfilmfestival.org.

NIGHTLIFE

Dallas has three areas where bars, lounges, nightclubs, and live music venues are concentrated: downtown's West End, the Deep Ellum neighborhood east of downtown, and along Lower Greenville Avenue in near East Dallas, south of Mockingbird Lane, where there are more than 50 establishments.

(Some, such as Sambuca Jazz Cafe, which could be listed in either chapter, are described in the DINING chapter.)

"Dallas club goers exhibit all the constancy of Emma Bovary," observes the *Dallas Morning News*. "Risk-averse and herd-positive, they like to go where it's easy to get to and where everybody else is going."

Smoking

The Dallas City Council voted in 2003 to ban smoking in all restaurants, hotel and motel guest rooms not designated for smoking, and private clubs with eating establishments. Smokers are allowed to light up on restaurant patios, as long as they are not enclosed.

The smoking ban was also extended to all Dallas museums, cinemas, libraries, bowling alleys, and bingo parlors. The only exceptions to the ban are specifically designated areas of stand-alone bars and pool halls, cigar bars, and outdoor patios.

Drinking establishments must derive 75 percent or more of their gross revenue each quarter from the sale of alcoholic beverages to allow smoking, and even they must provide no-smoking sections. Fines range from $25 to $500.

Addison

Flying Saucer
Memphis

Deep Ellum

Art Bar
Club Clearview
Blind Lemon
Club Dada
The Bone
The Door

The Gypsy Tea Room
Lizard Lounge
Main Street Internet Café
Trees
Xpo Lounge

Downtown

Dallas Alley
Euphoria
Gilley's
Umlaut

Greenville Avenue

Cuba Libre Café
The Dubliner
Mariano's Mexican Cuisine
Muddy Waters
Poor David's Pub
Red Jacket & Ruby Room

North Dallas

Dave & Busters
G.G.'s Jazz Club
Obzeet
Samba Room
Sipango
Times Square

Uptown

Hard Rock Café

Bars & Clubs

Art Bar/Blind Lemon/Club Clearview, 2803-2805 Main St., between Crowdus St. and Malcolm X Blvd., (214) 939-0077/0202. Oakland was renamed Malcolm X Boulevard in 1998. Open Wed- or Thu-Sat 6 PM or 7 PM-11 PM or 2 AM. Live music Thu-Sat. Dancing. One cover charge is all you need for all three clubs. You must be 21 to drink here. Located in Deep Ellum, just east of downtown Dallas. Also on the block is the Palm Beach Reggae Club.

Three hip bars in a 1992 collection of Deep Ellum venues, from national alternative to pop acts, from swing dance lessons to live lounge music. A popular meeting place, Blind Lemon, is named after the well-known Texas blues singer "Blind Lemon" Jefferson, who played Deep Ellum after moving to Dallas in 1917. Surprisingly, it does not even have a photo of Blind Lemon on the wall. Club Clearview, with a rooftop patio, is the oldest nightclub in Deep Ellum. Texas Poetry Slam regional competitions are held here.

The Bone, 2724 Elm St. and Crowdus St., Deep Ellum, (214)

744-2663, Internet www.thebone.com. *NCH*. Open Tue-Sat 8 PM-2 AM; closed Sundays and Mondays. There is live blues Tue-Thu, live music also Fri-Sat 6 PM-9 PM. No cover charge, but there might be a line on weekends to get in. Must be 21 or older to enter. Casual dress, but no tank tops for women.

A stylish bar located next to Club Dada and across the street from the Green Room that has a 2,500-square-foot (or 232-square-meter) rooftop patio with full bar and a view of downtown. Features pool tables. There are large television sets to while away your time.

A large club for a mostly younger clientele, although some in their 40s and 50s will also be found here. A "meat market," the *Dallas Observer* labels it. The Bone is owned by Ray Balestri, a cohort of Dallas billionaire Mark Cuban, who made Balestri a multimillionaire by getting him to invest early in Broadcast.com which was sold to Yahoo.

Club Dada, 2720 Elm St. at North Crowdus, (214) 744-DADA, Internet www.clubdada.com, e-mail info@clubdada.com. Open Sun 8 PM-2 AM, Wed-Thu 7 PM-2 AM, Fri-Sat 5 PM-2 AM; closed Mon-Tue. Live music nightly. Accommodates up to 225. Cover charge applies Fri-Sat after 9 PM.

Happy hour starts at 5 PM. You must be at least 21 years old to be admitted. Located in Deep Ellum, east of downtown Dallas, next to The Bone club (see entry). Established in 1986, this original and eclectic Deep Ellum club is one of the oldest in the area and leans toward traditional rock and blues. It has three stages—one outdoor—and three bars, also a back patio with lush trees so patrons can enjoy a drink outside in the spring or fall.

Cuba Libre Café, 2822 North Henderson Ave. at Willis Ave., (214) 827-2820. Open daily 11 AM-2 AM. Happy hour is Mon-Fri 4 PM-7 PM. The kitchen is open until 1:30 AM. Seats up to 140. Smoking on the patio. Wheelchair accessible. Parking available behind the building.

Opened in 2000 in an elaborately constructed two-story triangular building, located north of downtown and two blocks east of North Central Expressway (or U.S. Hwy. 75).

"A popular spot for the out-and-about crowd, this place swings into noisy-bar mode Thursday through Saturday nights," declares the *Fort Worth Star-Telegram*. Owned by the 30-something-old Tristan Simon, Cuba Libre caters mostly to a younger clientele.

(Cuba Libre is a popular mixed drink.) *D Magazine* labeled the café's signature cocktail as "a wimpy frozen blend of rum, Coke, and lime." "The drink is authentically Caribbean, while this bar and grill—albeit immensely festive—simply injects cute, technicolor island theme in decor and menu," claims the *Fort Worth Star-Telegram*.

Dallas Alley, 2019 North Lamar St. at Munger Ave. and Marker St., (214) 720-0170/2036, Internet www.dallasalley.com. Open Wed-Sat 7 PM-2 AM; closed Sun-Tue. One admission for all four bars. You must be at least 18 years of age on Thursdays and 21 on all other nights. Located next to the West End Market Place, a reconstructed turn-of-the-century candy and cracker factory with 50 specialty shops on five floors.

The Dallas Alley promotes itself as being "reminiscent of New Orleans' Bourbon Street," and consists of four piano, karaoke, oldies, and 90s bars, and video arcade with a variety of nightly entertainment. The ten alley sculptures by Texan William Easley honor ten Texas pop and blues legends: The Big Bopper, Blind Lemon Jefferson, Lefty Frizzell, Buddy Holly, Scott Joplin, Sam "Lightin'" Hopkins, Roy Orbison, Tex Ritter, T-Bone Walker, and Bob Wills.

Dave & Buster's, 8021 Walnut Hill Ln., (214) 361-5553, Internet www.daveandbusters.com. M. Open for lunch and dinner daily 11 AM-midnight. Those under the age of 21 must be accompanied by a parent or guardian. A new murder mystery, with audience participation, is shown each month with a performance every Friday evening, starting at 8 PM. Located northeast of downtown Dallas and NorthPark mall (see listing), in a small strip mall, just off North Central Expressway.

The Dallas-based Dave & Buster's was founded in 1982 by Dave Corriveau and James "Buster" Corley. The two lads once ran a restaurant and an entertainment center side by side in Little Rock, Arkansas. Seeing that many customers visited both, the entrepreneurs merged their businesses that now cater to adults ages 21 to 44 years.

There are many distractions in this friendly, large complex which opened in 1988 and caters to adults looking for children's play in more than one way. It includes games of chance and skill, virtual reality games, fake casino-style games, and several bars where patrons are likely to bump into an attractive member of the opposite sex. The handmade mahogany billiard tables cost $7,500 each, but the investment paid off handsomely, when in the mid-1990s pool became popular among the monied professionals, who arrive in their Lexuses and BMWs.

The original Dave & Buster's is located in Dallas' Restaurant Row, at 10727 Composite Dr. and Walnut Hill Ln. Another is in Frisco's Stonebriar Centre shopping center, 2601 Preston Rd. at Hwy. 121, where a 50,000-square-foot (or 4,645 square-meter) facility employs 250 and boasts 200 state-of-the-art arcade games.

The Door, 3202 Elm St. at Hall St., Deep Ellum, (214) 742-3667, Internet www.thedoorclubs.com. Open Thu-Sat 8 PM-1 AM. *CH*. Live music Thu-Sat. Not wheelchair accessible. Located in Deep Ellum east of downtown Dallas, across the street from the Bank of America.

An all-ages, three-room, 10,000-square-foot (or 929-square-meter) venue with a concert hall, coffeehouse, and theater. One of the few area clubs that feature Christian rock music.

The Dubliner, 2818 Lower Greenville Ave., (214) 818-0911. Open Mon-Fri 4 PM-2 AM, Sat-Sun 3 PM-2 AM. Happy hour Mon-Fri 4 PM-7 PM, Sat-Sun 2 PM-7 PM. The kitchen is open until 12:30 AM. Irish newspapers are available for perusal. Located in east Dallas, northeast of downtown, next door to the Grape (see entry) restaurant and across the street from the Blue Goose.

An Irish pub, owned and operated by two natives of Dublin. It might surprise you with its selection of imported whiskeys, stouts, porters, ales, and ciders. It has fabulous baked potatoes, as well as standard sandwiches, like roast beef, club, Reuben, and Welsh rarebit, most under five dollars each.

Other Irish hangouts, all located east of North Central Expressway and going southward from Mockingbird Lane, include:

- **The Blarney Stone,** 2116 Lower Greenville Ave. at Richmond, (214) 821-7099.
- **Cock & Bull,** 6330 Gaston Ave. at La Vista Court, (214) 841-9111.
- **Trinity Hall Pub & Restaurant,** 5321 East Mockingbird Ln. at North Central Expwy., (214) 887-3647. (See also entry Mockingbird Station in the SHOPPING chapter.)

For British fare, go to the **Londoner** (see listing), located in Addison.

Euphoria, 1400 Main St., between Field and Akard Sts., (214) 658-1400. *CH*. Open Mon-Wed 5 PM-10 PM, Thu-Sat 4 PM-2 AM. You must be 21 to drink here. Seats 800. Wheelchair accessible. Dress code is hip and trendy. Located in downtown Dallas, across the street from the bistro JeroboAM and down the road from the nightclub Umlaut (see individual listings).

The three-level, 8,000-square-foot (or 743-square-meter) dance club with a 35-foot (or 10.6-meter) water wall in the basement bar opened in 2002. It serves sushi. "Euphoria sticks to the basics," notes the *Dallas Observer*, "And the basics drift from average to sub par, mostly." Twenty-five varieties of sake are available. The *Dallas Morning News*, whose restaurant critic gives it only two of the possible five stars for its food, calls it "a Gothic funhouse," adding, "It's imposing, garish and somewhat bizarre, which is not exactly a condemnation."

Among its more unusual amenities, you will encounter caves, a Plexiglass-floor DJ booth, a private elevator, and a third-floor sushi bar surrounded by a $45,000, 1,500-gallon (or 5,678-liter) aquarium teeming with fish from the Florida Keys, including stingrays, sharks, blowfish, lionfish, and a four-foot (or 1.2-meter) moray eel.

Flying Saucer, 14999 Montfort Dr. at Belt Line Rd., Addison, (972) 934-2537, Internet www.beerknurd.com/addison. Open for lunch and dinner Mon-Wed 11 AM-midnight, Thu-Sat 11 AM-2 AM, Sun noon-midnight. Occasional live entertainment. Wheelchair accessible. Located in the Village on the Parkway (see entry), one block east of the Dallas North Tollway behind restaurants Bennigan's, El Fenix, and Steak and Ale.

Opened in 1996 by Dallas entrepreneur Shannon Wynne, the son of Six Flags Over Texas (see entry) creator Angus Wynne. He also started Flying Fish restaurant at the Village on the Parkway in Addison. This beer joint could make you believe it stocks every beer on the planet. It claims to have more than 100 varieties of brew on tap and stocks another 100-plus bottled kinds from dozens of countries. The food menu is rather short and limited mostly to food that makes it possible to handle more beer. There is an extensive selection of cigars.

G.G.'s Jazz Club, 5915 East Northwest Hwy. at Shady Brook, (214) 692-7088. Open Wed-Fri 5 PM-2:30 AM, Sat-Sun 8 PM-2:30 AM. Live music. Wheelchair accessible. Located northeast from downtown Dallas, a block east of North Central Expressway (or U.S. Hwy. 75) and across the street from Half Price Books (see listing). NorthPark (see entry) mall is just a few blocks west of here. A multi-level dance and jazz club with a balcony-style stage. A good place to listen to rhythm & blues.

The Gypsy Tea Room, 2548 Elm St. at Good-Latimer Exwy., Deep Ellum, (214) 744-9779, Internet www.gypsytearoom.com. *CH*. Live music Wed-Sat. Wheelchair accessible.

A former microbrewery that features country and rock acts. Operated by owners of the Green Room and Trees, it consists of a 10,000-square-foot (or 929-square-meter) ballroom with entrance on Main Street and a 2,500-square-foot (or 232-square-meter) performance spot you can enter from Elm. The interior has exposed brick walls and hardwood floors. "Gypsy Tea Room is the finest music venue in that grimy little world called Deep Ellum," claims the *Dallas Observer*. "It looks great, sounds good, has plenty of charm and now boasts a variety of talent, not playing favorites to one genre."

Hard Rock Café, 2601 McKinney Ave. at Routh St., (214) 855-0007, Internet www.hardrock.com. M. Open Sun-Wed 11 AM-11 PM, Thu 11 AM-1 AM, Fri-Sat 11 AM-midnight. Seats 250. Live music starts at 10 PM Thu-Sat. Valet parking is available. Located uptown across

Routh Street from the Paris Bistro, one block from the Italian-cuisine Avanti on McKinney, and the same distance from Arcodoro & Pomodoro.

The café was begun in 1971 by two Americans in London homesick for hamburgers and rock & roll. It was the place to be and to be seen in the 1970s and 1980s. Objects on exhibit include everything from guitars to "Madonna's now-classic bustier." The concept is similar to Planet Hollywood, the movie memorabilia restaurant chain begun in 1991 by Hard Rock's former president, except that Hard Rock stresses music and the Planet movies. Merchandise—from $16 boxer shorts to $230 leather bomber jackets—sometimes accounts for up to one-half of the business.

The 20-year-old café is situated in the building originally erected as a Baptist church in 1906, when the fiery Fort Worth preacher Frank Norris led the Baptists in opposing dancing and short skirts. Judging by the lines up the carpeted stairs to this rock & roll temple, with a working oil pump next door to it, this hamburger site must be on the itinerary of every passing tourist. The food is average and the music ear splitting.

Lizard Lounge, 2424 Swiss Ave., between North Central Expressway and Good-Latimer Expwy., (214) 826-4768. Open Thu-Sun 9 PM-4 AM. *CH*. For ages 18 and older. Smoking permitted. It has a patio. Located just north of the Deep Ellum Historic District, east of downtown Dallas.

A two-story, bordello-red, velvet-covered dance club. Features theme nights and video bar. The weekly *Dallas Observer* named it the city's best dance club. Thursday and Sunday nights, up to 500 pack the lounge for a get-together known as the Church, a masquerade party held every week by the same group of friends amid gothic culture that encourages fascination with horror. Dress code is strictly vampire: black clothes and white-powdered faces; fangs are optional.

Main Street Internet Café, 2656 Main St. at Good Latimer Exwy., (214) 237-1121. Open Mon-Sat 8 AM-2 AM, Sun 10 AM-midnight. It has a bar. Live music on Wednesdays. Located in Deep Ellum east of downtown Dallas.

Opened in 2000, this is one of the few Internet cafés in Dallas. It is owned by computer industry veteran Ed Quarles, whose family members also work here. The café has some 20 computers and Internet games. You can sit on one of the sofas or at the bar, where you will be served an espresso or an alcoholic drink. Flat customized screens hang from the ceiling for your Internet surfing. For every beverage that costs more than three dollars, you get complimentary 30 minutes on the Web.

Mariano's Mexican Cuisine, Old Town Shopping Center, 5500 Greenville Ave. at Lover Ln., (214) 691-3888. Open Tue-Thu 11 AM-10 PM, Fri-Sat 11:30 AM-11 PM, Sun 11:30 AM-10 PM. Located northeast of downtown Dallas, just west of North Central Expressway.

This is actually more of a Mexican restaurant than a watering hole, except that it holds a special place in Dallas' drinking annals. On May 11, 1971, Dallas restaurateur Mariano Martinez, Jr. created the world's first mass-produced frozen margarita here with the help of a converted ice cream machine.

A few months later, the Texas legislature made it legal for restaurants to sell liquor by the drink in their dining rooms, instead of separate private clubs. The area around here became popular with singles, and Mariano's has prospered ever since. The fact that Southern Methodist University is just a few blocks southwest of here did not hurt one bit. Several scenes for the television soap opera *Dallas* were filmed here. Even Frank Sinatra once stopped by. Martinez, who once played in a rock and roll band and graduated from Dallas' El Centro College, was 26 years old when he opened Mariano's with a margarita recipe from his father.

Memphis, 5000 Belt Line Rd., Addison, (972) 386-9517, Internet www.memphis-dallas.com. Open daily 4 PM-2 AM, Fri-Sat 7:30 PM-2 AM. *CH*. Features rock and jazz bands nightly. Happy hour Mon-Fri 4 PM-8 PM with complimentary buffet. Located a couple of miles (or 3.2 kilometers) north of the Galleria Mall, on the southwest corner of Belt Line and Dallas North Tollway.

Opened in 1982. Dim, noisy, and intimate, a favorite for members of the opposite sex who hunger for human contact. It has a Cajun restaurant that serves food until 1:30 AM.

Muddy Waters, 1518 Lower Greenville Ave., one block north of Ross Ave., (214) 823-1518. Open daily 6 PM-2 AM. Live music starts at 10 PM. *CH* on weekends. Located in east Dallas, just a mile (or 1.6 kilometers) or so from downtown.

Everything from blues to rock & roll can be heard at this unpretentious funky club nightly. "Muddy Waters is the perfect dark hole to crawl into when you just need a cold beer, good company, and uncomplicated music that cleanses your soul," claims *D Magazine*.

Obzeet, 19020 Preston Rd. at Lloyd, (972) 867-6126. Open Mon-Thu 10 AM-11 PM, Fri 10 AM-1 AM, Sat 10 AM-midnight, Sun 11 AM-8 PM. Plays live jazz Mon-Sat during warm months. You must be 21 years old to drink here. Located in far-north Dallas, between Frankford Road and President George Bush Turnpike. French-cuisine Lavendou Bistro (see listing under Chez Gerard) is situated across Preston Road.

Obzeet is South African slang for "groovy." During the day, Obzeet is a coffee bar; by night, it becomes a tropical spot with outdoor waterfalls and a creek that runs through the property. Serves more than a dozen varieties of ice-cold martinis. It has an outdoor patio with a fish pond. Food includes smoked salmon and salads. "The rambling combo antique shop and café opens to an outdoor garden that is a delight for the drinking class," observes the *Dallas Morning News*.

Poor David's Pub, 1924 Lower Greenville Ave. near Ross in east Dallas, (214) 821-9891, Internet www.poordavidspub.com. Open daily 7 PM-1 AM, music starts at 9 PM Mon-Sat; closed Sundays.

A prestigious club seating up to 200 whose decor, if you can call it that, consists of "exposed rafters and orange vinyl chairs covered with strips of electrical duct tape," according to the *Dallas Morning News*. "The floor is covered with a cobalt blue rug speckled with small stains, like liver spots." The menu is equally no-frills: nachos and sandwiches.

The original club, a dart-throwing bar really, stood on the corner of McKinney Avenue. When the lease was up in 1983, the owner, David Card, a former IBM computer salesman with an MBA, moved it to its current location. Some of the greatest folk and blues musicians, such as John Lee Hooker, Albert Collins, and Clarence "Gatemouth" Brown performed here. No pinball machines or jukeboxes, just good music.

Red Jacket & Ruby Room, 3606 Lower Greenville Ave., five blocks south of Mockingbird Ln., (214) 823-8333. *CH.* Open Wed-Thu 10 PM-2 AM, Fri-Sun 9 PM-2 AM. Live music Thursdays. Specials on drinks Fri-Sat before 11 PM. You must be 21 to drink here. Seats up to 150. It has a sunken dance pit. Wheelchair accessible. Located in east Dallas.

A dance club that tries to be all things to all people on different nights of the week to keep ahead of changes. It has theme nights and capitalizes on such quirky celebrities as Ron Jeremy of adult-film fame. Sundays radio station KDGE (94.5 FM) broadcasts gothic and new wave tunes from here. Pool tables, poker games, and go-go dancers are featured.

In 1998, Red Jacket expanded to include the Ruby Room, a "tacky" tribute to the nightclub owner who killed John F. Kennedy's alleged assassin. It includes a Kennedy bust and an enlarged photo of the fatally wounded and grimacing Lee Harvey Oswald.

Samba Room, 4514 Travis St. at Knox, Suite 132, (214) 522-4137. Open daily 5 PM-midnight, Sunday brunch noon-3 PM. It has a bar. Happy hour Sun-Thu 4 PM-7 PM. Located on the southern edge of Highland Park, three blocks west of North Central Expressway (or U.S.

Hwy. 75). Next door is the Italian-cuisine restaurant Il Sole, and across the street club Sipango (see individual listings).

A Cuban bar and Latin café stuffed with impossibly pretty people who do not know what to do with themselves or their time. There are more little black dresses here on a weekend night than at the Dallas Opera gala. Loud Latin music is the trademark of this joint. Brazilian fried calamari, Caesar's salad, Cuban chicken sandwich, and Argentinian-style skirt steak are some of the menu items.

"The Samba Room combines the sizzle of Havana with a cool Uptown address," notes *D Magazine*, while *Playboy* magazine describes it as "a swank club that takes you back to pre-Castro Cuba days." Samba Room's humidor stocks cigars.

(For **Sambuca Jazz Café,** please see entry in the restaurant chapter.)

Sipango, 4513 Travis St. at Knox St., (214) 522-2411, Internet www.sipango.com. *E*. Open for dinner Tue-Wed 6 PM-10:30 PM, and Thu-Sat 6 PM-2 AM; closed Sun-Mon. Live entertainment nightly, including dancing. The private Sellar nightclub, located under the restaurant, is open Fri-Sat only. Cover charge for men only starts at 9:30 PM. Located on the southern edge of Highland Park, a couple of blocks west of North Central Expressway (or U.S. Hwy. 75), between Knox Street and Armstrong Avenue. Italian-cuisine Il Sole, bar Samba Room, and French L'Ancestral restaurant (see listings) are located across the street.

A popular watering spot for singles, opened in 1994, with people-watching being a major feature that you may have to stand in line for. "Sipango is a place for the sveltely sexy; the conspicuously primped; the elegantly hip," once said the weekly *Dallas Observer*, which named it the best dance club for those over 21 years of age.

The 3,000-square-foot (or 279-square-meter) basement Sellar is an inner sanctum for star athletes, celebrities, and middle-aged men with wallets as fat as their owners. "The great draw of the place is that it keeps people out: You're in; somebody else is not," observes the *News*. The initiation fee for the Sellar, where even Monaco's Princess Stephanie displayed her assets, is $1,000. Service is particularly attentive if you are perceived as important or wealthy. The food is mostly entertainment and an excuse to socialize and drink.

Just south of Sipango, at 4501 Travis St., is located **Café Madrid,** a tapas bar.

Trees, 2707 Elm St. between Crowdus and Good-Latimer Expwy, in Deep Ellum, (214) 748-5014; events, 748-5099, Internet www.trees.com. Open Tue-Thu 8:30 PM-1 AM, Fri-Sat 9 PM-2 AM. You must be at least 21 to drink here. Cover charge when there is live music. Wheelchair accessible. Located in Deep Ellum east of downtown Dallas.

"Designed to look like an indoor forest (if you've had several drinks and the house lights are down)," says *D Magazine*. There are no trees, except for a few pillars "half-heartedly disguised as trees," but you will find upstairs and downstairs bars, pool tables, video games, and rock music.

This is perhaps the best-known Dallas rock & roll venue with local and national acts that can accommodate up to 900 patrons. Nirvana, Smashing Pumpkins, and Pearl Jam all played their first Dallas gigs at Trees. This was the club where the rocker Kurt Cobain sparked a near-riot in 1991 after his fight with a bouncer.

Brothers Brady and Brandt Wood of New Orleans took over Trees in 1991, six months after it opened. In Deep Ellum, they also own the Green Room restaurant, and downtown the French brasserie named Jeroboam (see listing).

Umlaut, 1602-B Main St., (214) 748-2368. *CH*. Open Mon-Sat 8 PM-2 AM. Has a disc jockey. Located downtown, between Ervay and Akard Streets, near the Neiman Marcus department store (see entry).

A 4,000-square-foot (or 372-square-meter) subterranean, futuristic club that includes a small dance floor and a patio, created by the "brothers of cool," Brandt and Brady Wood, who already own restaurants Jeroboam, a couple of blocks away, and the Green Room in Deep Ellum. The former cafeteria is named after the two-dot Germanic symbol. Umlaut sports lavender leather booths, cherry-red chairs, and light-blue couches. Feels like "a rich guy's apartment," claims the *Dallas Morning News*.

Xpo Lounge, 408 Exposition St., Deep Ellum, (214) 823-2329. Open Mon-Sat 5 PM-2 AM, Sun 8 PM-2 AM. Happy hour all day Sun-Mon. Located east of downtown, near Fair Park (see entry), in a renovated warehouse.

Details magazine named Xpo Lounge one of the best bars nationwide. It "hums with the artistic-hip vibe that rocked Deep Ellum before the yuppies came," notes the weekly *Dallas Observer*. David Quadrini, owner of Deep Ellum's Angstrom Gallery (see entry), hangs out here.

Country & Western Dance Clubs

Cowboys Red River Dance Hall, 10310 West Technology Blvd. at West Northwest Hwy., (972) 263-0404. *CH*. Open Wed-Thu 7 PM-2 AM, Fri 5 PM-2 AM, Sat 7 PM-2 AM, Sun 5 PM-11 PM; closed Mon-Tue.

Live music Wed-Sat starts after 9 PM. No alcohol is served. Dress code is casual. Minimum age is 18. Located just east of Loop 12, in this instance Walton Walker Boulevard, and west of Stemmons Freeway, also known as Interstate Highway 35 East. **Top Rail** (see listing), a nightspot of like kind, is located less than a mile (or 1.8 kilometers) north of here.

The circular wooden dance floor surrounding the bar is the most popular attraction in this 1980s-style club that can accommodate up to 3,000. A wide walkway separates the stage from the dance floor. Dance lessons are available. Off the dance floor, you will find blackjack, craps, and pool.

Gilley's, 1409 South Lamar St. at Cadiz, (214) 428-2919 or (888) GILLEYS, Internet www.gilleysdallas.com. Located downtown, within walking distance of the City Hall and the Dallas Convention Center (see entries), a block from a DART light-rail line.

There is practically nothing that pleases Dallasites more than being able to brag about something that is the biggest or grandest in the world. When Gilley's announcement was made in 2000, hired cowboys walked around a former warehouse in duster coats and shot blanks in the air.

After two years of planning, the largest honky-tonk in Dallas was promised for 2004. It was to sit on ten acres (or four hectares) of land. It just so happens that all those thousands of out-of-town conventioneers, dying for some Wild West fare, including Texas barbecue, are just a stone's throw away—and until now have gone to Fort Worth.

But the 45,000-square-foot (or 4,180-square-meter) outdoor rodeo arena is supposedly just the beginning of the $18-million, three-building, 91,000-square-foot (or 8,454-square-meter) entertainment complex. Retail shops selling boots, hats, and Western wear; theme bars; and restaurants are planned for. The Coors Light Showroom promises to seat 4,000 for concerts.

The original club, also run by country music singer Mickey Gilley, opened in Pasadena, Texas, in 1971 and was immortalized in John Travolta's 1980 film, *Urban Cowboy*. It closed in 1989 after a devastating and mysterious fire.

Sons of Hermann Hall, 3414 Elm St. at Exposition Ave., Deep Ellum, (214) 747-4422, Internet www.sonsofhermann.com. *CH*, cash only. Open Wed-Fri 5 PM-midnight, Sat 5 PM-1 AM. Live music Thu-Sat, usually starts after 9 PM. Wheelchair accessible. Located in the Deep Ellum Historical District at the corner of Elm and Exposition Avenue, the building is one of the oldest wooden structures in Dallas and is situated on land that originally cost just $6,500.

A saloon, dance floor, and country music museum that has been open since 1911, Sons of Hermann housed a German fraternal organization until 1982, when it opened to the public. The organization, composed of immigrants who formed to provide insurance for members, takes its name from Hermann the Defender, known as the first-century German folk hero who united the various Germanic tribes to successfully fend off the Roman army. The doors still have peepholes used by members to bar unwelcome visitors.

It is a favorite dance hall for those who enjoy offbeat bands and music that could include reggae, blues, Western swing, and gospel. Dance lessons can be had. Pool and shuffleboard tables are also available.

Times Square, 5640 Arapaho Rd. at Prestonwood Blvd., (972) 701-9751. Open Wed-Fri 5 PM-2 AM, Sat 8 PM-2 AM. *CH* for men Wed-Sat. Tennis shoes, baseball caps, and T-shirts are discouraged, but jeans with shirts and jackets are acceptable. Valet parking is available. Located in far-north Dallas, north of LBJ Freeway, three blocks east of Dallas North Tollway, and near the former Prestonwood Town Center mall at the site of a former AMC theater.

Formerly called City Streets, this club encompasses five separate entities: San Antonio Rose country bar, Bourbon Street karaoke room, South Beach dance club, Wall Street martini bar, and Stray Cats dueling piano bar. The $2-million, 21,000-square-foot (or 1,951-square-meter) megaclub was inaugurated in 2000 by a German-born Houston businessman.

There is a floor-to-ceiling painting of the Alamo in the San Antonio bar. The karaoke room has a replica of the New Orleans French Quarter landmark street painted by Dallas artist Frank Campagna. The martini bar has a 20-foot-long ticker tape with real stock market quotes from New York. The club is packed with up to 2,500 people on a weekend night. The age of the clientele hovers in the mid-30s around 10 PM, but drops to the mid-20s by 1 AM.

A Latin dance club is located on the other side of what was once Prestonwood Mall, **Blackberry's,** 15203 Knoll Trail at Arapaho Road, and is open Wed, Fri-Sat 9 PM-2 AM. You must be 21 or older to enter. No jeans or athletic wear allowed on Saturdays.

Top Rail, 2110 West Northwest Hwy. at Loop 12, (972) 556-9099. *CH*, except Tue and Thu. Open Mon 6 PM-midnight, Tue-Sat 11 AM-2 AM, Sun 5 PM-2 AM. Happy hour Tue-Fri 11 AM-7 PM. Live country music on weekends. Wheelchair accessible. Located west of Interstate Highway 35 East (also known as Stemmons Freeway), unfortunately among the topless bars, which detract from this venue.

In business since 1935, this "gritty Texas honky-tonk" is one of the state's oldest ballrooms and a top spot to enjoy country and western dancing. "Top Rail is less of a pickup spot than the more hormone-driven clubs, and the somewhat older clientele is more interested in dancing than pairing up," says the *Dallas Morning News*. "Even so, singles shouldn't have much trouble finding a partner to kick up with on the roomy dance floor."

Tuesdays when Cowboys Red River is closed, Top Rail is humming, also Fridays and Saturdays. Dance lessons are available. But if you don't care for them, you can enjoy pool or sit down at blackjack tables. Cowboys Red River (see listing), a similar venue, is situated less than a mile (or 1.6 kilometers) south of here.

SIGHTS & ATTRACTIONS

There is plenty to see and enjoy in Dallas, as long as you keep in mind that 50 years, not 500, means history in Dallas. Here are some of the better-known sights, listed in alphabetical order.

"Dallas architecture is not great, as a whole—certainly not on an international level, nor as compared to the fabric of archetypal American cities such as New York, Chicago, and Philadelphia," according to the Dallas chapter of the American Institute of Architects. "But if Dallas architecture is not great, it does indeed have its great moments." Such is the AIA's introduction to the *Guide to Dallas Architecture*, one of the better city guides "to the man-made structures," which you can purchase by calling (214) 742-3242, Internet www.dallasAIA.org.

"Dallas is a postwar American city, which means that much of its best architecture dates from the 1950s and 1960s, when the country was flush with money and optimism and people believed that the future was the place to be," observes the architecture critic of the *Dallas Morning News*.

The *San Antonio Express-News* claims that Dallas architecture, until a decade ago, was predictable. "It was the metropolitan equivalent of a social climber, projecting the outward form of wealth, breeding and sophistication, but a chicken-fried hayseed under the sequin."

Regardless of which definition you apply to the city, Dallas is not beautiful in the sense that Paris, London, Vienna, or Moscow, are. "Only five percent of poll respondents said they lived in the Dallas area because 'I find this region of the country attractive,'" according to the *Dallas Morning News*. "And only seven percent said they preferred it to other cities."

CH abbreviation indicates there is a charge, *NCH* that there is none.

1600 Pacific Place/LTV Tower, 1600 Pacific Ave., (214) 824-8500. Centrally located downtown, across the street from Thanksgiving Square (see listing).

This 33-story, 434-foot (or 132-meter) tall tower, formerly named

LTV Tower, was constructed for Ling-Temco-Vought in 1964 on the spot where one of several theaters facing Elm Street, on the other side of the building, was located decades ago. The sloping ground floor is still there to see. The 417,000-square-foot (or 38,739-square-meter) reinforced concrete tower sits atop a two-story, 200-car underground garage. An 18-foot-high (or 5.48-meter) lobby features a small reflecting pool in the building that feels dated. A nine-story, 500-car garage is adjoining the tower.

In 1966, an exclusive Lancers Club opened at the top of this tower, offering "fine quality food and first-class service in sophisticated settings for an exclusive membership to entertain family, friends, and business associates."

Texas entrepreneur James V. Ling (b. 1923) started Ling Electric Co. on January 1, 1947, with $2,000, "at first mostly installing doorbells and lighting fixtures," and merged it with Temco Electronics. In 1961, Ling Electric and Temco Electronics joined hands with the Connecticut defense contractor and aircraft designer Chance Vought, which made Ling's one of the 200 largest companies on the *Fortune* magazine list.

The merger almost sank Ling's ambition to build a Fortune 500 company, but it created Ling-Temco-Vought (LTV), which already had sales of $2.7 billion. By 1969, the conglomerate had acquired more than two dozen additional companies and kept changing their names. Ling was earning up to $375,000 a year, and his stockholdings once were valued at $80 million. In 1968, Ling-Temco-Vought acquired Jones and Laughlin Steel Co. for $425 million, the largest cash tender ever made until then. The successor became the 14th largest industrial enterprise in the United States, according to the *Fortune* ranking in 1969. By the end of the decade, it was providing 15,000 products and services and employing 29,000 workers. The company gradually acquired more than two dozen additional companies, including Braniff Airlines, National Car Rental, and the 110-year-old meat packer Wilson & Co., which was spun into several divisions. After financial difficulties, LTV's plants and other assets were later bought by W. L. Ross & Co., a private New York investment firm.

Ling was diagnosed with Guillain-Barre syndrome in 1981, but has recovered. Since 1992, he has been co-founder and chief executive of the privately owned Empiric Energy, Inc., a small oil and gas exploration company headquartered in Addison, a north Dallas suburb.

A. H. Belo Mansion/Dallas Bar Association, 2101 Ross Ave. at Olive St., (214) 220-0239/7449, Internet www.dallasbar.org. *NCH*. Guided tours Sep-May, second Tuesday of the month, 9 AM-11 AM.

Located in the northern part of downtown, across Pearl Street from

Belo Mansion, across the street from the Trammel Crow Center, Meyerson Symphony, and Cathedral Santuario de Guadalupe, is the only early-Dallas residence left standing in the central business district. It was built in 1890 by A. H. Belo, a Civil War officer and publisher of the Dallas Morning News. (Photo by Yves Gerem)

Cathedral Santuario de Guadalupe and Morton H. Meyerson Symphony Center (see entries). At the turn of the previous century, this was the silk-stocking district of Dallas and home to many of its business leaders. Today, this neoclassical revival mansion is a rare reminder of that opulent era.

Perhaps the only other outstanding historical structure remaining on Ross today is the Dallas Woman's Forum headquarters, at 4607 Ross. Built by a local banker in 1906, it was until then the most expensive mansion built in Dallas and considered one of the finest in the nation.

Ross Avenue, once a showcase Dallas street, was the first city thoroughfare to be paved, but today houses mostly fenced-in used-car lots with growling guard dogs. Most of the houses were built between 1880 and 1910, although some owners began moving away even before the last mansions were built. Belo's was one of the first Dallas homes to have electricity and indoor plumbing.

The Belo Mansion was designed by architect Herbert Green and stood on land once owned by Dallas banker, Capt. William Gaston. It is named after North Carolinian Alfred Horatio Belo (1839-1901), publisher of the *Dallas Morning News*.

"During the Civil War he served in every major engagement of Robert E. Lee's Army of Northern Virginia from Manassas to Appomattox," notes the Texas State Historical Association, and for his conduct at the battle of Bull Run was promoted to major. In 1862, he endeared himself to his regiment by dueling an officer of another regiment who cast doubt on North Carolinians' courage. Colonel Belo, who was severely wounded at Gettysburg in the summer of 1863, died in 1901 in his native Carolina.

He came to Texas in 1865 and went to work for the *Galveston News* as a bookkeeper. By 1876, Belo owned the newspaper that began publication in 1885 and is now the second largest daily in Texas, after the *Houston Chronicle*. Belo Corporation also publishes several other newspapers and owns television stations nationwide.

In the 1890s, Colonel Belo purchased a frame house here in his wife's name with $27,500 from her own funds. He built a luxurious structure with Corinthian columns and a pediment portico that resembled his family home in North Carolina. "The dark interior of the rooms with their handsome mahogany and oak paneling were considered 'hideous' by the Belo neighbors," according to the Bar Foundation's Web site.

The colonel's widow, Nettie Belo, lived in the mansion with her daughter-in-law and two granddaughters until her death in 1913. Belo's son, Alfred Jr., died of meningitis in 1906, and his wife, Helen Ponder of Denton, who had suffered from ill health, moved to the East Coast in 1922.

Four years later, the Sparkman family signed a 50-year lease on the building to use it as a funeral home downstairs, while they lived upstairs. In 1934, the bodies of bank robbers Clyde Barrow and Bonnie Parker were displayed here after being ambushed by Texas Ranger Frank Hamer and his lawmen. Ten thousand nosy Dallasites "nearly wrecked" the mansion trying to catch a glimpse of the outlaws. (For more details, please read the DALLAS PAST history chapter.)

Upon expiration of that lease in 1977, the colonel's granddaughter, Helen Belo Morrison, who was born in the mansion in 1902, agreed to sell it to the Dallas Bar Foundation, which restored it as the 14,000-square-foot (or 1,301-square-meter) Dallas Legal Education Center. The mansion is the only early-Dallas residence left standing in the central business district.

In place of its 60-space, street-level parking lot, the Bar Association built a 20,000-square-foot (or 1,858-square-meter), $12-million pavilion and a 250-car underground garage.

Bank of America Plaza/NationsBank Building, Internet www.baplaza.com, 901 Main St. at Griffin, Elm, and Lamar Streets.

Located in the western part of downtown, two blocks east of the Dallas County Historical Plaza with John Neely Bryan's Cabin, John F. Kennedy Memorial, and "Old Red" Courthouse (see individual listings).

Before several of the largest Texas banks went bankrupt in the oil and real estate collapse of the 1980s, this was known as the InterFirst Building and before that as the First Republic Bank Building. In the late 1980s InterFirst merged with its competitor, RepublicBank, but the new corporation failed within a year.

The Federal Deposit Insurance Corporation closed all of the holding company's banks in what was then the largest bank failure in the United States, pumping $3.2 billion into member banks to restore them to a zero-capital position.

Rising 921 feet (or 280 meters), or 72 stories, above the street level, this is the tallest building in Dallas and has 48 elevators and 1,585 steps on its stairwells. It houses up to 6,000 residents and perhaps 2,000 visitors, many of them high-priced lawyers, and 28 floors of bank employees. New York City's Empire State Building, in comparison, is 1,250 feet tall and has 102 floors. One of the five tallest buildings in Texas, until recently this was also one of the 40 tallest in the world, giving the attention-starved Dallasites plenty to brag about.

The $300-million tower, which was inaugurated in the fall of 1985, has 1.84 million square feet (or 170,936 square meters) of leasable space, making it the largest office building in the city. You will recognize it at night by its radiant 10,000-foot (or 3,048-meter) emerald-green argon-gas outline, which can supposedly be seen as far as 26 miles (or 42 kilometers) away. What appears as a solid green light from a distance is actually a chain of tubes that are powered by 158 transformers.

The original National Exchange Bank of Dallas was founded in 1868 and eventually became the First National Bank of Dallas. In 1895 the North Texas Building was erected on the very spot where the Bank of America tower rises today. It had six stories and held the distinction of being the tallest building in Dallas for three years, when it was topped by the seven-story Linz Building, also on Main Street.

The street-level plaza is joined by an overhead trellis, and in the center of the trellis garden is a sunken courtyard planted with trees. An underground concourse encompasses 80,000 square feet (or 7,432 square meters) of arcades, shops, restaurants, and cafés. The concourse is also part of the city's underground network, which connects the Bank of America building with the rest of the central business district.

The **City Club,** originally founded in 1918, is located on the 69th floor of this building, where lunch and dinner are served for up to 300 persons.

The **Texas Club** fitness center is located atop the 15-story Bank of

America Plaza parking building, at 800 Main St. and Lamar nearby, (214) 761-6300, Internet www.thetexasclub.guidelive.com. Open daily. Established in 1985, it provides aerobics classes and cardiovascular training. There is an indoor running track, a 20-meter heated indoor swimming pool, a full-size basketball court, and five racquetball courts. Sauna, whirlpool, and massage are available.

Bank One Center, Ervay, Elm, Main, and St. Paul Sts., (214) 658-1600. Centrally located diagonally across the street from the Neiman Marcus luxury department store (see listing).

The 60-story Bank One Center was designed by the Cleveland-born, award-winning architect Philip Johnson (b. 1906) and John Burgee of Chicago—who formed a partnership in 1967—and was completed in 1987 at a cost of $300 million. With 1.53 million square feet (or 142,137 square meters) of space, it is one of Dallas' largest office buildings and vies for the honor of one of the tallest.

One of the last downtown office structures born of the 1980s real estate boom, the tower was erected as the headquarters for Dallas' Momentum Bank. Its name was changed to Bank One Tower in 1989. In 1997, a Fort Worth-based real estate investment trust purchased the building for $238 million, until then the highest price paid for any downtown office tower. The same trust also co-owns the Fountain Place and the 50-story Trammell Crow Center (see listings).

Johnson's career took off in 1948, when he was hired to design a house for John and Dominique de Menil, the French émigrés who transformed Houston's cultural life. Although the de Menil house was a modest project by today's standards, it led to Johnson's designing of the Pennzoil Place and Transco Tower. After he met Ruth Carter Stevenson, who in 1961 asked him to design the Amon Carter Museum in Fort Worth, she described him as "an absolutely enchanting man."

Stanley Marcus handpicked Johnson to design the John F. Kennedy Memorial, which in turn led to commissions for Thanksgiving Square, Bank One, and Crescent Court (see individual entries).

"Texas has been his laboratory and his refuge, welcoming him when others tried to kick him out the door, and on several occasions saving his career," notes David Dillon, the architecture critic of the *Dallas Morning News*, adding, "Philip Johnson's greatest achievements, as even he acknowledges, are likely to be as critic and mentor rather than designer."

Calatrava's Suspension Bridge across the Trinity River. Located downtown and linking Woodall Rodgers Freeway on the east side of the river with Singleton Boulevard (named for a Dallas County commissioner) in west Dallas.

The city earmarked $1.2 million in public art funds for the bridge's design, and an anonymous donor gave $2 million. Sports impresarios Mark Cuban of the Dallas Mavericks basketball team, Tom Hicks, who owns the local baseball and hockey teams, and real estate developer Ross Perot Jr. reached into their pockets to cover the difference for what will probably be the most talked about bridge in Dallas history. All three are among the wealthiest people in Texas and nationwide.

"Dallas has never seen anything like it," promises the architecture critic of the *Dallas Morning News*.

The $73-million, six-lane, steel arch and concrete traffic deck bridge, when completed in 2007, will be 1,870 feet (or 570 meters) long and more than 200 feet (or 61 meters) high. Its most striking feature might be a parabolic arch soaring 300 feet (or 91 meters) above the Trinity bed, strung with a double line of cables that curve over the top of the supporting structure.

Calatrava's sleek, futuristic creations "are feats of dazzling mechanical and structural difficulty, demanding invention, always attempting something that has never been done before," notes the *Dallas Observer*, which claims that his "abstract sculpture resembles warmed-over Henry Moore."

"A descendant of aristocratic Spaniards and converted Jews," according to his biographer Alexander Tzonis, Calatrava (b. 1951) grew up in a village near Valencia, Spain. "At age 14, his mother sent him to Paris to learn French and, at age 17, to Zurich to learn German."

Calatrava was paid a hefty $5.9 million to design the Dallas bridge. The Zurich- and Paris-based architect has proposed designing four more bridges across the Trinity to bridge the divide between various Dallas neighborhoods. "Fifteen million people come to Dallas every year," he told the *News*. "The bridges will be the new civic gateways that create the image of your city."

Additional bridges are facing an uphill battle, although Dallas County Commissioners Court and an anonymous benefactor pledged $6 million each to cover the cost of a second suspension bridge's design. If an additional $50 million can not be raised from state, federal, and private sources, the Texas Department of Transportation will proceed with a basic bridge design to replace the older structures.

"It appears that people are not conscious of the very high symbolic significance of bridges," observes Calatrava. "In Dallas, people are accustomed to bridges that are strictly functional and, in some cases, built to be replaced at regular intervals."

He studied to be a painter before receiving degrees in architecture, civil engineering, and urban planning from the Federal Institute of Technology in Zurich. Calatrava has already designed more than 40 bridges, mostly in Europe. In 2002, he was selected to design the

Atlanta Symphony Center in Georgia. Some critics accuse him of being self-indulgent and exhibitionistic.

Calatrava received the Meadows Foundation's $50,000 Algur H. Meadows Award for excellence in the arts at a formal dinner on the campus of Southern Methodist University in 2000.

"The event seemed part of the courtship, not so much of Mr. Calatrava, who's more than willing, but of the Dallas elite who could help pay for the project," reported the *News*.

The bridge will serve as a backdrop for the American Airlines Center (see entry), the basketball and ice hockey teams' new home, which opened in 2001 and is located less than a mile (or 1.6 kilometers) away. The city contributed $125 million of the arena's cost, with the money coming from increased hotel and rental-car taxes.

Cathedral Santuario de Guadalupe, 2215 Ross Ave. at Pearl St., (214) 871-1362, Internet www.cathdal.org/dallasparishes.htm. Open daily 9 AM-3:30 PM. Located in the northernmost part of downtown, next to the Meyerson Symphony Center (see listing), on what was the most elegant Dallas street at the turn of the previous century.

The Catholic cathedral is 160 feet (or 48.7 meters) long, 104 feet (or 31.7 meters) wide, and can seat 1,100 persons. It was designed by Galveston's 19th-century architect Nicholas Clayton and was dedicated on October 26, 1902, although the building was not completed as planned because the money ran out. The architect died in 1916 and was apparently never paid for his work.

"The well-proportioned facades and prominent corner tower are enriched and unified through the architect's deft use of color and texture," observes a publication by the Dallas chapter of the American Institute of Architects.

The Diocese of Dallas was established in 1890, and the Sacred Heart Church became the Sacred Heart Cathedral.

In 2001, a seven-foot-tall (or 2.13-meter) replica of a 470-year-old image of the Virgin Mary, displayed in a Mexico City's basilica, was unveiled in the cathedral in her honor. A few months earlier, Pope John Paul II blessed the replica before thousands in St. Peter's Square.

Tradition holds that on December 12, 1531—one year after Copernicus announced his findings about the relationship between the planets and the sun—Our Lady of Guadalupe appeared near Mexico City to a poor peasant named Juan Diego, a devout Aztec and Christian convert.

She supposedly told him in the Nahuatl language of the Aztecs to instruct the bishop to build a church in her honor. When the bishop asked for proof, the peasant opened his cloak, where an image of the Virgin miraculously appeared. That cloak now hangs in the Basilica of Guadalupe in Mexico City.

Cathedral Santuario de Guadalupe, a Catholic church that can seat 1,100 and was dedicated in 1902, stands in what is today the city's Art District. Directly behind it is the Meyerson Symphony Center, which cannot be seen here. The tower in the center is the Federal Reserve building, which opened in 1992. The structure farthest to the left is the Crescent Court office building with a hotel and several restaurants. (Photo by Yves Gerem)

The first recorded mention of Juan Diego and his encounter came nearly 120 years after the fact in the writings of a Spanish priest who studied religious devotion in Mexico. Every year, an estimated ten million pilgrims visit the Mexico City basilica, where the original image hangs. The Dallas cathedral is named in the Virgin Mary's honor. Pope John Paul II canonized Juan Diego as America's first indigenous saint during his trip to Mexico in 2002.

A multi-million-dollar renovation of the Dallas cathedral was in the works, starting in 2002. Two spires, one with a 20-story tower for a 49-bell carillon with clavier, were also to be constructed. The final phase is to include installation of a new pipe organ and construction of a performance hall.

"If people can give millions of dollars to the American Airlines arena [see entry] to watch people get sweaty and smelly, then why not give something for the people to get closer to their God?" asks the cathedral's rector.

Thomas F. Brennan (1855-1916), a native of Tipperary, Ireland, was the first bishop of the Catholic Diocese of Dallas. His family arrived in the United States when he was eight years old, and Brennan received his doctor of divinity degree in 1876 at the University of Innsbruck in Austria. When the Vatican established Dallas as the third diocese in Texas, it encompassed 109 counties and 118,000 square miles (or 305,620 square kilometers). When he was named the first bishop of the new see the following year, Brennan was 35 and the youngest Catholic bishop in the country. He spoke seven languages and established himself as an exceptional orator.

The cathedral was paid for in large part with fees that Edward Joseph Dunne (1848-1910) earned by making lecture tours of the North and East. The second Catholic bishop of Dallas, also born in Tipperary, chose to live in a small room in the rectory rather than spend money on the elaborate episcopal residence.

The property where the Cathedral de Santuario is located was purchased for a mere $30,000. The cornerstone for the new cathedral was laid on June 17, 1898, and Father Jeffrey Aloysius Hartnett (b. 1859), ordained as the first priest in 1891. Also born in Ireland, Hartnett came to America at age four. He attended St. Mary's Seminary in Cincinnati, where he received a master's degree in art.

On the night between February 11 and 12, 1899, while a smallpox epidemic raged through the town, a blizzard hit Dallas. Hartnett walked to the pesthouse during the storm to administer last rights to a dying woman. He contracted smallpox and died the following month. Hartnett is buried at Calvary Cemetery in Uptown. His death deeply affected the Dallasites, and the priest became known as a "martyr to duty" and the subject of poems and stories.

Cathedral Santuario de Guadalupe is the largest congregation among the Dallas Diocese's 75 parishes and missions, and the largest Latino congregation in the country. It numbers 12,300 families, or about 49,200 individuals, 95 percent of them Hispanics. The weekend masses at the cathedral draw up to 10,000 Catholics. There are 630,200 parishioners in the Dallas Diocese, 402,000 of them Hispanic and 15,100 Asian.

Chateau du Triomphe, 10330 Strait Ln., between Royal and Walnut Hill Lanes. Located on Dallas' Billionaire Row, northwest of downtown Dallas, and west of Inwood Road and Dallas North Tollway.

The neighbors include the billionaire Ross Perot clan, telecom tycoon Kenny Troutt, and restaurateur Phil Romano, whose "kitchen in his house is larger than most restaurant lines and spills out onto a large pond, which Romano has stocked with bass," according to the weekly *Dallas Observer*. The family of Robert Dedman, the late founder of the privately owned ClubCorp, also lives on this street.

Big D would hardly be worthy of its name if it could not brag of having the largest French-style mansion in the whole of Texas, perhaps even the Southwest. It was inspired by the Loire Valley chateaux and named Chateau du Triomphe. Christie's auction house described it as "one of the reigning luxury properties in the U.S."

The chateau was initially commissioned in 1994 by George Perrin, founder of the bankrupt Paging Network, a company sold to Arch Wireless in 2000. Once the world's biggest paging company, it had ten million subscribers in the mid-1990s, but went belly up when paging customers threw out their pagers for mobile phones.

Although he supposedly had $28 million invested in the home and real estate, he listed the property at $14 million. Perrin sold the estate to an investor who offered $8.5 million in cash. "The Perrins walked away from almost $20 million and what had become a limestone albatross," observes *D Home* magazine.

Two years in design and seven years in construction, the estate was undergoing finishing touches before it was ready to be occupied. It was offered for $44.9 million as the largest and most expensive property in Dallas history.

Located in the exclusive Preston Hollow in north Dallas, the residence measured 43,169 square feet (or 4,010 square meters), excluding the 73,746 square feet (or 6,851 square meters) for a gatehouse, a guardhouse, servants' quarters, and covered verandas.

The Gothic-Renaissance-style, three-story mansion sat on 9.66 acres (or 3.9 hectares) and featured six bedroom suites, with the master bedroom alone measuring 1,794 square feet (or 167 square meters). It had 13 full baths, 11 half baths, nine wood-burning fireplaces, a 16-car garage with an indoor car-washing facility, an enclosed heated swimming pool, and a 6,200-square-foot (or 576-square-meter) natatorium. There was a moat around the entry gatehouse, a grotto, a wine cellar with tasting room, a home theater, ladies' and men's changing rooms—even a separate gift-wrapping room. And a 17,000-square-foot (or 1,579-square-meter) basement and technical control center.

Designed by architect Robbie Fusch, the chateau was ravaged in July 2002 by a spectacular six-alarm, 1 AM fire that kept 300 Dallas firemen busy for eight hours and caused an estimated $20 million in damage. Smoke hovered for days over neighborhoods south of the LBJ Freeway. Two months later, investigators declared that the fire started because of a buildup in the attic of liquid vapors from paint, floor finishing solvents, and wood varnish.

"It's like a museum burning down," noted the former Dallas Stars owner Norm Green, who seven years earlier sold the team to local businessman Tom Hicks for $84 million and lived next door to the charred mansion. He said he had recently completed work at his house to create a view to Chateau du Triomphe. Green became owner of the Minnesota North Stars in 1990 and moved the team to Dallas three years later.

"What's left of the house sits empty, its elegant windows occasionally blowing open in the breeze," reported the *Fort Worth Star-Telegram* almost a year later. "The grand room beyond the foyer is a cavernous hulk with a view of open sky and the back yard, where a lake was planned."

The chateau's actual replacement value was said to be about $70 million.

Cityplace Center, 2711 North Haskell Ave. at North Central Expwy., (214) 828-7517, Internet www.swres.com. Located about a mile (or 1.6 kilometers) north of downtown. A DART light-rail underground station opened here in 2000. Freedman's Cemetery (see entry) is situated diagonally southwest of here. Drive a few blocks around the Cityplace, and you will be stung by some of the worst poverty you have ever seen in a city that ceaselessly brags about being "world-class."

At 546 feet (or 166 meters) high and having 42 stories, this is one of the tallest building outside of downtown Dallas. Having 1.41 million leasable square feet (or 130,989 square meters) of space, it is one of the largest office buildings in the city.

Cityplace tower was built by the Southland Corporation, which operates more than 24,400 7-Eleven convenience stores in 17 countries—16,000 outside the United States—and has 1,000 of its own office workers in the headquarters located in this building. Typically 7-Eleven stores are staffed by people who encompass 200 nationalities and speak 100 languages.

The development became a high-profile victim of the 1980s real estate crash. The anticipated second tower on the west side of Central Expressway was never built. The first tower, which was completed in 1988, has underground garages with a parking capacity of 3,400 vehicles. Southland unveiled a 7-Eleven store on the ground floor here to cater to the tower's 3,400 office workers.

The 7-Eleven store concept started with an employee of the Southland predecessor, named Southland Ice Co., who began selling milk, eggs, and bread from an ice dock in Oak Cliff in 1927 as a convenience to his customers. Soon the idea caught on with other Southland Ice outlets. By 1928, Southland Ice operated 12 ice plants and 20 retail ice docks in Dallas and San Antonio.

The firm sank into receivership during the Depression, but recovered with the help of a local banker and the repeal of Prohibition, which allowed it to sell beer. The company owned 60 retail locations in the Dallas-Fort Worth area by 1939 and supplied Camp Hood, the nation's largest training camp, with ice during World War II.

It was renamed 7-Eleven in 1946 to let customers know when it was open, although, by 1963 7-Eleven stores began operating around the clock. Southland surpassed $1 billion in sales in 1971, and later that decade operated more than 5,000 stores.

When facing a hostile takeover by a Canadian entrepreneur, the Thompson family took the company private in a multi-billion-dollar leveraged buyout. With 12,700 stores, including 600 in Texas, the company filed for Chapter 11 bankruptcy in 1990.

Japanese interests bought nearly 73 percent of the stock the following year and provided an equity infusion of $430 million that enabled the company to restructure, although it had to divest itself of several businesses. For the first time in nearly 60 years the Thompsons lost the management of the company.

John Philip Thompson, who became 7-Eleven's president in 1961 at age 35, died of brain cancer in Dallas in 2003 at age 77. The oldest of three sons of the company's founder, he served as vice chairman until he was cast into retirement in 1996.

Next door to the Cityplace tower is a small shopping center. Across Haskell Avenue stands a 14-screen Loews Cityplace Theatre.

The Dallas Arboretum & Botanical Gardens, 8525 Garland Rd. on White Rock Lake, (214) 327-8263; event hotline, 327-4901, Internet www.dallasarboretum.org. *CH*, except children under age three, and parking fee. Open daily, except major holidays: Nov-Feb 10 AM-5 PM, Mar-Oct 10 AM-6 PM. Most gardens are wheelchair- and stroller-accessible. Only dogs assisting the handicapped are permitted on the grounds. Located on the southeastern shore of the 1,120-acre (or 453-hectare) White Rock Lake (see entry). Driving on Mockingbird Lane, turn right to Buckner Boulevard, and right again on Garland Road. The entrance is on the right, after Lakeland Drive. A DART bus stops in front of the Arboretum. A gift shop is on the premises.

The arboretum, which the city had purchased from Southern Methodist University, consists of 66 acres (or 26 hectares) on the shore of White Rock Lake. There are more than 5,000 cultivated varieties of plants to see throughout the year, and they are admired by more than 250,000 visitors annually. Among the arboretum's chief attractions are:

The **DeGolyer Mansion,** a 21,000-square-foot (or 1,950-square-meter) 13-room house in Spanish Colonial Revival style, now a museum, which is on the National Register of Historic Places and a historic landmark. The mansion, built in 1940, sits on an estate, once a dairy farm, that "still remains an island of peaceful beauty shielded from the hectic rush of Dallas traffic."

In 1910, while the 24-year-old Everette Lee DeGolyer worked his way through college as a geologist in Mexico, he guessed the location of an oil well that produced 130 million barrels of oil and made him a millionaire before his graduation from the University of Oklahoma. The Kansas native moved his office to New York in 1916, and in 1924 located what became the first oilfield discovered by geophysical methods.

DeGolyer was chief of the technical advisory commission to President Franklin D. Roosevelt at the Teheran Conference. He was director of the American Petroleum Institute for 20 years. DeGolyer assembled one of the nation's best libraries for the history of science and donated it to University of Oklahoma. For many years the world's leading oil consultant, he held seven honorary doctorates, and lectured at the Massachusetts Institute of Technology and at Princeton. He moved to Texas in 1936 and purchased this property three years later. His study, with floor-to-ceiling bookcases, once boasted 15,000 volumes, the rarest among them hidden in two rooms behind sliding bookcases. Many have been removed to the DeGolyer Library (see entry), which was donated to Southern Methodist University in 1974.

The 4.5-acre (or 1.82-hectare) **DeGolyer Gardens** are filled with roses, wisterias, and magnolias, as well as hundreds of annual and perennial flowers. The Sunken Garden component is a popular wedding site. Near the entrance to the Sunken Garden stands a 200-year-old pecan tree, the oldest tree inside the Arboretum.

The **Camp House** is an 8,000-square-foot (or 743-square-meter) mansion that Alex Camp built in 1938. It has a nice view of White Rock Lake. Designed by the prominent Houston architect John Staub, it was completed in 1938 at a cost of $80,000 and is now the arboretum headquarters. Its restoration in 1980 cost ten times its original cost. The house is a harmonious combination of Latin Colonial, English Regency, Tudor, and art deco architecture.

Alex Camp died about the time the house was completed. His wife, Roberta Coke, lived there until her death in the early 1970s. A Dallas Arboretum & Botanical Society board member and chairman of Texas Industries purchased the property and held the note until it was paid off by the society in 1982. The Camp and the DeGolyer estates were combined to become the Dallas Arboretum and Botanical Gardens, which are owned by the city.

The 6.6-acre (or 2.67-hectare) **Margaret Elizabeth Jonsson Color Garden** was designed by Dallas landscape architect Naud Burnett and opened in 1990. Jonsson Garden is planted with more than 15,000 chrysanthemums each autumn and more than 2,500 varieties of azaleas every spring. Picnicking is encouraged. Here you can see a bronze sculpture, titled *Grandi Amanti,* created by Giacomo Manzu and on permanent loan from the Dallas Museum of Art.

The **Eugenia Leftwich Palmer Fern Dell,** is a one-acre (or 0.4-hectare) home to 90 varieties of ferns, rhododendrons, and other shade-loving plans. The 2.2-acre (or 0.90-hectare) **Lay Ornamental Garden** at the northern end of the Arboretum showcases hundreds of perennial plants that are native or adapted to north-central Texas. A collection of Texas wildlife bronze sculptures, donated by the Trammell Crow family of Dallas, can be seen here.

A 1.8-acre (or 0.72-hectare), $1.6-million **Woman's Garden** was inaugurated on the slope behind DeGolyer mansion, overlooking White Rock Lake, in 1997. It was designed by landscape architect Morgan Wheelock and features a Mediterranean-style balustrade enclosing a poetry garden.

The 40,000-square-foot (or 3,716-square-meter), $20-million **Trammell Crow Pavilion,** designed by San Antonio architect Ted Flato, opened in 2003 near the main gate. **Bath House Cultural Center** (see entry) is located a good mile (or 1.6 kilometers) north of here.

After a visit to either one, you might want to have a bite to eat at **Franki's Li'l Europe,** Garland Rd. at Buckner Blvd., (214) 320-0426, located nearby in the southeast corner of the Casa Linda shopping center. The Eastern European cuisine restaurant has been here for more than 15 years.

Dallas Arts District, bound by Woodall Rodgers Frwy., Routh St., Ross Ave., and St. Paul St. Located in the northeastern end of downtown Dallas. A. H. Belo Mansion and Cathedral Santuario de Guadalupe (see entries) are also situated here.

The Arts District, where the Dallas Symphony Center (see entry) is located, was born in 1979, when the citizens voted to set aside 60 acres (or 24.2 hectares) in downtown Dallas for the arts and culture. The Dallas Museum of Art (see entry) emerged at one end of the district, while the Dallas Theater Center (see listing) began operating the Arts District Theater at the other.

Meanwhile, the Dallas Symphony Association began the site selection for its future home, which then was still in Fair Park. The new symphony center opened in the fall of 1989.

The **Trammell Crow Center** (see entry) sculpture collection is located at Ross Avenue and Harwood Street, and displayed around a 50-story granite skyrise, where 20 bronzes are featured in a one-block area. They include examples by several influential sculptors of the past 100 years, such as Aristide Maillol, Auguste Rodin, and Emile Antoine Bourdelle.

Also situated here is the **Trammell & Margaret Crow Collection of Asian Art** (see entry). Two pavilions on the Flora Street side of the building were reconstructed into a permanent display of 500 Asian art objects of metal and stone drawn from a collection of more than 7,000 that the Crows amassed over 30 years.

Nasher Sculpture Center (see entry), across the street from the Dallas Museum of Art, opened in 2003. Gathered over a period of 30 years, this modern sculpture collection is regarded as one of the most important ones still owned privately.

Built at a cost of $57 million, the 2.4-acre (or 0.97-hectare) sculpture garden displays up to two dozen artworks at a time, all owned by Raymond Nasher, who also runs NorthPark shopping center (see entry). His large collection by more than 40 artists includes works by Alexander Calder, Willem de Koonig, Aristide Maillol, Joan Miro, Henry Moore, and Auguste Rodin.

In 2002 the **Dallas Museum of Natural History** (see entry) tapped California architect Frank Gehry to design its $100-million, 150,000-square-foot (or 13,935-square-meter) building in the district.

The **Dallas Center for the Performing Arts** has been under discussion for more than a decade. The plan calls for a 2,400-seat lyric theater, to be named Winspear Opera House, for the Dallas Opera and other musical, theatrical, and dance groups. It is to be located between the Meyerson Symphony Center and Booker T. Washington High School. An 800-seat theater is to replace the temporary Dallas Theater Center stage on Flora Street.

Sir Norman Foster, "an ambitious lad in gritty Manchester who put himself through university selling ice cream," according to the *Dallas Morning News*, won the opera house commission. Foster (b. 1935) had restored the historic Reichstag in Berlin and designed the Great Court of the British Museum in London.

The Winspear Opera House is to be named after Margot (b. 1932) and William (b. 1933) Winspear, philanthropists and opera lovers who in 2002 committed $42 million toward the completion of the performing arts center. This is possibly the largest philanthropic gift for a public Dallas project in the city's history. The Winspears were both born in Edmonton, in the Canadian province of Alberta, and graduated from the University of Alberta. They were married in 1955.

Bill Winspear held various executive positions until 1975, when the couple moved to Dallas, where two of their five children also live. Here, he was president of Chaparral Steel and Associated Materials. He sold the majority interest in Associated Materials to the New York-based Harvest Partners Inc. for $436 million.

Rem Koolhaas, director of the Office for Metropolitan Architecture in Rotterdam, Netherlands, was to draft the adjacent 800-seat theater, budgeted at up to $60 million. A journalist and screenwriter before he was an architect, the "mercurial" Koolhaas (b. 1944) teaches at Harvard's Graduate School of Design. He won the prestigious Pritzker Architecture Prize in 2000. He is also designing a $650-million broadcast center for the 2008 Olympics in Beijing.

The $250-million center would fill a two-block site bounded by Flora, Ross, Routh, and Fairmount streets, on the east side of the Arts District.

A multimillion expansion of the arts-magnet **Booker T. Washington High School for the Performing & Visual Arts** is also planned here. Booker T. High, at 2501 Flora St., was built in 1922 replacing the old Colored High School, Dallas' first African-American high school, but closed in 1969 after federal courts ordered Dallas schools integrated. When courts issued another order requiring magnet schools for gifted students, the Dallas Independent School District put its arts magnet school in Booker T. Washington in 1976.

With some 700 students, the school accepts about 40 percent of students who apply as freshmen. Studies at Booker T. are divided into four disciplines: dance, theater, music, and visual arts. Grammy award-winners like singer Norah Jones (b. 1980), Soul queen Erykah Badu (class of 1989), and jazz trumpeter Roy Hargrove (class of 1988) are but three Booker T. graduates.

Dallas City Hall, 1500 Marilla St. at Young and Akard, (214) 744-1000. Mayor's Office is in Room 5-E North, (214) 670-0773; for City Hall tours call (214) 939-2701. Located in the southern part of downtown, adjacent west of the Dallas Convention Center and Pioneer Plaza (see individual listings).

The present City Hall, designed by architect I. M. Pei, whose partnership also drafted five other Dallas buildings, was inaugurated in March 1978 at a cost of more than $43 million. Six years late and $14 million over budget, it is one of the most distinctive structures in the city. The cantilevered seven-story building is 122 feet (or 37 meters) high and 560 feet (or 170 meters) long, claiming 691,000 square feet (or 64,193 square meters) of space. Sloping outward and upward at a 34-degree angle, it is held and balanced by a network of U-shaped cables in the floors and walls. Each floor is nine feet (or 2.7 meters) wider than the one below it. A spacious interior court extends from the second floor 100 feet (or 30 meters) to a vaulted ceiling, providing sunlight and spaciousness.

"Pei's dramatically tilted facade still intimidates some people," noted the *Dallas Morning News* in 1998, adding, "The building is a product of post-Kennedy-assassination Dallas, when the city was struggling to change its image as a backwater of bigotry and violence." The site was carved from a downtown warehouse district and was among the first attempts at urban renewal.

On the four-acre (or 1.61-hectare) plaza—"twice the size of St. Mark's in Venice, Italy"—in front of the Hall there are three enormous flagpoles with the American, Texas, and Dallas flags. A circular lake is

Dallas City Hall, designed by architect I. M. Pei, whose partnership drafted five other Dallas buildings. Inaugurated in 1978, it replaced the 1914 city hall on South Harwood Street in whose basement Lee Harvey Oswald was shot on live television. (Photo by Yves Gerem)

between the flags and the City Hall building, displaying two floating sculptures by Marta Pan.

Its predecessors include:

• The *first* City Hall opened in 1872 in a two-story frame building on the southwest corner of Main and Akard Streets; that part of Akard was then known as Sycamore. Ben Long, its mayor, was later murdered in a Dallas saloon.

• The *second* City Hall was built at the northwest corner of Commerce and Lamar Streets, with the city government being housed above a fire station, which later burned down. This building was sold to a local developer and the city moved to space rented from the Sarah Horton Cockrell family, whose patriarch, Alexander Cockrell, was killed by a Dallas city marshal in 1858. His 38-year-old widow was left to fend for herself with four small children. She continued her husband's business and started several new businesses. Upon her death in 1892, she owned nearly one-quarter of downtown Dallas, as well as several thousand acres throughout Dallas County.

• The *third* City Hall was installed on the northwest corner of Commerce and Akard Streets in 1889, at a cost of $80,000, and included a 1,000-seat auditorium on the third floor. The four-story structure was designed by A. B. Bristol. The Busch family of St. Louis bought this site in 1910 for the present Adolphus Hotel (see listing).

• The *fourth* City Hall was set in 1914 in a five-story granite and Indiana limestone Beaux Arts building, at 2014 Main Street, Harwood and Commerce Streets, which still houses some city offices and is now called the Police & Municipal Courts Building (see separate entry). Although Dallas taxpayers allocated only $475,000 for its construction, the final cost this time was more than $900,000, $585,000 of it for the building construction, the rest for land. It was in the basement of this building, nicknamed High Five, that Jack Ruby pulled the trigger on his .38-caliber Colt Cobra and shot the alleged Kennedy assassin Lee Harvey Oswald on live national television in 1963. The site has been significantly altered by construction of double doors on the spot where the shooting took place.

Dallas Convention Center, 650 South Griffin St. at Akard, (214) 939-2700/2724, Fax 939-2795, Internet www.dallascc.com. Located east of the Dallas City Hall and south of the Pioneer Plaza (see individual listings). There is a DART light-rail station on both Red and Blue lines at the center.

Outside the convention center stands the 6-foot-tall (or 1.8-meter) and 4-foot-wide (or 1.2-meter) gray granite Pearl Harbor monument in the Veterans Memorial Garden. Dedicated to the "ten boys from Dallas" who died aboard the USS *Arizona* in the December 1941 attack, it was dedicated in 2002.

Dallas Convention and Visitors Bureau once claimed that Dallas was the second largest convention city in the United States, although few ever took such statements at face value. Most seem to agree that Big D is more likely to be in sixth place or so nationwide, although it has arguable the best accessibility through the Dallas/Fort Worth International Airport (see entry). The first real convention took place in 1902, when 3,000 veterans of the Civil War and 100,000 other visitors came to Dallas for the Confederate Army Reunion.

Dallas Convention Center dates back to 1957, when the Dallas Memorial Auditorium was inaugurated. It now occupies an area of more than four city blocks and has more than one million square feet (or 92,900 square meters) of exhibit space. The center was originally designed by architect George L. Dahl, who had also supervised the construction of some 45 buildings for the 1936 Texas Centennial Exposition in Fair Park (see entry).

There are two ballrooms with 47,000 square feet (or 4,366 square meters) of space, 94 meeting rooms, and an arena for concerts and meetings that can seat 7,428. Also on the premises is a fully equipped theater with 1,770 upholstered opera-style seats.

"I am quite excited about the fact that we have the largest singular pillarless room in the world," confided the convention center president to the *Dallas Morning News*. He was talking about the 203,000-square-foot (or 18,859-square-meter) hall-with a roof that measures nearly five acres (or two hectares)—which is the centerpiece of the Dallas Convention Center's $128-million renovation completed in 2002.

"Dallas taxpayers did not pay for the renovation and expansion expenses of the convention center;" brags an advertisement following its recent upgrade, "the complex was paid for by the hotel occupancy tax."

"The Dallas Convention Center has been expanded so many times that it's more like an artificial mountain range than a building," observes the *News*. It "remains inscrutably vast and disconnected from the rest of the city." No stores, restaurants, or hotels line Young Street, in front of it, so "weary conventioneers exit into bleak parking lots and empty streets," says the *News*, adding that some of them pile into cabs and head for Sundance Square, a major tourist attraction in Fort Worth that is described in the *Marmac Guide to Fort Worth & Arlington*.

You may be tired of hearing this Dallas refrain, but the convention center wants you to know that it also has "the world's largest elevated vertiport," located atop the center, which can accommodate five helicopters and two vertically-landing aircraft at one time.

"Your Convention Center is one of the largest in the country but by all means is not the most memorable," writes the Massachusetts Institute of Technology-educated city planner Antonio di Mambro, whom the city has tapped as a consultant. "It's a warehouse in many ways."

Of the 20 largest American cities that have hotels within a mile (or 1.6 kilometers) of their convention facilities, Dallas ranks 16th in the number of rooms, according to the *News*. Dallas has about 4,840 rooms available in such proximity, compared with 6,320 in San Antonio.

Among the other Metroplex cities, the following convention facilities are available:

Addison Conference & Theatre Centre (built in 1992) has 40,000 square feet (or 3,716 square meters) of convention space, designed by Gary Cunningham. Addison also has 21 hotels with 150,000 square feet (or 13,935 square meters) of meeting space.

Fort Worth Convention Center (built in 1969) has nearly 300,000 square feet (or 27,870 square meters) of convention space, and major hotels have another 300,000 square feet of space. The convention center's renovation and expansion was completed in 2002. The city also owns the Will Rogers Memorial Center in the cultural district with 100,000 square feet (or 9,290 square meters) of space.

Grapevine Convention Center (built in 1988) has 23,500 square feet (or 2,183 square meters) of exhibit space. Eight Grapevine hotels have a total of 225,000 square feet (or 20,902 square meters) of space. The $450-million Opryland Hotel Texas & Convention Center on 77 acres (or 31 hectares) along the shores of Grapevine Lake, scheduled for completion in 2004, will have 400,000 square feet (or 37,160 square meters) of exhibit space.

Irving Convention Center (to be completed in 2004), a 38-acre (or 15.3-hectare) site at the southeast corner of State Highway 114 and Northwest Highway in Las Colinas will have a $104-million convention center with about 100,000 square feet (or 9,290 square meters) of exhibit space and a $60-million, 450-room hotel on 38 acres (or 15.3 hectares) of city-owned land. Eleven Irving hotels have another 200,000 square feet (or 18,580 square meters) of meeting space.

Plano Centre (built in 1990) has 86,000 square feet (or 7,989 square meters) of exhibit space. Another 200,000 square feet (or 18,580 square meters) of space are available at Plano hotels. The city is considering a 70,000-square-foot (or 6,503-square-meter) expansion.

Richardson Civic Center (built in 1980) has 13,000 square feet (or 1,208 square meters) of exhibit space. The Eisemann Center (see entry), next door to a DART light-rail station, is a 53,500-square-foot (or 4,970-square-meter) performing arts facility that opened in 2002. Richardson's three largest hotels have another 53,000 square feet (or 4,924 square meters) of space.

Dallas County Historical Plaza, located in downtown Dallas. The two-block plaza includes the **"Old Red" Courthouse,** which now houses a visitors center, a reproduction of Dallas founder **John Neely Bryan's cabin**, circa 1850, next to the neo-English Gothic revival Dallas County Records Building, constructed in 1928, and the **Kennedy Memorial**. They are bound by Elm, Market, Commerce, and Houston Streets. The Sixth Floor Museum and Dealey Plaza are across the street. Union Station and Hyatt Regency Hotel are still farther away. (See individual entries for details.) Discussions have been going on for years on how to enhance the plaza, which is divided by Main Street. "The area definitely needs more water, shade and inviting places to sit," opines the *Dallas Morning News*.

Dallas County Parks & Open Spaces, 411 Elm St., Third Floor, (214) 653-6653, Internet www.dallascounty.org. If you like to hike, check out this Web page of the Dallas County open spaces or pick up a map at the downtown visitors center, inside the "Old Red" Courthouse. It lists 21 preserves measuring about 3,000 acres (or 1,214 hectares).

The Dallas Market Center, 2100 North Stemmons Frwy., (800)

DAL-MKTS or (214) 655-6100, Fax (800) 637-6833, Internet www.dallasmarketcenter.com, e-mail info@dmcmail.com. Business hours are 7 AM-6 PM during market days, 8 AM-5 PM during non-market days. More than 14,000 parking spaces are available on the DMC campus.

Children under the age of 12 are not allowed, but YMCA childcare services are provided at a fee. Picture-taking is not permitted inside the showrooms without the owners' consent. (For details about the sculptures on display here, please see the Art in Public Places section of the VISUAL ARTS chapter.) The complex is located a few minutes northwest of downtown Dallas, between Harry Hines Boulevard and Stemmons Freeway (also known as Interstate Highway 35 East).

The Market Center is the world's largest wholesale merchandise mart. It features 50 markets annually and attracts more than 100,000 professional buyers from the United States and other countries every year. The five buildings comprise 2,200 permanent showrooms with 6.9 million square feet (or 641,000 square meters) of display space. The center employs 12,000. The 100-acre (or 40-hectare) complex was founded in 1957 and is controlled by the wealthy Crow family of Dallas, one of the largest commercial property managers in the United States. The company has 170 offices nationwide.

Trammell Crow was born in Dallas in 1914, the fifth among eight children, and grew up during the Depression. He launched his empire by building and leasing a small warehouse to a battery manufacturer in 1948. Crow pioneered the idea of "building on speculation" and used short-lease arrangements that permitted him to raise rents frequently. He and developer John Millard Stemmons (1909-2001) built more than 50 warehouses in Dallas alone, initially on reclaimed land, known as the Trinity Industrial District, in the western downtown area.

By the mid-1950s, Crow was Dallas' largest warehouse developer, and when he retired in the late 1980s also the largest commercial real estate developer in the country. Outside Texas, he built Atlanta's Peachtree Center and the Embarcadero mixed-use complex in San Francisco.

"My husband has Alzheimer's and has had it for several years," said his wife Margaret in 2002, when the family gave $1.1 million to establish a chair and support research at the University of Texas Southwestern Medical Center at Dallas.

Stemmons's father, **Leslie Allison Stemmons** (1876-1939) was born in Dallas and graduated from the University of Chicago. He developed several areas of Oak Cliff and led the construction of the Houston Street viaduct between Dallas and Oak Cliff. The Stemmons family donated much of the valuable right-of-way for the building of the Stemmons Freeway, also known as Interstate 35 East. While donating land that was worth "about 50 cents a square foot," before the freeway, it skyrocketed to "$10 a square foot" afterward.

The nineteen seventies and eighties were hard on Crow's enterprises, first because of high interest rates, then because of a glut of office space. Crow had to refinance 150 properties in 1990, when the number of employees was drastically reduced. The company nevertheless remains one of the nation's largest real estate services firm with some 7,000 employees.

Dallas Market Hall, at 2200 North Stemmons Frwy., (800) DMC-MKTS or (214) 879-8330, open since 1960, consists of three consumer exhibit halls with a total of 214,000 square feet (or 19,880 square meters) of space. It attracts more than 400,000 people to its 1,400 display booths. This is the only facility in the Dallas Market Center that is open to the public. Car and boat shows are but two annual events held at the Market Hall.

Dallas Trade Mart, located at 2100 North Stemmons Frwy., (214) 655-6100, which opened in 1959, has about one million square feet (or 92,900 square meters) of display space for the wholesale merchandising of gifts, decorative accessories, housewares, and lighting. It was designed by Harwell Hamilton Harris and is "probably the best of the Trammell Crow market buildings," in the opinion of the Dallas chapter of the American Institute of Architects.

World Trade Center, located at 2100 North Stemmons Frwy., (214) 655-6100, and dedicated in 1974, is a 15-story building with 3.1 million square feet (or 287,990 square meters) of space.

The ground floor of the 15-story atrium, which is open to the public, contains foreign trade commissions and buying offices, the International Development Center of the Greater Dallas Chamber of Commerce, a restaurant and a cafeteria, a bank with an automatic teller machine, and a post office.

Also located here is the largest permanent wholesale gourmet showroom in the nation. Its upper floors house showrooms for furniture and other household items, toys, and jewelry.

"Representing 1970s architecture at its most brutal, the exterior of the massive World Trade Center looks like a typical down-and-dirty Trammell Crow warehouse concept subjected to a very heavy steroid regimen," opines the Dallas branch of the American Institute of Architects.

International Apparel Mart, once located at 2300 North Stemmons Frwy., and the largest building of its kind in the nation, opened in 1964 at a cost of $15 million and had 1.8 million square feet (or 167,220 square meters) of display space covering four square blocks.

By the late 1970s, the weeklong seasonal shows were attracting 15,000 visitors. More than 12,000 lines of menswear, womenswear, and footwear were once exhibited here. "Like Neiman Marcus, the Apparel

Mart was a high-fashion outpost at a time when getting dressed up in Dallas meant putting on a clean shirt," notes the *Dallas Morning News*.

In *Logan's Run*, a 1976 science-fiction film, the mart and the water gardens in Fort Worth were used to represent life in the 23rd century.

The Apparel Mart anticipated closing in 2004, when some of its vendors would move into the nearby World Trade Center, which was reconfigured to hold the 600 showrooms of the Apparel Mart. The closing came because of the consolidation of department store chains, which often deal directly with manufacturers, a decline in independently owned stores, and an emphasis on private-label merchandise, which cuts out vendors and manufacturers' representatives.

The Menswear Mart, built in 1982, relocated to the International Apparel Mart in 2000 and ceded its space to the Children's Medical Center (see entry). The six-story building was renamed the Children's Pavilion.

International Floral Design Center, opened in 1999, is the rebirth of the Dallas Market Center's original building, the Home Furnishing Mart. The 440,000-square-foot (or 40,876-square-meter), two-story building is the only U.S. market dedicated to the permanent floral business and hosts two shows every year. Here professional buyers find everything from Christmas trees to collectables.

The DMC's sister mart is the 150,000-square-meter Brussels International Trade Mart, with 8,000 lines, 1,400 exhibitors, and 700,000 professional buyers.

Dallas Nature Center, 7171 Mountain Creek Pkwy. at Straus Rd., (972) 296-1955, Internet www.dallasnaturecenter.org. *CH* per each car. Open daily from sunrise to sundown, closed Mondays. Located southwest of downtown Dallas, east of Joe Pool Lake and Cedar Hill State Park, and 2.5 miles (or four kilometers) south of Interstate 20. The entrance is on the west side, just south of the Wheatland Road intersection.

The Dallas Nature Center, at 755 feet (or 230 meters) one of the highest elevations in the Metroplex, covers 633 acres (or 256 hectares) with 10 miles (or 16 kilometers) of hiking trails. The DNC's land, which was offered by Dave Fox of the Fox & Jacobs development company, is protected under conservation ownership by the center, the city, and the county.

The property was once a ranch owned by Dallas businessman and ambassador to Japan, Clayton Wyman, and purchased by Fox in the early 1970s. Opened in 1975, the facility was known as the Greenhills Experimental Center until 1978.

The preserve's founder, Geoffrey Stanford (b. 1916), who spent the last 25 years working and living at the nature center, died in his sleep in 2000. A transplanted Londoner, widely regarded as a pioneer in such fields as medicine, surgery, and the environment, he graduated at age 16 and became one of England's youngest medical students. After teaching for several years at the University of Notre Dame in the 1960s, Dr. Stanford took a teaching position at Rice University before being "lured to Dallas with the prospect of establishing the city's first protected open space."

The center maintains nine walking trails, the longest of which is 2.5 miles (or four kilometers) that include the moderately challenging Bluebonnet Trail and the rugged Fossil Valley Trail. The DNC, budgeted at $450,000, offers a variety of educational programs, such as aquatic tours, guided hikes, insect safaris, and fossil excavations. Each year some 80,000 people, including 10,000 schoolchildren, visit the center. There is a gift shop on the premises.

Dallas Police Memorial, Plaza at Young, Akard, and Marilla Sts. intersections.

Located in the southern part of downtown, east of the Pioneer Plaza & Cemetery, and in front of City Hall (see individual entries).

More than 20 years in the making, the memorial was dedicated in the spring of 2001. Standing on a 1.8-acre (or 0.72-hectare) site, it is built of 30 tons of stainless steel supported by nine columns with a canopy extending 40 feet (or 12 meters) over a grassy plaza. The memorial was designed by University of Texas at Arlington architecture dean Edward Baum and professor John Maruszczak.

"The memorial borrows some of its crisp geometry from I. M. Pei's plaza and its softness from the cemetery," observes the *Dallas Morning News*. "If a few details don't quite work, the overall design is quite powerful." Powerful enough to receive the 2001 honor award from the Dallas chapter of the American Institute of Architects.

The memorial is inscribed with the names of more than 75 Dallas officers who have died in the line of duty since 1892, and their badge numbers are projected onto the pavement. Having a premonition that more will come, the creators have left room for 110 more officers' names that are sure to follow.

Corporate and private donations paid for the $1.6-million memorial. A guiding force behind the memorial was former Dallas mayor Jack Evans, a grocery executive and banker who died in 1997 at age 74.

The first Dallas officer to die in the line of duty was C. O. Brewer, who died on May 24, 1892, at age 42, of a gunshot wound suffered while he tried to make an arrest at a saloon. Officer J. D. Tippit, killed by Lee Harvey Oswald shortly after the assassination of President John F. Kennedy on November 22, 1963, is also remembered here.

Dallas Streets & How They Were Named

Dallas has about 11,350 miles (or 18,265 kilometers) of streets. Here are some of the most prominent with the sources of their names:

Akard Street: Named after William Christopher Columbus Akard (1826-1870), an early Dallas merchant who came from Civil War-torn North Carolina in 1865 and died on a trip to Calvert, Texas, to get supplies for his store. Akard Street originally extended only to Commerce Street; from there to Ross Avenue it was named Sycamore. Akard's home stood at Wood and Akard Streets, where the old Federal Reserve Bank (see entry) is located today.

Bryan Street: Named after John Neely Bryan (1810-1877), founder of what is today Dallas, after his death.

Central Expressway: (See the TRANSPORTATION chapter).

Commerce Street: Original principal business street so named by John Neely Bryan.

Elm Street: Named for a grove of elm trees growing near the Trinity River. After 1911, when 110 streetlights were installed along it, Elm Street was also known as the Great White Way.

Ervay Street: Named after Henry Schley Ervay (d. 1911), a flower mill operator turned real estate owner. A native of Elmira, New York, where he was born in 1834, Ervay was the eldest of ten children and came to Texas at age 24. He served as a Dallas alderman from 1873 to 1877 and later as school board president. As Dallas mayor from 1870 to 1872, he was admired for choosing jail rather than carrying out the orders of the Reconstructionists.

In 1872, Texas governor E. J. Davis ordered Ervay to be removed from his office as mayor because he supposedly was not sufficiently loyal. Ervay Street was briefly renamed Johnson Street after Ervay's successor. Ervay refused to concede and was jailed until the Texas Supreme Court ruled that the governor did not have the power to remove officials from office. Ervay was back in office four days later.

Field Street: Named for Thomas William Field (b. 1847), a Missouri native and real estate developer who arrived in Dallas in 1872, the same year as the first railroad. The following year, he built Dallas' first opera house. He built for himself a house the size of an entire city block. Field began building "the most elegant hotel east of the Mississippi," the Oriental, in 1893. The city's first truly luxury hotel, located at Akard and Commerce Streets, was to cost $500,000 and have 150 fully electrified guestrooms. "Field's Folly," as it was referred to, bankrupted the developer and was completed by the beer baron Adolphus Busch of St. Louis.

Gano Street: Bordering the southeastern end of the Old City Park (see entry), this street is named after Richard Montgomery Gano (1830-1913), a descendent of French Protestants who escaped to America to avoid the persecution of King Louis XIV.

Born in Bourbon County, Kentucky, he graduated from medical school at age 22. Gano moved to the Lone Star State in 1857, obtained a Texas land grant, and began importing and raising registered Hereford and Guernsey cattle. His great-grandfather was an Army chaplain who baptized George Washington in the field.

After distinguishing himself on the Confederate side of the Civil War—although he owned no slaves—Gano became a minister of the Disciples of Christ. To support his family, he established a real estate company that also made him a millionaire. He is buried in south Dallas' Oakland Cemetery, along with many other well-known citizens. The weekly *Dallas Observer* claims Oakland, established in 1891 off what is now Malcolm X Boulevard, has the "best public sculpture" in the city.

Gaston Avenue: William Henry Gaston (1841-1927), one of the founders of Dallas, was born in Alabama. Upon his discharge as a captain from the Confederate Army, he moved to Dallas "with $20,000 in gold." He donated cash and land in 1871 to help bring the railroad into the village of Dallas.

Gaston, said to be responsible for the transformation of Dallas into a city, was one of the city's first millionaires. The avenue named after him bisects today's Old East Dallas neighborhood. Gaston's plantation became the town of East Dallas, which was annexed in 1890 and made Dallas the largest city in Texas. He gave 80 acres (or 32 hectares) to what became the State Fair of Texas (see entry) and built the first bridge in Dallas spanning the Trinity River. Gaston Bank, founded as the first permanent bank in 1868, was the predecessor of the RepublicBank, which in turn was sold during the 1980s real estate collapse to today's Bank of America at a cost to taxpayers of $3.6 billion.

Good-Latimer Expressway: This roadway gets its name from a lawyer who led a residents militia into Collin County, and the editor of Dallas' first newspaper.

In the summer of 1852, John Jay Good (1827-1882) led 100 armed residents in the Hedgecoxe War, which confronted a land-company agent who had challenged their land claims. The dispute was eventually resolved, and no one was hurt. John Good was elected mayor of Dallas in 1880.

James Weck Latimer (1783-1860), who came from Connecticut in 1833, was co-founder, editor and co-publisher of Dallas' first newspaper, named *Cedar Snag*, which later became the *Herald* and in 1885 was incorporated into the *Dallas Morning News*. Latimer was also chief justice of Dallas County. The two streets named after Good and Latimer were eliminated by the construction of North Central Expressway. In the fall of 1951, this road was named after them.

Greenville Avenue: This was the first major road between Dallas and the city of Greenville, about 30 miles (or 48 kilometers) to the northeast. From Garrett Park, near downtown, to Mockingbird Lane, the street is known as Lower Greenville, after that as Upper Greenville.

Both have one of the largest concentrations of shops, restaurants, and nightclubs.

Harry Hines Boulevard (or Old U.S. 77, now Spur 3540): Named after a former state highway commissioner, from 1935 to 1941, when Texas introduced driver's licenses. Hines, a meat packer, oil operator, real-estate company owner, and civic leader, made an unsuccessful bid for Congress in 1942. He died in 1954, and this road was named for him two years later.

Harwood Street: Alexander Harwood (1820-1885) was county clerk from 1850 to 1854. Born in Franklin, Tennessee, he walked from Shreveport, Louisiana, to Dallas in 1842. In 1845, he was one of 32 Dallas County delegates selected to vote on the proposed annexation of Texas into the United States, and cast one of three nay votes. Harwood supported secession in 1861 at the start of the Civil War and later helped the Confederate government establish a postal system. He died in the same year as Union general and president Ulysses Grant.

Haskell Avenue: Horatio Haskell, who fought with Zachary Taylor in the Mexican War, was alderman of East Dallas in the 1880s. After surviving a ten-man exploration of the Platte River in Nebraska, where most of the other men froze to death, he settled in Dallas.

Hord Street: Named after William Henry Hord (1809-1901), a Virginian who settled with his family west of the Trinity River in 1845. They were the first settlers of Hord's Ridge, which is known today as Oak Cliff, a neighborhood located southwest of downtown Dallas. Hord was justice of the peace in Dallas before he was elected county judge in 1848.

Houston Street: Named for Gen. Sam Houston, first president of the Republic of Texas.

Howell Street: Named for John M. Howell, the father of Dallas horticulture, who was born in Tennessee and came to Texas in 1870 with a wagon train of trees. Two years later, he opened Howell & Thomas, the first commercial greenhouse in Dallas County. Howell introduced peach trees to Parker County and magnolias to Dallas. He named five streets on his property between McKinney Avenue and Cedar Springs Road: Fairmount Avenue for Fairmount Park, the grounds of the Philadelphia Centennial exhibition; Routh Street for his father-in-law, the Rev. Jacob Routh; Thomas Avenue for his business partner; Maple Avenue for the trees; and Howell Street for his family.

Jackson Street: The only downtown Dallas street named after a U.S. president.

Lamar Street: Named for Mirabeau B. Lamar, second president of the Republic of Texas, 1838-41. Almost every Texas city has a Lamar Street.

Main Street: So named by Dallas founder John Neely Bryan. In the mid-1870s, Dallas' business district consisted of Main and Commerce Streets, but only as far east as Murphy Street, about where the 1968, 33-story, concrete One Main Place complex stands today.

Marilla Street: Named for Mrs. Marilla Ingram Young, wife of Rev. William C. Young. (See Young Street, below.)

McCommas Boulevard: Amon McCommas's family of nine children came from Kentucky in 1844. They settled on 640 acres (or 259 hectares), situated five miles (or eight kilometers) northeast of John Neely Bryan, who started Dallas on the banks of the Trinity River. McCommas helped organize the Dallas County government in 1845 and was the first county judge for the Commissioners Court.

McKinney Avenue: This was the road leading to McKinney, a city which was named after Collin McKinney, the oldest man to sign the Texas Declaration of Independence in 1836.

Munger Street: Named after Robert Silvester Munger (1854-1923), manufacturer of gins and East Dallas real estate developer who came from Birmingham, Alabama, in 1883, and made his fortune by improving Eli Whitney's cotton gin. In 1902, he sold his companies and went into real estate. The 50-block Munger Place was a real estate development begun in 1905 in East Dallas, with homes costing $10,000 or more on Swiss and Gaston Avenues at a time when an average home in Dallas cost about $2,000.

Pacific Avenue: Originally Burleson Street, it was renamed Pacific as an inducement for the Texas & Pacific Railroad to build the railroad here in 1872.

Record Street: Originally named for President Thomas Jefferson, then changed to honor James K. Polk Record (1834-1872), a prominent citizen during the post-Civil War era. A Tennessee lawyer, he became a Dallas district attorney in 1860 and six years later a state senator.

Ross Avenue: Named after William W. and Andrew J. Ross, Dallas fruit growers and wine merchants who owned large tracts of the land on both sides of the street. One of the oldest remaining buildings on the avenue outside the immediate downtown area that now sports mostly used-cars dealers is the former Fishburn's laundry complex built near Hall Street in 1907. It was converted into office space and apartments in 2000.

Routh Street: Named for Rev. Jacob Routh (1818-1879), a Tennessee native who first came to the area between today's Richardson and Plano in 1851. He brought his family in a four-horse wagon on a trip that took 45 days. There were no schools, stores, railroads, public roads, or churches nearby. He built a small log school in 1853 and became a Baptist minister.

St. Paul Street: Named by Barnett Gibbs, lieutenant governor of

Texas, 1884-1886, and a staunch proponent of Prohibition, although he himself liked a big nip now and then, to honor his favorite apostle, St. Paul, who wrote, "Drink no longer water, but use a little wine for thy stomach's sake."

San Jacinto Street: Named for the historic battle for Texas independence.

Skillman Street: In September 1927, Dallas threw a huge parade for aviator Charles Lindbergh and named a street after him for his historic flight across the Atlantic Ocean. However, by 1941 Dallasites were fed up with Lindbergh's pacifist sympathies and changed the name of the street to Skillman, after William Francis Skillman, a Dallas banker. Dallas named Lindbergh Drive for the pilot in 1975.

Wood Street: Named after George T. Wood, Texas governor from 1847 to 1849, who was liked by the citizens because he rode a mule.

Young Street: Named after Rev. William C. Young (d. 1921), a two-term Dallas County district clerk, a Methodist minister, and a Confederate missionary chaplain. It was originally named for President James K. Polk, who campaigned for Texas' annexation. Young is buried in Pioneer Cemetery (see entry) downtown.

Young named **Marilla Street** after his mother, **Canton Street** after his birthplace in Kentucky, and **Cadiz Street** for the Trigg County seat. Some Dallasites erroneously thought that Cadiz was named after a city in Spain and wanted to change it during the Spanish-American War.

Dallas streets also bear the names of 22 American states, from **Alabama** to **Virginia,** mostly in Oak Cliff.

Eighteen streets have names of Indian derivation: **Aztec, Brazos, Caddo, Cherokee, Chihuahua, Comal, Concho, Montezuma, Nakoma, Owega, Pocahontas, Powhattan, Sewannee, Swananoah, Taos, Tuskege, Watauga,** and **Wichita**.

World War I influenced the naming of streets, such as **Versailles, Belleau, Argonne, Bordeaux,** and **Lausanne,** mostly in Highland Park and University Park.

There are **Da Vinci Drive, Van Gogh Place,** and **Monet Place** in a north Dallas neighborhood off Kelly Boulevard. Also in north Dallas and off Royal Lane are **Cinderella Lane, Snow White Drive,** and **Peter Pan Drive**. There is also a **Pinocchio Drive**.

(For more details about Dallas highways and other major thoroughfares, please see the Private Car section in the TRANSPORTATION chapter.)

The Dallas World Aquarium, 1801 North Griffin St. at Hord St., (214) 720-2224, Internet www.dwazoo.com, e-mail info@dwazoo.com. *CH*, except children two years old and younger. Open daily 10 AM-5 PM, except Thanksgiving and Christmas. Restaurant open 11:30 AM-

2:30 PM. Wheelchair accessible. Parking is available across the street. Located in a two-story former warehouse, east of the West End Historic District downtown. The American Institute of Architects calls the building "one of the most sophisticated adaptive reuse projects in downtown."

Opened in 1993, the aquarium and rain forest, budgeted at more than $2 million a year, are visited by 500 children and adults daily. Starting with 12 tanks of fish and a penguin exhibit, it has since expanded to two warehouses. More than 85,000 gallons (or 321,800 liters) of saltwater exhibits are filled with bonnet head sharks, stingrays, cuttlefish, seadragons, jellyfish, and giant groupers, living in natural reef settings. There is a 22,000-gallon (or 83,280-liter) tunnel to experience a panoramic view of reef life.

In 1997, a 40,000-square-foot (or 3,716-square-meter) five-story, glass-enclosed tropical rain forest—twice the size of the aquarium—opened in a building next door, displaying poison dart frogs, Emerald tree boa constrictors and anacondas, jaguars, Peruvian squirrel monkeys, and toucans amid cascading waterfalls.

From the Australian Great Barrier Reef, you can admire Tridacna Gigas clams, a protected and the largest of its species that can weigh in excess of 300 pounds (or 136 kilograms). From Southern Australia comes the Leafy seadragon, a rare bony fish on display in only four aquariums in the world—Dallas's being the only one in the United States. Seadragons, which can be found only in Southern and Western Australia, have no teeth or stomach and feed on diets of msydopsis shrimp.

The aquarium, which is accredited by the American Zoo and Aquarium Association, also has several specimens from the only Lord Howe Island exhibit in the world. They include spectacled angelfish, comb wrasse, and painted goldie whose females are known to change sex in the absence of a male.

A pair of Orinoco crocodiles were brought to the aquarium in 1998 when they were the nation's only breeding pair. Miranda, the female, was 27 years old and weighed 300 pounds (or 136 kilograms). Juancho, the male, was about 20 and weighed 400 pounds (or 181 kilograms). Living in the fresh water of the Orinoco River in Venezuela, the Orinoco is one of the larger crocodilian species measuring up to 22.9 feet (or seven meters). The Orinoco population once totaled nearly one million, but most were killed by hunters for purses, belts, and shoes. Only about 1,000 are believed to remain.

In 2003, the Mundo Maya exhibit with a 400,000-gallon (or 1,514,120-liter) shark aquarium was inaugurated. It includes jaguars, sea turtles, hummingbirds, and butterflies.

Among the black-footed penguins on display in a 30,000-gallon (or

113,559-liter) habitat, three of them starred in the Warner Brothers film, *Batman Returns*. They and the green sea turtles hail from south Africa.

Eighteen-O-One restaurant features native dishes from the regions where the aquarium fish come from: Australia, British Columbia, Fiji, Indonesia, and Mexico. Open for lunch only, it is popular, despite the fact that patrons have to pay the museum admission even if they come just to eat.

The Dallas Zoo & Wilds of Africa, 650 South R.L. Thornton Fwy., (214) 670-5656/6826, Internet www.dallas-zoo.org. *CH*, except for children under the age of three; there is also a parking fee. Open daily 9 AM-5 PM, except Christmas. Average tour time 2-3 hours, monorail rides take place 10 AM-4 PM. Strollers and wheelchairs can be rented at the gift shop. ATM is available near the main entrance. Located three miles (or 4.8 kilometers) south of downtown Dallas, in the neighborhood of Oak Cliff, the Zoo is just off Interstate Highway 35 East, also known as Thornton Freeway. If you take DART's Red Line light-rail train from the West End, you will be there in about 15 minutes. The Clarendon Drive entrance is across the street from the DART rail station.

More than 380 species and 8,000 animals are displayed on 95 acres (or 38 hectares). The Zoo is owned by the city and managed on a budget of about $7 million by the Parks and Recreation Department. It boasts up to 600,000 visitors annually.

Snow leopards, red pandas, and okapis are among the rare and endangered species at the Dallas Zoo, which was established in 1888 with two deer and two mountain lions in the Old City Park (see entry), just southeast of downtown, and transferred to its current location in 1912. The Zoo has three of the no more than ten Texas ocelots in captivity, an endangered cat whose population in the wilds is estimated at fewer than 100.

A female black rhinoceros came from the Fort Worth Zoo in 2000. Three among fewer than 1,200 sand gazelles in the world were born at the San Diego Wild Animal Park, but otherwise originate in the Arabian Peninsula.

The 25-acre (or ten-hectare) **Wilds of Africa** section, separated from the main zoo by East Clarendon Drive, is part of a $100-million expansion program. It is one of the better zoo exhibits in the United States. In it, zoo visitors travel through six African habitats, where animals roam freely, while enjoying a three-mile (or 4.8-kilometer), 20-minute narrated monorail ride. More than 80 species of reptiles, mammals, and birds can be seen. Ostriches, okapis, and impalas are usually visible only from the monorail. The monorail is not air-conditioned so it might be shut down during the summer, when the temperature rises to 100 degrees Fahrenheit (or 38 degrees Celsius), and during the winter when it drops below 40 degrees (or four degrees Celsius).

Wilds of Africa also features a wooded quarter-mile (or 0.4-kilometer) nature trail, a walk-through aviary, and a two-acre (or 0.8-hectare) gorilla conservation research center, where the animals can be viewed without their knowledge. A rain forest is simulated.

In 1997, the zoo completed inside the Wilds of Africa a $1.9-million, 19,000-square-foot (or 1,765-square-meter), open-air Kimberly-Clark Chimpanzee Forest habitat that replicates the native African forest home for several chimpanzees. The site, with more than 40 species of vegetation, includes an artificial waterfall, a 20-foot (or six-meter) moat, and rocks that are heated in the winter and fan cooled during the summer.

A one-acre (or 0.4-hectare), $4.5-million ExxonMobil Endangered Tiger Habitat opened in 1999 as part of the **Zoo North** with several tigers. They include three Indochinese tigers—among only 1,500 still known to exist in the wild—born in the San Diego Zoo. Lions are not so fortunate. Not having a sponsor with Exxon's deep pockets, they live in a habitat built in 1936. The giraffes and elephants have had the same home since 1960.

Incidentally, Texas has as many as 2,300 captive tigers—kept either in zoos, as pets, or on exotic game ranches—or almost one-quarter of the world's entire tiger population. That's more than the tiger populations in Indonesia, Malaysia, Myanmar, Thailand, and Bangladesh, and more than that of Russia and China combined. Only India, with 3,000 to 4,000 tigers, has more of the big cats than Texas.

The Bird & Reptile Building in this area boasts a collection of 120 reptile and amphibian species. The Lacerte Family **Children's Zoo** displays pettable farm animals and educational activities.

If you have the stomach to eat in these surroundings, there is Ndebele Café in the Wilds of Africa and a sandwich shop in the Children's Zoo.

(For the story about the "tallest statue in Texas," located in front of the Zoo, see the Art in Public Places section in the VISUAL ARTS chapter.)

Dealey Plaza, Elm, Main, and Commerce Streets at Houston. Located in the western part of downtown, on the southern edge of the West End Historic District, north of Reunion complex, and adjacent to the former Texas School Book Depository. (For details about John F. Kennedy's assassination here, please see the Sixth Floor Museum and Kennedy Memorial entries in the VISUAL ARTS chapter.) A stretch of land located at Dallas' triple underpass of Elm, Main, and Commerce

Streets, west of Houston. Here was once the bed of the Trinity River, where the city of Dallas originated in 1841, when John Neely Bryan set his trading camp.

The plaza was built in the1930s by the Work Project Administration as a Depression-era project to address the problem of flood control. The river was relocated to its present channel, and Elm, Main, and Commerce Streets were realigned to converge into a triple underpass underneath the railroad tracks that led to Union Station (see entry).

The plaza is flanked by Bryan Colonnade, situated about where the founder of the city built his first log cabin, and Cockrell Colonnade, named after businessman Alexander Cockrell and his wife Sarah Horton, once the richest woman in Dallas.

The three-acre (or 1.21-hectare) plaza was named after George Bannerman Dealey (1859-1946), the founder of the *Dallas Morning News*, who had donated the land to the city.

Dealey was born in Manchester, England, of Irish parents, and emigrated with a family of eight children to Galveston, Texas, in 1870. At age 15, he took a job with the *Galveston News* as an office boy. Ten years later he was sent to Dallas, where he helped publish the first issue of the *News* in 1885. Dealey bought the *News* from the heirs of Alfred H. Belo in 1926.

Dealey's son Ted (1892-1969), who succeeded him as president in 1940, made national news in 1961 when "he impugned President John F. Kennedy's leadership ability at a White House luncheon."

G. B. Dealey's 12-foot (or 3.65-meter) 1948 bronze statue, created by the Austrian-American artist Felix de Weldon, faces the "Old Red" Courthouse (see entry) and twin reflecting pools. Behind the statue are bas-relief plaques mounted on a granite wall and depicting Dealey's contributions to Dallas.

The Vienna-born De Weldon (1907-2003) also sculpted the Iwo Jima Memorial on the hillside next to Arlington National Cemetery in Washington, D.C. The 100-ton 1954 sculpture took hundreds of assistants and more than nine years to complete.

The son of a wealthy Austrian textile manufacturer who was killed during Soviet bombing in World War II, de Weldon was regarded as an artistic genius from childhood. He received a master's degree from the University of Vienna and took a doctorate in architecture there at age 22. In 1973, Dr. de Weldon "declared bankruptcy after he was unable to repay a $1.5 million loan he had taken out to care for his wife, who had Alzheimer's disease and died in 1987," reports the *Washington Post*. He created more than 1,200 public works on seven continents.

Deep Ellum, Bounded by Elm, Main, Commerce, and Canton Streets; information line, (214) 747-DEEP, Internet www.ondaweb.com/deep_ellum. Located in the far-eastern end of downtown Dallas, south of the Baylor University Medical Center.

Deep Ellum has been described as a miniature Harlem, the African-American settlement in upper Manhattan in New York City. The name comes from the Southern drawled-out way of pronouncing the word Elm. Once an industrial neighborhood, where freed slaves first settled in the 1860s, this is now an alternative neighborhood in the shadow of one of America's more image-conscious cities. Henry Ford built a regional assembly plant here in 1913. It was for years filled with nightclubs, cafes, small hotels, pawn shops, shoeshine parlors, furniture stores, and domino halls.

The Grand Temple of the Black Knights of Pythias, in the 2500 block of Elm Street, was constructed here in 1916 on the design of William Sidney Pittman (1875-1958), "the first practicing black architect in Texas," who moved to Dallas in 1913 and stayed for 16 years.

While a student at Tuskegee Institute, he met Portia Marshall (1883-1978), the only daughter of educator Booker T. Washington, and fell hopelessly in love. Portia studied piano in Europe, but Pittman won her over through a "passionate correspondence," until the promising concert pianist sacrificed her studies and married him on Halloween of 1907.

Pittman moved to Dallas to escape his well-known father-in-law, but was plagued by financial problems throughout much of his marriage. When in 1928, in a "violent quarrel" with his daughter, Pittman struck the child, his wife left him and returned to Tuskegee, not coming back until 30 years later to attend the funeral of her former husband at Glen Oaks Cemetery in south Dallas. In the 1940s, Pittman was charged with mail fraud and spent two years in prison.

His wife outlived the architect by 20 years, and all three of her children. One of Pittman's children, Booker, became a jazz musician playing alto saxophone and spent the last 20 years of his life in Brazil, where he died in 1969.

After the completion of the first two miles (or 3.2 kilometers) of Central Expressway in 1948, Deep Ellum was suddenly cut off from the rest of downtown and went into decline. The resurgence came in the late 1970s, when artists took over what were then mostly manufacturing plants and boarded-up buildings. Today, its throbbing life begins after dark, and its welcome also extends to you, not just your wallet. There are some three dozen restaurants and nightclubs.

The legendary blues musicians "Blind Lemon" Jefferson and Huddie "Leadbelly" Ledbetter "joined forces, and with Huddie's mandolin and Lemon's Hawaiian guitar made a good living in the saloons and redlight district of East Dallas," according to the Austin, Texas-born folklorist Alan Lomax (1915-2002). That lasted until 1917, when Leadbelly was sentenced to 30 years in prison for killing a man in a dispute over a woman.

Leadbelly (1889-1949) hailed from Louisiana, the son of a black tenant farmer. He was pardoned in 1925 after having written a song in honor of Texas governor Pat Neff, but was back behind bars five years later. Married three times, he toured with Lomax and was particularly popular with white audiences.

Leadbelly claimed that he and Jefferson were so popular that "the women would come running, Lord have mercy. They'd hug and kiss us so much we could hardly play."

"Blind Lemon" Jefferson (1893-1929) was born blind near Wortham, south of Dallas, and received no formal education. He was a bootlegger whose wife would sneak two or three drinks at a time. When he would get home and find out what she had done, "he'd beat the hell out of her for that."

While playing in Deep Ellum, he was discovered by a talent scout and made 80 records, each of which is believed to have sold at least 100,000 copies. His songs were "personalized versions of traditional folk blues from East Texas that utilized proverbs and other elements of African-American folk speech."

Jefferson, who influenced such artists as Louis Armstrong and Bix Beiderbecke, was reported to have died of a heart attack on a Chicago street during a snowstorm.

Sam "Lightnin'" Hopkins (1912-1982), a Texan, made his first cigar-box guitar with chicken-wire strings at age eight. He recorded more than 100 records and became a hit in the folk-blues revival of the 1960s, when he performed at Carnegie Hall with Pete Seeger and Joan Baez. He played for Queen Elizabeth II during his 1970s European tour. Hopkins made some 90 albums and died of cancer of the esophagus.

Texas-born ragtime pianist **Scott Joplin** (ca. 1867-1917) played in the better clubs here, while the lesser-known blues singers performed for pocket change. In the 1930s and 40s, Deep Ellum attracted small businesses, pawnshops, and dry-goods stores, many run by largely Eastern European Jewish merchants.

"Although black businessmen in Dallas were essentially self-sufficient and able to meet the needs of their community, they did, by necessity, interact with Jewish shopkeepers in Deep Ellum," note Govenar and Brakefield in their 1998 history of the neighborhood. "Shopkeepers were generally sympathetic to the plight of African Americans, who, like them, were immigrants to Dallas and subjected to social discrimination and racism."

"The choice of restaurants in Deep Ellum is daunting," declares the *New York Times*, adding, "They range from dirt-cheap dives to pricey spots where reservations are required."

Caution: The later into the night the more careful you should be while in Deep Ellum or you might end up as a mugging statistic in the Dallas crime books.

FAIR PARK, 3809 Grand Ave. at Robert B. Cullum Blvd.; administration, (214) 670-8400; English-Spanish information line, 421-9600, Internet www.fairparkdallas.com. Bounded by Parry Avenue, Robert B. Cullum Boulevard, South Fitzhugh Avenue, and Union Pacific Railroad tracks. Several buses run from Commerce Street downtown to Fair Park and back.

Fair Park is a 277-acre (or 112-hectare) cultural and entertainment complex owned since 1903 by the city of Dallas in a mostly African-American neighborhood two miles (or 3.2 kilometers) east of downtown. It takes $4 million a year to operate the park, excluding the State Fair of Texas. More than 100 events take place in the park annually, but the biggest is the fair, which is now the largest state fair in the United States, attended by up to 3.5 million people. The fair is a private, non-profit corporation and is entirely self-supporting. (For more about it, please see below.)

The Fair Park complex includes the **African-American Museum of Life & Culture, Age of Steam Railroad Museum, Dallas Aquarium, Dallas Horticulture Center, Dallas Museum of Natural History,** Dallas Music Hall, **The Science Place,** Smirnoff Music Centre, **Texas Hall of State, Women's Museum,** and Texas Vietnam Veterans Memorial. (For details about museums in bold, please see individual entries elsewhere.)

There are six exhibition buildings with 338,000 square feet (or 31,400 square meters) of space on the fair grounds with 9,000 parking spaces:

- **Automobile Building** (84,500 square feet, or 7,850 square meters), a free-span roofed facility, which is adorned by three female allegorical 20-foot-high (or six-meter) figures that were created by the French-American artist Raoul Josset.
- **Centennial Building** (94,500 square feet, or 8,779 square meters) was originally constructed in 1905 as the first steel and masonry exhibition building at the fairgrounds. This structure burned after the centennial celebrations and was replaced by the current Automobile Building.
- **Creative Arts Building** (17,000 square feet, or 1,579 square meters) has a 256-seat theater.
- **Embarcadero Building** (27,000 square feet, or 2,508 square meters) also dates from 1936.
- **Food & Fiber Building** (25,000 square feet, or 2,322 square meters) was designed by the chief Centennial Exposition architect George L. Dahl, built in 1936, and restored in 1999.

• **Grand Place** (50,000 square feet, or 4,645 square meters), is dedicated to the women who served and died in the Civil War. Next to it is the Crafts Village, where during the fair there are exhibits of jewelry, leatherwork, textile art, woodcraft, and toys.

• **Tower Building** (40,000, or 3,716 square meters), a 179-foot-high (or 54.5-meter) triangular tower of the original U.S. Government Building that marked the geographic center of the Centennial Exposition. It was designed by George Dahl and Chicago Exposition architect Donald Nelson and built in 1936. The structure includes Raoul Josset's gilded, stylized eagle sculpture, and a bas-relief promenade of Texas history by Julian Garnsey.

You will also find here seven horse stables, and cattle, poultry, swine, sheep, and goat buildings that total almost 300,000 square feet (or 27,870 square meters).

The midway is an amusement park with more than 60 rides and games for all ages, including the 212-foot (or 64.6-meter) Texas Star Ferris wheel—now, listen up!—the tallest in North America. It was installed in 1985 by Buster Lee Brown (b. 1935), whose legs were paralyzed by polio in 1939 and who died at age 54 in a car accident in Wyoming.

The **Magnolia Lounge,** drafted by New York Architect William Lescaze, "introduced European Modernism to Texas in 1936." It served as the hospitality lounge for the Magnolia Petroleum Co. The building's overall image was different from that of any other structure at the Centennial Exposition.

The **Dallas Opera** performs at the 3,420-seat Music Hall, (214) 565-1116, Internet www.dallassummermusicals.org, mostly from November to February. The cavernous structure was designed by Lang and Witchell, constructed in 1925, and renovated in 1972. (For more information, please see entry in the PERFORMING ARTS chapter.)

At other times Broadway shows under the banner Dallas Summer Musicals (Internet www.dallassummermusicals.org), have been taking place at this hall since 1941.

The city-owned 24-hour all-classical radio station **WRR-FM,** (214) 670-8888, on 101.1 FM band, is also headquartered at Fair Park. It is the second oldest radio station in the United States and the only municipally owned commercial station in the country.

The **Cotton Bowl Stadium,** (214) 939-2222, is a 25,000-square-foot (or 2,322-square-meter) facility. Built in 1930 as a wooden, 15,000-seat football stadium, it is Dallas's largest outdoor stadium with a capacity for 71,500 spectators since its 1993 renovation.

Originally named Fair Park Stadium, it was renamed in 1936 after Dallas' former prominence as a big cotton market. The stadium with no suites or club seats has cramped seating, meager concessions, and narrow corridors. Until 1971, when Texas Stadium (see entry) opened in the suburb of Irving, the Dallas Cowboys football team played its home games here.

The **Coliseum,** (214) 670-0269, arena, where rodeos take place each year, measures 28,000 square feet (or 2,601 square meters) and seats 7,100. **Dallas Burn,** (214) 979-0303, the city's professional soccer team, also plays some games at the Coliseum, which accommodated World Cup soccer in 1994.

Across Pennsylvania Avenue, southeast of the Cotton Bowl, is the $8-million **Smirnoff Music Centre,** 1818 First Ave., (214) 421-1111, Internet www.hob.com, an outdoor performing arts venue with celebrity entertainment and the capacity to hold 20,100 persons. The city-owned facility, which is privately run and was previously known as Coca-Cola Starplex Amphitheater, is wheelchair accessible.

A Dallas city council member manipulated Smirnoff's guilt over associating alcohol with entertainment until the parent company, Guinness United Distillers, "contributed" $3.8 million for "social improvement efforts" in south Dallas. This on top of the $6 million that Smirnoff paid for naming rights for eight years. One Dallas County commissioner called it "blood money."

Also located near Fair Park is the **Martin Luther King Jr. Community Center,** at 2922 Martin Luther King Jr. Blvd., (214) 670-8372, named after the African-American clergyman and reformer who received the Nobel Peace Prize in 1964.

Fair Park's 1936 Centennial Exposition

In 1936, when Dallas had a population of 265,000, an extravaganza took place in Fair Park the likes of which have never been repeated. The 185-acre (or 74.8-hectare) grounds were transformed into a $25-million world's fair visited by 6.3 million. Dallas, Houston, San Antonio, and Fort Worth, they all wanted to host the exposition, but when asked whether they would carry on without any state or federal aid, only Dallas' civic leader R. L. Thornton replied without hesitation: "Dallas has already said 'Yes.'"

A Fort Worth representative noted tartly that holding a "Centennial Celebration at Dallas, is like celebrating Washington's Birthday at Buckingham Palace." Dallas, in fact, did not even exist a hundred years earlier.

The Minneapolis-born, Harvard-educated George Leighton Dahl (1894-1987) was hired at $1,500 a month as the chief architect of the fair complex, at a time when a "colored" porter earned $50 a month, and a good secretary received $125. He coordinated the work of 130 architects, engineers, and artists at Fair Park. Dahl came to Dallas in 1926, after spending two years in Rome as a fellow at the American Academy.

Among countless buildings, Dahl designed the Dallas Morning News building and the former Titche-Goettinger department store at 1900 Elm Street downtown, now the site of 129 lofts. Married twice, Dahl died of cancer in 1987 at the age of 93 at his Dallas home.

By May 1936, 10,000 men worked in three shifts to complete what seemed the impossible task of opening the exposition the following month. Seventy-seven buildings were completely remodeled or constructed just for the fair. After ten months of breakneck construction and $5.5 million in local funding, the gates were flung open on June 6.

The first day, 117,600 visitors came. The general admission price was 50 cents and the gates stayed open from 9 AM until midnight. Ginger Rogers and Lucille Ball, Clark Gable and Robert Taylor were just some of the personalities who came from Hollywood. Duke Ellington, Cab Calloway, and Tommy Dorsey brought their orchestras to entertain the fairgoers.

"While the exposition brought money and notoriety to Dallas, it proved destructive to the serious arts," observes Dallas cultural historian Ronald L. Davis. During the second year of the celebration, which was called the Pan American Exposition, the "local theaters and serious music had either been disrupted or totally ignored."

Meanwhile, Fort Worth businessman and civic booster Amon Carter felt that his beloved Cowtown must not be outdone and convinced his cronies that an unofficial Fort Worth Frontier Centennial Exposition, also to celebrate the state's freedom from Mexico, was just what Texas needed. He hired a New York showman, Billy Rose, at $100,000 for one hundred days, to put on the greatest extravaganza Fort Worth had ever seen "and teach those dudes over there [in Dallas] where the West really begins."

Rose went so far as to offer Ethiopian emperor Haile Selassie (d. 1975) $100,000 to appear in Rose's show with his lions. He engaged Sally Rand, a Quaker farm girl from Missouri and a nude dancer of some ill repute, who stirred a predictable local response, just the controversy Carter hoped would sell lots of tickets. It focused around the newly built Casa Manana, the world's largest open-air theater, which could seat more than 3,800.

But in spite of all the hoopla, the Fort Worth Frontier Fair was a financial flop, and only 986,000 showed up, mostly to be titillated by the sensuous music and the Quaker girl who really did not show much flesh after all.

Fair Park's State Fair of Texas, General information (214) 565-9931, Internet www.bigtex.com. The fair is held annually roughly between September 27 and October 20. Fair grounds are open daily 10

AM-10 PM. *CH*, except children under the age of two and elderly over 60 on Thursdays; some museums are free. Cash only, but ATMs are located at several locations. Parking for 8,000 vehicles. Wheelchair and stroller rentals are available. For DART city bus service to Fair Park, call (214) 979-1111.

State fairs have a long tradition in America, but their roots are traceable to Europe, where fairs were held along trade routes. The first American state fair took place in Syracuse, New York, in 1841. The first Dallas Fair, which had a strictly agrarian bent, was initiated in 1859 and attracted 2,000 visitors, followed by 11,000 the following year. The fair was suspended for the next eight years, when the Civil War got in the way.

Fair Park has been the site of the annual State Fair of Texas since 1886, the year when the Statue of Liberty was dedicated and the 49-year-old President Grover Cleveland married 21-year-old Frances Folsom. Fourteen thousand people attended the opening day of the first state fair here. By 1905, when the famed French actress Sarah Bernhardt performed here in a tent for 4,000 spectators, 300,000 fair visitors came through the gates. In 1916, attendance passed the one million mark, two million in 1949, and three million in 1968.

World War I was the reason for the 1918 State Fair to be canceled, and Fair Park was converted into a temporary army tent encampment named Camp Dick. The grounds were used to house German prisoners during World War II. President William Howard Taft visited the fair in 1909, and Woodrow Wilson delivered a speech there in 1911. President Lyndon B. Johnson came in 1961 and again in 1963. Former Soviet President Mikhail Gorbachev visited the fair in 1998 and enjoyed a corny dog that he declared similar to Russian fried sausage.

Elvis Presley Concert

After evading hundreds of screaming teenagers, some of whom drove from as far away as Florida to hear him, Elvis Presley gave a concert on October 11, 1956, at the Cotton Bowl Stadium nearby. One hundred policemen maintained order, while 26,000 fans, mostly girls, waited breathlessly for their Prince Charming. Lori Torrance described the event in part in her 2002 book, titled *Elvis in Texas*:

"At the end of his 35-minute stint, he jumped off the stage and crawled around in the grass singing, 'You ain't nothin' but a hound dawg' in his electric green sports jacket, white bucks, and black-and-gold striped cummerbund." The next day he left for nearby Waco. The *Fort Worth Star-Telegram* claimed at the time that, "besides a few government wheels like the President, Elvis Presley is probably the most closely guarded man in the U.S."

Enjoying the Fair

To enjoy the fair at its merriest, come with your children. The fair's Web site and the *Dallas Morning News* list the events daily. You will receive a map and guide to various activities upon entering the grounds.

The fair stands for rides, which now cost up to $20 each, or trying your luck at a game of skill, although you will seldom win anything worthwhile. It is parades and contests of every description. It is shows or just walking around and indulging yourself in many varieties of foods. It is the place to watch, listen, shop, browse, eat, and relax. And spend money. Lots of money. In cash.

In a long Texas tradition, thousands of steers, cows, horses, hogs, sheep, goats, rabbits, even broiler hens, are judged in the livestock arenas during the fair for prizes going into tens of thousands of dollars for those winning the first place. In recent years, hundreds of animals have been auctioned, raising more than $500,000, the proceeds going mostly for scholarships.

A 1,168-pound (or 530-kilogram) Grand Champion steer, aptly named Pot of Gold, sold for a record $75,000 at one fair. Its owner got to keep $25,000 for his college scholarship. The year before, a steer that weighed 1,327 pounds (or 602 kilograms) sold for $73,000.

Food, surprisingly, is the No. 1 reason visitors come to the fair. And the best-selling food item is the three-dollar corny dog, invented by brothers Neil and Carl Fletcher in 1942, when it cost 15 cents. Today, Neil's son "Skip" Fletcher Jr. (b. 1934) still mans five corny dog stands at the fair. More than $16 million in food and beverages at 200 concession stands is sold every year.

The Old Mill Inn, 1112 First Ave., (214) 426-4600, was built as an experimental flour mill "of the future" for the 1936 Texas Centennial and World Fair, with model kitchens and a tearoom. It is situated near the Big Tex statue and serves lunch and dinner during the fair, but is open 11 AM-3 PM only at other times.

Although police are visible on foot and on horseback, inside and around the park during the fair, petty crime abounds. Arrive early enough to park in a well-lighted area inside the fair grounds and walk with a group if possible. Police suggest that you carry with you as little as you can and do not display large amounts of cash or wear expensive jewelry.

The crowds can be crushing during the fair, and as many as 200 children get lost every year. Wear comfortable shoes because you could be walking all day. Most of the fair is accessible to the handicapped. Restrooms are scattered throughout the grounds.

The average stay, according to the organizers, is 5.2 hours, with 41 percent attending the fair annually. Female visitors, surprisingly, predominate. The fair produces more than $20 million in revenues and employs about 1,500.

Big Tex

Big who? Big Tex. Texas' contribution to the American folklore is a cowboy larger than life, and the Texas State Fair is the place where you will find Big Tex, the gigantic monument to the Western way of life. Since 1952—when Dean Martin and Jerry Lewis were here—he has been booming out, "Howdy, folks. Welcome to the State Fair of Texas," about 60 times a day.

The man speaking on behalf of Big Tex during the fair sits for hours every day behind a microphone in a cramped booth, working the controls that move the giant cowboy's head and hand. Big Tex was originally constructed in 1949 as a huge Santa Claus in the Navarro County town of Kerns, Texas, to lure shoppers downtown. The fair president, R. L. "Bob" Thornton, a former Dallas mayor, bought it two years later for $750.

Big Tex is 52 feet (or 15.8 meters) tall, has a 30-foot (or nine-meter) chest, and a 283-inch (or 718-meter) waist. It takes 132 square yards (or 110 square meters) of tent fabric for his shirt, 100 inches by 180 inches (or 4.57 by 4.57 meters), neck and sleeve, with the neck measuring more than 12 feet (or 3.6 meters) in diameter. His shirt buttons are five inches (or 12.7 centimeters) wide. An average man's size is 16 by 32.

Big Tex wears jeans that are 284 inches by 185 inches (or 7.21 by 4.7 meters), waist and inseam, with a 23-foot (or seven-meter) waist—most mortal men wear size 36 by 30. Tex's jeans take 71 yards (or 65 meters) of denim and weigh 65 pounds (or 29 kilograms). His hat can hold 75 gallons (or 284 liters) of Lone Star beer, and his boots are seven and a half feet (or 2.28 meters) high.

Federal Reserve Bank of Dallas Building, 2200 North Pearl St. Tours are available Mon-Thu during business hours by calling (214) 922-5250. A cafeteria and an automatic teller machine are located on the second floor, a post office on the ground floor. Located across Woodall Rodgers Frwy. (also known as Spur 366) in the historic State-Thomas neighborhood, just north of the Arts District.

The Dallas Fed opened its 17-story, 595,385-square-foot (or 55,311-square-meter) building, sitting on six acres (or 2.42 hectares) of land, in 1992. The project was recommended in 1988 to consolidate the offices which had overflowed from a downtown building, located across the street from the Dallas Public Library (see listing), to three additional sites.

The building project cost almost $160 million at a time when the banking, energy, and real estate industries were barely starting to recover from the depression of the Texas economy in the mid-1980s. More than 500 banks went bankrupt from the early 1980s through mid-1992 in the Dallas Federal Reserve Bank's 11th district, which includes Texas, northern Louisiana, and southern New Mexico.

The first-floor lobby measures 27,000 square feet (or 2,508 square meters) and includes a large fiberglass sculpture depicting a farmer and two oxen, called *Sodbuster*, by El Paso native Luis Jimenez. Other artworks by Texas, Louisiana, and New Mexico artists are also on display.

Most of the floors are of similar design, including the 14th executive floor. The floors appear to be of marble, but are travertine. The building has a five-story vault with 18-inch (or 45-centimeter) thick walls, the second largest in the country, where currency is stored in carts, each of which can hold 300,000 notes.

The original 280,000-square-foot (or 26,012-square-meter) Federal Reserve Bank building sits at 400 South Akard and Wood Streets on 2.9 acres (or 1.17 hectares) of land downtown, next to the SBC Communications office towers.

When the Federal Reserve System was created in 1913, Dallas was the smallest city selected as one of the 12 regional centers. It only had about 100,000 inhabitants. Federal officials were skeptical about placing the bank anywhere in Texas, which was then seen as farm country.

It was largely because of efforts by Nathan Adams (1869-1966), the "dean of Texas bankers," that the bank came to Dallas. Starting out as a general store cash boy in Tennessee, in 1887 Adams borrowed $75 to be able to come to Dallas, and in 1929 became president of the First National Bank of Dallas, by then the largest in the South.

The seven-story neoclassical-style building, with columns and portico, and with a towering lobby, was drafted by architect Graham Anderson and constructed in 1921. Following the 1933 banking system collapse and the scarcity of jobs during the Depression, the Dallas Fed issued a policy that no married women would be employed at the bank or any of its branches.

First Baptist Church, 1707 San Jacinto St. at North Ervay, (214) 969-0111. Located two blocks southeast of the Dallas Museum of Art and two blocks from the Fairmont Hotel (please see individual listings).

The First Baptist Church is one of the largest Baptist churches in the nation with a membership of more than 25,000, a staff of 300, and 40 ordained pastors. First Baptist was established in 1868, on the corner of Ervay and San Jacinto Streets, where the first one-room structure was erected in 1871, when Dallas had a population of 2,500. It was enlarged in 1890 when Col. C. C. Slaughter donated $60,000, or two-thirds of the cost, for the construction of a house of worship.

Col. Christopher Columbus Slaughter (1837-1919) was a Texas ranching pioneer and banker who had moved to Dallas in 1873. He volunteered his services in the 1859 outbreak of war with Indians and was in the expedition that unexpectedly liberated Cynthia Ann Parker (1825-1871), for 25 years a captive of the Comanches. Nicknamed the Cattle King of Texas, Slaughter became one of the country's largest landowners, holding a million acres (or 404,700 hectares) and 40,000 cattle by 1906. He was said to be for many years the largest individual taxpayer in Texas.

The church's first pastor was W. W. Harris, in later years knows as "Spurgeon" Harris, a reference to Charles Haddon Spurgeon of London, who was believed to be the greatest Baptist preacher of his time.

Today, the church complex covers more than five city blocks, and comprises real estate worth well over $100 million. Designed by the Cincinnati-trained architect Albert Ulrich, the brick and stone structure was the fourth Baptist church built in Dallas. This is the only downtown Dallas church still located on its original site where it encompasses twelve buildings. Up to 2,000 people can attend services in the church auditorium.

The church congregation is involved in a seven-day-a-week ministry and also serves the deaf, transient, incarcerated, and those in rehabilitation. In 2002, First Baptist unveiled plans to construct a $48-million, eight-story building at San Jacinto and Ervay streets. It was to include classrooms, office space, a prayer tower, a Christian bookstore with a coffee bar that would be open at night, a sports-theme snack bar, and a banquet hall.

Also part of the church is **Criswell College,** established in 1971, where one can earn a bachelor's or master's degrees in preparation for ministry. The block-long campus on the corner of Gaston Avenue and Haskell Street numbers about 450 students. Ruth Ray Hunt (d. 1999), the widow of oilman Haroldson Lafayette Hunt, gave the college $3.4 million in 1989.

(For more about the **First Baptist Academy,** Ervay at Patterson Sts., a kindergarten through grade 12 school, please see the education section of the NEW RESIDENTS chapter.)

Pastor W. A. Criswell

The First Baptist Church was led for almost 50 years by pastor Wallie Amos Criswell, one of the most powerful men of cloth in the Metroplex history.

As a boy, Criswell swept his father's small-town barbershop in Texline, on the Texas-New Mexico border, and once considered becoming an actor. Seven years out of seminary, Criswell (b. 1909), left a

Muskogee, Oklahoma, church and came to Dallas in 1944, when First Baptist had a couple thousand members.

Twelve years later, he said in impromptu remarks to the South Carolina Legislature that integration is a "thing of idiocy and foolishness." But in 1969, Criswell told his deacons, "I came to the profound conclusion that to separate by coercion the body of Christ on the basis of skin pigmentation was unthinkable, un-Christian, and unacceptable to God."

In 1968 he was elected president of the Southern Baptist Convention. The *Fort Worth Star-Telegram* called him "a paradoxical combination of a warm, gentlemanly personality and a hard critic to those who disagreed with his view on the inerrancy of the Bible."

Reverend Criswell, who also wrote 54 books, was so successful in his real estate business that in 1974 he returned more than $600,000 in salary to First Baptist. Dr. Criswell, who had played trombone while at Baylor University in Waco, was married to church pianist Betty Marie Harris for 66 years. The couple lived for many years on Dallas' historic Swiss Avenue. He had surgery for colon cancer in 1998 and died in 2002 at age 92.

"Dr. Criswell was an important spiritual leader for America," President George W. Bush said in a statement. He is buried at the Hillcrest Memorial Park Cemetery on West Northwest Highway.

First Presbyterian Church, 408 Park Ave., (214) 748-8051. Located downtown near the 1914 building also known as the Police and Municipal Courts Building, at 106 South Harwood and Young Streets.

The First Presbyterian Church of Dallas was founded with eleven members in 1856 and is believed to be the first Southern Presbyterian Church in the city. Lacking a formal place of worship, the church members met in private homes, even a blacksmith shop, a lumberyard, and the courthouse. Not until 1873 was the congregation able to erect its first building.

In 1882, First Presbyterian built its second home at Harwood and Main Streets, which was also the first brick church building in Dallas. In 1913, the congregation moved to its present home, which originally cost $150,000. So much was spent on the exterior that no money was left for stained glass, and the windows were donated over the years by individual parishioners. The neo-classical church edifice was designed by the once-prominent Dallas architect C. D. Hill, who also drafted the old city hall nearby. It was restored in 1989.

On the next block, at 508 Park Ave., stands the 1929 Zigzag Moderne-style **Warner Brothers Film Exchange Building,** where in the 1920s was located a film distribution center feeding Dallas' theaters on Elm Street. In June 1937, the legendary Delta blues singer Robert Johnson recorded his final 13 songs here. Fourteen months later, Johnson was dead, poisoned by the owner of a Mississippi roadhouse whose wife the singer had tried to seduce.

When Columbia released these recordings in 1961, it sold more than a million copies, and the blues fans were "hypnotized by his ethereal singing and wicked guitar playing—not to mention the mystery surrounding his short, ill-fated life," reports the *Dallas Morning News*. Most did not even know what Johnson looked like until the 1980s, when two black and white photos of him surfaced.

A block southeast from the First Presbyterian Church, at 500 South Harwood St., you will find the 1913 Beaux Arts-styled **Scottish Rite Cathedral,** a temple to freemasonry designed by architect Herbert M. Greene. Across the street from it, at 501 South Harwood sits the Masonic Temple, built 28 years later. On some days, up to a couple hundred mostly young homeless men sit aimlessly on the sidewalks south of here.

First United Methodist Church, 1928 Ross Ave at Harwood St., (214) 220-2727, Internet www.fumcdal.org. Located downtown in the Arts District, across the street from the Dallas Museum of Art, Trammell Crow Collection, and Nasher Sculpture Center.

Designed by architect Herbert M. Greene in 1924 and built two years later, when it was the first Dallas church structure to cost a million dollars. Greene also drafted the downtown Neiman Marcus department store and the 1913 Beaux Arts-style Scottish Rite Cathedral (see above).

First United Methodist goes back to 1846, when a group met in the area without a church of their own. The church's first building, Lamar Street Methodist, was erected in 1868 on a lot donated by Sarah Horton Cockrell, Dallas' first true female capitalist. Eleven years later, the church was destroyed by fire. The church's third home at Commerce and Prather Streets was built in 1887. The Trinity Methodist and First Methodist congregations merged in 1916 at the corner of McKinney Avenue and Pearl Street. By 1927, the membership had grown to 3,400.

The church, in addition to ministries helping the homeless, and music and arts programs, has a daycare center for children aged up to five years.

The Fountain Place, 1445 Ross Ave. at Field St., (214) 855-7766, Internet www.cei-crescent.com. Located in the northern part of downtown, on the same block as the Fairmont Hotel (see listing) and across Ross Avenue from the YMCA building, where you can exercise and swim.

The 1.2-million-square-foot (or 111,480-square-meter) Fountain Place, designed by architect I. M. Pei & Partners, is an enormous beveled-glass prism, completed in 1986. The following year, lenders foreclosed on what was then called the Allied Bank Tower, the first downtown real estate domino to collapse in the late 1980s real estate crash.

The Dallas chapter of the American Institute of Architects calls the Fountain Building "the most extraordinary of Pei's three Dallas towers built during the 1980s. As an object standing in isolation, the tower recalls similar bravura forms of Philip Johnson's Pennzoil Place in Houston."

The 60-story building, which is 721 feet (or 219 meters) high, vies with the Bank One Tower and JP Morgan Chase Tower (see entries) for the honor of being the second tallest city structure. "Depending on the direction from which it's viewed, this tower can appear to be razor thin, obelisk-like, inconspicuous or the jewel of downtown," one architect told the *Dallas Business Journal*. Local architect Frank Welch (b. 1928) calls it "the most extraordinary urban space in Dallas."

Once called the First Interstate Bank Building, this structure seems to be the object of adoration for many out-of-town visitors. Thousands come each year to admire its architecture and a collection of 200 computer-controlled water jets on the 5.8-acre (or 2.34-hectare) plaza, along with more than two hundred cypress trees, both of which offer a welcome respite from the summer heat. "Sure, Houston has fountains, but none are as enticing as Fountain Place in downtown Dallas," declares the *Houston Chronicle*, adding that the dancing waters drown out the urban noise.

There is an Italian-cuisine **Avanti Café** (Internet www.avantirestaurants.com), where lunch is served 11 AM-2 PM on the ground floor. Wells Fargo Bank in the lobby has an automatic teller machine in the tunnel that leads toward the Fairmont Hotel (see entry).

In 1997, the Fountain Place was purchased for $122 million by a Fort Worth-based real estate investment trust, which that year also bought the Bank One Tower and the Trammell Crow Center (see listings). The building has won several awards for its architectural merits.

A block northwest of here, at 1901 North Akard St. and Woodall Rodgers Fwy., stands the **Cumberland Hill School,** Dallas' oldest public school building still standing. It was built in 1888 and closed 70 years later.

Freedman's Cemetery Memorial, Freedman's Memorial Park, Uptown, (214) 760-6066, Internet www.freedmans.org. Located about one mile (or 1.6 kilometers) north of downtown Dallas, on the corner of North Central Expressway and Calvary Street, just south of Lemmon

Avenue. The 42-story Cityplace skyrise is diagonally across North Central Expressway. Temple Emanu-El, Calvary, and Greenwood Cemeteries are situated nearby. Eight Dallas mayors are buried at Greenwood.

The original four-acre (or 1.61-hectare) cemetery, dating back to 1869, served as a burial site for as many as 7,000 freed slaves and their descendants after the Civil War, but was condemned by the city in 1907.

"The site was first desecrated in 1872, when eminent domain was invoked to take part of the cemetery for the Houston railway, and again in 1949, with the construction of Central Expressway," observes the *Fort Worth Star-Telegram*. Almost a third of the cemetery was covered by the expressway construction and the rerouting of Lemmon Avenue. It was closed in the 1920s.

As part of a preservation plan at the cemetery, where more than 1,100 African-Americans were excavated and reburied between 1990 and 1994 to accommodate the North Central Expressway reconstruction, the memorial was completed in 2000.

A bronze-and-stone bas-relief sculptural ensemble of four male and female figures, conceived by sculptor David Newton of New York, is a reminder of African-American history, from freedom in Africa through emancipation in the United States. Newton won the commission in competition with 73 other artists nationwide. Poems are etched into the adjacent sunken circle.

The memorial's arched entryway is flanked by a female African *griot* (oral historian) and a male African warrior, the two figures who keep the story alive at the site so it will never be lost again, at least symbolically. Behind them, two other poetically recreated, but thought-provoking and disturbing in their simplicity, enslaved figures are chained in shame and sorrow. They are united by the news of emancipation in a sculpture standing at the center of the memorial.

The original Freedman's Town stretched from the intersection of Lemmon and McKinney Avenues through the area that later became known as Deep Ellum, observes the monthly *Texas Highways*, adding that Freedman's Town thrived just northeast of the Dallas city limits as a separate, self-contained town. It had shanty dwellers, a thriving business community, and a middle class complete with tea societies.

At Greenwood Cemetery near here, Sarah Horton Cockrell, once the wealthiest resident of Dallas, was buried in 1892. She was the wife of an illiterate businessman, Alexander Cockrell (b. 1820), who was killed by a Dallas city marshal in 1858.

Another area of Freedman's Town is located in a neglected ten-acre (or 4-hectare) neighborhood, part of the Tenth Street area of Oak Cliff. It also was a busy commercial and social hub for African-Americans, claiming stores, restaurants, and barbershops.

Infomart, 1950 North Stemmons Frwy., (800) 232-1022 or (214) 746-3500, Internet www.infomartusa.com. Open weekdays 9 AM-4:30 PM. Located a few minutes northwest of downtown Dallas on Stemmons (also known as Interstate 35 East) at Oak Lawn Ave.

Infomart is a seven-story, 1.16-million-square-foot (or 107,764-square-meter) white-metal and mirrored-glass building. It serves as a combination learning and information resource center, as well as an exhibit hall with permanent offices for 100 leading software, telecommunications, and office automation companies. Its architect is Martin Grovald.

In the wake of the terrorist attacks of September 11, 2001, when many corporations made finding back-up Web-hosting space a high priority, the InfoMart has also positioned itself as a back-up data management center.

It was built on 25 acres (or ten hectares) of land at a cost of $170 million by the wealthy Trammell Crow family in 1985 and sold to NeXcomm (www.nxcapital.com), a limited partnership in Southport, Connecticut, in 1999. NeXcomm leases space to telecommunications providers and Internet and e-commerce firms. The facility is physically located on the Dallas Market Center property (see listing) and open to the public and the trade. You can see live demonstrations of products and exhibits by leading hardware and software companies.

More than 1,000 meetings and shows are held here each year. There are 34 conference rooms, a 510-seat auditorium, and a post office located in the building. A Dow Jones Information Service kiosk, bookstore, florist, and automatic teller machine will also be found here.

Infomart building has been recognized by Great Britain's Parliament as official successor to the Crystal Palace, a structure that until 1936, when it burned down, was a landmark in London. The glass and iron London building was constructed in 1851 for the first World's Fair.

The **Crystal Palace** restaurant is one of the cafes on the premises and is open Mon-Fri.

Jack Evans Police Headquarters, 1400 South Lamar St. at Belleview, (214) 243-2126. Located in the Cedars neighborhood just across Interstate 30, not far from the Cedars DART light-rail station. Across the street are the 457 loft-style apartments in a former Sears catalog center (see entry Southside on Lamar), to be followed by a luxury hotel in the same block. Further north on Lamar, toward I-30, construction is taking place of a Gilley's entertainment complex (see entry), similar to the original honky-tonk in Pasadena, in south Texas.

The $59-million, six-story police station, completed in 2003, accommodates 1,360 officers and department employees, many of whom were previously located in the run-down police headquarters at

106 South Harwood Street and Main. Designed by architect Greg Schon, it is named for a former mayor who died in 1997.

The 358,000-square-foot (or 33,258-square-meter) brick and glass building was constructed around a 7,000-square-foot (or 650-square-meter) courtyard. "Instead of a civic monument," says the *Dallas Morning News* about its architectural execution, "the city is getting an overdressed office block that would look perfectly at home in Las Colinas or Addison."

The headquarters contains half a million dollars in public art. A kinetic sculpture or a giant metal flower-theme sundial, titled *Dallas Dahlia*, executed by New York artist Alice Aycock, sits in the courtyard. San Francisco artist Anita Margrill installed 30 glass panels featuring police-related photography in the lobby. New Yorker Gregg LeFevre embedded 19 300-pound (or 136-kilo) bronze relief panels depicting Dallas police history, such as the Kennedy assassination, into the concrete plaza outside the headquarters. LeFevre (b. 1946) has created 600 sidewalk panels in New York, Boston, Chicago, Miami, and Minneapolis.

A 4,000-square-foot (or 372-square-meter), $1-million law enforcement museum, (214) 670-0172 or 243-2126, with an antique Model A patrol car and other memorabilia, is planned for the building's second-floor area. It will tell the story of the Dallas police department since it was founded in 1881.

Dallas has 29 full-time police officers per each 10,000 residents, compared with 33 in Houston, 23 in Fort Worth, 21 in Austin, and 18 in San Antonio. Until relocating here, the police department was located in the five-story neo-classical 1914 building at the intersection of Main and Harwood Streets in whose basement the alleged Kennedy assassin Lee Harvey Oswald was shot by nightclub owner Jack Ruby. The 1914 portion of the building will be renovated for the municipal courts. The police headquarters is named after Jack Evans, a grocery executive and banker who served as mayor of Dallas between 1981 and 1983. In 2000, the city renamed a three-block stretch of Fairmount Street in the downtown Arts District in his honor.

Cedars, so named because it is located in an area once covered by a forest of cedar trees, was developed in the late 1870s as a wealthy residential area. A streetcar line and what is now known as the Old City Park only added to the value of the property. It was home to many Dallas Jewish merchants, such as Alex and Philip Sanger, founders of the Sanger Brothers department stores. But Cedars' exclusivity was short-lived. Ten years later, apartments appeared, and factories sprouted around the Victorian mansions. By the early 1920s most of the affluent residents were gone.

John F. Kennedy Memorial, Dallas County Historic Plaza, at Main, Record, Elm and Market Streets. Open 24 hours, lighted at night.

Located on the plaza in front of the "Old Red" Courthouse, as well as the new county courthouse on Commerce Street, one block east of Dealey Plaza (see individual entries). Where the memorial is now situated there once stood the West End Bakery, which was closed during the Depression. A dry-goods store also occupied the site of today's memorial at one time.

The memorial was designed by the Harvard-educated architect and Kennedy family friend Philip Johnson (b. 1906). The 50-foot-square, roofless, concrete, steel and marble cenotaph, 30 feet (or nine meters) high, is symbolic of an open tomb. The open-air cube, consisting of 72 wall elements joined by steel tendons, is sober and austere. "Because the room is open at the bottom and the top, one feels oddly exposed inside," observes the Sixth Floor Museum Web site. "There is the uncomfortable feeling that those outside the memorial will see only feet, which adds to the viewer's self-absorption, a necessary aspect of the ontology of the memorial."

The memorial was funded with about $175,000 given by 50,000 people nationwide, including a five-year-old girl who gave four pennies. It was dedicated at 10 AM on June 24, 1970, almost seven years after Kennedy's assassination. To make space for it, the John Neely Bryan Log Cabin (see entry) was moved one block north.

Philip Johnson's other Dallas commissions include BankOne, which was previously known as Momentum Place, the Crescent Court, and Thanksgiving Square. The Harvard graduate also reconstructed Fort Worth's Amon Carter Museum (see the *Marmac Guide to Fort Worth & Arlington*).

Hundreds of people stood to witness the dedication. Jacqueline Kennedy is said to have been consulted on the design, which was Johnson's first memorial commission. Sargent Shriver was the first member of the Kennedy family to view the memorial that same year.

A slab of black marble inscribed "John F. Kennedy" is located inside the memorial and also was erected with private donations. Until 1986, annual observances honoring Kennedy were held here until his family requested that such services be held on May 29, the anniversary of JFK's birth.

After the neglected and defaced memorial was repaired in 2000, Senator Edward Kennedy wrote to a Dallas County judge: "On behalf of all the members of the Kennedy family, please accept my gratitude for the care and concern you have shown in renovating your Memorial to President Kennedy. It means a great deal to know the citizens of Dallas County loved him, too."

Dallas historian A. C. Greene wrote in 1984: "The memorial doesn't say enough to the visitor. It is stark and barren of emotion. Though designed by noted architect Philip Johnson, it is a failure as a memorial.

Someday, perhaps, it will be symbol enough, but not now, and not so long as members of that generation remain who always remember where they were, what they were doing, when they heard the words: 'The president's been shot!'"

Dallas architect Gershon Canaan, a local cultural leader at the time, has been quoted as saying: "This ruin-like open square box without any content, constructed of a rough and crude material, is completely out of line and without the qualities so characteristic of the late president."

Across Market Street from here, at 701 Commerce Street, you can see H. A. Overbeck's 1912 seven-story terra-cotta and masonry MKT Building, which once served as the national headquarters for the Missouri-Kansas-Texas Railway Co., or the Katy in popular parlance.

John Neely Bryan Log Cabin, Dallas County Historic Plaza, at Main, Record, Elm, and Market Strees. Located one block east of Dealey Plaza and slightly farther from the Sixth Floor Museum. The John F. Kennedy Memorial is south of here. (Please see individual entries for details.)

In 1841, a Tennessee-born lawyer named John Neely Bryan (1810-1877) camped in this area and founded the settlement that grew into the city of Dallas. He built a one-room cabin overlooking the east bank of the Trinity River the following year. Bryan's alcoholism caused him to sell his remaining land to Alexander Cockrell by 1852. Three years later, he shot a man for a perceived insult of his wife and, believing he had committed murder, fled to the Creek Nation. He did not return to Dallas until 1861.

(For more about Bryan, please see the beginning of the chapter DALLAS PAST.)

While Bryan was absent on a trading expedition to what is today Preston Road, his first cabin was washed away by a rise in the Trinity River. This cedar-log replica, reconstructed in 1935 and now seldom open, is typical of cabins used by the settlers at that time. The cabin previously stood roughly where the John F. Kennedy Memorial (see entry) is located today.

In the spring of 1842, Bryan supposedly built a larger one-room cabin, close to where the "Old Red" Courthouse (see listing) stands today, and lived as a bachelor until February 26, 1843, when he married a daughter of his neighbor John Beeman, who had brought his family from Illinois.

While the Bryans were buying supplies in Clarksville, near the Oklahoma border, another flood damaged the cabin so badly that a third had to be constructed, parts of which are supposedly built into the current one on display. If the last of the three cabins, it would have served as the town's first post office, although mail, brought on mule from Bonham, seldom exceeded two letters.

In 1880, the Rev. Robert Cooke Buckner purchased 44 acres (or 17.8 hectares) east of Dallas. In a log cabin on the property the Buckner Orphan Home was dedicated. The preacher believed that this cabin was the original Bryan's home so it was known as the Bryan Cabin for a hundred years. An ordained minister at 17, Buckner was a Baptist preacher from Tennessee who came to Dallas in 1875.

In 2001, new cedar shingles, designed to look like the original ones, were installed on the roof of the Bryan cabin. They still have that rough, hand-split look even though the roofers manufactured them by machine.

J. P. Morgan Chase Tower/Texas Commerce Tower, 2200 Ross Ave. at Pearl St., (214) 979-6300. Located in the northern part of downtown, two blocks southeast from the Meyerson Symphony Center, across the street from the Catholic Cathedral Santuario de Guadalupe, and the former Belo Mansion (see individual entries for more details). Weekdays, roughly 9 AM-6 PM, you can go to the observation area on the 40th floor and enjoy a view of Dallas. The private Petroleum Club is on the 39th floor, known as the Sky Lobby.

Named after the fruit-growing brothers Andrew and William Ross from East Texas, who arrived in Dallas following the Civil War and also traded in wine, the upper end of this avenue was as desirable between 1885 and 1920 as Fifth Avenue in New York City, after which it was nicknamed.

This 55-story polished-granite and 738-foot-high (or 225-meter) tower, with 1.24 million leasable square feet (or 115,196 square meters) of office space and a 959-car garage underneath it, was built in 1987. Designed by Los Angeles architect Richard Keating, it is one of the half-dozen tallest and largest buildings in Dallas, supposedly the last boom-time skyrise in the late 1980s. In 2002, the tower was for sale at more than $200 million. A 75-foot-high (or 22.8-meter) and 27-foot-wide (or 8.2-meter) window cuts out the center of the 41st through 49th floors. Its 30-foot-high (or nine-meter) lacquered ceiling and limestone lobby houses a bank formerly known as Texas Commerce Bank.

Katy Trail, 3523 McKinney Ave., (214) 559-2180/3523. Located along the former MKT (or Katy for short), the Missouri-Kansas-Texas Railroad Co. railbed, and meandering from the American Airlines Center (see entry) downtown through Reverchon Park to Turtle Creek and Highland Park near Knox Street, then continuing to the Mockingbird Station (see entry) mixed-development and eventually to Lake Highlands.

The trail began as a pioneers' wagon and hiking path, followed by the railroad ties and steel of the old MKT Railroad Co. Trains with names such as Katy Flyer, the Limited, Texas Special, and the Bluebonnet transported thousands of Dallas residents to destinations throughout the Midwest. The last Katy train departed Dallas on August 11, 1988. The Union Pacific Railroad acquired the Katy and ran the service for several years, then donated the line. The trail has undergone a $7.6-million expansion that includes 11 access points and two major entrances.

The 3.75-mile (or six-kilometer) Katy Trail, which has up to 12-foot (or 3.65-meter) wide paths, with about two to four feet (or 0.6 to 1.2 meters) of clearance and unobstructed sight lines, is a 30-acre (or 12-hectare) linear city park utilized by up to 1,600 people a day. In 2002, the city received a $3.8-million state grant to extend the trail for another three miles (or 4.8 kilometers) from DART's Mockingbird rail station to the White Rock station. Construction could take three years.

The trail's initial segment opened in 2000. Bicyclists, skaters, walkers, and joggers are the only people permitted to use it, and they can do so without crossing a single street. No cars or motorcycles are allowed. The most often asked question about the trail is whether it is safe. Since its inauguration, crime has been minimal. "You need to take the same degree of caution you would anywhere else," advises a city planner. "If it's dark outside, don't go out there by yourself."

La Reunion Utopian Colony

Located three miles (or 4.8 kilometers) west of today's Reunion hotel complex downtown (see entry), on the bank of the Trinity River, just north of today's Interstate 30, this settlement was established in 1855. It was founded as a democratic, loosely structured communal experiment whose participants were to share in the profits based on the amount of capital invested and the labor performed.

Most of the colonists were French, Belgian, and Swiss, some of them believers in the socialist ideas of the French philosopher Francois Marie Charles Fourier (1772-1837) to whom La Reunion could be traced. Followers of Fourier established some 40 such colonies in America.

La Reunion's founder was **Victor Prosper Considerant** (1808-1893), a French-born engineer who was educated at the same lycée as Fourier. Considerant was contacted in France by agents of the Peters Colony and, after having been exiled and fleeing to Brussels for his participation in the abortive insurrection of 1849 against Napoleon Bonaparte, he visited America in 1852.

Considerant was enthusiastic about the land, climate, and people of Texas and sent his representative Francois Cantegral to purchase a 2,000-acre (or 809-hectare) tract of land west of the Trinity River for $7 an acre (or 0.4 hectare).

The first of some 200 colonists then sailed to America on two small vessels that took 60 days to reach the port of Houston. They thought they would continue on to Dallas on the Trinity River, but instead had to trudge all of April and May through 250 miles (or 402 kilometers) of bad roads with a few ox carts. From the very beginning the settlement had the reputation of being disorganized.

The original colonists arrived at Dallas in the summer of 1855 and were greeted by the entire population of Dallas. Only one Dallasite, Maxime Guillot, could speak both French and English. Considerant and his family soon followed.

The earlier Dallas settlers were usually farmers, while the La Reunion colonists were predominantly tradesmen, craftsmen, professionals, and artists. They included tailors, shoemakers, milliners, jewelers, watchmakers, weavers, vintners, brew masters, storekeepers, naturalists, philosophers, musicians, dance masters, poets, chefs, and butchers, as well as candle and soap makers.

The first director of La Reunion, **Francois Jean Contagrel** (1810-1887), went to Paris to study engineering and architecture, but befriended Considerant and began advocating Fourier's socialist theories. He, too, opposed Napoleon's force in Italy, and to avoid a penal colony in Algeria, settled in the United States in 1854. It was Contagrel who chose the site and hired the Americans to construct the first La Reunion buildings.

While the land was not the most productive, it could have sustained the new arrivals had they known how to farm. They were so short of implements that the first crops were harvested with swords. The colonists also underestimated the brutal Texas climate. They suffered a blizzard in May 1856, and the freezing of the Trinity River the following winter, followed by droughts and a plague of grasshoppers.

More than 350 colonists had come to La Reunion by 1859, but their settlement was by then already insolvent, in part because Considerant had overspent the colony's resources by purchasing large tracts of land elsewhere. Some La Reunion colonists relocated to Dallas, San Antonio, or New Orleans, while others returned to Europe.

Considerant went to San Antonio, where he tried to raise funds for another commune. He became an American citizen and farmer, but returned to Paris in 1869. Contagrel also lost his enthusiasm, resigned the directorship in 1856, and left for Europe the following year.

He was replaced by **Allyre Bureau** (1810-1859), a writer, musician, and composer, who was not able to reverse the colony's deterioration. Bureau contributed to the colony's reputation for its musical entertainment. He died of yellow fever near Houston while returning to France.

Three other men with large influence on La Reunion and Dallas were Maxime Guillot, Julien Reverchon, and Augustin Savardan.

Guillot (1824-1889) trained as a carriage builder in Angers and left France in 1847 to seek his fortune in New Orleans. Three years later, he met Maj. Ripley A. Arnold, who hired him as wagon maker for the military post at Fort Worth.

Guillot moved to Dallas in 1852 and opened a well-regarded carriage shop, believed to be the first manufacturing plant in the city. While not an official La Reunion resident, the bilingual Guillot was the principal intermediary between the colonists and the somewhat suspicious Dallas citizens. During the Civil War, he served the Confederate Army as superintendent of a wagon factory in nearby Lancaster.

Botanist **Reverchon** (1837-1905), born in Diemoz, France, came from a family with a long involvement in French politics. His father Jacques (1810-1878) was also a Fourier disciple and together with his son joined the Dallas commune at the end of 1856, when La Reunion already showed signs of distress.

Reverchon's father later bought a small farm nearby, and there Julien studied the local plants and in later years contributed specimens to the U.S. Agriculture Department and Smithsonian Institution. He taught botany at the Baylor University College of Medicine at Dallas during the last ten years of his life. His collection of 2,600 species and 20,000 specimens of Texas plants went to the Missouri Botanical Garden in St. Louis.

Savardan (1822-1893) earned his medical degree at the College of Medicine in Paris in 1846 and in the process fell under the spell of the utopian socialist Fourier. He was one of the first 43 settlers who arrived at La Reunion in June 1855.

Savardan gained a reputation as an outstanding physician and also served the colonists as their chief magistrate and justice of the peace. He became disenchanted with Considerant and his management of La Reunion in 1856 and returned to his native France the following year.

Most visual reminders of La Reunion's existence are gone now. A small memorial sits on the back of a tee box at Stevens Park golf course. Farther west, on Fort Worth Avenue, a few graves of these European settlers might still be found in La Reunion Cemetery at Fish Trap Lake Park.

And there is Reverchon Park in the Oak Lawn neighborhood that was opened in 1915 and benefited from public works projects initiated during the Great Depression.

Las Colinas Development, Irving. Located between north Dallas and D/FW International Airport, off John W. Carpenter Freeway (also known as State Highway 114).

Las Colinas is a 12,000-acre (or 4,856-hectare) commercial, residential, and recreational development situated east of the D/FW

Airport. It is home to more than 2,000 companies, including some 20 of the nation's largest corporations that can draw on more than 21 million square feet (or 1.95 million square meters) of available office space.

Thousands of homes and apartments are clustered on the west side of the 125-acre (or 50-hectare) man-made Lake Carolyn, which gives the development its personality. There are stores, restaurants, several hotels and banks, even a few services, yet the feeling you get walking haphazardly is closer to being in Brasilia than in a supposed European village.

A billion-dollar Dallas Cowboys stadium and related tourist attractions were proposed in 2003 for a 300-acre (or 121-hectare) area near Lake Carolyn.

John W. Carpenter (1881-1959), father of the founder of Las Colinas, Ben Carpenter, established a ranch in this area in 1928 that grew to 6,000 acres (or 2,428 hectares). Utility and insurance executive and rancher, Carpenter worked for General Electric and came to Dallas in 1918 to become general manager of Dallas Power and Light Company. He managed or organized two dozen major companies in the Southwest, including 11 utilities.

The Las Colinas (The Hills) ranch was managed by Carpenter's son Ben and his partner Dan C. Williams. After plans for the D/FW Airport were announced, Carpenter and Williams began developing a planned community, which originally encompassed 7,000 acres (or 2,832 hectares) and which eventually took 20 years to complete.

Ben Carpenter envisioned the Urban Center as the downtown of the Las Colinas development, a high-density community where people could live, work, and play. But the construction has stalled since the real estate crash of the mid-1980s.

The Urban Center's Canal Walk was the central part of this planned development. The tree-lined cobbled walkway, which winds around the Urban Center into Lake Carolyn and back, has a slight resemblance to a quasi European village, except that many shops once attracting visitors are now gone, and an eerie absence of pedestrians stands out.

In 1986, Las Colinas developer, Southland Corporation, was forced to restructure its debts, and unable to service them, had to sell some of its holdings. It took until the early 1990s before the development began recuperating. By 2002, entire floors of office space stood vacant again.

Actually, it was not until a DART light-rail line was plotted through the Urban Center that developer interest picked up for land on Lake Carolyn's eastern side. About 100 acres (or 40 hectares) of the Urban Center have been set aside for the transit mall that is to be built around the DART station scheduled to open in 2008.

A 1.4-mile (or 2.25-kilometer) people-mover, elevated up to 30 feet (or nine meters) from the ground, navigates the Urban Center. You can ride electric cars, free of charge, all within half a mile (or 0.8 kilometer) of the Williams Square Plaza, where the massive *Mustangs of Las Colinas* bronze ensemble is located. (For details, please see entry in the section Arts in Public Places in the VISUAL ARTS chapter.) The transit system is operational Mon-Fri 10:30 AM-2:30 PM only. For details call (972) 556-0625.

Williams Square, whose four towers comprise 1.396 million leasable square feet (or 129,688 square meters), is named after Southland Corporation's officer Dan Call Williams, the lake after his wife Carolyn.

After a three-year hiatus, gondolas returned to Las Colinas in 2002, even if there are few takers. Their return is part of an effort to revitalize the office-heavy Urban Center, where few people will be found on its streets. Gondola Adventures, Inc. of Irving, (972) 506-8037, is offering 30-to-90-minute cruises around the lake, the Mandalay Canal, and connecting waterways by appointment. The service is available daily, and the boats can accommodate up to six passengers. The rides on two gondolas—which cost $50,000 apiece and were handmade in northern California from mahogany—range from 50-dollar, 30-minute excursions to 300-dollar, 90-minute dinners and cruises for four.

"Is this Venice?" asks a writer from the *Dallas Morning News* tongue in cheek, answering: "No, it's Irving."

The Dallas County Utility Reclamation District, which oversees Lake Carolyn, previously operated water taxis on the lake from 1982 to 1999. Unfortunately, except for golfing, eating, or lying at your hotel's swimming pool, there is almost nothing to do in Las Colinas. Instead of suggesting to visitors what they can do, they are constantly confronted by signs telling them what not to do, where not to park or smoke. It is grotesque to visit so huge a development and have such a hard time finding free parking.

Harold Clayton's *Bluebonnet Hill Cows* sculptural ensemble is on display near the Urban Center, on the north side of State Highway 114 at Rochelle Boulevard.

Magnolia Building & Pegasus Plaza, Bounded by Akard, Commerce, and Main Streets. Located west of the Adolphus Hotel (see entry) and across from Akard Street in downtown Dallas. Until the mid-1870s, the Dallas business district consisted of Commerce and Main Streets, but only as far as this building and the adjacent plaza.

Completed in 1922, this limestone-clad Renaissance Revival skyscraper housed the offices of Magnolia Petroleum Co., later Mobil Oil Co. and now ExxonMobil. The 29-story building was designed by Sir Alfred C. Bossom, a noted British architect, author, and statesman, and

The 27-story Magnolia Building was designed by a noted British architect and built for what was later Mobil Oil in 1922. It remained the tallest city structure for more than 20 years. In 1934, the Flying Red Horse, a revolving neon sign weighing 15 tons, was placed atop the building and quickly became a local landmark. (Photo by Yves Gerem)

built at a cost of $4 million. The 16th tallest skyrise in the United States when constructed, it was the tallest structure in Dallas for more than 20 years, reflecting the city's increasing economic importance.

In 1934, a revolving neon sign was placed atop the building. The Flying Red Horse, a trademark for Magnolia Products, which weighs 15 tons, quickly became a local landmark that can still be seen today. Actually, this is a $700,000 reproduction. The original horse—a pair of two-story sheet-metal cutouts mounted ten feet (or three meters) apart—too worn and rusted to keep, is located behind the Plexiglass in a shed at the Dallas Farmers Market (see entry). The horse, consisting of 1,160 feet (or 353 meters) of neon, is 30 feet (or nine meters) high, and stands on a 50-foot (or 15-meter) steel tower. The building was entered in the National Register of Historic Places in 1978, two years after Mobil moved its headquarters out of downtown, and the Pegasus sign was given to the city. In July 1999, Pegasus was dismantled, and as the New Year began, a new image relighted to the cheers of about 45,000 downtown revelers.

Vacant for several years, the building was bought in 1997 by a Denver developer who turned it into the Magnolia Hotel (see entry).

The rectangular **Pegasus Plaza,** constructed in large part through the generosity of the Irish-born film actress Greer Garson, who had lived in Dallas on and off since 1949 and died here in 1996, is a bit of an eyesore. Instead of serving as an oasis of greenery amid burning downtown concrete sidewalks, this sliver of land piles up still more stone.

The 16,000-square-foot (or 1,486-square-meter) plaza was built at a cost of almost $3 million on the lot that once sported the Southwestern Life Insurance Co. Building, the tallest Dallas structure from 1913 to 1918. On it, sculptor Brad Goldberg contributed a mythic design of nine granite boulders, each engraved with the name of a Greek muse, and a limestone fountain. Goldberg had previously been commissioned for public works in Austria, France, and Japan.

Majestic Theatre, 1925 Elm St. at St. Paul, (214) 880-0137. Located in the eastern part of downtown, one block north of the Aristocrat Hotel (see entry).

The $2-million, five-story Majestic reopened on April 11, 1921, as a vaudeville house on Elm Street, which had been known as Dallas' Theater Row. Theater Row extended from Harwood to Akard Streets and was the entertainment center of Dallas between the 1920s and 1960s. Interstate Amusement Co., the theater chain that built the Majestic, spared no expense to impress the public. The theater included a three-level auditorium, Italian-style Vermont marble floors, twin marble staircases, and a fountain copied from one in the Vatican gardens in Rome.

Initially, the Majestic offered seven vaudeville acts twice daily during the winter and movies during the summer. Among the entertainers who appeared here were Mae West, Bob Hope, and George Burns, as well as Duke Ellington and Cab Calloway. Joan Crawford, James Stewart, and John Wayne made their appearances at the Majestic, and Ginger Rogers began her career in this theater.

The Majestic was selected to hold the world premiere of MGM's *Cabin in the Sky*, which featured Louis Armstrong and Lena Horne, in 1943. Before each performance ushers entered the lobby in military formation, did a right face, and fell out as they were assigned to a station, according to Dallas cultural historian Ronald L. Davis. They treated patrons with supreme courtesy and made each one feel that the show could begin once they were in their seats. Davis claims that the Majestic was the only downtown theater that accommodated Africa-Americans, and even there they were restricted to the upper balcony. Seats in the "colored balcony" were cheaper, and there was a special box office for black patrons. White children were not uncommon up there.

There was a playroom for children with a petting zoo and next to it a nursery with infant cribs, nurses, and free milk so parents could enjoy the shows undisturbed. The theater building originally included 20,000 square feet (or 1,8585 square meters) of office space on the upper four floors.

The first Majestic was built on the corner of Commerce and St. Paul Streets in 1905. After it perished in a 1916 fire, the well-known Chicago theater architect John Eberson designed a replacement that was completed in 1921.

The Majestic, with its marble fountain and mahogany stair rails, was one of the 165 theaters nationwide founded by **Karl St. John Hoblitzelle** (1879-1967) through the Interstate Amusement Co., which he founded in 1905.

Born in St. Louis and one of 13 children, he worked in a soap factory after completing grammar school to help support his family. "A tall, courteous man of aristocratic bearing, always impeccably groomed, the showman was determined to provide wholesome, inexpensive entertainment suitable for the entire family," writes historian Ronald Davis. Hoblitzelle introduced motion-picture theaters with air-conditioning, which allowed him to screen films during the sizzling Texas summers. In 1929, he sold his theaters to RKO and retired. When two years later he returned with his wife, a former Broadway starlet, from a cruise to Europe, RKO and Paramount were bankrupt. It took a Hoblitzelle to make the businesses successful again. Through the auspices of Hoblitzelle Foundation, he helped form what is now the University of Texas Southwestern Medical Center.

The theater closed in 1973 and was given to the city three years later. In 1983, the 1,650-seat renovated Majestic reopened as a home to the Dallas Ballet, which went out of existence in 1996. The Majestic has been restored to its former splendor after a $5-million renovation, but no one seems to know what exactly to do with the theater, which is too small for some events and too large for others. A smaller Experimental Theatre is located in the basement of the Majestic.

Mary Kay Cosmetics, 16251 North Dallas Pkwy. at Keller Springs, Addison, (800) MARY-KAY or (972) 687-6300, Internet www.marykay.com. Located three miles (or 4.8 kilometers) north of the LBJ Freeway, in the eight-story rose-and-black marble atrium of a far-north Dallas skyrise, east of Addison Airport.

Tours are given Mon-Fri 9 AM- 4:30 PM and include a museum, which opened in 1993. Reservations can be made 48 hours in advance by calling (972) 687-5720. Guided tours of the manufacturing facility at 1330 Regal Row are available Mondays at 2 PM; Tuesdays through Thursdays, 10:30 AM and 2 PM; and Fridays at 10:30 AM by calling the above number. The *Houston Chronicle* claims that the museum is "a fitting end for any wretched excess tour" of Dallas, "a little gaudy but fun, just like its founder and guiding spirit, Mary Kay Ash."

On Friday, September 13, 1963, after resigning from her job in direct sales, Mary Kay began her cosmetics firm, Beauty by Mary Kay, in a 500-square-foot (or 46-square-meter) storefront in downtown Dallas, with the help of her 20-year-old son, and her life savings of $5,000. She bought the formulas for a batch of skin care products from a hide tanner's daughter.

Her key to success was to find a sales force of independent women and to sell them 200 beauty products at wholesale prices. They, in turn, would sell them at a 40-50 percent markup. The company had nearly $200,000 in revenues the first year. Four years later, she was able to award the first of her 10,000 pink Cadillacs to motivate her sales force and still pocket handsome profits.

Today, hundreds of thousands of women—and a few men—sell $2 billion worth of Mary Kay products in 33 countries, including Kazakhstan. Internet transactions now account for three-quarters of the sales. Mary Kay calculates that more than 150 Mary Kay women have earned at least $1 million working for the company, which also claims to have 17 percent of the men's skin market. About 70,000 such "beauty consultants" live in Texas, with 45,000 in the Metroplex. One Dallas saleswoman, 66-year-old Dorothea Dingler, says she has earned more than $9 million during her 37 years working for the company.

The company was listed on the New York Stock Exchange in 1976, but Mary Kay's family bought it back in a $390-million leveraged buy-out in 1985 because "Mary Kay's dream is too important to be held by the public," according to her son Richard Rogers (b. 1943), who had left in 1992, but took control of the company in 2001. In 1991, the company settled for $3 million with the Internal Revenue Service to end a $29-million claim by the IRS. By then it was on the Fortune 500 list of the largest American enterprises.

Mary Kathlyn Wagner (1918-2001) was born in Hot Wells, a hamlet 25 miles (or 40 kilometers) northwest of Houston that does not exist any more. By age six, she cared for her father, who was seriously ill with tuberculosis, while her mother worked in a restaurant 14 hours a day. She married Houston radio personality Ben Rogers at 17, but he left her after a three-year stint in the Army.

Mary Kay took a job in direct sales with Stanley Home Products in Dallas in 1938 "to make enough money to enable herself and her first husband to move out of her mother's house," according to the Texas State Historical Association, which adds that "she was taking pre-med classes at the University of Houston when her husband deserted her."

She left Stanley Products in 1953, after being denied the title of unit manager in favor of a man whom she had trained. She joined the World Gift Company in Dallas, where she was eventually made a member of the board of directors, but earned half of what the men were making.

In 1963, Mary Kay married one George Hallenbeck, but he died of a heart attack a month later. She married Mel Ash, a retired wholesale manufacturer's representative, three years later, but he passed away of lung cancer in 1980. Her daughter Marilyn, one of three Ash children, died of pneumonia in 1991.

Mary Kay retired as chairwoman of the company in 1987, suffered a stroke in 1996, and rarely left her famous 19,000-square-foot (or 1,765-square-meter) pink mansion on Douglas Avenue in north Dallas' Preston Hollow neighborhood after that.

Mary Kay Museum

The museum's 1967 pink Cadillac with a heart-shaped rear window, similar to Cadillacs Mary Kay originally gave to some of her top saleswomen, was sold to charity in 2002 and is no longer on display.

Unless you want to read a lot of framed old newspaper clippings, see fuzzy photos of Mary Kay that make her years younger than her true age, and yawn over an assortment of knick-knacks, do not bother going, because it is a long way from downtown Dallas on a tollway where few speed limit rules are obeyed. OK, there are also Mary Kay's gowns.

In 2002, some 25,000 saleswomen received pink Cadillacs, red Pontiac Grand Ams, and white Pontiac Grand Prixs and Chevy Blazers. Others got vacations, jewelry, china, crystal, and cash, all as a reward for good sales. In Germany, the top Mary Kay sales award is a pink Mercedes.

A company cafeteria in the lobby leads to a dining area with teak tables. It is open to the public. "The prices are inexpensive, and the food high-quality, so pig out and end the tour with this valuable lesson: wretched excess doesn't always have to cost a lot," notes the *Houston Chronicle*.

Actress Shirley MacLaine ably portrayed Mary Kay Ash in an otherwise shallow made-for-television CBS film, titled *Hell on Heels: The Battle of Mary Kay*, which was released in 2002.

Medieval Times Tournament & Dinner, 2021 North Stemmons Frwy., (214) 761-1800, Internet www.medievaltimes.com. *CH* includes live show, dinner, and beverages. Show times Tue-Sun, hours vary. Reservations required. Located just northwest of downtown, off Stemmons Freeway and Market Center Boulevard exit, across from Market Hall and behind Sheraton Suites hotel (see individual entries).

You can enjoy an evening of family entertainment based on the history of Middle Ages. The year is 1093, and you are a guest of the royal family. The lord of the castle has invited 1000 friends, including you, neighbors, and foes to a royal tournament.

There is pageantry, horsemanship, swordplay, falconry, sorcery, and jousting tournaments among the knights that are usually picked from among students, Marines, welders, and such. Every detail has been recreated for your entertainment on the 65,000-square-foot (or 6,038-square-meter) facility with an arena seating 1,000.

"The present show is historically based if not historically nitpicky," observes *D Magazine*. "Each fight begins with a joust and ends in two-footed highly choreographed fury."

A four-course meal, which includes whole roasted chicken or spare ribs, is served during the festivities in medieval fashion. "Eat your meal with your hands and cheer on your favorite knight as he jousts for the title of champion," advises SMU's *Daily Campus* newspaper. The dinner and tournament last more than two hours.

Medieval Times began with two dinner theaters in Spain. It now has operations in several cities. Although the smallest, its Dallas show is attended by more than 200,000 visitors a year.

Mercantile National Bank Complex, Main, Ervay, Commerce, and St. Paul Streets. Centrally located across Main Street from Bank One downtown.

The original 36-story limestone and brick Mercantile National Bank Building was the tallest high-rise in the city and one of the tallest in Texas when it opened in 1943. When the Mercantile Bank was established, its headquarters were in today's Magnolia Hotel (see entry) building.

The Merc was constructed by Robert Lee Thornton (1880-1964), a candy salesman, banker, and four-term Dallas mayor who served in that capacity from 1953 to 1961. The design is by the same New York architect, Walter Ahlschlager, who also drafted Manhattan's landmark Roxy Theater. This is one of the four buildings on the block—constructed between 1942 and 1972—that stood vacant from 1991 to 2003 because they contained asbestos. Other parts of the complex include the 16-story 1949 Securities Building, the 20-story 1958 Dallas Building, and the five-story 1972 Securities Annex Building.

"Although downtown Dallas has the West End, Deep Ellum and a surge of new residential development, much of the city's core is viewed as an eyesore with no substantial retail element," the *Fort Worth Star-Telegram* quoted a Dallas assistant city manager, who added, "It tends to be dark, dirty and blighted."

Mesquite Championship Rodeo, 1818 Rodeo Dr., Mesquite, (800) 833-9339, (972) 222-BULL or 285-8777, Internet www.mesquiterodeo.com. *CH* and parking fee. Open April 4 through October 4, Fri-Sat 8 PM-10 PM. Located at LBJ Freeway and Military Parkway, behind the Trail Dust Steakhouse.

You can recapture the flavor of the West at the 5,500-seat, covered Resistol Arena, where some of the most daring cowboys show their stuff with often uncooperative and potentially deadly livestock. The 74 luxury suites are for those who want to display their financial might.

Mesquite rodeo, established in 1957 by Neal Gay of Terrell, Texas, is to Dallas what ballet is to the Bolshoy Theater in Moscow. You will see saddle and bareback riders, calf ropers, steer wrestlers, bronc and bull riders perform with courage and skill that you have seen before only on the movie or television screen. Prize money for competitors exceeds $200,000.

While sitting in the stands, you can try cotton candy. The carnival atmosphere is enhanced by barrel racers, clowns, and country music. Televised on a delayed basis, the rodeo is carried on Fox Sports Net. There are so many first-timers at the Mesquite rodeo that organizers explain each event's rules and scoring procedures.

Businessman Tom Hicks, who also owns the Texas Rangers baseball and Dallas Stars hockey teams, bought the show for $10 million in 1999. Arena Brands Inc., the Garland-based maker of Resistol hats and other Western wear, is paying $5 million for the right to name the arena.

Bull riders score points for style and skill, not just for staying atop the fierce animals for at least eight seconds. If you want to know how the real cowboys of yesteryear handled their daily chores, watch for steer wrestling, where the cowboy leaps from his galloping horse, grabs a 600-pound (or 272-kilogram) animal by its horns, and wrestles it to the ground in about four seconds using leverage and strength.

In calf roping—whose roots date to the Old West when a calf might be injured and had to be immobilized quickly for treatment or for branding—the contestant ropes a calf, gets off his horse, throws the animal to the ground, and ties any three of the calf's legs together using a pigging string he carries in his teeth.

Saturday and Sunday nights, you can also watch Cowboy Poker, where four players sit in chairs around a table in the middle of the arena. The fifth "player" is a snorting, 900-pound (or 408-kilogram) Mexican fighting bull, who does not care for gambling or humans. The last man to leave his seat, voluntarily or otherwise, wins the $400 pot.

Durango Skoal is the one bull that has developed a reputation by tossing more than 200 riders, in less than eight seconds on average. The one exception was former world champion Cody Custer, when Durango had an "off day," says his owner. At Mesquite's arena, Durango is a designated "bounty bull," meaning the first cowboy to beat him gets $100,000. The bull, which was eight years old in 2002, weighs 1,800 pounds (or 816 kilograms).

The bull stole the show at the National Finals Rodeo in Las Vegas, where it threw every contender it faced. While most opponents are tossed so far away there is little fear Durango will stomp them, one 21-year-old cowboy "needed 104 stitches in the face after his match with Durango, and several other challengers have been carried out of the ring on stretchers, with everything from severely cricked necks and separated shoulders to concussions and ruptured spleens," according to *D Magazine*.

Come early enough—between 6:30 PM and 7:30 PM—and you can sit down to a hickory-smoked barbecue sandwich, barbecued brisket of beef, or sliced smoked sausage, before the show starts and then work off the calories by visiting the gift shop nearby. For children there are a petting zoo, pony rides, and a calf-catching contest.

More than a quarter-million spectators come every year. Texas has more professional rodeos than any other state, 110 a year, compared with about 62 in the second-ranked California. If going to the rodeo on your own sounds too complicated, call a tour company through your hotel.

A $28-million Rodeo Center was completed nearby in 1998 and includes a 35,000-square-foot (or 3,251-square-meter) exhibit hall, and a 160-room Hampton Suites hotel and convention center.

The Movie Studios at Las Colinas, 6301 North O'Connor Blvd., Bldg. 1, Irving; (800) 914-0006 or (972) 869-3456, Internet www.studiosatlascolinas.com. *CH*, except children under three years of age.

Monday through Friday the one-and-a-half-hour tour takes place at 12:30 PM; Saturdays and holidays at 10:30 AM, 12:30 PM, 2:30 PM, and 4 PM; Sundays at 12:30 PM, 2:30 PM, and 4 PM. Located south of Lyndon B. Johnson Freeway (also known as Interstate Highway 635) at Royal Lane, not far from the nine bronze *Mustangs of Las Colinas* on Williams Square.

The 112-acre (or 45-hectare) communications complex was built by the Trammell Crow interests, one of the wealthiest Dallas families, in an Irving office park in 1982. Standing like "a concrete cathedral," it includes the National Museum of Communications. The $10-million production center was built to compete with Hollywood. One of the sound stages measures 15,000 square feet (or 1,393 square meters).

These are often advertised as the only working film studios between the East and West coasts where production work can be done daily. Almost a hundred film, video, and television service companies once operated here, but many have left. Among the last major features filmed here was Steve Martin's *Leap of Faith* in 1992.

Producers of the popular children-oriented television series, *Barney & Friends*, occupied Stages A and C from 1994 to 1999, but left for its own Carrollton plant because of insufficient office and support space. Social events also irk local filmmakers who want the facility to drop the tours and parties.

In 1991, Texas Commerce Bank foreclosed on the Las Colinas studios' acreage. The current owner, Chris Christian, a former Nashville singer, bought it the following year for $1.25 million. It was he who came up with the studio tour of film memorabilia.

The studios have fallen on lean times with the cancellation of two major television shows, *Barney* and CBS' hour-long drama *Walker, Texas Ranger,* staring Chuck Norris, which aired for eight seasons. The Dallas-based series contributed $50 million annually to the local economy. At its ratings high point of 1995-96, Walker averaged 19.4 million viewers.

The guided tour takes you behind the scenes at a motion picture and television sound stage. The studios served as the interior of the nuclear power plant in the 1983 film *Silkwood,* the first major production at the studios, with Cher and Meryl Streep.

You can see the 20-foot-long (or six-meter) wooden model submarine used in *The Hunt for Red October* and the Oval Office set from Oliver Stone's film *JFK*. Julie Andrews' costumes from the *Sound of Music* and Christopher Reeve's *Superman* garb are also on display, as are costumes from the films *Batman* and *Star Trek.*

Several longtime employees—one with the studios for 18 years—alleged in 2001 that fake memorabilia have been displayed and sold at the museum's auctions for years, and at least one manager "created the letters of authenticity himself." The museum replies that "the studio has always made every effort to accurately represent the memorabilia on its tour, that 95 percent of those items were bought or acquired with the understanding that they were authentic, and that the few replicas are designed to enhance the tour experience."

Old City Park, 1717 Gano St. at South Harwood, (214) 421-5141, Internet www.oldcitypark.org. Open Tue-Sat 10 AM-4 PM, Sun noon-4 PM; closed Mondays and major holidays. Guided one-hour tours are available. *CH*, except children under three years of age and the wheelchair-bound. An additional charge for audio tours. Wheelchair accessibility is limited.

Located just outside the immediate southeastern downtown area, across from the R. L. Thornton Freeway (also known as Interstate Highway 30 East), and near the Farmer's Market. The main entrance to the park is on Gano, which connects Harwood and Ervay Streets. Ramada Plaza Hotel (see listing) is just west of here.

This site was part of a larger tract purchased in the late 1840s by Lucy Jane Browder and her two sons. Nearby, there was a freshwater spring, known as Browder's Spring, which supplied water to neighboring residents for almost 100 years. In 1876, the city acquired about 19 acres (or 7.68 hectares) around the spring for $600 and established the first municipal park. The city's first zoo was started here in 1888, when two deer and two mountain lions were housed in the park. Tennis courts and a swimming pool were removed when construction of the R. L. Thornton Freeway sliced nearly five acres (or two hectares) from the north side of the park in the early 1960s.

The 13-acre (or 5.26-hectare) Old City Park, shaded by oak, elm, and pecan trees, is an accredited outdoor historical museum and home to some of the oldest structures in north Texas. Its 38 restored Victorian-era homes, buildings, and shops date back to the 1840s.

An 1886 railroad depot, an 1890 doctor's office originally located in the Oak Cliff section of Dallas, an 1888 one-room schoolhouse built in Renner—now part of Dallas—and used until 1919, the 1895 Pilot Grove Church, a 1906 print shop constructed near Sherman, the 1904 McCall's general store built near McKinney, the 1904 Worth Hotel, an 1847 oak and cedar log cabin, and the 1905 Citizens' Bank, built near Fort Worth and supposedly robbed by Bonnie Parker and Clyde Barrow in their 1932-34 crime spree, are all part of the museum village that provides a look back into the 19th century. A tipi tent, such as used by the Caddo, Cherokee, and Kiowa Native Americans during the first half of the 19th century, is also on display.

Then there is Millermore, an antebellum mansion built by a Dallas pioneer William Brown Miller, who arrived in Texas in 1846 with his family and four slaves. Millermore House was dismantled in 1966 and reassembled here two years later from its original site on the banks of the Trinity River, where it was constructed between 1855 and 1861.

Adapted after the Greek Revival architecture popular at the time, it has a symmetric facade with an original Doric portico, while its Ionic columns were added during a 1912 reconstruction. This was among the first Dallas County homes with glass windows. Miller once controlled 1,284 acres (or 519 hectares) of land in Dallas' Oak Cliff subdivision. In the mansion you will see an 1851, 31-star American flag donated in 2002 by Helen Eaton, then the 84-year-old great-granddaughter of pioneer William Brown. She lived in the Millermore House until she was five years old.

All buildings are open for self-guided tours. You can observe craftsmen—a blacksmith, printer, potter, an Indian, and cook—demonstrate everyday activities of the early settlers.

Lunch is available at the 65-seat **Brent Place,** (214) 421-3057, an 1876 farmhouse restaurant, which provides picnic lunches, Tue-Sat 11 AM-2 PM. In a compromise to modernity, there is also a McDonald's fast-food restaurant nearby, at South Harwood and Gano. Gano Street, incidentally, is named for Richard Montgomery Gano (1830-1913), a Kentucky physician, soldier, and minister, who moved to Dallas County in 1870. (For more details, please see entry under Dallas Streets & How They Were Named, in this chapter.)

The city of Dallas has 400 parks totaling 21,526 acres (or 8,711 hectares). They include 146 miles (or 235 kilometers) of trails, 125 neighborhood parks, 96 community parks, 26 miniparks, 22 linear parks, 18 metropolitan parks, six regional parks, six conservancy parks, and 68 special facilities, such as Fair Park, the Dallas Zoo, and the Dallas Arboretum. These facilities include 267 playgrounds, 254 tennis courts, 154 outdoor basketball courts, 130 soccer fields, 104 picnic pavilions, 81 softball fields, 46 recreation centers, 30 baseball fields, 28 gyms, 24 community pools, 19 volleyball courts, 11 football fields, and six golf courses.

The city's largest park is Trinity River Greenbelt, measuring 3,476 acres (or 1,406 hectares), the smallest Stone Park, measuring 0.10 acre (or 0.04 hectare). The Old City Park is the oldest such facility; Jubilee Park, established in 2000, is the newest.

"Old Red" Courthouse, Dallas County Historical Plaza at Houston St., between Main and Commerce Sts. Located west of John F. Kennedy Memorial and southwest across from Main Street and a replica of the John Neely Bryan Cabin (see listings), when he settled here.

Starting in 2004, a $38-million, 16,000-square-foot (or 1,486-square-meter) Museum of Dallas County History (see entry) was expected to occupy the entire second floor here. The Dallas Convention & Visitors Bureau is also located here.

This is perhaps the most prominent structure in the two-square-block Dallas County Historical Plaza. The "Old Red" Courthouse was built at a cost of $300,000 from 1890 to 1892 in a Romanesque Revival style of rough-cut, red Pecos sandstone, trimmed with Arkansas blue granite. Its cornerstone was laid on the property that Dallas founder John Neely Bryan had donated in 1850.

What some still consider "a decayed monument to the grandiose and ornate taste of the nineties" was designed by Maximilian A. Orlopp, Jr. of Little Rock, Arkansas. Orlopp was born in Brooklyn, New York, in 1859 and graduated from the U.S. Naval Academy in Annapolis as a civil engineer. After this courthouse, already labeled an "architectural monstrosity" in the 1940s was completed, Orlopp moved to Fort Worth and joined the prolific firm of Sanguinet & Staats, where he designed several more courthouses.

The newer, white-marble Dallas County Courthouse is located south of here, across Commerce Street. Opened in 1966, it became the **George L. Allen Sr. Courts Building** in 1992, the first downtown building named after an African-American area resident. It houses civil courts, family courts, and the 5th Court of Appeals.

Allen (d. 1991) was appointed the first African-American city councilman in 1968. In the early 1950s, he was instrumental in starting the Round-Up Players theater for blacks, which closed after a couple of years. "After the Supreme Court ruling in 1954 [declaring the doctrine of separate but equal unconstitutional in the Brown vs. Board of Education decision] George Allen felt that he could no longer be so closely identified with whites," notes Dallas cultural historian Ronald L. Davis.

Several previous courthouses preceded the "Old Red" on the site. The original ten-by-ten log courthouse was built in 1846 on the northeast corner of the square, "so as not to disturb John Neely Bryan's crops," when Dallas County was created. The structure was burned down by drunks on Christmas Day in 1848.

Until 1850, court is said to have been held in Bryan's cabin; then a larger, but similar structure was built. A two-story brick building was erected five years later, at a cost of $7,400. In 1871, the building of 1855 was condemned as unsafe and sold for $465. By 1874, a two-story granite structure was erected, but it burned badly in 1880 and had to be rebuilt the next year. Just ten years later, this fifth building was constructed by architect James Flanders at a cost of $100,000. It was believed to be the first fireproof courthouse in the city's history, but was completely gutted by fire. The sixth and present courthouse was built in 1892 at a cost of $276,967. It included a massive two-ton, 90-foot (or

27-meter) clock tower, which was removed in 1919 when it became unstable. A $22-million renovation is expected to be completed in 2004.

Pioneer Plaza & Cemetery, Young & Griffin Streets. The 4.2-acre (or 1.7-hectare) plaza is adjacent to the Pioneer Cemetery in front of the Dallas Convention Center and west of the Dallas City Hall (see individual listings), just east of Interstate Highway 35 East.

This group of 44 six-foot-tall (or 1.82-meter) bronze longhorn steers and three 11-foot-tall (or 3.3-meter) cowboys, each weighing more than a ton, riding along waterfalls and across a water stream is—as you would, naturally, expect by now—another largest sculptural ensemble in the whole wide world. The fact that Irving claims the same for its *Mustangs of Las Colinas* (see entry in the section Art in Public Places), is immaterial in Dallas, where everything must surely be the biggest and the best. Titled ***Trailing Longhorns,*** it was created by sculptor Robert Summers (b. 1941) from the nearby town of Glen Rose to fulfill developer Trammell Crow's vision for an expanded Convention Center.

"I apologize for the apparent boastfulness," Crow told the *New York Times* in 1994, "but ten years from now, this is absolutely going to be one of the greatest monuments in the world." He added that the longhorns would someday be what Eiffel Tower is to Paris and the Coliseum is to Rome. The weekly *Dallas Observer* already called it the "best cheesy public sculpture."

The first longhorn was unveiled in 1993, amid some derision from Fort Worth, where such Western symbols are taken even more seriously. The entire project assumed its current shape the following year and has become one of the most photographed Dallas sights. Those six-foot-tall (or 1.82-meter) steer horns have been calculated to withstand 400 pounds (or 181 kilograms) of rascally swinging kids each and comments, such as that of a former director of the Dallas Museum of Art who called the steers "lumpy bronze longhorns with their politically-correct cowboy escorts."

There was nothing but a flat, asphalt Convention Center parking lot, where a wooded, grassy slope with a waterfall and the sculptures stands today. Three thousand truckloads of soil were brought in to create a hill.

Pioneer Plaza and its display are said to be located near the historic Shawnee Cattle Trail that began in 1854 and led through Dallas and on to Missouri, and the Chisholm Trail, which cut through Fort Worth and on to Kansas.

The sculptures memorialize these cattle drives that supposedly took place on the trail that we know today as Preston Road (or State Highway 289), one of the main Dallas roads, named for William G.

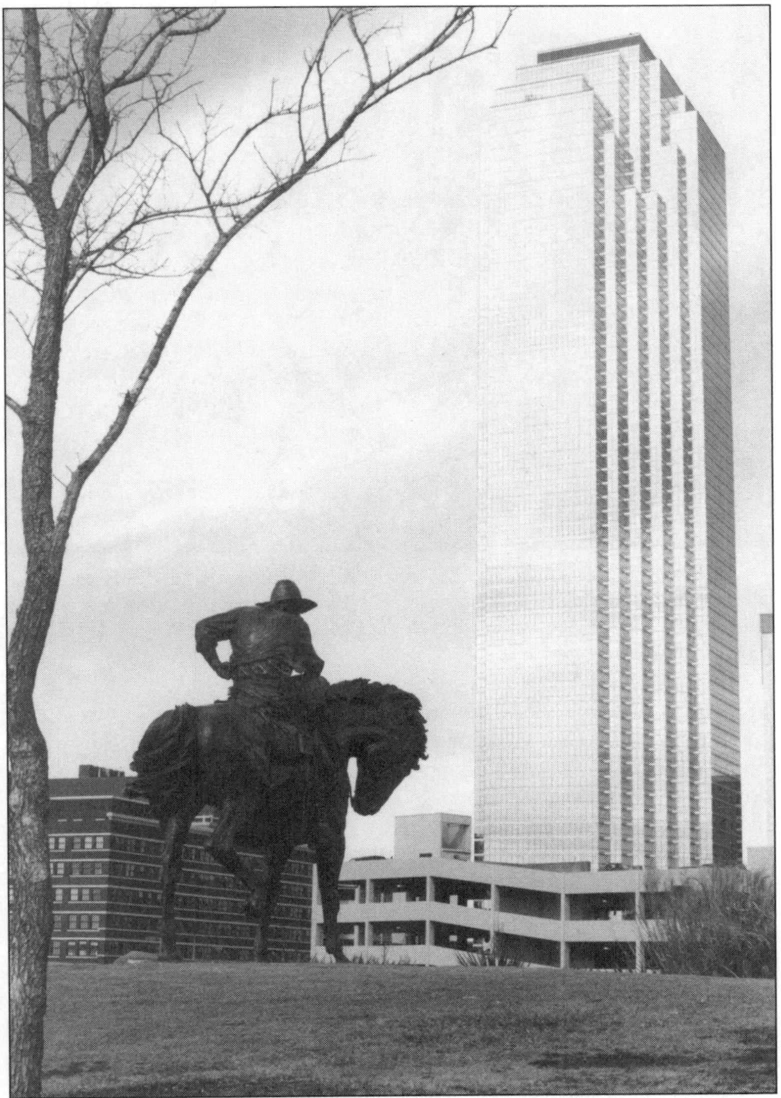

One of three horseback riders from the Pioneer Plaza & Cemetery downtown and toward the 72-story NationsBank tower, the tallest building in Dallas and one of 50 tallest in the world. Thirty-eight more longhorns are also located in front of the Dallas Convention Center. (Photo by Yves Gerem)

Downtown Dallas viewed from the Pioneer Plaza & Cemetery hill. Only one of the 39 six-foot-tall longhorns and one of the 11-foot-tall horseback riders can be seen here, located downtown and in front of the Dallas Convention Center. (Photo by Yves Gerem)

Preston, a Republic of Texas army captain. Pioneers moving west and cowboys herding thousands of beef cattle to the markets north used the Shawnee Trail. They are said to have crossed the Trinity River at a ford downtown—where the Hyatt Regency Hotel stands now—just a few blocks west of Pioneer Plaza.

Skeptics claim, however, that Dallas only briefly hosted a minor cattle drive and was much more an Eastern mercantile and financial center than an outpost of the Old West. A sculptor from the University of Texas at Dallas unsuccessfully sued to stop the project in 1993. He was quoted as saying:

"People photograph anomalies, things they can't believe they are seeing. You could have a big bronze herd of insurance salesmen coming across the river with briefcases or Neiman Marcus bags, and that would be just as relevant. The history of Dallas is fascinating, but you'd never know because we've obscured it with this mockery."

Under the red oaks along Griffin and Young Streets, you can also see 38 granite panels detailing the history of cattle ranching and branding in Texas, with etchings of 36 brands that go all the way back to the 1700s.

Adjacent to the Convention Center's Ceremonial Drive and Griffin Street is the **Pioneer Park Cemetery,** composed of the remnants of four graveyards. Dating from the 1850s, when the population of Dallas was about 1,000, the cemetery holds the remains of Dallas' early settlers and civil leaders, including four mayors.

Here lies John McClannahan Crockett (1816-1887), a relative of the Alamo hero Davy Crockett, who started one of the city's first law offices. A lieutenant governor of Texas during the Civil War, he returned to Dallas and became mayor. Tennessee lawyer James Polk Record (1834-1872) became Dallas' district attorney in 1860.

Here are the remains of Alexander Harwood (1820-1885), who came from Tennessee in 1844, and James Weck Latimer (1783-1860), the editor in 1849 of the first Dallas newspaper, the *Cedar Snag*. Latimer, a New London, Connecticut, native, and his wife brought one of the first pianos to the growing city. Also lying here is John Jay Good (b. 1827), who was elected Dallas mayor in 1880, two years before his death.

Some local historians believe that the earliest graves here come from the city's original cemetery just northwest from the West End Historic District (see entry). Prominent white families arranged for reburials once the Masonic cemetery opened at Griffin Street.

There are more than 100 gravestones and monuments scattered over the hill shaded by oak trees. The most imposing monument is the 60-foot-tall (or 18.2-meter) Confederate War Memorial of Italian marble and Texas granite, created by the German-American artist Frank Teich. Unveiled in 1897, this is the oldest public sculpture in Dallas. It includes life-size statues of the Confederate generals Robert E. Lee, Stonewall Jackson, and Albert Sidney Johnston, and the president of the Confederate States, Jefferson Davis, along with a Confederate private. Robert Edison, a local African-American historian was quoted as saying that the war memorial clearly lionizes men who fought, killed, and died to make the South a separate nation and preserve slavery, but he would never advocate altering or dismantling it. "They have as much right to honor those dead as we have to honor Martin Luther King." The Confederate Memorial was originally dedicated in April 1897 at Sullivan Park, now known as Old City Park (see listing). The monument was moved here in 1961 because it was in the way of the construction of the R. L. Thornton Freeway.

By 1956, the east side of the cemetery was used by the city to build the $8-million Dallas Memorial Auditorium, the precursor of today's convention center.

Plaza of the Americas, 700 North Pearl St., (214) 720-8000/8060, Internet www.trizechahn.com. It has 1,031 parking spaces, and a

DART light-rail station is situated next door. Located between San Jacinto and Bryan Streets, on the northeastern edge of downtown, two blocks southwest of the Meyerson Symphony Center and almost as close to the Dallas Museum of Art to the west (see individual listings).

This is a small, but elegant mixed-use development, consisting of two 25-story office towers on the north and south ends of the block, with a mall around a 15-story atrium with large palm trees. Each tower has more than 500,000 square feet (or 46,450 square meters) of space.

Built in 1980, Plaza of the Americas sports a striking interior with French grey Grimaldi marble floors accented with mahogany woods. The plaza is owned by Trizec Properties, a real estate investment trust which also manages the downtown Bank One Center and Renaissance Tower (see entries).

There are more than 40 shops, restaurants, and personal services on the two-level 5.5-acre (or 2.22-hectare) plaza. More than one automatic teller machine is at your disposal. If you are looking for anything that resembles a bookstore, sadly, Valley View News here may be the closest thing that you will find downtown. There is Kareer Kids, (214) 720-0168, a child development center licensed for up to 120 children.

A bronze of a female on a pedestal overlooks the **America's Ice Garden** skating rink, (214) 720-8080, Internet www.icesk8aig.com, where skate rentals are available. There are white-marble statues in classical style at the entrance to each office tower.

In 2002, the nonprofit Greater Dallas Chamber of Commerce moved to the 12th floor of the north tower. **Le Meridien Hotel** with its 650 North restaurant overlooks both Pearl Street and the two-level plaza, which is connected by skybridges to the J. P. Morgan Chase Tower and the Adam's Mark Hotel (see entries).

Across the street is the Cancer Survivors Plaza, financed by the owners of H & R Block tax service. The landscaped plaza has benches, mosaic brick paths, and bubbling water.

Municipal Courts Building/Old City Hall, 106 South Harwood St., between Main and Commerce. Located in the eastern part of downtown, diagonally across the street from the Aristocrat Hotel (see entry), and two blocks from Central Expressway, or U.S. Hwy. 75.

"In 1914, Dallas' majestic new City Hall must have had an architectural impact similar to what I. M. Pei's replacement [see entry] had 64 years later," observes an architectural guide to Dallas by the American Institute of Architects. "As the state's finest Beaux-Arts monument, City Hall demonstrated the mature Neo-Classical prowess of architect C. D. Hill." Hill also drafted the First Presbyterian Church, at 408 Park Avenue nearby (see entry).

Constructed at a cost of $700,000, the building was considered state of the art. Regretfully, the edifice is hardly known for its classical beauty, which can still impress today, provided it is admired from outside. Instead, it is known as the structure in whose basement the alleged Kennedy assassin, Lee Harvey Oswald, was shot on live television by nightclub owner Jack Ruby. The site was altered years ago by the construction of double doors where the shooting took place. Since the brutal terrorist bombing of New York's World Trade Center on September 11, 2001, the glass doors in the garage, through which Jack Ruby walked down the ramp before shooting Oswald, have been barred to unescorted visitors. The insides of the Old City Hall are decrepit and not well maintained. Those getting traffic violation tickets have to pay them in this building.

In 2003, many of the city employees and police officers vacated this building for the Jack Evans Police Headquarters (see entry) at 1400 South Lamar Street

Renaissance Tower, 1201 Elm St. at Field St., (214) 571-6220, Internet www.trz.com. Located in downtown Dallas.

The Renaissance tower, 56 stories high and soaring 710 feet (or 216 meters) above the street level, was built in 1974 and renovated in 2003. It was Dallas' first "glass box" tower and Texas' tallest building until 1981. The tower's exterior is a distinctive silver-blue with green glass. Having 1.9 million square feet (or 176,510 square meters) of leasable space makes it one of the largest office buildings downtown. It includes 176-foot (or 53.6-meter) communications and decorative rooftop elements. The dual-tiered lobby features a 35-foot-high (or 10.6-meter) rotunda. The building's original architect was Helmuth, Obata & Kasselbaum.

Originally named First International Building, this was the tallest Dallas building when constructed, until surpassed by the 72-story InterFirst Building, now known as Bank of America/NationsBank Building (see listing).

Dallas has I. M. Pei's City Hall, but the closest it comes to Pei's 71-foot (or 21.6-meter) pyramid in the Louvre's courtyard in Paris is a nine-story glass pyramid with an atrium, named Crystal Court, adjacent to the Renaissance tower, and featuring a bank, various shops, and several inexpensive restaurants, all located below the ground level.

Republic Center Towers, 300 North Ervay., between Bryan and Pacific. The St. Paul DART light-rail station is situated one block away. It is centrally located downtown, across the street from Thanksgiving Square and the 1929-built U.S. Post Office (see individual entries).

The 49-story, 598-foot (or 182-meter), and the 36-story, 452-foot (or 138-meter) Republic Towers were designed by Wallace K. Harrison—architect of the United Nations headquarters in New York—and built in 1955 in an ongoing competition with Interfirst Corporation "for the preeminent position in Texas banking." By then Republic had grown to $60 million in capital. "Harrison cloned his earlier Alcoa Building in Pittsburgh," claims the Dallas chapter of the American Institute of Architects, "reutilizing its aluminum panel cladding in this bankerly conservative and elegant complex."

The initial building design was quickly approved by Republic's executives, but the architect was "incredulous" when the bankers asked that the $25-million building be crowned by a scale replica of the Statue of Liberty. Harrison was completely opposed to such desecration, but did not want to lose his commission and proposed an illuminated steel and aluminum rocket spire covered in neon. The rocket also made the building taller than the nearby Mercantile Bank, which also had a lighted rooftop tower. The beacon pulsated and flashed until 1980, when it was turned off because pilots from nearby Love Field complained.

"The old Republic Bank Building made the boldest design statement on the skyline of any project in the city's history, albeit diminished in time by taller and less noteworthy structures," one architect told the *Dallas Business Journal.* "The story of Republic Center is the story of Dallas and what makes this city great."

Founded as the Guaranty Bank & Trust Company in 1920, Republic Bank was once the largest bank in Texas. One of its officers was Fred Farrel Florence (1891-1960), who rose from janitor to president of a small bank in Alto, Texas, and was later hired by Republic. Republic National Bank of Dallas under Florence financed cotton and was among the first to give loans to oilmen against their oil reserves. Florence, who was born in New York City of Lithuanian immigrants, led Republic from 1929 to 1957.

In the 1970s and 1980s, Republic made significant loans to the real estate interests in the Metroplex and statewide. The quality of Republic Bank's loan portfolio fell in tandem with real estate in the late 1980s. The bank was badly in need of reorganization by 1987.

Believing that its major rival, Interfirst Corporation, had survived the worst of its credit problems, Republic merged with its former foe, and the combined bank was renamed the First RepublicBank Corp. First Republic was bought by NationsBank, which later merged with Bank of America. Interfirst's financial condition was no better than Republic's, and the new entity failed within a year. The Federal Deposit Insurance Corporation closed all of the holding company's banks in what was then the largest bank failure in the United States at a cost to taxpayers of more than $3 billion. Seven of the ten largest commercial banks in Texas failed between 1987 and 1990.

In 1995, a flood in the basement caused severe electrical problems and vacated the entire complex. The 49-story tower underwent a $75-million refurbishment and by 2001 claimed 866,500 square feet (or 80,498 square meters) of leasable space.

One of the Republic Towers' tenants is RTKL Associates, one of the country's largest architectural firms, which designed the Mockingbird Station (see entry). The owners are to spend another $25 million converting the second tower into housing.

Instead of the abstract paintings by the New York artist John Zinsser, on display before the renovation, you can now check out Andy Warhol's art in the ground-floor lobby.

The 150-foot (or 45-meter), three-legged illuminated rocket spire perched on Republic Tower One was lit again in 2000.

The Reunion Complex, 300 Reunion Blvd. and South Stemmons Frwy. Reunion Tower hours Sun-Thu 10 AM-10 PM, Fri-Sat 10 AM-midnight; *CH* to go to the Tower. Located in the extreme southwest corner of downtown Dallas, off South Stemmons (also known as Interstate Highway 35 East). You can walk to the Union Station (see listing) train depot by following signs through an underground tunnel. From here, you will be within walking distance of the Dallas County Historical Plaza and the site of John F. Kennedy's assassination. The West End Historic District (see listing), farther north, is also reachable on foot.

The complex, designed by Welton Becket Associates of Los Angeles, consists of the Hyatt Regency Hotel, Reunion Tower, and Reunion Arena (see listings). Inaugurated between 1978 and 1980, it was built by Dallas billionaire Ray Lee Hunt (b. 1943), the eldest child of the second family of Texas oil magnate H. L. Hunt, in cooperation with the city.

"If you were to name one person who has done more for this city and taken less credit than anyone, Hunt Oil chairman Ray L. Hunt would be the man," gushes a *Dallas Morning News* columnist. "Despite countless acts of civic, international and charitable largesse, the son of oil legend H. L. Hunt keeps a lower profile than a secret agent."

It is named in honor of the European colonists of the failed utopian La Reunion colony (see entry) whose 200 members from Belgium, France, and Switzerland arrived to the banks of the Trinity River, where Oak Cliff stands today, around 1854. All land and profits from their individual labors went into the central treasury, with each member sharing equally—until the late 1850s, when the community broke up.

Reunion Tower, (214) 712-7145. *CH*. A popular visitors attraction and, aside from the Pegasus Flying Red Horse atop Magnolia Building (see entry), perhaps the most recognizable symbol of Dallas. It opened on April 15, 1978. The 23,600-ton tower consists of four concrete cylinders topped by a geodesic dome covered with aluminum triangles. The dome measures 118 feet (or 36 meters) in diameter, has 260 lights, and contains more than 100,000 separate parts. The 560-foot (or 170-meter) tower is one of the 15 tallest structures in the city. The tower's observation deck is located 52 stories above the city. A 360-degree view is accessible from both indoor and outdoor observation areas. To get to the top, you can spend 70 seconds in an elevator, or walk up the 837 steps separated by 61 landings.

You can enjoy cocktails and appetizers at the informal Top of the Dome revolving lounge, or have lunch and dinner at a more upscale Antares revolving restaurant (see entry). Food and refreshments in the lounge are probably overpriced, unless you stay for 55 minutes, while the dome makes a slow 360-degree rotation, and you feel you have got your money's worth by seeing the entire Dallas panorama. The prices at Antares restaurant are just as dizzying.

The tower is a popular spot for men to pop that eternal question, hoping that their intended future wives will says yes, perhaps for the lack of oxygen.

Scottish Rite Cathedral, 500 South Harwood St., between Young and Canton, (214) 748-9196. Located downtown, three blocks north-east from the Dallas City Hall and a similar distance northwest from the Farmers Market (see individual entries). The Dallas Scottish Rite was initially organized in 1898 and in just a few years claimed more than 6,000 members. The Rite is a fraternal organization of Freemasons who are members of a recognized Grand Lodge. The 1913, neoclassic Greek Revival-style cathedral was designed by architect Herbert M. Greene, who also drafted the downtown Neiman Marcus department store (see listing). Its construction began in 1907 and cost more than $300,000.

Six Flags Over Texas, 2201 Road to Six Flags at State Hwy. 360, Arlington, (817) 530-6000 or (817) 640-8900, Internet www.sixflags.com. Open daily 10 AM-10 PM during the summer, on weekends in spring and fall closing times vary. Admission for the whole family is steep, although discounts are available. Plan to spend more than $200 for a family of four. Individual season passes cost about the same as a medium-quality child's bike, but kids under the age of two enter free of charge. Some rides have height requirements. Admission fee includes most of the rides and shows. There is also a parking fee, about the price of a good lunch. Lockers, strollers, and wheelchairs can be rented. Automatic teller machines are located in several locations.

Shirts and shoes must be worn at all times. Coolers and picnic baskets are not allowed in the park, but water bottles are not discouraged. No smoking is allowed.

Six Flags and Hurricane Harbor are owned by an Oklahoma City-based company that owns 39 other parks and employs 2,700. This is probably the most popular entertainment park in the Metroplex. With almost three million visitors a year, it is also the second most popular attraction in Texas, just behind the Alamo in San Antonio. Arlington's Six Flags is among the 20 or so largest theme parks in the United States, behind Disney's California Adventure in Anaheim, California, but ahead of Six Flags Fiesta Texas in San Antonio. The six flags—Spanish, French, Mexican, Republic of Texas, Confederate, and U.S.—which are fewer than half in number that have actually flown over Texas, are commemorated in the name of this amusement park, one of the earliest American theme parks. Opened in the summer of 1961 on 65 acres (or 26 hectares) of empty prairie land as a temporary measure to make money from some vacant land, the park has since quadrupled in size.

In 18 months, its owner, Angus G. Wynne, made back the $3.5 million he spent to build the park. He got the idea for the park after visiting Disneyland in California with his children. The park attracted half a million visitors between August 5 and Labor Day during its first year. He sold Six Flags in 1969. His son, Shannon Wynne, started such well-known restaurants as the Flying Saucer and 8.0.

In 2003, a $10-million, 315-foot (or 96-meter) three-tower complex, **Superman Tower of Power,** was built on the grounds. It launches 1,200 riders hourly 30 stories high at speeds exceeding 50 miles (or 80 kilometers) per hour in three seconds. Each compressed-air ride lasts one minute and 15 seconds.

The Six Flags' attraction of 2001 was the $12-million **Titan,** the tallest, fastest, wildest, longest, and curviest scream ride in Texas. But in Texas even these superlatives are not enough; the Titan is also "one of the top ten roller coasters in the world," in the words of the *Fort Worth Star-Telegram.* It took 3.2 million pounds (or 1,451 tons) of steel—enough to built 16,000 automobiles—for the coaster that can carry 1,600 riders an hour. Ascending the 240-foot (or 73-meter) hill, amid the clackety-clack sounds that will scare novices, the five-car orange train made in Switzerland plunges at a 60-degree angle more than 25 stories and through a 120-foot (or 36.5-meter) totally dark tunnel. It then climbs toward its second drop. Soon the track threads through the carousel steel supports, causing some riders to want to duck. The next twisting, turning, and diving section of the track might disorient you. One helix will have you nearly on your side, and it will be here that you will feel the strongest force of gravity. By now you will probably be grateful that the one-mile-long (or 1.6 kilometers), 55-miles-an-hour (or 88 kilometers) ride that lasts three minutes is over. Waits can easily exceed one hour.

"This ride knocked my socks off," declared the publisher of *Amusement Today*, a local trade magazine. Your child has to be at least 48 inches (or 122 centimeters) tall to ride it.

Before the Titan, **Mr. Freeze,** 236 feet (or 72 meters) high, was billed as the state's most technologically advanced roller coaster. It is built with a technology that uses linear induction motors, which give the trains enough momentum to top steep hills alone, as opposed to traditional coasters which require chains and cables to pull the trains uphill before gravity takes over. Linear induction launches the trains from a standstill to more than 70 miles (or 112 kilometers) per hour in less than four seconds. After boarding, you will experience a launch through a 190-foot (or 58-meter) tunnel, unexpectedly corkscrew straight up in the air, then careen straight down backward. There is just one problem: you may have to wait for up to one hour, first in the boiling sun and then in the dark corridors, for a ride that lasts about 45 seconds.

You might also enjoy older, less hair-raising roller coaster rides, like the 14-story wooden **Texas Giant,** whose 143-foot (or 43.5-meter) climb is followed by a 62-mile-an-hour (or 100-kilometer-per-hour) ride. It is believed to be one of the best wooden roller coasters in the country. There is a 17-story parachute drop, called **Texas Chute-Out, G-Force,** with gondolas dropping like falling elevators, and the **Shock Wave** double-loop roller coaster, the world's first vertical back-to-back looping roller coaster.

The **Flashback** is another ride that drops from a 125-foot (or 38-meter) tower and careens through three loops at speeds of 55 miles (or 88 kilometers) an hour—and again, but backwards. There is also the **Grand Canyon Blaster, Runaway Mountain, Judge Roy Scream,** and **Runaway Mine Train**. The **Right Stuff,** a supersonic aviation jet fighter race challenging the sound barrier, was replaced in 1999 with an animated thrill ride.

There are Western shows at the **Crazy Horse Saloon** and pop concerts at the 10,000-seat **Music Mill Amphitheater**. The 1.5-acre **Looney Tunes USA** area is for younger children who enjoy interacting with characters, such as Bugs Bunny, Daffy Duck, and Sylvester the cat. There are several rides that let parents accompany their children on the rides.

Food is plentiful, but expensive. There are nearly 20 restaurants, ice cream parlors, and similar establishments. You will have plenty of opportunities to overpay for souvenirs and T-shirts. Facilities are clean and employees courteous.

For those who prefer water over air, there is **Hurricane Harbor,** across the highway from the Ballpark and Six Flags, at 1800 East Lamar

Blvd., (817) 265-3356. It is open daily 10 AM-10 PM during summer, and weekends in September. Admission is just as steep, but you get free parking.

Whatever Six Flags does on the ground and in the air, Hurricane Harbor does in the water. Opened in 1983, this might be the most popular water theme park in the Metroplex, especially in July and August, when the asphalt melts in the scorching sun. More than 500,000 visitors come to the park every summer.

Bearing the Wet & Wild moniker for 14 years, the park was renamed Hurricane Harbor in 1997. The 47-acre (or 19-hectare) park has pools, 20 giant vertical slides, and other rides from heights of up to six stories. Rafting is replicated on a man-made river with waterfalls. There are also water playgrounds for younger children. Lifeguards are on duty throughout the park. Water for rides on the east side of the park is heated in early and late season.

Hurricane Harbor has not added a new attraction in its park since 1999. It "and other water parks are hamstrung by a limited operating season that makes it hard to justify significant capital spending on new attractions," says Hurricane Harbor's general manager, as quoted by the *Fort Worth Star-Telegram*.

The former FunSphere entertainment park was also incorporated into Hurricane Harbor. It includes a four-court sand beach volleyball area, two volleyball courts in waist-deep water, basketball, and horseshoes. There are two 18-hole miniature golf courses.

The only other water park that even comes close is the 17-acre (or seven-hectare) **NRH2O Family Water Park,** at 9001 Grapevine Hwy. and Precinct; (817) 427-6500, in North Richland Hills.

Southfork Ranch, 3700 Hogge Rd., Parker; (800) 989-7800 or (972) 442-7800, Internet www.southfork.com. *CH*. Open daily 9 AM-5 PM, with the last tour at 4:30 PM. Closed on Christmas and Thanksgiving Day. Located 20 miles (or 32 kilometers) northeast of downtown Dallas and five miles (or eight kilometers) from Plano or Richardson. Go north on North Central Expressway (or U.S. Highway 75) to Exit 30, at Parker Road, then continue east for about 6.5 miles (or ten kilometers) and turn right on FM 2551, or Hogge Road.

Depicting an improbable lifestyle—at least for most Dallasites—the television show implied to 350 million viewers in 96 countries and in 43 languages (including Swahili) that *Dallas* was Dallas. It was not, but it was fun pretending, even if interior scenes were filmed on a sound stage in Hollywood. Only shots of the outdoor pool, patio, and exterior of the home were filmed here.

The five-episode pilot started on Sunday, April 2, 1978, and generated enough interest for CBS to order a full season. The show dealt with two generations of the fictional, dysfunctional Ewing family, whose fortunes had been made in the oil business. All of them supposedly lived at this ranch in the fictional Braddock County. The critics were both appalled and intrigued. The show became the second-longest-running dramatic series ever, only *Gunsmoke* lasted longer. *Knots Landing, Dynasty,* and *Falcom Crest* were just three among the soap operas that tried to cash in on *Dallas*' popularity.

"Everything is bigger in Texas, and *Dallas* was larger than life, symbolizing the excesses of the eighties and establishing Texas as the bold and swaggering place the rest of the world already imagined it to be," observes *Texas Monthly*.

The show was so popular it is credited with toppling Communism in Romania, where the insane dictator Nicolae Ceausescu allowed *Dallas* to be shown on television to illustrate the decadence of capitalism. Romanians went crazy about it, even if electricity sometimes went off in the middle of the show. There is now a Southforkland theme park in Transylvania.

By the 1989-90 season, the 13th, not even exteriors were filmed in Dallas, and the series finished in 43rd place. A total of 356 episodes were filmed. Actor Larry Hagman (b. 1931), portraying J. R., was one of only two continuously serving members left from the original cast. In 2001, Texas legislators proclaimed the Fort Worth, Texas-born Hagman a "bona fide Texas treasure" for so successfully playing a "wheeling-dealing, lying, cheating, no-good, double-crossing scoundrel," recalled one state senator.

"In some ways, the success of J. R. put us back 100 years," bemoans Dallas Mayor Laura Miller, speaking of the stereotype.

Following the series, Hagman admitted to heavy drinking that almost left him at death's door, according to the *Dallas Morning News*. Hagman received a 15-hour liver transplant surgery in 1995 that saved his life. His colleagues have gone their own ways:

Linda Gray (b. 1940), who played the part of Sue Ellen Ewing, lives outside Los Angeles and serves as the goodwill ambassador for the United Nations Population Fund. She made her stage debut in *Love Letters* with Hagman at the Canon Theatre in Beverly Hills. Gray won Germany's Bambi award and Italy's Il Gato for best television actress.

Patrick Duffy (b. 1949), who was Bobby Ewing, lives on his Oregon ranch. After *Dallas*, he was featured in a sitcom co-starring Suzanne Somers. Duffy could also be seen in the film *The Enola Gay*.

Victoria Principal (b. 1950 in Japan), a.k.a. Pamela Ewing, or J. R.'s sister-in-law, lives in Beverly Hills and manages a profitable line of skin-care products. She studied acting at London's Royal Academy of Dramatic Arts, but impressed no one in Hollywood.

Charlene Tilton (b. 1959), who played Lucy Ewing Cooper, J. R.'s svelte niece, lives in Los Angeles and writes a Hollywood gossip column for the rag *Globe*. While in *Dallas*, she was described as "95 pounds of bosom, boots, and blond hair." Her television wedding to Mitch Cooper was the show's second-highest rated episode, just behind the one titled, "Who Shot J.R.?" Tilton, who had a No. 1 hit single in Germany, has gone through three marriages.

Barbara Bel Geddes (b. 1923), who played matriarch Miss Ellie Ewing, lives in New York illustrating children's books and designing Christmas cards. She left the series in 1984 to undergo heart surgery, but returned the following year and remained with the series until 1990. Her father was the brilliant theatrical set designer Norman Bel Geddes.

Jim Davis (b. 1916), who played Jock Ewing, died of complications after surgery for a gastric ulcer in 1981, at the age of 65. He had made numerous guest appearances on other popular TV shows, such as *Bonanza*, *Gunsmoke*, and *Perry Mason*.

Dallas originally was filmed at the Box Ranch in nearby Frisco, but when Lorimar, the production company, lost the filming rights there, the show moved to Southfork, after the owner stipulated that only the exterior shots be filmed and only in the summer. For six years, no cast member set foot inside the house.

Once a working ranch, the 41-acre (or 16.5-hectare) Southfork was built in 1970 by a real Dallasite, J. R. (no kidding) Duncan, who sold it 14 years later because the crush of tourists overwhelmed him. In the show the ranch measures 100,000 acres (or 40,470 hectares). In 1992, when the new owner went bankrupt, it was bought at auction by Arizona developer Rex Maughan for $2.6 million and extensively renovated to include a 63,000-square-foot (or 5,853-square-meter) conference center, rodeo arena, Oil Baron's Ballroom, and Miss Ellie's Delicatessen shop. The beds in each of the four bedrooms were handmade by Dallas artisans.

"But the main attraction is J. R. and Sue Ellen's bedroom suite," claims *D Home* magazine. "Colored in Texas topaz (the state stone), it's outfitted with his sauna, her Jacuzzi, a double shower with 24-karat gold fixtures, and their canopied nuptial bed of Napoleonic proportions set upon a massive raised platform and spotlighted by an overhead crystal globe."

The tour includes an exhibit hall that features Lucy's wedding dress and a "convoluted" diagram of the Ewing family tree, while outside visitors can gawk at Jock Ewing's original 1978, 19 feet (or 5.8 meters) long Lincoln Continental. The ultimate absurdity on display, however, is "the gun that shot J. R." A tram takes visitors along a quarter-mile (or 0.4-kilometer) route, past some 20 grazing longhorns and a pack of quarter horses.

At its height, in 1984, the ranch attracted a million gawkers; that's more than visit the Alamo in San Antonio. Up to 300,000 tourists a year still come to the Ewing family 7,500-square-foot (or 697-square-meter) home, supposedly the second-most visited Metroplex sight after the Sixth Floor Museum (see entry). Now, if that doesn't scare you, nothing in Dallas will.

Southfork is owned and operated by Forever Resorts, a national resorts company with 23 properties across the United States.

Swiss Avenue Historic District, on and around Swiss Ave., northeast of downtown, in East Dallas.

East Dallas was originally settled by a group of Europeans from the socialist colony La Reunion, located west of Dallas, whose idealistic enterprise failed by 1859. Some among its French and Swiss immigrants decided to stay in the area, and they bought land east of downtown.

A muddy country lane in 1857, when Swiss immigrant Dr. Henri Boll (1830-1904) named it after his native Switzerland, Swiss Avenue was originally named White Rock Road, after the lake whose shore starts a couple of miles (or 3.2 kilometers) northeast of here. Becoming part of an exclusive 140-acre (or 56-hectare) residential area, Munger Place, developed by cotton gin manufacturer Robert Munger, the avenue was paved in 1905. Boll Street north of downtown is named after Dr. Boll, who sailed to Galveston with 25 other colonists from Bremen, Germany.

Plans to bring Swiss Nationals to Texas date back to 1819, when a group of Swiss merchants in Philadelphia proposed to settle 10,000 of their countrymen in Texas, although nothing came of it. The first substantial group of Swiss came to the Dallas area with the La Reunion (see entry) settlers in the 1850s. One of them was Benjamin Lang, who was the post-Civil War mayor of Dallas and the U.S. commissioner for the district.

Listed by the National Register of Historic Places since 1974, this 22-block district has been revitalized, restored, and preserved in more than 100 Georgian, Spanish, Mediterranean, English Tudor, and Prairie School homes in the heart of old East Dallas that you can see here. They were originally owned by wealthy merchants, bankers, doctors, and other professional types like Munger.

"By the 1970s, the mansions were crumbling," says the *Dallas Observer*, "and Swiss Avenue was to be razed to make way for high-rise apartments." It was then that the neighborhood fought to have the area designated a historic district, which was approved by the Dallas city council in 1973.

It was Dorothy Savage (d. 1999), the wife of the respected former Dallas mayor Wallace Savage (d. 2000) who helped establish this historic district in 1973, although she and her husband had worked on it since the 1950s, when the homes along Swiss Avenue were threatened to be razed in favor of apartments.

"Swiss Avenue probably would have looked like Gaston Avenue if not for the Savages," once said a city mayor pro tem, referring to dilapidated apartments on Gaston. In 1998, the city dedicated the Dorothy & Wallace Savage Park at 5500 Swiss Avenue.

The restored Victorian homes date from 1898 to 1902 and command high prices. The Wilson Block Historic District includes the five homes built on the 2900 block of Swiss Avenue by Frederick Wilson, an English-Canadian magnate, whose Wilson Building (see listing) still stands downtown, as well as part of the 2800 block, where other homes were moved and restored. The Wilson House, 2922 Swiss Avenue, "the lone survivor of the great Victorian mansions that once covered east Dallas in the late 19th century," was built in 1898 and restored by the Meadows Foundation in 1981. Also notable are Haroldson Lafayette Hunt's Aldredge House, at 5500 Swiss Avenue, and a "more subdued Mediterranean cottage," at 5314 Swiss. Both were designed by Dallas architect Hal Thomson (b. 1882).

In addition to Swiss Avenue, Munger Place, and Peak's Suburban Addition, all of which border on each other in East Dallas, the city claims seven other residential areas that are formally designated as historic districts:

• Edison/La Vista Court, located just north of the above three residential areas.

• State-Thomas, in Uptown, located north of downtown and across Woodall Rodgers Freeway, was a freedman's town after the Civil War, a place where former slaves settled. In less than a dozen years, the area evolved from a simple neighborhood with a couple of hundred homes to a bustling urban venue with restaurants, shops, and 2,500 apartments.

• Winnetka Heights, located in north Oak Cliff, southwest of downtown Dallas.

• Lake Cliff, located in Oak Cliff, west of Interstate 35 East and north of the Dallas Zoo.

• Tenth Street, located a few blocks southeast of Lake Cliff and northeast of the Zoo.

• South Boulevard/Park Row, located southeast of downtown, just east of Interstate 45.

• Whitley Place, located southeast of downtown and south of Fair Park.

Texas Discovery Gardens/Dallas Horticulture Center, 3601 Martin Luther King Jr. Blvd., (214) 428-7476. *NCH*. Interior gardens open Tue-Sat 10 AM-5 PM, Sun 1-5 PM. Visitors Center is closed Mondays. Located inside Fair Park, between King Boulevard and Pennsylvania Avenue, as well as between First and Second Avenues.

The 7.5-acre (or three-hectare) non-profit center, founded in 1941, is the second oldest horticulture institution in Texas, superseded only by Fort Worth's Botanical Garden. Built for the Texas centennial celebrations in 1936 and extensively renovated since then, the former Horticulture Museum bears the least resemblance to its original appearance. Its most notable feature is the minimalist glass Blanchy Conservatory, added in 1971. It consists of ten thematic gardens featuring rare native Texas plants and colorful floral displays, a collection of African flora in the 6,800-square-foot (or 632-square-meter) climate-controlled glasshouse, a 5,000-square-foot (or 464-square-meter) educational greenhouse complex, and the Centennial Home, which was also built in 1936 but is usually closed to the public.

A $3-million butterfly house and insectarium are also planned for.

Texas Hall of State at Fair Park, 3939 Grand Ave. at Second St., (214) 421-4500, Internet www.hallofstate.com. *NCH*. Open Tue-Sat 9:30 AM-5 PM, Sun 1 PM-5 PM. Situated in Fair Park east of downtown Dallas.

The Hall, also known as the State of Texas Building, is centrally located between the Cotton Bowl stadium and Centennial Building, which was constructed in 1905 as the first steel and masonry exhibition building on the fairgrounds. It lies at the head of the Esplanade, a 700-foot-long (or 213-meter) promenade along a reflecting pool and fountains.

Built during the Texas centennial of the state's independence from Mexico, in 1936, as a memorial to Texas revolutionary heroes, and constructed of Texas limestone in the shape of an inverted T, this four-story art deco-style building was the architectural centerpiece of the Texas Centennial Exposition (see under Fair Park). Designed by 11 Texas architects and constructed by the state at a cost of $1.25 million, it was the most expensive and the most symbolic structure erected for the centennial. It boasts stenciled ceilings and verde marble floors.

"A team of international, national, and regional artists was assembled to augment the Art Deco architecture, a collaborative effort that produced some of the most splendid and inspiring interior spaces in the U.S.," opines the Dallas chapter of the American Institute of Architects in its *Guide to Dallas Architecture*.

Former governor Pat Neff described it as "the Westminster Abbey of the Western World." Well, not quite, but it is indeed monumental and impressive in its simplicity. Inside, the Great Hall's 94-foot-long (or 28.6-meter) murals, executed by Eugene Francis Savage, depict the history of Texas, from the advent of the first Europeans to the Alamo and

San Jacinto battles on one side and the state's development on the other.

Savage (1883-1978) was born in Covington, Indiana. In 1912, while studying at the Chicago Art Institute, he won the Prix de Rome in painting, enabling him to study at the American Academy in Rome. He received his master of fine arts degree from Yale University, where he taught for 28 years. His other murals are located in Connecticut, Illinois, Indiana, and New York public buildings.

The hall is a museum, archive, and reference library managed by the Dallas Historical Society. The G. B. Dealy Library in the West Texas Room, (214) 421-4500, is open by appointment only.

The Hall of Heroes displays, ensconced on marble pedestals, six bronze statues of heroes of the Republic of Texas—Stephen F. Austin, Gen. Sam Houston, Col. Mirabeau B. Lamar, Thomas Jefferson Rusk, Col. James Walker Fannin, and Col. William Barret Travis—created by the Italian-born Pompeo Coppini.

In 1946, a bust of Fleet Adm. Chester W. Nimitz (1885-1966) became the first addition to the hall, and the only living Texan to be so honored. He led the Allied naval forces to victory in the Pacific in World War II. The West, East, North, and South Texas Rooms depict the accomplishments of the four Texas regions. Outside is a statue of the former four-time Dallas mayor, R. L. Thornton.

The Historical Society hopes to have an underground museum built under the Hall's front lawns and walkways to exhibit up to six million objects, from a Confederate Army banjo made with bobcat hide to the desk upon which the Republic of Texas constitution was signed. The 800-member society is trying to raise $25 million for a two-level 60,000-square-foot (or 5,574-square-meter) addition.

At the entrance is a sculpture, *Tejas Warrior*, by Allie V. Tenant (please see section Art in Public Places in the VISUAL ARTS chapter for more details).

Texas Theatre, 231 West Jefferson Blvd. at South Zang Blvd. Located in southwest Dallas between Madison Avenue and Zang Boulevard.

An Oak Cliff landmark, designed in Italian Renaissance style by theater architect W. Scott Dunne and built by Howard Hughes, it opened in the spring of 1931 at a cost of $250,000. Some claim it was Dallas' first suburban air-conditioned theater. For a nickel, here you could have seen *Red Dust*, with Clark Gable and Jean Harlow, the following year.

Lee Harvey Oswald, a 24-year-old employee of the Texas School Book Depository, was arrested in this cinema around 2 PM on November 22, 1963. He was charged with the murders of John F.

Kennedy and Dallas policeman J. D. Tippit (b. 1924), who stopped him for questioning.

Austin's Barbecue, at 404 East Tenth Street nearby, where Tippit worked part time, became a popular restaurant in the years following the shooting. The restaurant closed for business in 2000 and was torn down, then replace by an Eckerd drugstore.

Oswald allegedly shot Kennedy from a sixth-floor window of the downtown book depository, which now houses the Sixth Floor Museum (see entry). Oswald's apartment at the time of the assassination, located at 1026 North Beckley Avenue, also in Oak Cliff, still functions as a boarding house. His room has been converted to its original use as a family library by the daughter of Oswald's landlady, Mrs. Fay Puckett, who still has the bed and furniture used by him. The apartment, where the alleged assassin was photographed holding the rifle used to murder Kennedy, at 214 West Neely Street, is still a residence. A female tenant downstairs charges visitors five dollars to borrow a toy rifle and pose in an Oswaldesque pose in his former back yard.

Jack Ruby's apartment at the time of the assassination, situated at 223 South Ewing Street in Oak Cliff, was gutted by fire in the fall of 1999. The Circle Inn, where Ruby lived at the time he killed Oswald, burned down in 1999, when an enraged woman "tried to get back at her boyfriend."

The Texas Theatre has undergone several renovations, including one by movie director Oliver Stone for his film *JFK* in 1991. The theater was damaged by fire in 1995. After sitting idle for five years, it was purchased in 2001 for $400,000 by the Oak Cliff Foundation, which renovated the structure and opened it the following year as a community center and playhouse. The foundation, a nonprofit arm of the Oak Cliff Chamber of Commerce, bought it from a California company. The purchase money came largely from the U.S. Department of Housing and Urban Development whose preservation guidelines the foundation had to follow.

Thanksgiving Square, Pacific Ave., Bryan and Ervay Streets, (214) 969-1977, Internet www.thanksgiving.org. *NCH*. Open Mon-Fri 9 AM-5 PM, Sat-Sun 1 PM-5 PM.

Located almost exactly in the center of downtown, the Square is surrounded by the 50-story and 36-story Republic Towers, built in 1954, and the old 1929-built U.S. Post Office on Ervay Street, former the ARCO building now known as the Energy Tower on Bryan Street, and Thanksgiving Tower (see entry) on Pacific Avenue. It is not a square at all, but rather a narrow triangle.

The Thanksgiving Foundation was initiated in 1961, the land bought seven years later. Designed by architect Philip Johnson (b.

1906) and his partner John Burgee, the square was dedicated in 1976 in observance of the 200th anniversary of the Thanksgiving holiday. Some claim it borrows elements from Johnson's Fort Worth Water Garden, about which you can read in the *Marmac Guide to Fort Worth & Arlington*.

The Thanksgiving Square has been a destination of world religious leaders, ranging from the Dalai Lama to the Archbishop of Canterbury, for more than twenty years. It is a quiet place to reflect and give thanks for your blessings. An underground museum is near the fountain. You may also want to visit the 90-foot (or 27-meter) spiral Chapel of Thanksgiving, featuring stained glass by Gabriel Loire, to pray and reflect.

And if your feet ache, and you are hot at summer's height, sit down anywhere in the shade of the trees and recharge your body. This spot is popular with the downtown lunchtime crowd. Three bronze bells are hung from a 50-foot (or 15-meter) bell tower over the Court of All Nations at the apex. There is a feeling, however, that more recent additions to the square have cluttered and diminished its original architectural message.

Tatyana Androsov (b. 1947), the Belgian-born daughter of World War II refugees who has worked for the United Nations in Cambodia, Cameroon, Mozambique, and South Africa, was chosen as the square's executive director in 2002. She replaced Elizabeth Espersen, the former nun who helped make the square an international landmark for interfaith work.

Peter Stewart, its founder and longtime chairman, is now chairman emeritus. It was Stewart, a wealthy businessman and well-connected to the Dallas power structure, who "dreamed of a place, a park, a center in Dallas dedicated to some universal value," according to the *Dallas Morning News*. "The value he settled on was thanksgiving—a common element in the world's major faiths."

Thanksgiving Tower, 1601 Elm St. at Pacific Ave., (214) 267-0400, Internet www.macfarlan.com. Located in the central part of downtown Dallas and overlooking Thanksgiving Square (see entry) on Pacific Avenue.

Where the tower stands today there was a popular gathering spot, Mayer's Beer Garden, located in the 1880s, one of the first establishments to have electric lights. To amuse his patrons, Simon Mayer maintained a brass band and a small menagerie of animals and birds. Beer cost five cents a glass.

The 50-story, 645-foot (or 196-meter) building was constructed by Hunt Development in 1982 and a decade later underwent a $6-million renovation. Hunt interests, going back to the patriarch Haroldson

Lafayette Hunt (1889-1974), still occupy some of the premises. It was H. L. Hunt and his wildcat well Daisy Bradford No. 3 in Texas' Rusk County that provided the financial base for Hunt Oil Company in 1934. Following his death, his youngest son Ray Lee Hunt became Hunt Oil's chairman.

The building's architect was the Chicago-born Harwood K. Smith (1913-2002), who also designed the Plaza of the Americas, Reunion Arena, and Texas Scottish Rite Hospital for Children (see individual entries). He came to Dallas in 1936 and sought a job with the well-known architect George Dahl, who designed much of Fair Park. "I don't need anybody," replied Dahl. Smith went back day after day asking, "Do you need anybody?"

"I don't need anybody," kept replying Dahl. The persistent Smith would not take no for an answer. Finally, Dahl told him, "If you aren't going to leave, then, yes, I'll hire you."

The building boasts 1.35 million leasable square feet (or 125,415 square meters) of office space, a sunset-red granite lobby, and six levels of underground parking. Hunt Petroleum Corp. is a major tenant. In the lobby is a larger-than-life-size bronze of the oil magnate H. L. Hunt, created in 1979 by Katherine Speed Ettl.

Trammell Crow Center building in the downtown arts district. (Please see Trammell Crow Center Sculpture Collection entry in the museum section.)

The Trinity River rises in three principal branches: the East Fork, the Elm Fork, and the West Fork. A shorter fourth headstream is known as the Clear Fork. The East Fork of the Trinity River rises in central Grayson County, the Elm Fork in eastern Montague County, the West Fork in southern Archer County, and the Clear Fork in northwestern Parker County.

The Trinity is 715 miles (or 1,150 kilometers) long from the confluence of the Elm and West forks to the northernmost part of Galveston Bay, making it the longest river having its entire course in Texas.

The Trinity (La Santisima Trinidad or the Most Holy Trinity) was a name first given to a river near present day Midway, Texas, by Gen. Alonso de Leon in 1690 while searching for an outpost, St. Louis. The Trinity was discovered two days before the Feast of the Most Holy Trinity. Rene Robert Cavelier, Sieur de la Salle, called it the River of the Canoes in 1687.

Beginning around 1836, packet boats steamed up the Trinity River, bringing groceries and dry goods and carrying down cotton, sugar, cowhides, and deerskins. Before 1868, some of these boats came within 50 miles (or 80 kilometers) south of Dallas, with their movements sometimes impeded by snags or sand bars, or halted by low water.

Around 1852, one James A. Smith built a flatboat and loaded it with cotton bales destined for Houston. It took him four months to navigate 70 miles (or 112 kilometers) so Smith shipped his cotton by wagon. In 1867, another boat piloted by Capt. James McGarvey reached Dallas after a yearlong voyage from Galveston.

John Neely Bryan, the Dallas founder, began operating a ferry across the Trinity in 1846.

Many schemes to make the Trinity navigable have been proposed over the last century, but the dream of a port of Dallas seems unattainable. By 1915, the federal government had spent $2.1 million on the river until it was determined its navigation was impractical.

In the great flood of 1908, the river reached a depth of 52.6 feet (or 16 meters) and a width of one and a half miles (or 2.4 kilometers); five people drowned, and 4,000 fled their homes. "Dallas was completely dark for three days, all telephone and telegraph service was down, and rail service was canceled," observes the Dallas Historical Society. "Oak Cliff could only be reached by boat."

The city realized that something had to be done. Planner George Kessler proposed that the Trinity River's course be moved farther west through the use of levees, and the project began in 1930. The river's course was moved between one-half and three and a half miles (0.8 and 5.6 kilometers) westward of its original course. It took three and a half years to move some 21 million cubic yards (or 16 million cubic meters) of dirt.

To continue overseeing the river's flood control and conservation, the Trinity River Authority was established in 1955 by the state legislature.

The Trinity River Project is a vast, multi-billion-dollar public works plan to provide recreation, new roads, and added flood protection along the Trinity River downtown. It has been the cause of more intensive lobbying at Dallas City Hall, in Austin, and in Washington, D.C., than practically any other local issue in recent memory.

In 1998, Dallas voters approved a $246-million bond issue for the project whose official name then was the Dallas Floodway Extension Project. This investment was to "leverage" almost one billion dollars in state and federal funds, or as the former Dallas Mayor Ron Kirk promised in an op-ed piece in the *Dallas Morning News*: "We will invest $246 million and receive $953 million from other government agencies." Since the project was approved by voters, debate has been mired in the quicksand of either-or, observes the *Dallas Morning News*: Either it must be a road project or a park project. Either the road must be an eight-lane tollway or a four-lane parkway. Either the park must be a manicured urban space or a nature preserve.

As of 2003, "the possible cost of the project is in the multiple billions, and the city's share is estimated as high as $1.2 billion," according to the weekly *Dallas Observer*. President George W. Bush initially struck this program from his 2003 budget, but the Congress included moneys for Trinity River floodway extension. The city establishment "want(s) this project done, president or no president. It's money for them," claims the *Observer*.

"There is probably no one project more anticipated by the people of Dallas, least understood, more perplexing and more complex than this one," said former Mayor Kirk. "But it will happen."

Well into 2003, the redevelopment plan was still being evaluated by consultants, but already the briefing material prepared for the city council said—here goes Texas optimism again—that the result would be "the largest urban park system in America."

Underground Walkways in downtown Dallas. Open weekdays roughly 6 AM-6 PM.

There are now almost three miles (or 4.8 kilometers) of underground tunnels connecting 35 major downtown office buildings with each other and 250 underground businesses, which sell everything from neckties to flowers and popcorn. There are banks with automatic teller machines, dry cleaners, and some 50 restaurants. There is a general physician here, even a dentist. Five hotels with seven restaurants are also connected in this way. The post office under the 1968 concrete-and-glass One Main Place, at 1201 Main Street, is open weekdays 8:30 AM-5 PM.

The walkways are air-conditioned and will be a welcome relief during the summer when sidewalks melt from the heat. They are heated in the winter, when icy winds blow down Commerce Street. You can now walk from the Texas Club building housing the Bank of America Plaza parking, near El Centro College, to One Main Place, from the Fairmont Hotel to One Dallas Centre tower, without having to worry about January sleet or July heat.

In the 1960s, urban planner Vincent Ponte, who worked as a city contractor, advocated the city tunnels as a way of relieving congestion, with busy intersections crowded with crossing pedestrians tying up traffic. Downtown property owners, who now believe they could lease out retail space on street-level at higher rates, have become advocates of street life in recent years.

Union Station, 400 South Houston St., (214) 712-7270. Open daily 5:30 AM-1:30 AM. Located in the extreme southwestern part of downtown, it lies between the Hyatt Regency Hotel (see entry) and Ferris Plaza park, which opened in 1925 west of the Dallas Morning News old building.

Union Station, which was inaugurated in 1916, when it combined five railroad depots and could handle more than 100 trains and 50,000 passengers a day. Hyatt Regency Hotel and Reunion Tower are located behind it, the Dallas Morning News building across the street. (Photo by Yves Gerem)

The plaza is named after banker Royal Andrew Ferris (1851-1929), president of the American Exchange National Bank in the early 1900s, who moved from Waxahachie in 1884. The land was bought by the city in 1920 to serve as an extension of the terminal itself. Designed by architect Jarvis Hunt of Chicago, the Union Station was built in the Beaux-Arts style in 1916 at a cost of $6.5 million, until then the costliest Dallas building. It was once the hub of train transportation for the Southwest, something akin to Grand Central Station in New York. It could handle 50,000 passengers a day and combined five separate depots that were until then scattered all over the business district. At its peak, more than 100 trains each day brought in thousands of passengers through the terminal. A 1950 renovation took place under the supervision of the noted Fort Worth architect Wyatt C. Hedrick. In 1954 and 1955, the complex served as a temporary public library, while the new facility was being built at the other end of downtown.

Today, DART light rail, Amtrak, and Trinity Railway Express operate from the station, while a pedestrian tunnel from here leads to Hyatt Regency. Union Station's current surroundings were molded by the Dallas billionaire Ray Lee Hunt who built the Reunion Complex (see listing) in the late 1970s and made it part of this 30-acre (or 12-hectare) downtown development. He and his three sisters inherited Hunt Oil Co.

U.S. Post Office & Courthouse, 400 North Ervay St. at St. Paul. Located in the central downtown area, across the street from Thanksgiving Square, Energy Plaza Tower, RepublicBank Tower, and Thanksgiving Tower. (Please see individual entries for more details.)

"Chief architect Louis Simon was responsible for this featureless and mundane federal building with its minimal Renaissance Revival detailing," claims the Dallas chapter of the American Institute of Architects. "To make for its myriad architectural deficiencies, including the absence of a suitable entrance, the building was awkwardly dressed with overly-detailed belt course and comic strip-like terra-cotta panels."

A local architect, however, described the structure to the *Dallas Business Journal* thus: "This building is a subtle architectural treasure of the highest magnitude. This building takes itself very seriously for what it is without the pretentiousness of what it wants to be."

The five-story structure, which was completed in 1930, once housed office of the U.S. District Judge Sarah T. Hughes, who swore in Lyndon B. Johnson as president aboard Air Force One soon after John F. Kennedy was assassinated. Its exterior has murals depicting the evolution of the Postal Service from the Pony Express through the early 20th century. Inside, it has marble walls, with carved, arched entryways on the east and west sides of the building.

The U.S. Post Office, which owned the 190,000 square-foot (or 17,651 square-meter) building until 2002, tried to demolish it to make space for a 45-story office tower, but, fortunately, never succeeded. In 2002, a developer agreed to construct loft-style rental units on the top four floors of the building. Construction of the one- and two-bedroom Lofts at Thanksgiving Square, scheduled to open in 2004, was to cost about $14 million.

West End Historic District, Bounded by Market Street, Pacific Avenue, Woodall Rodgers Freeway, and McKinney Avenue, (214) 741-7180; events line, 741-7185, Internet www.dalaswestend.org. Located near Dealey Plaza, the West End is convenient to many downtown hotels and to the Dallas Market Center (see entry). This area, also known as the warehouse district, is rich in buildings that date back to the turn of the twentieth century. It is part of the original town of Dallas going back to 1846.

The 36-block area generates $100 million a year in sales and employs 10,000. This 55-acre (or 22-hectare) district boasts some 40 restaurants and nightclubs, and almost twice as many shops. The Old

Spaghetti Warehouse restaurant was one of the first to be renovated and is still going strong. Other well-known restaurants include the Palm and Morton's of Chicago steakhouses (see entries), Lombardi's Italian cuisine, Landry's Seafood House, and Tony Roma's barbecue and ribs.

Up to four million visitors a year stop by in the district. Caution: Dallas can be as rough a city at night as any and that includes the West End. Watch where you go and what you do, particularly if you are alone and have had a few drinks.

The shops at West End MarketPlace are located at 603 Munger Ave. at Market St., (214) 748-4801, Internet www.westendmarketplacedallas.com. They are open Mon-Thu 11 AM-10 PM, Fri-Sat 11 AM-midnight, Sun noon-6 PM. Some are handicapped accessible.

A reconstructed turn-of-the-century Brown Cracker & Candy and Company building has 50 specialty retail shops on four floors, as well as several eateries. Wild Bill's Western Wear store is just one of them. The 250,000-square-foot (or 23,225-square-meter) retail center opened in 1986.

The adjoining Dallas Alley (see entry), (214) 720-0170, on the 800 block of Munger St., consists of four clubs and piano and karaoke bars.

Ten sculptures created over a period of four years, beginning in 1992, by Texan William Easley, are on display in the alley to honor ten Texas pop and blues legends: The Big Bopper, Blind Lemon Jefferson, Lefty Frizzell, Buddy Holly, Scott Joplin, Lightin' Hopkins, Roy Orbison, Tex Ritter, T-Bone Walker, and Bob Wills.

The Wilson Building, Elm, Ervay, and Main Streets. Located downtown across the street from Neiman Marcus upscale department store, as well as from Bank One Tower (see listings).

The Wilson Building, until 1997 when it was closed and known as H. L. Green discount department store, was built in 1903 by Dallas rancher and banker John B. Wilson and was patterned after the Grand Opera House in Paris, which was designed by Charles Garnier in 1874.

The "splendid" building was designed by the Fort Worth architects Sanguinet and Staats and originally housed the department store Titche-Goettinger on the ground floor, with offices above it. The store later relocated a block west, to 1900 Elm Street, and into a George Dahl-designed 1929 building, where 129 lofts now beckon.

When it opened, at a cost of $600,000, the Wilson Building was considered the finest office building west of St. Louis, with mahogany doors and marble floors. With eight stories, it was one of the tallest Dallas structures when built, just ahead of the Linz Building, with seven.

Some believe that, aside from the "Old Red" Courthouse (see

entry), this is the most important historic building in downtown Dallas. It certainly is a lot more aesthetic. The Wilson is considered to be one of the nation's best surviving examples of Second Empire architecture.

Post Properties of Atlanta (Internet www.postproperties.com) turned it into a residential development in 2000 consisting of one- and two-bedroom loft apartments. Restaurants are located on the ground floor.

Businessman John B. Wilson, known to most as simply "J. B.," was born in Toronto, Canada, in 1847 and arrived in 1872 in Dallas, where he raised five daughters. He was a key participant in the early development of downtown Dallas. When Wilson died in 1920, he was one of the richest men in the Southwest.

VISUAL ARTS

According to the *Forbes* list of the 400 wealthiest Americans, there are more than a dozen Dallas families or individuals worth at least $600 million each, which is the magazine's rough cutoff for tracking the super rich. Fort Worth has ten, Houston and San Antonio half as many as Dallas. Probably only the Internal Revenue Service keeps score on the countless other multimillionaires in Dallas. Excluding the generosity of a handful, such as the Crows, you would be hard pressed to find many who have made a visible dent on the Dallas cultural horizon.

One Dallasite, Ray Nasher, who owns the NorthPark mall (see entry), did make a recent list of the ten most generous Americans, as compiled by *Fortune* magazine. Billionaires Robert and Nancy Dedman—who gave more than $77 million to Southern Methodist University—Gerald J. Ford, even multimillionaire H. R. "Bum" Bright, were other Dallasites among the top 40 *Fortune* gift-givers.

One cannot help but speculate on how quickly Dallas could have been transformed into the Florence on the Trinity if all its wealthy donors like these contributed to the arts in like proportion. But Dallas' monied are not the Medicis, of course, so the artistic wealth of this city resembles that of a mid-sized city.

But let's be practical. There is still plenty to do, to see, and to hear in the city, even if the quality is a bit uneven. The Dallas Visitors Bureau claims there are 160 museums, galleries, and artistic attractions in Dallas and more than 100 live performances each night. The claim about the live performances seems a bit inflated, unless the high schools are included, but let's give the bureau the benefit of the doubt.

For reviews of visual arts events in the Metroplex, see the daily *Dallas Morning News* and the *Fort Worth Star-Telegram*, the weekly *Dallas Observer*, the monthly *D Magazine*, or visit the Web sites mentioned in this chapter.

MAJOR METROPLEX MUSEUMS

The history of art in Dallas is not dissimilar from that of many other Southwestern American cities. Dallasites were often preoccupied with more immediate concerns about their survival than having time to fret about artistic inclinations of the few among them. Artistic expression was usually limited to portraits of the well-to-do who could pay for them. Texas' struggle for independence was another favorite subject.

In the summer of 1887, Prof. Richard Lentz, a German painter, displayed his painting, *View of Dallas from Oak Cliff*, and attracted a "perfect crush of spectators" to his gallery. It was traded for a town lot of land on Seventh Street, between Cliff and Eads Avenue in Oak Cliff. The numbers of visitors to Lentz's studio so impressed the local civic leaders that they added the first fine-arts exhibition to the State Fair of Texas in 1887.

Born in 1857 in Koenigsberg, East Prussia, now known as Kaliningrad on the Baltic, Lentz is generally considered the first professional artist in Dallas. He was a member of the Munich School of artists and had his own studio at 911 Elm Street downtown. The Lentz brothers returned to Germany following the financial panic of 1893.

In 1900, industrialist Andrew Carnegie provided $50,000 for a public library, where the second floor served as home to the first free public art gallery in Texas. The first art exhibition was held there the following year. In 1903, the Dallas Art Association was formed, and in 1936 the Fine Arts Building in Fair Park was completed to celebrate the centennial of the state's independence from Mexico. The first private art gallery opened in 1921 on Knox Street in Uptown.

(The description of the Sixth Floor Museum and Kennedy's assassination follows Dallas' art museums. Other museums are listed alphabetically.)

Dallas Museum of Art, 1717 North Harwood St. at Ross Ave., (214) 922-1200, Internet www.dallasmuseumofart.org. *CH*, except children under 12 years of age. Open Tue-Sun 11 AM-5 PM, Thursdays until 9 PM. No admission the first Tuesday of each month and Thursdays 5 PM-9 PM. Closed Mondays and major holidays. Tours are held Tue-Fri at 1 PM, Sat-Sun at 2 PM. Gallery Talks are Wednesdays at 12:15 PM. A variety of family and children's programs are available. A café and a restaurant are on the premises. Have your parking ticket validated at the museum garage. The bookstore sells art books, gifts, and toys. Located in the Arts District on the north side of downtown, between Harwood and St. Paul Streets. Situated across the street from the Nasher Sculpture Center, Crow Collection of Asian Art, as well as Trammell Crow Center and its outdoor sculptures (see individual entries).

The 230,000-square-foot (or 21,367-square-meter) main limestone building was completed in 1983 when the museum relocated from Fair Park. Its architect was Edward Larrabee Barnes, who with the DMA "has produced a work of great simplicity, integrity, and elegance," claims the architectural guide of the Dallas chapter of the American Institute of Architects.

Ten years later, a 140,000-square-foot (or 13,006-square-meter) Nancy & Jake Hamon Building, also designed by Barnes, was added to the original facility with $20 million from the philanthropists. The addition provides a large atrium for public events, and is home of the museum's installation of American art of the Western Hemisphere, which includes a collection of ancient American art. Other than its minimalist design, the museum's most distinguished architectural feature is the Barrell Vault, located near the sculpture garden. The museum, which claims about 22,000 objects—about 10 percent of them American art, and 1,200 paintings—is the cornerstone of the Dallas Arts District (see entry). Each year, up to 400,000 people visit the DMA, the only general art museum in north Texas.

The Dallas Art Association, a precursor of the Dallas Museum of Art, was formed on January 19, 1903, in the art room of the first Carnegie Library downtown. (see entry Dallas Public Library.) Its first acquisition that year was titled *September Moonrise* and was painted three years earlier by the American Frederick Childe Hassam. It was followed in 1909 by Robert Henri's *Dutch Boy Laughing* from 1907. With a few exceptions, the museum acquired nothing but American art during its first 25 years. In 1909 the Association's artworks were given to the city, and the 14 paintings and one sculpture were moved to the new Free Public Art Gallery of Dallas on the State Fair grounds. To guard the possessions of the gallery, a local artist served in this capacity from 1910 to 1923 at $25 a month and "the purchase of an overcoat." In 1928, its glass dome was destroyed by hail, and the collection was moved to the Majestic Theatre (see entry). After more than 15 years of the Association's lobbying for a new building, the new Dallas Museum of Fine Arts opened in Fair Park during the Texas Centennial in 1936. Today the building houses The Science Place (see entry).

From 1943 to 1964, while teaching art at Southern Methodist University, the museum director was Jerry Bywaters (1906-1989), a well-known Texas artist whose oil *On the Ranch* (1941) could be seen at the DMA. He was appointed for one year, but stayed for 21. Under his leadership, the museum acquired works by George Grosz, Thomas Hart Benton, Edward Hopper, Alexander Calder, and Benton's pupil, Jackson Pollock. Bywaters himself was one of the Dallas Nine, a group of regional painters with some reputation.

In March 1950, Bywaters and the DMA "faced accusations that the museum was exhibiting works by 'Reds' or communist artists," notes the Texas State Historical Association, adding that "Bywaters and the trustees of the Dallas Art Association clung to the standard of freedom of expression and professionalism." The museum did "temporarily remove works by Pablo Picasso, Diego Rivera, and other ideologically suspect artists from display." Also around that time, "the Dallas park board was accused of planting 'Picasso poppies' (because of the flowers' bright red color), and some townspeople saw them as a sign that leftist political sentiments were seizing control," writes Ronald L. Davis in his 2002 cultural history of Dallas. "Eventually the city council got involved in the controversy that ensued, and the flowers were dug up."

The Dallas Museum for Contemporary Arts—which opened in 1957 at 5966 West Northwest Highway and two years later relocated to 3415 Cedar Springs Road—merged with the Dallas Museum of Fine Arts in 1963. The contemporary arts museum was co-founded by Lupe Murchison (1925-2001), who was an arts patron and one-time co-owner of the Dallas Cowboys with her brother-in-law, team founder Clint Murchison Jr. "The contemporary arts museum provided a safe place for controversial artists [such as Picasso] until the McCarthy era passed," claims an editorial in the *Dallas Morning News*.

The arrival of energetic Harry S. Parker III as director in 1974 marked the museum's most dramatic surge in growth. It was during his watch that the museum moved from Fair Park to its current location. He was succeeded by Richard Brettell, who created the Museum of the Americas, and in 1993 by Jay Gates.

Dr. John R. ("Jack") Lane, for ten years the director of the San Francisco Museum of Modern Art, was named the DMA's director in 1999. A native of Chicago, with a doctorate from Harvard University, Dr. Lane (b. 1944) was director of Pittsburgh's Carnegie Museum from 1980 to 1987. As a boy, he helped herd sheep on his family's Idaho ranch near Ketchum, the onetime mining town, where poet Ezra Pound was born in 1885 and writer Ernest Hemingway committed suicide in 1961.

His parents were friends with the late sculptor Electra Waggoner Biggs (1914-2001), the granddaughter of Fort Worth cattleman and oilman William Thomas Waggoner. He "stumbled" into art at Williams College and attended business school at the University of Chicago. Dr. Lane succeeded Jay Gates, who had left DMA in 1998 to head the Phillips Collection in Washington, D.C.

DMA hired Bonnie Pitman, the former executive director of the Bay Area Discovery Museum in Sausalito, California, an interactive learning center for children and families, as the museum's deputy director.

Stake Hitch

Perhaps the best-known piece of art at the museum has been Claes Oldenburg's monumental 1984 *Stake Hitch*, a giant rope extending from the ceiling and tied around a huge red stake that appeared to be driven through the floor. It was reminiscent of the stakes used to anchor circus tents.

Made of aluminum, painted steel, reinforced resin, and urethane foam, it was created jointly with his Dutch-born wife, Coosje van Bruggen, his teammate since 1976. *Stake Hitch* was designed to make it appear as if rope attached to the Barrel Vault gallery's ceiling were pulled taut by the gigantic red stake driven into the museum's limestone floor.

The artists went to great lengths to follow the wishes of the museum's architect, Edward Larrabee Barnes, in their execution. They, for example, abandoned their initial plan for a giant nail that would appear to pierce the roof and penetrate the ceiling of the Barrel Vault. But the sculpture still ended in the basement loading dock below it, with a 12.5-foot (or 3.8-meter) element visible only by request.

The 5,500-pound (or 2,495-kilogram) sculpture was commissioned to honor the museum's longtime patron John D. Murchison. It extended 53 1/2 feet (or 16.3 meters) at an angle from floor to ceiling and reportedly limited the use of the 44-foot-high (or 13.4-meter) Barrel Vault gallery, the museum's largest and architecturally possibly the grandest gallery.

In 2002, the museum decided to dismantle and place the artwork in storage, supposedly because of lack of exhibition space. "But if space were the only consideration, there's lots that's wasted in this museum," observes an art critic of the *News*. "And if the museum wants to rid itself of obtrusive objects, it should take down the garish Dale Chihuly glass piece in the Atrium, another cavernous space in need of art."

The *Stake Hitch* creators were not happy and had this to say from their home in the French Loire Valley:

"We assumed it was permanent since it was clearly intended for the Barrel Vault as part of the architecture." While they did not object to a temporary storage, "if this entails the destruction of a work of art, and if the nature of that work is not taken into account, then I feel we are on a much more dangerous path," said van Bruggen. "The *Stake Hitch* was made for one place only and has no value elsewhere." It was the artists' first site-specific sculpture commissioned by an American museum and the only one located indoors.

Oldenburg and van Bruggen have completed 32 such site-specific projects for public spaces worldwide. They include the monumental *Cupid's Span* in San Francisco, the 50-foot (or 15-meter) *Saw, Sawing in Tokyo*, and the 96-foot (or 29-meter) *Batcolumn* in Chicago. The *Stake Hitch* is the only one ever to be removed.

The DMA, which "invested significant resources" for its de-installation, claims it will exhibit the sculpture at its original location for at least a year before 2010. "Personally, I'm disappointed because I am very conscious of the symbolism the *Stake Hitch* initially had for Dallas," said former DMA director Harry S. Parker, who now oversees the Fine Arts Museum of San Francisco.

The Icebergs

In 1979, Lamar and Norma Hunt—Lamar being the offspring of the first marriage of billionaire Haroldson Lafayette Hunt—donated the $2.5-million, 6-foot-by-9-foot (or 1.82-by-2.74-meter) oil arctic landscape, the *Icebergs*, by Frederic Edwin Church (1826-1900), to the museum anonymously.

Created in 1861, following Church's month-long sketching trip off the coast of Newfoundland, the canvas is said to be valued at twice that much today. It was hailed as "the most splendid work ever produced in America" when displayed for the first time.

The painting was originally bought by Sir Edward Watkin, a railroad magnate and Member of Parliament, who had lived in Manchester, England, and died in 1901. His residence, Rose Hill, eventually became a boys' school, where the painting was discovered on an attic staircase. It was supposedly sold to the Lamars over the phone during a Sotheby's auction on New York's Madison Avenue on October 25, 1979.

"One story has it Lamar intended *Icebergs* for his home, but discovered after the purchase that there was no place to hang the huge work," writes the Texas historian A. C. Greene, who died in 2002. In 1998, the landscape sustained a 40-inch horizontal scratch by vandals.

American Galleries

The American galleries highlight cultures of North America from 1000 B.C. to A.D. 1945. In 1986, the museum received the Bybee Collection of American Furniture, which comprises articles from the 18th and 19th centuries, and the following year the Hoblitzelle Foundation's gift of a 550-piece collection of British silver. The collection of American art includes paintings, sculpture, and decorative arts, including works by Thomas Hart Benton, Mary Cassatt, Stuart Davis, Charles Demoth, Winslow Homer, Edward Hopper, George Inness, Georgia O'Keefe, and Andrew Wyeth.

John Singer Sargent, who on the request of the British government to serve as its official World War I artist, went to the Western Front at age 62 and lived in trenches, is also on display here. Two portraits of the wealthy New Hampshire merchant Woodbury Langdon and his wife Sarah, painted in 1767 by John Singleton Copley (1738-1815), the foremost American painter of the 18th century, can also be seen. They were acquired from the Langdon family in 1997 after a year of negotiations. The museum also has an extensive collection of works on paper, including Winslow Homer's 1889 watercolor, titled *Casting in the Falls*.

And while on the DMA concourse, have a look at William Wetmore Story's 1873 life-size marble sculpture, titled *Semiramis*. Personifying the Assyrian queen, who lived around 800 B.C. and who ruled for 15 years after her lover poisoned her husband, the work is cut from a single block of Italian marble. Semiramis died at the hands of her own son who avenged his father's death. The work was originally created for the wealthy American collector William Blodgett and his New York City home.

The Latin American galleries display works such as an oil of Dr. Otto Ruhle (1940) by Diego Rivera, and five oil paintings by Mexican artist Gunther Gerzso (1915-2000). Sculptor Octavio Medellin (b. 1907), who died in Dallas in 1999, is represented by a 1955 black walnut sculpture, titled *Moses*, and *Conceived* (1950) made of wild cherry wood.

Contemporary Galleries

These galleries house a collection of post-1945 contemporary art including that of the Armenian-born Arshile Gorky, Alexander Calder, Mark Rothko, David Smith, pop artists Robert Rauschenberg and Claes Oldenburg, as well these works:

- *Untitled* (1977), an oil by Willem DeKooning.
- *Large Interior Notting Hill* (1998), an oil by Lucian Freud.
- *Device* (1962), by Jasper Johns.
- *Orange, Red and Red* (1962), and *Block White* (1967), oils by Ellsworth Kelly.
- *Elegy to the Spanish Republic* (1966), an oil by Robert Motherwell.
- *Portrait and a Dream* (1953), an oil by Jackson Pollock.
- *Valparaiso Green* (1963), a metallic paint on canvas by sculptor Frank Stella.
- *Electric Chair* (1964), a polymer on canvas by Andy Warhol.

David Smith's steel sculpture, *Voltri VI* (1962), and bronze *Skin of Leaves* (2000), by Italian Giuseppe Penone (b. 1947), might not be far away.

The late merchant Stanley Marcus, of Neiman Marcus fame, gave the museum Alberto Giacometti's 1949 bronze, *Three Men Walking*, and helped it acquire other works, including Jackson Pollock's 1947 "drip" enamel and aluminum paint on canvas, titled *Cathedral*, Rufino Tamayo's mural *El Hombre*, and a group of Japanese prints. The prints were given to him by architect Frank Lloyd Wright as collateral for a loan, according to the DMA, and Marcus gave them to the museum when the architect could not repay it.

"I have the simplest taste," once declared the wealthy Marcus, "I am always satisfied with the best." He was an art collector whose taste ran from Latin American art to antiquities. He owned a stabile by Alexander Calder, glass pieces by Dale Chihuly, tabletop sculptures by

Jim Love of Houston, drawings by Henry Moore and Saul Steinberg, ceramics by Picasso, watercolors by Diego Rivera, and oils by Rufino Tamayo. In 2002, Sotheby's auctioned the late retailer's artwork that included Giacometti's *Figure Walking Between Two Houses* that Marcus bought from the sculptor for $750 in 1951. It sold for $1.9 million. In 2003, a group of local collectors bought *The Cloud Club*, a mixed-media sculpture made of a piano, plastic, potatoes, concrete, and sterling silver, valued at up to $1 million, by an "internationally acclaimed" New York artist, Matthew Barney.

Also at the museum is a 30-foot (or nine-meter) piece consisting of 50 back-to-back mirrors supported by piles of beach sand, titled *Mirrors and Shelly Sand*, and created in 1970 by Robert Smithson, a leading practitioner of earth art. Smithson died in a plane crash in Amarillo, Texas, at age 35 in 1973. *Mirrors and Shelly Sand* is estimated to be worth $1 million.

A black, white, and gray aerial view of Munich, Germany, titled *Stadtbild Mu* and painted by Gerhard Richter (b. 1932) in 1968, was purchased in 2002 in partnership with two Dallas couples. The museum has a 40 percent interest in the painting that is "fraught with irony and ambiguity" and presumably showing the city after World War II.

A more Impressionistic 1988 Richter oil, titled *Apples*, can also be seen at the DMA. Dallas private collectors own some 20 other paintings created by this leading artist of Germany's postwar generation.

In 2001, the DMA also acquired a monumental 1996 painting, *This Dark Brightness Which Falls From the Stars*, by the internationally renowned German artist Anselm Kiefer. The 17-by-18-foot (or five-by-5.48-meter) canvas was purchased from a London gallery for an estimated $500,000.

European Galleries

The second-floor European Galleries are much too modest for a city of wealth that Dallas indisputably is and include paintings, sculpture, mosaics, metals, works on paper, and textiles from classical antiquities to modern works.

"The DMA's holdings in old masters and antiquities are so sparse there's no hope of doing anything significant," claims the *Dallas Morning News*.

There are 25 etchings by Rembrandt, a 1498 engraving by Albrecht Durer, six lithographs and an oil by Honore Daumier, a couple of works each by Edouard Vuillard and Odilon Redon, a 1750 oil by Jean-Baptiste-Marie Pierre, an 1816 etching by Goya, and an 1868 oil by Pierre-Auguste Renoir.

The museum's "pathetic" European collection (according to the *Dallas Observer*) contains paintings from the 16th century on, including art by Canaletto. Mostly secondary works by other well-known European artists include:

- *Still Life* (1912), an oil by Georges Braque.
- *At the Swimming Hole* (1878), an oil by German artist Max Liebermann.
- *Portrait of Isabelle* (1879), an oil by Edouard Manet.
- *The Seine at Lavacourt* (1880), *Valle Buona*, (1884), and *Water Lilies* (1908), oils by Claude Monet.
- *Bust* (1908) and *Bottle of Port and Glass* (1919), oils by Pablo Picasso.
- *Apple Picking* (1888), an oil by Camille Pissarro.
- *River Bank in Springtime* (1887), an oil by Vincent van Gogh.

Among the sculptures, you can see a 1911 bronze, *The Masseuse*, by Edgar Degas, bronzes *The Sculptor and His Muse* (1895) and *The Slade* (1880) by Auguste Rodin. Another Rodin is on exhibit in the museum's sculpture garden.

(Rodin's sculpture is also featured at the Trammell Crow Center Sculpture Collection—see listing—at Ross Avenue and Harwood Street nearby.)

Henry Moore's life-size plaster, *Reclining Mother and Child* (1976), is on display inside, while his monumental bronze, *Two-Piece Reclining Figure No. 3*, dating from 1961, is prominently displayed in front of the museum's north entrance. Moore (1898-1986) is well known for his undulating reclining nudes which you can also admire on the Dallas City Hall plaza downtown and at the Meadows Museum (see entry) in University Park. A classical marble *Figure of a Young Man from a Funerary Relief* (c. 330 B.C.) is shown near the *Reclining Mother*.

One recent DMA acquisition is a five-foot-square (or 1.5-by-1.5-meter) mosaic panel, titled *Orpheus Taming Wild Animals*, showing the Greek poet-musician seated on a rock playing his lyre. The panel, valued at $250,000, was created during the third century in the eastern Roman Empire, in what is now Turkey,

Frenchman Jean Arp is represented by a 1958 bronze, titled *Star in a Dream*, while Jacques Lipchitz could be judged by his 1925 bronze, *The Bather*. (You can compare this Lipchitz with his bronze displayed at the Meadows Museum on the campus of Southern Methodist University.)

The 20th-century collection includes works by Russians Vassily Kandinsky, with his 1908 oil *House in Murnau*, and Nataliya Goncharova. Frenchmen Rene Magritte and three oils by Fernand Leger are also on display.

The collection of a dozen paintings and paper works by the Dutchman Piet Mondrian, including the more traditional *The Winkel*

Mill (1908) and *Windmill* (1917), is one of the better examples of the museum's thoughtfulness.

The Reves Collection

A somewhat tacky Reves Collection opened in 1985. It consists of 1,400 paintings, furniture and porcelain pieces, rugs, and European decorative art collected by Emery Reeves (1904-1981) and his wife Wendy that was originally displayed in their home on the French Riviera.

Villa La Pausa, located on the hillside near Monte Carlo, with a view of the Mediterranean, was designed by European architect Robert Streitz (1901-1984). It was built in 1927 by the Duke of Westminster, cousin to King George V of Great Britain, for the French fashion designer Coco Chanel. In 1930, Chanel's relationship with the duke ended. She closed the house in 1947 and left for Switzerland. The Reveses purchased it in 1953.

Marshall, Texas, native Wendy Russell Reeves was a fashion model and met her future husband, a fashion retailer, in 1945. After his death, she gave the museum $35 million worth of items on the condition that they be displayed in a replica of the French villa where they lived and entertained men as important as Winston Churchill and Albert Einstein.

"So museum officials spent $6 million to reproduce six rooms atop the museum roof and display the items exactly as Reves instructed," observes the *Houston Chronicle*, pointing out as an example of questionable taste "a pair of Reves' slippers casually cast off on the floor at the side of the bed in her reconstructed bedroom."

Included in the make-believe great hall, salon, library, bedroom, and dining room are mostly smaller works by many well-known French and other European artists.

Two marble works and an 1882 bronze by Auguste Rodin, and an 1890 oil by Vincent van Gogh will be found in the great hall. In the salon, there are five oils by Pierre-Auguste Renoir, an 1889 glazed *Vase in the Shape of a Woman's Head* by Paul Gaugin, an Edgar Degas 1897 pastel, and three oils by Camille Pissarro.

Two oils by Henri de Toulouse-Lautrec, an 1887 Paul Cezanne, and works by Pierre Bonnard, Edouard Manet, Claude Monet, Alfred Sisley, and Edouard Vuillard are on display in the Reves library. In the bedroom, aside from the two pairs of footwear on the floor, there was a photographic reproduction of Edgar Degas' 1897 pastel and charcoal, *Bathers*, in 2003. A fake 1908 Edouard Vuillard was on display in the dining room, in addition to a genuine Manet. A small room on the side displays four oils by Sir Winston Churchill, all from the 1950s.

The museum director who pandered to Reves is gone, but her collection remains as a permanent reminder of the museum's priorities.

A Paul Gauguin 1890 painting, titled *Farm at le Pouldu* (or *The Blue Roof*), that was on long-term loan here from Mrs. Reeves since 1984, was sold for $5.286 million in 2000.

More Beds

Then, in 2001, the museum went out and spent $450,000 for a 19th-century, "flamboyant example" of a Gothic Revival-style, eight-foot-long (or 2.4-meter) and seven-foot-wide (or 2.1-meter) bed of Brazilian rosewood designed for the one-time presidential candidate Henry Clay.

"A big bed in Big D is creating a big fuss," noted the *Fort Worth Star-Telegram*.

Clay was believed a shoo-in in the 1844 presidential elections, but lost support after he opposed annexation of the Republic of Texas. Neither Clay nor the bed made it to the White House, but the 13-foot-tall (or four-meter) bed, instead ended in the impressionable Dallas after 150 years on a Louisiana plantation.

"Museum visitors are agog when they view the bed," reports the *Star-Telegram*, quoting one as saying, "It could be in a church as an altar almost."

By 2002, the museum "has virtually dedicated itself to the proposition that art can be anything: candy on the floor, or little piles of pollen, or even, as in the current Great Masters of Mexican Folk Art exhibit, tourist-trade tchotchkes," noted the *Dallas Observer*. "The result is a Neiman Marcus fortnight masquerading as a major museum show, a corporate PR job that raises the commodification of folk art to new heights, and last but probably not least, a cynical, cheap, politically correct bid to raise the DMA's profile and membership in the Hispanic community."

Arts of Africa, Asia & the Pacific

These galleries opened in 1996 on its renovated third-floor galleries, which display some outstanding works. From 1990 until 2002, the collection included ancient Egyptian and Nubian art, some 400 objects of which were on a long-term loan from the Museum of Fine Arts in Boston. In its place, the museum displays a growing collection of South Asian art, along with a modest display of Egyptian objects.

The Asian collection includes Buddhist and Hindu sculptures, bronzes from the Himalayas, and ceramics from China and Japan. Here you will find, for example, the *Shiva Nataraju*, a rare 11th-century three-foot (or 91-centimeter) bronze that depicts the Hindu god Shiva and is valued at $2.5 million, a 2000 museum acquisition.

The Pacific galleries highlight the traditional arts of Indonesia and Oceania. In 2001, the DMA acquired a group of seven Indonesian sculptures dating from between the 11th and early 20th centuries. They are part of the museum's collection of about 300 works from the Indonesian islands. The DMA began collecting in this area in 1980.

The Sculpture Garden

Aside from the sculptures located throughout the museum's four levels, a portion of its sculpture collection is also displayed in the garden, which is divided into galleries by a series of waterfalls:

• *Granite Settee*, a 1983 granite abstraction by Scott Burton (d. 1989).

• *Ave*, a 1973 painted bright-red I-beam sculpture by Mark Di Suvero (b. 1933), whose giant works you may have seen in Paris or New York, is located at the museum's south entrance. Facing the north entrance, aside from a Henry Moore, is a 1954 glass mosaic, *Genesis, Gift of Life*, by Miguel Covarrubias (1904-1957) of Mexico City.

• *Figure for Landscape*, a 1960 bronze, and *Sea Form (Atlantic)*, from 1964, both by the British artist Barbara Hepworth (1903-1975). Another Hepworth is on exhibit in the main lobby of the Dallas Public Library (see entry).

• *Untitled*, a stainless-steel abstract created by New Yorker Ellsworth Kelly in 1983 as a commission for the newly inaugurated museum. Kelly (b. 1923) became an abstractionist around 1950.

• *Amphion*, a 1957 bronze by French artist Henri Laurens (1885-1954).

• *Flora*, a 1911 bronze by French sculptor Aristide Maillol (d. 1944), whose work can also be seen at the Trammell Crow Center Sculpture Collection (see entry), across North Harwood Street from here.

• *Jean d'Aire*, an 1886 bronze from the Burghers of Calais, created by French sculptor Auguste Rodin (d. 1917). Other Rodins are situated inside the museum.

• *Untitled*, a 1971 Cor-Ten steel sculpture by Richard Serra (b. 1939).

• *Cubi XVIII*, a 1963 stainless steel sculpture by the Indiana-born David Smith (1906-1965). Smith's *Cubi VIII*, created just a year earlier, can be seen at the Meadows Museum (see entry) on the campus of Southern Methodist University.

• *Willy*, a 1978 steel sculpture by former architect Tony Smith (1912-1980) whose work can be seen at the National Gallery of Art in Washington, D.C., and the Whitney Museum of American Art.

• *Flower*, a 1982 oak and welded steel sculpture by Texas artist James Surls (b. 1943), who has also exhibited at the Meadows Museum (see entry).

The "blunt-spoken and soft-mannered" father of seven children was born in Terrell and raised in Athens, both in Texas. In 1969, he bumped into Bill Verhelst, a sculptor and Southern Methodist

University art instructor, who was looking for a summer replacement. Surls remained at SMU through 1975 and met his future wife there.

"She had seen one of my sculptures, a cradle, in a faculty art exhibit and decided to take my course as an elective," he told the weekly *Park Cities People*. "It was absolutely electric when we first met." Surls moved to Colorado in 1997.

My Curves Are Not Mad, a 1971 Cor-Ten steel monumental sculpture by Richard Serra, was for years on loan from Dallas collector Raymond Nasher. The artwork was moved to the Nasher Sculpture Center (see entry) nearby in 2002.

The museum's endowment is less than half that of Fort Worth's Kimbell Museum. "At present," noted *D Magazine* in the late 1990s, "the DMA does not win Dallas what it wants: the bragging rights that come with a 'world-class' museum." It is safe to add that every world-class museum has a European art collection of greater note.

"One of the many ironies of the DMA is that, until it can let go of the boosterish blather," opines the *Observer,* "it will never provide the interesting sophisticated entertainment or the worthwhile scholarship that are a good museum's only legitimate products."

Seventeen Seventeen, one of the top five museum restaurants in the United States, according to *Modern Maturity* magazine, is located on the second floor and open for lunch Tue-Fri 11 AM-2 PM only. The restaurant takes its name from the museum's address. Seven-foot (or two-meter) windows, cypress-wood screens around the kitchen, cable-hung lights, and mahogany chairs will remind you that you are in a house of culture, although no artwork is on display in the restaurant.

Chilean sea bass and barbecue beef tenderloin are two among the entrées served. "Our entrée was the finest chicken dish in memory," gushes the *Texas Monthly,* adding, "Impressive."

For those in a hurry, there is the museum's Atrium Café, where a brunch is served on Sundays.

Meadows Museum, Southern Methodist University, 5900 Bishop Blvd. at Mockingbird Lane, (214) 768-2516/3511, Internet www.smu.edu/meadows/museum. *NCH*, except for special exhibits. Open Mon-Tue and Fri-Sat 10 AM-5 PM, Thu 10 AM-8 PM, Sun 1 PM-5 PM; closed Wednesdays and major holidays. A simple, 80-seat restaurant serves lunch daily from 11 AM to 4 PM. Art books, T-shirts, and the like are sold in the gift shop. Located on the southern end of the SMU campus in the town of University Park, three blocks west of North Central Expressway, and across the street from the Highland Park United Methodist Church.

Free gallery tours are offered every Thursday at 6 PM and every Saturday and Sunday at 2 PM. Guided one-hour tours for adult groups and children in English, French, and Spanish are available at a charge by calling (214) 768-2740 three weeks in advance. Parking, always scarce at SMU, can be had in the 500-car garage under the museum, where 100 spaces are set aside for museum visitors. You can also take the DART light-rail train from downtown to Mockingbird Station, then DART bus #21 to Bishop Boulevard.

SMU initiated the construction of the $28-million museum near the main entrance to the campus in 1997 so that most of its Spanish art could be on permanent display. There are eight permanent galleries on the second floor, each one dedicated to a particular era in Spanish art.

The Meadows was inaugurated in the spring of 2001, when King Juan Carlos I (b. 1938) and Queen Sofia of Spain, a member of the Greek royal family, attended opening festivities. The king, who was born in Rome and married in 1962, assumed the throne when dictator Francisco Franco died in 1975. He quickly restored democracy and left himself with only symbolic power. At SMU, the king received an honorary doctorate of arts, thus joining former presidents Lyndon B. Johnson, Gerald R. Ford, and George Bush, who have been given the same honor. A bronze portrait of the king by Spanish sculptor Miguel Zapata was unveiled at the museum to commemorate the visit.

The two-story, 66,000-square-foot (or 6,131-square-meter) museum is housed in a Georgian red brick building and made possible by a $20-million gift from the Meadows Foundation. It was designed by the architectural firm of Hammond Beepy Rupert Ainge, which also drafted the James A. Baker III Institute for Public Policy, at Rice University in Houston. It is six times the size of the previous museum that was built just a block away.

"The problem with the Meadows Museum is not that it is a classical building as much as that it is such a plodding classical building," observes the architectural critic of the *Dallas Morning News*. "Its classicism is skin deep and strictly pro-forma, warmed-over Palladio mixed with collegiate Georgian and Spanish Colonial." The founding director of the Meadows called the building "ugly."

The Meadows houses one of the better collections of Spanish art of the 15th through 20th centuries outside Spain. It has examples, sometimes "second-rate," of almost every Spanish artist of note, including El Greco, Francisco Goya, Murillo, Ribera, Velazquez, and Zurbaran, "works on par in some cases with those in Madrid's famed Prado Museum," claims the *News*'s art critic. "Weak points such as still lifes become evident along with strengths—including five pictures each by Murillo and Goya, among them the latter's famous *Yard with Madmen* from the startling insane asylum series." Linger at the Yard awhile for it will give you an insight into Goya's debilitating illness that left him permanently deaf.

"Up to the 15th century, the results are spotty at best," says the *Dallas Observer,* about the collection, insisting that "the Meadows' greatest strength is in Spanish painting under the Hapsburgs, especially the Baroque and its variants, including El Greco."

There is an almost impressionistic *Female Figure* created around 1648 by Diego Rodriguez de Silva y Velazquez, and a wood panel, titled *Saint Sebastian,* by Valencia native Fernando Yanez de la Almedina, painted around 1506.

Were it not for the innocent young model looking at you, you might feel like an unwelcome voyeur approaching Antonio Maria Esquivel's seated *Woman Removing Her Garter*. The Seville-born artist lost his sight to herpes in 1838. Contemplating suicide, the 36-year-old painter was sent to a famous German eye specialist. His vision restored in 1841, Esquivel painted this daringly sexual oil on canvas the following year.

The 20th-century galleries feature Diego Rivera's 1915 Cubist oil portrait of Russian writer Ilya Ehrenburg, who died in 1967. There is Picasso's 1915 oil on canvas *Still Life in a Landscape,* Juan Gris's 1917 *Cubist Landscape,* and Joan Miro's 1929 *Queen Louise of Prussia* and 1937 tempera and oil, titled *The Circus*.

The 550-piece permanent museum collection, "formed with an eye for posterity," is valued at well beyond $110 million. "The Meadows' budget is embarrassingly slim," points out the *News,* claiming it gets only $300,000 a year for exhibitions from the Meadows Foundation, its major source of funding. In 2003, the Meadows approached Ted Pillsbury, for nearly 18 years the director of the prestigious Kimbell Art Museum in Fort Forth, to be its next director. A sophisticated perfectionist who has afterwards had a partnership in Dallas' Gerald Peters Art Gallery (see entry), Pillsbury must have had his doubts for he told the *News,* "I think they really want me to fund-raise." He also reminded the daily that "the Meadows is a relatively small institution." But he took the job anyway.

Algur Hurtle Meadows (1899-1978), the third of seven children, was born in Vidalia, Georgia, and earned a law degree from Centenary College in Shreveport, Louisiana, in the early 1920s. He became rich by acquiring oil-producing properties he developed in a scheme that "involved three parties in the purchase transaction to minimize tax liability and the use of interest-bearing oil payments to meet a large percentage of the purchase price." By 1959, General American Oil Co. had acquired almost 3,000 oil wells in the United States and Canada and was drilling for oil in Spain.

In the early 1950s, Meadows was granted exclusive rights to explore for oil in Spain. During his trips there, the oilman—after whom the museum and school of the arts were named in 1969—spent many hours at the Prado Museum in Madrid. "Meadows was so smitten with art that he purchased *Adoration of the Shepards* by Pedro Orrente knowing that he could not take the painting out of the country," notes *D Magazine*. "Instead, he donated it to the Spanish government." The Prado's collection of Spanish masterpieces inspired Meadows to begin his own collection of Spanish art.

Following his first wife's death in 1961, Meadows remarried the following year, but his second wife apparently did not care for the religious art so typical of Spain. He donated his collection of paintings and prints to SMU and gave it a million-dollar endowment to establish a museum of Spanish art in memory of his first wife, Virginia Garrison Stuart Meadows, whose portrait is on display here.

In the mid-1960s, on his second wife's suggestion, Meadows began collecting paintings by French Impressionists and post-Impressionists. When contacting a local dealer about selling a few pieces, he was confronted with a shocking discovery that some 38 of the 58 works in his collection were forgeries. His humiliating experience was the basis for Clifford Irving's best-selling novel, *The Fake,* in which the businessman was portrayed as an "out-of-control" Texas tycoon.

"With characteristic generosity, Meadows immediately gave the museum a million dollars to replace the questionable works," notes the Texas State Historic Association. "The people who once laughed at him fell down dead on how he reacted to his misfortune," recalls the museum's first director, Bill Jordan. "He became one of the most respected and admired collectors in the world."

Meadows was killed in an automobile accident and entombed at Hillcrest Mausoleum, about two dozen blocks north of here. The Meadows Foundation has given well over $200 million toward charitable causes.

Spanish art reached its zenith during Spain's Golden Age in the 16th century, when that country was the most powerful economic, political, and cultural force in the world. The Meadows Museum owns major works dating from the Middle Ages to the present, including a 1937 Picasso, *The Dream and Lie of Franco.*

Another recent addition to the museum, Luis de Morales' *Pieta,* radiating a "sublime emotional expression," reflects the mysticism of mid-16th-century Spain. In this small, but arresting version, the Virgin Mary embraces the dead body of her son that makes it impossible to avert your gaze. The museum also possesses 200 works on paper by Goya.

The subject of the first exhibit at the new Meadows was the well-known Spanish architect Santiago Calatrava, whose railway stations you can see in France, Portugal, and Switzerland. A suspension bridge by Calatrava is being considered for inclusion in Dallas' Trinity River improvement plan. One can only imagine what Calatrava, who recently completed the $100-million Milwaukee Art Museum, could have done with the Meadows Museum building.

Calatrava also designed the $1.5-million, perpetually moving 26-by-68-foot (or 7.9-by-20.7-meter) bronze sculpture, titled *Wave*, atop a 40-by-90-foot (or 12-by-27-meter) reflecting pool. Lighted from below at night, it is located on Bishop Boulevard, just south of the staircase leading to the museum. It was inaugurated in the fall of 2003, with the participation of the artist and the Spanish ambassador to the United States. The SMU president said at the time that Calatrava is the Michelangelo of this century.

The *Wave* features a four-inch-deep (or ten-centimeter) pool with slow undulating steel arms that seem to transfer water from one end to the other in a continuous wave. The sculpture consists of 129 green-patinated bronze bars that pivot back and forth in sequence to create an impression of waves. The bars, which rise up to six feet (or 1.82 meters) then descend over the black granite pool, weigh 440 pounds (or 199 kilograms) each and are actually made of reinforced hollow steel.

Within two weeks of its inauguration, an SMU student rode the *Wave* as a nightly prank and bent or broke six of the pins supporting the sculpture, then ran away, but was caught by a video surveillance camera. The *Wave* seems to be more often motionless than functioning.

Much to the displeasure of the *Dallas Observer*, one of the first Meadows' exhibits consisted of Mexican silver sculptures exhibition which the weekly described as "a PR event from the start to gilt finish, the 'collection' crassly commercial and self serving." The *Observer* claims that since opening, the Meadows "has seemed to envision itself less as a real museum than as Big D's cultural ambassador, a promoter of Spanish tourism and designer bridges."

The old museum featured the Elizabeth Meadows Sculpture Garden, which opened in 1969 in honor of Meadows' second wife, a bust of whom is also on display. The new Meadows has transferred all but two sculptures to the new Doolin Plaza Gardens out front or inside the new building. The plaza is named for Dallas artist Kaleta Doolin. The two pieces remaining in their original space are:

• Isamu Noguchi's (1904-1988) *Spirit's Flight*, in black Japanese basalt and stainless steel, dating from 1979.

• Claes Oldenburg's (b. 1929) *Geometric Mouse II*, created in 1969-70 for the Meadows Garden by the Swedish-American artist whose taller variation on this work is exhibited at Houston's Central Library. It was Oldenburg's first all-metal sculpture. (For more about Oldenburg's *Stake Hitch*, please see Dallas Museum of Art, above.)

The artworks transferred to the new location include:

• Jacques Lipchitz's (1891-1973) well-known 11-foot-high (or

3.35-meter) bronze *La Joie de Vivre* (The Joy of Life), created in 1927 by the Lithuanian-born artist who emigrated to the United States in 1941, after the German occupation of France. Edition 4 out of 7 was for sale in 2003 at New York City's Marlborough gallery. Lipchitz moved to Paris in 1909 and after meeting Pablo Picasso and Juan Gris began working in the Cubist style. He died on the Isle of Capri, Italy. His bronze, *Sacrifice*, can be seen at the Meyerson Symphony downtown.

• Aristide Maillol's (1861-1944) larger-than-life-size work cast in lead, *The Three Graces*, from 1937-1939, by the French tapestry designer who went blind temporarily from this meticulous labor in artificial light and devoted himself to sculpture at age 40. He is also on exhibit at the Trammell Crow Center (see listing), at 2001 Ross Ave. downtown, as well as the nearby Dallas Museum of Art.

• Marino Marini's (1901-1980) *Crouching Woman*, 1934, and *Horse and Rider* from 1951, by the Italian sculptor well known for his expressionistic horse-and-rider series, as well as for portraits of painter Marc Chagall and composer Igor Stravinsky.

• Henry Moore's (1898-1986) *Three-Piece Reclining Figure*, completed in 1962 by the well-regarded Yorkshire sculptor known for his monumental nudes in bronze and stone. You can also see one on the plaza in front of the Dallas City Hall, and another at the north entrance of the Dallas Museum of Art (see entry) downtown.

• Alberto Giacometti's (1901-1966) 1956 bronze *Femme de Venise* in the museum atrium by the Swiss painter and sculptor who lived in Paris and was influenced by Egyptian and primitive art, as well as Surrealism. Another Giacometti bronze is on display at the Dallas Museum of Art (see entry) downtown.

• Auguste Rodin's (1840-1917) *Eve in Despair*, from 1915, is supposedly the only Rodin marble sculpture in the Southwest. Other Rodin bronzes can be seen at the Trammell Crow Center downtown and the Dallas Museum of Art (see entries).

• David Smith's (1906-1965) *Cubi VIII*, created in 1962 by the Decatur, Indiana-born sculptor. This was one of the first in his well-known Cubi series. *Cubi XVIII*, a stainless steel sculpture that he authored the following year, can be seen at the Dallas Museum of Art (see entry) downtown.

• Fritz Wotruba's (1907-1975) *Figure with Raised Arms*, done in 1956 by the Austrian sculptor who gained prominence in the 1950s.

Nasher Sculpture Center, 2001 Flora St. at North Harwood and Olive Sts., (214) 891-8570, Internet www.nashersculpturecenter.org. Located on a former parking lot downtown, across the street from the Dallas Museum of Art and a block from the Meyerson Symphony Center (see listings).

Gathered over a period of 30 years in partnership with Nasher's wife Patsy, who died in 1988, this modern collection is regarded as one of the most important among those still owned privately.

Nasher kept the city in suspense until 1997, when he announced at City Hall that he planned to build, at his expense, a $57-million sculpture garden on a 2.4-acre (or 0.97-hectare) site. Up to 25 of his 200 outdoor sculptures—some of them true masterpieces—are rotated in a landscaped environment costing more than $1 million a year to maintain and financed by the Nasher Foundation, which owns the art.

The Tate Gallery in London, the Solomon R. Guggenheim Museum in New York, the National Gallery of Art in Washington, D.C., and the Fine Arts Museum of San Francisco, all have salivated over Nasher's outdoor collection by more than 40 artists. He is one of three Dallasites singled out as one of the world's top 200 art collectors, according to ARTnews.

Among the artworks on display in the garden could be Alexander Calder's *The Spider* from 1940 and *Three Bollards*, Alberto Giacometti's three bronze and hand-painted busts of his brother Diego, Willem de Koonig's *Seated Woman*, Aristide Maillol's *Night*, Henri Matisse's 1925 *Reclining Nude*, Joan Miro's *Caress of a Bird*, Henry Moore's *Reclining Figure*, *Angles*, and Auguste Rodin's *Eve*.

Richard Serra's *My Curves Are Not Mad*, a Cor-Ten bent steel sculpture on loan to the Dallas Museum of Art nearby from Nasher since 1988, was installed here in the fall of 2002. Serra (b. 1939) created the two curved slabs of steel, each 14 feet (or 4.2 meters) high, more than 40 feet (or 12 meters) long, and weighing 50,000 pounds (or 22,680 kilograms), in 1971.

In 2001, Nasher paid $3.1 million for the great Henri Matisse bronze *The Serf*, which will be on display here. Dated around 1900-1904, it is the first of Matisse's sculptural masterpieces.

The year before the sculpture center opened, Nasher acquired a ten-foot-tall (or three-meter) Pablo Picasso sculpture, titled *Tete de Femme* (Head of a Woman), that might be displayed here periodically. The concrete and gravel head mounted on a thin column was created in 1958 and bought through a Paris dealer. It was the first of 20 concrete and gravel works the artist created. Until bought by Nasher, the sculpture had not been seen in public because it was made for a Norwegian family that kept it in their Oslo garden.

The artwork, which must be viewed from 360 degrees to appreciate it, is valued at more than $3 million. Even before this acquisition, Nasher had already owned half a dozen other Picasso sculptures, making it one of the largest private collections. He also owns a cast of a 1908 bronze, *Two Negresses*, by Henri Matisse. Nasher possesses key works by Jonathan Borofsky, Tony Cragg, Jeff Koons, and Richard Long. His first sculpture acquisition supposedly was a Jean Arp's torso.

The garden's five-pavilion design belongs to Genoa-born Italian architect Renzo Piano and American landscape architect Peter Walker. It includes a 55,000-square-foot (or 5,109-square-meter) building with an indoor gallery, a café, a library, and offices of the Nasher Institute for Modern Sculpture.

Piano called it a "'generous, provocative and almost mad idea' to place a sculpture garden in a parking wasteland next to an expressway," according to the *Dallas Morning News*. A year later he told the daily: "It is absurd really, this idea of a noble ruin in the middle of a busy downtown, but that is what makes it powerful."

The surrounding walls of the Nasher center are made of warm-colored travertine stone giving the appearance of an archeological site. Instead of sidewalks, there are stone paths to wander around. Regional trees, such as cedar elm, red oak, and crape myrtle provide shade to shelter visitors from the broiling sun. A "fountain" on the Flora Street end of the garden has single drops of water falling at intervals so that when the concentric ripple reaches the edge, another drop falls. A sophisticated system of outdoor climate controls combats the deadly Dallas heat. Copenhagen, Denmark, Minneapolis, and Washington, D.C., also have outdoor sculpture gardens, but none downtown.

"The project, more than any other, will help Dallas achieve its long-time desire to be considered an international city," the *News* quoted one local notable. "The collaboration between Renzo Piano and Peter Walker brings together an architect who makes poetry out of technology and one who turns landscape into art," observes the *News*.

The "spectacularly charming" Piano (b. 1937) is also winner of the 1998 Pritzker Prize and designer of Houston's Menil Collection. The *New York Times* chose him to design its new 40-story headquarters in the Times Square area of New York City. His most breathtaking commission, however, is the Paris-based Centre Pompidou, which he designed as "an act of loutish bravado" in 1977.

There are parallels between the Nasher Center and the $45-million Beyeler Foundation Museum in the Basel suburb of Riehen in Switzerland. The art dealer Ernest Beyeler has gathered some 200 similar objects—with large holdings of Giacometti, Picasso, and Ferdinand Leger—that have been on display since 1997. The Beyeler, too, was designed by Renzo Piano.

Dr. Steven A. Nash (b. 1944), former deputy director and chief curator at the Dallas Museum of Art (see entry) was named the center's first director. He left Dallas in 1988 to join former DMA director Harry Parker at the Fine Arts Museum in San Francisco. Dr. Nash graduated from Dartmouth College and has a doctorate in art history from Stanford University.

Trammell Crow Center Sculpture Collection, 2001 Ross Ave. at

North Harwood St., (214) 749-6753. Located in the Arts District of downtown Dallas, across from the Dallas Museum of Art (see entry). From 1885 to 1920 the upper end of Ross Avenue was known as the Fifth Avenue of Dallas and was as desirable a residential address as its New York City namesake.

The elegant 50-story polished and flamed granite Trammell Crow Center, which is 686 feet (or 209 meters) tall, with 1.12 million square feet (or 104,000 square meters) of office space and a six-level, 1,180-car garage underneath the tower, was built in 1984, renamed for Crow in 1987, and sold to a Fort Worth-based real estate investment trust for $162 million ten years later.

The structure is the first of architect Richard Keating's three downtown office buildings. One local architect calls it "an absolute classic skyscraper with a drop-dead lobby." The tower was originally constructed for LTV Corp., then one of the nation's largest conglomerates run by Dallasite James Ling.

(For more about Ling and LTV, please see entry 1600 Pacific Place/LTV Tower in the SIGHTS & ATTRACTIONS chapter.)

The building is the headquarters of Trammell Crow's commercial real estate operations, with 170 offices in the United States and Canada managing more than 510 million square feet of space, and employing 7,000. Robert Jordan, the founding partner of the Dallas law firm of Baker Botts, was located here before President George W. Bush named him the U.S. ambassador to Saudi Arabia.

On the mezzanine of this building is located the **Aija** restaurant and bar with floor-to-ceiling windows, open for lunch and dinner Mon-Fri 11:30 AM-7:30 PM. The prices are reasonable, until you factor in the underground parking, which is free after 4:30 PM. The lunch buffet is self-serve.

This is not a museum in the usual sense of the word, but it will be treated as such for its wealth of sculpture inside and out. Dallas developer Trammell Crow is one among a handful of Dallas multimillionaires who have shared some of their art with the city.

Twenty bronzes of French art, from the late 19th century to the present, are displayed around the one-block tower, its pavilion, and the landscaped garden that are all pleasant to look at. You can stop by almost any time of the day and spend as much time as you like.

The collection includes examples by several of the most influential sculptors of the past one hundred years. If you should make a clockwise circle around the building, starting at the Ross Avenue entrance, you can see the following works:

• Aristide Maillol (1861-1944) devoted most of his life to exploring the beauty and poetry of the female form. On either side of the entrance to the building are two of his well-known works, *Port-Vendres*, from 1921, and its companion lead piece of 1912-25, *Monument to Cezanne*, facing one another, as Maillol conceived them. The only other place in the world where they are to be seen together is in the gardens of the Louvre Museum in Paris.

• Continuing east on the Ross Avenue side are these four works: *Woman Walking*, by Jean Carton (b. 1912), from 1984-85; Maillol's *Nymph with Flowers*, created in 1931; *Genius of Eternal Rest*, from 1898, and his *Cybele* from 1889, both by Auguste Rodin (1840-1917). Going north, on the Harwood Street side, there are two more Rodin bronzes, the 1909 *Prayer* and the 1882 *Large Torso of a Man*.

• The next four bronzes are by Emile Antoine Bourdelle (1861-1929), Rodin's assistant until 1910: a *Horse for Alvear* study, from 1913-1915; the 1911 *Torso of Fruit*; the 1912 *Penelope*; and the 1909 *Hercules the Archer*, which is 98 inches (or 2.49 meters) high and perhaps his best known work. They are followed by *Young Girl Carrying Water*, a 1910 work by Joseph Bernard (1866-1931), and his 1925 *Mother and Child*.

• On the corner of Olive Street and Ross Avenue, you will encounter Bourdelle's monumental *Horse for Alvear*, so huge and imposing that it needs twice the space it has. Close to it is his 1906-1907 *Crouching Bather*, a 1930-1931 *Meditation* by Robert Wlerick (1882-1944), Bourdelle's 1907 *Monument to Debussy*, and *Lucile* from 1984 by Stephan Buxin (b. 1909), who was Wlerick's student.

• Back to Ross Avenue, the collection is rounded out by three more Rodins: *Jean de Fiennes*, *Pierre de Wiessant*, and *Meditations*, all three dating from 1885.

• On the patio below street level and near the corner of Flora and North Harwood Streets, you can also admire the sculpture *Men Against Man*, a disturbing 1986 work by Norwegian-American artist Kaare K. Nygaard, otherwise also a practicing surgeon at the Mayo Clinic in Rochester, New York. This is the only non-French outdoor sculpture here.

OTHER MUSEUMS

Following the Sixth Floor Museum, all remaining museums are listed alphabetically.

The Sixth Floor Museum, 411 Elm St. at North Houston St., (214) 747-6660, Internet www.jfk.org, e-mail jfk@jfk.org. *CH*, except children under six years of age. Audio tour recordings are available in English, French, German, Italian, Japanese, Portuguese, and Spanish at an additional cost. Open daily, except on Christmas Day, 9 AM-6 PM.

The entrance to the museum is on Houston Street. Only up to 300 visitors at a time are admitted so there may be a wait. No photography is allowed inside the museum. There is a security detector at the entrance.

Located downtown on the southwestern edge of the West End Historic District and across the street from the three-acre (or 1.21-hectare) Dealey Plaza, in the former Texas School Book Depository Building. The Museum of Dallas County History (see entry) was to open one block southeast of here, inside the "Old Red" Courthouse.

The site of the building was originally owned by the founder of Dallas, John Neely Bryan, and during the 1880s the French-born Maxime Guillot operated a wagon shop on the property. The Rock Island Plow Co. of Illinois built a five-story building here in 1898, but a fire destroyed it in 1901, and the plow company rebuilt it and added the sixth and seventh floors, which are noticeably different.

Colonel David Harold Byrd, whose cousin was admiral and polar explorer Richard E. Byrd (1888-1957), bought the property in 1937 and leased it to several tenants over the years. In the early 1960s, the building was leased to the Texas School Book Depository Company, a private firm that supplied textbooks to Texas schools. The structure was designated a national historic landmark in 1993. The bottom five floors are occupied by county agencies.

On November 22, 1963, President John F. Kennedy was assassinated in front of this building, an event that remains one of the most remembered and controversial in the last century. Each year up to two million tourists flock to Dealey Plaza from around the world to try to understand how and why it happened. The Sixth Floor Museum, which is located on the floor where a sniper's nest was found after the shooting, examines the life, death, and legacy of President Kennedy.

Prelude to the Assassination

Here is the sequence of events that led to the killing and what followed. (A 154-page summary, titled "November 22, The Day Remembered," published by the *Dallas Morning News*, was one of the several references consulted for this chronology.)

The second of nine children, John F. Kennedy served 14 years in Congress before he ran for president in 1960. His maternal grandfather served in Congress and as mayor of Boston. His father was ambassador to England until 1940. He married Jacqueline Lee Bouvier (1929-1994), a Rhode Island socialite, in 1953.

Four days before the 1960 presidential elections, Lyndon Johnson (1908-1973) and his wife Lady Bird attended a Democratic Party luncheon at the Adolphus Hotel in Dallas. As they were about to cross Commerce Street from what was then the Baker Hotel, they were mobbed by several hundred protesters, some carrying placards. It was suggested that Johnson use a side door to avoid the crowd, but he refused. It allegedly took the Johnsons 45 minutes to cross the street. They described the scene the following night: "We were hissed at and spat upon, and two women were hurt in a mob scene that looked like some other country. It was hard to believe that this was happening in Dallas and in Texas." Lady Bird Johnson claimed that she was never so scared for her life.

On October 24, 1963, a United Nations Day was planned for in Dallas, and the U.S. ambassador to the United Nations, Adlai Stevenson, was scheduled as a keynote speaker. He was hit on the head with an anti-U.N. placard and spat on by a college student. While giving his speech, Stevenson was continuously interrupted and booed. Dallas merchant Stanley Marcus escorted the ambassador to a waiting car, and once he was inside, the protesters started rocking the car before it sped away.

Dallas was embarrassed, and the *Dallas Morning News*, although until then "unswervingly conservative," published an editorial extending a "community apology" to Stevenson. The *Dallas Times Herald* published a front-page editorial that was headlined "Dallas Disgrace." Telegrams signed by some 100 civic leaders, saying that Dallas was "outraged and abjectly ashamed," were sent to Kennedy and Stevenson.

The day that Stevenson spoke, handbills were passed out around the city displaying Kennedy's pictures with the words, "Wanted for Treason. This Man is wanted for treasonous activities against the United States." *Time* magazine called Dallas "A City Disgraced."

Several Dallas civic leaders, merchant Stanley Marcus among them, thought of dissuading President Kennedy from visiting the city, fearing that harm may come to him. The mayor asked the city to show the president its customary Southern hospitality. Even Richard Nixon, the former vice president, urged Dallas to give the president a "courteous reception."

Kennedy flew to Texas to attend several official functions and to help reunify the Democratic party in the Lone Star State. Also to raise money for the 1964 presidential campaign. The tour was to end with a fund-raising dinner in Austin.

The day of infamy that Dallas may never outlive came on November 22, 1963. Ironically, the dugout of John Neely Bryan, the founder of Dallas, was at the spot where, 122 years later, Kennedy was assassinated.

The previous day, Thursday, November 21, Kennedy spent the last afternoon of his life in San Antonio. He made the Alamo City his first stop on a two-day visit to five Texas cities. It was 78 degrees when John and Jacqueline Kennedy began their 26-mile (or 42-kilometer) motorcade to Brooks Air Force Base, while some 125,000 spectators greeted them along the way.

Texas governor John B. Connally (1917-1993) and his wife sat in the presidential limousine and smiled approvingly. Kennedy had named him Secretary of the Navy, but he had resigned to come home and win the Democratic gubernatorial nomination in 1962.

The president spoke to 10,000 present at the dedication of a $6-million addition to the Brooks' School of Aerospace Medicine. A tanned, smiling Kennedy then boarded Air Force One and left the Alamo City for Houston at 3:55 PM.

"President Kennedy has spent two hours and 25 minutes of his last afternoon soaking in the warmth of San Antonio and its citizens," observed the *San Antonio Express* in an article published on the day that the assassination took place 274 miles (or 441 kilometers) away.

After a quick visit to Houston and a Kennedy speech at Rice University, Air Force One landed at Carswell Air Force Base in Fort Worth at 11:07 PM. "A large crowd, estimated in the thousands, had waited near the runway for more than four hours," noted the *Fort Worth Star-Telegram*.

Kennedy spent his last night at what was then known as Hotel Texas. He was the first sitting president to visit Fort Worth since 1936, when Franklin D. Roosevelt rode in an open touring car down Main Street. Also part of his entourage were again Connally and his wife Nellie, who was 84 years old in 2003; the Connallys had lived in Fort Worth during the 1950s and early 1960s.

The following morning, Friday, November 22, Kennedy made a quick speech in the parking lot across the street, while standing amid light drizzle on the flatbed of a truck, with Vice President Lyndon B. Johnson and Governor Connally looking on.

He was honored at a Fort Worth breakfast gathering for 2,500 business leaders. An even larger crowd chanted, "Where's Jackie? Where's Jackie?" He apologized for his wife's tardiness, saying, "She is busy organizing herself. It takes her longer because she is prettier than the rest of us."

Following is a moment-by-moment account of what took place next.

The Assassination

Kennedy departs Carswell on Air Force One at about 11:20 AM and arrives in Dallas at 11:40 AM. Vice President Johnson follows on Air Force Two. Large and enthusiastic crowds, estimated at 250,000, cheer as Kennedy rides in a motorcade from Love Field Airport on his way to the Dallas Trade Mart, where he is to speak at a luncheon for 2,600. He leaves the airport in his Lincoln Continental limousine and travels downtown via Mockingbird Lane and Lemmon Avenue. The temperature is in the mid-60s.

He halts the motorcade at the intersection of Lemmon and Lomo Alto Drive to greet a group of children. One girl carries a sign saying,

"Mr. President, will you please stop and shake hands with me?" He does, then continues down Lemmon, turns on to Turtle Creek Boulevard, and then Cedar Springs Road until approaching Harwood Street, just outside downtown.

By noon, when the motorcade reaches Ervay Street, the crowds are "very thick and very friendly," according to then-U.S. Attorney Barefoot Sanders. Lyndon Johnson approves, too, noting years later: "I was very impressed and very pleased with the crowds."

Kennedy travels down Main Street at a speed of about eleven miles (or 17.7 kilometers) per hour with his wife Jacqueline at his side. At about 12:29, as the motorcade is about to turn north on Houston Street and pass the Dallas County Courthouse, Nellie Connally supposedly turns to the president and says, "Mr. Kennedy, you can't say that Dallas doesn't love you."

About a minute later, perhaps at 12:30 PM, as the entourage proceeds west on Elm Street and travels down the slope in front of the Texas School Book Depository, inside the three-acre (or 1.21-hectare) Dealey Plaza, shots ring out, from the sixth floor of the book depository, it is believed. Kennedy lurches forward and slumps in his seat, with his wife falling on him, shouting, "Oh, my God, they have shot my husband. I love you, Jack."

Governor Connally has but one thought, "Oh, no, no, no. My God, they are trying to kill us all." Mrs. Connally thinks her husband is dead until he moves his hand. Although lethally wounded with the side of his chest blown out, he survives.

Several bystanders point to the upper levels of the book depository and police rush into the building. Deputy Sheriff Buddy Walters kicks the grass, muttering, "Oh, damn. Oh, damn."

At about 12:33, the phone rings in the emergency room of Parkland Memorial Hospital informing the staff that the president has been shot and is on the way there, at about 80 mph.

Soon afterward, the United Press International transmits a12-word bulletin worldwide: THREE SHOTS WERE FIRED AT PRESIDENT KENNEDY'S MOTORCADE TODAY IN DOWNTOWN DALLAS. Some suspect it might be a Russian plot.

The president's body reaches Parkland Hospital at 12:36 or so. Mrs. Kennedy sits with her husband's head in her lap, saying, "They murdered my husband. They murdered my husband." The Secret Service rushes at Johnson and forms a ring around him, one addressing him, "Mr. President."

Dr. C. James Carrico (d. 2002), a first-year surgical resident at Parkland, is the first physician to tend to the president. He inserts a tube into the barely breathing man's trachea and stays at Kennedy's side for 25 minutes.

Among the five physicians who work on Kennedy in the frantic minutes after he is shot is Dr. Paul C. Peters (1928-2002), who in 1964 performed the first kidney transplant ever in Texas. He was chief of urology at the University of Texas Southwestern Medical Center at Dallas from 1971 to 1993.

Doctors work on the president for about 35 minutes. Kennedy never regains consciousness and is pronounced dead from wounds in the neck and head at about 1 PM. The emergency room staff members stop being doctors and nurses and become citizens shedding tears, like the rest of the nation.

Hours later, the *Dallas Times Herald* displays this headline across its special edition front page: PRESIDENT DEAD, CONNALLY SHOT.

Mayor Earl Cabell stands in Parkland's surgery area and keeps repeating, "It didn't happen. It didn't happen." U.S. Representative Henry B. Gonzalez (d. 2001), a San Antonio Democrat, cries uncontrollably. Near him, an attendant opens the door, and on the bed lies Kennedy's body covered with a linen sheet. Mrs. Kennedy comes in, she kisses her husband, takes off her ring, and puts it on the president's finger.

Earl Jay Watson (d. 2001), the program director at WFAA-TV (Channel 8), who watches the presidential motorcade travel through the intersection of Houston and Main streets a moment before the assassination, is among the first local newsmen who report the killing to north Texas television viewers. Interrupting a cooking show, his eyes are "wide with alarm" as he addresses the viewers:

"Good afternoon, ladies and gentlemen. You'll excuse the fact that I'm out of breath, but about 10 or 15 minutes ago, a tragic thing, from all indications at this point, has happened in the city of Dallas." He reads wire service dispatches and interviews witnesses, such as Abraham Zapruder, the amateur photographer whose name is now synonymous with his home film of the assassination.

In a post-presidential interview with CBS, Lyndon Johnson tells broadcaster Walter Cronkite that he had never been convinced that a lone gunman killed Kennedy. Immediately after the taping of the interview, Johnson and his staff convince CBS to delete those comments from the broadcast version for reasons of "national security."

Police rush inside the book depository and begin a floor-by-floor search of the warehouse. They uncover a barricade of boxes, three spent bullet cartridges, and a rifle. Finger and palm prints on the 1940 Italian Mannlicher-Carcano rifle with a telescopic sight are later identified as Lee Harvey Oswald's. The rifle is hidden amid the boxes in the northwest corner of the sixth floor.

Marina Oswald, Oswald's Russian-born wife, hears of the shooting from her neighbor at about 12:40 PM. A few minutes later, her husband arrives at his rooming house in Oak Cliff, grabs his pistol, and leaves.

At 1:15 PM, Dallas police officer J. D. Tippit is shot in Oak Cliff. The book depository officials poll their employees and discover that the 24-year-old Oswald, an order clerk, who has only been hired five weeks earlier, is missing.

A worker behind the concession stand at the Texas Theatre on Jefferson Boulevard in Oak Cliff neighborhood sees Oswald running in at about 1:45 without buying a ticket. *Cry of Battle* with Van Heflin and Rita Moreno is featured at the theater. Police arrive a few minutes later and search the patrons.

"Get on your feet," one of them orders Oswald, but is punched between the eyes with Oswald's left fist. Another officer arrives, and Oswald is brought from the theater. There are about a dozen people outside, some supposedly yelling, "Kill that son of a b____!"

At about 1:31 PM, a news conference is held at Parkland, where White House spokesman Malcolm Kilduff (1928-2003) tells shocked reporters:

"President John F. Kennedy died at approximately 1 PM, Central Standard Time, today here in Dallas. He died of a gunshot wound in the brain."

A short time earlier, the young assistant press secretary breaks the news to Vice President Lyndon Johnson and his wife, Lady Bird. Fearing a plot against other top-ranking officials, Johnson orders Kilduff to withhold the announcement of Kennedy's death until he is safely aboard his plane.

Lyndon B. Johnson boards Air Force One at 1:33 PM, but refuses to leave for Washington without Mrs. Kennedy, who says, "I'm not leaving without Jack." Her dress is stained and her right glove caked with her husband's blood. At about 2:08 PM, Kennedy's body leaves Parkland in a bronze casket and is placed aboard Air Force One. Kennedy staffers refuse to let the slain president's body remain for an autopsy in Dallas and remove it by force.

Oswald is taken to police headquarters, where detective Gus Rose is assigned to interrogate him about Tippit's death. Oswald is belligerent, curses, and refuses to identify himself: "You're the detective, you figure it out," he taunts.

Mrs. Kennedy comes from the rear of the plane, composed but quivering, to be present for Johnson's presidential oath. For security reasons, all the shades are lowered. He is sworn in as the next president of the United States, at about 2:38 PM, by the U.S. district judge Sarah T. Hughes at Love Field Airport in a cracked voice, her hands shaking. The jet's idling engines nearly drown her voice.

Air Force One is airborne by about 2:47 PM. Kennedy aides sit with Mrs. Kennedy next to the casket in the back of the plane that is returning to Washington, D.C.

At 3:30 PM, Oswald is still being questioned at Dallas police headquarters. His room is searched. Detectives are dispatched to Irving where his wife Marina Oswald is staying, watching the assassination on television. To their surprise, she tells them that she is a Russian citizen and does not speak English. The woman with whom Mrs. Oswald stays volunteers to interpret. Both are taken to City Hall to give statements.

Erik Jonsson, president of the Dallas Citizens Council, and other civic leaders remain at the Trade Mart discussing what the assassination may do to the reputation of Dallas. Governor Connally is being operated on at Parkland Hospital.

Air Force One approaches Andrews Air Force Base near Washington shortly before 5 PM, Dallas time. Robert Kennedy meets the plane. A Navy ambulance takes his brother's coffin to Bethesda Naval Hospital for an autopsy of the body.

President Johnson addresses the nation at about 5:10 PM, saying: "This is a sad time for all people. We have suffered a loss that cannot be weighed. I will do my best. That is all that I can do." The new president then takes a helicopter to the White House.

Shortly after midnight, Oswald is shown to the reporters and declares that he is not guilty of anything.

Instantly, Dallas gains the reputation of Hate City. Its former four-term mayor, the 84-year-old Robert L. Thornton, tells the city's top leaders, who meet in private to discuss ways to improve the city's image: "Don't do anything. Dallas hasn't done anything. Dallas is a great city, and we have nothing to be ashamed of. Forget it and go about your business." He dies the following year.

Most activities stop.

Aftermath of the Assassination

The day after the assassination, CBS broadcaster Bob Shieffer went to Dealey Plaza, reporting that "hundreds of people seemed to wander aimlessly, occasionally talking to anyone who happened by. Some left flowers; some just stared."

The Dallas Opera's performance of Verdi's *Un Ballo in Maschera* was postponed. "Even the company's Italian members were devastated by the tragedy, crying as they sat in front of television sets watching the events that followed, immobile like everyone else," writes Dallas cultural historian Ronald L. Davis. Author Conover Hunt claims that "one Japanese family walked 18 miles to the American Embassy in Tokyo to pay its respects."

The charity ball was canceled. Restaurants and stores closed, as did most of the offices in the city. Jack Ruby's burlesque nightclub, Carousel, at 1312 ½ Commerce Street (where the former Southwestern Bell, now SBC Communications building now stands), across the street from the Adolphus Hotel, closed for the weekend.

Oswald was charged with the murder of John Kennedy and Dallas policeman J. D. Tippit (b. 1924), who stopped him for questioning. He allegedly shot Kennedy from a sixth-floor window of the depository.

Born in New Orleans and placed in a Lutheran orphanage at the age of three, Oswald came to Texas with his mother in 1944. Moving between Louisiana and Texas, he received spotty education, "became a chronic truant and was placed under psychiatric care" in 1952.

A former Marine in Japan and California, Oswald defected to Russia in 1959. He tried to commit suicide when the Soviets ordered him out of Russia, but was allowed to stay and work in a Minsk, Belarus, radio factory. In 1961 he married Marina Nikolayevna Prusakova, whose first daughter was born the following year, when the disillusioned Oswald was permitted to return to America with his Russian wife.

He lived in Fort Worth until October 1962, then moved to Dallas. In April 1963, Oswald attempted to kill Maj. Gen. Edwin A. Walker (1909-1993), a fanatical anti-communist, in his Dallas home, missing by a few inches.

The investigative Warren Commission, established by President Johnson, concluded in its report, issued in 1964, that Oswald acted alone, although many conspiracy theories have flourished ever since.

Two days after the assassination, Oswald was shot in the basement of the old police station, at 106 South Harwood Street. The shooting was carried live on NBC television, while he was being transferred from the city to the county jail. President Kennedy's funeral was held on November 25, 1963. His now-deceased son, John Jr., was three years old that day.

Flanked by two detectives—one of them an easily recognizable Jim Leavelle (b. 1919) in his Resistol hat and a second-hand tan Neiman Marcus suit—Oswald entered the basement around 11:21 AM on Sunday, November 24. Less than a minute earlier, **Jack Ruby** had entered the basement with a .38-caliber Colt and picked his spot behind a detective.

"You son of a b____," Ruby allegedly cursed the prisoner in "an unnatural and excited voice" seconds later, shooting Oswald, who was pronounced dead less than two hours later. A *New York Times* editorial called it "an outrageous breach of police responsibility."

The killer was "the cheesy little hood," who owned the Dallas nightclub Carousel, where his women hustled $1.98 bottles of champagne for up to $75. Born in 1911 of Polish immigrants as Jacob Rubenstein in Chicago, he was placed in a foster home upon his parents' separation in 1921. He dropped out of school at 16 and at one time delivered sealed envelopes for gangster Al Capone at a dollar an errand.

In 1947, he moved to Dallas and later that year changed his name to Ruby. He ran several nightclubs over the next 16 years and was arrested eight times by the Dallas police. The most recent arrest was at the Carousel Club, one of three such establishments in downtown Dallas, which employed strippers, a band, and three or four waitresses.

Oswald's mother, Marguerite (1907-1981), briefly worked as a nurse for a *Fort Worth Star-Telegram* executive before the assassination. When her son was arrested after Kennedy's assassination, she saw his name on Channel 8 and called the *Star-Telegram* city desk asking if anyone could give her a ride to Dallas.

"Lady, this is not a taxi, and besides, the president has been shot," Bob Schieffer, then a young police reporter, who later made a name for himself at CBS News, told her none too diplomatically.

"I know," she said. "They think my son is the one who shot him." Schieffer and another reporter lost no time in picking her up and giving her a ride to Dallas, while she railed about how Oswald's Russian-born wife would get sympathy, while no one would remember her and that she would probably starve.

"Do you think he did it?" A magazine writer once quoted her as saying: "Now, maybe Lee Harvey Oswald was the assassin. But does that make him a louse?"

Mrs. Oswald "later took to selling pieces of Oswald's clothing to support herself and peddled autographed business cards reading 'Marguerite Oswald, mother of Lee Harvey Oswald' to tourists near Dealey Plaza for $5," according to the *Morning News*.

She "sued one national magazine for libel because an article had referred to her son as a 'son-of-a-b . . .'" according to the *Star-Telegram*. After a lonely struggle with cancer, she died in 1981 and was buried next to her son at Shannon Rose Hill Memorial Park on Fort Worth's east side. The site is noted by a simple marker, a flat granite stone with one word only, OSWALD.

Ruby claimed he shot Oswald because he wanted to spare Kennedy's wife from having to return to Dallas to testify at Oswald's trial. His jurors were selected from a pool of 900 candidates in February. Ruby was convicted of murder with malice on March 14 and sentenced to die in the electric chair. The conviction was later overturned, and the defendant awaited a new trial.

In December 1966, Ruby was admitted to Parkland Hospital and diagnosed with terminal lung cancer. He died at Parkland, like Kennedy and Oswald, on January 3, 1967, of a blood clot in his lungs. Ruby maintained to the end that he killed Oswald "on impulse from grief and outrage."

The cell, where Oswald once sat, was part of a jail on the fifth floor of the old city hall building. The hallway where Ruby shot him remains a blank corridor between a records office and a garage. No sign tells visitors where they are walking. The Dallas City Council raised the possibility of turning the neglected Beaux Arts-style building into a museum that would make the cell and basement corridor into public monuments.

When Parkland Hospital refurbished its emergency facilities in the 1970s, the dismantled Parkland Hospital Trauma Room No.1, where Kennedy died, was relocated to a secure vault at the National Archives & Records Administration warehouse in Fort Worth. Tiles off the floor, the clock that showed the time when Kennedy died, the machine that took his blood pressure, everything was moved, to keep it out of the hands of souvenir hunters, and stored in a 30-by-30-foot room with 12-inch-thick walls, behind a steel door. It will not be accessible to the public within the foreseeable future.

In 1968, Kennedy's brother, Senator **Robert F. Kennedy** (b. 1925), was killed in Los Angeles, and black civil rights leader, **Martin Luther King, Jr.** (b. 1929), was assassinated in Memphis, Tennessee. Hundreds of books have been written about John Kennedy's assassination. Camelot was no more. America and Dallas lost their innocence and have never been the same.

Following the assassination, the building was closed to the public for 25 years. The School Book Depository, then one of two textbook distribution sites for the state, was first leased and then bought by Dallas County from Colonel Byrd for $400,000 in 1977. The museum opened on February 20, 1989, to meet a widespread desire for information about Kennedy and this tragic event. It is operated under the auspices of the Dallas County Historical Foundation, a non-profit organization established in 1983. The 9,000-square-foot (or 836-square-meter) museum takes visitors back to the 1960s, through the trip to Dallas, the assassination, and the quarter-century of investigations that followed. About 400 photos, interviews, artifacts, and displays, along with a 40-minute documentary—one of several—will help you to relive this tragedy.

The window, from which Oswald allegedly killed Kennedy, is encased in Plexiglass in the southeast corner of the museum, a few feet from where the crime was supposedly perpetrated. It was donated to the museum by Byrd's son in 1995. The window is open to the position it was that day, and empty boxes in front stand in for the original ones, which contained schoolbooks.

In 2002, a $1.8-million addition on the seventh floor doubled the facility's exhibition space to 19,000 square feet (or 1,765 square meters). Instead of focusing on the events surrounding the Kennedy assassination, the seventh floor showcases the American presidency and similar temporary exhibitions. The seventh-floor addition is also popular for corporate dinners and receptions.

"It's a really nice space but also a truly weird place to have a reception with people drinking and guffawing and making jokes," says the publisher of *D Magazine*, as quoted by the *New York Times*.

Film director Oliver Stone used the seventh floor window with the view of Dealey Plaza when he recreated the assassination for his 1991 film *JFK*.

On the sixth floor, you can see Kennedy and his wife arrive at Love Field Airport, their ride on Main Street downtown, and the unexpected conclusion that ended in a national mourning. Americans who have seen many documentaries on this subject will find the darkened museum more of a chapel to reflect than an observation point to see anything new. It is almost anticlimactic, except for the opportunity to look from the sixth floor down to the site where Kennedy was shot. This was the fourth presidential assassination in American history.

Should you look through the window, you will see streetlights and a road sign that were not there in 1963. Perhaps the biggest change outside is the oak tree with its leafy branches that have grown over Elm Street, obscuring somewhat the view that Oswald would have had of Kennedy's motorcade. The 1961 Lincoln Continental limousine in which Kennedy was assassinated is on display at the Henry Ford Museum in Dearborn, Michigan.

On some days the crowds are so thick it is uncomfortable to move around the sixth floor. Some 400,000 visit the museum every year. No original evidence is included among the exhibits; all such documents are housed at the National Archives in College Park, Maryland.

On the plaza, half a dozen self-styled conspiracy theorists peddle their crude grainy-photos newspapers on weekends and, when ticketed, complain of a government cover-up to get rid of them.

At the northeast corner of Main and Houston Streets, there stands the eight-story, 124-foot-tall (or 37.8-meter) Dallas County Criminal Courts building that was constructed between 1913 and 1915.

If you look southeast from the Sixth Floor Museum, across Elm and Houston, you will also see the 1928 Records Building, where Jack Ruby was jailed in Room 6M-35 after killing Oswald. The infamous bank robber Clyde Barrow was also held here on the sixth floor.

Dealey Plaza—once the ceremonial gateway to Dallas—was built as a Works Progress Administration project and is one of the most visited sites in the city. Many among the tens of thousands of tourists who visit the plaza and the museum are foreign nationals. Take time to walk around the plaza, which was laid out in 1935-1937 and still looks much as it did in 1963, except for the trees, which are 40 years older. The spot where the first bullet hit the president is marked with an X.

Jeffrey West (b. 1958) has been the museum director since 1993. Born in Tuscaloosa, Alabama, a licensed Baptist minister early on, he ran the Shakespeare Festival of Dallas from 1986 to 1988, then served as managing director of the Dallas Theater Center.

African-American Museum of Life & Culture, 3536 Grand Ave. at First Ave., (214) 565-9026. *NCH*. Open Tue-Thu noon-5 PM, Fri noon-9 PM, Sat 10 AM-5 PM, Sun 1 PM-5 PM. Free parking. Located in the western part of Fair Park, at the Grand Avenue entrance, near the Magnolia Lounge, two miles (or 3.2 kilometers) east of downtown Dallas.

Conceived at the now-defunct Bishop College, the 38,000-square-foot (or 3,530-square-meter), $6.5-million museum was founded in 1974 and has operated independently since 1979. It explores African-American life through exhibits and displays, including historical artifacts and arts, through four galleries. Some 350,000 people visit the museum every year. The weekly *Dallas Observer* calls it "the best place to learn about black Dallas history."

The museum's African art collection includes masks, sculptures, and textiles. Its folk art collection features works by Johnny Banks, David Butler, Bessie Harvey, Clementine Hunter, Sister Gertrude Morgan, Mose Tolliver, Willard "The Texas Kid" Watson, and George White. There is a lecture hall, community center, and a theater on the premises. This is one of only eight major African-American museums in the United States. The three-story structure was designed by Art Rogers of Dallas. Wings emanating from a central core form the shape of a cross with the limestone-covered exterior. In the lobby, a combination of glass, tile, bleached wood, and steel makes the 60-foot-high (or 18.2-meter) rotunda feel like an atrium.

After eight years of delays, the African-American Museum opened in 1993 in the same area where 66 years earlier the Hall of Negro Life had stood to celebrate black Texans' achievements and culture during the state's Centennial Celebration in 1936. It was torn down two years later to make space for a whites-only swimming pool. The Hall of Negro Life at the Texas Centennial Exposition was funded by the federal government at the urging of the Dallas Negro Chamber of Commerce. Dallas architect George L. Dahl designed the building that had a figure with broken chains sculpted by the French artist Raoul Josset, who had studied with the noted Antoine Bourdelle and also worked in New York. Thirty-two states and the District of Columbia contributed to the hall.

Age of Steam Railroad Museum, 1105 Washington Ave. at Parry Ave., (214) 428-0101, Internet www.dallasrailwaymuseum.com. *CH*, except children under three years of age. Open Wed-Sun 10 AM-5 PM; closed Mon-Tue. Limited wheelchair access. Located at Fair Park, about two miles (or 3.2 kilometers) east of downtown. There is talk of moving the museum to the West End Historic District.

The museum opened in Dallas' 1903 Houston & Texas Central

Railroad depot. It is a nonprofit, not-city-funded museum started by the DeGolyer family in 1963. Dallas' oldest train depot, which was built in 1930, is on display here, along with 32 passenger cars, freight trains, and engines from 1900 to 1950 that are exhibited behind the Centennial Hall building.

Union Pacific's 1942 Big Boy No. 4018, at 1.2 million pounds (or 544,320 kilograms) laying claim to being the world's largest steam locomotive, can also be seen. Twenty-five of the locomotives were built in 1942 to haul heavy equipment and troops over the Continental Divide during World War II. "It was the biggest, grandest, most powerful steam locomotive," says the museum's executive director. Eight Big Boys, including No. 4018, still survive. Before being retired at age 20, the 132-foot-long (or 40-meter) locomotive chugged more than a million miles. In the late 1990s, a group of Dallas film-makers wanted to rebuild Big Boy and have it star in an epic train blockbuster, but nothing came of it.

But not all are steam engines. In 2000, the museum acquired a 1942 diesel-electric locomotive donated by TXI Corp., the former Texas Industries cement company. Built by American Locomotive Co. of Schenectady, New York, in 1942, the 256,000-pound (or 116,121-ton) unit was purchased by the New York Susquehanna & Western Railway. It was one of 13 locomotives requisitioned by the War Department in 1942, when it was used in Europe as part of the emergency relief effort to Russia out of Iran. TXI purchased unit No. 8000 as war surplus and operated it at its Midlothian, Texas, cement plant for 25 years. Also in 2000, the museum acquired from a used-railway equipment dealer in Chicago an F-7 diesel locomotive built by General Motors in 1952.

Kids and adults will also enjoy a first-hand look at the luxurious 1910 Glengyle, the nation's oldest Pullman all-steel sleeper that formed part of the 1945 funeral train of President Franklin D. Roosevelt. There are other steam and early diesel-electric locomotives. You can look inside several of the trains.

The electric locomotive No. 4903, which pulled the funeral train of Sen. Robert Kennedy—who was assassinated in Los Angeles—from New York to Washington on June 8, 1968, is also on display. The museum's newest locomotive is the 1967 Santa Fe 3,600-horsepower diesel-electric engine that carried first-class passengers at 90 miles (or 144 kilometers) an hour from Chicago to Los Angeles.

An elegant twice-yearly Dinner in the Diner is held in a restored 1937 Katy Railroad dining car, an early air-conditioned Goliad, at the museum. Such cars could be seen in Billy Wilder's 1959 film *Some Like it Hot*, with Marilyn Monroe, Jack Lemmon, and Tony Curtis.

The Switchman's Corner gift shop is located in a 1905 vintage depot. The museum is owned and operated by the non-profit Southwest Railroad Historical Society.

American Museum of Miniature Arts/Dollhouse Museum of the Southwest, Sharp Gallery in the Texas Hall of State, Fair Park, (214) 969-5502, Internet www.minimuseum.org. *CH*, except children under the age of three years. Open Tue-Sat 9 AM-5 PM, Sun 1 PM-5 PM; closed Mondays. Located in Fair Park two miles (or 3.2 kilometers) east of downtown Dallas.

This is the only miniature museum of its kind in Texas. Until 1997 known as the Dollhouse Museum of the Southwest, it originally opened in 1988 in a 1920's two-story Uptown Victorian house. For lack of funding, it later moved to the West End Historic District, and in 2001 to the Texas Hall of State (see entry) at Fair Park. The museum, which once displayed ten rooms of dollhouses furnished to scale, anticipated relocating to the Children's Medical Center, north of downtown Dallas, in 2004.

The miniature arts museum strives to preserve an art form that has been practiced by craftsmen since the early Egyptian days. On exhibit are English and American dollhouses, trains, and handcrafted miniatures, and dolls of all sizes, some supposedly valued up to $1 million. Displays also include tiny houses, workplaces, streets, and cities built to scale, such as a replica of the home that Benedict Arnold (1741-1801), American Revolutionary general and traitor, bought for his bride. Or a 1939 replica of MGM's Stage 27 set for the film *Wizard of Oz*. The Biehl House, for example, was designed by Marie Biehl and built by Bill Matherson in 1969. It is furnished with 165 furniture pieces, 485 accessories, and 21 dolls, and is six feet (or 1.82 meters) tall, 48 inches (or 122 centimeters), and 28 inches (or 71 centimeters) deep. The ballroom floor has 1,300 pieces. The Georgian-style house is a partial replica of the home of John Hayes, who was ambassador to England.

You will admire antique hand-painted toy soldiers—each with historically accurate clothing and weapons—barely two inches tall, yet with all the detail in their faces and clothing, including eyebrows no thicker than a thread. Here you will find militaria dating from 300 B.C. to the present.

Biblical Arts Center, 7500 Park Ln. at Boedeker St., (214) 691-4661, Internet www.biblicalarts.org. *CH*. Open Tue-Sat 10 AM-5 PM, Sun 1 PM-5 PM; closed major holidays. Located six miles (or 9.7 kilometers) north of downtown Dallas, near the northwest corner of the NorthPark shopping center (see listing) and behind the Hillcrest Memorial Park Cemetery.

The center was founded by Dallas philanthropist Mattie Caruth Byrd (d. 1972), who did not live to see it completed. It is operated by the Miracle at Pentecost Foundation as a nondenominational, nonprofit organization and helps visitors understand the events of the Bible through contemporary artworks and ancient archeological artifacts.

The museum, which features works of art with a Biblical theme in several galleries, evokes Paul's Gate in Damascus with its limestone entrance. Highlights of the Arts Center include *Miracle at Pentecost*, a life-size mural by Torger Thompson presenting a historical interpretation of the day of Pentecost. Measuring 124-by-20 feet (or 37.8-by-6 meters), it depicts more than 200 Biblical characters. The mural is unveiled daily through light and sound presentations that take place on the half-hour. There is a life-size replica of Christ's Garden Tomb at Calvary.

The center publishes a monthly *Christianity and the Arts* magazine.

In 2000, the center canceled an exhibit of paintings by the Oklahoma-born Edward Knippers, an Episcopalian artist from Arlington, Virginia, in large part because of their Rubenesque nudity. "I'm trying to make people face their humanity in its fullness," noted the artist, who invites comparisons with Michelangelo, German romanticism, and baroque styles. "We don't come before God dressed in our Sunday best." Knippers (b. 1946) received his master of fine arts degree from the University of Tennessee.

Cavanaugh Flight Museum, Addison Airport, 4572 Claire Chennault, Addison, (972) 380-8800, www.cavanaughflightmuseum.com. *CH*, except children under five years of age. Open Mon-Sat 9 AM-5 PM, Sun 11 AM-5 PM. Located west of Addison Road and south of Westgrove Drive, less than ten minutes from the Galleria, on the grounds of the Addison Airport.

Opened in 1993, the museum consists of four hangars containing 40 vintage aircraft, including 32 that are airworthy, and covers nearly 40,000 square feet (or 3,716 square meters). Cavanaugh is entirely funded by Dallasite Jim Cavanaugh, who has made millions as the founder of Jani-King, the world's largest commercial cleaning franchise.

"In a country whose liberty often has been protected through bravery in the skies," begins a pamphlet about the museum, "in the heart of a region rich with aviation history, the Cavanaugh Flight Museum preserves and protects the flying machines that have earned the U.S.'s reputation as the leading air power in the world."

At the museum, historic warbirds, trainers, fighters, jets, and other aircraft chronicle heroes, battles, and technological advances span more than seven decades. From World War I fighting aircraft like the Sopwith Camel, to modern military jets like the fierce F4 Phantom, more than 30 aircraft fill 50,000 square feet (or 4,645 square meters). The museum offers 30-minute rides in two warbirds, the N2S-4 Stearman and the AT-6 Texan, to passengers 18 year or older.

The 360-acre (or 145-hectare) Addison Airport started out as a private dirt strip in 1952 and was sold to the town in 1976.

Connemara Sculpture Show, Connemara Conservancy Meadow, 6625 Ridgeview Circle near Tatum Dr., Allen, (214) 351-0990, Internet www.connemaraconservancy.org, e-mail connemara1@compuserve.com. *NCH*. Open daily between March and May from sunrise to sunset. Not wheelchair accessible. No bicycles or motorized vehicles are allowed, and dogs must be on leash. Located in Collin County, between Plano and Allen, northeast of downtown Dallas, west of North Central Expressway, and north of the Chase Oaks golf course.

An annual spring sculpture show was held in the 72-acre (or 29-hectare) meadow for 22 years. In 2002, artists from Texas, California, Connecticut, and Utah exhibited. The show, which attracted national attention, was temporarily suspended in 2003 because it apparently negatively affected the very land the trust is supposed to preserve.

Connemara Conservancy, a land trust founded in 1981, is one of the oldest land trusts dedicated to the preservation and protection of open spaces in North Central Texas. It relies on land donations by those who wish to protect their lands from development. About 805 square miles (or 2,201 square kilometers) of land—nearly the size of Dallas County—have been protected statewide through national and grass-roots organizations.

Frances Montgomery Williams, Connemara's benefactor and founder, died in 2002 at age 77 after a long illness. "She was a champion for a cause before we knew it was a cause," her daughter told the *Dallas Morning News*. "She knew it before we did."

Williams graduated from the Hockaday School (see listing) in Dallas, received her bachelor's degree from Vassar College, and a master's from Harvard Business School. The meadow was part of a larger family holding that was originally a gift from Williams' father to her mother in 1919.

The Conspiracy Museum, 110 South Market at Commerce Streets, (800) 535-8044 or (214) 741-3040, Internet www.conspiracymuseum.com. *CH*. Open daily 10 AM-6 PM. Located in downtown Dallas, in the historic 1912 MKT, or Katy Building, across the street from the John Kennedy Memorial (see entry), and one block farther from his assassination site. "Old Red" Courthouse and John Neely Bryan Cabin are also nearby (see entries).

A small private museum established by a retired architect, it tries to shed light on assassinations in America since 1835, including those of Abraham Lincoln, James Garfield, William McKinley, Martin Luther King, Jr, and Robert Kennedy.

It speculates that "in 1960, the Central Intelligence Agency, spawned by the cold war, changed the U.S. foreign policy in the downing of the U2 spy plane over Russia. Three years later, the CIA, with the assistance of the Mafia and the FBI, publicly murdered President John Fitzgerald Kennedy in Dealey Plaza, Dallas." The museum's Web site claims that this coup d'état established the professional war machine, "which even today controls the presidency by political assassination." Some exhibits are hand drawn. There is a bookstore on the premises, where you can also buy Who Shot JFK? shot glasses or two 6.5-mm slugs, one fired, one not.

Dallas Aquarium at Fair Park, 1462 First St. at Martin Luther King Jr. Blvd., (214) 670-8443, Internet www.dallas-zoo.org. *CH*, except for children under three years of age. Open daily all year 9 AM-4:30 PM; closed major holidays. Located at Fair Park, about two miles (or 3.2 kilometers) east of downtown Dallas.

The aquarium's original art deco building opened to the public on June 6, when the 1936 Texas Centennial Exposition was inaugurated. It was designed by architects Marion Fooshee of Weatherford and James Cheek of Hillsboro, both in Texas, who had also drafted Highland Park Village, the first self-contained shopping center in the nation. The saltwater section was added in 1964.

The aquarium shelters 400 species and 6,000 aquatic animals, including freshwater and marine fish, reptiles, amphibians, and invertebrates, making it one of the larger inland aquariums in the United States. It is part of the city's Park and Recreation Department and is managed by the Dallas Zoo (see entry).

Note the expanse of blank wall surfaces incorporating a series of alternating brick planes and recessed sculptural panels by artist Allie Tenant, who also sculpted the *Tejas Warrior* in the nearby Hall of State.

A lemon shark from the Gulf of Mexico residing in the 7,000-gallon shark tank is the top attraction. There are fish from Australia, the Pacific reef, the Caribbean and Red Seas, as well as amphibians, reptiles, and invertebrates. The five-foot (or 1.52-meter) electric eel and venomous lion fish are also on display. Your kids can watch the deadly piranhas being fed every Tuesday, Thursday, and Saturday at 2:30 PM, and sharks Wednesdays, Fridays, and Sundays at the same time.

The newest aquarium addition is also the largest exhibit: the Amazon flooded forest, a 10,500-gallon (or 39,745-liter) tank featuring some 30 species of fish found in the Amazon River, including the prehistoric-looking black armored catfish and the fearsome freshwater stingray. There are several tanks of fish from Texas fresh and saltwater areas, including giant Texas varieties of catfish, and Texas gamefish.

"Generally, the public perception of the 70-exhibit city aquarium seems to be that it is still a small, dark and musty building that cannot even really be compared to the private and more popular multistory Dallas World Aquarium & Zoological Garden [see entry]," notes the

Dallas Observer. The aquarium's budget is under $400,000 a year, about half of that generated from entry fees. The Dallas World Aquarium's budget, in comparison, is more than $1.5 million.

The American Zoo and Aquarium Association notified the Dallas Aquarium that its accreditation had not been renewed in 2001 and that the Dallas Zoo's accreditation would be tabled for one year to give the city a chance to make improvements to the facility. The problems cited were aging infrastructure and a wide range of needed repairs, not concerns about animal care. More than $1.6 million in repairs were required at both to comply with the standards.

Some 200 zoos and aquariums across the country are accredited, including the privately owned Dallas World Aquarium. The designation shows that a zoo or aquarium meets a list of specific standards, and it helps determine which facilities receive sought-after or endangered species. Accredited zoos and aquariums are reviewed every five years.

Dallas Children's Museum, 308 Valley View Center, Second level, Preston Rd. at Lyndon B. Johnson Frwy., (972) 386-4191, reservations 386-6555, Internet www.dallaschildrens.org, e-mail dcminfo@dallaschildrens.org. *CH*, except children under two years of age. Groups must have one adult for every five children. Open Mon-Fri 9 AM-6 PM, Sat 11 AM-6 PM, Sun noon-6 PM; closed Thanksgiving, Christmas, and Easter Sunday. Located north of downtown Dallas, on the northwest corner of Preston and LBJ, inside Valley View shopping center (see entry), and next to the J.C. Penney department store, the museum is designed to introduce young children to arts, crafts, science, and cultural diversity.

Established in 1998 in Inwood Village shopping center (see entry). The following year, the Meadows Foundation gave it a three-year grant and made it possible for the DCM to open six days a week. In 2000, the museum moved to its current location that encompasses 6,500 square feet (or 604 square meters) of exhibit, office, classroom, and party room space for children ages two to ten.

Among the permanent exhibits, the kids will find everything from a scorpion to a fox, courtesy of the Dallas Museum of Natural History (see entry). Presbyterian Health Care System established a hospital and community health exhibit to help children deal with their fears about doctors and hospitals, illness and injury. A Kroger grocery store, sponsored by the Quaker Oats Co., features child-size shopping carts, cash registers, and scanners, and helps kids learn about food and nutrition, as well as math skills. The Dairy Farm exhibit, sponsored by Southwest Dairy Farmers, features a Holstein cow that children can milk. The Arts District includes a center where children can create their own works using art supplies and recyclable materials. Music classes for infants, preschoolers, and their parents are taught weekly. There is also a technology center with computers.

Dallas Firefighters Museum, 3801 Parry Ave., (214) 821-1500. *NCH*. Open Wed-Sat 9 AM-4 PM, Tuesdays by appointment only. Located in Fair Park on the northwest corner of Parry Avenue and Commerce Street.

The Firefighters Museum is situated inside the Old No. 5 Hook and Ladder Co. Station, which was built in 1907 and is now a Dallas historical landmark. It contains antique horse-drawn, hand-drawn, and motor-driven fire apparatus. Also on display are antique fire helmets, fire tools, and photos.

The nearest eating facility is the Old Mill Inn, which started out as a flour mill during the 1936 Texas Centennial. The vintage stone structure is usually open 11 AM-3 PM.

Dallas Holocaust Memorial Center, 7900 Northhaven Rd. at North Central Expwy., (214) 750-4654, Internet www.dallasholocaustcenter.org. *NCH*. Open Mon-Fri 9:30 AM-4:30 PM, Sun noon-4 PM. Located in north Dallas, less than two blocks west of North Central Expressway (also known as U.S. Highway 75), on the lower level of the Aaron Jewish Community Center of Dallas, where cultural entertainment is also offered. NorthPark mall (see listing) is situated across the street.

This museum, which opened in 1984, is a tribute to the memory of the millions who perished during the Holocaust. Its origins go back to 1977, when some 200 Jewish Holocaust survivors formed an organization called Holocaust Survivors in Dallas. It was conceived by Mike Jacobs, a survivor of the Auschwitz/Birkenau death camps, along with several other Holocaust survivors. He has been a guide at the center for more than 50 years. Jacobs was born in Poland and lost his entire family—both parents, two sisters, and three brothers—at camps in Treblinka.

The displays begin on the stairway leading down to the museum. At the bottom of the stairs, you will find yourself in a shortened railroad boxcar, donated by the National Belgian Railways. It is an actual boxcar used to transport Jews and other undesirables to concentration camps. From the boxcar, you will enter the rooms filled with the pictorial evidence of horrors endured by the prisoners.

The first room contains 12 marble pillars, each engraved with the name of a camp, with all of them bound by barbed wire. The walls of the Memorial Room are inscribed with hundreds of names of Holocaust victims, survivors, and others who risked their lives to help someone.

The 4,000-square-foot (or 372-square-meter) facility was in the process of being expanded to 15,000 square feet (or 1,393 square meters) in 2003 at a cost of $2.8 million. The Holocaust center's library was to merge with two other community center libraries in a 10,000-square-foot (or 929-square-meter) addition at the building's north end. Some 35,000 school children, but fewer than 5,000 walk-ins, visit the museum each year. To increase attendance, the center considered a relocation downtown in 2003.

Elliott Dlin (b.1942), a native of Canada, who has spent 20 years at Israel's Holocaust memorial center in Jerusalem, became the Dallas center's director in 2002.

Dallas Museum of Natural History, 3535 Grand Ave. at First Ave., (214) 421-3466, Internet www.dallasdino.org. *CH.* Always free for children under 3, for adults Mondays until 1 PM. Open Mon-Sun 10 AM-5 PM. Handicapped accessible. Located in Fair Park, two miles (or 3.2 kilometers) east of downtown Dallas, the museum is situated between the African-American Museum and The Science Place (see entries). The building was designed by Mark Lemmon and Clyde H. Griesenbeck "as a monolithic, rectangular box, with little architectural detail."

In front of the museum, you will be greeted by a 13-foot-high (or 3.96-meter-high) bronze of *The Dallas Mammoth*, by Tom Tischler, whose work can be seen from Ethiopia to Switzerland. Three chrome-bumper dinosaurs are also lurking around the building. (For more details, please see the Fair Park entry in the Art in Public Places section in the VISUAL ARTS chapter.)

The museum's collection of some 280,000 items supposedly includes the largest exhibition of Texas wildlife habitats in the nation. It also boasts the first reconstructed Texas dinosaur, an interesting collection of Texas pollinating insects, and the most complete collection of mounted cats and bears in the state. There are four halls of realistic dioramas of native Texas wildlife on the ground floor, displaying Texas mammals and birds. You can see mountain lions from the Davis Mountains, pelicans fishing in the Gulf of Mexico, and a large alligator.

Upstairs are the halls of prehistoric Texas, where you can see the state's dinosaurs going back millions of years: tyrannosaurus rex, acrocanthosaurus, tenontosaurus, torosaurus, and alamosaurus. There are also the Trinity River mammoth and glyptodont from the Ice Age.

In 2001, 5,000 pounds (or 2,268 kilograms) of fossilized dinosaur bones were brought to the museum after a five-year excavation of a remote wilderness area of Big Bend National Park in west Texas. Seven giant neck bones from an alamosaurus, one of the last great dinosaurs to roam North America, were discovered in 1999. The largest vertebrae weigh 1,000 pounds (or 453 kilograms). Some Big Bend-area residents wanted the bones to stay in the park, but were overruled. First airlifted to a flatbed truck, the fossils were then ferried to Dallas, where they are to go on display sometimes in 2005. Alamosaurus was the last known sauropod in North America before all dinosaurs went extinct about 65 million years ago.

The 50,000-square-foot (or 4,645-square-meter) museum opened to the public in 1936, during the celebration of the Texas Centennial, and became a private institution in 1993. The museum is a Smithsonian Institution affiliate. Twenty-five percent of its $2.1-million annual budget comes from the city.

The museum announced plans for a new 175,000-square-foot (or 16,257-square-meter), $175-million facility that would be designed by the well-known California architect Frank O. Gehry and located in the Dallas Arts District (see entry) downtown. It would be surrounded by ten acres (or four hectares) of greenery and include interactive exhibits, a digital theater, shops, and a restaurant. Gehry, who has won the Pritzker Prize and the American Institute of Architects Gold Medal, is the architect of the Guggenheim Museum in Balboa, Spain.

The selection of Gehry, notes *D Magazine* tartly, "follows a Dallas tradition: hiring out-of-town architects with outsized reputations to build monuments to themselves with Dallas money."

Frontiers of Flight Museum, Love Field Airport, 8008 Cedar Springs Rd. at Mockingbird Lane, (214) 350-3600/1651, Internet www.flightmuseum.com, e-mail fofm@iglobal.net. *CH*. Open daily 10 AM-5 PM, Sun noon-5 PM. Located in northwest Dallas, at the city's first commercial airport, where aviator Charles Lindbergh arrived in his *Spirit of St. Louis* on September 27, 1927, just 27 days after the state's first commercial passengers service. Love Field was originally built as a Navy air base in 1917, was declared surplus two years later, and reopened for civilians in 1923.

The Metroplex played a vital role in the aviation phase of World War II. At this museum you will see displayed more than 200 aircraft models representing United States involvement in this conflict. Artifacts are mostly from the University of Texas at Dallas's Collection of Flight, one of the largest aviation archives in the nation. Models and placards describe the history of flight from Leonardo da Vinci to the Space Age.

Another display explains dirigibles, like the LZ-129 *Hindenburg*, which was 803 feet (or 244 meters) long—nearly the size of the Queen Mary ocean liner—and was filled with seven million cubic feet of hydrogen. It carried 100 passengers across the Atlantic 37 times non-stop before any airliner managed the task. The crossing time from

Frankfurt to Lakehurst, New Jersey, was three days and two nights at 77 mph. On exhibit here is the radio operator's chair from the *Hindenburg* that survived the crash at Naval Air Station Lakehurst on May 6, 1937. Also Adm. Richard Byrd's parka, and china from the German airship *Graf Zeppelin*. There are full-scale models of historically significant planes.

In the museum gift shop, you will find books, clothing, toys, and collectibles.

A board member of this museum is Paul Thayer (b. 1920), chairman and chief executive officer of the now-defunct LTV Corp. from 1970 to 1982, when it was still based in Dallas. After he left LTV, he was U.S. Deputy Secretary of Defense. Once a top-gun test pilot, who survived eight crashes, he developed macular degeneration in his eyes and has not flown since 2000.

A new, $9-million museum is planned for on Lemmon Avenue, at the eastern edge of Love Field, on land occupied by a World War II-era B-29 hangar. The hangar is to be replaced with a 100,000-square-foot (or 9,290-square-meter), three-story structure big enough to house several aircraft, a 200-seat auditorium, and an education center. Up to 60,000 visitors a year are expected in the new museum which was to be completed in 2004.

Heard Natural Science Museum & Wildlife Sanctuary, One Nature Place, McKinney; (972) 562-5566, Internet www.heardmuseum.org, e-mail heardmuseum@texoma.net. *CH*, except children under the age of two. Open Mon-Sat 9 AM-5 PM, Sun 1 PM-5 PM; closed on major holidays. Partially wheelchair accessible. Guided trail tours are available Sundays from 1:30 PM to 3:30 PM. Located northeast of downtown Dallas, one mile (or 1.6 kilometers) east of State Highway 5, on the north side of FM 1378, and on the southeastern edge of McKinney.

The museum was founded in 1967 by Miss Bessie Heard (1884-1988) an avid collector of everything from butterflies to nature prints. She inherited wealth from her father, a founder of the Heard Mercantile Co. The complex is dedicated to preserving a portion of Collin County land, with its native wildlife and vegetation, in as natural a condition as possible. The sanctuary is a haven for more than 240 species of birds, mammals, reptiles, and amphibians, as well as 150 species of wildflowers and other plants. Throughout the 289-acre (or 117-hectare) wildlife sanctuary there are three miles (or 4.8 kilometers) of nature trails, including one for wheelchairs. A 25,000-square-foot (or 2,322-square-meter) science museum and a 4,000-square-foot (or 372-square-meter) Raptor Rehabilitation Center are also on the premises. A 50-acre (or 20-hectare) wetlands features a 3,750-square-foot (or 348-square-meter) outdoor learning center with an observation deck, a floating study laboratory, and a boardwalk. Bessie Heard's collection of seashells, gems, and minerals is on display in several exhibit areas.

Before leaving McKinney, shop one of more than 100 shops and eateries that surround the old Collin County Courthouse, which dates to 1876, and is part of the town's historic district. Quite a few specialize in American and European antiques.

Heritage Farmstead Museum, 1900 West 15th St. at Pitman Dr., Plano, (972) 424-7874 or 881-0140, Internet www.heritagefarmstead.org. *CH*, except children under three years of age. Open June 1-August 1: Tue-Fri 10 AM-1 PM; August 1-May 31: Thu-Fri 10 AM-1 PM; all year: Sat Sun 1 PM-5 PM; closed Mondays and major holidays. Located 20 miles (or 32 kilometers) north of downtown Dallas if you travel on North Central Expressway (also known as U.S. Highway 75), 1.3 miles (or two kilometers) west of Expressway on 15th Street, one block east of Custer Road.

Turn-of-the-century farming on the Blackland Prairies of north Texas is captured in this four-acre (or 1.61-hectare) complex with row crops, gardens, a windmill, and an 1891 Victorian farmhouse with 12 original outbuildings. The 365-acre (or 147-hectare) farmstead was built by Hunter Farrell, a businessman from Collin County, for his wife Mary Alice and their daughter Ammie. After the Farrells' divorce in 1928, Mary Alice and her daughter retained ownership of the homeplace, which they ran as a farm until 1972. Ammie married twice, the second time for 53 years, and was known as a champion sheep breeder. Upon Ammie's death in 1972, the Plano Heritage Association was formed to preserve the home and its grounds. The Heritage Farmstead opened to the public after a $1.2-million restoration that took seven years.

The farmhouse is a good example of a late Victorian structure and retains its original colors. The smokehouse is an outbuilding illustrating how home-butchered hogs were cured. There are several barns that were used to house sheep, hogs, horses, mules, and cows. The pole barn, made of bois d'arc trees, sheltered wagons, feed, hay and equipment. A 1905 open-geared windmill helped the family to pump and store water. What was once the foreman's cottage now houses the museum offices.

Plans were afoot to transfer here an 1880s three-gabled, two-story Plano house built by John Young of cypress planks and held together by hand-forged nails. Gladys Young, his daughter, lived in it without indoor plumbing until her death in 1997 at age 94, although her executor said "she had $100,000 sitting in the bank." Her grandfather came from Illinois in 1844.

International Museum of Cultures, 7500 West Camp Wisdom Rd.,

Duncanville, (972) 708-7406, Internet www.sil.org. *CH*. Open Tue-Fri 10 AM-5 PM, Sat-Sun 1:30 PM-5 PM; closed Mondays. Located on a wooded ridge in Duncanville, near the 7,740-acre (or 3,132-hectare) Joe Pool Lake, and the Nature Center in south Dallas County. The IMC is situated in a 6,000-square-foot (or 557-square-meter) building designed by Philip Henderson of Dallas and funded in part by the Trammell Crow and Hunt families.

The museum's mission, according to its Web page, is "to be a window on indigenous people of the world and to create greater appreciation for ethnic and cultural diversity, thereby furthering mutual respect and peace between peoples."

This ethnographic museum opened in 1981 on the International Linguistics Center campus in southwest Dallas and is basing its exhibits from around the world on the research conducted by linguists, anthropologists, and translators from the Summer Institute of Linguistics (SIL).

The IMC is an anthropological museum focusing on ethnology to foster appreciation for the rich cultural diversity and creativity of indigenous, contemporary societies living in remote areas of the world. The highlights of the museum's collections stretch from Papua New Guinea in the South Pacific to the jungles of Ecuador and Peru. You can see early Quichua pottery from Amazonian Ecuador and hear a story of a young Shipibo bilingual educator from Amazonian Peru.

SIL was founded in 1934 in Sulphur Springs, Arkansas, to apply linguistics to the problems of understanding unwritten languages and translating the Bible into those languages. SIL became affiliated with the University of Texas at Arlington in 1972. In the early 1980s, the SIL organization worked in 30 countries with more than 5,000 workers. By the mid-1980s, the New Testament had been translated into 221 languages. SIL has been recognized internationally, including by the UNESCO.

A gift shop, selling books and music, wood and leather objects, and ethnic jewelry, and a cafeteria are also on the premises.

Interurban Railway Station Museum, 901 East 15th St., Plano, (972) 941-7250/2117, Internet www.planoparks.org. *NCH*. Open Mon-Fri 10 AM-2 PM, Saturdays noon-5 PM. Guided tours are available. Located in downtown Plano in a building that served as a primary stop on the Texas Electric Railway line from Denison to Dallas.

The Interurban Museum is situated inside one of the original electric cars that ran on the tracks through Plano, beginning in 1908, with the last run in 1948. The station remained closed until 1990, when a complete restoration of the building took place. Exhibits placed inside the former railway Car 360 tell part of the Interurban story. The museum is sponsored by the City of Plano.

J. C. Penney Museum, Legacy Park, 6501 Legacy Dr. at Dallas North Tollway, Plano, (972) 431-TOUR or (972) 431-1000. *NCH*. Open Mon-Fri 9 AM-4 PM. Located inside the J.C. Penney corporate headquarters, north of downtown Dallas.

The museum tells the story of the national department store that was founded by James Cash Penney. It features a recreated first shop that Penney opened in Kennemore, Wyoming, in 1902 and called the Golden Rule Store. A Penney Museum & Boyhood Home is located in Hamilton, Missouri.

MADI Museum & Gallery, Kilgore Law Center, 3109 Carlisle St. at Bowen St., Uptown, Dallas, (214) 855-7802, Internet www.madimuseum.com. Open Tue-Wed & Fri-Sat 11 AM-5 PM, Thu 11 AM-8 PM, Sun 1 PM-5 PM; closed Mondays. *NCH*. Located north of downtown Dallas.

The MADI was founded in 2003 by Highland Park natives Bill and Dorothy Masterson. They became acquainted with MADI art in the early 1990s while visiting the home of the Uruguay-born Florida resident and artist Volf Roitman, who is now the museum's artistic and visual director. More than two dozen other art galleries are located in Uptown.

This is believed to be the world's first permanent museum entirely dedicated to the MADI art movement, which includes visual art, poetry, and music, and is noted for its playful, nonrepresentational approach. Here you will find moveable pieces on wood, globes filled with floating shapes, and irregularly shaped paintings.

MADI (pronounced mahDEE) was founded in Argentina in 1946, during the rule of Juan Peron, by artist Carmelo Arden-Quin "as a protest against the government control of the arts in Buenos Aires." After the artist moved to Paris, the movement—which now consists of about 70 sculptors, painters, architects, and musicians around the world, most still alive—spread to Europe. Counting some 80 artists worldwide, the movement encompasses paintings and sculptures, at times combining the two together with poetry and music. The MADI style is distinguished by polygonal forms, contoured surfaces, and asymmetrical geometric influences. One observer calls it "an energetic form of modern art featuring bright colors and geometric shapes." A collection of MADI art is on display near Milan, Italy, and there is a traveling exhibition based in Hungary. A museum in the process of being built in Maubeuge, France, also has a sizeable MADI collection.

The law firm of Kilgore & Kilgore, a "boutique litigation firm" of which Bill Masterson is a partner, occupies the second floor of the Kilgore Law Center. Roitman created the two-story building's red, blue, green, yellow, and silver laser steel cut-outs on the facade of the 1970s building.

"Housing a serious law firm in a wild-and-wacky building isn't without some risks," the *Dallas Business Journal* quoted one Kilgore partner, who cheerfully acknowledged, "to me it's just a marketing opportunity," and "a way to distinguish ourselves from the myriad of other law firms out there."

Museum of Dallas County History, "Old Red" Courthouse, Second Floor, Dallas County Historical Plaza, 100 South Houston Street, between Main and Commerce Sts. *CH*. Located just west of the John F. Kennedy Memorial and across from Main Street and a replica of the John Neely Bryan Cabin (see listings). The Dallas Convention & Visitors Bureau is situated on the courthouse's ground floor.

The most prominent structure in the two-square-block Dallas County Historic Plaza, the courthouse was built 1890-1892 in a Romanesque Revival-style. Its cornerstone was laid on the property that Dallas founder John Neely Bryan had donated in 1850. The 16,000-square-foot (or 1,486-square-meter), $38-million museum of Dallas County history was to occupy the entire second floor of the historic courthouse and was slated to open in 2004. It was to tell the story of the entire county, which includes cities such as Carrollton, Farmers Branch, and Lancaster. Some of the artifacts were to come from the Dallas Historical Society.

The museum's designer is Gallagher and Associates of Washington, D.C., the firm that created the Museum of Jewish Heritage in New York City, and a hall of African history and culture at the Smithsonian Institution.

National Scouting Museum, 1329 West Walnut Hill Lane at North MacArthur Blvd., Irving, (800) 303-3047 or (972) 580-2100, Internet www.bsamuseum.org. *CH*. Open Tue-Wed & Fri 10 AM-5 PM, Thu & Sat 10 AM-7 PM, Sun 1 PM-5 PM. Located northwest of downtown Dallas, east of the D/FW International Airport, and across the street from the Boy Scouts of America headquarters. Previously based in Murray, Kentucky, this hands-on museum relocated to Irving, its national headquarters, in 2002 for lack of visitors.

The 50,000-square-foot (or 4,645-square-meter) museum is situated in a renovated building that formerly housed the Boy Scouts business operations. It documents the history of an organization that was founded in 1910 and has touched the lives of more than 100 million American children and adults.

There is a knot-tying wall, a virtual-reality mountainside rescue area, a six-lane Pinewood Derby racetrack, a stockade fort, an interactive Eagle Scout display, and full-size replicas of campsites from 1910, the 1950s, and today.

The museum also features a gallery of paintings by American artist Norman Rockwell (1894-1978), whose first paid job was as an illustrator for *Boys' Life*, a monthly publication of the Boy Scouts, in 1913. The museum owns 61 original Rockwell works, the largest such collection anywhere. It includes 40 oil paintings and 21 charcoal and pencil drawings. The museum's Rockwell holdings are second only to those of the Rockwell Museum in Stockbridge, Massachusetts.

The Science Place & IMAX Theater, 1318 Second Ave., (214) 428-5555, Internet www.scienceplace.org. *CH*. Open Mon-Sat 9:30 AM-5:30 PM, Sun noon-5:30 PM. Cafe open Tue-Fri 10 AM-2:30 PM, Sat-Sun 10:30 AM-4:30 PM. Located in Fair Park, about two miles (or 3.2 kilometers) east of downtown Dallas, near Robert B. Cullum Boulevard, named after the Dallas civic leader and founder of the Tom Thumb grocery chain. Except during the State Fair of Texas there is free parking in the area.

(Cullum, former Dallas mayor Earle Cabell, and billionaire philanthropist Robert Dedman are all alumni of the 80-year-old North Dallas High School, at North Haskell Ave and McKinney, designed by architect William B. Ittner of St. Louis.)

Established in 1946 as the Dallas Health Museum, it was the first to be devoted entirely to public health education. The museum opened in a 10,000-square-foot (or 929-square-meter) space leased from the Dallas Park Department in 1947.

Its name was changed to Dallas Health and Science Museum in 1958 and The Science Place in 1981. The *Dallas Business Journal* claims it is the oldest continuously operating science museum in the Southwest. The Science Place attracts up to 800,000 visitors annually.

Housed in the building that until 1983 had been occupied by the Dallas Museum of Fine Arts, The Science Place has been an attraction for children of all ages for more than three decades. *Dallas Child* magazine named it the "best museum for families." There are permanent and special exhibits, about whales or the Etruscans, that will always challenge your intellect.

The museum is dependent on admission fees for 70 percent of its income. Less than 10 percent of its funding comes from the city of Dallas. The remainder is coaxed from corporations, such as the $1-million gift from Plano-based Electronic Data Systems Corp. (EDS), and individual sponsors.

Kid's Place is of particular interest to children up to age seven. They can try out computers or make music on a walk-on piano. Since 1994, it also includes a $20-million, 60,000-square-foot (or 5,574-square-meter) addition with a specially built surround-sound **Omni Theater,** where kids can study technology displays.

The Planetarium, which is included in the Science Place admission price, is housed on First Street at the foot of the Texas Star Ferris wheel. Both the Science Place and the Planetarium are wheelchair accessible.

The headline event in 1996 at Fair Park was the summer opening of the **Texas Instruments Founders IMAX Theater,** also made possible in part by the EDS. The 329-seat theater has a 79-foot (or 24-meter) domed ceiling and a starfield floor inlaid with planets, constellations, and Halley's Comet. You need a separate ticket for the IMAX theater.

Another IMAX theater is located at **Cinemark 17 IMAX,** 11819 Webb Chapel Rd. at Lyndon B. Johnson Frwy., (972) 888-2629, Internet www.cinemark.com. It has stadium seating for 256, a food court, and a video arcade.

Telephone Pioneer Museum of Texas, One Bell Plaza/2nd Floor, 208 South Akard St. at Commerce St., (214) 464-4359. *NC*. Open Mon-Fri 9:30 AM-3:30 PM. Wheelchair accessible. Call ahead for a guided tour by a Bell volunteer or you may find a locked door. Located downtown, across the street from the Adolphus Hotel and the Magnolia Building (see entries). Once you enter the lobby of the One Bell Plaza building, look for the elevators that go to the museum's second floor only.

Bell Plaza is a collection of "monotonous, volumetric, travertine-clad towers" comprising the regional headquarters of the former Southwestern Bell telephone company, now SBC Communications, around a landscaped public plaza accented with art.

If you are interested in the telephone history of Texas, this is the place to go. The museum was renovated in 2003. Through the audio-visual displays, you will learn the story of the telephone from its Alexander Graham Bell beginnings until today.

The newly invented telephone was first demonstrated at the Centennial Exposition at Philadelphia in 1876. Dallas was the first Texas city to have an operating telephone in 1879. The first switchboard here opened in June 1881 with 38 subscribers. Phone numbers were one and two digits long. By 1898 the Dallas system counted 4,000 subscribers.

At 1312 ½ Commerce Street, where one of the SBC Communications buildings is situated today, there once stood the Carousel Club, with "burlesque girls," owned by Jack Ruby, who shot Lee Harvey Oswald after the John F. Kennedy assassination in 1963.

Trammell & Margaret Crow Collection of Asian Art, 2010 Flora St., between Harwood and Olive, (214) 979-6430, Internet www.crowcollection.com, e-mail education@crowcollection.org. *NCH*. Open Tue-Sun 11 AM-6 PM, Thu until 9 PM. Wheelchair accessible. Visiting scholars, audio tours, and monthly lectures are scheduled. Located downtown across the street from the Dallas Museum of Art and the Nasher Sculpture Center, on the north side of the Trammell Crow Center, with its outdoor sculpture collection, and across the street from the Belo Mansion (please see individual entries).

In 1999, a pavilion on the Flora Street side of the Trammell Crow Center, measuring 12,000 square feet (or 1,114 square meters), was reconstructed into a permanent three-level display. Shown are more than 500 Asian art objects of metal and stone drawn from a collection of more than 7,000 that Trammell Crow and his wife Margaret amassed over 30 years. She acknowledged in 2002 that her husband "has Alzheimer's and has had it for several years."

The artworks date from 3500 B.C. to 1900 and cover a wide geographic expanse, from Chinese lacquers, ivory, and jade to Indian medieval sculpture, from Mogul architecture to Japanese literati painting and Khmer sculpture. Most objects were displayed in Crow family homes, offices, and commercial properties, but can now be seen free of charge.

Women's Museum, Peter Wolf Building, 3800 Parry Ave. at Haskell, (214) 915-0860, Internet www.thewomensmuseum.org, e-mail 411@thewomensmuseum.org. *CH*, except children under five years. Open Tue-Sat 10 AM-5 PM, Sun noon-5 PM; closed Mondays and major holidays. Located in the northwest corner of Fair Park, a 277-acre (or 112-hectare) cultural and entertainment complex owned by the city of Dallas, two miles (or 3.2 kilometers) east of downtown Dallas. This is Fair Park's ninth museum. (For the other eight, please see listings under Fair Park.) The Meridian Room restaurant and bar, which serves Sunday brunch, is practically across the street.

In 1997 the mayor of Dallas announced plans for a $30-million privately funded Women's Museum: An Institute for the Future. SBC Communications contributed $10 million, with additional one-million-dollar contributions from Johnson & Johnson, State Farm, and Lucent Technologies.

Hillary Rodham Clinton and Texas Republican Senator Kay Bailey Hutchison were among the first to join the museum's sponsors. "Women are poised for greatness in the new millennium," said former Texas governor Anne Richards (b. 1934), "This is not just about what others think of us, but how we think of ourselves."

When you walk in the door you will receive a Mentor Phone as a tour guide. Designed for the museum by Lucent Technologies, the hand-held phones allow visitors to enter an exhibit number on the keypad and hear a presentation about the corresponding exhibit. Presentations are given in both English and Spanish. Vistors can also leave a voice message for the museum on the phone.

The 70,000-square-foot (or 6,503-square-meter) three-story museum, which was finished in the fall of 2000, is affiliated with the Smithsonian Institution in Washington, D.C. Attendance is spotty, and were it not for schools it probably would not exceed 100,000 visitors a year. With the help of high-technology gadgetry, visitors can participate in a suffragist march or hold "virtual reality" conversations with Cleoparta and Joan of Arc.

Museum inductees also include novelist Pearl S. Buck, Polish-French chemist Marie Curie, vice-presidential candidate Geraldine Ferraro, actress Katharine Hepburn, former congresswoman Barbara Jordan, anthropologist Margaret Mead, Supreme Court justice Sandra Day O'Connor, painter Georgia O'Keeffe, astronaut Sally Ride, former First Lady Eleanor Roosevelt, sportswoman Wilma Rudolph, feminist Gloria Steinem, and television host Oprah Winfrey.

In the Poetry and Music Listening Room, one of 17 permanent exhibits on two levels, you can touch a screen to select one of about 70 poets, composers, and musicians, and hear a brief biography. The Pathways to Health exhibit, financed by the Johnson & Johnson pharmaceutical giant, makes it possible to explore women's health issues. Presentations give a historical look at women's health and explore medical advancements and the future of women's health.

You will learn at the museum that it was Grace Murray Hopper who developed the COBOL computer language and that women invented refrigeration, the windshield wiper, Liquid Paper, and the square-bottom paper sack used in grocery stores. In the entertainment field, there is Lucy Ricardo, Carol Burnett, and Phyllis Diller. Actress Farah Fawcett is still fetching in her swimsuit poster that sold millions of copies.

"The strength of the Women's Museum is that it reveals the wide variety of ways women have taken their fates into their own hands," observes the *San Antonio Express-News*, adding that "a dramatic cantilevered staircase to the second level is the structure's design tour de force."

But even before its first anniversary, a well-compensated New York feminist who for two years researched and wrote much of the text that appears in the museum, criticized the museum for omitting mention of unconventional feminists and faulted museum officials for deleting references to abortion. In an article in *Ms*. magazine she claims "the directive was to 'avoid male-bashing.'" The museum's executive director agreed that some scripts were edited because "some of the feminist men associated with the museum found them offensive," according to the *Dallas Morning News*.

The two-story museum is housed in one of the oldest buildings at Fair Park. Designed by architect C. D. Hill, it was built in 1910 and had a facade added in 1936 for the Texas Centennial Exhibition marking the 100th anniversary of Texas' independence from Mexico. Erected as Dallas' first municipal coliseum, the building was constructed by the State Fair mostly for livestock shows. It was used as a cattle auction barn by day and an opera house at night.

In 1935, the Centennial Exposition's architect George Dahl renovated the coliseum into the exposition's Hall of Administration Building. Only the building shell was preserved for the Women's Museum.

The "kitschy" 20-foot-tall (or six-meter) statue of a woman rising from a stylized saguaro cactus, titled *The Spirit of the Centennial*, is by Frenchman Raoul Jean Josset (1892-1957), who created several other artworks at Fair Park. The Tours, France-born Josset, who during the First World War had served as an interpreter for the American forces in France, died at Dallas' Baylor Hospital. It was this statue that seized the attention of Dallas businesswoman Cathy Bonner as she scouted locations to celebrate the lives of women in America.

ART IN PUBLIC PLACES

Estimates have it that there are as many as 200 pieces of art on public display in Dallas, not an extraordinary number when you consider that almost as many could be seen in Loveland, Colorado, which has a population of only 40,000, but probably more than many would expect to find in any Texas city.

A handsome if not very durable walking tour map of Dallas sculpture is published by the Dallas Foundation and is available by calling (214) 741-9898. You can also access it on their Web site, www.dallasfoundation.org. It is available at the Dallas Visitor Center in the "Old Red" Courthouse, and in the lobby of the 17-story Belo Corporation executive offices, both downtown.

Dallas/Fort Worth International Airport –

The $560-million Terminal D at D/FW, expected to be completed by 2005, will include a "world-class art collection to impress airport visitors and show them that they have reached a destination like no other," according to the *Fort Worth Star-Telegram*.

A $6-million allowance for art has been set aside in the airport budget and 24 artists—most of them from north Texas—were selected in 2002. Individual contracts range from $60,000 to $500,000. Unlike the cramped, existing terminals that have little artwork, Terminal D's "crystal palace" design will feature high ceilings with 70-foot (or 21-meter) walls as a gigantic showroom.

The 20-foot (or six-meter) cast bronze wishbone by sculptor and painter Terry Allen of Santa Fe, New Mexico, will go in the middle of the North Ticket Hall. His works have been exhibited from Boston to Bangkok, and he has been awarded several public commissions for sculptures.

"The wishbone could be to D/FW Airport what the Blarney Stone is to Ireland, the omamori is to Japan or the mezuza is to Jewish culture," observes the *Star-Telegram*.

In the South Ticket Hall, 20-foot-tall (or six-meter) metal-and-glass bluebonnets, designed by Arlington artist Celia Munoz , were to hang from the ceiling like chandeliers. But before the project was completed, D/FW officials withdrew the $200,000 commission amid concerns that she copied a similar art project at the Robert Mueler Municipal Airport in Austin, Texas, which closed in 1999, and whose art no longer exists except in photographs.

D/FW instead commissioned Anitra Blayton of Fort Worth to create a 16-foot (or 4.8-meter) cast bronze, acrylic, and terra cotta sculpture, titled *Applause*, for the south ticket entrance hall.

Fort Worth painter Dennis Blagg's acrylic rendition of Big Bend will be 14 feet (or 4.2 meters) high and 42 feet (or 12.8 meters) across and will cover a terminal wall. His work will be one of the largest he has ever undertaken.

Downtown

On the **Dallas City Hall** plaza, at 1500 Marilla Street, there is a three-piece, typically massive 16-foot-high (or 4.87-meter) bronze sculpture by Henry Moore (1898-1986), supposedly the largest he ever created. Commissioned in 1976 at a cost of $450,000 and titled *The Dallas Piece*, it weighs 13 tons. Art patron W. R. Hawn funded the pieces in memory of his wife Mildred.

Cast in England, the sculpture was assembled in a hangar at Love Field Airport, and dedicated on December 6, 1978. Until restored by a team of conservators from the Henry Moore Foundation in the United Kingdom in 1996, the work "was covered with graffiti and used by homeless men as a urinal."

The Dallas Piece is an enlarged, reconfigured version of an earlier Moore work, *Three Piece Sculpture: Vertebrae.*

In the **Dallas City Hall** lobby, you will find a larger-than-life statue of the former mayor *John Erik Jonsson* (1901-1995), which sculptor Barvo Walker, a Highland Park resident, created in 1994. Born in New

Orleans, Walker graduated from the Baylor College of Dentistry in 1960, but could not warm up to pulling teeth. Initially a portrait painter and book illustrator, he never took formal lessons in sculpting, but learned by looking at masterpieces in Italy, particularly by his favorite sculptor, Giovanni Lorenzo Bernini (1562-1629), who was born in Naples.

(For details about the sculptural ensemble, titled *Trailing Longhorns*, by Glen Rose sculptor Robert Summers, please see entry Pioneer Plaza & Cemetery in the SIGHTS & ATTRACTIONS chapter.)

At the **Dallas Convention Center,** near the bronze longhorns, *Lightstream*, an 800-foot-long (or 243-meter) work installed in 2003 by Portland, Oregon-sculptor Ed Carpenter will be seen in the north lobby. Suspended not quite parallel to the ceiling are hundreds of white metal tubes encasing thousands of small individual lights. The lights shine through and reflect from strips of tinted glass attached at various angles. They are computer-programmed to go on and off in sequence. The artist's other work is on display in Alaska, California, Colorado, Florida, Illinois, Minnesota, Wisconsin, and Japan.

There is a 1996 abstract steel sculpture, *Steel Wave*, by Tom Orr on the plaza in front of the 17-story 1985 **Belo Building,** at 400 South Record Street, across Young Street from the WFAA (Channel 8) television studios, a Belo station. A mural from 1949 by Perry Nichols and his assistants is on display inside the lobby. In 1997, New York artist Richard Haas installed two new murals, continuing the Belo story.

Next to the Belo tower, there is **Lubben Plaza,** a one-block park developed by Belo in 1985 to commemorate the centennial of the Belo daily, the *Dallas Morning News*. There are monumental abstract sculptures by Linnea Glatt of Dallas, Jesus Bautista Moroles of Rockport, Texas, and George Smith of Houston, on the plaza. Glatt's 1992 *Harrow* is a motorized steel cone that turns on a circular track completing one revolution every 24 hours.

At the **Dallas Public Library,** a 1971 suite of four panel serigraphs on mirror-coated Plexiglas, titled *Star Quarters, I-IV,* by Robert Rauschenberg (b. 1925), can be seen on the landing of the stairway to the second floor. For more of his work visit also the Dallas Museum of Art (see entry). On the library's third floor there is *Morning News*, a 1979 bronze sculpture by the British artist Harry Marinsky. A 1982 relief print, titled *TR-16*, by the German Juergen Strunck will be found on the fourth floor, along with *Music Stand*, a 1956 wooden piece by Frank Lloyd Wright. Other works are scattered throughout the library.

In the main lobby you can see *Square Forms with Circle*, a 1963 bronze abstract sculpture by the British artist Barbara Hepworth, which was unveiled the year after the library opened. Other Hepworths are on exhibit in the sculpture garden of the Dallas Museum of Art (see entry).

(For information about a 1776 copy of the Declaration of Independence, Shakespeare's 1632 *First Folio of Comedies, Histories & Tragedies*, Frank Reaugh's 1883 pastel *Scene on the Brazos*, a Babylonian clay tablet, a 1493 *Nurenberg Chronicle*, a 1450 Catholic prayer book, and Navajo rugs, please see the listing Dallas Public Library.)

Across the street from **Thanksgiving Square** and former LTV Building (see entries), on TXU Plaza's narrow stone courtyard, between Bryan, Akard, and Federal Streets, you can see the *Four Chromatic Gates* (1984), an abstract aluminum sculpture painted in red, white, blue, and yellow, by the Austrian-American architect Herbert Bayer. You can enter from Bryan or Federal Streets.

The original 49-story, 629-foot (or 191-meter) **Energy Plaza Building,** constructed for the Atlantic Richfield Co., and now occupied by TXU Corporation/Oncor Group, was designed by I. M. Pei's partner Henry Cobb and built in 1983.

Overlooking Thanksgiving Square from the Pacific Avenue side of the Thanksgiving Tower (see entry), you will find Gerald Balciar's *Forever Eagles*, a copper-colored bronze eagle that is about as relevant as the statue of Charlie Brown in Santa Rosa, California. "Those of us who prefer more provocative art shouldn't forget that there's a place for the schlock that some people think is art," says Minnesota sculptor Welles Emerson.

Just east of the **Wilson Building,** across from Neiman Marcus, on the Stone Place pedestrian walkway between Elm and Main Streets, is a stylized life-size bronze, titled *Lot's Wife*, which was created in 1965 by the Belgian sculptor Mark Macken.

Until the 1960s, the thoroughfare was called Stone Street. Two historic structures on Stone Place, one of them the F. W. Woolworth Building from the 1920s, were restored as a retail and restaurant complex named Stone Street Gardens.

While you are near the famed **Tolbert's Texas Chili Parlor** (see entry), at the corner of St. Paul and Bryan Streets and diagonally across from the U.S. Post Office Building, catch the sight of Dimitri Hadzi's massive granite sculpture, *Bishop's Triad*, on the St. Paul Street side of the tower, and across the street from the Republic Towers, one of the ten largest office complexes in the city.

Tolbert's son, also Frank X. Tolbert (b. 1945), is now a well-known painter living in Galveston, south Texas. His work can be seen at the Gerald Peters Art gallery (see entry). His wife, photographer Ann

Stautberg (b. 1954), exhibits at Dallas' Barry Whistler gallery (see entry) in Deep Ellum.

On the southwest corner of the 40-story **Bryan Tower,** at 2001 Bryan St., is an arresting 11-foot-high (or 3.35-meter) bronze sculpture, titled *Pegasus and Man,* created by the Swedish-born artist Carl Milles, who lived in France and who became an American citizen in the 1940s. Shipped from Stockholm, it was installed in 1972. Milles knew and was influenced by Rodin.

Across the street from here and in front of the 36-story, 483-foot (or 147-meter) **Harwood Center,** also on the corner of Bryan and Harwood Streets, you will find a 22-foot (or 6.7-meter) abstract *Red Twist,* created in wine-red Turkish marble by the American artist Walter Dusenberry specifically for this location.

On the Olive Street side of Bryan Tower is J. Seward Johnson's 1983 life-size bronze, titled *Aftermath.* Johnson, who began his artistic career as a painter, is a grandson of one of the founders of the pharmaceutical giant Johnson & Johnson. A similar Johnson bronze, *The Right Light,* depicting a painter is located on Flora Street, between the the Nasher Sculpture Center and the Crow Collection of Asian Art (see entries). And two blocks southeast of here, on Olive Street, just south of Ross Avenue, behind the Northern Trust Bank and across the street from San Jacinto Tower, there is a Johnson bronze of an elderly woman knitting on the bench, titled *Getting Involved.* Still another Johnson bronze of a policeman issuing a traffic ticket, titled *Time's Up* (1984), will be found in front of the Barnes & Noble bookstore in Lincoln Center, across Northwest Highway from NorthPark Mall (see entry).

Displayed on the north side of the 1980 **KPMG Centre** (formerly Maxus Energy Tower), and the original home of the Diamond Shamrock energy company, at 717 North Harwood and San Jacinto Streets, is a 13-foot-high (or 3.96-meter) abstract sculpture, *Bear Mountain Red* (1982). It was carved from a 12 1/2-ton block of sunset-red Texas granite by New York native Alice Maynadier Bateman (b. 1944) in her Fort Worth studio. Maxus Energy Corp. became part of a Spanish-Argentine company in 1999.

Located across the street from the KPMG Centre, in front of its parking garage, is Anna Debska's 1980 steel sculpture *Colts in Motion.* Real estate developer Trammell Crow commissioned several sculptures from her and arranged for Debska to come from Warsaw, Poland, and work in Dallas for several months in 1979.

Inside **Plaza of the Americas,** at North Pearl, San Jacinto, and Bryan Streets, you can see a larger-than-life bronze of a female in flowing robe,

On the southwest corner of Bryan Tower downtown is this arresting 11-foot-high bronze sculpture, entitled Man and Pegasus, *created by the Swedish-born Carl Milles, who became an American in the 1940s. Shipped from Stockholm, it was installed in 1972.* (Photo by Yves Gerem)

sculpted by Richard McDermott Miller in 1992, overlooking the ice skating rink.There are two classical-style 12-foot (or 3.65-meter) white-marble female figures at the entrance to each of the two Plaza of the Americas office towers, created by the Transylvanian-born artist Marton Varo, who also authored the 48-foot (or 14.6-meter) angels on the facade of the $65-million Bass Performance Hall in downtown Fort Worth.

Internationally known for his draped female figures, angels, and cubes with drapery fragments, Varo was born and brought up in a frontier region which was then Hungarian territory, but is now part of Romania. He studied art at the Ion Andresccu School of Fine Arts in Cluj, Romania. A Fullbright Scholarship made it possible for him to come to the United States in 1988. His other works are on display in Brea and Palm Desert, both in California, as well as in Greece, Holland, and Norway.

On the **Cancer Survivor Plaza,** across the street from Plaza of the Americas, at Pearl and Bryan Streets, you will find five life-size bronze figures walking tentatively into a squared-off coil that represents cancer treatment. At the other end of the coil, a trio of smiling survivors emerges. The design was the work of Mexican sculptor Victor Salmones, who was found to have cancer two weeks after finishing the sculpture, and died shortly afterward.

At Pearl and Live Oak Streets, there is *Portal Park Piece* by Robert Irwin, at **John W. Carpenter Plaza,** 2200 Pacific Avenue.

(For details about a sculpture titled *John William Carpenter*, by Robert Berks, please see entry Adam's Mark Hotel in the LODGING chapter.)

Nearby, on Commerce Street, between Central Expressway and Good-Latimer, there is **Julius Schepps Park** with a nine-foot (or 2.74-meter) bronze sculpture of citizen Schepps. Created by Michael Pavlovsky, the sculpture was dedicated in 2002 by Dallas Mayor Laura Miller. Pavlovsky is also on exhibit at the Texas Sculpture Garden (see entry) in Frisco.

Schepps (1895-1971) was one of Dallas' most prominent Jewish civic leaders. He started Schepps Brewing Co. in 1934 and Schepps Wholesale Liquors the following year. He attended Texas A & M on a basketball scholarship, but had to withdraw after a few weeks, when it came to light that he had no high school diploma.

In front of the **Morton H. Meyerson Symphony Center** in the Arts District, at 2301 Flora Street, you can see two 15-foot-high (or 4.57-meter) oxidized iron abstract, 73-ton elements, titled *De Musica* (1989), which were created by the leading Spanish sculptor Eduardo Chillida, who died in 2002 at age 78. The artist attended the sculpture's dedication. A longtime resident of the northern Spanish coast near San Sebastian, Chillida yearned for peace in his beloved, violence-ridden Basque region through such monumental works as *The Comb of the Winds*, displayed on a ridge overlooking the ocean at San Sebastian. His other works are on display in Barcelona, Berlin, Frankfurt, and Paris. Falling prey to Alzheimer's disease, his 50-year career ended in 1999.

Also in the symphony center garden is an abstract bronze, titled *Les Ondines*, by the French artist Henri Laurens (1885-1954), whose bronze *Amphion* is on display in the Dallas Museum of Art sculpture garden.You will also find there the four-foot-high (or 1.21-meter) bronze *Sacrifice III*, by the French-American sculptor Jacques Lipchitz (1891-1973), whose even more modernistic *La Joie de Vivre* is on display at the Meadows Museum on the Southern Methodist University campus.

The most recent addition occupies a grassy lot north of the Meyerson Center, on the corner of Pearl Street and Woodall Rodgers Freeway. In the fall of 2002, the celebrated American sculptor Mark di Suvero came to Dallas to oversee the installation of his 60-foot-tall (or 18.2-meter) piece, titled *Proverb*, which alludes to a metronome.

The bright-red I-beam sculpture is on loan from the artist for at least three years as part of a collaboration between the Nasher Sculpture Center nearby, whose owner arranged the loan, and the Dallas Symphony Orchestra. Nasher himself owns a couple of this artist's works.

This is di Suvero's second big sculpture downtown. The Dallas Museum of Art owns an I-beam construction, titled *Ave*, from 1973, which sits in front of the Ross Avenue museum entrance downtown. One museum director describes his work as part engineering, part abstraction, and part metaphor.

The son of an Italian naval officer, di Suvero (b.1933) was born in Shanghai, China, and raised in San Francisco. He moved to New York in the late 1950s and began creating his open I-beam constructions some ten years later. In 1975, di Suvero became the first artist to have a solo show in the Tuileries Gardens at the Louvre in Paris. Venice honored him in 1995.

Less than a block northeast of the **Majestic Theatre,** which is located at 1925 Elm St., in the tiny traffic island in the 2000 block of Pacific Avenue, and next to DART's east transfer center, you can see a 12-foot-high (or 3.65-meter) 1968 abstract cast aluminum sculpture, titled *Astral Flower*, by the Spanish artist Jose Luis Sanchez.

The art of a hundred artists was considered before five were selected to exhibit on the plaza at the **Bank of America/NationsBank Building,** the city's tallest, at 901 Main Street at Griffin and Elm. *Venture*, a 38-foot-high (or 11.58-meter) steel sculpture in front of the building was created in 1985 by the Kiev-born American painter and sculptor Alexander Liberman (1912-1999). Born to a wealthy timber merchant, his comfortable life was thrown asunder by the 1917 Russian Revolution. His colossal abstract works were often constructed from discarded tank drums, boiler heads, giant pipes, and steel beams. His work is on display at the Smithsonian American Art Museum.

Airscape Trio, created in 1985 by William Martin, is a focal point art piece in the lobby. Four larger-than-life-size frogs, titled *The Quorum*, created in 1985 by the Omaha, Nebraska, native John Kearney from chromium-plated automobile bumpers, sit in the Bank of America reflecting pond. Born in 1924, he is one of the founders of the Contemporary Art Workshop in Chicago, whose director is Lynn, his wife for more than 50 years.

Next to them is Michael Todd's 1985 *Sunami*, an overgrown daddy longlegs spider made of steel and dancing to water sounds. The 1985 fabric sculptures called *Fanfare*, by Ina Kozel, were modeled after techniques taught by Japanese kimono makers. The Lithuanian-born resident of Oakland, California, studied wax painting in Kyoto, Japan. Her vintage art-to-wear pieces were sold at Barney's clothing store in New York for five-figure sums.

At **One Bell Plaza,** 208 South Akard St., you can see *Neon for Southwestern Bell*, a multicolored neon tubing, created in 1984 by Stephen Antonakos (b. 1926), an American artist born in a Lakonia mountain village in Greece in 1926. It is part of a landscaped courtyard, where a man-made pool of water flows down a terraced slope.

Antonakos immigrated to New York City, where he lives and works, when four years old. One of his earliest exhibitions took place in 1970 in Fort Worth. His permanent installations are also located in the San Antonio, Texas, Public Library, at the University of Dijon, France, in Frankfurt, Germany, and in Tokyo, Japan.

Nearby are *Two Open Rectangles Horizontal*, a 20-foot-high (or six-meter) stainless steel sculpture created in 1984 by New York painter and kinetic artist George Rickey. Born in South Bend, Indiana, in 1907, he grew up and was educated in Scotland, where his father was transferred when his son was four years old. He began creating moveable structures such as this in the late 1940s and is now represented by the Guggenheim Museum and the Museum of Modern Art, both in New York, as well as the Tate Gallery in London.

A few blocks southwest of Bell Plaza, at 570 Young Street, you can see a Texas history mural in the lobby of Belo Corp.'s TXCN (Channel 38) that funded its $170,000 restoration. The 22-by-34-foot (or 6.7-by-10.3-meter) painting by James Buchanan "Buck" Winn, Jr. was originally commissioned for the Highland Park Village Theatre (now

Regent Highland Park), at Mockingbird Lane at Preston Road, which opened in 1935. When the theater was remodeled in the early 1980s, the mural was removed and donated to the Dallas Historical Society. The most prominent figure in the painting is French explorer *Rene-Robert Cavelier, Sieur de La Salle*, who is shown at Matagorda Bay on the coast of Texas in 1685. Buck Winn (1905-1979), a native of Celina, Texas, studied in Europe and spent his early career in Dallas as a member of the group of artists known as the Dallas Nine that also included Jerry Bywaters (1906-1989), who was the director of the Dallas Museum of Art from 1943 to 1964. Winn, who studied art and architecture at the Academie Julien in Paris, France, also created murals and relief sculptures in Dallas for the Mercantile Bank, and, together with Eugene Savage, the Hall of State (see entry) art at Fair Park.

North of the downtown business district, in the Oak Lawn neighborhood, bounded by Hall, Hood, and Lemmon streets and Turtle Creek Boulevard, there is a tiny **Robert E. Lee Park,** named after the Confederate Army general. In 1928, the Dallas Southern Association raised $50,000 and commissioned sculptor A. Phemister Proctor to execute a larger-than-life bronze equestrian statue of *Gen. Robert E. Lee* with his orderly. This bronze was originally planned for Dealey Plaza downtown.

Seated in the back of an open touring car, President Franklin D. Roosevelt unveiled the statue on June 12, 1936, as part of the Texas Centennial of the state's independence from Mexico. Two years later the ground was broken for Arlington Hall, which was finished in 1939 with the help of the Works Progress Administration. The 10,000-square-foot (or 929-square-meter) facility, reportedly a two-thirds scale replica of Gen. Lee's Virginia residence, underwent a $2.8-million facelift in 2002.

Proctor (1860-1950) was born in Canada and spent his early years in Denver, Colorado. After studying in Paris, he moved to Oregon in 1915 and created numerous monuments nationwide. His last work was a commission for the Mustangs at the Texas Memorial Museum of the University of Texas, although it was not installed until two years after his death.

The shoppers at **NorthPark Center** (see entry) enjoy the art owned by the mall's proprietor Ray Nasher, even if some would better appreciate more traditional sculptures. The wealthy Nasher, whose parents were immigrants from Russia, displays much of his valuable sculpture collection in the Nasher Sculpture Center (see entry) downtown.

Among the works that you can see at the mall might be *Torus Orbicularis* by American John Newman, or the ten 1985 silkscreen prints, titled *Ads*, by the Pittsburgh-born Andy Warhol (d. 1987), the king of American pop.

British-born Anthony Caro's 1972 painted abstract steel sculpture, titled *Fanshoal*, might also be on display. Sir Anthony Caro (b. 1924), who studied engineering at Cambridge and sculpture at the Royal Academy Schools in London, was an assistant to Henry Moore from 1951 to 1953. He was knighted in 1987.

At one time or another you could admire up to three dozen works of the 20th-century masters, such as Frank Stella's 1982 color print *Talladega Three II*, all from the owners' private collection. The British-born Antony Gormley (b. 1950) is the author of an ensemble of three well-known 1983 gray, lead, fiberglass, and plaster sculptures, titled *Three Places*, molded from the artist's own body in various positions.

Particularly popular with the shoppers is Jonathan Borovsky's 16-foot-high (or 4.87-meter) steel *Hammering Man*, with a motorized right arm hammering a piece of metal held in his other hand, while the other steel man seems to be looking on.

Among the permanent sculptures at NorthPark is the 1971, 236-foot-long (or 72-meter) earthwork by Beverly Pepper, titled *Dallas Land Canal*, on the Northwest Highway side of the mall. Inside, Nasher might display Pepper's 1967 stainless steel and black enamel paint abstraction, titled *Black Angel*. Pepper (b. 1924) was raised in Brooklyn, New York, and attended Pratt Institute. She has lived for extended periods in Italy.

At **Dallas Love Field Airport** (see entry), an 18-foot-high (or 5.48-meter) bronze of a winged male on a 30-foot (or nine-meter) plinth, titled *Spirit of Flight*, which soars from a water fountain with 18 birds aflight, will be found just before reaching the terminals. It was created by Charles Umlauf in 1961. A seven-foot-high (or two-meter) Umlauf bronze of a reclining muse, is located at the water fountain in front of the Hilton hotel, at LBJ Freeway and Dallas North Tollway.

Artwork displayed in a glass-enclosed, 1,500-foot (or 457-meter), third-floor concourse leading to the 4,000-space parking Garage B was created by Dallas artists Philip Lamb and Susan Magilow. The photo displays are made of 860 vertical, 9 feet (or 2.7 meters) tall aluminum slats that are installed perpendicular to the concourse wall. Each of the five 60 to 120 feet (or 18 to 36.5 meters) long panels has images on one side and color on the other. As travelers move toward the main terminal, they see gigantic photographs of Texas that disappear as the viewers behold the flip side of the panels.

At the **Dallas Zoo,** three miles (or 4.8 kilometers) south of downtown, a 67.5-foot (or 20.5-meter) bonded bronze-and-Plexiglas giraffe statue was unveiled at the crest of a hill near the zoo's main entrance in 1997 by the St. Louis artist Bob Cassilly. It is—well, you already know by now—the tallest sculpture in Texas. The artist originally designed the giraffe to be 60 feet (or 18 meters) tall, with a two-foot (or 0.6-meter) tongue, but when the zoo administrators heard about the 67-foot-tall (or 20.4-meter) statue of Sam Houston in Huntsville, Texas, which was inaugurated in 1994, they asked Cassilly to make their statue even taller. Luckily, the zoo administrators did not know about the 164-foot (or 50-meter) Millenium Dome in Greenwich, England, or the giraffe's tongue would be even longer.

Also at the zoo are works by the Dallas artist Wayne Amerine, three sculptures by the Huntsville, Texas-born David Cargill (b. 1929), a life-size lamb by the Dallas artist Mary Jean Jaynes, and bronzes by artist Tom Tischler.

A bovine herd, titled *A Long Way Home* (1985), will be found in Trinity Lake Park at Sylvan Avenue, west of downtown Dallas. Texas sculptor Harold Clayton carved five 4.5-to-five-foot (or 1.37-1.5-meter) bovines in marble and stone, each one weighing four tons. The two cows in black Spanish marble, and the remaining ones in Italian marble or stone, were donated to the city by the real estate developer Trammell Crow. Clayton's *Bluebonnet Hill Cows* are on display at Las Colinas Urban Center, Highway 114 (or John W. Carpenter Freeway East) and Rochelle Road.

On the west side of the **Shelton apartment building,** at 5909 Luther Lane and Dallas North Tollway, two blocks south of West Northwest Highway and next to the Park Cities Hilton Hotel (see listing), there stands a life-size equine sculpture, *Stallion with Mare,* created by Santa Fe, New Mexico, resident Veryl Goodnight. Her seven-ton bronze monument to freedom, *The Day the Wall Came Down,* consisting of five horses, one stallion and four mares running through the rubble of the collapsed Berlin Wall, is located in Berlin and at the George Bush Presidential Library. Her sculpture is on display in private and corporate collections in the United States and Europe.

Fair Park

At the entrance to the Esplanade of State, you will see the *Winged Horse and Siren,* two 27-foot-high (or 8.2-meter) cement frescoes, featuring a mythological winged horse on one and a siren on the other, created by the French-American Pierre Bourdelle, the son of the sculptor Antoine Bourdelle, who died in 1966.

At the Parry Avenue entrance there is a 13-foot-high (or 3.96-meter) bronze and granite memorial fountain, created by Clyde Giltner Chandler (b. 1879), honoring Captain Smith, who was the first secretary of the State Fair, from 1886 to 1912. Also in the area there is an 85-foot-high (or 26-meter) pylon with a stone sculptural frieze, titled *Buffalo Hunt*, designed by Texan James Buchanan "Buck" Winn and realized by architect George Dahl, who supervised the construction of 45 buildings for the Texas Centennial Exposition.

Nearby stands the stone *State Fair of Texas Statue* sculpted by the French-American artist Jose Martin (1891-1984). Born in the village of Miery, in the Jura district of France, Martin came from a family of artists. He went to Paris and enrolled at the Ecole des Beaux Arts, but his studies were interrupted by the First World War, and Joseph Camille Martin had to enlist in the army. In 1920, he met his lifelong friend Raoul Josset, with whom he worked at Fair Park. Martin lived in Seattle, Washington, during the Second World War, returned to Dallas in 1947, married a local woman, and lived for several years at 616 Exposition Avenue, near Fair Park.

In front of the Women's Museum (see entry), there is a 20-foot-high (or six-meter) "sublimely kitschy" plaster statue of a nude woman rising from a stylized saguaro cactus, titled *Spirit of the Centennial*, or *Venus on a Cactus* in the local vernacular, realized in 1936 by French artist Raoul Jean Josset, "the debonair ladies' man," who could not sustain a lasting relationship with a woman. Georgia Carroll, then a 16-year-old Texas-born model, posed for the statue's face and went on to a modeling career and singing for bandleader Kay Kyser.

A student at Dallas' Woodrow Wilson High, Carroll (b. 1920) competed in the Texas Centennial Exposition Bluebonnet contest to select a young woman who was to guide Eleanor Roosevelt when the First Lady visited the fair. She did not win the top prize, but caught the eye of the French sculptor Pierre Bourdelle, a Rodin student, who asked her to sit for a painting.

"It was just my head," says Carroll, who now lives in Chapel Hill, North Carolina. "I didn't pose in the nude at 16 for the statue." She modeled for *Redbook*, *Vogue*, and *Cosmopolitan* until Warner Bros. signed her on in 1940, then joined the big band of Kay Kyser. Her career ended when Kyser, then her 15-years-older husband, decided to retire at age 44. Kay Kyser died in 1985.

Josset, whose artwork for the 1933 exposition in Chicago led to his being engaged at Fair Park, is also the author of the *United States, France and Mexico*, the three 20-foot-tall (or six-meter) stone figures at the Automobile Building. Ten years later, he executed a bronze statue of Gen. Marquis de Lafayette (1757-1834) that stands on the Esplanade of the Philadelphia Museum of Fine Arts.

His *Spirit of the Centennial* is located in front of an arched opening with a mural painted in 1936 by the Italian-born artist Carlo Ciampaglia (1891-1975), who had won the Prix de Rome prize, making it possible for him to study at the American Academy in Rome with architect George Dahl. He returned to the United States in 1933 and maintained studios in New York and New Jersey. Ciampaglia's artwork on the Centennial and Food & Fiber buildings was painted out in 1942 and many years later restored by 19 conservators over a two-year period at a cost of $3 million.

Josset had less luck with his seven-foot-tall (or 2.1-meter) gold-plated nude, *Ula Girl,* another of his plaster creations, that he supposedly also made in 1936. Ula Girl was first displayed at the Art Institute of Chicago in 1936. Later it was acquired by a Dallas real estate investor, who donated it to the Dallas Museum of Art, where it was consigned to storage. In the late 1970s, the real estate man reacquired the nude and installed it in his Highland Park home.

On his death, he willed the statue to his great-nephew, who had bronze copies cast and offered the original to the Friends of Fair Park and other art associations. They politely declined, as did the Texas Discovery Gardens. The Women's Museum replied it did not need any more sculpture. Said the president of the Friends of Fair Park: "I'd take her home with me, but I'm a married man."

Across from Josset's companion works, you will find, at the Centennial Building, the three 20-foot-high (or six-meter) concrete figures, titled *Spain, The Confederacy,* and *Texas,* by Lawrence Tenney Stevens (b. 1896). Stevens, born in Brighton, Massachusetts, won the Prix de Rome competition in 1922, which earned him three years of studies at the American Academy in Rome. An accomplished artist, he died on board the liner *Michelangelo* in 1972 on voyage home from Italy.

Near the Texas Hall of State, you can see a larger-than-life-size bronze bust of *Prospero Bernardi,* the Italian hero of the Battle of San Jacinto. It was created by the Italian-born, San Antonio-based sculptor Pompeo Luigi Coppini (1870-1957), who grew up in Florence. The 26-year-old Coppini arrived in the United States "with very little money and no knowledge of English" in 1886 and married two years later. Hearing that sculptor Frank Teich sought an assistant, he moved to Texas in 1901. His 36 public monuments, 16 portrait statues, and 75 busts will be found all over the country, including his cenotaph to the defenders of the Alamo in San Antonio. (For more about Coppini and a controversy about his art, please see the *Marmac Guide to San Antonio.*)

You will also see nearby a small statue of a bear given by the people of Berlin to Dallas.

On the plaza, there is a larger-than-life-size bronze sculpture of *Robert Lee Thornton* (1880-1964), a Dallas businessman, civic leader, and president of the State Fair, 1945-1963, as well as a four-term mayor of Dallas, 1953-1961. The sculptor was Waldine Tauch (1892-1986), a native Texan who worked with the well-known Pompeo Coppini in San Antonio and was the first female artist commissioned for a war memorial, the Indiana War Memorial. Coppini was so impressed with her talent that he taught her free of charge on the condition that she must never wed. She never did marry and continued working into her 80s.

Thornton was instrumental in bringing the Texas Centennial Exposition to Dallas, when Houston and San Antonio also bid for the event in 1936.

Born near Hico, Texas, Thornton got an eighth-grade education and in 1904 became a traveling candy salesman for a St. Louis company. With $6,000 in cash and $12,000 in notes, in 1916 he began a private bank, which during the Depression became the Mercantile National Bank (see entry in the SIGHTS & ATTRACTIONS chapter). Thornton was the first Dallas banker to make automobile loans.

The entrance Texas Hall portal features *Tejas Warrior*, an 11-foot-high (or 3.35-meter) gilded-bronze gold-leafed statue of an Indian warrior taking aim with his bow, by Allie Victoria Tennant (1898-1971). A native of St. Louis, she came to Dallas as a child, kept a studio, and died here at age 73. In 1936, she also created decorative reliefs for the Dallas Aquarium at Fair Park (see entry). You can see Tennant's black marble sculpture, *Negro Head* (1935), at the Dallas Museum of Art, where a dateless *Woman's Head* is also displayed.

Sculptor Lawrence Tenney Stevens also designed a playful and larger-than-life statue of the *Woofus* for the 1936 exposition. It consisted of the head of a sheep, the horns of a Texas longhorn steer, the neck and mane of a stallion, the body of a hog, the tail of a turkey, and the wings of a duck. The *Woofus* mysteriously disappeared soon after the exhibition.

Starting in 1997, developer and art collector Craig Holcomb raised $30,000 to have the statue recreated. Sculptor David Newman, known locally for the friezes on the Freedman's Cemetery memorial (see entry), was commissioned to do the job. After eight months of work, he sent the molds to the Bryan Foundry near Azle, Texas, in mid-1999.

Shortly afterwards, a fire at the Bryant Foundry destroyed the molds. The *Woofus* fund-raising continued until another $15,000 was collected, and Newman started from scratch. The bronze statue covered with metallic patina and weighing 3,000 pounds (or 1,360 kilograms) was installed in the fall of 2002. The *Woofus* is nine feet (or 2.7 meters) tall and stands near Fair Park's Swine Barn.

There is a seven-and-a-half-foot-high (or 2.28-meter) statue of civil rights leader *Dr. Martin Luther King Jr.* in the front courtyard of the King Community Center, near Fair Park. It was designed by Texan Walter Winn (b. 1930) and completed by Detroit sculptor Oscar Graves. The street on which the center stands was named for him in 1981.

Around the Dallas Museum of Natural History (see entry) there are three *Chromosaurs*, dinosaur replicas made entirely of chrome automobile bumpers and created by sculptor John Kearney (b. 1924). A life-size replica of *Tyrannosaurus rex* towers 20 feet (or six meters) tall, while *Triceratops* and *Stegosaurus* are each more than 32 feet (or 9.7 meters) long. They have been on loan to the museum since 1998. Kearney and his wife, married for more than 50 years, are founders of the Contemporary Art Workshop in Chicago. He discovered the medium by chance. His work can be seen in private and public collections, from the estate of the billionaire John D. Rockefeller in West Virginia, to writers Norman Mailer and Studs Terkel. Francoise Gilot (b. 1921), who met the 62-year-old Picasso at age 21 and became his wife, an artist in her own right, also collected his works.

In front of the museum entrance, you will be greeted by a 13-foot-high (or 3.96-meter) bronze of *Dallas Mammoth*, by Tom Tischler, whose work can be seen in several countries.

Also facing the museum is the Leonhardt Lagoon, named after philanthropist Dorothea Leonhardt and built by the federal Work Progress Administration in 1936 at the site of the Texas Centennial Exposition. Artist Pat Johnson was commissioned to develop environmental sculptures for the lagoon. Completed in 1986, they are built of gunite, a type of concrete sprayed over a steel foundation. Crushed firebrick was mixed with the concrete to create its terra-cotta color.

Market Center

For tours of the **Dallas Market Center,** call (214) 749-5414, at least two weeks ahead.

That pair of monumental granite horses in front of **Infomart** (see entry), at 1950 North Stemmons Frwy., dates from the Han period (206 B.C.-A.D. 25) and is believed to be one of the first stone sculptures created in China.

In front of and around the **World Trade Center,** 2050 North Stemmons Frwy., are the following pieces of art:

• A 1961 life-size water fountain with a stone sculpture, titled *The Bear,* by the Danish-born Mogens Boggild. It was dedicated that year by the chargé d'affaires of the Danish embassy.

• A black metal sectional sphere, titled *Cortens*, by Dushan Dzhamonya (b. 1928), a Macedonian-born Croatian sculptor from the former Yugoslavia.

• A 1964 nine-foot-tall (or 2.74-meter) bronze, titled *Grand Double*, by Alicia Penalba (b. 1918) of Buenos Aires, Argentina. Until 1975 this work was displayed at the Dallas Museum of Fine Art. At the entrance stands watch a pair of hand-carved 19th-century antique stone elephants from China, while inside the lobby lie two marble lions.

Located on the grounds of the **Dallas Trade Mart,** 2100 North Stemmons Frwy., is a surprisingly varied collection of art, including:

• A stone sculpture of a king and queen from a palace of the Kerala region of southern India, titled *Indian Prince with Royal Consort*, which is believed to date from the 19th century.

• A six-foot-tall (or 1.82-meter) lava rock abstract sculpture, titled *Figure IV*, by the Zurich-born sculptor Hans Aeschbacher (b. 1906), also going back to 1963.

• A seven-foot-tall (or 2.13-meter) bronze with two human figures, titled *Endangered Species*, by the prolific Texas sculptor David Cargill.

• A 1964 bronze, titled *The Eagle*, by Elizabeth Frink (b. 1930), a British sculptor whose public commissions can be seen throughout England. *The Eagle* here is one of only five castings with a plaque reading, "Placed in Memorial by the Friends of President John F. Kennedy Who Awaited His Arrival at the Dallas Trade Mart on November 22, 1963."

• A bronze by the Egyptian sculptor Samuel Henri Honein, entitled *The Pots Carrier* and dating from 1963.

• Bronzes *World Trade* and *Cera Perdida Vertical*, both created in 1969 by Jose Maria Subirach (b. 1927) of Barcelona, Spain.

• A 1963 bronze *The Singing Man*, created by the Austrian artist Elisabeth Turolt (b. 1902). Nearby is a time capsule to be opened on April 1, 2017.

Displayed outside the former **International Apparel Mart,** north of the Renaissance Hotel (see entry) and across North Stemmons from the Mariott Suites, is a Burmese bronze *Hong Bird*, dated circa 1650. Part of the Apparel Mart has been concerted into Children's Hospital, whose main facility is nearby.

The granite *Foo Lion* nearby dates from the Chinese Han Dynasty period (206 B.C.-A.D. 220). Also on display here is David Cargill's 1979 *Longhorn Rider* bronze. Cargill is a native Texan.

A nearly life-size solitary bronze, titled *Laughing Man*, in front of the **Market Hall,** at 2100 North Stemmons Frwy., is a work by the London-born artist Harry Marinsky, whose work can also be seen at the Dallas Public Library (see entry).

Irving

The Mustangs of Las Colinas, the nine bronzes sculpted by Robert Glen of Nairobi, Kenya, at 5205 North O'Connor Boulevard in Irving, appear as though they gallop through a stream of water in the middle of the Williams Square Plaza in Las Colinas.

The plaza is almost the size of two football fields side by side and paved with Texas pink granite. A visitors center in the west tower on the plaza is open Wed-Sat 11 AM-5 PM and has a souvenir shop managed by the city of Irving. Six other sculptures of Glen's African wildlife are also on display here. Mustang Café (see entry) is located next door.

Glen (b. 1939), a wildlife artist of Scotch ancestry who was born in Kenya, East Africa, and maintains a studio on the outskirts of Nairobi, was commissioned to create this ensemble in 1976. Casting at a foundry near London, which at one time also served sculptors Barbara Hepworth and Henry Moore, was completed in 1981.

At Heathrow Airport, the 17-ton cargo of nine bronzes was loaded onto a 747 cargo plane and flown to Kennedy Airport in New York. From there an American Airlines 747 freighter took them to Dallas. An 8,000-pound (or 3.6-ton) concrete plinth was made as a base for each horse, while a pumping system was designed to suggest the splashing of water around the hooves of the horses, crossing in midstream.

Dedicated in September 1984, the five mares, two colts, a young and an older stallion, took seven years to create. They are advertised as the world's largest equestrian ensemble, although Dallas makes the same claim for its *Trailing Longhorns* at Pioneer Plaza downtown (see entry). A former director of the Dallas Museum of Art calls the mustangs "the delightfully reassuring kitsch of Las Colinas."

(For more about the area, please see entry Las Colinas in the SIGHTS & ATTRACTIONS chapter.)

Frisco

Texas Sculpture Garden, Hall Office Park, 6801 Gaylord Pkwy. at Dallas Pkwy., Frisco, (972) 377-1100, Internet www.texassculpturegarden.org and www.hallofficepark.com. *NCH*. The garden is open daily from dawn to dusk, lobby weekdays 9 AM-5 PM. Guided tours are available through the concierge or via e-mail at tours@texassculpturegarden.org. Restrooms and drinking fountains are accessible during business hours. Located 30 miles (or 48 kilometers) north of downtown Dallas, on the western side of Dallas Parkway, and north of Highway 121. It is also situated near Stonebriar Country Club and Tom Fazio golf course, and adjacent to the Stonebriar Centre Mall.

Hall Office Park is a 162-acre (or 65-hectare), seven-building real estate development of the Hall Financial Group, an investment and development company founded in 1970 by entrepreneur Craig Hall (b. 1950). He also owns the Kirby apartment building (see entry) in downtown Dallas. With some four million square feet (or 371,600 square meters) of space, it is one of the dozen largest office parks in the Metroplex.

Hall bought 175 acres (or 71 hectares) of land here in 1989 for about $25,000 an acre (or 0.4 a hectare), and he voluntarily handed over about 15 acres (or six hectares) to the Turnpike Authority a few years later, effectively inviting the tollway to his doorstep, observes the *New York Times*, adding that the road is now used by 312,000 cars a day.

The four-acre (or 1.61-hectare) Texas Sculpture Garden, focusing on contemporary living Texas sculptors, contains some 37 works in the park. It also includes other works of art inside the buildings. The garden was inaugurated in the spring of 2001 and contains "the most ambitious collection of contemporary Texas art in the state," according to *D Magazine*. It features:

• Frances Bagley (Dallas): *The First Crusade* (1986), made of cedar.

Married to Dallas artist Tom Orr, Bagley has exhibited throughout the nation and abroad.

• Joe Barrington (Throckmorton): *4 Ravens Nevermore!* (2000), steel and glass.

• Betsy Daves Bass (Dallas): *Bird Window* (2000), bronze and oak.

• Alice Bateman (Fort Worth): *Saturnia—La Rocca* (1996), black Italian marble.

Born in New York City, Bateman studied painting at the University of Guadalajara in Mexico. She received her degree in fine arts from the Byam Shaw School of Painting in London, England. She has worked and exhibited nationwide and in Europe. At North Harwood and San Jacinto Streets, in downtown Dallas, you can see her 13-foot-high (or 3.96-meter) abstract sculpture, *Bear Mountain Red* (1982).

• Jim Bowman (Dallas): *Bluebonnets* (2001), blown glass.

Bowman received his master of fine arts degree the from California College of Arts in Oakland and has exhibited nationally.

• James B. Cinquemani (Dallas): *Arbor* (2001), forged iron.

• Roger Colombik (Wimberley): *Poetry Series II* (1998), limestone and steel.

• Jerry Daniel (Sanger): *Dancers* MM (2000), concrete and steel.

This showcase piece is a 30-foot (or nine-meter) sculpture at the entrance. "I'm bound and determined to make this guy famous," Hall told the *Dallas Business Journal*. Daniel has a fine arts degree from Texas Tech University and has also exhibited in Austria and Germany.

- Jerry Dodd (Commerce): *Trident Marker* (1995), steel.
- Eliseo S. Garcia (Farmers Branch): *Maternal Caress* (1999), stone.
- Harry Geffert (Crowley): *Downside Up* (1999), bronze.
- Polly Gessell (Dallas): *Art Conference* (2000), glass.
- David Graeve (Houston): *Window #36—Iris 2* (2001), glass.
- Joseph Havel (Houston): *Two Starched Shirts* (2001), bronze.

Havel received his master's degree in fine arts from the University of Minnesota. He exhibited at Whitney Museum in New York in 2001. His work is in the collections of the Dallas Museum of Art (see entry) and the Contemporary Art Museum in Honolulu.

- T. Paul Hernandez (Austin): *Reincarnation of Farmer Bradly* (1999), concrete and steel.
- David Hickman (Dallas): *Prairie Falls* (2001), bronze, copper, and marble.
- David Iles (Bolivar): *H.O.P. Rabbits* (2000), bronze.
- Paul Kittelson (Houston): *Staples* (2001), stainless steel.
- Arthur Koch (Dallas): *Elements of Change-series* (1995), mixed media.
- Ken Little (San Antonio): *Coast (Walking Coyote)*, bronze.
- Heather Marcus (Dallas): *Green Ray* (1993), oil on aluminum.
- David McCullough (Dallas): *Celtic Spirit Catcher* (2000), mixed media.

McCullough received his degree from the Kansas City Art Institute and has exhibited nationwide. The Indianapolis Museum of Fine Arts and the Solyn Museum in Omaha are but two places where his work can be found.

- John Brough Miller (Argyle): *Dolphin Rhythm* (1998), steel.

Miller has taught for almost 30 years at the Texas Women's University in Denton. His commissions will be found at the Los Angeles International Airport and the Movie Studios at Las Colinas (see entry).

- Jesus Bautista Moroles (Rockport): *Black Spirit* (2000), black granite.
- Richard Neidhardt (Sherman): *Clock Rider* (1987), bronze.
- Tim Nentrup (Fort Worth): *Bird Window* (2000), bronze and oak.
- Michelle O'Michael (Houston): *La Mujer Roja* (2000), steel.
- Tom Orr (Dallas): *Black Bend. Wood Bend* (1986), wood, glass, and laminate.

The husband of Frances Bagley, Orr has a degree from the Rhode Island School of Design. He has attained a considerable following in Japan, where he has exhibited over several years.

- Sherry Owens (Dallas): *Coming Out of the Circle* (1999), steel.
- Michael Pavlovsky (Fort Worth): *Perseverance* (2000), bronze.
- Damian Priour (Austin): *Temple* (2000), fossiliferous limestone and glass.

• Art Shirer (Dallas): *The Wiz* (2001), steel.

• Isaac Smith (Dallas): *Panther* (2001), wood, acrylic, and mixed media.

Smith is a self-taught woodcarver, who grew up in Louisiana. His favorite subject for 40 years has been wildlife. He is represented by the Cidnee Patrick Gallery (see entry) in Uptown Dallas.

• James Surls (Dallas): *Three and Three and Seven Flower* (1999), poplar and steel.

• James Sullivan (Dallas): *Figure Aloft* (1995), straw, plaster, and steel.

• Karl Umlauf (Lorena): *Legend Series* (1986), cast paper.

Umlauf teaches art at Baylor University in Waco, south of Dallas. His exhibitions took place at the Metropolitan Museum of Art and Modern Museum of Art, both in New York, the Philadelphia Museum of Art, and the New Orleans Museum of Art.

• Mac Whitney (Ovilla): *Blanco #17* (n.d.), steel.

• Marla Ziegler (Dallas): *Office Party* (1999), clay and glaze.

Patricia Meadows, the Hall Financial Group senior vice president who oversees the project, is founder of the Dallas Visual Art Center, which was established in 1981.

Craig Hall "owned his first building at 18, after a childhood marred by epilepsy and a feeling of often being an outcast," according to the *Dallas Morning News*. His mother was an elementary school art teacher. Hall moved from Michigan to Dallas in 1981.

"He later endured bankruptcy and a bitter divorce before finding himself in a romance with Ms. Hall," who was previously married to Texas Democratic senator David Cain of Dallas. The couple also owns hotels in Paris and vineyards in California's Napa Valley. Hall, who had supposedly lost "an estimated $1 billion in the 1980s," has been collecting art for 30 years.

Frisco's Central Park, at Parkwood and Warren Parkway, is the site of a herd of bronze steers and stone sculptures by Fort Worth artist Anita Pauwels. They depict the history of the Shawnee Trail. As you stroll along the winding walk to the top of an eight-acre (or 3.23-hectare) park, you learn about the trail drive by reading text embedded in the walkways and looking at the relief murals.

ART GALLERIES

The Metroplex is not London, Paris, or Rome, not even Moscow, when it comes to art galleries. You do not come here to look for Picassos, although several Henry Moores are scattered over the city. But you will always find some good regional art, particularly with depictions of the West, in various media. Uptown, especially Routh and Fairmount Streets, has a large concentration of galleries and antique stores.

"Dallas is a growing adolescent," says the owner of the Photographs Do Not Bend gallery. "Time will take care of it," he notes, while his wife adds, "It's not the warmest place for art." These comments were published in a weekly, which also quoted Edith Baker, a former long-time owner of the respected Edith Baker Gallery (since renamed Cidnee Patrick Gallery), as saying, "Dallasites are most interested in buying big names, and for something that'll match their sofa."

"Texas has more artists per capita than any other state," continued Baker, who supported Texas art by representing such regional artists as Reg Loving, Tom Pribyl, and Norman Kary, "yet they must leave the state to make a name for themselves."

One of the first private galleries in Dallas was the home of artist and art patron Katherine Lester Crawford (1864-1947), who at the turn of the 20th century displayed some 300 paintings and statuary at her elegant mansion at 3709 Ross Avenue. The Mississippi-born artist moved to Paris, France, in 1887 and studied at the Academie Julien. She returned to the United States five years later and moved to Dallas as an art instructor. In 1895, she established an art school at 189 San Jacinto Street. After remarrying the following year, her family lived in an elegant Eastlake mansion on Ross Avenue, where she displayed works of European and American artists.

To see unconventional creations of younger, emerging artists, your best bets are **500X Gallery, Gray Matters,** and **McKinney Avenue Contemporary** in Dallas. Consider also the annual Fall Gallery Walk, held in mid-September, (214) 855-5101, Internet www.dallasartdealers.com. Up to three dozen local galleries, mostly in Uptown and around Fair Park, lure art lovers with artworks, wine, and cheese snacks.

Only galleries that are open at least three days a week are listed here:

500X Gallery, 500 Exposition Ave., (214) 828-1111, Internet www.500X.org. Open Sat-Sun 1 PM-5 PM, or by appointment. Located in a former 1916 tire factory and air-conditioning warehouse in Deep Ellum, just east of downtown Dallas.

The gallery was established in 1978 by a Massachusetts artist, Will Hipps, who came to Dallas to teach, and a local painter, Richard Childers. This nonprofit, artist-run cooperative gallery serves mostly emerging artists. It exhibits contemporary painting, sculpture, and photography in a space that measures 3,000 square feet (or 279 square meters).

Since 1981, 500X Gallery has featured an annual Open Show for new artists, where the "works range from insane to inspired." All media and styles are represented. Participating at the show could be artists from lands as varied as Romania and El Salvador. 500X Gallery artists include Brennen Bechtol, Robert Boland, Iris Bustillos, C. J. Davis, Jennifer Pepper, Luke Sides, Charlotte Smith, Takako Tanabe, and Kyle Cock Wadsworth. Prices range from $75 to $5,000.

Across the street from here is **Xposure Gallery,** 507 Exposition Ave. There are another half-dozen art galleries within a few blocks.

Adani Gallery, 5330 Alpha Rd. at Noel, Suite 300, (972) 503-5662, Internet www.adanigallery.com, e-mail adani@adanigallery.com. Open Tue-Sat 11 AM-6 PM, Sun 1 PM-5 PM. Located in a two-story, red-brick office building in far-north Dallas, north of Lyndon B. Johnson Frwy., east of Dallas North Tollway, and around the corner from the Galleria shopping center (see entry).

Mexico City physician and retired professor of microbiology at the University of Texas' Southwestern Medical Center, Jacobo Kupersztoch (b. 1945) is so passionate about Latin American art that he initially opened this gallery out of his home in 1999. His small exhibit space features artists such as Gilberto Aceves-Navarro, Jose Luis Cuevas, Gunther Gerzso, Berta Kolteniuk, Kurt Larisch, Carlos Merida, Guillermo Meza, Nicolas Moreno, Xiao Ling Peng, Luis Rizo-Rey, Sergio Rodriguez, David Alfaro Siqueiros, Rufino Tamayo, Francisco Toledo, and Francisco Zuniga.

"The quality of the work itself, which ranges from a 1939 Rivera pastel to a 2001 acrylic by Sergio Rodriguez, is wildly uneven," claims the *Dallas Observer*.

Afterimage Photographic Gallery, The Quadrangle, 2828 Routh St., Suite 141, Uptown, (214) 871-9140, Internet www.afterimagegallery.com, e-mail images@afterimagegallery.com. Open Mon-Sat 10 AM-5:30 PM. Located on the Laclede Street side, just north of downtown Dallas.

Established in 1971, this is one of the oldest Texas art galleries devoted exclusively to photography. Photographs and books by the well-known photographer Ansel Adams (1902-1984), for example, are bought and sold here for up to $25,000 each.

Other photographers, whose works are available and often priced into the thousands of dollars, include Berenice Abbott (1898-1991), Edward S. Curtiss (1868-1952), and Edward Weston (1886-1958). The gallery also sells quality photography books and photographic posters. There are also photos by the French artist Henri Cartier-Bresson (b. 1908), Peter Cattrell (b. 1959) who lives in England, Keith Logan (b. 1950) who now lives in Canada, David J. Osborn (b. 1961) in Australia, and Willy Ronis (b. 1910) in France.

Its owner, Ben Breard, a native Dallasite, became interested in photography while majoring in journalism at Northwestern University. He opened the Afterimage upon receiving a master's degree in communications photography from Syracuse University.

Altermann Galleries, Internet www.altermann.com, e-mail tony@altermann.com. For 25 years located in the Uptown neighborhood, across the street from the Quadrangle mall, Altermann closed its Dallas gallery in 2003 and now serves its north Texas clients through its Web page.

The Altermanns, specializing in 19th-, 20th-, and 21st-century American paintings and sculpture featuring Western artists such as Frederick Remington and Charles Russell, now manage their galleries in Santa Fe, New Mexico.

The gallery's lawn across the street from the Quadrangle mall for years exhibited sculpture by Texan Glenna Goodacre—who designed the Vietnam Women's Memorial on the Mall in Washington, D.C.—a 2003 recipient of the Texas Medal of Arts. Goodacre (b. 1939) also designed the U.S. Mint's new gold-alloy, one-dollar coin that features the image of Sacagewea, the young Shoshone Indian who accompanied explorers Lewis and Clark to the Pacific Ocean in 1805. As payment for her work, Goodacre received 5,000 of the specially minted coins from the U.S. Mint. She sold half of them—one at a time—for $200 a piece, ringing up $500,000.

Angstrom Gallery, 3609 Parry Ave. at First Ave., (214) 823-6456, Internet www.angstromgallery.com, e-mail angstromtx@earthlink.net. Open Wed-Sat noon-5 PM, or by appointment. Located east of downtown Dallas, in a storefront across from Fair Park. Next door is the Meridian Room restaurant and bar.

Created by two graduates of the bachelor of fine arts program at the University of North Texas in 1996, this is a cutting-edge gallery that displays the work of Texas and international artists. It is owned by David Quadrini, who planned to enter graduate school, but the gallery was so successful that he changed his mind about his advanced degree.

"He lives and breathes cutting-edge art," claims the *Paper City* monthly newspaper. "Quadrini has an uncanny ability to discover artists (mainly from Texas), nurture them and, eventually, see them exhibited at major shows worldwide or in avant-garde galleries in New York or Los Angeles."

A former director of the McKinney Avenue Contemporary (see listing), who advises Angstrom, Quadrini also keeps the dialogue going with the mostly abstract exhibitions.

Angstrom exhibits artists such as the Irving, Texas, native Jeff Elrod

(b. 1967), who has already exhibited at the Whitney Museum of American Art in New York City. Other featured artists include Aaron Baker, Tim Bavington, Jay Davis, Bill Davenport, Inka Essenhigh, Jack Hallberg, Steven Hull, Daniel Johnston, Giles Lyon, Robin O'Neal, Aaron Parazette, Jack Pierson, Victoria Reynolds, Susie Rosmarin, Christian Schumann, Sean Slattery, Hills Snyder, and Erik Swenson. Also featured here is Dallas artist Ludwig Schwartz, who, the owners believe, is "the best painter in the state."

The price range of art sold at the gallery, which measures 10,000 square feet (or 929 square meters), is $300 to $12,000.

Nearby, at 3603 Parry Ave. in Expo Park, is located **Forbidden Gallery & Emporium,** (214) 887-5939, established in 2000. The weekly *Dallas Observer* once named it the "best alternative art space" in the city.

ArtCentre of Plano, 1039 East 15th Street at Avenue K, Plano, (972) 423-7809, Internet www.artcentreofplano.org, e-mail info@artcentreofplano.org. *NCH*. Open Tue-Sat 10 AM-6 PM. Free parking.

A nonprofit organization housed in a renovated 19th-century building in historic downtown Plano. The ArtCentre, founded in 1981, consists of two art galleries and exhibits mostly local and regional visual arts. The 160-seat Plano Repertory Theatre, established in 1975, is located behind the ArtCentre.

Cliff Redd, a former director of the Shakespeare Festival of Dallas, was named director of the ArtCentre in 2001. A Houston native, he founded Theatre Arlington in 1972 and ran it for 18 years. He directed the Shakespeare Festival from 1989 to 1997 and again from 1999 to 2001.

An exhibition of artworks by 48 Vietnamese artists at the ArtCentre in 1998 was delayed after Vietnamese-Americans and Vietnam War veterans objected to the alleged pro-communist message. "Opponents of the Vietnamese exhibit say it is nothing more than propaganda for a brutal communist regime," noted the *Plano Star Courier*. Some 100 Vietnamese-Americans protested at a Plano city council meeting.

"The idea of putting on a communist art show is insensitive to the Vietnamese community," said at the time U.S. Congressman and former Vietnam prisoner of war Sam Johnson.

"Pressure from the same people protesting the Plano exhibition" kept the show from opening a year earlier in Dallas, where it was rejected by the mayor.

The exhibition of Vietnamese art, organized by the nonprofit Meridian International Center (Internet www.meridian.org) in Washington, D.C., was the first cultural exchange project to be organized since the United States reestablished diplomatic relations with its former foe. The same exhibit created "a torrent of protest from Vietnamese-Americans" in other American cities.

Around the corner, at the downtown Plano ligh-rail DART station, you can see a life-size bronze sculpture titled *Ironhorse,* created by Tom Askman. Nearby, at 914 Eighteenth Street, you will find the art studio of the Indiana-born potter Tony Holman (Internet www.holmanpottery.com), whom you can observe at work weekdays 10 AM-5 PM.

Banks Fine Art, 1231 Dragon St. at Cole, (214) 352-1811, Internet www.banksfineart.com, e-mail bob@banksfineart.com. Open Mon-Fri 9 AM-5 PM. Located in the Dallas Design District, about one mile (or 1.6 kilometers) west from the American Airlines Center (see entry).

Appraiser Bob and his wife Maloree Banks have been in the wholesale business since 1980. Their 10,000-square-foot (or 929-square-meter) gallery sells antique oil paintings, as well as landscapes, still lifes, and portraits of living artists. They stock up to 2,000 paintings, dating from the 19th century to the present. The sales are mostly to interior designers and other galleries. The works featured could be as different as those of Norman Rockwell and Pablo Picasso. An Impressionist floral painting by the St. Petersburg-born Maria Rosenberg would cost you from $3,600 to $6,000 here.

"Their showroom, under the direction of partner Michael Serrecchia, is spacious, smart, and very SoHo," claims *D Magazine*.

Also in the Design District is **American Fine Art,** 1611 Dragon St. at Oak Lawn Ave., (214) 749-7749, Internet www.americanfineart.com, e-mail sales@americanfineart.com. Open Mon-Fri 9 AM-5:30 PM, Sat 10 AM-4 PM. A contemporary gallery featuring original works on paper and canvas, fresco, sculpture, and pottery by international and regional artists, priced from $200 to $25,000. It was established in 1982.

Another gallery situated in the Design District is **Beaux Arts,** 1505 Hi Line Dr. at Edison St., (214) 741-5555. Open Mon-Sat 9 AM-6 PM. Located within walking distance of the American Airlines Center (see entry). Established in 1988 and at this location since 1993, it features 18th- and 19th-century oil paintings and watercolors; 16th- through 19th-century antique prints, lithographs, and rare maps; 1890-1950 posters; and 20th-century contemporary artworks, including posters. Prices range "from a few hundred to several thousand dollars."

Carlyn Galerie, Preston Center, 6137 Luther Ln. at Preston Rd., (214) 368-2828, Internet www.carlyngalerie.com, e-mail carlyng@earthlink.net. Open Mon-Sat 10 AM-6 PM, Thu 10 AM-8 PM, Sun noon-5 PM. Located north of downtown Dallas and south of West Northwest Highway, on the edge of University Park.

Established in 1989 and at this address since 1993, fine American crafts, such as turned wood, handblown glass, handcrafted jewelry, and ceramic art pieces are the focus in this gallery owned by Cindi Ray and Wendy Dunham. Started as a college hobby, Ray named the gallery after her youngest daughter.

The featured artists include ceramicists Irina and Nicholas Zaitsev. Cheryl Williams works in clay. Fiber artists for sale here include Valerie Guignon, Serena Mann, Jeanne Shackelford, and George Westbrook. Jewelry is made by Terri Logan, a self-taught former psychotherapist. Glass artists include Leon Applebaum, Chris Heilman, Michael Hopko, Susan Longini, Debra May, Dimitri Michaelides, Australian-born James Minson, Roger Paramore, John Phillips, Harry Stuart, former baker and chef Christian Thirion of France, and Craig Zweifel.

"This is the best selection of art glass in the city," claims *D Magazine*. Prices range from $2 to $2,000.

Columbia Arts Center, 5501 Columbia Ave. at Augusta St., (214) 823-8955 or 824-3377, Internet www.docarts.com, e-mail info@5501.com. *NCH*. Open Thu-Fri 11 AM-5 PM, Sat-Sun noon-5 PM during exhibitions. Located in east Dallas, north of Fair Park.

Operated by the non-profit Documentary Arts and Contemporary Culture, Columbia is home to an array of exhibitions, art workshops, creative collaborations, and cutting-edge projects. It includes a large gallery, a book arts gallery, studios for sculpture, and neighborhood art workshops.

Documentary Arts located here administers the Texas African-American Photography Archive, a collection of 32,000 prints and negatives taken mostly by African-American photographers.

This 1918 two-story brick former firehouse was designed by H. A. Overbeck, and a studio addition is by architect Dan Shipley. The arts center was founded in 1992 by folklorist Alan Govenar and his wife.

Conduit Gallery, 1626 Hi Line Dr. at Oak Lawn Ave., Suite C, (214) 939-0064, Internet www.conduitgallery.com, e-mail conduit@airmail.net. Open Tue-Sat 10 AM-5 PM. Located northwest of downtown, in Dallas' Design District, home to high-end, wholesale furniture showrooms.

A Deep Ellum pioneer established in 1984 as one of the first commercial spaces along Elm Street, Conduit moved to a renovated warehouse on Main Street in 1991, and to its current location off Stemmons Freeway (or Interstate 35 East) in 2002. It claims 4,600 square feet (or 427 square meters) divided into two galleries.

Deep Ellum was the right place to be when she moved there, then it was time to move on, gallery owner Nancy Whiteneck told the *Fort Worth Star-Telegram*. "It's a great time to move to this neighborhood. There are lots of things happening down here."

Conduit focuses on paintings, sculpture, works on paper, and photography by some two dozen established Texas and regional contemporary artists, such as James Sullivan, Vincent Falsetta, and Lance Letscher. Another is Robert Jessup, a nationally recognized Denton artist and professor at the University of North Texas whose "densely packed layers of colors from both ends of the spectrum are applied in stippled fashion to produce a constantly shifting array of abstract patterns," according to one critic.

Another would-be Denton-based artist, Vincent Falsetta, an art teacher at the same university for 25 years, "isn't gluing pens on tin cans and calling it art; isn't listening to grumpy gallerists. Here's a guy who could raise your art-scene standards from the dead, Dallas; if only he weren't so darn quiet, unassuming, and ego-less," says the weekly *Dallas Observer*.

Prices range from $400 for small drawings to $17,000 for the gallery's best work.

Joel Cooner Gallery, 1605 Dragon St. at Oak Lawn Ave., (214) 747-3603, Internet www.joelcooner.com, e-mail joel.cooner.gallery@airmail.net. Open Mon-Fri 10 AM-5 PM. Located in the Dallas Design District, about a mile (or 1.6 kilometers) west of the American Airlines Center.

Established in 1979, the gallery measures 4,700 square feet (or 437 square meters). Authentic tribal, Asian, and pre-Columbian art is for sale by Joel Cooner, who once lived in Japan and traveled throughout Asia. This is the only Dallas gallery where you will find African weapons and shields.

Prices range from $300 to $200,000.

The Craighead-Green Gallery, 2404 Cedar Springs Rd. at Maple Ave., Suite 700, Uptown, (214) 855-0779, Internet www.craigheadgreen.com, e-mail director@craigheadgreen.com. Open Tue-Fri 10 AM-5:30 PM, Sat 11 AM-5 PM. Located in the Oak Lawn neighborhood, just north of downtown Dallas, across the street from the Crescent Court Hotel (see entry) and next to the Cidnee Patrick Gallery (see entry).

Established in 1992, the gallery measures 2,000 square feet (or 186 square meters). Owned by Kenneth Craighead, an attorney, and Steve Green, an interior designer, it features contemporary works by predominantly regional and international artists in all media. It also runs an annual new talent exhibition. Prices range from $800 to $40,000.

Among the artists represented are Gregg Coker, Connie Connally, Marci Crawford-Harnden, David Crimson, Gail Cadman Dawson, Yrjo Edelman, Brad Ellis, Dallasite Lee Harrington, Dana Ruth Harvey, Mike Hill, Mary Hood, Aaron Karp, Ann Kobdish, Josep Navarro-Vives,

Carole Pierce, Ron Pokrasso, Susan Sales, Gary Schafter, Dallasite Rusty Scruby, Scott Simons, Shawn Smith, Delos Van Earl, Jeff Wenzel, Jeff Wilson, Gordon Young, and Maria Ziegler.

Dallas Center for Contemporary Art, 2801 Swiss Ave., Suite 100, (214) 821-2522, Internet www.dallasvisualart.org, e-mail thecontemporary@mindspring.com. Open Mon-Fri 9 AM-5 PM, Thu 9 AM-9 PM, Sat noon-4 PM. Located northeast of downtown Dallas in the historic Wilson district, between Liberty and Texas Streets.

Founded by Patricia B. Meadows in 1981, when it was one of the city's first alternative art spaces, and housed in a building funded by the Meadows Foundation, DCCA is an information center and a gallery for Texas artists and collectors. Its members include working artists, collectors, curators, and donors. Until 2002, it was known as Dallas Visual Art Center and before 1995 as D'Art.

Its director, Joan Davidow, a native New Yorker, is a former art critic for the Dallas public radio and an assistant curator at the Dallas Museum of Art. Until 2001, she was in charge of the Arlington Museum of Art.

Featured artists include Frances Bagley, Harry Geffert, Joe Harel, John Hernandez, Annette Lawrence, Mary McCleary, Melissa Miller, Celia Munoz, Pamela Nelson, Dallasite Tom Orr, Linda Ridgway, and Julie Speed.

In 2002, the center awarded Dallas painter Benito Huerta its 10th annual Legend Award, given to the backbones of the Texas art community. That year, Huerta completed artwork for a DART rail station in Richardson. He is also one of the two dozen artists selected to produce artwork for the new international terminal at the Dallas/Fort Worth International Airport.

David Dike Fine Art Gallery, 2613 Fairmount St., between McKinney Ave. and Cedar Springs Rd., Uptown, (214) 720-4044, Internet www.daviddikefineart.com, e-mail ddfa@aol.com. Open Mon-Fri 10 AM-5 PM, Sat 11 AM-5 PM. Located just north of downtown Dallas, a couple of blocks from the Crescent Court Hotel (see entry) and next door to Riddell Rare Maps & Fine Prints (see entry). Established in 1986.

"I love being from Texas and love Texas art," the owner, who attended Texas Christian University and studied finance, told the *Dallas Morning News*. "I thought I'd be a banker or something like that, just like my friends." A part-time job at Ron Hall Gallery, then located in Fort Worth, opened a new world to him.

David Dike specializes in late 19th- and early 20th-century American and European paintings, emphasizing the works of Texas artists. Prices range from $400 to $200,000.

Among the featured artists you might find Jose Arpa, Reveau Bassett, Charles T. Bowling, Dawson Dawson-Watson, Otis Dozier, William Lester, Florence McClung, Julian Onderdonk, Frank Reaugh, Porfirio Salinas, Everett Spruce, and Olin Travis.

Dunn & Brown Contemporary, 5020 Tracy St. at McKinney Ave., (214) 521-4322, Internet www.dunnandbrown.com, e-mail dcb@dunnandbrown.com. Open Tue-Sat 11 AM-5 PM; closed Mondays. Located north of downtown Dallas, on the southeastern edge of Highland Park, two blocks west of North Central Expressway, and close to Javier's restaurant.

Operated by Talley Dunn and Lisa Hirschler Brown, both of whom come from the former Gerald Peters Gallery (see listing). Dunn, an art history graduate from Smith College, is a former president of the Texas Fine Arts Association in Austin. The gallery sells contemporary paintings, sculpture, drawings, prints, and photographs. Several of its artists are former Whitney Biennial participants.

In 2001, the owners bought and renovated the U-shaped warehouse, in which the 6,000-square-foot (or 558-square-meter) gallery is located, at a cost of $1 million. A garage was converted into a rectangular gallery with a 12-foot (or 3.65-meter), exposed-beam ceiling. Prices range from $500 to $200,000.

Featured artists include Helen Altman, Forrest Bess, Julie Bozzi, Vernon Fisher, Brian Fridge, Sam Gummelt, Trenton Doyle Hancock, Houston sculptor Joseph Havel, Annette Lawrence, Lisa Ludwig, David McGee, Melissa Miller, Amy Myers, Nic Nicosia, Sam Reveles, Linda Ridgway, Laurence Scholder, Christian Schumann, Matthew Sontheimer, Myron Stout, and Liz Ward.

Among the recent events here was an exhibit of Dallas-born painter and sculptor David Bates' "idiosyncratic blends of painting and sculpture, form and substance." The weekly *Dallas Observer* named Bates "far and away the best living Texas artist" in 2002.

(For additional information, see also entry Gerald Peters Art Gallery in this section.)

European Art Gallery, 3012 Fairmount St. at Carlisle St., Uptown, (214) 468-0683, Internet www.european-artgallery.com, e-mail info@european-artgallery.com. Open Tue-Sat 9 AM-6 PM. Located in a 12,000-square-foot (or 1,115-square-meter) four-wing colonial-style building just north of downtown.

Established in 2000 by European art lover and U.S.-based businessman Danny Wettreich, this is "the largest fine art gallery in Texas, and the largest European paintings gallery in the U.S.," according to its owners. EAG sells mostly British artists, Impressionist paintings, as well as artworks by living European artists. It offers 19th- and 20th-century art and displays hundreds of works, starting at about $3,000. One of them is Pierre-Auguste Renoir. EAG is affiliated with Hahn Gallery of Piccadilly, London, art dealers since 1870.

Florence Art Gallery, 2500 Cedar Springs Rd. at Fairmount, Uptown, (214) 754-7070, e-mail floartgal@earthlink.net. Open Tue-Fri 10 AM-5 PM, Sat noon-5 PM; closed Mondays. Located within walking distance of the Quadrangle mall, two blocks north of the Crescent Court Hotel (see entry), and across from the Gerald Peters Gallery (see entry).

The gallery was established in 1974. Measuring 4,000 square feet (or 372 square meters), it focuses on abstract and traditional paintings and sculpture by American and European artists such as Anton Arkhipov, Clemens Briels, Romero Britto, Amanda Dunbar, Peter Max, Henrietta Milan, Jay Miller, David Shear, Rufino Tamayo, and Bruce Tinch. Prices range from $650 to $12,000.

The Romanian-born Alexandra Nechita (b. 1985) exhibits here her contemporary paintings that "routinely sell for tens of thousands of dollars." She began drawing in pen and ink at age two, graduated to watercolors at five, and oils at seven. The following year, Nechita had her first solo show in Los Angeles, where she was dubbed the "petite Picasso." Sales of her artwork have already surpassed $5 million.

Galerie Kornye, 2530 Fairmount St., between McKinney Ave. and Cedar Springs Rd., Uptown, (214) 954-4475, Internet www.kornye.com, e-mail art@kornye.com. Open Mon-Sat 10 AM-5 PM. Located just north of downtown, one block east of the Crescent Court Hotel (see entry) and next to Christy Stubs Gallery. Several other galleries and restaurants are situated in the area.

Kornye, named after its owner George W. Kornye, specializes in 19th- and 20th-century American and European fine art, which he buys, appraises, and consigns. Established in 1969, the gallery's prices start at $2,000. Artists featured include D. Buckley Good, Robert Johanningmeier, Stapleton Keams, Rich Penny, Stokely Webster, and J. Sun Yan.

"The charming Monsieur Kornye doesn't *sell* paintings—he *presents* works of art," declares *D Home*, an offshoot of *D Magazine*, quoting the proprietor: "Buy with your heart, not with your purse—the way you pick a wife for life."

Ivanffy-Uhler Gallery, 4623 West Lovers Ln., between Lemmon Ave. and Inwood Rd., (214) 350-3500, Internet www.ivanffyuhler.com, e-mail info@ivanffyuhler.com. Open Tue-Sat 10 AM-6 PM, Sun 1 PM-6 PM.

Located east of Love Field Airport and three blocks west of Inwood/Lovers intersection.

Established in 1996, the gallery measures 2,000 square feet (or 186 square meters) and is owned by Agnes Ivanffy and Paul Uhler. It features internationally established contemporary European painters, sculptors, and graphic artists such as Maria Bozoky, Lajos Dobos, Francois Gall, Pal Gerzson, Romeo V. Tabuena, Elizabeth Zaremba, Andras Kiss-Nagy, Janos Kass, and Rufino Tamayo.

Prices range from $150 to $25,000.

William E. Johnson Fine Art Gallery, 2525 Fairmount St. at McKinney Ave., Uptown, (214) 871-1197, e-mail wejohnsonfineart@aol.com. Open Tue-Fri 10 AM-5 PM, Sat noon-4:30 PM; closed Sundays and Mondays. Located in a restored Victorian house one block east of the Crescent Court Hotel (see entry).

Established in 1976, this is one of the oldest Dallas galleries. It showcases paintings and sculpture from the 17th to the early 20th century, with special emphasis on American, European, and early Texas artists. You might also find here Flemish, Italian, and French paintings.

Prices range from $500 to $75,000.

Karen Mitchell Frank Gallery, 4532 Cole Avenue at Knox St., (214) 559-4700, Internet www.karenmitchellfrank.com, e-mail kmsgallery@ibm.net. Open Tue-Sat 10 AM-6 PM, Sun noon-5 PM. Located Uptown near the Highland Park Pharmacy.

Established in 1995, although it changed its name and location three years later, it is a 3,400-square-foot (or 316-square-meter) contemporary gallery featuring traditional and abstract art in all media by regional and national artists. *D Magazine* believes it to be "the most accessible entry into the Texas art market."

Artists represented include Tom Bacher, Dominique Boisjoli, Fort Worth native Lisa Laughlin Boyd, Maysey Craddock, Janos Enyedi, Jose Guerrero, Martha Hinojosa, Paul Hunter, Angus Macpherson, Dallas painter Jay Maggio, Louisa McElwain, Roger Moore, Elisa Pasquel, J. Alex Potter, David Rainey, Maria Elena Villalon, Darlene Wall, and Gregory Zeorlin.

Prices range from $500 to $16,000.

Thomas Kinkade at Weir's, 3219 Knox St. at Henderson St., (214) 528-0321. Open Mon-Fri 10 AM-9 PM, Sat 10 AM-6 PM; closed Sundays.

There is no escaping this purveyor of sweet, idyllic images whose stores nationwide are multiplying like mushrooms after rain. Much ink has been spilled about Kinkade, the "painter of light," but for what you could pay for some of his serial work, one might prefer the art that has withstood the test of the centuries. Weir's furniture store seems an appropriate place for this kind of work.

Kinkade (b. 1958) was born in Sacramento, California, and grew up in the foothills of the Sierra Mountains. After attending the University of California at Berkeley and the Art Center College of Design in Pasadena, California, he "studied" Rembrandt and Caravaggio before starting to make a name for himself.

One Web site maintains that "Kinkade is America's most collected living artist," with his "art-based products" estimated to have topped sales of $300 million in 2000. His "originals"—in effect digitally replicated original images hand-highlighted by either an apprentice or Kinkade—sell for tens of thousands of dollars.

Kinkade is the leading brand name of Media Arts Group, Inc., a publicly traded New York Stock Exchange company that posts $130 million in sales. Its Web site claims that "through our aggressive sales and marketing efforts, Thomas Kinkade has become the most widely recognized and best selling living artist in the world."

Kittrell/Riffkind Art Glass Studio, Village on the Parkway, 5100 Belt Line Rd., Suite 820 , (888) 865-2228 or (972) 239-7957, Internet www.artglass.guidelive.com, e-mail artglass@kittrellrifkind.com. Open Mon-Sat 10 AM-6 PM, Thursdays 10 AM-8 PM; closed Sundays. Located north of downtown Dallas, on the southeast corner of Dallas Parkway and Belt Line Road, a school is located above the store.

Established in 1990, the focus in this Addison gallery is on the work in fine-art glass by 300 emerging and established regional and national artists. Items featured are sculpture, jewelry, goblets, scent bottles, wall pieces "and hundreds of other treasures, large and small," according to the gallery.

Prices range from $25 to $15,000, although most objects cost between $100 and $500.

Christopher H. Martin Gallery & Studio, 2702 McKinney Ave. at Boll St., (214) 880-9667, Internet www.christopherhmartin.com, e-mail chmgallery@sbcglobal.net. Open daily 11 AM-6 PM, Sundays 1 PM-5 PM. Located Uptown, across the street from the S & D Oyster Company restaurant.

Established in 1997, it has been at this location since 1999. An artist-run gallery that measures 1,800 square feet (or 167 square meters) and features paintings by Christopher Martin, sculpture by Jerry D. Sanders, Dallas artist Patricia Shannon, California sculptor Rick Carpenter, and other regional talent. One of Martin's commissions can be seen at 1401 Elm Place downtown.

Prices range from $100 to $7,000.

One block west from here stands a home named after the Tennessee-born feed dealer Ahab Bowen (1807-1900). The house was built in 1874 and is one of the few remaining wood frame homes from that era still standing.

McKinney Avenue Contemporary, 3120 McKinney Ave. at Bowen St., Uptown, (214) 953-1212, Internet www.the-mac.org, e-mail info@the-mac.org. Open Wed-Sat 11 AM-10 PM, Sun 1 PM-5 PM. Located just north of downtown Dallas.

The purple brick MAC building on lower McKinney Avenue is owned by businessman and art collector Claude Albritton. The 18,000-square-foot (or 1,672-square-meter) building with a 2,800-square-foot (or 260-square-meter) gallery, renovated in 1994, was once the home of the Potts Longhorn Leather Company.

This cutting-edge contemporary, noncommercial art gallery was founded by a former Dallas Museum of Art board member in 1994. *Texas Monthly* calls it "Dallas' frisky alternative space." Other events here include films, poetry readings, dance, and music. The building also houses the Kitchen Dog Theater (see listing), the resident theater company of the MAC.

Meadows Museum (please see entry under Major Art Museums in this chapter).

Mulcahy Modern, Bishop Arts District, 408 West Eighth St. at Bishop Place, (214) 948-9595, e-mail modgallery@aol.com. Open Wed-Sat 11 AM-5 PM; closed Mondays and Tuesdays. Located in a restored, three-block, award-winning north Oak Cliff neighborhood southwest of downtown Dallas in which semi-derelict houses and commercial buildings were given new lives as a home for artists and designers, gift shops, and restaurants. The city and the federal government invested more than $2.5 million in improvements that include new streets, brick sidewalks, old-fashioned street lamps, and landscaping.

Owned by Cynthia Mulcahy, her contemporary gallery emphasizes Texas artists. In 2001, Ted Pillsbury, once co-owner of the Gerald Peters Gallery (see entry) snatched Richard Stout and Frank X. Tolbert, two up-and-coming Texas artists, from her gallery.

Among her featured artists are Christine Bisetto, Rosalyn Bodycomb, Nate Cassie, Corbin Doyle, Celia Eberle, Robert Hamilton, Jin-ya Huang, Patrick Kelly, Page Kempner, Meg Langhorne, the Houston-born Monica Pierce, Gary Retherford, Derrick Saunders, and Tom Sime, who writes on art for the *Dallas Morning News*.

Most of the art on sale here can be had for under $1,000.

Pan American Art Gallery, 3303 Lee Parkway at Hall, Suite 100, (214) 522-3303, Internet www.panamericanart.com, e-mail panamericanart@aol.com. Open Tue-Fri 10 AM-6 PM, Sat noon-6 PM; closed Mon-Tue. Located north of downtown Dallas, west of North Central Expressway and across from Robert E. Lee Park.

Established in Los Angeles, the Pan American has been in Dallas since 1993 and claims 4,000 square feet (or 372 square meters) of space inside a suite of spacious storefront rooms.

Among some 75 Cuban artists represented are Umberto Castro (b. 1957), Victor Manuel Garcia (d. 1969), and Manuel Mendive (b. 1944). The 60 or so Haitian artists include Burton Chenet (b. 1958), the Ecole Nationale Superieure de Beaux Arts-educated Edouard Duval-Carrie (b. 1954), and Philome Obin (d. 1986). Carl Abrahams (b. 1913), Eric Caden (d. 1995), and George Rodney (b. 1936) represent some 40 Jamaican artists on exhibit here. Other artists whose works are available at the Pan American Art Gallery come from throughout the rest of Latin America. Prices range from $500 to 50,000.

Cidnee Patrick Gallery/Edith Baker Gallery, 2404 Cedar Springs Rd. at Maple Ave., Suite 300, Uptown, (214) 855-5101, Internet www.cidneepatrickgallery.com, e-mail info@cidneepatrickgallery.com. Open Tue-Fri 10 AM-5:30 PM, Sat 11 AM-5 PM; closed Sundays and Mondays. Located just north of downtown Dallas, above it is situated the private club Opus Room, developed by Dallas restaurateur Phil Romano.

Contemporary paintings, works on paper, and sculpture are available with emphasis on Texas artists. The former Baker Gallery was renamed in 2002, when Cidnee Patrick (b. 1971) bought it, although Baker continues playing an active role. Except for a brief stint at the Arlington Museum of Art, Patrick has been director of the Baker gallery since 1996. She received a bachelor of arts degree in French and foreign service from Baylor University, and a master of arts degree in art history from Southern Methodist University in 1999.

Artists represented include Bruno Andrade, Deborah Ballard, Vera Barnett, Brian Bosworth, Denise Brown, Frank Brown, Sandi Seltzer Bryant, Kate Budd, Chong Keun Chu, Hyun Ju Chung, Tim Coursey, Rob Douglas, Lisa Ehrich, Patricia Forrest, Ginger Henry Geyer, Heather Gorham, Houstonian J. Hill, Libby Johnson, Norman Kary, Liu Liu, Tom Pribyl, Marty Ray, Henry Rayburn, Nancy Rebal, Gary Richardson, Richard Rosebury, Steve Seinberg, Gail Siptak, Dallas woodcarver Isaac Smith, Mark Smith, Arkansas art professor Kern Stout, Cecil Touchon, Vanita Smithey, and Judy Youngblood.

Another of the gallery's artists is Pamela Nelson (1947), a native of

Oklahoma City and a graduate of Southern Methodist University, who received the Dallas Visual Arts Center 2000 Legend Award. She designed three DART light-rail stations and teaches art to the homeless at the First Presbyterian Church Stewpot, a downtown social-services agency. He husband Bill gave up a computer consultancy job to conduct monorail tours at the Dallas Zoo.

Baker, herself a sculptor, for years featured contemporary paintings, sculpture, and works on paper by established and emerging Texas and Metroplex artists. A native of Sofia, Bulgaria, where she was born in 1923, Baker arrived in Dallas in 1951. She opened her first gallery in 1977 and moved it to its current location ten years later.

Photographs Do Not Bend, 3115 Routh St. at Carlisle, Uptown, (800) 284-4042 or (214) 969-1852, Internet www.photographsdonotbend.com, e-mail gallery@photographsdonotbend.com. Open Tue-Sat 11 AM-6 PM. Located in a house with creaky hardwood floors just north of downtown Dallas, north of the Crescent Court Hotel, and behind the Brazilian-cuisine restaurant Texas de Brazil.

This Uptown gallery specializes in contemporary photography, rare books, and monographs. Established in 1995, it stocks some 5,000 photos and exhibits three dozen at a time. The *Dallas Observer* opines it "may be Dallas' best commercial gallery per square foot." The gallery also buys photographs from the 19th to 20th centuries, including the work of Diane Arbus, Dorothea Lange, Paul Strand, and Edward Weston.

Gallery artists include Shelby Lee Adams, John Albok, Karl Blossfeldt, Marta Maria Perez Bravo, Debbie Fleming Caffery, Keith Carter, Carlotta Corpron, Jack Delano, Don Donaghy, Rafael Doniz, Janna Smith Fulbright, Earlie Hudnall, Michael Kenna, George Krause, Ida G. Lansky, Barbara Maples, Delilah Montoya, Eduardo Munoz, Luis Gonzalez Palma, Patricia Richards, Walter Rosenblum, Lorry Salcedo, Jeffrey Silverthorne, Thomas Tulis, Jan van Leeuwen, Cassio Vasconcellos, and Ryan Weidman.

Prices range from $150 to $10,000.

Gerald Peters Art Gallery, 2913 Fairmount St. at Cedar Springs Rd., Uptown, (214) 969-9410, Fax 969-9023/9410, Internet www.gpgallery.com. Open Mon-Fri 10 AM-6 PM, Sat 11 AM-5 PM; closed Sundays. Located north of downtown Dallas, a couple of blocks north of the Crescent Court Hotel and almost as far from the Quadrangle mall (see entries). The four-star American-cuisine Lola the Restaurant, with 2,000 wines on its list, is situated next door.

Begun in Santa Fe, New Mexico, in 1974, its Dallas branch opened in 1985. It features paintings, sculpture, and photographs by regional and national contemporary artists such as Magdalena Abakanowicz, John Alexander, Dale Chihuly, Jim Dine, Virgil Grotfeldt, David Hockney, Bill Komodore, Jim Love, David McManaway, Andrea Rosenberg, George Segal, Al Souza, Richard Stout, James Surls, and Tom Wesselman. You might also find here Degas oils, Maillol sculptures and drawings, Matisse drawings, Henry Moore tabletop sculptures, and Picasso paintings.

There is also a Peters gallery in New York City. The Dallas gallery is the smallest of the three, and Santa Fe's, at 32,000 square feet (or 2,973 square meters), is the largest.

Its owner, Gerald Peters, "jets coast-to-coast in his Lear 55, negotiating seven-figure deals that put Picassos, Bierstadts and O'Keeffes on the walls of virtually every major contemporary art museum in the country," notes the *Dallas Morning News*. "His reputation has afforded the native Coloradan a high cachet, opening the doors and checkbooks of America's private mega-millionaire art collectors, a clientele whose names appear on corporations, buildings and foundations."

Before her death in 1986, painter Georgia O'Keeffe chose Peters as her primary dealer, and he probably handled more of her artwork than anyone else. After the 99-year-old O'Keeffe died in New Mexico, 28 of her supposedly "lost" watercolors, dating back to 1916-1918, were offered for sale and eventually bought by Peters for $1 million in 1988. Millionaire banker R. Crosby Kemper paid Gerald Peters $5 million for 24 of them and made the watercolors, titled *Canyon Suite*, the first donation to his own museum in Kansas City in 1993.

Six years later, the National Gallery of Art in Washington, D.C. notified the Kemper Museum of Contemporary Art that the watercolors were not authentic because their paper was not available before the 1930s. Gerald Peters was forced to refund the money to the museum.

Edmund P. "Ted" Pillsbury was the co-owner of this gallery until 2003. He was for nearly 18 years the director of the Kimbell Art Museum in Fort Worth, which is believed to be one of the ten wealthiest in the United States. Pillsbury, an Italian Renaissance scholar and former curator of European art at Yale University's Art Gallery, was, at about $450,000 a year, perhaps the highest-paid museum director in the world.

Earlier, Peters and Pillsbury reconfigured the Dallas gallery into a full partnership, with Pillsbury in charge in Dallas, while Peters handled the strategic planning. In 2002, the gallery took over a location next door and spent $3 million to triple its exhibit space to 6,000 square feet (or 557 square meters), and add a landscaped sculpture garden.

Two of the galleries include marble fireplaces, while a 1,000-square-foot (or 93-square-meter) contemporary space has a glass wall and 11-to-16-foot-high (or 4.87-meter) ceilings. Swiss architect Thomas

Kraehenbuehl, who has worked with several European museums, designed the new galleries.

"The reason for having this gallery with these beautiful spaces is to make people understand that this is a serious business and we're dealing with the best art, often of museum quality," Pillsbury told the *Dallas Morning News*, while the *Fort Worth Star-Telegram* quoted him as saying: "I still think the best technique of selling any work of art is to pay attention to what is important to the buyer—quality or history or even how it works with a buyer's sofa or curtains."

In 2001, Peters acquired the neighboring **Kristy Stubbs Gallery,** at 2606 Fairmount St., specializing in Impressionist and contemporary paintings, prints, and sculpture by artists such as Edgar Degas, David Hockney, Roy Lichtenstein, Henri Matisse, Camille Pissarro, Robert Rauschenberg, Pierre-Auguste Rodin, and Alfred Sisley. In recent years, you could have seen here Picasso's ceramics, paintings, and drawings—such as the $2.5-million *Arlequin au Bicorne*—mobiles by Alexander Calder, works by British artist David Hockney, and sculptures by Texan James Surls. Prices range from $500 to $3 million—dollars, that is.

One of an increasingly more popular gallery artists is painter Frank X. Tolbert (b. 1945), whose father was a long-standing *Dallas Morning News* columnist and chili promoter. Tolbert took art lessons from Otis Dozier, one of the so-called Dallas Nine artists at the old Dallas Museum of Fine Arts in Fair Park. "For a long time, however, Mr. Tolbert's artwork didn't sell enough to pay many bills," notes the *News*. "So the artist spent his days cooking chili at his dad's restaurant [see entry Tolbert's Texas Chili Parlor in the DINING chapter] and his nights drawing and painting."

His wife of more than 20 years is art photographer Ann Stautberg (b. 1954), exhibiting at Barry Whistler Gallery in Dallas' Deep Ellum district east of downtown. The couple lives on the beach in Galveston, in south Texas, in a former Fort Crockett barracks.

Talley Dunn, until mid-1999 the manager of the former Gerald Peters Gallery, opened her own gallery, **Dunn and Brown Contemporary** (see entry), with colleague Lisa Hirschler. Some of the Gerald Peters Gallery's top artists, such as David Bates, Vernon Fisher, Joseph Havel, and Sam Gummelt, followed Dunn to her new gallery.

Plush, Paradise Studios Bldg., 1404 South Akard St. at Griffin St., (214) 498-5423, Internet www.plush01.com. Open Thu-Fri 3 PM-6 PM, Sat noon-5 PM. Located in a bare-bones warehouse four blocks south of City Hall (see entry).

Established in 2000, this "eccentric" gallery is one of several exhibit spaces in what is commonly called the Paradise Art complex. One reviewer claims it possesses "a messy funkiness that makes it seem more like an alternative than a commercial gallery." The works shown include everything from Garland housewife Marcia Alaniz's "family portraits" of tomatoes and her pet chihuahua, to skateboard paintings and used clothes. Prices range from $50 to $3,000.

"It's a labor of love," run by Dallas artist and Richland College gallery director Randall Garrett, notes the *Dallas Morning News*, adding that "underground art movements are rare in conservative Dallas, where the stamp of approval is greatly prized."

On at least one occasion, the owner chained himself to a chair and had the audience of apprehensive onlookers splatter him with paint balloons and glitter to let the creativity flow.

Sharing the entrance, but not necessarily a joint venture, is Joe Allen's gallery **Purple Orchid,** (214) 826-8016.

R. L. Riddell Rare Maps & Fine Prints, 2611 Fairmount St., between Cedar Springs and McKinney Ave., (214) 953-0601. Open Tue-Sat 10:30 AM-6 PM; closed Sun-Mon. Located in Uptown, about a block north of the Crescent Court Hotel (see entry), it shares the building with David Dike (see entry).

Established in 1988, its owner, Royd Riddell, sells antique maps and fine prints from the 16th century through the Civil War. He also has antique globes, Republic of Texas maps, Audubon and Gould prints. Prices range from $50 to $10,000.

Roughton Galleries, 3702 Fairmount St. at Welborn St., Uptown, (214) 871-1096, Internet www.roughtongalleries.com, e-mail brian@roughtongalleries.com.. Open Mon-Sat 10 AM-5 PM and by appointment. Located five blocks from the Mansion on Turtle Creek Hotel (see entry).

This gallery was established in 1974, when Newbern Gallery on Oak Lawn had burned to the ground. Brian Roughton, who had managed Newbern and supplied its frames, was suddenly jobless. With the help of his father and a bank loan, Roughton opened his gallery with about $13,000.

Roughton features 19th- and early 20th-century American and European paintings by regional, national, and international artists such as Albert Bierstadt, A. T. Bricher, William M. Chase, Edouard Cortes, Frederick Childe Hassam, Raymond Kanelba, Eugene Galien-Laloue, Thomas Moran, Hovsep Pushman, Daniel Ridgway, and Knight Thomas. Prices range from $20,000 to $500,000.

After being located for 15 years at 2925 Fairmount St., Roughton moved to this location in 2001. The Spanish-style building with terra-cotta roof and Texas stone walls was constructed in 1931 by architects

James Cheek and Marion Fooshe to serve as their offices. The pair is perhaps best known for designing the Highland Park Village shopping center.

Southwest Gallery, 4500 Sigma Rd. at Welch, (800) 960-8935 or (972) 960-8935, Internet www.swgallery.com, e-mail sales@swgallery.com. Open Tue-Sat 9 AM-6 PM, Sun 1 PM-6 PM; closed Mondays. Located in north Dallas, a little over a mile (or 1.6 kilometers) northwest from the Galleria shopping center (see entry).

Established in 1969, and measuring 16,000 square feet (or 1,486 square meters), the gallery features American and European oils, as well as sculpture, in a variety of styles, including Western and Southwestern.

Among its artists it counts Antoine Blanchard, Bogomir Bogdanovich, Edouard Cortez, Hennie de Korte, L. Gordon, Greg Harris, R. W. Hedge, Harold Kraus, James Rizzi, W. A. Slaughter, Rufino Tamayo, and Xiang Zhang. Prices range from $200 "to hundreds of thousands of dollars."

Stephanie Ward Gallery, 2546 Elm St., between Good-Latimer Expwy. and Central Expwy., (214) 752-5588, Internet www.stephaniescollection.com, e-mail gallery@stephaniewardgallery.com. Open Tue-Sat 11 AM-7 PM; closed Sun-Mon. Located in Deep Ellum, east of downtown Dallas, two blocks west from the Sambuca Jazz Café (see entry).

In 1990, Ward "anticipated the art niche aimed at affluent African-Americans would do well and opened Stephanie's Collection in Plano," notes the *Dallas Business Journal*. "After traveling stints in Europe and New Mexico, Ward's taste in art evolved, and she changed the focus of her gallery to fit her new tastes."

The Ward Gallery features "modern, contemporary abstracts and originals by both mainstream and Third World artists" such as Steve Bartu, Horace Beal, Anna Cool, Wendy Johnson, Kareem Jones, Patrick Lewis, Sylvia Marie, Tim Scott, and Stephen S. Vaneck.

"An especially good place to see the work of Texas artists," says the *New York Times* about her 2,500-square-foot (or 232-square-meter) gallery. Prices range from $50 to $2,000.

Valley House Gallery, 6616 Spring Valley Rd., between Preston Rd. and Hillcrest Rd., (972) 239-2441, Internet www.valleyhouse.com, e-mail kvogel@valleyhouse.com. Open Mon-Sat 10 AM-5 PM; closed Sun-Mon. Located in a far-north Dallas residential area, northeast of the Valley View Mall (see entry).

A family-run gallery, it is surrounded by four and a half acres (or 1.82 hectares) of landscaped greenery, a pond, and fountains. "The beauty of the garden is multifaceted: it's quaint, not huge and is well insulated from urban noise," observes the *Dallas Morning News*. The gallery was built as the owner's home and studio in 1954.

Valley House features 19th- and 20th-century paintings, sculpture, drawings, and graphics. In addition to many American artists, you will also find here the work of Europeans Albert-Benjamin Andre, August-Henri Berthoud, Francoise-Marius Granet, Edmund Daniel Kinzinger, Henry Moore, Lucien Ott, Henri Riviere, Sergio Signori, Claude Venard, and Edouard Vuillard. Prices range from $200 to $1 million, although much of the art sells at $3,500 to $5,000.

The Vogels exhibited Alexander Calder, Catalan artist Joan Miro, and Pablo Picasso before most local galleries would even consider them. This was also one of the first Dallas galleries to promote Texas artists.

The **Valley House Sculpture Garden,** designed by Clarence Roy in 1959, includes works by Mike Cunningham, David Hayes, Nat Neujean, Frederich Sotebier, Charles Umlauf, and Charles Williams.

Donald S. Vogel (b. 1918) started painting watercolors in Cry, Illinois, at 12. He moved to Dallas after two years at the Art Institute of Chicago and founded the gallery 50 years ago. He had exhibited at the Dallas Museum of Fine Arts, which is now the Dallas Museum of Art, in 1941. Vogel built the gallery "into an internationally renowned venue while maintaining an active painting career of his own." The business evolved from the Betty McLean Gallery established in 1951, one of Texas' first galleries dealing in modern art. Now his son Kevin and his wife run the gallery.

Victorian Gallery, 2722 Fairmount St. at Howell, Uptown, (214) 871-2474, Internet www.thevictoriangallery.com, e-mail vicart1@swbell.net. Open Mon-Fri 8:30 AM-5 PM, and by appointment. Located just north of downtown Dallas. Established in 1970 by Robert Potts, who started the gallery as a hobby.

Nineteenth- to early 20th-century British and European oil paintings and watercolors are featured. Many paintings are obtained from English estates and art dealers who attend the weekly British country sales. Prices run from $500 to $100,000.

The Victorian represents Matthew Alexander, John Cook, Lorraine Christie, Darrell Davis, Diane Flynn, Jay Maggio, Roy Petley, and Henry Scott.

Barry Whistler Gallery, 2909-B Canton St. at Malcolm X Blvd., (214) 939-0242, Internet www.barrywhistlergallery.com, e-mail info@barrywhistlergallery.com. Open Wed-Sat noon-5 PM. Located in Deep Ellum, east of downtown Dallas, and less than a mile (or 1.6 kilometers) northwest from Fair Park (see entry).

Established in 1986, the gallery, whose owner's involvement in Dallas art goes back to the 1970s, focuses mostly on contemporary Texas painters, sculptors, and photographers. They include Scott Barber, Ed Blackburn, Ted Kincaid, Jody Lee, Doug MacWithey, Skeet McAuley, Michael Miller, John Pomara, Allison V. Smith, Lorraine Tady, John Wilcox, and Danny Williams. Prices range from $300 to $5,000.

"One of the most knowledgeable and best-connected art dealers in Texas, Barry was the first to open a gallery in Deep Ellum," observes *D Magazine*. "Representing both emerging and established artists, he is a great source for Texas art."

In this gallery you could have seen the "rigorous yet poetic geometric abstractions" by the 100-year-old Dorothy Antoinette "Toni" LaSelle, who was born in Beatrice, Nebraska, and who died in 2002 in a Denton nursing home. When 16 years old, she attended Chicago sculptor Lorado Taft's lecture and sculpting of a clay bust, then went home and cried in frustration when "I realized how ignorant I was."

Another Whistler Gallery artist is photographer Ann Stautberg (b. 1954), the wife of painter Frank X. Tolbert, who in turn is the son of a well-known late *Dallas Morning News* columnist. She grew up in Houston, the daughter of an independent oilman, and majored in painting at Texas Christian University in Fort Worth.

"She waitressed to get by financially," observes the *Dallas Morning News*, and taught art at the Greenhill School (see entry) and at local community colleges. When they met in 1975, "the attraction was immediate," and "they eventually eloped on Valentine's Day 1978." The Tolberts live in south Texas.

In 2002, First Lady Laura Bush stopped by at the gallery to admire Stautberg's work.

SHOPPING

"While the locals go mad over ice hockey and are known to be crazy about professional football, the real sport of Dallas is shopping," claims the *Houston Chronicle*. NorthPark, Galleria, and Grapevine Mills are the three "most popular Metroplex attractions," according to the *Dallas Business Journal*, which says that NorthPark leads with 19 million visitors, followed by Galleria with 16 million.

When the Houston & Texas Central Railroad began service to Dallas in 1872, a group of merchants also came along selling their wares. Among them were the five Sanger brothers, who had emigrated from German Bavaria to avoid the Prussian military service, and made the retailing here an art. The Sangers opened their first store in a brick building on the courthouse square, then in 1910 relocated to an eight-story Lang & Witchell structure, a block east to Main and Lamar Streets, where El Centro College is housed today. This is "Dallas' finest example of the Chicago School of high-rise commercial architecture," claims the Dallas chapter of the American Institute of Architects. The Sangers were the first in Texas with a buyer in New York and could boast 21 departments by 1880. Free home delivery to Dallas customers was also a Sanger first. Sanger Bros. was also the first to introduce monthly retail charge accounts and employee fringe benefits. "One such benefit was a delivery wagon to take unmarried female employees home after work, with Alex Sanger, one of the brothers, as guardian," notes one historian. By the turn of the century, Sanger Bros. had become the largest dry-goods company west of the Mississippi. The last of the Sanger brothers, Alexander (b. 1847), died at Baylor Hospital in Dallas in 1925. The St. Louis-based Stifel, Nicholaus & Co. purchased Sanger Bros. in 1926, although its name survived until 1987, when Federated Department Stores, owner of Foley's, changed its name.

The legendary Herbert Marcus, founder of another celebrated emporium, trained at Sanger's and left because, when asking for a pay raise, received only two dollars more a month. Frank James, brother of the outlaw Jesse James, was one of Sanger's early salesmen.

Today, Dallas is said to have more shopping centers per capita than any other large American city, and still new malls are being planned for or built. If you do not like Dallas shopping centers, you just hate shopping. Period.

The Dallas City Council voted in 2003 to ban smoking in all

shopping malls, department and grocery stores. Also in restaurants, hotel and motel guest rooms not designated for smoking, and private clubs with eating establishments. The smoking ban also applies to all Dallas museums, cinemas, and, of course, hospitals and schools. The only exceptions to the ban are specifically designated areas of stand-alone bars, pool halls, cigar bars, and outdoor patios.

Chances are some stores will not take your personal checks if you come from out of town or abroad, but your Visa, MasterCard, or American Express cards will be quite welcome, as will your travelers checks. Cash, too, but we advise you to carry around a minimum of it.

So if you feel blue, if something is missing in your life, if you have a toothache or are trying to get over your divorce, and nothing has worked so far, do what your Dallas friends might do, brighten your day by going shopping.

But, officially at least, you have not been to Dallas until you have shopped at the downtown Neiman Marcus, as far as Dallasites are concerned the one and only store in the world, even if you only buy a worthless item with the store's name on it. Sadly, Neiman's is the only department store left downtown, even if the suburbs are filled with them. There are few cafés, no bookstores, few shops where one would actually want to spend money. "Downtown Dallas has become the poster child for the exodus of retail business from urban centers," observes a *Dallas Morning News* editorial.

After you have bought your obligatory $20 coffee mug at Neiman's, you can proceed to the most glittering shopping centers in north Dallas, where prices are sometimes just as lofty.

Neiman Marcus Department Store, 1618 Main and Ervay Sts., Dallas, (214) 741-6911, Internet www.neimanmarcus.com. Open Mon-Sat 10 AM-5:30 PM; closed Sundays. Complimentary parking in valet parking lot next door. The NorthPark store is also open Sundays noon-6 PM.

According to the company legend, in 1907—when the city had 86,000 people and 222 saloons—"Herbert Marcus, Sr., his sister Carrie Marcus Neiman, and her husband A. L. Neiman founded Neiman Marcus with the concept of offering the finest, most carefully selected merchandise in the world. It was said that one would have to visit 40 stores in New York to find the variety of designer names represented under one roof at Neiman Marcus.

"Over the years, under the leadership of Herbert's son, Stanley Marcus, the scope of the store was expanded to include fine jewelry and furs; glassware, linens, and silver; men's clothing; epicurean items; and contemporary, traditional, and antique gifts and art objects for the home."

Herbert Marcus (1878-1950) was born in Kentucky and at age 15 followed his brother Theodore to Hillsboro, Texas, working as a janitor and clerk in a general store. On coming to Dallas in 1899, he sold men's pants wholesale and then Buster Brown boys' clothes. He joined his brother-in-law, A. L. Neiman, in a sales promotion in Atlanta.

"The success of this venture brought Marcus and Neiman two offers for their business, one of $25,000 in cash and the other of the Missouri or Kansas franchise for a new product, Coca-Cola," says the Texas State Historical Association, adding that "They chose $25,000 and used the money to stake themselves in a specialty shop in Dallas."

The "flamboyant and egotistical" **Abraham Lincoln Neiman** (1875-1970) hailed from Chicago and was raised at the Cleveland Jewish Orphans Home. He and Carrie Marcus were married around 1907, when good quality ready-to-wear clothes were a novelty and an idea waiting to be exploited.

After the store, initially located several blocks farther west, at today's One Main Plaza, at Elm and Murphy streets, burned in 1913, Neiman persuaded New York investors to finance the building of today's shop. The original four-story building was erected in 1914 and soon expanded by another four floors, and later two more.

After many disagreements with his partners, Neiman sold his share of the business for $250,000 and divorced his wife. Following several other business ventures and his marriage to a Chicago fashion model, Neiman returned to Texas and died penniless in a Masonic home in Arlington, "with a cuff link in a cigar box as his sole remaining possession."

"A woman of impeccable tastes," **Carrie Marcus Neiman** (1883-1953) did not finish high school and worked as a saleswoman at A. Harris & Company department store. A hard worker, she was among the highest paid working women in Dallas by age 21. As a buyer for Neiman Marcus, "she displayed a fashion awareness and an uncompromising demand for quality" while buying the store's merchandise in New York.

Upon Herbert Marcus' death in 1950, she became chairman of the board and reluctantly agreed for the store to open shops in the suburbs. More than 200 pieces of apparel from her personal collection became the basis of the Dallas Museum of Fashion, located at the University of North Texas in Denton. She is buried at Temple Emanu-El Cemetery in Uptown.

The Harvard University graduate **Harold Stanley Marcus** (b.1905), the venerable Mr. Stanley, as he was known in his old age, came into the business in 1926. "Tensions between my father and uncle Al continued to mount, caused no doubt, in part, by my presence in the business," Stanley Marcus wrote in his book titled *Minding the Store*.

The store opened on Monday morning, September 10, 1907, and

made money from its first year of operation. Stanley Marcus caused a stir in 1934, when the store became the first retailer outside of New York to advertise in *Vogue* magazine.

Along the way he met and married the St. Louis-born sportswear buyer Mary Cantrell, who gave him three children, including the only son, Richard (b. 1939), who succeeded his father at Neiman Marcus in the 1970s. She died in 1978 at their home at One Nonesuch Road in Lakewood. The following year, Marcus married a woman 30 years his junior.

The second-generation Marcus, the oldest of four sons, long an advocate of desegregation, Stanley headed the store from 1950 to 1977, when he retired as chairman emeritus. He attended a public grammar school, "many of whose students came from a rough and tough adjoining area, and many a day I was run home by a gang of schoolmates shouting, 'little Jew-boy.'" As a freshman at Amherst, he again encountered religious discrimination.

Although "celebrities from Coco Chanel to John Wayne all fell under his spell," claims the *Dallas Morning News*, he listed among his unfilled desires "one for Sophia Loren, but my wife and her husband wouldn't let me have her." He played host to the Italian film actress during Neiman's Italian Fortnight in 1975.

Marcus, a regional arbiter of style and taste, took Spanish lessons at 88 and developed a fondness for computers after that, but "was always one for a pretty leg," observed his former merchandise manager and later president of Stanley Korshak, another pricey emporium. "He was a flirt." Marcus "dressed Mamie Eisenhower and Lady Bird Johnson," and convinced Grace Kelly that she should buy her bridesmaids dresses at Neiman Marcus. He attended her wedding in Monaco to make sure that everything was all right.

"I don't think clothes have ever been uglier," he told the *News* in 1994. "I also think they are excessively priced for what they are." He said that Calvin Klein's clothes looked like attire for prison inmates. Marcus died in his sleep at age 96 in 2001. Two thousand attended a memorial at the Morton H. Meyerson Symphony Center, the Dallas Symphony Orchestra played Elgar's and Gershwin's music, and its conductor Andrew Litton flew from London to double as piano soloist.

"Stanley Marcus has had an enormous impact on the cultural and economic development of Dallas, perhaps more than any other single person, as well as on the worlds of fashion and retailing," observes the director of retailing studies at Texas A & M University. Says the weekly *London Economist*: "He never let up his mission to save the very rich from the wasting disease of boredom."

Neiman Marcus merged with Broadway-Hale Stores of Los Angeles in 1968 and became part of Carter Hawley Hale Stores in the 1980s. In

1987, the Neiman's chain was sold to Harcourt General, based in Chestnut Hill, Massachusetts. Two years later, Harcourt's 54 percent controlling interest was sold to shareholders, and the corporation is now independent.

The Neiman Marcus Group Inc., parent company of Neiman Marcus Stores, formally changed its corporate address from Massachusetts back to Dallas in 2001. With about $3 billion in sales, the retailer ranks as one of the top 25 Metroplex companies. It includes 33 Neiman Marcus stores in 19 states, two Bergdorf Goodman stores in Manhattan, and the company's catalogue and online business based in Irving. Horchow Finale discount stores are also part of Neiman's.

"In Texas, a visit to Neiman-Marcus is as de rigueur as visits to the Vatican, the Louvre and the Tower of London are in Europe," wrote Nan Tillson Birmingham in 1978 in her book about Neiman's, titled *Store*.

The *Houston Chronicle* notes that the "'mother ship' of the upscale specialty chain is not quite as impressive as it once was since lavish retail stores have fled to the suburbs, but it's still special." Its downtown building was drafted by architect Herbert M. Greene and erected in 1914, following a disastrous fire a few blocks west, where it was previously located.

Today, Neiman's at times appears to be just another corporation pushing the most expensive and sometimes nonsensical objects, like His & Hers Camels, or His and Hers Mummy Cases through Neiman's catalogue, that only an idiosyncratic Dallas millionaire who has never suffered privation would buy.

The first mail-order catalogue came out as a six-page brochure in 1915, His & Hers for the socially conscious started in 1960 with His & Hers Beechcraft airplanes that year, $4,125 camels in 1967, a dinosaur safari in 1975, not to mention a $7,500 day at the circus.

Anyone doubting the insanity of some Neiman's products need go no farther than its cosmetics counter, where a 16.5-ounce (or 467-gram) tub of Creme de la Mer Moisturizing Cream, nestled in a signed silver platform by Henry Dunay, sells for $1,200. Or a small Cipolla pewter cat bowl for $235, which qualified for the honor of a "stupid pet gift" by the *Fort Worth Star-Telegram*.

There is a pleasant New American-cuisine **Zodiac,** (214) 573-5800, on the sixth floor, a café on the Commerce Street side of the building, and an espresso bar inside, also on the ground floor. Open since 1953 and desegregated in the 1960s, when it was not popular to do so, the Zodiac is a place of tradition, consistent and dependable for some shoppers.

The Zodiac is open Mon-Sat 11 AM-3 PM. For a recorded message about its daily entrées, call (214) 573-5801. Your lunch will begin with a complimentary demitasse of clear chicken consommé and a basket of hot rolls. The menu includes salads, entrées, sandwiches, and desserts, all geared mostly toward the suppressed appetites of its female shoppers. Once a downtown dining gem with a pianist, the Zodiac has lost some of its prominence, although the *Dallas Morning News* gives its food four out of the possible five stars.

The person with the largest imprint on the Zodiac was the Irish-American Catholic, Helen Corbitt, a native New Yorker, who managed the restaurant from 1955 to 1969 and died in Texas in 1978. She had worked at the Houston Country Club and the well-known Driskill Hotel in Austin before coming to Neiman's. Her meals were supposedly so scrumptious that President Lyndon B. Johnson wrote to her: "Dear Helen: I can't understand how in the world you can admonish me about my weight and at the same time tempt me with crab bisque and seven-layer cake."

Considering the astronomical sums that can be dropped at Neiman's, the Zodiac is affordable to many and so pleasant you might, for a moment at least, forget that you paid $2,000 for those silly silver earrings.

THE MEGA SHOPPING CENTERS

The first Dallas store was opened in 1842 by John Beeman, one of the earliest settlers whose daughter Margaret married Dallas founder, John Neely Bryan, the following year. He stocked it with tobacco, gunpowder, and whiskey. In 1845, a tiny trading post was established at what is today Cedar Springs Road, in the Oak Lawn neighborhood, where buffalo hides were traded for gunpowder and food.

The first suburban shopping centers in America appeared in 1907, and Highland Park Village (see below), built in 1931, was a prototype. Today, Dallas has a dozen large malls that constantly compete for supremacy.

The Galleria, Lyndon B. Johnson Fwy. at North Dallas Pkwy., Dallas, (972) 702-7100, Internet www.dallasgalleria.com. Open Mon-Sat 10 AM-9 PM, Sun noon-6 PM. Located in far-north Dallas, off Dallas North Tollway—whose service road is called Dallas Parkway—between Alpha Road and Lyndon Johnson Freeway (also known as Interstate Highway 635). The Shops at Willow Bend (see entry) mall is seven miles (or 11.3 kilometers) north of here.

Galleria, some will swear, is the most fantastic shopping center on the face of the earth, although it brings in fewer shoppers than its cousin, NorthPark Center (see entry). Where else will you find 200 specialty shops, men's and women's clothing and shoe stores, home and electronics shops, and then, just as you are ready to collapse from exhaustion and hunger, two dozen eateries? Have you ever experienced anything more exhilarating? All right, go ahead, laugh and call it silly, but before you leave Dallas, you, too, will be addicted, and then I will have the last laugh.

Galleria's beginnings go back to 1964, when cow pastures and cornfields were transformed into the LBJ Freeway. When, in 1968, it linked with the North Central Expressway (or U.S. Highway 75), this thoroughfare became the gateway to north Dallas. The Galleria's doors flew open on October 30, 1982, when "15,000 people turned out to see the newest temple to Texas shoppers," according to the *Dallas Morning News*. The night before, singer Dionne Warwick had entertained at a black-tie ball for more than 1,300 VIPs.

Architecturally, Galleria traces its roots back to the original legend, Milan's Galleria Vittorio Emanuelle, which was built in 1867. The Milan's 160-foot-high (or 48.8-meter) glass-and-iron dome inspired the 960-foot-long (or 293-meter) glass-vaulted skylight that culminates in a 100-foot-high (or 30-meter) dome over the ice center at the Dallas Galleria.

The Dallas namesake sits on a 42-acre (or 17-hectare) tract of land and covers 1.9 million square feet (or 176,510 square meters). Also situated here is a 431-room **Westin Hotel** (see listing), and a 160-by-80-foot (or 55-by-24-meter) ice skating rink that is open daily. Sixteen million shoppers throng its passageways every year and nearly every third shopper is a tourist. Among the foreign visitors, the most likely ones are from Mexico, Canada, the United Kingdom, Germany, or Japan. Although there is space to park 9,600 automobiles, the traffic congestion can be horrifying, and you may spend more time looking for a parking place than shopping.

"If you haven't seen Galleria, you haven't seen Dallas, " proclaims a mall's public relations tract, claiming that the shopping center is the second most visited tourist attraction in Dallas, after the Sixth Floor Museum (see listing) downtown.

The stores are located on four levels, with some among the most prestigious, like **Macy's,** (972) 851-5185; the 225,000-square-foot (or 20,902-square-meter) **Nordstrom,** (972) 702-0055; and **Saks Fifth Avenue,** (972) 458-7000, occupying anchor positions on three levels.

Elsewhere, you will find more than three dozen women's apparel and accessories shops, such as Ann Taylor, Casual Corner, DKNY, Guess, Gucci, Harold's, Lillie Rubin, The Limited, Limited Too, Louis Vuitton, Original Levi's Store, Petite Sophisticate, Talbots, and

Victoria's Secret. No fewer than 30 stores sell jeans, and another 15 petite sizes for women.

One of the newer ones is the "spare, modern and luxe" MaxMara's first Dallas store, in the center court of the first level, where white cotton shirts go for $150 each, and camel's-hair blazers start at $900. Near Banana Republic, you will find a 3,700-square-foot (or 344-square-meter) men's and women's clothing store, Club Monaco, whose fans supposedly include actresses Salma Hayek, Sarah Jessica Parker, and Susan Sarandon. Founded in Toronto in 1985, it was purchased by Polo/Ralph Lauren in 1999. Another 20 apparel stores, like bebe Outlet, BOSS Hugo Boss, Brooks Brothers, Express, Gianni Versace, Levi's, and Tommy Hilfiger, sell men's and women's apparel. Elizabeth Arden and Nordstrom department store run expensive spas and skin-refurbishment salons.

Gap took over the entire three-story, 127,600-square-foot (or 11,854-square-meter) space once occupied by Saks Fifth Avenue to open in 2002 individual Gap, Banana Republic, and Old Navy stores that also sell GapKids, BabyGap, and GapBody products. In addition to those already mentioned elsewhere, half a dozen other shops cater to children, such as clothing purveyor Gymboree and the Children's Place. The area around Gap is now populated with a teen-oriented cluster of stores that also include American Eagle Outfitters, Wet Seal, and fye music store. The old Gap's 40,000-square-foot (or 3,716-square-meter) store is occupied by the Abercrombie & Fitch teen store, Celine boutique, and Dunhill men's couture store.

You can go to Shakespeare Beethoven bookery, (972) 387-1720, and a dozen other shops to buy cards, stationery, and gifts. Located on the Galleria's third level, Shakespeare Beethoven measures about 5,000 square feet (or 464 square meters) and stocks books and classical and jazz CDs. It also has a large selection of French, German, Italian, and Spanish-language magazines. Children's books will be found in the back of the store.

Film and cameras can be had at Wolf Camera. Tiffany & Co., which in 1997 was joined by the august Cartier, is one among ten jewelry stores that also include the ever-present Zales chain of 2,300 stores that was founded in 1924.

For leather goods, you can go to Bag 'n Baggage, Coach, Louis Vuitton, and several other shops. More than two dozen stores, such as Enzo Angiolini, Foot Locker, Johnston & Murphy, Kenneth Cole, and Tommy Hilfiger, sell men's and women's shoes.

If coming from abroad, you can have a part of your sales tax refunded. (Please see details about TaxFree Shopping Ltd. under NorthPark Shopping Center, below.)

Add to this a business center, a drugstore near the Old Navy clothing store, a bank, and an American Express foreign currency exchange, (972) 233-9291, on the third level, and you get an idea why Galleria has so many fanatical followers.

On the lower level there is the **Ice Skating Center,** (972) 392-3361, where America's and Olympic ice skating darling, Tara Lipinski, once spinned free of charge. The mall often brags about the "largest indoor Christmas tree in the U.S." that is usually located here.

Food at the Galleria: As if this were not enough, there are two dozen restaurants, candy and coffee shops. Surrounding the ice rink, you will find Bennigan's, Bistro China, Café Sbarro, La Madeleine French Bakery & Cafe, Tex-Mex Mi Cocina, Johnny Rockets, and Steak Escape. Nicola's Ristorante, an "excellent authentic Italian restaurant," and Sonny Bryan's BBQ will be found on the third level, along with Uncle Tai's, a 20-year-old Chinese cuisine restaurant, which is situated near Macy's department store. The Seattle, Washington-based Nordstrom department store has its own Café Nordstrom. The Corner Bakery is located on the second level, near the Westin Hotel. Other eateries on the third level include the Russian Island Gift Shop & Café (www.russianisland.com), located on the balcony overlooking the ice rink, and McDonald's fast-food restaurant. Russian Island sells icons, lacquer boxes, and make-believe Faberge eggs.

UBS Realty Investors purchased the Galleria for $300 million in 2002. That same year, a Chicago investor bought the 93,987-square-foot (or 8,731-square-meter) Galleria North specialty center, located across from the Galleria, where the Container Store and Crate & Barrel are located.

But don't go away yet, here is another shopping center just as beloved by Dallasites:

NorthPark Center, 8080 North Central Expwy. at West Northwest Hwy., Dallas, (214) 361-6345 or 363-7441; security, 363-8347; management office, 363-7441; no Internet site. Open Mon-Sat 10 AM-9 PM, Sun noon-6 PM. A newer, but much smaller addition to NorthPark shopping lies just south of here, across Northwest Highway. Located in north Dallas, just west of Central Expressway (also known as U.S. Highway 75), between Northwest Highway and Park Lane. Park Lane light-rail station is on the east side of Central Expressway. For those taking a DART light-rail train from downtown or from Plano, a complimentary DART trolley runs from the Park Lane station, at Greenville Avenue, to NorthPark, Mon-Sat 9 AM-10 PM, Sun 11 AM-7 PM, about every 15 minutes.

When it opened in 1965, NorthPark was the largest such air-conditioned facility in the country. Natural light is provided by translucent skylights placed above deep beams to reduce glare. On a busy Saturday, up to 100,000 shoppers might visit the mall and up to 19 million come annually. NorthPark attracts shoppers from 40 foreign countries, and its directory is printed in several languages.

> International travelers can enjoy tax-free shopping thanks to TaxFree Shopping 'Ltd., (214) 368-9067, Internet www.shoptexastaxfree.com, e-mail info@shoptexastaxfree.com. The Web site gives the details of the services available in English, French, German, Italian, Portuguese, and Spanish.
>
> This service is available to all foreign visitors who can shop anywhere in Texas, then come to the TaxFree Shopping office on the north side of Dillard's department store, which is open Mon-Sat 10 am-8:30 pm, and Sundays noon-6 pm.
>
> Upon submission of the visitors' passport, airline ticket, and original invoices, TaxFree Shopping will provide the necessary paperwork to refund the state's 8.25 percent sales tax and credit it to their credit card. Jewelry, for example, is eligible for a sales tax refund, but only if it is not worn during the visit to Texas. Restaurant and hotel bills are not eligible for such sales tax refund.
>
> The processing fee is 2.5 percent of the purchase amount and the refund will be made within six weeks of departure from the United States. Foreign visitors must have purchased items within the last 30 days and must take their purchases with them when leaving the United States.

Among the 160 shops on the first and second level, are the anchor department stores, such as **Dillard's,** (214) 373-7000, with an automatic teller machine just inside its entrance; **Neiman Marcus,** 363-8311; and **Lord & Taylor,** 691-6600, owned by St. Louis-based May Department Stores. It took the developer two years to convince Neiman Marcus to open its first store here outside of downtown.

There are no fewer than 70 men's and women's fashion apparel and accessories shops, although many, like Anne Klein, Brioni, Calvin Klein, Chanel, DKNY, Dolce & Gabbana, Donna Karan, Emanuel Ungaro, Escada, Hermes, Giorgio Armani, Jean Paul Gaultier, Montblanc, Ralph Lauren, or St. John, are part of these department stores. Others include Ann Taylor, Banana Republic, Brooks Brothers, Express, Gap, J. Crew, Liz Claiborne, Talbots, Timberland, and Victoria's Secret.

The 1,900-square-foot (or 177-square-meter) Jaeger boutique here, the venerable British company started in 1884 by German professor Dr. Gustav Jaeger, sells clothing designed by Bella Freud, great-granddaughter of Sigmund Freud and daughter of painter Lucian Freud. One of the newer entrants is the 1,300-square-foot (or 121-square-meter) Lacoste boutique, where black Lacoste polos with silver crocodile logo go for $100 a pop. The brand was started in 1933 by Rene Lacoste, a popular French tennis star.

Although it was already one of the most successful malls in Texas, the wealthy Nasher family, which owns it, has also lured the Houston-based retail chain, **Foley's,** (469) 232-3600, part of May stores, which opened a three-level 250,000-square-foot (or 23,225-square-meter) store in 2000.

Except for Neiman's, you will have a hard time distinguishing the merchandise at the remaining three department stores because their once-distinct personalities seem to be gone, not unlike the personality many small and mid-size American towns lost with the arrival of fast-food restaurants and chain stores.

In 2004, a new 240,000-square-foot (or 22,296-square-meter) **Nordstrom** will cap the Northpark's count at 200 stores and make it one of the largest malls in Texas. Nordstrom already runs its subsidiary here, the Nice, France-based Faconnable men's and women's apparel boutique, where jeans start at $70, and a lambskin dress costs $800.

For teenagers and twenty-somethings, there is Abercrombie & Fitch, where the rock music can be so loud that those over the age of 29 can get an instant headache. Also popular with such crowds might be Gap, Guess, and Rampage clothing stores, Record Town disc and video store, and EBX video and computer games shop.

The department stores, an upscale Oilily, Disney Store, and Gymboree all sell children's apparel, but FAO Schwartz toy seller left the mall in 2002. Brookstone, Charlotte's Room, and Steuben Glass at Neiman's are just three of some 20 stores selling home furnishings and accessories. A 12,000-square-foot (or 1,115-square-meter) William-Sonoma Grande Cuisine emporium, next to Tiffany's, provides everything from cooking demonstrations to new user-friendly fixtures.

At least two dozen NorthPark shops, such as Easy Spirit, Enzo Angiolini, Foot Locker, Johnston & Murphy, Kenneth Cole, Nine West, Pappagallo, Salvatore Ferragamo at Neiman's, Timberland, and Via Spiga offer men's and women's shoes. The *Dallas Observer* claims that Dillard's here has the best women's shoe store in the city. Shoes account for more than 10 percent of sales at 340 Dillard's stores in 29 states.

Jewelry is available at Bailey Banks & Biddle, Bulgari at Neiman's, Faberge at Richard D. Eisman Jewels, James Avery Craftsman, Paloma Picasso at Tiffany & Co., and several other shops. If you liked the diamond bracelet design worn by Julia Roberts in the film *Ocean's Eleven*, Tiffany's can probably sell you another one for $60,000. The family-owned Eisman Jewels, one of the original NorthPark tenants, sells baubles and timepieces that go for up to $100,000 each and has not had a markdown sale in more than 20 years. Richard Gere wore a $3,000

Baume & Mercier watch borrowed from Eiseman in the film *Dr. T and the Women*, part of which was filmed at this mall.

You will find luggage and leather goods at Bag 'n Baggage, Coach, and Dooney & Bourke; also at Neiman Marcus's boutiques Bottega Veneta, Gucci, Louis Vuitton, and Prada. Among the cosmetics and beauty shops at NorthPark is Clinique at Dillard's. An expensive Estee Lauder Spa is situated at Neiman Marcus.

Also part of NorthPark is Le Theatre de Marionette, (214) 369-4849, Internet www.ltdm.com, a young children's puppet theater, where such classics as Jack and the Beanstalk, The Little Mermaid, and Pinocchio can be seen Saturdays and Sundays.

What pleases the upscale shoppers, many of whom come from the nearby University Park, Highland Park, and Preston Hollow neighborhood in north Dallas, are the frequent displays of artwork. You never know when you might find a work by Marc Chagall, Henry Moore, Frank Stella, Claes Oldenburg, Andy Warhol, or Roy Lichtenstein, all from the owners' private collection.

Raymond Nasher, NorthPark's owner, was among the first real estate developers in the United States to install original artworks in commercial and retail complexes. (For a few examples of his NorthPark art, please the Art in Public Places section in the VISUAL ARTS chapter.)

Books, unfortunately, take a back seat at NorthPark. The only mall bookstore is Rand McNally, which has a large selection of travel-related books and accessories only. A few children's books will also be found at the Museum Company. The Dallas Museum of Art Store sells art objects and art books in the mall. For a much wider selection of books, consider Barnes & Noble (see entry) in the Lincoln Park Shopping Center, across Northwest Highway, just south of here. Cheesecake Factory, where dinner plates are the size of truck tires, and Blue Mesa (see entry) restaurants will also be found there.

NorthPark Center Concierge, (214) 361-6345, is located on the lower level, behind Dillard's. In addition to providing information about NorthPark stores, restaurants, and events, and helping with restaurant, salon, and spa reservations, it also sells gift certificates and stamps, rents wheelchairs and strollers, as well as checking coats and packages.

It is at NorthPark that Corpus Christi-born actress Farah Fawcett, according to the *Dallas Observer*, is "losing her mind and, eventually, her clothes as she takes a dip in a fountain that does little to cover Fawcett's outstretched nude body," in Robert Altman's 2000 film *Dr. T and the Women*, with Richard Gere and Helen Hunt. The film features Gere as a gynecologist who devotes his practice to Dallas socialites. *The Fort Worth Star-Telegram* judged the movie "more than a little myopic when it comes to its representation of Dallas society." Added the *Dallas Morning News*: "Dr. T may be the silliest thing to happen to Dallas since [the television soap opera] *Dallas*."

Food at NorthPark: The mall lacks a food court, affording limited opportunities to sit down with your friends and family during or after shopping. The restaurants and food shops include Corner Bakery, the Italian Sbarro, and La Madeleine French Bakery & Café (see entry). P. F. Chang's large China Bistro (Internet www.pfchangs.com) serves lunch and dinner. Near it is McCormick & Schmick Seafood Restaurant. Neiman Marcus has the Zodiac, which is open Mon-Sat 11 AM-3 PM. Starbucks Coffee is also on the premises. For a more serious lunch or an early dinner, try Maggiano's Little Italy, (214) 360-9061, which serves steaks, chicken, lamb, and fish.

Highland Park Village, Mockingbird Ln. at Preston Rd., (214) 559-2740. Open Mon-Sat 10 AM-6 PM, Thu 10 AM-8 PM, Sun noon-5 PM. ATM is situated at Tom Thumb supermarket. Located north of downtown, between the towns of Highland Park and University Park. The private Dallas Country Club is situated across Preston Road from here.

Built in 1931 and patterned after the Plaza in Kansas City, the Village shopping center is one of the most prestigious in the city. It was the first such American facility in which shops faced inward. The mall's builders were Texas architects James B. Cheek and Marion F. Fooshee, who became partners around 1920. Cheek and Fooshee were one among the firms involved in the design of the Hall of State at the Texas Centennial Exposition in Fair Park (see individual entries). They traveled to Barcelona and Seville in Spain, California, and Mexico in search of a suitable design for Highland Park Village and settled on a Mediterranean Spanish look.

Designed by a Beverly Hills planner, Wilbur David Cook, the shopping center took almost 20 years to complete because the Depression was ravaging the country, and tenants were difficult to attract. When it finally opened in 1931, many businesses were reluctant to move to what they considered too far north and away from downtown Dallas. Sanger Bros., a prestigious downtown institution since 1872, when 2,500 people inhabited Dallas, became the first Dallas department store to open a suburban branch here in 1941.

By the mid-1960s, the center had fallen into disrepair and could not be sold until realtor Henry S. Miller snapped it up for a mere $5 million in 1976. In 2000 the 9.9-acre (or four-hectare), 200,000-square-foot (or 18,580-square-meter) mall was designated a national historic landmark by the Secretary of the Interior Department on recommendation of the National Park Service.

A neighborhood shopping center, it has everything from a supermarket to a barbershop, from restaurants to multiple cinemas housed in a domed, three-story stucco tower built in 1935. Among its 80 stores and restaurants are some exclusive shops, like Bottega Veneta, Calvin Klein, a 5,000-square-foot (or 465-square-meter) Chanel Boutique, Christian Dior, Escada, Harold's, Luca Luca, Polo/Ralph Lauren, St. John Boutique, and Ultimo. Prada closed its store here in 2002.

The luxury Paris-based children's apparel merchant, prim-and-proper Jacadi, is also situated here, selling girls' velvet dresses for $80 or more. One of 14 Hermes stores in the United States is located here and managed by a woman who readily acknowledged to the *Dallas Morning News* that "you don't need anything in this store." A Hermes beach towel can cost you $400, a dog collar $310, and a matching leash $380. Want a Hermes Birkin bag? The wait is two years. But if you need to know its price, you probably cannot afford it.

The middle-class Gap and Banana Republic, Cooter's Village Camera, Gerald Tomlin Antiques, and Williams-Sonoma are also situated here. Women can now buy $250 bodysuits at the Wolford Boutique. Beretta Gallery, the 475-year-old Italian firearms manufacturer, also pushes sport clothing for men and women, and fashion accessories in the Village.

There is Heritage Rare Coin Galleries, one of the nation's largest auctioneers.

For women unable to confine themselves to $500 dresses, there is Lilly Dodson boutique, where they can spend from $3,500 to $12,000. First Lady Laura Bush had her inaugural gown done here by designer Michael Faircloth (b. 1959), who also caters to the wives of Ross Perot Jr. of Dallas and Lee Bass of Fort Worth. "Not bad for a boy who grew up in the southeast Texas town of Yoakum, population 5,533," observes the *Dallas Morning News* about Faircloth. "But like a lot of youngsters in tiny Texas towns, he got a heaping helping of strong work ethic served alongside his chicken-fried steak." In 2002, Faircloth moved into a 4,700-square-foot (or 437-square-meter) studio on Edison Street, in Dallas' Design District, near Oak Lawn Avenue and Interstate 35 East, to capitalize on publicity and launch his first ready-to-wear collection.

Food at the Village: If Tom Thumb supermarket ready-to-eat foods are too low in social status for you, there are several eateries in the Village, including Phil Romano's Who's Who Burgers, which the *Dallas Morning News*, amazingly, judged one of the 100 best restaurants in the Metroplex. You will find here Mi Cocina, a Tex-Mex restaurant. Patrizio and Café Pacific are also good choices to display yourself and show that you make oodles of money. A Starbucks, too.

Also situated here is **Larry North Total Fitness,** (214) 526-6784. North, whose inflated promises can be heard on late-night infomercials, is the prince of Dallas fitness gurus with a location befitting his popularity. A born salesman, he will easily sell you on lifetime happiness—as long as you exercise in one of his gyms. "On the radio, in books, in speeches, and on infomercials, Larry has inflated his name into a multimillion-dollar brand, with himself as the smiling figurehead," observes the *News*.

The son of a "compulsive gambler who spent his life in and out of prison and psychiatric hospitals," a "degenerate" as North described him to the *News*, he, his brothers, and his mother drove a beat-up green Chevy Impala from New York toward Houston to escape the old man. The car broke down at Spring Valley Road and Central Expressway, and the family stayed in Big D, where in the 1980s North worked as a shoe salesman and a nightclub bouncer. He opened this center in 1990.

For the rest of us who are embarrassed to show ourselves at the North Fitness center, there is an intimate, small but handsome, European-style Doubleday bookstore.

Valley View Shopping Center, 2040 Valley View Center, Lyndon B. Johnson Frwy. at Preston Rd., Dallas, (972) 661-2424/2425, Internet www.shopvalleyviewcenter.com. Open Mon-Sat 10 AM-9 PM, Sun noon-5 PM. It has automatic teller machines, a service center, strollers, and disability access with wheelchairs. Located in far-north Dallas, west of Preston Road and north of LBJ Freeway (also known as Interstate Highway 635). The Galleria shopping center is farther to the west.

Valley View is owned by the Macerich Company of Santa Monica, California, a real estate investment trust that claims a portfolio of 40 malls.

Sears Roebuck opened a freestanding store in this area that in 1965 was surrounded by pastureland. The LBJ Freeway had not yet been constructed. Valley View opened in 1973, when a Sanger-Harris store (now Foley's) was added and connected to Sears with a corridor of specialty shops. It was the first shopping center north of LBJ, renovated in 1999. Seen from the outside, the mall may remind you of an industrial plant somewhere in Baghdad, with lots of concrete and hardly any greenery. Valley View has 170 stores occupying 1.6 million square feet (or 148,640 square meters) of space, arranged on two levels around an atrium.

The four anchor department stores that surround the mall are **Dillard's,** (972) 458-3500; **Foley's,** 385-6996; a 233,000-square-foot (or 21,646-square-meter) **J.C. Penney's,** 726-1821, located in a former Bloomingdale's space; and **Sears,** 458-3500. This was one of the first Dillard's department stores in Dallas.

Among the great variety of stores, more than 20 of them sell apparel and accessories for women, including A Gaci, American Eagle, Ann

Taylor Loft, Bebesh, Casual Corner, Charlotte Ruse, Denim Underground, Express, Gap, J. Harris, La Diva, Lane Bryant, Lerner New York, The Limited, Motherhood Maternity, Old Navy, Petite Sophisticates, and Victoria's Secret. Half that many shops offer men's apparel or accessories, such as Gadzooks, Georgio for Men, Gingiss Formal Wear, and Milano's for Men. There are several children's apparel stores, including The Gap Kids and Gymboree. Kay Jewelers, Gordon Jewelers, and Zales are among a dozen jewelry stores. Footwear merchants include Champs, Jarman, Lady Footlocker, Florsheim Shoes, Naturalizer, and Stride Rite for kids.

The Milwaukee-born craftsman James Avery (b. 1921), who started his jewelry business in Kerrville, Texas, in 1964 with a help of a Small Business Administration loan, sells his well-known stylized crosses, doves, and other religious symbols. It was James Avery Craftsman that hand-hammered the Communion chalice created for Pope John Paul II when he visited San Antonio in 1987.

Specialty stores include Bag & Baggage, Bath & Body Works, Brookstone, Eyemaster and Lenscrafters, Lego and KB Toys, RadioShack, Ritz Camera, Sunglass Hut, and a severely limited Waldenbooks bookstore. There is the City Golf indoor facility for kids with arcade games and billiards.

Food at Valley View: You will not go hungry at Valley View, although the food is rather pedestrian. There are more than a dozen food shops and restaurants, including the reasonably priced Luby's Cafeteria, Camille's Sidewalk Café, Charlie's Steakery, Colter's Bar-B-Q, Great American Cookie Co., McDonald's, Sbarro, and Taco Bell. The sole white-tablecloth eatery is European Chocolate Café, located near J.C. Penney and the children's play area, where desserts can be had after sandwiches, soups, and salads. Chuck E. Cheese's children's restaurant, one of 400 nationwide, vowing kids with unbearable noise, rides, games, and pizza, is located at Montfort Drive and Alpha Road nearby.

(For more information about the **Dallas Children's Museum,** located on the mall's upper level, next to J.C. Penney, please see the museum entry in the VISUAL ARTS chapter.)

Grapevine Mills Mall, 3000 Grapevine Mills Pkwy., Grapevine, (888) 645-5748 or (972) 724-4900, Internet www.grapevinemills.com. Open Mon-Sat 10 AM-9:30 PM, Sun 11 AM-7 PM. There is parking for 8,500 cars. Located 21 miles (or 33.8 kilometers) northwest from downtown Dallas, at the intersection of State Hwy. 121 and Farm Road 2499 in northeast Grapevine, a two-mile (or 3.2-kilometer) drive north of the D/FW Airport. Out-of-town shoppers can use a shuttle service from the airport. The minimum one-way taxi charge within a seven-mile (or 11.3-kilometer) radius of the airport is $15.

Grapevine Mills is, of course, in Grapevine, but it is included here because it is conveniently situated just northwest of the D/FW Airport. With 1.5 million square feet (or 139,350 square meters) of retail space, it is also one of the largest malls in the Metroplex. The racetrack-shaped mall boasts up to 13 million shoppers annually. The $200-million project encompassing a 175-acre (or 71-hectare) mall with more than 200 specialty and outlet stores, two ice skating arenas, and a 30-screen AMC movie theater, opened in 1997.

Bed, Bath & Beyond, J.C. Penney Outlet Store, Marshalls, Old Navy, and **Virgin Megastore** are this mall's anchors.

Women's apparel merchants include 5-7-9, Anchor Blue Clothing Co., Ann Taylor Loft, bebe Outlet, Big Dog Sportswear, Burlington Factory, Casual Corner Annex, Charlotte's Room, Chico's, Coastal Cotton, Donna Karan, Dress Barn Outlet, Gap Outlet, Guess Factory Store, Levi's Outlet, Motherhood Maternity Outlet, and Polo Jeans Factory Store. But women have other excuses to stop at Grapevine Mills: more than half a dozen health and beauty shops, just as many home furnishings stores, and twice that many jewelers.

Brooks Brothers Factory Store, Casual Male Big & Tall, Dockers Outlet, Haggar Clothing Co. Izod, S & K Menswear, Tommy Hilfiger, Van Heusen, and Wilson Leather Outlet sell men's clothing.

Children's apparel can be bought at Carter's for Kids, the Children's Place Outlet, and the OshKosh B'Gosh Outlet. Build-a-Bear and K-B Toys sell children's toys. If you have unruly kids with too much energy, send them to Chuck E. Cheese's nearby for pizza, lots of games, and unbearable noise.

Looking for footwear? Man or woman, you can buy it at the Athlete's Foot Outlet, Banister Shoe Studio, Foot Locker Outlet, Just for Feet, Liz Claiborne Shoes, Naturalizer, Nine West Outlet, Payless Shoe Source, or Sketchers.

There are half a dozen luggage and handbag shops, including the Samsonite Company Store and Leather Loft. Golf America and the Dallas Cowboys Pro Shop sell athletic apparel. Books-a-Million, Brookstone Outlet, and a couple of optometrists are also here. Other merchants include Kenwood Stereo and Bose Factory Store for music fanatics, RadioShack that sells a little of everything, Ritz Camera, and Western Warehouse.

Some stores may disappoint you. "Off Fifth more closely resembles a mini Mervyn's than its tony parent Saks Fifth Avenue," according to one critical review, while the Off Rodeo Drive racks might turn out to be "a jumble of unexceptional sportswear from labels such as Fubu, XOXO, FiFi, CK Jeans and Adidas."

In 2002, Neiman Marcus opened a 32,000-square-foot (or 2,973-square-meter) Last Call clearance center in a free-standing building, near Rainforest Café, where Neiman's merchandise from the company's 30-plus high-end stores across the country is sold at up to 80 percent of its original price. You might find here Chanel boots, Manolo Blahnik sandals, Versace shirts, Prada bags, Fendi coin purses, or Lauren jackets.

Food at Grapevine Mills: There are two dozen eateries on the premises, including Corner Bakery, Dick Clark's American Bandstand Grill, Dickey's Barbecue Pit, Kelly's Cajun Grill, Paradise Bakery & Café, and Sbarro Italian Eatery. Steak 'n Shake, the Indianapolis-based chain of 400 distinctly Midwestern restaurants serving shakes and sirloin burgers, is also here. Desperate transplanted addicts, who before had to drive to Arkansas, now can get their sirloin burger fix here. The Steak 'n Shake (Internet www.steaknshake.com) legend began in 1934 in the Illinois hamlet of Normall, where restaurateur Gus Belt invented the steakburger.

For those seeking fun at night, there is a 23,000-square-foot (or 2,137-square-meter), $2-million nightclub called Corte that can accommodate up to 2,000.

A privately owned 40,000-square-foot (or 3,716-square-meter) **ESPN X Games Skate Park,** (972) 539-4340, Internet www.xgamesskatepark.com, is open daily.

"Toddlers will be entertained by the robotic animals at the Rainforest Café," notes the *Dallas Morning News*. "Older kids will happily blow weeks' worth of allowance at GameWorks, a sensory-overloading arcade of video and virtual reality games."

AmeriSuites and Homewood Suites hotels, Bennigan's restaurant, Discount Tire, and the Trail Dust Steak House are all located nearby. There is also the huge Bass Pro Shops Outdoor World, (972) 724-2018, Internet www.basspro.com.

OTHER DALLAS SHOPPING CENTERS

Crescent Court Shops, Cedar Springs Rd. at Maple Ave., Dallas, (800) 828-4772 or (214) 871-3232. Located in Uptown, just across Woodall Rodgers Freeway from downtown.

Opened in 1985 in a ten-acre (or four-hectare) office complex, Crescent is owned by Caroline Rose Hunt, the youngest of five children from oil baron Haroldson Lafayette Hunt's "first family." She is said to be worth $600 million and has a soft spot for the English countryside, antiques, and knicknacks, which she sells at the Primrose shop here along with tea. She claims to abhor aloof service and loves to travel economy class.

Stores like Boehm Porcelain Gallery, Cathy's Antiques, and Pratesi Linens ring a three-level open atrium. Fashion shops, such as clothier Stanley Korshak, with a 400-square-foot (or 37-square meter) Valentino boutique, and a similar Korshak Kids department will be found here. Korshak, where clothes from the self-professed fashion designer Susan Dell—the wife of computer billionaire Michael Dell—are sometimes shown, is now owned by Crawford Brock, who had run the specialty boutique for 15 years. "Korshak is a stark-looking clothing store where overly friendly salespeople eagerly offer drinks while you shop for a $2,000 suit," observes the *Houston Chronicle*. *Men's Health* magazine once named it one of the best places to shop in America. The magazine's advice: "Make sure you bring a ten-gallon wallet."

The Crescent Court Hotel and Beau Nash restaurant (see below) are located here, as well as Creole-Cajun-cuisine Gumbo's, the Capital Grille steakhouse, and Palomino.

Beau Nash, (214) 871-3240, is open daily and has live jazz Thu-Sat nights. The restaurant is named after Richard "Beau" Nash (1674-1762), a dandy born in Wales who studied at Oxford. "He then made a shifty living by gambling, but in 1704 became master of ceremonies at Bath, where he conducted the public balls with a splendor never before witnessed," according to a British Web page. Although he died a pauper, he was buried with pomp in Bath Abbey, England's last great medieval church that was begun in 1499 by Bishop King.

Well-dressed "beautiful" people who live on the admiration of others like to eat at this brasserie with mahogany paneling. "Center stage is the open kitchen, where, like actors, the chefs masterfully deliver New American cuisine, which changes daily according to the freshest ingredients available," claims the Crescent's Web page. The large open bar attracts singles in the evening.

The most expensive piece of dinner meat might be the prime New York strip steak, followed by filet of beef, grilled swordfish, and pan-seared striped bass. The *Fort Worth Star-Telegram* opines that "the food is as beautiful as the sleek interior."

The development also includes 1.3 million square feet (or 120,770 square meters) of office space in a 19-story tower flanked by two contiguous 18-story buildings and 160,000 square feet (or 14,864 square meters) of atrium space. Many of Dallas' old-line companies and families have offices here.

Among them is investment firm Hicks, Muse, Tate & Furst, one of the largest private equity companies in the nation, led by Tom Hicks, who was instrumental in building the American Airlines Center (see entry) nearby. In the 1980s, he and his partners financed the purchase of Dr Pepper, 7-UP, and A&W Root Beer. They took A&W public in

1987 and merged Dr Pepper with 7-Up the following year, selling it to Cadbury Schweppes for $700 million in 1995.

According to *Forbes* magazine, Hicks is one of the 15 richest people in Dallas and among the top 400 in America. Hicks (b. 1946), who reportedly earns $15 million a year, enjoys a lavish lifestyle that includes a 24,438-square-foot (or 2,270-square-meter) mansion valued at $50 million on Walnut Hill Lane, west of the Dallas North Tollway, in north Dallas. Hicks and his family live on the estate designed by architect Mario Fatio of Palm Beach, Florida, and named for an Italian cotton broker. Count Pio Crespi and his wife Florence constructed a 14,950-square-foot (or 1,389-square-meter) French chateau beginning in 1939 and through World War II. When the Dallas North Tollway was built, it bisected the Crespi estate. Florence Crespi survived the count, and her second husband, and died in the 1990s when she was close to 100 years old. To shield himself and his neighbors from the tollway traffic noise, Hicks is reported to have paid $650,000 to the North Texas Tollway Authority to build a ten-foot-tall (or three-meter) sound-absorption wall beside his 25-acre (or ten-hectare) property that features woods and a creek.

Also located at Crescent Court are offices of the Dallas billionaire Sam Wyly (b. 1935), who has spent four decades battling mammoth competitors and building companies like University Computing, Sterling Software, Michaels Stores, and the Bonanza restaurant chain. A Louisiana native with a master of business administration degree from the University of Michigan, he came to Dallas in 1958 and worked for five years as a salesman at IBM and Honeywell before founding University Computing.

"Not Philip Johnson's best work, to be sure, but still worthy of its landmark status," observes the Dallas chapter of the American Institute of Architects about the Crescent Court. "Ironically, the Crescent represented the height of opulence and conspicuous consumption in Dallas when it was built—the same time that the city and state were tumbling into a near depression that would last for the rest of the 1980s."

"No longer shining like a new penny, the Crescent has a timeless look that gives it a stateliness and grace one would expect from a well-designed, established, traditional building," claims one local architect speaking at a *Dallas Business Journal* forum.

Dallas Design District. Located two blocks west of Interstate 35 (or Stemmons Fwy.) and bound by Oak Lawn Ave., Hi Line Dr., Slocum St., and Industrial Blvd. Many showrooms are open until 6 PM on weekdays, as well as on Saturdays.

You once had to be an interior designer or architect to gain admission.

Now the neighborhood is no longer a gated community, but remains home to high-fashion furnishings merchants. Several showrooms, including those that feature contemporary furniture, fabrics, lighting, and ceramic tiles, are open to the public.

The original Decorative Center—several one-story showrooms on the corner of Hi Line Drive and Slocum Street—opened in 1955 with a dozen tenants. By 1967, the center occupied six buildings. (Four Design District's art galleries are featured in the VISUAL ARTS chapter.)

There are some 30 antique dealers on Slocum Street alone, many of whom came to escape higher rents elsewhere. The Mews and Mews II, at 1708 Marker Center and 1333 Oak Lawn Ave., together feature almost 100 dealers. Four kitchen showrooms opened in the district in 2002 alone.

Bella Italia, 1548 Slocum, imports antiques and art from villas and castles. Connie Williamson Antiques, 1313 Slocum, sells 18th- and 19th-century furniture. Debris showroom, open since 1999 at1205 Slocum, represents 50 national and international dealers with goods from England, France, Italy, Tibet, and the United States.

The Gathering, 1515 Turtle Creek Blvd., is one of several high-end antique malls representing some 50 dealers, and also has a café. Ligne Roset, 190 Decorative Center, sells contemporary furniture by Europe's best designers, crafted in France. Philip Maia Antiques, 1209 Slocum, imports 18th- and 19th-century provincial antiques from France, Portugal, and Spain.

Directly south of the Design District is the Trinity Design District, which caters to the design-related companies, production studios, photographers, printers, and other arts-related businesses.

Inwood Village Shopping Center, Lovers Ln. and Inwood Rd., Dallas, (214) 745-1701. Many stores are open Mon-Sat 9 AM-6 PM, Sat-Sun 10 AM-5 PM. Located on the western edge of the Highland Park and University Park townships.

"The Miracle Mile," a string of 1950s Lovers Lane shopping strips that actually continues for a quarter of a mile only, runs through this area. Its most distinguishing features are the lack of parking and enough stores to keep the wealthy University Park residents busy on weekends.

Begun in 1949, this was one of Dallas' first retail neighborhood shopping centers. The Caruth family sold Inwood Village in the 1980s. The Gap and St. Bernard Sports are among the anchor stores. St. Bernard, (214) 357-9700, Internet www.stbernardsports.com, maintains a large ski and clothing shop, where you can spend into the hundreds if not the thousands. The mid-sized Bookstop, (214) 357-2697, is quiet and pleasant and a good place to stop by before or after seeing a quality film at the Inwood cinema next door which in 1949 was one of the first tenants.

There are apparel, art and antique, accessories and furniture, collectibles, fitness and beauty, jewelry, footwear, and gift shops in this upscale 14.5-acre (or 5.8-hectare) shopping center that spills over several blocks.

Byzantine, Mary Nash, and Turtletique women's clothing and accessories stores are located here. There is Sebastian's footwear and handbag store near the Gap. You will also find nearby a rather expensive Children's Place clothing and footwear store and Right Start toy store. Pier 1 Imports home furnishings store is situated on the north side of Lovers Lane.

Several popular restaurants are located here, including the Mexican-cuisine Cantina Laredo whose roots go back to 1949. Café Istanbul, serving Turkish foods, is also in the neighborhood. City Café (reviewed in the DINING chapter) and Hofstetter's Spargel are located on Lovers Lane nearby. On the other end of the shopping center, you will find Bali Bar, where the dishes are influenced by French cuisine.

Le Passé, a 3,000-square-foot (or 279-square-meter) store specializing in country French pottery and antiques, opened in the center in 1989 and has expanded twice. Texas Art Gallery is situated in Suite 396, (800) 783-4278 or (214) 350-8500, Internet www.txartgallery.com. It is an 8,000-square-foot (or 743-square-meter) gallery that opened in 1964 and sells mostly American and Western paintings and sculpture.

William W. Caruth (1912-1990), a descendant of a prominent local family that settled in Dallas in 1848, built this shopping center in the mid-1940s on what was then the northeast edge of the city limits. His father donated the land for the Southern Methodist University campus a year after Caruth Jr. was born. Junior graduated from SMU in 1933 and went on to Harvard. He got his start at age 21, when his father gave him $1,000 (a little over $10,000 in 2002 dollars) for not smoking or drinking until 21.

People "laughed and told him he was an idiot," and predicted he would lose his shirt because there were no buildings at the time in the immediate area, according to his wife, Mabel Morrow Peters Caruth, a descendent of a Harvard founder, who died in 2000 at the age of 86.

Mabel Caruth met her husband at a dance when he was a student at Harvard Business School, and they married in 1936. The couple gave generously to hospitals and medical facilities in the area. The Caruths once owned 30,000 acres (or 12,141 hectares) stretching from downtown Dallas to Forest Lane. The family's homeplace, located west of Central Expressway and south of West Northwest Highway, includes a 19th-century mansion where William Barr Caruth settled with his family in the mid-1800s. Nearby is the Mabel Peters Caruth Center, which houses the Communities Foundation of Texas, one of the area's largest philanthropic organizations.

Knox-Henderson Streets & Vicinity, Uptown Dallas. Most shops are open daily, except Sundays. A shopping area located between Knox Street and Armstrong Avenue, Travis Walk and McKinney Avenue that goes back to the 1950s, when it was the place to find the latest electrical devices, television sets, and air-conditioners.

Knox Street once featured a regularly scheduled trolley. This is an area slowly evolving into what might resemble slightly a European-style promenade favored by those tired of mega malls. You can park your car and keep busy for a whole afternoon, then have a good meal in the evening. Anchored by the $6-million, 37,000-square-foot (or 3,437-square-meter) Crate and Barrel store that opened in 1997, Weir's Furniture Village, and Ed Kellum appliance and video store, there are some three dozen home and garden furnishing stores, specialty and antique shops. The 22,000-square-foot (or 2,044-square-meter) Weir's Furniture store opened in 1948 and has been run by J. Ray Weir (b. 1911), who started it with $16,000, half of it from his father.

Highland Park Antiques & Nauticals, Peacock Alley bedding, and Morgen Chocolate are just a few area stores. The upscale Sur la Table kitchenware store on Travis Walk is also the one where you can take cooking classes for . . . dogs. Forty Five Ten, named for its address on McKinney Avenue, across the street from Abacus restaurant (see entry), sells home furnishings, clothing, jewelry, and accessories, where Sartor art gallery once exhibited Gaugins.

The newest addition here is the **Knox Park Village,** an 88,000-square-foot (or 8,175-square-meter) office and retail complex that occupies the southwest corner at Knox Street and Central Expressway. The central district office for the American Automobile Association is located here.

"The proximity to businesses and growing residential neighborhoods has made Knox Street one of Texas' hottest retail strips since developers first began renovating the area in the early 1990s," reports the *Dallas Morning News*.

Among the eateries in this area are Abacus, Adelmo's, Chez Gerard, Sipango, Tarazza, and Ziziki.

When Knox Street crosses North Central Expressway it changes its name to Henderson Avenue, which is also a popular dining and shopping street with "what may be the only pedestrian-friendly highway overpass in the state." Here you will find crafts, hand-forged chandeliers, jewelry, a garden market, Nick Brock Antiques, Collage designer furniture, La Mariposa folk art, and Canterbury Antiques. The weekly

Dallas Observer claims that Emeralds to Coconuts, at 2730 North Henderson, is the "best women's clothing store" in Dallas. Next door is the Pandemonium Limited vintage clothing store. A *Texas Monthly* shopper assumed that "this trendy neighborhood in North Central Dallas would be a victim of Crate and Barrel-ization," but was "thrilled to discover that the shops on the Henderson end of the street have plenty of personality."

For diners there are Italian-cuisine Alfredo's, Boat House restaurant, East Side Grill, and Tei Tei Restaurant on Henderson Avenue. Also Barley House, Cuba Libre, and Old Monk drinking establishments. Parking is scarce.

Mockingbird Station, 5307 East Mockingbird Ln., Dallas, (214) 252-1183 or 421-LOFT, Internet www.mockingbirdstation.com. An eclectic, mixed-use village with a bridge to the DART light-rail station at East Mockingbird Lane and North Central Expressway, on the edge of the affluent Park Cities. A ten-acre (or four-hectare) $100-million urban-chic village with 595,000 square feet (or 55,275 square meters) of shops, restaurants, and theaters, developed in 2001 by a graduate of Southern Methodist University, which is situated on the other side of Central Expressway.

Where there was once a decrepit three-story Western Electric building, there are now 200 loft apartments with a rooftop swimming pool. Some tenants pay up to $5,000 a month. There is a 900-car underground garage and 1,600 more spaces next door.

The development includes a 25,000-square-foot (or 2,322-square-meter) Virgin Megastore selling recorded music. There is Dallas' only Urban Outfitters clothing store, the "best example of capitalism gone mad," according to *D Home* magazine, as well as Ann Taylor, Bath & Body Works, Gap, and Victoria's Secret. Park Cities Bank is also located here. Movida, launched by a former Latina J.C. Penney buyer, sells women's clothing, shoes, and jewelry from trendy Los Angeles venues.

Among the restaurants, you will find Rockfish Seafood Grill, Starbucks, and an Irish pub, Trinity Hall (Internet www.trinityhall.tv), whose interior is a traditional Irish pub with the design based on the provost's home at Dublin's Trinity University that dates back to 1592. With the exception of the wooden flooring, practically everything else was brought from Ireland. Sample their "hearty" Irish breakfast on weekends, until 2 PM. There is live music on some nights.

Next door to the pub is Angelika Film Center, with eight theaters having from 100 to 180 stadium seats and featuring mostly independently produced films. Lobby areas include a bar and a respectable offshoot of the Dallas restaurant Parigi, named Angelika Cafe, with terrace seating. The self-service restaurant Café Express, on the other end and with outdoor seating, overlooks Mockingbird Lane and Central Expressway.

Across Mockingbird stands the severe, almost Soviet-style, 400-room Hotel Santa Fe, owned by the Maharishi School of Vedic Science, which was founded by 1960s spiritual icon Maharishi Mahesh Yogi. Farther east from it is the Mockingbird/Central Plaza strip mall, with the Pocket Sandwich Theatre (see entry), Whole Earth Provision Co. for backpackers and hikers, and Premiere Video (see entry).

Old Town Village Shopping Center, 5500 Upper Greenville Ave., Dallas, (214) 750-1517. Located between East Lovers Lane and Southwestern Boulevard, and across Greenville from DART's Lovers Lane light-rail station. During the 1970s and 1980s the area along Greenville Avenue was mostly a nightclub strip that has largely been rehabilitated.

A 1970 development, where hip singles congregate, particularly at the Borders bookstore, which stocks up to 100,000 titles. The shopping center has more than 40 other stores and restaurants, including a Tom Thumb supermarket which also is a popular meeting place for thousands of singles from the adjacent Village apartment community.

A 20,000-square-foot (or 1,858-square-meter) Michaels Arts and Crafts store, overlooking Greenville Avenue, opened in 2002. Dive West, one of the first scuba diving specialty stores in the city in 1977, opened next to Wolf Camera and across Greenville Avenue from the Black-Eyed Pea restaurant. A bike shop and a couple of clothing stores can also be found here.

There are several inexpensive restaurants in the area, including Baker Bros. Deli, Fuddruckers, Humperdink's. Miami Grill, Pizza Inn, Texadelphia, Two Rows Restaurant & Brewery, and Wing Daddy's. If you enjoy Thai cuisine, Royal Thai restaurant, at 5500 Greenville Avenue here would be a good choice. Open Mon-Fri for lunch from 11 AM to 2:30 PM, it serves dinner from 5 PM to 10 PM.

Across Lovers Lane and south of here, the San Antonio-based H.E. Butt Grocery Co. built an 75,000-square-foot (or 6,967-square-meter) Central Market "food emporium" (see entry) in 2002 that attracts up to 20,000 shoppers weekly on the 12-acre (or 4.8-hectare) site.

To make the traffic congestion even worse, Lincoln Property, the area landlord, also brought in a 3,000-square-foot (or 279-square-meter), 24-hour drive-through Krispy Kreme doughnut shop, whose product causes Dallasites to behave as though they are about to get a free Swiss gold watch.

Diagonally across from Old Town is the post office, an Eckerd Pharmacy, and Office Depot.

Preston Center West, Berkshire Ln. at Westchester St., Dallas. Located on the edge of University Park, south of West Northwest Hwy., between Preston Road (or State Highway 289) and Dallas North Tollway, Preston Road is one of the oldest Dallas streets, which between 1840 and the coming of the railroad three decades later, was the principal immigrant route into northern Texas.

This 385,000-square-foot (or 35,766-square-meter) shopping area has more than a hundred stores and restaurants serving the affluent neighborhoods of Highland Park and University Park around it. It was one of the first major retail centers in north Dallas when opening in the 1950s. More than a dozen property owners control the center. There is covered complimentary parking in the square.

What was originally built as a Sanger Brothers department store that later became Foley's has since moved to NorthPark shopping center (see entry) nearby. The three-level, block-long building was converted into a "vertical urban mall," titled the Preston Center Pavilion, which opened in 2002 at a cost of $70 million.

It now houses shoe retailer DSW Shoe Warehouse, with 31,000 square feet (or 2,880 square meters) of space, located on the ground floor and facing Berkshire Lane. Marshall's MegaStore has 50,000 square feet (or 4,645 square meters) in the basement. The second floor includes a large day spa and several off-price apparel retailers.

Facing the corner of Douglas Avenue and Berkshire, the Pavilion developer created a two-level store for Sun & Ski Sports. There is a 30-foot (or nine-meter) high rock-climbing wall that faces the windows. Restaurants are located on the ground floor.

Stride Rite children's footwear and Duxiana bedding, where you can spend thousands on a Swedish-style bed, are some of the other stores situated in Preston Center West.

(For more about the well-regarded Tramontana Mediterranean bistro here, please see the DINING chapter.) La Madeleine French Bakery & Café (see entry) is also situated in this area.

And located nearby is the **Park Cities Hilton Hotel** (see entry) on Luther Lane near Dallas North Tollway, which technically is in Dallas, not the tony Park Cities—but who could resist the temptation when naming a hotel so close to wealth?

A couple of blocks east of the Hilton, there is Café Expresso, 6135 Luther Ln. at Preston Rd., not well-known, but boasting such luminaries as the Ross Perot extended family, the Dickeys of barbecue fame, the supermarket Cullums, retailer Roger Horchow, and oilman T. Boone Pickens as its patrons. George W. Bush ate here when he lived in Dallas. It is run by the German-born Dieter Paul, who had cooked in Switzerland, Manila, and Hong Kong before coming to Dallas' Fairmont Hotel. Just south of here is steak, fish, and pasta restaurant, Sevy's, a large "gorgeous and impeccably maintained" eatery, according to the *Dallas Morning News*.

East of Preston Center, across Preston Road, there are 40 more shops at the **Plaza at Preston Center,** (469) 232-0000, located in an eight-building village and renovated in the mid-1980s. The Plaza is part of the Caruth family holdings.

Situated here is the Storehouse furniture mart, where the old Neiman-Marcus stood before moving to NorthPark (see entry) nearby in 1965. American Express travel and foreign exchange office, (214) 363-3219, is also located on this side.

Sound Warehouse, Tom Thumb supermarket, and Biz Kid children's clothing store will be found here. Several clothing stores, such as Betty Reiter, Carla Martinengo, and Tootsies, and restaurants, including Houston's, Momo's Italian Specialties, and Taco Diner, are located in this shopping area previously known as Preston Center East.

Both Preston Center developments sit within minutes of three million square feet (or 278,700 square meters) of office space. The owners of the shopping centers estimate that more than 120,000 people live within a three-mile (or 4.8-kilometer) radius of here and that their average income is well above $100,000 a year.

The Quadrangle, 2800 Routh St. and Howell St., Uptown Dallas, (214) 871-0878. Located midway between McKinney Avenue and Cedar Springs Road, north of the Crescent Court Hotel (see entry). Built in 1965 on the street named after the Baptist preacher Rev. Jacob Routh.

A four-acre (or 1.61-hectare) courtyard center with shops, galleries, and restaurants designed for pedestrians, who seem to have cooled to the area, it includes 129,000 square feet (or 11,984 square meters) of office space in an eight-story tower.

Ruggeri's Italian-cuisine restaurant is located here. There is a Dream Café with what some would generously describe as a children's playground. Sigel's 8,000-square-foot (or 743-square-meter) gourmet food and liquor store is also located here.

Theatre Three (see entry) has owned its building in the Quadrangle since the 1980s.

"The Quadrangle was revolutionary when it was constructed—its intimate scale and unpredictable layout an appealing alternative to the generic shopping centers that were taking hold of the suburbs," observes the Dallas chapter of the American Institute of Architects.

By 2000, the weekly *Dallas Observer* called it "Uptown's ghost town," where "your voice simply echoes past the fountains and off the concrete."

In the words of Dallas painter Lynn Noelle Rushton, who defiantly proclaims, "You won't catch me scraping hair off famous people's sofas, putting it in little bottles and calling it art," Quadrangle was once "a place where artists gathered in the now-dismal courtyard on the weekends for open-air painting, and friendly exchanges with shoppers and neighbors out for a stroll."

The Shops at Legacy, Legacy Dr. between Dallas North Tollway and Parkwood Blvd., Plano, (972) 239-6966. Located north of downtown Dallas and Park Cities, east of Dallas North Tollway, and north of Tennyson Pkwy. Legacy is situated 1.8 miles (or 2.9 kilometers) south of the Stonebriar Centre and 3.2 miles (or five kilometers) north of the Shops at Willow Bend (see listings) regional malls. A 2.4-acre (or 0.97-hectare) lake in Bishop Park features fountains, strolling paths, and a gazebo.

With a daytime population of more than 40,000, Plano's Legacy corporate campus in northwest Plano is bigger than many Texas towns. Its corporate residents include Dr Pepper/Seven Up, Electronic Data Systems, The Frito-Lay Company, J.C. Penney, and Marriott International.

The 150-acre (or 60-hectare) Legacy Town Center includes a 400-room Doubletree hotel, a three-building, mid-rise luxury apartment complex, restaurants, and shops. Post Properties maintains 384 apartments, while 100 townhomes are on the planning board. The $55-million mixed development was financed by Instanbul, Turkey-born Fehmi Karahan (b. 1956), who received his master of business administration degree from the University of North Texas while waiting tables.

There are two TLC Child Development Center daycare facilities, a Southern Methodist University campus, and a 57,000-square-foot (or 5,295-square-meter) YMCA fitness facility at Tennyson Parkway and Windcrest Drive. A five-screen, 30,000-square-foot (or 2,787-square-meter) Angelika Film Center & Café, similar to that at Dallas' Mockingbird Station (see entry), was built in 2003, the first art-house cinema in Collin County.

Patterned after an urban shopping center, the handsome 23-acre (or 9.3-hectare) high-density, mixed-use development opened in 2001. Designed by Florida urbanist architect Andres Duany, it is laid out on a small-town street grid with tree-lined sidewalks, a variety of storefront architecture, and ample landscaping.

Circa 2000 menswear store, Creative Leather furniture of Scottsdale, Empowered Women's Golf, Images of Nature gallery, Robb & Stucky furniture store, Sara Gates Frame & Gallery are a few of the retailers featured here.

Among the restaurants, you will find a 7,000-square-foot (or 650-square-meter), 270-seat Bob's Steak and Chop House (see entry) on Legacy Drive, Café Express, Cliff's Grill of Houston, Half Shells

Seafood Grill, Jasper's Steakhouse, Kathleen's Art Café, Main Street Bakery, Mi Cocina, Rice Boxx, Starbucks Coffee, and Barumba Latin Lounge

The 2,660-acre (or 1,076-hectare) Legacy complex is owned by Electronic Data Systems Corp., which has some 10,000 employees in the area. Started in the early 1980s, Legacy is one of the Southwest's largest and most successful campus-style business parks. Only Las Colinas (see listing) in Irving is larger in the Metroplex.

Snider Plaza. Bound by Hillcrest Ave., Lovers Ln., Dickens Ave., and Daniel St., University Park. Located close to the geographical center of University Park, north of downtown Dallas. "Certain buildings along this shopping center approach architectural significance, but the overall atmosphere of these five blocks is their real gift," observes the Dallas branch of the American Institute of Architects.

C. W. Snider of Wichita Falls, Texas, developed the plaza in 1927 and sold it in 1977. The plaza features more than 80 antique, home furnishings and clothing stores, restaurants, and other specialized shops facing each other from the opposite sides of the plaza and side streets. Tom Thumb supermarket is located on the northern edge of the plaza.

Sebastian's is an offshoot of a similar store in Inwood Village (see entry) with a footwear selection that's "one of the best in town," according to the *Dallas Morning News*.

You will find G. Stanton art gallery across the street from Bubba's Cooks Country, a down-home, biscuits-and-gravy shelter for those who miss their mother's cooking. At Allie-Coosh boutique near the fountain, whose proprietor is from Newfoundland, women can choose the fabric and pattern and have their clothes made to order.

The 4,500-square-foot (or 418-square-meter) Learning Express toy store, one of 16 locations in Texas, carries a large assortment of educational toys for children up to age 12. The *Dallas Observer* named it the best toy store in Dallas. Sarkis Oriental rug store is nearby.

"Snider Plaza has one-of-a-kind individually owned shops and restaurants where local residents are the mainstay," observes the *News*. Some residents of the Park Cities feel it is one of the few places in Dallas that has character.

Among the more than half a dozen other restaurants on the plaza, you will find Kuby's, serving German-cuisine, Italian-cuisine Penne Pomodoro, and a couple of hamburger spots. Marc Hall has owned Amore Italian Restaurant, Cisco Grill, and the well-regarded Peggy Sue BBQ since 1975. Picardy's serves seafood, particularly shrimp specialties. Burger House on Hillcrest Avenue claims "secret seasoning" created in 1951 by its founder, Prometheus "Jack" Koustoubardis, who died in 2001. The previously mentioned Bubba's overlooks Hillcrest Avenue and has been here since 1980. A 1927 Texaco service station, it has a drive-through window, too. The film *Breaking Home Ties*, with actor Jason Robards, was filmed here in 1987.

A nine-story, $50-million, 112-foot (or 34-meter) office tower, between Daniel and Hursey streets, has been proposed for the south end of the plaza. It would replace the existing 70-foot-high (or 21.3-meter) J.P. Morgan Chase bank building, and would include a public library, and six levels of underground parking.

A $15-million Park Cities Medical Plaza opened in 2002. The three-story center, owned largely by doctors, has day surgery facilities for patients who do not require hospitalization.

West Village, bound by McKinney and Lemmon Aves., Cole St. and Blacburn Ave., Dallas, (469) 547-9666, Internet www.westvil.com. Located on the property previously owned by Cityplace (see entry) in Uptown. A three-block landscaped boulevard was built to connect West Village from McKinney to the Cityplace DART subway station on the west side of North Central Expressway.

A $60-million, two-block, mixed-use development designed to offer pedestrian-oriented shopping and dining, as well as a small-town feel, opened in 2001. West Village integrates luxury urban apartment lofts with a 150,000-square-foot (or 13,935-square-meter) retail, restaurant, and entertainment district that to some resembles Soho in New York City.

National retailers, such as Ann Taylor Loft, Banana Republic, Gap, Tommy Bahama, and a 4,200-square-foot (or 390-square-meter) Ralph Lauren Polo Sport store, where a basic sweater costs $175, are situated in several buildings. Trumeau sells Mediterranean-influenced furnishings and decorative items. The little black dress at Sara Lasier shop starts at $225. You can also freshen up at Avalon/Aveda Spa & Salon.

Bella Bella store sells trendy women's clothing, accessories, and shoes. The Glass Slipper features upscale women's clothing lines, accessories, and jewelry. Women's Rock Star jeans will be found at the laid-back Lucky Brand store. The Italian-based company Piaggio sells spunky scooters—popularized by Audrey Hepburn in the film *Roman Holiday*—under the Vespa brand, the first Vespa store in Dallas since the scooter was created in 1946.

A Tuscan-style, loft-like Ferre Ristorante e Bar, and Cru wine bar next door, both having the same owner, have opened to great fanfare here. They are both meant for the recklessly porous wallets of the young; most wines at Cru cost more than $10 a glass. A bohemian basement vodka Euro-bar, Club Nikita (named after La Femme Nikita, not Nikita Khrushchev), serves dinners and cocktails. French cuisine can be had at the pet-friendly Paris Vendome Brasserie, which has pretensions of being a relative of the Place Vendome eateries in Paris.

Celebrity Café & Bakery, Tex-Mex Taco Diner, Starbucks, and one of the several Paciugo Italian gelato parlors will also be found here.

There is a 1,000-seat, five-screen Landmark Theater's **Magnolia Cinema** (Internet www.magpictures.com), on the upper three floors of a building at Lemmon Avenue East and Cole. An 850-car parking garage is placed out of sight inside the perimeter of shops.

Developed by Henry Miler Interests and Phoenix Property Co., the development consists of six buildings designed by architect David M. Schwartz, who also drafted the American Airlines Center (see entry).

An Addison Shopping Center

Village on the Parkway, Southeast Corner of Dallas Tollway and Belt Line Rd. Open daily 10 AM-9 PM, Sundays noon-6 PM.

A Mediterranean-style shopping center with a hundred shops, restaurants, bars, and services. Among the anchor stores are Bed Bath & Beyond and Brook Mays Music Super Store. Kristi's and Liz Morgan sell women's apparel in suites across the street from each other. One of the three very expensive MallaSadi men's boutiques is located here. Sebastian's Closet, another men's clothier, is a couple of doors away from Travelex/Thomas Cook travel services, where foreign currencies can be exchanged.

Kittrell/Rifkind Art Glass Gallery (see entry) sells exquisite glass objects priced at up to $15,000. As so often the case in American shopping centers, there is no general bookstore in this one either. But you will find three jewelry stores and three spas, including Grand Spa International, where you can order a 20-hour, $1,625 bridal package, spread over six weeks prior to your wedding. 24-Hour Fitness and home furnishings salons like Fitz & Floyd and Interior Design Studio are located here.

Among the restaurants here and across Montfort Drive (and reviewed in the DINING chapter) are: Blue Mesa, Chamberlain's Steak & Chop House, El Fenix, and La Madeleine French Bakery & Café. The weekly *Dallas Observer* claims that the Tin Star here is the city's best restaurant for kids. But there are others, including Bennigan's, Celebrity Café & Bakery, Dream Café, Spanish tapas restaurant El Patio Flamenco, Enchilada's Tex-Mex, Flying Fish, Flying Saucer, Houston's, MoMo's Pasta, The Original Pancake House (which closes daily at 2:30 PM), TGI Friday, and Yoshi's Japanese fast-food restaurant.

To dance to live music from the 1960s and 1970s, head for Ernie's of Dallas, which opened in 1989 and attracts mostly an older clientele. Mercy wine bar stocks 150 wines, 80 of them by the glass, "And it's the best wine bar we have so far," declared the *Dallas Observer* in 2003. For those who have no one to share drinks with, there is even Elite Singles D/FW (Internet www.elitesinglesdfw.com) dating service, which might lead to Logan's bar and the British pub Sherlock's Baker Street nearby, which the *Dallas Morning News* calls "one heck of a bar."

A Frisco Shopping Center

Stonebriar Centre Mall, 2601 Preston Rd. at State Hwy. 121, Frisco, (972) 668-4900 or 668-6255, Internet www.generalgrowth.com. Open daily 10 AM-9 PM, Sundays noon-6 PM. More than 7,350 parking spaces are available. Located in south Frisco, on the border with Plano, east of The Colony, Frisco lies on State Highway 289 (or Preston Road) and is situated about 12 miles (or 19.3 kilometers) north of Dallas. Also nearby is Tom Fazio Golf Course, one of the most expensive in Texas. About a dozen miles (or 19.3 kilometers) away is Collin Creek Mall (see entry) in Plano in one direction, and Vista Ridge Mall in Lewisville in another.

The two-level regional mall that opened in 2000 was the first shopping center built in 19 years in Collin County. The *Dallas Morning News* calls it "the epicenter of North Texas' retail universe." Stonebriar has 1.64 million square feet (or 152,356 square meters) of space.

Stonebriar is anchored by **Foley's,** (972) 731-3600; **J.C. Penney,** 712-2707; **Macy's,** 731-9211; **Nordstrom,** 712-3794; and **Sears,** 731-3400.

The 160-plus tenants include women's apparel merchants Ann Taylor, bebe Outlet, Body Shop, Cache, Casual Corner, Charlotte Russe, Chico's, Coldwater Creek, Express, Lane Bryant, Rampage, and one of the 800-plus Talbots stores nationwide. Other apparel sellers having stores here are Abercrombie & Fitch, Banana Republic, Eddie Bauer, Fossil, The Gap, Guess, and J. Crew.

Among its ten jewelry stores, you will find Gordon's and Zales. Bag 'n Baggage and Coach sell leather goods; Stride Rite kid's shoes, the Children's Place, and Gymboree offer kid's apparel. The Dallas Cowboys football team sells it wares here, as does a Dell computer kiosk.

Teen-age-oriented retail row—with stores such as American Eagle Outfitters, Gadzooks, and Watchamacallit—is located on the second level. If bookstores are a stepchild of most Texas malls, Stonebriar is an exception. A comfortably large, two-level Barnes & Noble is located here at 2601 Preston Road and includes a café and a children's section.

Home furnishings are sold at the Bombay Company, Haverty's Furniture, Pottery Barn, and Williams-Sonoma Grande Cuisine. You can buy home entertainment and electronics equipment at Bose, RadioShack, Sam Goody, and SBC Communications stores.

There is a Bank of America here, Eyemasters, Lenscrafters, and Sterling Optical Laser Center, and a couple of hair salons. Godiva Chocolatier will satisfy your favorite addiction. Also here is Victoria's Secret intimate wear, two maternity stores, Discovery Channel, Kay-Bee Toys and Noah's Ark when children follow.

The Cheesecake Factory, Dave & Buster's (see entry), California Pizza Kitchen, Chili's, Paradise Bakery & Café, Sbarro's, and Steak Escape are some among the restaurants. The food court can seat up to 1,000 shoppers and has a full-sized carousel with 32 colorful horses and 24,000 lights. Another two dozen eateries are clustered near the mall.

There is a National Hockey League-size ice rink (Internet www.stonebriarice.com), open daily, a 24-auditorium AMC cinema complex, and 1,000-square-foot (or 93-square-meter) children's play area sculpted from soft foam.

General Growth, its manager, with 136 properties in 39 states, including Town East Mall (see entry) in Mesquite, is the nation's second-largest mall developer.

North of here, near the northwest corner of Preston and State Highway 121, are an additional 1.2 million square feet (or 111,480 square meters) of retail space in the $66-million **Centre at Preston Ridge,** which caters to retailers, such as Best Buy, DSW Shoe Warehouse, Linens N' Things, Marshall's, Old Navy, PetsMart, Pier One Imports, Ross Dress for Less, Staples Office Supply, Stein Mart, SuperTarget, and T.J. Maxx. More than half a dozen restaurants, including Bennigans, Chili's, Colter's Barbecue, and Texas Land and Cattle Co., will also be found here. The 126-acre (or 51-hectare) center is part of the 719-acre (or 291-hectare) Frisco development.

With sales averaging $425 per square foot, the only dark cloud on the Stonebriar's horizon are The Shops at Willow Bend (see entry), another upscale shopping center that opened a year later five miles (or eight kilometers) away. There are some 140,000 households with an average annual income of $100,000 within a five-mile (or eight-kilometer) radius. Stonebriar Centre targets mostly women 20 to 45 years of age.

West of the Stonebriar Centre, along the east side of the Dallas North Tollway, just north of State Highway 121, the city of Frisco built a minor league baseball park and a $20-million Dallas Stars training facility. The park, completed in 2003, anchors a $300-million, 72-acre (or 29-hectare) mixed-project that includes more than a million square feet (or 93,000 square meters) of new office, retail, and residential space. A 350-room Embassy Suites hotel and conference center is also planned for the area.

The Frisco RoughRiders (Internet www.ridersbaseball.com), a Texas Rangers affiliate, uses the $30-million, 8,800-seat Dr Pepper/Seven Up stadium, designed by architect David Schwartz. In 2002, Hicks' Southwest Sports Group, which operates the Frisco team, moved the former Swamp Dragons from Shreveport, Louisiana, where the professional team had played for 35 years. The Frisco StarCenter, one of five in the Dallas area, will have two National Hockey League-size ice surfaces and will become the chief training facility for the Dallas Stars when completed.

An Irving Shopping Center

Irving Mall, 3880 Irving Mall, North Belt Line Rd. at Hwy. 183, Irving, (972) 255-0571, Internet www.shopsimon.com. Open Mon-Sat 10 AM-9 PM, Sun noon-6 PM. Wheelchairs are available at no charge, while strollers can be rented at a fee. Situated near the Dallas/Fort Worth International Airport. Free shuttle is available from many Irving hotels.

Irving Mall is owned by Simon Property Group, which has interest in shopping centers in the United States and Europe. It features 150 stores, including anchors such as **Dillard's,** (972) 258-4968; **Foley's,** 257-4800; **Mervyn's**, 258-8955; and **Sears,** 570-8400.

Among the women's fashions merchants, you will also find 5-7-9, American Eagle Outfitters, Casual Corner, Express, Gap, Lane Bryant, Lerner New York, Old Navy, and Rave. Men's clothing is sold at Avanti, Gadzooks, and Structure. Footwear is available at Bakers, Famous Footwear, Foot Locker, and the Athlete's Foot. Barnes & Noble Booksellers and Bath & Body Works are also located on the premises. General Cinema maintains a 14-screen theater with stadium seating here.

The 13-unit food court includes Chicago-Style Hot Dogs, Colter's Bar-B-Que, Fuddruckers and McDonald's hamburgers, Phil's Philly Steaks, and Pietro's Pizza.

Not far from here, the Dallas County Sheriff's Department organized the first ambush on bank robber Clyde Barrow and his moll Bonnie Parker, while the pair tried to meet their families in the 1930s. Clyde drove up to their relatives' car, but, on a hunch, kept going. As soon as he passed their car, the officers opened fire.

A Mesquite Shopping Center

Town East Mall, 2063 Town East Blvd. and Lyndon B. Johnson Frwy.,

Mesquite, (972) 270-2363/4431, Internet www.generalgrowth.com. Open Mon-Sat 10 AM-9 PM, Sun noon-6 PM. Located east of downtown Dallas, between Interstate Highways 30 and U.S. Hwy. 80.

Built in 1971 on 99 acres (or 40 hectares) of land, it has since almost doubled to more than 180 stores, 20 of which have been in the mall since the beginning. Automatic teller machines, copy and fax services, safety escorts, strollers and wheelchairs are among the services available.

Town East is the largest employer in Mesquite. About 20 million shoppers visit it annually. There are 7,220 parking spaces available.

The stores on two levels, anchored by **Dillard's,** (972) 681-9231; **Foley's,** 681-6996; **J.C. Penney,** 279-4100; and **Sears,** 686-3500, occupy 1.3 million square feet (or 120,770 square meters) of retail space.

Among the women's apparel merchants, you will find Abercrombie & Fitch, 5-7-9, American Eagle Outfitters, Casual Corner, Express, GAP, Lane Bryant, Limited, and Wilson Leather. Children's clothing is available at Baby GAP, the Children's Place, Gymboree, and Limited Too. Athlete's Foot, Bakers, Florsheim, Jarman, Ked's, Lady Footlocker, Naturalizer Shoes, and Stride Rite are some among the footwear retailers.

Specialty stores include Bag 'n Baggage, Cutlery & Collectibles, Isis Bridal, Motherhood Maternity, Ritz Camera, and Sunglass Hut. There is a skimpy B Dalton Bookstore, Sam Goody, and Warehouse Music for recorded music. Gordon's, Samuel's, and Zales sell jewelry.

Food merchants to be found here include Charlie's Steakery, El Chico, Frullati Café & Bakery, Great American Cookie Co., Luby's Cafeteria, Marble Slab Creamery, McDonald's Express, Original Cookie Co., Sbarro, and Subway.

Adjacent to the mall is Sheplers, Internet www.sheplers.com, which started out as a single store in Wichita, Kansas, but now claims to be "the world's largest Western store," selling boots, jeans, Western hats, shirts, and accessories.

Two Plano Shopping Centers

Collin Creek Mall, 811 North Central Expwy. at West Plano Pkwy., Plano, (972) 422-1070; customer service desk, (817) 361-8340; management office, (972) 422-1070. Open Mon-Sat 10 AM-9 PM, Sun noon-6 PM. Located northeast of downtown Dallas and north of Richardson, just west of U.S. Hwy. 75, also known as Central Expressway.

The 1.1-million-square-foot (or 102,190-square-meter) indoor mall features more than 160 specialty stores and is anchored by **Dillard's,**

(972) 423-6902; **Foley's,** 422-8910; **J.C. Penney,** 578-8666; **Mervyn's California,** 578-8188; and **Sears,** 422-8534. American Express Travel is located on the upper level, near Dillard's and Sears.

Those looking for men's, women's, or children's clothing have these choices available at Collin Creek: Ann Taylor Loft, August Max Woman, Casual Corner, Children's Place, Dallas Cowboys Pro Shop, Eddie Bauer, Express, Gadzooks, Gap, Gingiss Formalwear, Gymboree, Lane Bryant, The Limited, Limited Too, Motherhood Maternity, Petite Sophisticates, Structure, and Wilson leather.

Footwear will be found at Bostonian Shoes, Foot Locker, Jarman, Johnston & Murphy, and Stride Rite. Jewelry is sold at Bailey Banks & Biddle, Crown Jewelers, Friedman's Jewelers, Gordon's Jewelers, Helzberg Diamonds, James Avery Craftsman, Key Jewelers, and Zales.

Bag 'n Baggage sells luggage, Brookstone the stuff you can get addicted to, General Nutrition Center vitamins, KB Toys children's toys, LensCrafters and Pearle Vision glasses, Ritz Camera photographic equipment, Victoria's Secret intimate wear, and Waldenbooks what the name says.

Luby's Cafeteria is located between Mervyn's and Sears; Tino's Mexican Restaurant between J.C. Penney and Dillard's. You will also find here Arby's, Frullati Café & Bakery, Colter's Bar-B-Q, Hot Dog on a Stick, McDonald's, Sbarro, and Steak Escape, even Godiva Chocolatier if you have a sweet tooth.

About 88 percent of Collin Creek Mall shoppers are said to be Caucasian, some 55 percent ages 20 to 50, more than half have at least some college education, and 60 percent earn $50,000 or more annually.

The Shops at Willow Bend, 6121 West Park Blvd. at Dallas North Tollway, Plano, (972) 202-4900, Internet www.shopwillowbend.com. Open Mon-Sat 10 AM-9 PM, Sun noon-6 PM. Two concierge centers are at shoppers' disposal. Parking is available on a two-level parking deck with space for 6,358 vehicles. Located north of downtown Dallas, less than a mile (or 1.6 kilometers) north of the President George Bush Turnpike (or State Highway 190), and immediately west of the tollway.

The upscale, $200-million, 1.5-million-square-foot (or 139,350-square-meter) regional mall opened in 2001 and is situated about five miles (or eight kilometers) from the Stonebriar Centre mall, Valley View, and the Galleria (see entries), which is located seven miles (or 11.3 kilometers) south of here.

The Willow Bend sits in the zip code 75093, one of the wealthiest areas of metropolitan Dallas, where homes start at about $250,000. Populated by corporate executives and managers, zip code 75093 is also home to such prominent country clubs as Gleneagles and Prestonwood.

There are six-foot-tall bronze weeping willows whose leaves "weep" water droplets into the courtyard reflecting pool and 2,200 trees shading parking areas and sidewalks. The mall also has an unusual carpeted children's play area filled with large-sized food items, such as a plate of steak and eggs that measures 15 feet (or 4.5 meters) across, a ten-foot-tall (or three-meter) bottle of Tabasco sauce, and what might be Texas' largest grapefruit. It is located near the Lord & Taylor department store. The area is a godsend for parents who need something for their kids to wear them out by the time the shopping is over.

"Willow Bend's aesthetic is not the aristocratic, European grandeur of so much of upscale Dallas but a deceptively simple, elegant American style," observes *D Magazine*.

A three-level, 250,000-square-foot (or 23,225-square-meter) **Dillard's,** (972) 202-4730; a three-level marble and specialty wood-floor **Foley's,** (469) 366-3790, one of the largest in the area; a three-level, 150,000-square-foot (or 13,935-square-meter) **Neiman Marcus,** (972) 629-1700; and a two-level, 140,000-square-foot (or 13,006-square-meter) **Lord & Taylor,** (972) 202-8333, are the anchor department stores. They might be joined by a three-level, 130,000-square-foot (or 12,077-square-meter) **Saks Fifth Avenue** in or after 2004. The grounds include almost a million square feet (or 92,900 square meters) of grass, 2,000 trees, and 25,000 plants.

More than 125 pieces of art from the company's collection are displayed at the Neiman's store. The collection is dominated by works from contemporary Texas artists and includes sculptures, works on paper, blown glass, and limited edition prints. Take note of the store's center escalator, which is filled with 25,000 white silk butterflies and small round mirrors.

On Neiman's third level is Mariposa (Butterfly) restaurant, which features a 40-foot-long and five-foot-high (or 12-by-1.5 meter) glass wall by designers Jim Bowman and Mary Lynn Devereux of Dallas. On the first floor, Neiman's also sports a NM Café.

The mall, two years in the making, boasts 140 designer and specialty store retailers, almost half of which opened their first Texas stores here. They include clothiers American Eagle Outfitters, Ann Taylor, Betsey Johnson, Giorgio Armani Collezioni, bebe Outlet, Bernini, Burberry, Cache, Casual Corner, Diesel, Escada, Express, Forever XXI, Hugo Boss, Jacqueline Jarrot, J. Crew, J. Harris, J. Jill, Limited Too, Lucky Brand, Nicole Miller, Petite Sophisticate, Reference, St. John, the Massachusetts-based Talbots, Talbots Woman, and Talbots Shoes, and Wolford. The Baoviet Collection store features authentic Vietnamese fashions and specializes in hand-woven silk women's clothing, handbags, and shoes.

Children's apparel is sold at April Cornell, Gymboree, Jacadi Paris, Strasburg Children, Zutopia; kid's shoes at Sketchers and Stride Rite. Doll Haven and KB Toys also cater to children.

Agatha Paris, Michel Quiniou's only French jewelry boutique in Texas, located on the lower level near Neiman Marcus and one of seven nationwide, sells "well-made, well-priced bijoux." Enameled pins start at about $70 each, and lariat necklaces in sterling silver or gold plate at about half as much. Lancel, a 127-year-old Parisian boutique that sells handbags and luggage, opened in 2002.

Footwear retailers Aldo, Allen-Edmonds, Bruno Magli, Charles David, Johnston & Murphy, Nine West, and Rangoni Firenze, as well as sneakers merchant Foot Locker, will also be found here. And, by the way, the seated figure in woven reed in Neiman Marcus's shoe department is Texas artist Frances Bagley's work created in 2000.

The Lalique French boutique sells crystal objets d'art, jewelry, and "to-die-for" handbags. Health and beauty products can be bought from Aveda, Bath & Body Works, the Body Shop, Caswell-Massey, and Crabtree & Evelyn. An Elizabeth Arden Red Door Salon & Spa will also be found at Willow Bend.

Godiva Chocolatier, Mont Blanc writing implements, gourmet franks and sausage house Frank & Stein, women's swimwear store Everything But Water, and Ritz Camera photo retailer are also located in this mall. Accessories merchant Coach has a store here.

Japanese Weekend, on the second level, across from Dillard's, has nothing to do with Japan. It is a San Francisco-based maternity shop that sells everything from dresses to bikinis. Nursing tops sell for up to $80. A couple of opticians and twice as many optical shops will be found here also.

Texas' first Apple computer 6,300-square-foot (or 585-square-meter) store, On Willow Bend's southern periphery, is "so popular that customers sometimes have to endure Six Flags-type lines to gain admission." Costco Wholesale retail warehouse and Home Depot are located across Park Boulevard.

Among the seven full-service and ten fast-food restaurants along the 30,000-square-foot (or 2,787-square-meter), 650-seat food court, you will find **The Mercury,** a smartly appointed top-of-the-line food destination. "Hip decor, attentive service, and delicious food finally give Plano diners an alternative to its typical family fare," observes *D Magazine*, while the *Dallas Observer* claims that "The Mercury's decor is as good as the food—very good indeed." The *Dallas Morning News*, which gives The Mercury no fewer than four and a half out of the possible five stars, notes that "you expect to find a restaurant like the Mercury in a world-class hotel . . . but in a suburban shopping center?" (Do not confuse The Mercury with an equally respectable The Mercury Grill, also a New American eatery, but located on Preston Road at Forest Lane in Dallas.)

Tenaya Mexican Café & Grill is an American Indian-theme steak and wild-game restaurant. Also located here are California Pizza Kitchen, Napa Valley Grille, Le Petit Bistro, and Richie's Neighborhood Pizzeria, which on its opening day was visited by actress Raquel Welch, who is married to one of the pizza chain's owners.

Cultural pursuits, as usual, have been limited to a mall-style Waldenbooks bookstore and the Museum Company. There are ATMs, strollers, and wheelchairs available.

The shopping center is the first such Metroplex facility developed by Taubman Centers, a real estate developer from Michigan. The company is run by the sons of A. Alfred Taubman, who in 1983 bought a controlling stake in the auction house Sotheby's Holdings.

Nearby is the 145,000-square-foot (or 13,470-square-meter) Shops at Park Place retail center.

A Richardson Shopping Center

Richardson Square Mall, 501 South Plano Rd. at East Belt Line Rd., Richardson, (972) 783-0117; management office, 783-0118; Internet www.shopsimon.com. Open Mon-Sat 10 AM-9 PM, Sun noon-6 PM. Wheel chairs are available free of charge and strollers at a charge. Located northeast of downtown Dallas, north and west of Garland.

The mall counts more than 80 specialty shops. **Dillard's,** (972) 783-2598, with one of its first area stores here in the late 1970s, and **Sears,** 470-5500, are the anchor department stores.

There are apparel vendors, such as Bugle Boy, Casual Corner, Lane Bryant, Lerner New York, The Limited, Old Navy, Ross Dress for Less, and Stein Mart. Bath & Body Works, Foot Locker athletic shoe vendor, Frederick's of Hollywood, KB Toys, Kay Jewelers, and Merle Norman Cosmetic Studios will also be found here.

Oshman's SuperSports, Pearle Vision, RadioShack, Ritz Camera, Sam Goody music merchant, Stride Rite footwear manufacturer, Sunglass Hut, and Zales jewelers are still other providers of what you often seek in an average mall.

You will seldom find two bookstores in one mall. Barnes & Noble Booksellers and Waldenbooks are both situated here.

Several eateries in a 364-seat, seven-unit food court will also be found at Richardson Square Mall, which was refurbished in 1998 and includes a large wildflower sculpture at center court.

Richardson Square Mall is owned by Simon Property Group, headquartered in Indianapolis, Indiana, which has interest in some 250 shopping centers nationwide.

BOOKS & MUSIC

While Dallas has its share of mega-sized bookstores in the suburbs, its downtown area fell on lean times, and there has not been a single full-sized general bookstore located there for almost a decade. One cannot imagine a "world-class city," which Dallas aspires to be, without several such bookstores downtown.

The best selection at full-price stores will be found at Borders, Barnes & Noble, and Bookstop. The latter two issue discount cards that will save you up to 20 percent on some book, magazine, and newspaper purchases. One of the 40 locations of Blockbuster Video is the overpriced "monster of recorded media," according to *D Magazine*.

However, if you have the time, want to save money, and do not mind getting your hands dirty a bit, there are also several discount book and music shops located in Dallas, particularly the Half Price Books.

If you have young children, check with the bookstores near you about the story times. Many Barnes & Noble and Borders locations, to name but two, hold readings on weekends. *Dallas Child* magazine named Barnes & Noble the "best" kids' bookstores.

Antiquarian of Dallas, 2609 Routh St. at McKinney, Uptown, (214) 754-0705, Internet www.abebooks.com. Open Tue-Sat 11 AM-5 PM; closed Sundays and Mondays. Located north of downtown Dallas, across the street from the Hard Rock Café (see entry). Opened in 1988, it claims to be the second oldest bookstore in Dallas, which shows how precarious book selling is in this city.

The 650-square-foot (or 60-square-meter) Antiquarian features a variety of old and rare books, including hard-to-find first editions, Texana, history, and children's literature. Some historical documents sell for as much as $10,000.

Barnes & Noble Booksellers, Lincoln Park, 7700 West Northwest Hwy. at North Central Expwy., (214) 739-1124, Internet www.bn.com. Open Mon-Sat 9 AM-11 PM, Sun 10 AM-9 PM. Located north of downtown Dallas, just south of the NorthPark shopping center. Parking can be scarce at times.

A handsome location with a helpful staff. Not one of the largest Barnes & Noble stores, but big enough to spend an evening contemplating your purchases. It has a compact disk department downstairs, and a children's section with a few toys upstairs. There is a decent selection of books about Texas and travel destinations, and plenty of magazines. Browsing is encouraged. A Barnes & Noble discount card entitles you to discounts.

A small café is attached to the store, but next door there are also the Southwestern-cuisine Blue Mesa (see entry) and one of the popular Cheesecake Factory restaurants.

Other area B & N locations, among the more than 500 nationwide, include:

• 14999 Preston Rd. at Belt Line Rd. in far-north Dallas, (972) 661-8068. It has a music store, a children's section, and a café.

• Las Colinas, 7615 North MacArthur Blvd. at Las Colinas Blvd., (972) 501-0430. It has a café and a music store.

• 3634 Irving Mall, Northwest corner of Belt Line Rd. at State Hwy. 183 (or West Airport Freeway), Irving, (972) 257-8320. It has a music store, a children's section, and a café. This is the second worst intersection in the nation, with some 250 accidents annually, according to the State Farm Insurance Co.

• 501 South Plano Rd. at Belt Line Rd., at Richardson Square Mall in Richardson, (972) 699-7844. It has a music store, a children's section, and a café.

• 2201 Preston Rd. at West Park Blvd. in Plano, (972) 612-0999. It has a music store.

• 801 West 15th St., west of North Central Expwy., in Creekwalk Village mall, just north of the Collin Creek Mall, (972) 422-3372. It has a Starbucks Café attached and a Black-Eyed Pea restaurant nearby.

• Stonebriar Mall, 2601 Preston Rd. at State Hwy. 121, Frisco, (972) 668-2820. It has a music store, a children's section, and a café. One of the largest mall bookstores in the city, but it stocks no foreign-language newspapers.

Black Images, 230 Wynnewood Village Shopping Center, Illinois Ave. West at Zang Blvd. South, (800) 272-5027 or (214) 943-0142, Internet www.blackmages.com. Open Mon-Sat 10 AM-7 PM, Sun 1 PM-6 PM. Located in Oak Cliff, southwest of downtown Dallas, and west of Interstate 35 East, also known as R. L. Thornton Freeway.

Opened in 1986 by the former social worker Emma Rodgers and Ashira Tosihwe, it claims to be the oldest Afrocentric bookstore in the Metroplex. "It's not the only black bookstore around, but it is the largest," notes the *Dallas Morning News* about the 2,600-square-foot (or 242-square-meter) store that offers 20,000 titles "about and mostly by African-Americans."

The bulk of the title stock consists of Afrocentric fiction, although one store's entire wall is also devoted to histories, biographies, and theoretical texts. The children's section includes the life stories of such well-known African-Americans as jazz player Miles Davis and writer Alex Haley. A few foreign language books are available. There is a small selection of music. Book signings are held each month.

The Book Tree, 702 University Village strip shopping center, on the northeast corner of Plano and Belt Line Roads, (972) 437-4337, across the street from Richardson Square Mall (see entry), which houses a Barnes & Noble superstore, as well as a Waldenbooks. Open Mon-Sat 10 AM-6 PM, Sun noon-5 PM.

A popular used-books store, with a small selection of new paperbacks and hardcovers, owned by twin brothers who claim they stock 150,000 volumes, mostly mass-market paperbacks, which sell for half the cover price. It has a good selection of mysteries. Collectibles start at about $50.

The *Dallas Morning News* labeled it "cheerfully cluttered" and "a haven for readers who crave not only the written word, but also the homey atmosphere and conversation with fellow book lovers." Free coffee and tea are available.

Borders Books & Music, 5500 Upper Greenville Ave. at Lovers Ln., (214) 739-1166, Internet www.borderstores.com. Open Mon-Sat 9 AM-11 PM, Sun 9 AM-9 PM. Located in the Old Town shopping center in east Dallas, across the street from the huge Central Market food emporium.

Solid and down-to-earth, comfortable, to some even cozy, Dallas Borders locations are just as inviting as anywhere. This is one of 350 Borders stores worldwide founded by the brothers Borders in early 1970s in Michigan. Most have cafes attached and plenty seating to peruse your latest acquisition even before you leave the store. This and other Borders locations are among the few in the city that carry British, French, German, Italian, and Spanish newspapers.

Borders also owns 850 smaller Waldenbooks stores, many located in shopping centers, but with a much more limited selection.

Other area Borders locations include:

• 10720 Preston Rd. and Royal Ln., (214) 363-1977, in north Dallas. It has one of the best selections of French-language magazines in the city. There is a small café. In front of the Gap clothing store nearby, you can see a replica of Frederick Remington's horse rider.

• 15757 Coit Rd. at Arapaho, (972) 458-0400, southwest of the University of Texas at Dallas.

• 1601 Preston Rd. at West Parker Rd., (972) 713-9857, in Plano.

• 2403 South Stemmons, Lewisville, (972) 459-2321.

CD World, 5706 East Mockingbird Ln. at Lower Greenville Ave., (214) 826-1885. Open daily 10 AM-10 PM, except Sun noon-8 PM. Located northeast of downtown, diagonally across from Kroger supermarket and Phoenix Apartments, and in the building that also houses 24-Hour Fitness.

"It's got an unbeatable selection," says *D Magazine,* which voted it as the best place to buy new or used CDs, primarily rock & roll, but also some jazz and classical music. A "Buy 10, Get 1 Free" card helps keep customers loyal.

Another location is at 5000 Belt Line Rd., in Addison, (972) 386-6565.

Doubleday Book Shop, 18 Highland Park Village, at Preston Rd. and West Mockingbird Ln., (214) 528-6756. Open Mon-Sat 10 AM-9 PM, Sun noon-6 PM. Located north of downtown Dallas, inside the exclusive Highland Park township, and next door to a pricey Hermes shop.

An elegant boutique Barnes & Noble bookstore, the last Doubleday remaining in the Metroplex, in an elegant mall with civilized service. A bit small, and the selection is limited, but if you love books you will want to linger. This is perhaps the only Metroplex bookstore that will remind you of a European bookshop. A Barnes & Noble discount card entitles you to lower prices for books, magazines, and newspapers.

Half Price Books, 5803 East Northwest Hwy. at Shady Brook Ln., (214) 379-8000, Internet www.halfpricebooks.com.Open daily 9:30 AM-11 PM. Located north of downtown Dallas, two blocks east of North Central Expressway (or U.S. Hwy. 75).

Established in 1972 in an abandoned self-service laundry at Lemmon Avenue and Inwood Road, with 2,000 books from the founders' personal libraries, it has moved twice. The privately held company with sales of more than $100 million a year is now headed by the daughter of a co-founder. It is one of the 50 largest private businesses in the Metroplex.

Half Price carries more than a quarter-million new and used books, some valuable, some barely worth the paper they are printed on. Note that there could be several dollars difference in price among what look like identical titles. About half of Half Price Books' merchandise is bought directly from publishers and is new. Tapes and CDs are sold as well, but you need to be even more discriminating not to gum up your equipment.

If you don't mind the dust, you can spend half your lifetime browsing among books on every conceivable subject. The Russian history section, for example, is probably the most extensive in the Metroplex, outside of major libraries. Price is one-half of the original price or less. Children can keep busy in a corner of their own. There is a coffee shop on the premises.

Half Price was started by Pat Anderson (d. 1995) and a self-described "corporate dropout" Ken Gjemre (1921-2002), who in 1972 borrowed $4,000 from her to open a store. Born near Groverton, Indiana, to Norwegian immigrants, he earned a science degree from Purdue University and a master of liberal arts degree at Southern Methodist University. Gjemre rose through the ranks at Zale Corp., where he became a senior vice president, then dropped out of corporate life.

"[I] got tired of selling people things they didn't need and couldn't afford," he said in 1991, when he retired from Half Price Books. He died at age 81 of prostate cancer and donated his body to the medical school at the University of California at Los Angeles. The chain is now run by Anderson's daughter, Sharon Wright.

If you have books to sell, you can unload them here, but do not expect to get anything near what you think you might. Call (214) 890-0850. For several other, smaller Half Price locations throughout the city, please see the white business pages telephone directory. About half of its 75 stores are located in Texas.

The History Merchant, 2723 Routh St., between McKinney Ave. and Cedar Springs Rd., (214) 979-0810, Internet www.historymerchant.com. Open Mon-Sat 10 AM-4:30 PM, Sun 12:30 PM-4:30 PM. Located in Uptown, diagonally across from Ruggeri's Ristorante in Quadrangle mall (see entries).

Set in a Victorian-era building with a winding staircase and balcony, this store's stock is mostly history, with some biographical and classical literature titles thrown in. Owner Richard Hazlett has recreated a London bookstore with rare, out-of-print books and autographed portraits of world leaders. Look for fine rare books by and about Sir Winston Churchill, prints, autographs, hard-to-find books about World War II and its leaders. The Merchant's Web site will help you locate one of those rare volumes.

Once you have stepped inside the world of the History Merchant, notes the *Dallas Morning News*, you will not want to leave.

A Likely Story, 4801 West Park Blvd., Suite 417, at Preston Rd., in Preston Town Crossing mall, Plano, (972) 964-8838. Open Mon-Sat 9:30 AM-6 PM; closed Sundays. Located north of downtown Dallas and north of President George Bush Turnpike.

An independent 1,500-square-foot (or 139-square-meter) children's bookstore, established in 1990, it caters to all, from newborns to young adults. Also carries educational toys, tapes, and videos. Since the Enchanted Forest store closed in 2002, it claims to be the best children's bookstore in town.

The founder and owner is Judy Chaiken (b. 1941), who had opened her first bookstore in Miami in 1978.

Premiere Video, 5400 East Mockingbird Ln. at North Central Expwy., (214) 827-8969. Open Mon-Sat 10 AM-10 PM, Sun noon-10 PM. Located north of downtown Dallas, across the street from the Mockingbird Station shopping center and lofts (see entry), and across North Central from Park Cities and Southern Methodist University.

One of the few local stores where videos for cinema connoisseurs will be found, including hundreds of foreign films. Perhaps the only store in town where films are displayed by directors and countries. Premiere will even lend you a special PAL player that plugs into your TV set so you can watch original Australian, British, Chinese, French, Japanese, Iranian, and Spanish DVDs.

"Still the best video rental joint in Dallas, no one compares to Premiere Video—which is what makes it, duh, premier," claims the *Dallas Observer*.

The Movie Trading Co. is a good choice for used videos and DVDs. There are two locations: 6109 Greenville Ave. at Southwestern Blvd., (214) 361-8287, and 3211 Oak Lawn Ave. at Cedar Springs Rd., (214) 219-2252.

Rand McNally Map & Travel Store, 211 NorthPark Shopping Center, at North Central Expwy. and West Northwest Hwy., (214) 987-9941. Open Mon-Sat 10 AM-6 PM, Sun noon-6 PM. Located inside the mall across from La Madeleine French Bakery & Café, which is a good place to linger over books, and next to Dillard's department store.

It has a good selection of travel guides, atlases, maps, luggage, and travel accessories. If you are looking for an electric-converter kit, for example, and cannot find it here, try Brookstone next door.

This is just about the only store in the mall and the city that sells travel books exclusively. Pity that one of the most desirable malls in the Metroplex cannot muster anything in the way of a general bookstore.

SMU Bookstore/Barnes & Noble, 3060 Mockingbird Ln. at Airline Rd., (214) 768-2435, Internet http://smu.bkstore.com, e-mail smu@bkstore.com. Open Mon-Fri 8 AM-9 PM, Sat 10 AM-9 PM, Sun 11 AM-7 PM. Barnes & Noble discount cards are honored. Located north of downtown, on the edge of Park Cities, a block west of North Central Expressway and next door to the original La Madeleine French Bakery & Café (see listing).

Across Mockingbird from here there once stood Mrs. Baird's bakery, which was built in 1953, when Mockingbird was the northern limit of Dallas, but in 2002 it relocated its operations to Fort Worth. The 5.64-acre (or 2.28-hectare) sliver of land on which it stood awaits a developer who wants to capitalize on its wealthy neighborhood.

The bookstore opened in 2001, when it relocated from the Southern Methodist University campus across the street. The store, which is operated by Barnes & Noble Booksellers, occupies 22,000 square feet (or 2,043 square meters). It stocks more than 50,000 titles, including college textbooks, SMU Press and other university press titles, and trade books. Periodicals, newspapers, and SMU merchandise are also sold, as are children's books.

A seating area for reading is available in an adjacent coffee shop inside the store.

Virgin Megastore, Mockingbird Station, 5307 East Mockingbird Ln. at North Central Exwy., (214) 615-3887. Open Sun-Thu 10 AM-11 PM, Fri-Sat 10 AM-midnight. Located north of downtown Dallas, across Central Expressway from the well-to-do Park Cities and Southern Methodist University.

The 25,000-square-foot (or 2,322-square-meter) superstore has three dozen listening stations, and hundreds of kids searching for rock of every shade on compact disks or DVD. The Virgin store also has a fair selection of children's videos.

Because of the blaring music, this is not the best place to search for classical music, although some is available. Nor am I enamored of the bare concrete floors. A limited selection of music- and cinema-related books is also available.

CLOTHING

Choices for Women

Shopping centers, such as Galleria, NorthPark, Highland Park Village, and Valley View in Dallas, the Shops at Willow Bend in Plano, and Stonebriar Centre in Frisco probably have most of what women need in the way of work and casual clothes or formal wear.

Among the upscale women's specialty clothing stores, **Forty-Five Ten,** at 4510 McKinney Ave. and Knox Street, (214) 559-4510, is bandied around as a place to check out. You will find here everything from a $30 T-shirt to a $1,000 cashmere coat. It also serves simple lunches worthy of a *Texas Monthly* review.

Lilly Dodson, (214) 528-0528, is described under Highland Park Village shopping center. The privately owned **Stanley Korshak,** at 500 Crescent Court; (214) 871-3600, is located uptown and equated with Neiman Marcus downtown.

Another choice would be **Tootsie's,** 8300 Preston Rd. at West Northwest Hwy., (214) 696-9993, where the Park Cities crowd shops for Via Spiga shoes, and Nicole Miller, BCBG, Parallel, D&G, Moschino, and Trina Turk clothing.

Next door is the popular boutique by Italian doyenne **Carla Martinengo,** (214) 522-9284, which boasts a selection of hard-to-find European designers.

Mid-priced, funky, and fashionable are women's clothing and shoe stores such as:

• **Ahab Bowen,** 2641 Boll St. off McKinney Ave., Uptown, (214) 720-1874.

• **Avant,** 2716 Lower Greenville Ave. at Vickery, (214) 824-0260. While here, check out also **HD's,** at 3014 Greenville, (214) 821-8900.

• **Cotton Island,** 6601 Hillcrest Ave. at Daniel, University Park, (214) 373-1085. Also sought after by women who cannot resist the latest fashion fad is nearby **Studio Sebastian,** 6730 Snider Plaza, (214) 360-9001.

• **Elements,** 4400 Lovers Lane, between Dallas North Tollway and Douglas Ave., (214) 987-0837. At 5600 West Lovers Lane is **Primrose,** (214) 352-1333.

• **The Graye Concept,** 8314 Preston Center Plaza, (214) 750-7463. It sells shoes, apparel, and accessories.

Women are also raving about the shoes at **Organicity,** 3028 Hall Street at McKinney Ave., behind Primo's restaurant; (214) 953-0330. It is open for lunch daily 10:30 AM-3 PM, for dinner 6:30 PM-10:30 PM, Wed 6 PM-midnight, Thu-Sat 6:30 PM-10:30 PM, Sun 6 PM-midnight. Live jazz music is offered Fridays, starting at 8 PM.

What, a lunch and dinner in a shoe store? Yeah, and you will probably have to come in to make up your mind whether you like it or not.

Organicity features traditional Greek-Macedonian low-fat cuisine and wine. The costliest dish is the $29 veal prime steak, but the dinner menu also includes moussaka (eggplant, potatoes, and ground beef), chicken, fish, and lamb kebabs, and Greek burgers.

Most lunches are under $15 and include several salads. Wines are available by the glass, while you try on clothes and shoes. *D Magazine* picked it as one of the ten best new restaurants.

Gino Nikolini and his wife Olina came to Dallas from Thessaloniki to open a shoe boutique in 2000, then added a Greek restaurant and wine bar. Nikolini shoes, belts, and bags have caused quite a stir in the city that seems to have a thousand women's shoe, belt, and bag stores. Shoes that go up to $350 a pair are made in the store by Nikolini, while clothes come from Milan and Florence.

Nikolini shoes are also available at **Nordstrom,** which the *Dallas Business Journal* picked as the best local place to shop for women's shoes.

Other expensive, but popular city shoe stores include:

• **E.G. Geller,** Preston Center, 8411 Preston Rd., Suite 116, (214) 373-8066, Internet www.egeller.com. Sells European comfort shoes.

• **Krista de la Harpe Shoe Salon,** 2609 Hibernia St., (214) 220-0243. By appointment only. De la Harpe designs all the leather shoes in her Uptown Victorian home.

• **Steven Spodek,** Inwood Village, 5600 West Lovers Ln., (214) 350-3883. Sells Anne Klein, Casadei, Calleen Cordero, Henry Beguelin, Icon, and Stuart Weitzman shoes.

Choices for Men

For men and boys, one of the choices would be **Culwell & Son,** at 6319 Hillcrest Ave. at McFarlin, across from the SMU campus, (214) 522-7000, Internet www.culwell.com. W. E. Culwell, who opened the University Park store in 1920, also has a Plano location, at 1900 Preston Rd., (972) 964-7000. His grandson now runs the business.

You can get three suits and three custom-tailored shirts, starting at $1,200, or three made-to-measure suits and three custom-made shirts for $1,800. Off-the-rack suits start at $250 and go as high as $6,000 for Hickey Freeman and Oxford brands. Dress shirts are priced from $50 to $150. Quality formal and casual shoes are also sold.

Both locations have hair-cutting salons for men and boys, one of the city's best, according to the *Dallas Observer*. Hair salon customers can enjoy complimentary soft drinks or coffee. The *Dallas Business Journal* considers Culwell's one of the best men's clothing stores around.

For men who do not need any more clothes, but want a suit priced from $3,000 to $20,000, there is one of the three **MallaSadi Men's Boutiques**. Owned by Mallas Osafo (b. 1950) from Ghana and Sadi Ertekin (b. 1959) from Istanbul, Turkey, the stores provide clothing for men who can afford a $15,000 Brioni suit. The two men met in 1987 at a clothing store in the Old Town Shopping Village. They worked side by side as tailors six days a week for eight years before they combined their $50,000 in savings and loaded up on credit cards to be able to start a business in 1995. Their boutiques are located at 3309 Oak Lawn Ave. at Lemmon (214) 526-2727. Also at Village on the Parkway, 5100 Belt Line Rd. at Dallas Parkway, and at the Hotel Inter-Continental (see entry), 15201 Dallas Pkwy., Addison.

The Western Wear

So you wanna be a cowboy, eh? All right, cover that belly, get your money ready, and we'll see what we can do for you. First the hat. If you plan to be a cowboy, it should be your fly swatter and a horsewhip. And in Texas you almost never take it off. John Stetson of Philadelphia introduced what is today the classic design in the 1850s with a hat made of felt. It has a wide brim to protect the eyes from the sun and a high crown to keep the top of your head cool. Cowboys also use it as a drinking vessel, to carry water to their horses, even to fan a fire. There's the Dude Stetson, Rodeo Stetson, and Joe Bob Stetson, Cowboy or Panama Straw, Oilman's Special, the Cattleman, and Baroness for his daughter.

You can't be a cowboy without the bandanna, always of bright red cotton to wipe your sweat after you have initiated a conversation with a cute blonde Texas lass or a handsome fella. You can wear it as a hatband, use it as a napkin or a handkerchief, or as a dog collar.

Now the Western shirt. Until the first livestock shows and rodeos in Fort Worth, the cowboy's shirt was just that. Afterwards it became a high fashion item with pearl snap closings, instead of buttons. Now, check out the shirt design and see what you want: Bull Rider, Honky-Tonker, Cowpoke, Rodeo Plaid, or City Slicker to wear under a suit to your Chicago office. And for you, ladies, Calico Cowgirl print in red.

Then there are the jeans. You'll never be anything beyond a circus clown without jeans. Not just anything from Guess at the Galleria or NorthPark will do. There are only three brands in which to show your stuff: Levi's, Lee, or Wrangler, the real Americana. What do these fashion-conscious Italians know about jeans! The back hem should just cover your heels, and straight leg is the only authentic cut.

The boots. You may have but three strands of hair left on your head, but you can be a cowboy. Wear anything but real boots, and you'll look like a Covent Garden ballerina. Try Studio boot if you have cinematic aspirations, or the Muleskinner if you want to be taken seriously. And you, ladies, can try the Urban Cowboy boot that gained prominence after the film with actor John Travolta.

Boots should never feel painful, no matter what a store clerk might tell you about "needing to break 'em in," according to the president of the American College of Foot & Ankle Orthopedics & Medicine. Off-the-shelf boots can be had for as little as $100 a pair. Prices for custom-made boots typically start at about $500, while boots made from exotic skins can go into thousands of dollars.

"The place to buy custom boots is Texas, which is home to more than 100 of the best bootmakers on earth—though you'd never know it; most custom bootmakers don't advertise, as word of mouth brings in all the business they can handle," observes *Texas Monthly*, the magazine that only singles out one Metroplex bootmaker among the supposedly 25 best in Texas: Carman Allen, at 8616 Quebec Dr., Fort Worth, (817) 367-7976.

Hold your horse, cowboy, you ain't done yet. You need a replica of Texas state seal buckle on a cowhide belt, a bolo tie, and if you reeeely want to look the part, silver spurs.

And where can you find all this? Try one of these stores:

Boot Town, 2821 Lyndon B. Johnson Frwy. at Josey Ln., Farmers Branch, (972) 243-1151, Internet www.boottown.com. Located on the north side of LBJ Freeway and the west side of Josey. Open Mon-Sat 9 AM-9 PM, Sun 11 AM-6 PM.

Boots, sizes 4-15, such as Justin and one of its subsidiaries, Tony Lama, Acme, Laredo, Lucchese, or Nocona, and Western clothes are sold.

The Nocona Boot Co., which once employed 400, shut down in 1999 after 74 years in business. It was replaced the following year by the Montague Boot Co., also located in Nocona, a north Texas town of 3,200 residents, whose boot-making operation was the town's largest business. Dallas leather supplier Jim Williams and his brother Bill now employ 40 craftsmen, some of them from the old Nocona Boot Co., who turn out 600 pairs of boots a week. They sell for $400 to $700 a pair.

Other Boot Town stores are located at 5909 Belt Line Road at Preston, (972) 385-3052, at 1328 West Centerville Rd. and LBJ, (972) 279-6886, next to the Target store, as well as in Garland and Plano.

Western Warehouse, 2475 North Stemmons Frwy. (or Interstate Hwy. 35 East), between Wycliff and Motor Streets, (214) 634-2668. Open Mon-Sat 9 AM-9 PM, Sun 11 AM-6 PM. Located northwest of downtown Dallas, near the Dallas Market Center (see entry). Wyndham Anatole Hotel (see entry) is about half a mile (or 0.8 kilometer) away.

Sells all kinds of Western apparel, claims to have 50,000 pairs of boots in stock, including Lucchese. Call for a courtesy car pick-up from major hotels near one of the stores. "We will beat any competitor's price," claim the store's ads. The weekly *Dallas Observer* named it the best Western wear store in Dallas. Another store is located at 10838 North Central Expwy., (214) 891-0888, between Royal Ln. and Meadow Rd. in north Dallas.

Wild Bill's Western Store, West End MarketPlace/3rd Floor, 603 Munger Ave., (214) 954-1052/1053, Internet www.wildbills1.com. Open Mon-Thu 11 AM-9 PM, Fri-Sat 11 AM-10 PM, Sun noon-6 PM. Located in the West End Historic District downtown, a few blocks from the Sixth Floor Museum (see entry).

Wild Bill has been selling hats, boots, buckles, jeans, and other Western paraphernalia since 1954. "Lowest prices guaranteed in writing (even after the sale)," is his motto.

Now that you are outfitted, you can try some real Western living. Check out Southfork Ranch, from the television series *Dallas*. And, of course, you cannot say you have been in Texas unless you go to at least one rodeo. Put on your Levi's and gallop over to the Mesquite Championship Rodeo. (For details, please see listings in the SIGHTS & ATTRACTIONS chapter.)

FOODS

Gourmet & Health Foods

Central Market, 5750 East Lovers Ln. at Greenville Ave., (214) 234-7000, Internet www.centralmarket.com. Open daily 8 AM-10 PM. Wheelchair accessible. Located one block east of North Central Expressway and about half a dozen blocks north of Mockingbird Lane.

Up to 20,000 customers squeeze in every week and at times the dearth of parking is so severe that you may have to park across the street and walk over. Next door is Dallas' first location of the Krispy Kreme doughnut shop, which only adds to the traffic congestion. A Tom Thumb supermarket is across the street as is a Borders bookstore. A souped-up Kroger Signature store is located less than two miles (or 3.2 kilometers) south of here.

Opened in the summer of 2002, the Central Market measures 75,000 square feet (or 6,967 square meters) and claims 50,000 fresh foods. It boasts a dozen varieties of onions, 15 types of tomatoes, 30 varieties of apples, 40 kinds of bread, 60 types of fresh sausages and mustards, 80 varieties of saltwater and fresh-water fish, 100 different brands of olives, 300 brands of beer, and several hundred varieties of cheese and wine. The store's greens are grown in specially allotted fields in California, Colorado, and Texas. Central Market's bananas are given a bath after harvesting to clean the surface of the peel, according to the weekly *Dallas Observer,* which asks: "And why do we need California wine grape leaves at $15.99 per pound anyway?"

The Central Market concept—pioneered by the 100-year-old San Antonio-based H.E. Butt Grocery Co.—began in 1994 in Austin, Texas, where 6,000 people were interviewed for 350 Dallas jobs. There are 600 employees in the Dallas store, where you will not find the everyday staples such as Tide detergent, Budweiser beer, or Ruffles chips.

A Central Market costs 40 percent more to build, and each store must bring in $800,000 a week to break even. That's three times the average weekly sales of a conventional supermarket. With $10 billion in sales, HEB is among the nation's dozen largest food retailers and the 13th largest private company in the United States.

Cooking classes—some complimentary and some with celebrity chefs like Stephan Pyles costing up to $125—are held often, and wine tastings are included in many evening classes.

A 76,000-square-foot (or 7,060-square-meter) Central Market is located at 320 Coit Rd. and George Bush Turnpike, across the street from Sam's Club, in Plano, (469) 241-8300.

Eatzi's Market & Bakery, 3403 Oak Lawn Ave. at Lemmon, (214) 526-1515 or (888) 468-8405; catering, 528-6100, Internet www.eatzis.com. Open daily, except Thanksgiving and Christmas, 7 AM-10 PM. Wheelchair accessible. Located north of downtown, in the Oak Lawn neighborhood, two blocks west of Turtle Creek Boulevard. Marty's (see listing), a competitor, is situated a block away.

Take-out gourmet market and bakery, it seats a couple dozen only. Opened in 1996, it has become so popular it may be difficult to elbow your way to the counter at certain times of the day or night. Thirty chefs cook and supervise the serving stations.

The 8,000-square-foot (or 743-square-meter) store sells some 1,500 food items and serves more than 2,000 persons daily. It sells 5,000 pounds (or 2.2 tons) of turkey every Thanksgiving holiday. The store squeezes out an amazing $17 million in annual sales. There are 75 varieties of cheeses, pâtés, and meats, 50 entrées—from grilled tenderloin and poached raspberry salmon to meat loaf, lasagna, and pasta salads—and 30 varieties of bread freshly baked throughout the day. You can order two dozen kinds of salads, soups, and sandwiches, and up to 50 varieties of desserts. Wine, beer, and some 20 varieties of coffee are available. A family of three, if selecting carefully, can pick up enough ready-to-eat food—meat, vegetables, salad, and dessert—for a satisfying picnic or home meal for under $30, excluding wine. Some picnic meals go as high as $50 for two persons, also without wine.

D Magazine named it the "best new eating concept" in the mid-1990s. "In truth, much of the food Eatzi's offers can be had at your local supermarket," observes the *Texas Monthly*. "But you won't feel as good shopping for it and you won't have nearly as much fun."

Eatzi's concept was created by the New York-born restaurateur Phil Romano, who in 2002 personally delivered free food weekly for some 300 homeless people in downtown Dallas. Romano claims Eatzi's sells the world's best meatloaf. Until 2003, the concept was part of Brinker International, a Dallas-based company whose Chili's, Macaroni Grill, On the Border, Maggiano's, and Corner Bakery locations add up to 1,200 restaurants in 48 states and 22 countries.

Norman Brinker (b. 1932), its mastermind, retired in 2000 and settled down in his $1.8-million, 5,988-square-foot (or 556-square-meter) home on Dallas' Robledo Drive. Born in Depression-era New Mexico, he supported himself at an early age by raising rabbits and picking cotton. At age 14, Brinker began trading horses and won a spot on the 1952 U.S. Olympic equestrian team. He moved to Dallas in 1983 and started his empire by buying Chili's, a small restaurant on Greenville Avenue at Walnut Hill Lane.

Empire Baking Co., 4264 Oak Lawn Ave. at Prescott Ave., (214)

526-1343. Open Mon-Fri 8 AM-5:30 PM, Sat 9 AM-4 PM, Sun 9:30 AM-2 PM. Located in the neighborhood of Oak Lawn, north of downtown Dallas, and a few blocks from Eatzi's Market & Bakery (see entry).

Empire supplies bread to 150 restaurants and hotels in the Metroplex, including Al Biernat steakhouse, Houston's, and the Palm downtown, where its owner spends more than $3,000 a month on the food item that he basically gives away.

"We're the custodians of the process," says the firm's proprietor, New Yorker Robert Meyer Ozarow, who left a lucrative career in investment banking to bake bread in Dallas. "You can't squeeze it, push it or mess with it to make it take less time, use less-expensive ingredients, or need less-skilled workers."

By 1991, Ozarow, whose Jewish immigrant grandparents came from Russia and Poland, was 40 years old and burned out, so he and his wife raised $650,000 to open a bakery named after the state he came from.

"Everyone knows their bread is the best," opines *D Magazine*, also raving about Empire's cheese sticks, "lengths of buttery dough twisted with grated cheese and baked till fabulously golden brown and crunchy."

Other Empire Baking Co. locations will be found at:

- 5450 West Lovers Lane at Inwood Rd., (214) 350-0007.
- 6059 Forest Lane at Preston Rd., (972) 851-5711.
- 18208 Preston Rd. at Frankford Rd., (972) 769-1600.

Marty's, 3316 Oak Lawn Ave. at Cedar Springs Rd., (800) 627-8971 or (214) 526-4070, Internet www.martysdfw.com, e-mail gourmet@martysdfw.com. Open Mon-Sat 9 AM-10 PM; closed Sundays. The Bistro is open 5 PM-10 PM, with live music starting at 7 PM. Accommodates about 80 patrons at a time. Located in the Oak Lawn neighborhood north of downtown Dallas and a block southwest from competitor Eatzi's (see listing).

Founded in 1943, Marty's is one of the oldest gourmet establishments in Dallas. It serves foods and beverages at its Bistro restaurant, as well as providing take-outs. The chef "turns out brilliantly prepared bistro fare," claims *D Magazine*. The *Dallas Morning News* reviewer, who proclaimed the $20 herb-marinated lamb chops "a perfect medium-rare with tender pink meat clinging to the bone," gives the Bistro four stars. The *Dallas Observer* proclaimed Marty's pepper-seared buffalo ribeye "sublime."

With its knowledgeable and friendly service, it competes with Eatzi's in ready-to-eat meals that can be taken out or eaten on the premises. Salads start at about $7, and pastas $13. Among its costliest entrées are the center-cut filet of beef, ribeye steak marinated in garlic, and pan-fried loin, each priced at about $23. Sevruga, osetra, and beluga caviars start at $60 an ounce (or 28 grams).

After selling liquor for 54 years, owner Larry Shapiro voluntarily gave up the store's liquor license in 1997 to open a restaurant and focus on wine sales. The store is now able to sell wine by the glass on the premises. In addition to 2,000-plus wines, Marty's also sells 100 kinds of cheeses, many varieties of meats and sausages, and desserts. Coffees and teas are also sold.

Whole Foods Market, 4100 Lomo Alto Dr. at Lemmon Ave., Highland Park, (214) 520-7993. Open daily 8 AM-10 PM. Located on the southwestern edge of the wealthy Highland Park, the first business in that town in more than eight years. It is situated only about a mile (or 1.6 kilometers) south of Eatzi's and Marty's (see listings), competitors in the Oak Lawn neighborhood.

An Austin-based supermarket chain selling all-natural meats, groceries, fruits, and vegetables that supposedly are free of chemicals. This 35,600-square-foot (or 3,307-square-meter) store, part of the nation's largest natural-foods grocer, opened in 2002.

"The new Highland Park location is bright and cheerful, full of high exposed ceilings; warn neutral tones; and plenty of kale for the whole Park Cities family and their platinum cards," proclaims *D Home* monthly magazine.

The health-food chain opened its initial Greenville Avenue store in 1986. "Whole Foods has ample square footage devoted to fresh produce, whole grains, chef-prepared takeout foods and organic this and that," notes the *Dallas Observer*. "But it doesn't seem to have the sex appeal that Central Market or Eatzi's possesses."

Whole Foods cafés feature healthy foods, such as spinach and cheese lasagna or chicken sandwiches with alfalfa sprouts, to eat on the premises or take out. Aside from a delicatessen, which has a wood-fired pizza oven, there is a large selection of imported beer and wine.

Still other Whole Foods Markets are located at:

• 2218 Lower Greenville Ave. at Belmont, (214) 824-1744. Open daily 8 AM-10 PM. Located in east Dallas close to downtown. This was originally a Bluebonnet Café taken over by Whole Foods. It measures nearly 10,000 square feet (or 929 square meters).

• 2201 Preston Rd. at Park in Plano, (972) 612-6729.

• Coit Rd. at Belt Line Rd. in Richardson, (972) 699-8075.

Markets

Dallas Farmers Market, 1010 South Pearl St., (972) 556-9900. Open daily 7 AM-6 PM. A four-block area located in the southeastern part of downtown, west of North Central Expressway, and south of Commerce Street. Wheelchair accessible.

It measures 11 acres (or 4.45 hectares). The first shed was installed in 1941, followed by the second one five years later. In the mid-1950s the market became a year-round operation. An enclosed shed was built in 1993, but it became practically unusable because it had no insulation and was too hot for produce. "A public asset with nearly two million customers a year instead led to some colossal miscalculations that the market is still recovering from ten years later," comments the *Dallas Morning News*, quoting one insider as saying, "'It was just a comedy of errors. A really tragic comedy, I might say.'"

Mayor Laura Miller was quoted by the *Dallas Business Journal* as saying that the current market is an "unbelievable mess" marked by junk furniture, rusted-out equipment, live chickens—and rats. In addition, said the mayor, "most of the people selling grapefruit and tomatoes are actually the big produce folks from next door. Their produce either goes to [the upscale supermarket] Simon David, or the little vendors take their carts over there and load up on the warehouse produce and sell it as though it just came off the farm."

The number of farmers selling their produce has dropped to just over a dozen. Most vendors sell shipped produce or buy from the farmers who arrive before dawn to sell wholesale. Others offer fresh fruits and vegetables, cheese, Texas honey, bread, flowers, and more.

SPORTS

The city of Arlington initially bid to host the 2012 Summer Olympic Games in 1997, then joined Dallas and Fort Worth to compete for the games as one entity the following year. The Olympic Village location was to coincide with the construction of the University of North Texas' Dallas campus, the first public four-year university inside the Dallas city limits. That campus is scheduled for completion in 2006.

In 2002, on the same day that Lockheed Martin in Fort Worth won a $200-billion, 40-year Pentagon contract for a new joint strike fighter jet, Dallas—along with several other cities—was eliminated from further consideration.

SPORTS TO SEE

Even so, if you love sports, Dallas is perhaps one of the best places in the nation to live. Dallasites are sports fanatics, and the city will reward you with a large selection of spectator sports activities.

Among the better known native Dallas-area athletes is Michael Johnson, who during the Sydney Olympic Games in 2000 became the first man to win back-to-back Olympic gold medals in the 400 meters. Four years earlier in Atlanta, he became the first man to win the 200- and 400-meter races. Johnson (b. 1967) also claims nine gold medals in world championships.

Missy Ryan, a rower who lives in Dallas and who won a silver medal in Atlanta in 1996, received a bronze medal in Sydney. Dallasite Chryste Gaines won a bronze medal in the 4X100 relay. Paul Wylie (b. 1964), another native who attended the local St. Mark's School (see entry) and received an MBA from Harvard University, was the 1992 Olympic figure skating silver medalist in Albertville, France.

Three-time University Interscholastic League shot put state champion Michael Carter, now living in Red Oak, won seven National Collegiate Athletic Association shot put titles at Southern Methodist University, then won an Olympic silver medal in shot put in Los Angeles in 1984.

Although born in Tulsa, Oklahoma, Jerry Heidenreich qualified as a Dallas resident through more than two decades as a swimming coach here. Most knew him as the winner of two gold medals at the 1972 Olympics in Munich, Germany, where even the legendary Mark Spitz was in awe of him. "Jerry Heidenreich was the reason I was great," once declared Spitz.

The ten highest-paid athletes in the Metroplex are seven Texas Rangers baseball players, two Dallas Mavericks basketball players, and one hockey player, each one earning more than $7 million a year. The top 24 area athletes earn at least $3 million a year. The best-paid Dallas Stars player, Mike Modano (b. 1970), signed a six-year, $43.5-million deal in 1998. "A filthy-rich, world-class athlete with GQ [*Gentleman's Quarterly* magazine] looks, a full head of hair and a cool house with a big TV, the Star center remains the desire of the most eligible bachelorettes and the envy of most men," declares the *Fort Worth Star-Telegram*.

Auto Racing

Texas Motor Speedway, State Hwy. 114 and FM 156, Justin, (817) 215-8500; hotel reservations, (888) FW-SPEED; tickets, 215-8500, Internet www.texasmotorspeedway.com. Open Mon-Sat 8:30 AM-5:30 PM. Call for calendar of races. Located west of Interstate Highway 35 West in Denton County, northwest of a 23-acre (or 9.3-hectare) lake, and about 15 miles (or 24 kilometers) north of Fort Worth. From central Dallas or Irving, take State Highway 183 west to Interstate Highway 35 West north to Speedway.

It is suggested that you arrive at least one hour before races start. There are 1,595 seats for the handicapped. The largest sport facility in the Metropelx can accommodate up to 60,000 vehicles, and includes 26,000 free paved spaces. Parking is a headache, but there are trams from the parking lot to the ticket gate.

Completed in 1997, this is the first NASCAR (National Association for Stock Car Auto Racing) facility in Texas. The 150,060-seat Speedway, which is spread over 950 acres (or 384 hectares), cost $110 million to build and is the largest spectator-sport facility in Texas and the third largest in the world, behind the Indianapolis Motor Speedway and the Maracana soccer stadium in Rio de Janeiro, Brazil. More than 200,000 attend the NASCAR Winston Cup race and more than a million over a year's worth of events. The speedway is now valued at $250 million. Its 153 luxury suites, seating up to 60 people each, sell for $65,000 to $100,000 a year. The 2002 Cup purse was $5,487,000.

The 100-acre (or 40-hectare) infield is large enough to contain 91 football fields. The speedway is a one-and-a half-mile (or 2.4-kilometer) asphalt track that has a double-dogleg front stretch and 24-degree high-banked turns. NASCAR racers ride high on the banks to take advantage of centrifugal force, which lets them maintain top speeds as they make turns. Drivers race around the track for several hundred miles at an average speed near 200 miles (or 322 kilometers) per hour.

Bring earplugs or headphones—especially for children—a scanner to eavesdrop on drivers' radio conversations, and binoculars. The campground on the north end of the speedway can accommodate 20,000 campers. Fans are allowed to bring in coolers, presumably filled with liquids ranging from Gatorade to beer, a decision which costs TMS about $12 million in lost sales. In a typical year, the owners earn more than $10 million in revenue from non-racing events, such as parties and conventions.

O. Bruton Smith (b. 1927), a former stock-car driver and chairman of Speedway Motorsports Inc., picked north Texas for the facility in 1995. He paid for most of the cost of building the speedway and sold the track to the Fort Worth Sports Authority, a non-profit agency created by the Fort Worth City Council as an independent economic development corporation. The sports authority leased the speedway back to Smith for 30 years. The track is exempt from most property taxes, tax breaks that could exceed $100 million over 30 years. The speedway, however, is one of the largest taxpayers in the area and has so far generated more than $20 million for the local school district, the city of Fort Worth, and the state. In addition to those in Fort Worth, Speedway Motors also owns speedways in Charlotte, North Carolina, and Atlanta, Georgia. Smith owns 69 percent of the company's stock.

There are 76 luxury Lone Star Tower condominiums at the track. Measuring 1,000 to 2,400 square feet (or 93 to 223 square meters), they all have floor-to-ceiling glass walls facing Turn 2 and sell from $250,000 to $750,000. Floors six through nine have theater-style seating in front of the glass, and penthouses on the ninth floor have roof access. Owners have clubhouse access, a Texas-shaped pool, and a tennis court. There is a golf course across the street and a helicopter landing pad north of the speedway. A three-story, 78-unit Sleep Inn & Suites hotel opened in Roanoke nearby.

In 2000, the veteran 35-year-old racecar driver Tony Roper of Missouri was the first track fatality since it opened. Following a crash, Roper died of a severe neck injury at Parkland Hospital in Dallas the following day, October 14.

Baseball

The Ballpark in Arlington Stadium, 1000 Ballpark Way at Randol Mill, Arlington, (817) 273-5222; tickets, 273-5100; tours, 273-5099,

Internet www.texasrangers.com. Museum is open Mon-Sat 9 AM-6:30 PM, Sun noon-4 PM. Wheelchair accessible. Tickets are priced for children age 6-13, for adults, and for combination visits to the museum and the Ballpark. Located in Arlington, halfway between Dallas and Fort Worth.

The Rangers season runs Apr-Oct. Parking costs up to $20 for valet parking. Smoking is prohibited in all seating sections and rest rooms. Surrounding the field are two restaurants, radio facilities, shops, and offices. One-hour guided tours of the Ballpark are available. No metal cans, glass containers, or alcoholic beverages are permitted, but fans can bring sodas and water in plastic bottles. Coolers, backpacks, and bags over 12 inches by 12 inches are not allowed.

The four-level Ballpark Stadium, which seats 49,178, was designed by David M. Schwartz, who also drafted the American Airlines Center in Dallas (see entry), and inaugurated it in 1994. It is the home of the **Texas Rangers,** the Metroplex baseball team, in the American League. The Washington Senators became the Texas Rangers in 1972, when the Dallas Cowboys were the only big-time franchise.

The Rangers have never won a playoff series, much less the World Series. "For 30 years, the little red-shoed Rangers have been on the unhappy side of mediocrity," observed *D Magazine* in 2002. "In that time, they have won 2,285 games and lost 2,483." The team attracts 2.5 million fans annually. The stadium is part of a $200-million complex that has 129 luxury suites costing from $30,000 to $200,000 a year.

The city receives about $4 million a year in direct payments from the Rangers on a taxpayers' investment of $135 million. While many envisioned a development combining hip retail stores with condos, corporate towers, and pedestrian-friendly public spaces, the park is still surrounded by more than 200 acres (or 81 hectares) of mostly vacant land.

"This stadium is the house that [George W.] Bush built—and the one that allowed him, in a sense, to become a presidential candidate," opined the *New York Times* before Bush became president. "As the owner of a baseball team in Arlington, a Dallas suburb, Mr. Bush laid the groundwork for his race for the governor's mansion, and that in turn may prove his stepping stone to the White House."

As an owner, George W. Bush supposedly proved himself "an outstanding manager, still remembered fondly by the players who pitched and batted for him." He is said to have helped turn the Rangers "into a greatly improved team, and he presided over the complex arrangements for the new ballpark, one of the finest in major league baseball."

Dallas businessman Tom Hicks (b. 1946), who had already paid $84 million for the **Dallas Stars** hockey team (see entry) in 1995, purchased the Rangers and their entire complex for $250 million three years later.

Forbes magazine estimates that the Rangers are now worth more than $330 million, although the team has lost millions over the years.

The three-storied, 15,658-square-foot (or 1,455-square-meter) **Legends of the Game Baseball Museum,** (817) 273-5059, located on the Randol Mill side of the Ballpark, is the only museum of its kind in a major-league park. It presents a general history of baseball, as well as the story of this game in Texas. On the first floor, the museum displays the nation's legendary players and their achievements. Worn gloves, jerseys, trophies, autographed balls, and photos are shown. On the second floor, Texas baseball is explored from the founding of the Texas League in 1888 until now. On the third floor, baseball-related games and entertainment are featured, complete with interactive computer games, baseball cards, and other memorabilia. The kids can play a game in which a virtual Nolan Ryan pitches a ball at them. A visiting exhibit from the National Baseball Hall of Fame and Museum in Cooperstown, New York, is also featured. In 2003, Congress doled out $750,000 to the Baseball Hall of Fame, prompting one Arizona lawmaker to suggest a Pork Barrel Hall of Fame.

Basketball

Dallas' basketball team is the **Dallas Mavericks,** which until 2001 used the city-owned Reunion Arena, part of the Reunion complex, next to the Hyatt Regency Hotel (see listing). The Mavericks are now located at the American Airlines Arena, 2500 Victory Ave.; ticket information, (214) 747-MAVS; team shop, (214) 665-4852, Internet www.dallasmavericks.com.

The team belongs to the Midwest Division of the Western Conference of the National Basketball Association. It became the 23rd member of the NBA in May 1980, when owner Donald Carter's Dallas National Basketball Association was awarded a franchise. This franchise is valued at more than $300 million and has revenues of $60 million a year. Ross Perot Jr., the son of billionaire and twice unsuccessful presidential candidate of the same name, bought the Mavericks in 1996 for $110 million. The team, which came to Dallas in 1980, plays more than 50 games each season, from October through April or May.

The dot.com billionaire **Mark Cuban** (born 1959), who had co-founded Broadcast.com Internet business, purchased the team for $280 million in 2000. The "incredibly, unfathomably rich" Cuban, who grew up in Pittsburgh, is successful in most of his endeavors. He bought and sold stamps when he was 16 years old, making enough money to finance his class trip to Russia and his first year of college. When Cuban bought the Mavericks, the team was such a losing entity that "even mediocrity seemed far off." They had not had a winning record or made the playoffs since the 1989-90 season. The billionaire owner changed all that.

"He is at the games, cheering and giving his players high-fives from his seat near the bench," observes the *Dallas Morning News*. "He is criticizing the referees with icy glares and cutting comments." The new owner purchased a $50-million Boeing 757 airplane, which he "customized to meet his players' special needs." He also answers some of the e-mails sent to mark.cuban@dallasmavs.com. If you see a jet-black Lexus SC 430 with a license plate MFFL (Mavs Fan for Life), that's Cuban.

After the 2001 terrorist attacks on the World Trade Center and the Pentagon, he made a $1-million donation on behalf of Dallas to benefit the families of firemen and police officers who lost their lives. He said simply, "It was just the right thing to do. There was no other reason."

But Cuban is not going bankrupt anytime soon. *Forbes* magazine estimates his wealth at $1.3 billion, which would easily make him one of the 400 richest people in the world.

French native Tariq Abdul-Wahad, who joined the Mavericks in 2002, created a foundation that exposes youth to art and history. "I want to show you stuff that comes from a completely different culture," he told a group of sixth-, seventh-, and eight graders, while showing them the Renaissance works at the Fort Worth's Kimbel Art Museum. "You have to understand there are things much bigger than Texas."

In addition to Abdul-Wahad, the Mavericks also employ a Canadian and a Mexican player. The seven-foot-tall (or two-meter), media-shy German, Dirk Nowitzki, who was recruited for six years at $79 million in 1998, when 20 years old, became a basketball sensation in 2002. Michael Finley, Nick Van Exel, and Raef LaFrentz all have seven-year contracts for $102 million, $77 million, and $69 million respectively.

The city's first professional basketball team, whose record was so miserable it drew only 200 fans to its final home game, was called the Chaparrals. In 1973, after six seasons, the team was leased to San Antonio businessman Red McCombs for $1 and renamed the Spurs. By the season's end, he and his partners exercised their option to buy the team for $750,000. McCombs gained sole control of the team for $47 million in 1988 and sold the Spurs for $79 million in 1993. Dallas was without a professional basketball franchise until 1980, when it got the Mavericks. The Spurs eliminated the Mavericks from the NBA playoffs in 2001.

Reunion Arena, 777 Sports St., off Interstate Highway 35 downtown, (214) 800-3000; box office, 800-3089; coming events, (214) 670-1395. The box office on the north side of the arena is open Mon-Fri 10 AM-5 PM. There is parking for 6,380 cars.

The 85-foot-high (or 26-meter) arena, which sits on 6.2 acres (or 2.5 hectares) of land, opened in 1980 at a cost of $27 million and is named after a 19th-century Utopian colony, La Reunion, which was established nearby. It was designed by the Chicago-born architect Harwood K. Smith (1913-2002), who also drafted the Hockaday School, Plaza of the Americas, and Thanksgiving Tower (see individual entries).

The arena now hosts rock & roll and county & western music concerts, ice skating performances, and other events. It can seat 16,900 to 19,200 spectators, depending on the event. Upon the completion of the American Airlines Center (see below), about a mile (or 1.6 kilometers) away, the number of its events dropped to 100 a year.

The arena was part of a much larger real estate development envisioned by billionaire Ray Lee Hunt (b. 1943) for downtown Dallas that never materialized. Hunt is the chairman of the Dallas-based Hunt Oil Company and one of the richest local residents who lives in a relatively modest $3-million home off Preston Road in far-north Dallas.

Football

Texas Stadium, 2401 East Airport Fwy., Irving, (972) 785-4000; tickets, Mon-Fri 9 AM-4 PM, 579-5100, Internet www.dallascowboys.com. Open daily. Parking gates open three hours before kickoff, stadium gates two hours before. Pre-season and regular season games begin in August and end in December. Located northwest of downtown Dallas and bound by State Highway 183 (or East Airport Freeway), State Highway 114 (or John W. Carpenter Freeway), and Loop 12 (or Walton Walker Boulevard North). It is the third largest sports facility in the Metroplex.

The Stadium is best known as the home of the **Dallas Cowboys** football team, the five-time Super Bowl champion of the National Football League, which moved from the Cotton Bowl in 1971. The Cowboys are identified by their silver and blue helmets and uniforms. The stadium, which now seats 65,850, along with its parking facilities, occupies 140 acres (or 56 hectares) and employs more than 2,000. The Dallas Cowboys offices are located at One Cowboys Parkway in Irving, (972) 556-9900. The team operates 23 Dallas Cowboys Pro Shop stores throughout Texas.

One of its legendary players was quarterback Roger Staubach, who played for ten years and guided the team to two Super Bowl victories, and now owns a large Dallas-based real estate company. Another was wide receiver Robert Lee "Bullet Bob" Hayes (1942-2002), who spent ten years with the Cowboys. Hayes burst onto the scene in the 1964 Olympics in Tokyo, where he won two gold medals, including the 100 meters in a world-record-tying time of 10.05 seconds. "As a former Olympic hero, he was the Cowboys' first international superstar," declares the *Fort Worth Star-Telegram.*

Clint Williams Murchison, Jr. (1923-1987), a Dallas businessman, purchased the Dallas Cowboys, a National Football League expansion franchise, for $600,000 in 1959, at age 36. He co-owned it with his sister-in-law, Lupe Murchison (1925-2001), also an arts patron and regent for the University of North Texas. The Dallas native, who received an electrical engineering degree from Duke University and a master's in mathematics from the Massachusetts Institute of Technology, was the son of the legendary oilman Clint Murchison Sr.

Texas Stadium—which now has 379 luxury suites priced from $30,000 to $125,000—was Clint Murchison's idea. His wealth was once estimated at $350 million by *Fortune* magazine, but he was hit by falling oil prices in the mid-1980s and went bankrupt. Murchison sold the Cowboys for $80 million in 1984 (including $20 million for Texas Stadium), then a record price for an NFL franchise, to H. R. "Bum" Bright, an Oklahoma-born businessman. As the Cowboys' performance declined during the 1980s, Bright sold it and the lease on the stadium to Arkansas oilman Jerry Jones for $140 million in 1989.

"By the time he entered the University of Arkansas on a football scholarship in 1959, Jones, just 18, was making $1,000 a month from selling insurance," notes the *Dallas Business Journal.* "His first day on campus, he met Eugenia Chambers, the then-reigning Miss Arkansas," and married her in his junior year. *Forbes* magazine lists Jones (b. 1942) as one of the 300 richest people in America and among the dozen wealthiest in Dallas.

Jones fired the team's legendary coach Tom Landry (b. 1924) in 1989. Landry helped the Cowboys win two Super Bowls, led the team to 270 victories and 20 consecutive winning seasons, and coached it for 29 seasons. He died in 2000 from leukemia. Landry was born in South Texas' Rio Grande Valley and graduated from the University of Texas. In 1954, the New York Giants football team asked him to become an assistant coach. He was 35 years old when the Cowboys made him the youngest coach in the National Football League.

The Cowboys became members of the National Football League in 1960 and are the second most valuable football franchise among the NFL teams in the United States, valued at $800 million, just behind the Washington Redskins.

Also part of the Texas football craze are the now-famous **Dallas Cowboys Cheerleaders,** a group of young, enthusiastic, and pretty women who have performed since 1972, for the benefit of the television cameras and mostly male audiences. About 1,000 cheerleading candidates show up at Texas Stadium every spring for preliminary tryouts, but only two or three dozen finalists are retained. A yearly photo calendar and other promotional work seem to have invested them with a glamour that has become the envy of thousands of American girls.

"The Dallas Cowboys Cheerleaders are international icons," declares an otherwise sober *Texas Monthly*. "They're also the reason Dallas women are perceived as some of the most gorgeous creatures on earth."

Cotton Bowl Stadium, 3809 Grand Ave., Fair Park, (888) 792-BOWL or (214) 939-2222, Internet www.swbellcottonbowl.com, e-mail mail@swbellcottonbowl.org. Open Mon-Fri 8 AM-5 PM. All gates open two hours prior to game time. Handicapped accessible at all gates, except 2 and 7. Located about two miles (or 3.2 kilometers) east of the downtown business district.

This is the city-owned stadium in which the annual Cotton Bowl Classic football game has been played since 1937. An attempt was made to build a wooden stadium in the 1890s, but it took until 1921 before one with a seating capacity of 15,000 was constructed. The next one, finished in 1930, could seat 46,000 and was later expanded to 72,000. Today, it is the second largest such facility in the Metroplex.

The stadium was used during the Texas Centennial Exposition in 1936 for an outdoor play with 250 actors. President Franklin D. Roosevelt also spoke here that year. Elvis Presley and Frank Sinatra both appeared at the Cotton Bowl. The Dallas Cowboys played here from 1960 until the Texas Stadium was completed 11 years later.

Gerald J. Ford Stadium, 5800 Ownby Dr. at Mockingbird Ln., (214) 768-2866; ticket information, (214) 768-2902, Internet www.smumustangs.com. On-campus parking is a confusion of color-coded parking zones, each of which has a specific point of entry. Free off-campus parking is available at DART's Mockingbird Station across the North Central Expressway. Located in University Park, just north of downtown Dallas.

The Mustangs, the Southern Methodist University football team, played their home games at Ownby Stadium, on the south side of the campus, until 1995. They then switched to the Cotton Bowl (see entry) at Fair Park to which they were committed by contract through the 1999 season, which runs from September to December.

The $60-million, horseshoe-shaped, red-brick Gerald Ford stadium was built on the site of the old Ownby Stadium in 2000. Ownby was constructed in 1926, when booster Jordan Ownby gave $10,000 toward the $190,000 cost of the facility. SMU's desperately needed first library, Fondren, in comparison, had to wait another dozen years before it was built in 1939.

The Ford Stadium seats about 32,000 spectators, but seldom attracts anywhere near that number. Attendance has been dropping as the novelty of the new stadium began wearing off. The field is recessed 25 feet (or 7.6 meters), with 24 rows of seats below ground and 24 rows above it. The two-acre (or 0.8-hectare) stadium has 29 sections in the upper and lower bowls, and seven entry gates. Seventeen luxury suites go for $25,000 each, while 540 club-level seats cost $275. The adjacent sports center houses training facilities and weight rooms.

Ford (b. 1944), the stadium benefactor, "grew up on a Texas wheat farm, but made his money in banks," according to *Forbes* magazine, which estimates his wealth at about $1 billion. His $14-million Turtle Creek estate is situated across Goar Park in University Park.

Northeast of the stadium lies the Doak Walker Plaza. It features an eight-foot-tall (or 2.43-meter) bronze statue of the All-American football player, 1948 Heisman Trophy winner, and pro-football Hall of Fame running back who brought national attention to the university in the late 1940s. The $150,000 statue was executed by Blair Buswell of Utah. Walker died in 1998 after complications from paralysis caused by a skiing accident.

Some of the athletic and other events are held at the nearby Moody Coliseum, 60204 Airline Rd., (214) 768-2106, which measures 124,000 square feet (or 11,520 square meters) and has a capacity of nearly 9,000. First Lady Laura Bush—an alumna of SMU who also serves on its board of trustees—celebrated her 56th birthday here in the fall of 2002, along with her husband.

Hockey

Dallas Stars, 211 Cowboys Pkwy., Irving; tickets, (214) GO-STARS or 467-8277; business office, (817) 273-5222, Internet www.dallasstars.com. Located about two miles (or north of the intersection of MacArthur Boulevard and Interstate Highway 635 (or LBJ Freeway).

A $254-million National Hockey League franchise, according to *Forbes* magazine, which estimates the team's revenues at $96 million a year. The Stars' season runs from September through the middle of April.

The first ice hockey game in Dallas took place on November 6, 1941. The game day an advertisement promised, "You can't use a gun in ice hockey, but practically nothing else is barred." The 1950 demise of the Texas Hockey League kept professional ice hockey from Dallas for 18 years. After that, the Dallas Blackhawks played here for 16 seasons, but never generated enough fan interest to remain a viable team.

Norman Green (b. 1935), "who grew rich as a real estate investor" in Calgary, Canada, became the sole owner of the Minnesota North Stars in 1990. He moved the team to Big D three years later, when there were only three ice rinks in the city. Tom Hicks, chairman of a Dallas-based private investment firm, bought the Stars from Green, who "encountered financial problems with his Canadian real estate," for $84 million in 1995.

In the summer of 1999 the Dallas Stars won the Stanley Cup title in triple overtime in Game 7 against the Buffalo Sabres. Afterward, Stars center Mike Modano, the team's highest paid player, stood in front of his locker "bawling like a baby." The city threw a parade for the Stars, and some 115,000 fans celebrated downtown. The Stars let the trophy slip away the following year, when they lost to the New Jersey Devils 2-1.

One of the most sought-after players on the team is the quiet, Moscow-born Sergey Zubov (b. 1971), who was acquired by the Stars in 1996 from the Pittsburgh Penguins and who earns $5 million a year. "If playmaking is art, Zubov is Monet," the *Star-Telegram* characterized him. The Stars have won five consecutive divisional titles since acquiring Zubov. The team also has a Swede, three Finns, and several Canadian players.

StarCenters. West of the Stonebriar Centre mall (see entry), along the east side of Dallas North Tollway, just north of State Highway 121, the city of Frisco is building a $20-million training facility for the Dallas Stars. The park, which is to be completed by 2004, will anchor a $300-million mixed-project that is also to include a $22-million, 9,000-seat minor-league baseball park, office, retail, and residential space.

The Frisco StarCenter—one of five in the Dallas area—will have two National Hockey League-size ice surfaces, costing $20 million, and will become the chief training facility for the Stars when completed.

(For more details about the Dr Pepper StarCenters, Internet www.drpepperstarcenter.com, please see entry Ice Skating and Skateboarding in the SPORTS TO DO section.)

The American Airlines Center, 2500 Victory Ave.; event information, (214) 665-4200; box office, 665-4797; Mavericks tickets, (214) 747-MAVS; Stars tickets, (214) GO-STARS, Internet www.americanairlinescenter.com. Box offices with 24 ticket windows are located at the east and south entrances, and are open Mon-Sat 10 AM-5 PM and two hours before and during events. If you can, buy the tickets for any event here because the Ticketmaster's Internet or phone surcharges are high.

Fans are not allowed to bring in food, beverages, weapons, or firearms. No smoking is allowed inside the center. Shuttle buses run from the West End to the arena about every ten minutes beginning two hours before major events and for an additional hour afterwards. A light-rail and commuter station is open on the arena's western side.

The 840,000-square-foot (or 78,036-square-meter) arena is located on the 46-acre (or 18.6-hectare) site of a former rail yard and electric power plant, east of Stemmons Freeway (also known as Interstate 35 East), and north of Woodall Rodgers Freeway and the West End entertainment district. The Crescent Court Hotel (see listing) and shopping center is within walking distance.

The former Little Mexico is also the area where the "dirt poor" Dallas-born Latino singer Trini Lopez grew up in the 1930s and 1940s. A protégé of Frank Sinatra, Lopez (b. 1937) recorded 50 albums in the late 1950s and afterward, 14 of which reached the charts. His top hits were titled "If I Had a Hammer," "Lemon Tree," and "La Bamba."

Designed by the Los Angeles-born architect David Schwartz (b. 1951), who also drafted the Ballpark in Arlington, the center opened in 2001 and seats 19,200 for basketball, 18,500 for hockey, or 20,020 for center-staged events. Changing over from one configuration to another, once a 12-hour chore, can now be accomplished in less than three hours, and two different events can be scheduled on the same day. The center hosts 200 events annually.

Comparing it with I. M. Pei's Dallas City Hall and Frank Gehry's Guggenheim Museum in Spain, David Dillon, a *Dallas Morning News* architectural critic, notes that the center "sends a less inspiring message about Dallas: that it is more comfortable with the past than the present, that it is better to be big than bold. The south lobby, facing downtown, features a mobile of American airlines planes that looks like a gigantic mockup of a 10-year-old boy's bedroom ceiling." Paris, Texas-born architect Frank Welch (b. 1928), who designed the St. Alcuin Montessori School on Churchill Way, calls it "a tarted-up hangar. Terribly expensive and a great embarrassment to Dallas."

In 1997, after four years of talks to replace the aging Reunion Arena (see entry), Dallas voters narrowly approved investing $125 million in a new $420-million downtown arena for its basketball and hockey teams.

The **Dallas Mavericks,** (214) 972-988-3865, and the **Dallas Stars,** (214) 467-8277 (see individual entries), invested $105 million, agreed to remain at this facility for 30 years, and will pay the city $3.4 million in annual rent.

American Airlines is paying the two sports teams $195 million for the right to name the arena, which is the most expensive such facility in the United States. Los Angeles' Staples Center, in comparison, cost $400 million. The entire Crescent Court development, a couple of blocks from here, cost $400 million in 1985.

Attractions such as Ringling Brothers and Barnum & Baile, Circus or Disney on Ice can be seen here when they come to town. Also the Sidekicks indoor soccer games and rodeo. The Eagles pop group interrupted its European tour to inaugurate the arena with a concert whose tickets were bid up to $3,000 each. The 66-year-old Luciano Pavarotti sang here in 2002.

The arena contains 2,000 "Platinum Club" seats, which sell for $7,000 to $18,000 a season, including tickets to Dallas Mavericks and Dallas Stars games and other events. The 142 luxury, 425-square-foot (or 39-square-meter) suites go for up to $300,000 each, while less than $3 million has been spent on public art, such as terrazzo floor designs by Colorado artist David Griggs and sculptor David Newton's exterior cast-stone friezes whose execution was delayed. Reunion arena, half the size of this venue, was the last of the no-frills, no-luxury-boxes arenas that created an intimacy between fans and players, and spectators were part of the action.

Several restaurants and bars, serving everything from $4 hot dogs to $40 prime beef or sea bass, are on the premises. A 2,000-car parking garage is reserved for occupants of the arena's luxury suites and Platinum seats, although the center has a total of 5,300 arena-owned parking spaces. Dr Pepper Bottling Co. is paying $35 million over ten years for a sponsorship that includes an exhibit hall.

The city has been financing its share of the cost by raising hotel-room taxes by 2 percent and car rentals by 5 percent, since mid-1998, to generate about $12 million a year. "We think people are going to love" it, claimed a vice president of Hillwood Development Corp., one of the arena's developers, just before it opened. "It will feel more like a performing arts hall or a sacred building."

The surrounding mile-long, 70-acre (or 28.3-hectare) property, known as Victory, is under development by its owners, Ross Perot Jr. and the Dallas Stars owner Tom Hicks. It is to contain, eventually, offices, restaurants, and shops. Several hundred upscale apartments are on the periphery of Victory, including Jefferson at the North End, on Field Street, just south of the arena, where rents start at $1,100 a month and include a concierge. There is almost nothing within an easy walking distance to see or do, if you exclude the El Fenix Mexican restaurant at 1601 McKinney Avenue (see entry in DINING chapter).

The debate goes on as to what Dallas got for its $125-million investment. By building the arena, Dallas did clean up, however, one of the region's worst contaminated areas at the edge of downtown. "Rising from ashes of a 100-year-old city dump, a railroad maintenance facility, an aging power plant and a row of abandoned grain silos, the Victory project is a $1 billion development catering to road-weary Dallasites who want to live, work and play downtown," observed *Time* magazine. "Chances are no one will be giving a second thought to the toxic mess that was here just four years ago—an industrial wasteland of asbestos and lead, arsenic and benzene and the carcinogenic remains of a 19th century crematory."

Dallas Citizens Council. The *Dallas Business Journal* explained as early as 1998 that the center was backed by the Dallas Citizens Council (DCC), which "pushed through a bed tax to pay for a new sports arena." The DCC, according to the business weekly, was also instrumental in the construction of the Dallas Convention Center, the North Central Expressway, the downtown tunnel system, the Dallas North Tollway, "and the all-time mother lode, Dallas/Fort Worth International Airport."

The council's founder was the former mayor, Robert L. Thornton, who headed one of the largest local banks, the Mercantile, and started the council in 1937. It originally consisted of the 100 most powerful businessmen, whose top 24 representatives could make quick decisions. They, aside from Thornton, included the men in charge of banks, like Republic National Bank and First National Bank, the future mayor J. Erik Jonsson, the late merchant Stanley Marcus, supermarket executive Robert Cullum, even the president of Southern Methodist University.

After seeing the turmoil in many other Southern cities over desegregation, the council, in the interest of public image, bypassed the resistance to desegregated restrooms, drinking fountains, schools, transportation, and other public facilities in the early 1960s. It arranged for the exclusive lunch counter at Neiman Marcus and other formerly whites-only locations to start serving African-Americans.

Officially dissolved in the 1970s, the council lost much of its prestige after the Kennedy assassination, when "the national news media turned a critical glare upon Dallas and its leadership." Dallas voters also became suspicious of the DCC and its motives. The courts eventually transformed the city's at-large election model into today's 14-1 system, where only the mayor is elected by an at-large vote.

Horse Races

Lone Star Park, 1000 Lone Star Pkwy., Grand Prairie, (800) 795-RACE or (972) 263-RACE, Internet www.lonestarpark.com. Thoroughbred season features about 70 racing days over 15 weeks between the beginning of April and mid-July. First live race weeknights starts at 6:35 PM, weekends at 1:35 PM. The minimum wager is $2. Parking is available for 6,000 vehicles. Located a little over ten miles (or 16 kilometers) west of downtown Dallas, on Belt Line Road, one-quarter mile (or 0.4-kilometer) north of Interstate Highway 30 and five miles (or eight kilometers) east from the Ballpark in Arlington (see entry). It is just a few miles from the old Arlington Downs racetrack that closed in 1937.

The 315-acre (or 127-hectare) racing facility, which opened for live racing in 1997, has a one-mile (or 1.6-kilometer) oval dirt track and the seven-eighths of a mile turf course inside it, both built at a cost of $110 million. By 2001, the park's attendance established it as the tenth leading racetrack in the nation in terms of average daily attendance. Lone Star can seat 8,000 in the grandstand and another 1,500 in the Post Time Pavilion, although the total attendance capacity is more than 40,000. It was designed by the same architect as the Ballpark in Arlington and the American Airlines Center (see entries). Lone Star Park is the area's only legal gambling option other than the Texas Lottery.

A seven-story, glass-enclosed, climate-controlled grandstand features 48 penthouse suites on levels five and six, a terraced trackside dining room, box seats, and outdoor seating, and measures 280,000 square feet (or 26,012 square meters) in all. The 283 pari-mutuel windows and 176 self-bet machines are scattered on the ground floor and other levels of the grandstand, as well as inside the Post Time Pavilion.

The Paddock, a landscaped European-style garden area with a fountain, is where horses are saddled and ridden through a grandstand tunnel to the track. The walking ring gives you a chance to see jockeys and horses before placing a bet. The Post Time Pavilion, adjacent to the grandstand, offers wagering on live racing via simulcast from several other racecourses nationwide, even during the live meets. It features Las Vegas-style racebook, sports bar, and restaurant complete with 175 television monitors and wagering windows. Next to the Pavilion is a 15-acre (or six-hectare) park and entertainment center with playgrounds for children, picnic gazebos, a petting zoo, and pony rides. Three restaurants, concession stands, and bars are located throughout the complex. One of them is the 1,200-seat Silks Dining Terrace that serves up to 1,200 meals in three hours.

Lone Star Park was selected to host the 2005 Breeders' Cup champion series—now called the World Thoroughbred Championships—an eight-race event that attracts horses, trainers, and jockeys from around the world. One of the races, the Breeders' Cup Classic, has a $4-million purse, making it the richest race in the country. In 2002, Lone Star, whose management rights were largely owned by the Trammell Crow family, was bought by Magna Entertainment Corp. of Ontario for about $99 million. Magna already owns major tracks near Los Angeles and between Miami and Fort Lauderdale.

GPX Skate Park & Entertainment Center (see listing) opened at Lone Star in 2001. **Texas NextStage,** a 6,350-seat, $65-million amphitheater owned by the city of Grand Prairie, is located southeast of the grandstand, near Interstate 30 and Belt Line Road.

Soccer

Dallas' Cotton Bowl (see entry) was one of the six U.S. venues for the World Cup soccer championship in 1994, when 64,000 paid to see the Brazil-Holland quarterfinal. The American team, which finished last in the 32-team field at the 1998 World Cup in France, shocked the soccer world at the 2002 Cup in South Korea, when it defeated Portugal, ranked fifth in the world, with a 3-2 victory. The Americans went on to the quarterfinals by beating Mexico 2-0, but lost to the Germans.

Compared with football, baseball, and basketball, even car and horse racing, soccer appears to be a stepchild of the Metroplex sports with grownups, although 70 teams form the Dallas Soccer Association adult league. Some 44,000 children in north Texas play on club soccer teams, even if the sport seems to cater mostly to kids of the well-to-do who can afford the club dues, uniforms, skills camps, and travel expenses.

Dallas Burn, 2602 McKinney Ave., Suite 200, (214) 979-0303, Internet www.dallasburn.com.

Dallas' professional outdoor soccer team is one of the ten that make up Major League Soccer, America's first topflight pro soccer league, which was organized in 1996 as a result of the 1994 World Cup.

Organized in 1996, the franchise, which claims an average attendance of 13,000, has been operating in the red since then. Until 2003, the Dallas Burn played its games in the cavernous Cotton Bowl (see entry) during the season that spans from April through October. It then moved to Southlake, in Tarrant County. The City of Frisco, Collin County, and the Hunt Sports Group agreed to build a 93-acre (or 37.6-hectare), $65-million soccer complex for the team at the northeast corner of Dallas Parkway and Main Street. It was to include a 20,000-seat professional soccer stadium slated for completion in 2005.

The Burn has made the playoffs every year since it was established, but it has never reached the MLS championship stage. Major League Soccer teams are owned by the league but controlled by owner-operators who buy into the league.

Dallas Sidekicks, 777 Sports St., (214) 653-0200; ticket information, 653-0297, Internet www.dallassidekicks.com.

The city's indoor soccer team of the Major Indoor Soccer League plays its games at Reunion Arena, the Cotton Bowl in Fair Park, and occasionally at American Airlines Center, from September through June. It was formed in 1983. The Sidekicks won the 2001 World Indoor Soccer League title.

The team's Brazilian soccer import Antonio Carlos Pecorari, nicknamed Tatu (or armadillo in Portuguese), was with the team for 18 seasons as a player and five as its coach until he retired in 2003. At that time, Tatu (b. 1962) was the longest tenured Dallas professional athlete. The 5-foot-6 (or 1.67-meter) forward was known for throwing his jersey into the crowd whenever he scored a goal, which he did more than 700 times.

Until 2002, the Sidekicks franchise was owned by Minyard Food Stores president Sonny Williams and former Mavericks owner Donald Carter, who relinquished his 50 percent interest to Williams.

SPORTS TO DO

Bicycling

The City of Dallas maintains bike trails throughout the city. You can check an interactive bike map at www.DallasCityHall.com, the Public Works & Transportation Department Web page. For more details call the District Engineering Office, 1500 Marilla St., (214) 670-4039.

One of the longest and most popular is a 12-mile (or 19.3-kilometer) jogging and bike path encircling White Rock Lake (see entry) and its surrounding park in northeast Dallas. While at the lake, you can also rent a bicycle daily 9 AM-7 PM from **Jack Johnston Irish shop** at 9005 Garland Rd., (214) 328-5238, about one-half mile (or 0.8 kilometer) from the Dallas Arboretum (see listing).

A free permit is required to carry bicycles on DART trains and buses. Bikes are permitted aboard light-rail trains, except from 6 AM-9 AM and 3 PM-6 PM weekdays. They should be taken to the wheelchair area in the last car. Bicycles are also allowed aboard Trinity Railway Express trains at all times. They could be taken on express-service buses and should be stored in cargo holds to be unloaded only at DART transit centers and in downtown Dallas.

There are more than 500 bicycle parking spaces in downtown Dallas, including those at Reunion Arena, Pioneer Park, Old City Park, Deep Ellum, the Arts District, City Hall, Convention Center, Dallas Central Public Library, and central business district, at the 600-1800 blocks of Elm, Commerce, and Main Streets, and the 1400-2100 blocks of Ross and San Jacinto.

The Frisco Superdrome, 9700 Wade Blvd. at College, Frisco, (888) 4-DROME-1 or (972) 377-1082, Internet www.superdrome.com. *CH.* Open daily for year-round events. Located on land donated by the Collin County Community College on its Preston Ridge Campus, about five miles (or eight kilometers) north of the EDS headquarters in Plano.

A $4-million training site for professional and amateur cyclists, with full public certification, rental and training programs for all experience levels. The world cycling championship was held here in 1999. When it opened in mid-1998, this was the country's most expensive velodrome. There are now 22 such venues in the United States.

The 6,000-square-foot (or 557-square-meter) Superdrome has a 250-foot (or 76-meter) circumference and leans in at 45 degrees on the curves. Constructed of marine-grade plywood panels, the track seats 2,000, features the timing technology of the Dallas electronic giant which sponsored it for one year, and was built by the same firm that constructed the velodrome for the 1996 Summer Olympics in Atlanta.

The city-owned Superdrome occasionally showcases the nation's cyclists in the U.S. Olympic trials. In 2003, the World Cup trials were held here.

Bowling

Don Carter's All-Star Lanes West, 10920 Composite Dr. at Walnut Hill Ln. and Stemmons Frwy., (214) 358-1382, Internet www.doncarterbowling.com. Located across the street from the 550-seat Old San Francisco Steakhouse, and near the 600-seat Trail Dust Steak House.

It has 58 lanes and is open 24 hours. The *Dallas Observer* named it the best bowling alley in the city. League bowling is available every night except Saturdays. Tuesday nights and weekends there are black lights for Lightning Strikes that will remind you of disco. The Professional Bowlers Association Tour has been held here in the past.

Other bowling venues include:

Fun Fest, 3805 Belt Line Rd., between Marsh Ln. and Midway Rd., Addison, (972) 620-7700. Open Sun-Thu 11 AM-midnight, Fri-Sat 11 AM-2 AM. It has 30 lanes with computer scoring and lots of "family entertainment." There are also video games, laser tag in a maze, and eight billiard tables. Lane Side Café and a bar with big screen television are on the premises.

Showplace Lanes Garland, 1950 Plaza Dr., at Lyndon B. Johnson Frwy. and West Northwest Hwy., (972) 613-8100. Open 24 hours a day, except Sundays until 4 AM. Fifty-eight lanes with automatic scoring, private club serving alcohol, cafe, game room for older children, and playroom for tots.

Fencing

Fencing Institute of Texas, 3501 North MacArthur Blvd., Suite 410, Irving, (972) 870-5756, Internet www.fenceintexas.org. Located in MacArthur Commons Business Park, between Highways 114 and 183.

FIT, established in 1998, is a non-profit member club of the U.S. Fencing Association and the largest training facility for fencers in north Texas. Its instructors teach all three Olympic weapons and encourage competitive team as well as recreational fencing. Dry practice equipment is provided to students at no additional charge. Group and private lessons are available. Five practice strips are located on the premises.

Irina Dolgikh, the Ukranian-born 1976 Junior World Champion in Women's Foil, when she was 20 years old, joined FIT as a guest coach in 2000. "We fell in love with her and asked if she wanted to stay," notes FIT's Web site. She did. Her countryman, coach Volodymyr Yefimov, is also on the institute's team.

Lone Star Fencing Center, 2636 Walnut Hill Ln., (214) 352-3733, Internet www.lonestarfencingcenter.com. Fencing lessons for children and adults are available daily, except Tuesdays. Other local fencing facilities are located at Hockaday and St. Mark's private preparatory schools (see entries).

Fishing & Hunting, Hiking & Sailing —

Call **Texas Parks and Wildlife,** (800) 792-1112 or (800) 895-4248 for details. For more information about fishing, boating, hunting, camping, and Texas state parks, check also the state's Internet sites, www.texas.gov and www.tpwd.state.tx.us.

The catch around Dallas is mostly bass. Resident and non-resident **fishing licenses** can be purchased at many tackle and sporting goods stores. Deer, turkey, pheasant, dove, duck, and quail will be found in north Texas. Resident **hunting licenses** cost about the same, and there is also a combination hunting and fishing license. A non-resident hunting license is available by the week or for the whole year.

The **first Saturday in June** is the Texas Parks and Wildlife Department's annual Free Fishing Day in Texas, and no license is required. About one million hunting licenses are issued annually in Texas contributing up to $3 billion to the state economy. Fewer than 6 percent of Texans go hunting.

For those needing camping, backpacking, or biking equipment, head for REI, 4515 Lyndon B. Johnson Fwy., Farmers Branch, (972) 490-5989.

Bachman Lake, 3500 West Northwest Hwy., (214) 670-4100. Open daily 5 AM-midnight. Rest rooms are at its Northwest Highway entrance. Located northwest of Love Field Airport, along Northwest

Highway. Robberies and rapes are not uncommon at night, so do not stay after dark.

The lake was named after the John B. and William F. Bachman families, who settled here in 1845. The 205-acre (or 83-hectare) Bachman—half of it water surface—with more than three miles (or 4.8 kilometers) of shoreline, is the only large natural lake in the area. Others were created by civil engineers.

Bachman has a bike and hike trail alongside it. It can be quite crowded on Sundays. There is a recreation center with paddleboat and skate concession. Pierre's by the Lake Continental restaurant, situated in a former private home, is located at 3430 Shorecrest Dr., (214) 358-2379.

The area starting just northwest of here, particularly Harry Hines Boulevard, between West Northwest Highway on the south and Walnut Hill Lane on the north, has been overwhelmed by prostitutes and adult theaters for years. The stretch of Northwest Highway between Lombardy Lane and Denton Drive has perhaps the highest concentration of nightclubs, dance halls, and topless clubs in Dallas, making it unsuitable for families after sunset.

In 1986, the city banned sexually oriented businesses from locating within 1,000 feet (or 304 meters) of homes, churches, parks, hospitals, or other topless clubs, "but instead of closing, club owners fought the law, in many cases winning the right to operate until they had recouped their investments," according to the *Dallas Morning News*, which also quotes a police officer calling the Bachman area "the red-light district of Dallas."

White Rock Lake, 8300 East Lawther Dr., Dallas, (214) 670-4100. Open daily 6 AM-midnight. Do not stay after dark. Located about five miles (or eight kilometers) northeast of downtown Dallas and surrounded by a park, this is a popular, city-owned recreational facility. It is accessible on the south end from Highway 78 (South Garland Boulevard) or from the north end via Loop 12 and South Buckner Boulevard.

The lake was built in 1911 as Dallas' first water supply at a cost of $2 million. It was recommended by George Kessler, a city planner from Kansas City, who also suggested flood control and land reclamation of the Trinity River. The reservoir was created by the damming of White Rock Creek, a stream originating in a pasture near Frisco, Collin County. It reached capacity in 1914.

"By the early 1920s, when it became clear that White Rock was becoming inadequate to meet the growing city's demand for water, construction began on a larger reservoir, to be called Lake Dallas, in neighboring Denton County," observes *Legacies*, the city's historical journal.

In 1923, a scenic road encircling the White Rock reservoir was built by Dallas city jail prisoners and named after Mayor Joe E. Lawther. The following year sailboats were allowed in the lake. A $122,000 bathhouse, with 268 steel dressing rooms, 908 steel lockers, and 29 showers was inaugurated in the summer of 1930. White Rock Lake became a park in 1929, after the city switched to Lewisville Lake for its water supply. Between 1935 and 1942, under President Franklin Roosevelt's New Deal programs, Civilian Conservation Corps erected buildings, bridges, tables, and benches.

Residential construction around the lake increased in the early 1930s, when the city began developing the lake shores into a municipal park. In 1944, the government used the barracks at Winfrey Point to house up to 400 German prisoners of war who had served as noncommissioned officers in Rommel's Afrika Korps. During the 1953 drought, the city used White Rock Lake for municipal water again and prohibited swimming in the lake. The bathhouse was closed in 1981.

Swiss immigrant Jacob Buhrer and his family purchased 350 acres (or 141 hectares) of land alongside the lake in 1891. He established a dairy farm, most of which is now under water, which was acquired by the city through condemnation. He owned 50 cows, and his Swiss Dairy delivered fresh milk to customers in East Dallas twice a day in a horse-drawn wagon. Buhrer's house survived the construction of the lake but was torn down in the early 1960s.

White Rock Lake Park consists of 1,088 acres (or 440 hectares) of lake and 2,956 acres (or 1,196 hectares) of surrounding park land, which shelters 49 species of trees, 190 wildflower species, 210 species of birds, and 33 species of mammals. Even without the lake, White Rock is more than twice as big as New York City's Central Park.

White Rock Lake has 9.3 miles (or 15 kilometers) of trails and jogging paths. The bike trail, which encircles the lake, is closed to automobiles. No camping is allowed. There are two sailing clubs on the lake, although a ten-horsepower limit on power boats is in effect. The public boat ramp is on the west side of the lake, off West Lawther Drive. Largemouth bass and crappie fishing from 12 piers and elsewhere is good, but you will need a license and will have to follow length and limit regulations. In 1998, a two-year dredging of the lake brought its minimum depth to eight feet (or 2.4 meters). Swimming has not been allowed since 1953 so the old Bath House Cultural Center (see entry), located on the northeast shore of the lake, at East Lawther Drive and Northcliff, is now a theater, gallery, and educational center.

(For more about the Dallas Arboretum & Botanical Garden, which is located on the lake's southeastern shore, south of the Bath House, please see a separate entry.)

The lake's parks have increasingly become a destination for persons cruising for anonymous sex to the point that Dallas police recommend that parents not let their children go into the public restrooms unescorted. The area has been listed on Web sites devoted to sexual tourists, police and residents say. More than 100 arrests for public lewdness and sexual activity are made each year.

Golf

Texas golf courses are not highly thought of outside the state. The Colonial Country Club is one of the few Texas facilities listed among *Golf Digest*'s top 100 courses. May is professional golf month in Dallas. Two well-known professional tournaments are held in the Metroplex.

Perhaps the best-known is the 30-year-old **Byron Nelson Championship,** tickets (972) 717-1200, played at the Tournament Players Club at Irving's Four Seasons Resort & Club (see listing) in Las Colinas, Irving. It is held one weekend in mid-May and televised. Tickets, which go on sale in January, have sold out since 1997. Texas Stadium parking lots in Irving can accommodate about 15,000 vehicles. Shuttle buses run to the tournament site.

The winner of the 2003 tournament was the 40-year-old Vijay Singh, who won $1 million.

The tournament is the only PGA tour event named for a player, the legendary golfer Byron Nelson, who won 18 victories in the 1945 season and 11 consecutive victories that same year, both PGA records. He won 52 titles at PGA Tour events and 61 tournament victories, including the 1955 French Open.

Nelson, who was born on a cotton farm just outside Waxahachie, south of Dallas, turned 91 in February 2003. He retired to his ranch in Roanoke, a few miles north of downtown Fort Worth, in 1946, and buried his first wife Louise who after a 50-year marriage died of a stroke in 1985. Since 1986, he has devoted himself to Peggy Simmons, an advertising writer whom he met in Dayton, Ohio, and his second wife nearly 33 years his junior. They celebrate monthly anniversaries because, as Nelson likes to put it, "I'll never have enough time to be with you."

Bank of America Colonial, tickets (817) 927-4280, held in the second half of May at the Colonial Country Club along the Trinity River in Fort Worth, is more than 50 years old and also televised. The purse in 2003 was almost $5 million. Kentuckian Kenny Perry (b. 1961) claimed $900,000 of it as the winner of the 57th Colonial. Arnold Palmer earned only $7,000 here as recently as 1962.

The Stockholm-born Annika Sorenstam—a 43-time winner on the

LPGA Tour-created a huge controversy by becoming the first woman to play in a Professional Golfers Association Tour event in 58 years. Sorenstam (b. 1970) ended in the 95th place among the 111 players on the second day of the competition.

During both, the Byron Nelson Championship and Bank of America Colonial, no cell phones are permitted on either golf course, and pagers must be on vibrate. No backpacks, signs, or banners are allowed, and no alcoholic beverages may enter or leave the tournaments. Cameras, video cameras, and coolers are also prohibited.

Arnold Palmer Golf Academy, The Golf Club at Castle Hills, 699 Lady of the Lake Blvd., Lewisville, (972) 899-2750, is believed to be one of the best golf instruction facilities in the area. It opened in 1999. The driving range is 500 yards long and 210 yards wide, with a hitting area 80 yards deep. There is a three-hole practice course. Instructors are accredited with the Professional Golf Association.

Also popular with Metroplex residents is **Hank Haney** instructional facility at 3636 McKinney Ave., across North Central Expressway from CityPlace and West Village, (214) 520-7275, Internet www.hankhaney.com. Another Haney facility is at 8787 Park Lane, (214) 341-9600. There is also his 56-acre (or 22.6-hectare) headquarters in McKinney, at 4101 Custer Rd., (972) 529-2221. *Golf Digest* magazine named Haney (b. 1955), a native of Chicago, the best golf teacher in Texas and among half a dozen best nationwide.

There are more than 75 golf courses in the area, among them:

Bear Creek Golf Course, 3500 Bear Creek Court, Dallas/Fort Worth Airport; (972) 456-3200. It has a grill, snack bar, and pro shop. Located less than a mile (or 1.6 kilometers) from the airport and 19 miles (or 30.6 kilometers) northwest from downtown Dallas.

Designed by architect Ted Robinson and opened in 1980. Par 72, yardage (from the back tees) 6,690 West course, 6,670 East course. Slope rating 130 West, 127 East. Course rating 72.7 West, 72.5 East. It has two 18-hole championship courses, East and West. Rated as one of the top 50 resort courses in America. The *Dallas Morning News* named it one of the top ten public courses.

"Bear Creek is still the same challenging and picturesque course it was when Ted Robinson built it in 1980," observes the *Dallas Business Journal*. "Rolling terrain, tall trees and small greens define both the West and East courses." The one disadvantage is the roar of jetliners coming and going from D/FW Airport.

Cedar Crest Park Golf Course, 1800 Southerland, Dallas, (214) 670-7615, Internet www.cedarcrestgolf.com. Located in Oak Cliff, east of Interstate 35 East and off Illinois Avenue. Par 71, yardage from back tees 121, course rating 71.

Dallas' most historic municipal golf course, built in 1919 as a country club, went out of business shortly after the Great Depression and sat dormant until the city bought it in 1947. It was the site of the 1927 PGA competition, with Walter Hagan the winner.

A 6,550-yard-long, 18-hole, full-service municipal course, designed by the legendary architect A. W. Tillinghast, it has a scenic hilly layout and a panoramic view of Dallas. Its small greens will test your skill and accuracy.

A new $2.3-million, two-story clubhouse was built in 2001. The 14,786-square-foot (or 1,374-square-meter) building features a pro shop, restaurant, and tournament room. Golf lessons are available.

Cowboys Golf Course, 1600 Fairway Dr., Grapevine, (817) 481-7277, Internet www.cowboysgolfclub.com, e-mail cowboys@eaglgolf.com. It has an 18-hole, par-72 course measuring 7,017 yards (or 6,416 meters). Located four miles (or 6.4 kilometers) north of D/FW Airport, off State Highway 26, about one-quarter mile (or 0.4 kilometer) west of Grapevine Mills Mall (see listing), and adjacent to the Opryland Hotel & Conference Center.

The 159-acre (or 64-hectare) site, bounded by Lake Grapevine, includes wildlife habitats and a pecan grove. The owners love to tell you that this is "the world's first and only National Football League-themed resort-style golf course."

One of the better recently constructed courses in the area, designed by Jeff Brauer, who moved to Arlington, Texas, in the 1980s and made a name for himself by designing the Tangle Ridge Golf Club in Grand Prairie. The $12-million Cowboys' course, completed in 2001, has interesting holes, good elevation changes, and plenty of challenges. A 12,000-square-foot (or 1,115-square-meter) Austin-stone clubhouse accommodates 200 guests and includes a conference center, dining room, sports bar for 40, and full-service pro shop.

The all-you-can-eat-and-play greens fees go beyond $125, but many find it a terrific idea for entertaining clients, friends, and family. The price includes all the food and non-alcoholic drinks you can handle before, during, and after the round. The dress code mandates a collared shirt and "proper length shorts; no cutoffs, denim or gym shorts."

Coyote Ridge Golf Club, 1680 Bandera Dr., Carrollton, (972) 939-0666. Par 71, slope rating (from back tees) 130, course rating (from back tees) 72.8, yardage (from back tees) 6,795. Located northwest of downtown Dallas and bordering on Lewisville.

Opened in 1999 to solid critical reviews. "After a flat, wind-swept front nine, Coyote Ridge undergoes a Sybill-like transformation into a rolling, tree-lined course," observes the *Dallas Business Journal*. "The flip-flop from links-style to quarry-style golf challenges players to adjust accordingly." It has a grill and snack bar, pro shop, practice facility, and meeting facilities.

Coyote Ridge was designed by Forefront Golf International/Steven D. Plumer Design, which was established in Arlington, Texas, in 1992. The firm also designed the Hidden Creek golf course in nearby Burleson and the Links at WaterChase in Fort Worth.

A couple of miles (or 3.2 kilometers) southeast of here is **Indian Creek Golf Course,** 1650 West Frankfort Rd., (972) 492-3620. Par 72, yardage 7,045. It is a championship 36-hole course, tree-lined, with bent-grass greens. Designed by Dick Phelps, Indian Creek opened in 1984 and was rated one of the better Texas municipal courses.

Firewheel at Garland, 600 West Blackburn Rd., Garland, (972) 205-2795. It has two 18-hole courses, trees, creeks. and hills.

Demand at Firewheel was so great that the city had to add the 27-hole, $12-million Bridges at Firewheel in 2001.

The $3.5-million, 8,000-square-foot (or 743-square-meter) clubhouse, which opened in 2002, offers Internet service, a conference room, and secretarial services. A full-service restaurant, the Branding Iron, serves chicken-fried steak, grilled salmon, and pasta primavera.

The original course started as an 18-hole golf facility in 1983. The *Dallas Morning News* rated both in the top ten among the municipal courses in Texas.

Four Seasons Resort & Club at Las Colinas (please see entry in the LODGING chapter.)

Keeton Park Golf Course, 2323 Jim Miller Rd., between Bruton and Scyene, Dallas, (214) 670-8784, Internet www.keatonpark.com. A 24-hour cancellation notice is required. Located in Pleasant Grove, in southeast Dallas, and south of Interstate 30.

An 18-hole municipal, par-72, 6,520-yard golf course designed by David Bennett. It features pecan tree-lined fairways and 12 small ponds on 15 holes. There is a snack bar and pro shop on the premises of this municipal golf course. It has a golf school for children and adults.

L. B. Houston Golf Course, 11223 Luna Rd., Dallas, (214) 670-6322. Located in northwest Dallas, south of LBJ Freeway (or Interstate 635).

An 18-hole, 72-par, 6,705-yard golf course built in 1960. It features tight fairways, rolling greens, and an abundance of trees and water. The clubhouse has a pro shop, a snack bar, and tennis courts.

South of here is L. B. Houston Nature Trail, a bicycle and hiking trail opposite the Texas National Guard building, also south of West Northwest Highway. The 4.3-mile (or 6.9-kilometer) loop takes you through a wooded preserve with glimpses of the Trinity River.

Northwood Club, 6524 Alpha Rd., between Preston and Hillcrest, Dallas, (972) 934-0544. Par 71, yardage 6,861 (from the back tees), slope 131, rating 72.9. Located north of downtown Dallas, north of LBJ Freeway (or Interstate 635), and about a mile (or 1.6 kilometer) northeast from the Valley View Mall (see entry).

Designed by William Dibbel, Northwood celebrated the 50th anniversary of the U.S. Open being staged here in 2002. The club was only seven years old when it staged the first and only national championship of golf to be held in Dallas. In 1990, designers Jay Morrish and Tom Weiskopf touched up the course.

While the 18-hole Northwood remains private, it hosts several tournaments each year. A large practice facility is also part of the club.

Pecan Hollow Golf Course, 4501 East 14th Street, Plano, (972) 941-7600. Located within a two-mile (or 3.2-kilometer) radius of the private course Los Rios Country Club, the upscale Pete Haney-run practice center, and the Golf Center of Plano.

Formerly known as Plano Municipal Golf Course, and at one time the only public golf course in the city, it is tucked away in the pecan and oak trees of Rowlett and Cotton Creeks.

The key at this par-72, 6,772-yard course is to "keep the ball in the very generous fairways, stay away from the small number of trees and water, make a few putts on the Bremuda greens and you're on your way to a record round," observes the *Dallas Business Journal.*

Stevens Park Golf Club, 1005 North Montclair, Dallas, (214) 670-7506. Located in Kessler Park, west of downtown, south of Interstate 30, and off Colorado Blvd.

An 18-hole, par-71, 6,005-yard municipal course that opened in 1924 as Dallas' second golf course. Golf lessons are available. It has food and beverage service.

"Stevens Park may not dazzle or even impress first-timers, but will introduce a bit of history and a new way to play the grand old game of golf," observes the *Dallas Business Journal.*

Tangle Ridge Golf Course, 818 Tangle Ridge Dr., Grand Prairie, (972) 299-6837. Par 72, 6,835 yards. Located southeast of downtown Dallas, near Joe Pool Lake and Cedar Hill State Park.

One of the better municipal courses in the area. The *Texas Monthly* rated it one of the top 20 in the state, the *Dallas Morning News* one of the five best newer courses in the Dallas area. "The unique bunkering, the variation in the length and shape of the holes, and the emphasis on decision-making captivated many players," observes the *News*.

Tangle Ridge was designed by Arlington, Texas-based Jeff Brauer (b. 1955), who played his first round of golf at age 12 and received his landscape architecture degree from the University of Illinois. He has also completed more than 30 golf courses outside Texas since 1995, including courses in Kansas and Minnesota.

"The layout has the feel of a Hill Country course with elevation changes of over fifty feet [or 15 meters], gently rolling hills and trees guarding every hole," notes the course's Web site.

Tenison Highlands Golf Course, 3501 Samuell Blvd. at East Grand Avenue, Dallas, (214) 670-1402. Located in east Dallas, just over three miles (or 4.8 kilometers) from downtown.

Tenison was Dallas' first public golf facility. It has two 18-hole courses: East, 6762 yards, sits on a hill, bisected by White Rock Creek; West course, 6,872 yards, is wooded and hilly. This was for years the training ground for golf superstar Lee Trevino.

The municipal course underwent a $4.7-million renovation by Plano golf pro D. A. Weibring in 2000. It now has five new lakes, 37 sand traps, undulating fairways, fast greens, and a "luxury feel not traditionally found on municipal courses," according to the *Dallas Morning News*.

The initial acreage was acquired by the city in 1923, a gift from Edward O. Tenison, who stipulated that it be used for a public park.

Ice Skating & Skateboarding

Dr Pepper StarCenters, Internet www.drpepperstarcenter.com, where skating, hockey, ice dancing, and figure skating lessons are available. They are located in Duncanville, Euless, Farmers Branch, Frisco, and Plano. All come with cafés, souvenir shops, and party rooms. The StarCenters, like the Dallas Stars hockey team, are owned by Dallas businessman Tom Hicks.

• **Dr Pepper StarCenter—Frisco,** located west of the Stonebriar Centre mall (see entry), along the east side of the Dallas North Tollway, just north of State Highway 121. This StarCenter is to have two National Hockey League-size ice surfaces and will become the chief training facility for the Dallas Stars. This $20-million training facility for the Dallas Stars was being built by the city of Frisco and scheduled for completion by 2004. It will anchor a $300-million mixed-project that might also include a $22-million, 9,000-seat minor-league baseball park, office, retail, and residential space.

• **Dr Pepper StarCenter—Valley Ranch,** 211 Cowboys Pkwy., Irving. Opened in 1986, this facility was scheduled to close in 2004, when the Valley Ranch center was to close upon the completion of the Farmers Branch facility (below).

• **Dr Pepper StarCenter—Farmers Branch,** Interstate 35 at Valley View Lane. Located in a 95,000-square-foot (or 8,825-square-meter) former Word of Faith Church, whose pastor Robert Tilton had his religious broadcasting center located here. It houses two National Hockey League regulation-size rinks and has a concession area and a pro shop. Farmers Branch bought this facility, situated on 14.2 acres (or 5.75 hectares), for $6.3 million. The center's second floor doubles as a conference center.

• **Dr Pepper StarCenter—Duncanville,** 1700 South Main St., (972) 283-9133, is located at the intersection of South Main St. and U.S. Hwy. 67, about two and a half miles (or four kilometers) south of Interstate Highway 20. Opened in 2000, it has 1,000 bleachers.

• **Dr Pepper StarCenter—Euless,** 1400 South Pipeline, (817) 267-4233, is located about one-half mile (or 0.8 kilometer) west of the intersection of South Pipeline and FM 157 in south Euless. Opened in 2000, it has 1,000 bleachers and a 3,500-square-foot (or 325-square-meter) pro shop. The 95,000-square-foot (or 8,825-square-meter), $9-million municipal complex with two ice rinks is located at the $500,000 Parks at Texas recreation area, along with a soccer and T-ball field. The city bought the complex from the Dallas Stars and leases it back to the hockey team.

• **Dr Pepper StarCenter—Plano,** 4020 West Plano Pkwy., (972) 758-7528, is located about two miles (or 3.2 kilometers) west of U.S. Hwy. 75 (or North Central Exwy.) on Plano Pkwy. It has 800 bleachers.

Eisenbergs Skatepark, 930 East 15th Street at G Ave., Plano, (972) 478-5171 or 509-7725, Internet www.eisenbergs.com. *CH*. Open Mon-Thu 10 AM-10:30 PM, Fri-Sat 10 AM-midnight, Sun 10 AM-10:30 PM. Unlimited annual passes cost $500. Patrons must sign a waiver, releasing the park from liability in case of injury. No alcohol or smoking allowed. Located northeast of downtown Dallas, about a quarter-mile (or 0.4-kilometer) east of North Central Expressway, in the heart of Historic Downtown Plano. Eisenbergs faces the Plano Police Department. Collin Creek Mall (see entry) is just across Central Expressway.

Opening in 1997 and measuring 30,000 square feet (or 2,787 square meters), it features a street course and a 12-foot (or 3.65-meter) vertical ramp. A retail shop, video lounge, and arcade are on the premises.

Equipment rentals are available, including the mandatory helmets. The best skateboarding facility in Dallas, claims the weekly *Dallas Observer*.

GPX Skate Park & Entertainment Center, 1000 Lone Star Pkwy. at Belt Line Rd., Grand Prairie, (972) 237-4370, Internet www.gpxsk8.com. *CH*. Open Mon-Thu 2 PM-10 PM, Fri 2 PM-midnight, Sat 10 AM-midnight, Sun 10 AM-10 PM. Local live bands play on weekends. Located west of downtown Dallas and next to Lone Star Park (see entry).

The $1.2-million, 40,000-square-foot (or 3,716-square-meter) park opened in 2001 and features a street course and a 12-foot (or 3.65-meter) vertical ramp. The park is owned by the city of Grand Prairie, and operated by Lone Star Park (see entry). It includes wooden ramps, pyramids, and other obstacles for up to 300 skateboarders, in-line skaters, and BMX bikers a day. There is a roller-hockey area, sand volleyball court, and pro shop, where mandatory helmets, as well as elbow pads, lockers, and hockey sticks can be rented.

A video surveillance system monitors all the courses so someone in the pro shop can see what is happening on a ramp. "We always have a skate guard, we always monitor who comes on our property, and we cut off registration if the course gets too crowded," the Lone Star general manager told the *Fort Worth Star-Telegram*. Year-round passes are available.

Ice Training Center Richardson, 522 Centennial Blvd. at Whitehall, Richardson, (972) 680-7825, Internet www.icetrainingcenter.com. *CH*. Open daily 8 AM-11 PM. Located northeast of downtown Dallas, about a mile (or 1.6 kilometers) east of North Central Expressway (or U.S. Hwy. 75).

This no-frills style ice rink opened in 2002. The 51,000-square-foot (or 4,738-square-meter) facility has two regulation-size hockey rinks and locker rooms. Funded by private firms, it hosts hockey clinics and summer camps, and provides skating lessons. The center is designed as a gymnasium with ice rinks rather than a family entertainment center.

Polo & Horseback Riding

Las Colinas Equestrian Center, 600 Royal Ln. at O'Connor Blvd., Irving, (972) 869-0600, is mostly a boarding stable for horses. Open Tue-Sun 7 AM-9 PM. Located across from the 112-acre (or 45-hectare) Dallas Communications Complex, which includes the Movie Studios at Las Colinas (see entry).

The 60-acre (or 24.2-hectare) equestrian center, constructed in

1982, provides riding lessons and hosts competitions. Outdoor season is held May through November. To check for Texas equestrian news and events at the Las Colinas Equestrian Center, log in on the Web site www.showsecretary.com.

Las Colinas Polo Club, which was established in 1996, holds tournaments on the club's two competition fields hugging the banks of the Trinity River. For details, please call (214) 373-8855 and ask for the polo information line, or visit their Web site, www.lascolinaspolo.com. Spectator games are held Friday and Sunday evenings.

North Texas Equestrian Center, 3110 Country Club Dr., Wylie, (972) 442-7544, Internet www.uswarmblood.com, e-mail kaihandt@uswarmblood.com. It has a full-service tack shop. Private and group English riding lessons are available for both adults and children.

Styled after a Spanish military riding academy, NTEC sits on 45 acres (or 18.2 hectares) near the western edge of Lake Lavon, northeast of downtown Dallas, on the border between Lucas and Wylie in northeast Collin County. Four long stucco barns are home to as many as 100 horses. There are covered and outdoor arenas for jumping and dressage. The 250 students at the center range in age from 5 to 60 years.

"Better known overseas than in Collin County, the NTEC is home to one of the world's top rider-trainers, and it supplies horses to customers around the world and throughout the U.S.," claims the *Dallas Morning News*. The head trainer and owner is German Kai Handt (b. 1960), a European champion who came to Texas in 1985 and lives at the center. He flies to Europe every month to train competitors and to sell and buy horses. Handt bought the center in 1986 and now specializes in the sales and training of imported warmbloods whose prices start at $25,000.

Park Lane Ranch, 8787 Park Lane at Abrams Rd. Located northeast of downtown Dallas, east of North Central Expressway and NorthPark Mall. The land abuts some 12,000 acres (or 4,856 hectares) of park land stretching from White Rock Lake north into Plano.

Park Lane Ranch, a one-time Dallas equestrian center reemerged in 2002 on the 31 acres (or 12.5 hectares) of land once owned by the Caruth family. A riding center and 120 private boarding stalls are available. There is a 16,000-square-foot (or 1,486-square-meter) banquet hall. Adjoining Park Lane Ranch is a 16-acre (or 6.4-hectare) Hank Haney's golf center.

If looking for equestrian gear, try **Las Colinas Tack Shop,** 600 East Royal Ln., Irving, (972) 556-1977, or **Newmarket Saddlery,** 7529 Campbell Rd. at Coit, Dallas, (972) 713-6613.

Rugby

Among the best known clubs is **Dallas Harlequins** (Internet www.quins.com), which was formed in 1971 and is named after the well-known Harlequin Football Club of London, England. The club has hosted teams from most countries where rugby is popular.

The Harlequins, located at 5207 McKinney Ave., 526-3586 or 739-1440, train Tuesday and Thursday nights at 6:30 PM, at Glencoe Park in Dallas, just east of North Central Expressway at McCommas, south of Mockingbird Lane. Home games are also played at Glencoe Park.

Dallas Rugby Football Club, (972) 738-9011, Internet http://dallas-rugby.org, trains Tuesdays and Thursdays at 7 PM at Griggs Park, east of North Central Expressway and south of Freedman's Cemetery Memorial (see entry). Established in 1968, it is the oldest area rugby club.

Tennis

Dallas was an important address in tennis during the 1970s and mid-1980s. World Championship Tennis, the Virginia Slims women's tour, and the Association of Tennis Professionals were all based in the area. Dallas hosted several annual "world-class" events that featured stars such as Bjorn Borg, Jimmy Connors, and Martina Navratilova.

Ken Rosewall's five-set victory over Rod Laver at SMU's Moody Coliseum in 1972 captured the public's imagination. Dallas was one of the best tennis towns in America. When the Texas economy hit the skids in the late 1980s, the corporate sponsorships for professional tennis evaporated, and the sport's popularity nosedived.

Neighborhood tennis courts are on a first-come-first served basis. For reservations, call:

- **Fair Oaks Center,** 7501 Merriman Pkwy. in northeast Dallas, (214) 670-1495.
- **Fretz Center,** 14700 Hillcrest Rd. in far-north Dallas, (214) 670-6622.
- **Kiest Center,** 2324 West Kiest Blvd. at Kiest Park in Oak Cliff, southwest of downtown Dallas, (214) 670-7618.
- **L.B. Houston Center,** 11223 Luna Rd. in northwest Dallas, (214) 670-6367.
- **Samuell-Grand Center,** 6200 East Grand Ave. in east Dallas, (214) 670-1374.

Among the private clubs, consider **T Bar M Racquet Club,** 600 Dilbeck Ln., (972) 233-4444/1415. It is located amid 12 acres (or 4.8

hectares) of oak trees, north of Lyndon B. Johnson Freeway (or Interstate 635), off Preston Road and on the eastern edge of the Valley View Mall.

A family membership with all privileges runs about $2,500 a year. Single members pay a $1,500 initiation fee and about $150 a month. The facility has 30 indoor and outdoor tennis courts, an Olympic-size swimming pool, restaurant, and bar. The staff includes 20 instructors. A 6,000-square-foot (or 557-square-meter) basement was transformed into a fitness center with massage therapy and a Pilates program. More than half of the membership is under 45 years old, and the roster includes 600 families.

T Bar M, named for three Dallas families, was founded in 1970. It was bought in 1997 by a former Microsoft executive Glen Agritelley, who sank millions into improving an aged facility and now also owns the Mercy wine bar in north Dallas.

In Plano, there is **High Point Tennis Center,** 421 West Spring Creek Pkwy., between Alma Dr. and North Central Expwy. (or U.S. Hwy. 75), (972) 941-7170. It has 20 lighted tennis courts. Lessons are available.

SPECIAL EVENTS

Please check the *Dallas Morning News, Dallas Observer,* or *D Magazine* for exact dates and times of these events. Also helpful is the area tourism council Web site www.visitdallas-fortworth.com. Be prepared for extreme heat with the outdoor events held during the summer.

January

The **Cotton Bowl Classic Football Game & Parade,** (214) 634-7525, a New Year's Day event, is shown on national television. In the morning, families line the streets of downtown Dallas for a free parade, featuring floats, marching bands, and drill teams, starting at City Hall. In the afternoon, those football fans lucky enough to have tickets converge on the Cotton Bowl in Fair Park, two miles (or 3.2 kilometers) east of downtown, for a bowl game between two nationally ranked teams.

KidFilm Festival, (972) 395-9034, Internet www.usafilmfestival.com, the largest children's film and video festival in the United States, is sponsored by the USA Film Festival. The program includes features shorts and animated work as a tribute to children's art. Showings are usually held one weekend in mid-January at Angelika Film Center, East Mockingbird Lane at North Central Expressway. *CH*.

From the end of January through the first day of February, it is also time for the annual **Dallas Boat Show,** (469) 549-4105, Internet www.dallasboatshow.net, one of the largest in the nation, featuring the latest equipment and supplies, at the Market Hall, Interstate Highway 35 (or Stemmons Fwy.) and Wycliff Ave. *CH*.

Martin Luther King, Jr. Birthday events are held at the King Recreation Center, a south Dallas cultural center, and area colleges and community centers.

February

February is **African-American History Month**. Check newspapers for various activities.

The annual **Texas Home & Garden Show,** (800) 654-1480,

Internet www.texashomeandgarden.com, has been held for more than 25 years at the Dallas Market Hall, 2200 Stemmons Freeway at Wycliff, in late February and again in September. *CH*.

An annual **Tri Delta Charity Antiques Show,** (214) 939-2700, one of the largest in the United States, is held at the Convention Center this month. *CH*.

Meanwhile, you may want to attend a **Dallas Stars** professional hockey, **Dallas Mavericks** professional basketball, or **Dallas Cowboys** professional football game.

Irving Symphony and **Las Colinas Symphony** give concerts at Irving Arts Center, 3333 North MacArthur Blvd at Rochelle Blvd., Irving, (972) 252-7558 or 256-4270, Internet www.ci.irving.tx.us/arts/index.htm, e-mail minman@ci.irving.tx.us.

March

During an early March weekend, the **North Texas Irish Festival,** Internet www.ntif.org, (214) 821-4174, is held at Fair Park, with more than 40 musical groups on eight stages, and plenty of Irish food and drink. Established in 1982, this is believed to be the second-largest annual Irish festival in the country, drawing upwards of 20,000 people.

In downtown Dallas, a **St. Patrick's Day Parade,** (972) 991-6705, Internet www.irishparade.com, is held this month, starting in the early afternoon at Young and Houston streets and proceeding toward City Hall. More than 85,000 usually attend.

On Lower Greenville Avenue, another **St. Patrick's Day Parade,** (214) 368-6722, takes place at about 11 AM from Blackwell Street to Yale Boulevard. Try not take your car because residents along Greenville are unhappy with unruly crowds that can exceed 15,000. DART shuttle buses run from the Mockingbird Station to the party between 10 AM and 6 PM.

Shamrock Music Festival, (214) 652-4300, at Knox-Henderson streets (which connect east and west Dallas at North Central Expressway), is held on St. Patrick's Day. (Dallas has the sixth largest percentage of Irish among American cities, after Boston and Philadelphia, but ahead of Chicago and New York).

You can attend the annual **Dallas Video Festival,** (214) 428-8700, Internet www.videofest.org, usually held at the Dallas Museum of Art and the Angelika Film Center (see entries) during the first week of the month, when some 200 programs are screened. *CH*.

Still in Dallas, **Dallas Blooms,** (214) 327-4901, Internet www.dallasarboretum.org, a display of 200,000 tulips, daffodils, and other flowers, takes place in late March and early April at the Dallas Arboretum &

Botanical Gardens overlooking White Rock Lake. More than 100,000 visitors attend the event. A traditional Easter egg hunt is also held this month. *CH*.

There is a four-day **Dallas Auto Show,** (214) 939-2700, Internet www.dallasautoshow.org, one of the largest such events in the United States, which draws 300,000 visitors late this month. Some 500 domestic and foreign cars and trucks of every description are on display at the Dallas Convention Center downtown. *CH*.

April

In an annual rite of spring that has become as regular as tornado warnings and bluebonnets, April is heaven for sports fanatics. During this month, hundreds of thousands of local fans are within a short drive of auto racing, baseball, basketball, hockey, horse racing, rodeo, and soccer competitions. And that does not include those sporting events shown on television.

In Addison, a three-day annual **North Texas Jazz Festival** is held during the first week of this month. *CH*. A collaborative effort between the town of Addison and the University of North Texas Department of Jazz Studies, several jazz-related events are held at Addison venues. Call (972) 450-6232, or visit www.addisontexas.net.

Deep Ellum Arts Festival, Internet www.meifestival.com, (214) 855-1881, initiated in 1994, takes place on eight blocks of Main Street between Good Latimer and Hall Streets, during an early April weekend. More than 150 painters, sculptors, potters, and jewelers exhibit. There is entertainment and food. Up to 100,000 visitors show up. Deep Ellum is a historic neighborhood located just east of downtown Dallas. *NCH*.

Also this month, the **USA Film Festival,** (214) 821-FILM, Internet www.usafilmfestival.com, is held for a week at the Angelika Film Center & Café, East Mockingbird Ln. at Central Expwy. *CH*. Started in 1970 by filmmaker L. M. "Kit" Carson, the festival screens new independent American and foreign films. The misunderstood genius Wim Wenders was honored for his lifetime work here, and Hyatt Bass, daughter of the Fort Worth billionaire Sid Bass, debuted her feature, titled *75 Degrees in July*, at the festival.

At the Resistol Arena in Mesquite, the annual Rodeo Parade kicks off the **Mesquite Championship Rodeo** (see entry), (972) 285-8777, Internet www.mesquiterodeo.com, season, which runs each Friday and Saturday, from April to September. Barrel racing, calf roping, and bronc and bull riding are featured.

At 2511 Farm Road 66, near Waxahachie, a town about a 30-minute drive south of Dallas, there is **Scarborough Faire,** (972) 938-3247, Internet www.scarboroughrenfest.com, an annual Renaissance festival recreating a 35-acre (or 14-hectare), 16th-century English village. You can watch knights in armor, marvel at the falconer and his birds of prey, or watch jugglers, sorcerers, and jesters. Henry VIII, the king of England from 1509 to 1547, has been played for years by a 40-something-year old Army/Air Force Exchange Service employee from Dallas.

One hundred and forty costumed entertainers and 200 merchants are on hand weekends only, 10 AM-7 PM, rain or shine, from mid-April until early June. "We bring you everything from the 16th century except the plague," claims the fair's general manager. Some visitors, however, complain that some shows are sexually inappropriate for young children. *CH*, but free parking.

In Denton, north of Dallas, an annual three-day **Denton Arts & Jazz Festival,** (940) 565-0931, Internet www.dentonjazzfest.com, is held this month at the Denton Civic Center Park, 321 East McKinney St. Up to 80,000 now attend the 25-year-old event. *NCH*.

May

Six Flags and **Hurricane Harbor** (see entries) amusement parks in Arlington open this month. (Please see the SIGHTS & ATTRACTIONS chapter for more details.)

In Dallas, the annual **Cinco de Mayo** (Fifth of May) celebration has been held for 60 years at Pike Park, at the beginning of this month, on the edge of the Little Mexico area, which is located at Harry Hines Boulevard, just north of downtown. A Mexican celebration that marks the defeat of Napoleon III's forces in east Mexico in 1862, it includes mariachi bands, folk dances, games, and food. *NCH*. Similar events are held throughout the Metroplex.

Swiss Avenue Historic District Tour, (214) 826-1967, is held on Mother's Day weekend in mid-May, starting Saturday at noon. It consists of visits to several of the old and restored homes along Swiss Avenue. *CH*.

Also around that time, the annual **Asian Festival,** celebrating Asian and Pacific American Heritage Month, takes place at Annette Strauss Artist Square downtown. It is the largest festival of its kind in north Texas and attracts some 10,000 people. (The Asian population in north Texas is estimated at 250,000.) Call the Asian American chamber of commerce at (972) 241-8250, Internet www.gdaacc.com for more details. *NCH*.

Up to 250 artists and craftsmen display paintings, pottery, jewelry, and porcelain at **Artfest,** (214) 361-2036 or e-mail info@500inc.org, one of the largest arts and crafts festivals in the city, held at Fair Park's Centennial Hall building and along the Esplanade walkway around the Memorial Day weekend this month. Some 75,000 visitors attend. Outdoor performances by the Dallas Symphony and smaller musical and theater groups can also be seen and heard. Proceeds go to Dallas arts organizations. *CH*.

In Fort Worth, the quadrennial **Van Cliburn International Piano Competition,** (817) 335-9000, Internet www.cliburn.org, one of the world's most prestigious classical music and pianistic events, takes place from the last week of May through early June. The next piano competition will be held in 2005.

Since 1997, and every three years thereafter, the **Dallas International Organ Competition** takes place, and the first-prize winner appears as a soloist with the Dallas Symphony Orchestra, which hosts the event. The competition is open to organists 30 years old or younger. First prize includes a $30,000 cash award.

In 2003, the first prize went to Bradley Hunter Welch (b. 1976), the Tennessee-born organist of Highland Park Presbyterian Church in Dallas, who also took the third prize in 2000. British organist Sarah Baldock took the second prize of $10,000. The events take place in the Caruth Auditorium at Southern Methodist University where a C.B. Fisk Opus 101 organ is available. For tickets and other information, call (214) 692-0203, or go to www.dallassympnhony.com.

In Las Colinas, Irving, an international golf event, the **Byron Nelson Golf Classic Tournament,** (972) 717-0700, at Four Seasons Resort & Club (see entry), is held one week in mid-May. Since 1968, some of the best golfers in the world have come here, usually more than 150 of them. The event is televised and named after a well-known Texas golfer. Some 1,700 volunteers run the event.

In Addison, also in the second half of this month, you can sample food from more than 40 area restaurants in the town's annual **Taste Addison** festival, (800) ADDISON, Internet www.addisontexas.net. Booths with arts, crafts, and promotions are set up at Addison Circle, in addition to an auto show, live music entertainment, and activities for children. More than 15,000 participate in the two-day event. *CH*.

June

Irving Heritage Festival, (972) 753-4824, has been held for more than a dozen years on a Saturday in the first half of this month in downtown Irving, at Main and Second streets. The event helps raise money for a heritage museum with live music, arts and crafts, a transportation display, and games for children. *NCH.*

Dallas International Festival, (972) 661-5140, Internet www.dallasinternational.com, is held free of charge Tue-Thu in the middle of the month at the Majestic Theatre downtown, 1925 Elm St. The annual artistic showcase for north Texas' ethnic organizations may start with a mass naturalization ceremony. (There are now more than 1,400 local ethnic and national groups in the metropolitan area.)

At least half a dozen events in Dallas alone celebrate **Juneteenth,** or June 19, 1865, known as Texas Emancipation Day. On that day Union general Gordon Granger arrived at Galveston, Texas, proclaiming U.S. authority over Texas, two and a half years after President Abraham Lincoln signed the Emancipation Proclamation. Other events are held throughout north Texas.

As the second oldest Shakespeare festival in the United States, founded in 1972, the **Shakespeare Festival of Dallas,** (214) 559-2778, is held from mid-June to the end of July, at Samuell-Grand Park in east Dallas, which can accommodate 5,000. One performance of the bard's two plays can be seen every evening, except Mondays, in an outdoor setting. You can bring your own picnic. Seating is first-come, first-served, and free of charge, although a $5 donation is requested.

July

Cotton Bowl Fireworks begins in the evening of July 4th at Fair Park, two miles (or 3.2 kilometers) east of downtown Dallas, along with live entertainment. Daytime festivities, including a parade that starts at 1 PM, are also held at the Old City Park, southeast of downtown.

Trinity Fest got off to a flying start in 2002, with 300,000 revelers downtown that brought in $1 million for the city's Park and Recreation Department. A fireworks display is held at the **Old-Fashioned Fourth of July** in Old City Park, just across R. L. Thornton Freeway, while the **Freedom Fest** takes place at Starplex in Fair Park.

In Dallas' downtown Historic West End District, near Ross and Market Streets, there is the **Taste of West End** festival held during a three-day weekend, when food is plentiful and entertainment not forgotten. It attracts more than 20,000 adults and children.

Since 1977, a rock & roll extravaganza, **Texxas Jam,** takes place one Saturday in mid-July at the Cotton Bowl stadium in Fair Park. Gates open at 11 AM, music starts a couple hours later.

In Highland Park and University Park, collectively known as Park Cities, which are completely enveloped by the city of Dallas, there is an annual **Fourth of July Parade** and picnic, which starts at Highland Park Town Hall and ends at Goar Park in University Park.

In Mesquite, there is an annual **Balloon Festival,** (972) 285-0211, held in Paschall Park, off New Market Road and near the Town East shopping mall, where up to 50 hot-air balloonists from all over the United States participate in this three-day event. More than 100,000 spectators also attend, and a variety of amusements can be enjoyed.

August

By August, Ringling Brothers, Barnum & Bailey **Circus** is usually already in town and giving up to two performances a day at the American Airlines Arena (see entry). **Six Flags Over Texas** and **Hurricane Harbor** amusement parks (see entries) in Arlington are in full swing and a welcome relief from the oppressive heat.

Meanwhile, Texas Rangers baseball and Dallas Sidekicks soccer competitions continue in Dallas, as does the Rodeo in Mesquite. **Dallas Summer Musicals** at Fair Park are still going strong.

September

In mid-September, the annual **Fall Gallery Walks** are held in up to three dozen art galleries located mostly in Uptown, Deep Ellum, and around Fair Park, (214) 855-5101, Internet www.dallasartdelares.org. Organized by the Dallas Art Association, they expose Dallasites to mostly local art, while treating them to hors d'oeuvres and wine. *NCH*.

The three-day annual **Greek Festival of Dallas,** (972) 233-4880, Internet www.greekfestivalofdallas.com, has been held since 1957 at Holy Trinity Greek Orthodox Church, 13555 Hillcrest Rd. at Alpha. *CH*. Some 20,000 people attend to sample Greek food and pastry, shop the marketplace, watch traditional dances, and tour the church and its traditional Byzantine architecture.

In Addison, there is the annual **Oktoberfest,** (800) ADDISON, Internet www.addisontexas.net, a four-day recreation of the well-known German festival, although, inexplicably, it is held in September, not October. You will enjoy authentic German food and drink, music and dancing, arts and crafts, and children's activities on Addison Circle Drive. *CH*.

In Grapevine, there is **GrapeFest,** (800) 457-6338 or (817) 410-3185, on a weekend in the middle of the month, one of the largest wine festivals in the Southwest. More than 100,000 visitors toast the Texas wine industry during this annual event benefiting Grapevine's historic preservation projects. It features carnival rides, live music entertainment, and wine tasting competitions. Free parking and shuttle service are available at the Grapevine Convention Center, 1209 South Main St., Internet www.grapevinetexasusa.com. *CH*.

In Plano, a **Hot-Air Balloon Festival,** (800) 81-PLANO or (972) 867-7566, www.planoballoonfest.org, is held at Collin County Community College's Spring Creek Campus, Oak Point Park, 6000 Jupiter Rd. Up to 100 hot-air balloonists participate in this three-day event. You can get to the festival from Collin Creek shopping mall (see entry). *CH* and parking fee.

The festival, which started in 1979, attracts up to 200,000, some paying $250 for an hour-long balloon ride. The balloon festival is one of the largest such events in the country. *Dallas Child* magazine votes this one of the best festivals in the area for kids.

October

(For the **Texas State Fair,** (214) 565-9931, which starts at the end of September, please see listing under Fair Park in the SIGHTS & ATTRACTIONS chapter.)

In Fair Park's Cotton Bowl, the **Texas-OU Football Game,** (214) 421-8716, is held in the first half of this month. In a long-standing rivalry between the University of Texas and the University of Oklahoma, the two teams square off and earn $1.5 million for each college. About 80,000 visitors come to Dallas and spend $20 million at hotels, restaurants, and bars. Fans go wild and cause a lot of commotion downtown the night before the game. Tickets go for up to $1,000 each.

In Dallas' West End Historic District (see entry) a **West End Cattle Drive,** (214) 741-7185, is held in recognition of past Texas cattle drives.

Also in Dallas, the annual **American-Indian Art Festival & Market** is held in the second half of October by the American Indian Art Council, (214) 891-9640, at the Annette Strauss Artist Square downtown near the Arts District, with up to 200 artists selling their work at more than 100 booths.

(Those interested in films from India, in Tamil, Malayalam, and Hindi languages, can head for the Everest Theaters at Plymouth Park Shopping Center, Story Rd. at Irving Blvd. West, in Irving. It is the only area movie house to schedule Indian-language films every day of the week. This is one of only six Indian theaters in Texas.)

November

In November, sometimes late in October, the **SMU Literary Festival** is held on the campus of Southern Methodist University in the town of University Park. Well-known American and other writers participate at meetings and lectures throughout the week.

Also at SMU in November, the Algur H. Meadows Award ceremony for excellence in the arts is held on the campus. Swedish film director Ingmar Bergman, American dancer Martha Graham, Russian-American cellist Mstislav Rostropovich, American dancer Merce Cunningham, American playwright Arthur Miller, American opera singer Leontyne Price, and Spanish architect Santiago Calatrava are among the past recipients. First awarded in 1981, it carries a cash prize of $50,000.

In the first half of this month, **Dallas Blooms Autumn,** (214) 327-4901, Internet www.dallasarboretum.org, takes place at the Dallas Arboretum (see entry) on Garland Road and overlooking White Rock Lake. *CH*. Among its attractions are 20,000 chrysanthemums, a pumpkin patch, horse-drawn wagon rides, and a hay-bale maze for children.

On Thanksgiving Day, in November, an eight-mile (or 12.8-kilometer) **Turkey Trot,** (214) 954-0500, is held in downtown Dallas. The race, which starts and finishes at City Hall, is the largest of its kind in the area, attracting some 10,000 participants.

And, of course, everyone is already in the Christmas spirit.

December

Christmas Lights extravaganza is held from the second week in December, through New Year's, on Armstrong Drive, between Preston Road and Douglas Street, in the town of Highland Park. Mansions along these and other neighborhood streets are laden with thousands of colored lights, some tastefully and some not. Many other communities have similar Christmas shows.

At the Old City Park, southeast of downtown, there are **Candlelight Tours,** (214) 421-5141, held during the second week in December. Their Christmas celebrations are old-fashioned, in keeping with the spirit of the park.

The 15-year-old Neiman Marcus/Adolphus Hotel **Children's Parade,** Internet www.childrensparade.com, also takes place around this time downtown. The parade, designed specifically for children, starts at 9 AM at Dallas City Hall Plaza and moves east down Commerce Street. It is broadcast on television on 200 stations across the country. All proceeds go to the Children's Medical Center hospital. *NCH*, except to view the parade from bleachers.

In mid-December a certified 26.2-mile (or 42-kilometer) **White Rock Lake Marathon** in Dallas has been held for more than 30 years. It starts at the American Airlines Center downtown, goes up McKinney and Turtle Creek into Highland Park and east to the lake.

Circling White Rock Lake, the race continues down Swiss Avenue, San Jacinto, and back to the Center.

To participate, you must register by the first week in December. Up to 5,000 runners of all ages take part. For details, call (214) 372-2068 or got to www.runtherock.com.

SELF-GUIDED TOURS

A fairly lengthy walking tour of downtown is sketched below, in addition to a driving tour that will introduce you to a few neighboring communities.

DOWNTOWN WALKING TOUR

This is just one of many ways to sightsee downtown. I have picked a route to introduce to you a large number of sights that are highlighted in **bold,** and you will find described in more detail in the SIGHTS & ATTRACTIONS and other chapters. Overseas visitors, particularly European visitors, accustomed to seeing priceless architectural gems on many a corner at home, should brace themselves for a hideous block of downtown real estate here and there, interspersed with a few buildings that would be a credit to any city.

Stanley H. Brown, a biographer of Texas conglomerate king Jim J. Ling, who had literally invented LTV Corp., wrote in 1972: "Dallas is a hard-edged community, a kind of new frontier town even though it is more than a century old. Old buildings offend people there." While that is still true, some things that Brown noted elsewhere did change drastically: "And the downtown streets seem so clean that a man may carry a cold cigar butt for blocks until he feels sure nobody is watching him ditch it in an immaculate gutter."

Wear a comfortable pair of shoes and plenty of suntan lotion if you take this tour in the summer, when the downtown streets are as hot as a boiling cauldron.

Depending on your pace, this tour could take two hours or longer. If you have a choice, I recommend it on a weekday, when there are more people about, and you will not stand out as sharply against the deserted weekend streets. Numerous restaurants are listed in case you need refreshment or want to sit down to a full meal.

Begin at the Sixth Floor Museum

Perhaps you have just visited the **Sixth Floor Museum** (see listing) and are standing on the corner of Elm and North Houston Streets, only

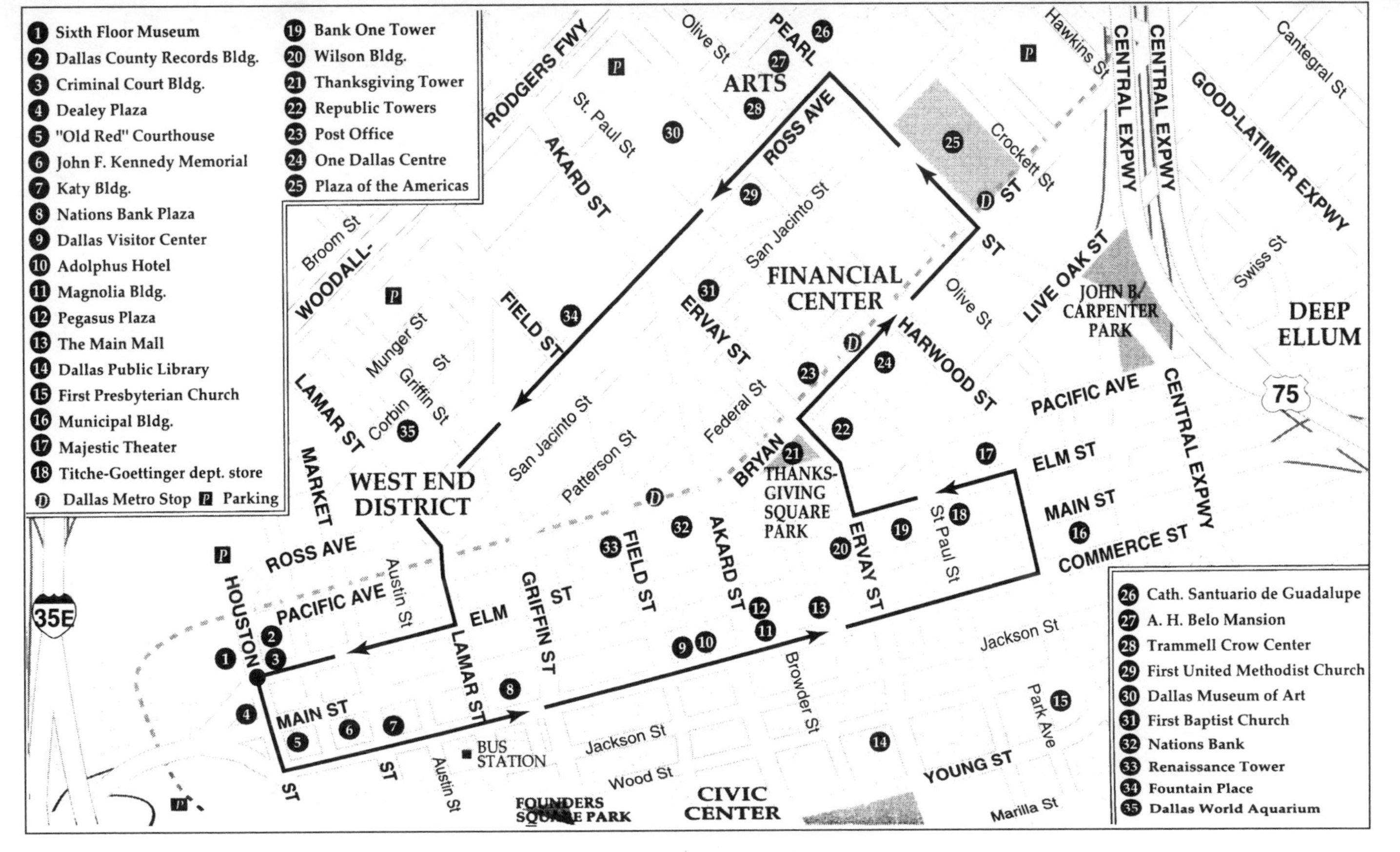
1 Sixth Floor Museum
2 Dallas County Records Bldg.
3 Criminal Court Bldg.
4 Dealey Plaza
5 "Old Red" Courthouse
6 John F. Kennedy Memorial
7 Katy Bldg.
8 Nations Bank Plaza
9 Dallas Visitor Center
10 Adolphus Hotel
11 Magnolia Bldg.
12 Pegasus Plaza
13 The Main Mall
14 Dallas Public Library
15 First Presbyterian Church
16 Municipal Bldg.
17 Majestic Theater
18 Titche-Goettinger dept. store
D Dallas Metro Stop
P Parking
19 Bank One Tower
20 Wilson Bldg.
21 Thanksgiving Tower
22 Republic Towers
23 Post Office
24 One Dallas Centre
25 Plaza of the Americas
26 Cath. Santuario de Guadalupe
27 A. H. Belo Mansion
28 Trammell Crow Center
29 First United Methodist Church
30 Dallas Museum of Art
31 First Baptist Church
32 Nations Bank
33 Renaissance Tower
34 Fountain Place
35 Dallas World Aquarium
ARTS
FINANCIAL CENTER
WEST END DISTRICT
DEEP ELLUM
CIVIC CENTER
JOHN B. CARPENTER PARK
THANKS-GIVING SQUARE PARK
FOUNDERS SQUARE PARK
BUS STATION
RODGERS FWY
WOODALL-RODGERS FWY
CENTRAL EXPWY
GOOD-LATIMER EXPWY
75
35E
PEARL ST
ROSS AVE
PACIFIC AVE
ELM ST
MAIN ST
COMMERCE ST
LIVE OAK ST
HARWOOD ST
ERVAY ST
AKARD ST
FIELD ST
GRIFFIN ST
LAMAR ST
MARKET ST
HOUSTON ST
YOUNG ST
BRYAN ST
Olive St
St. Paul St
St Paul St
San Jacinto St
Federal St
Patterson St
Munger St
Griffin St
Corbin St
Broom St
Austin St
Jackson St
Wood St
Browder St
Park Ave
Marilla St
Crockett St
Hawkins St
Cantegral St
Swiss St

steps from where John F. Kennedy was assassinated in 1963. This is a good spot from which to start a downtown walking tour. If you face east, or toward the **Dallas County Records Building**—built in 1928 to contain deed records and county statistical data—and the **Dallas County Criminal Courts Building,** going back to 1913, the Sixth Floor Museum is on your left, or north from you. Both Lee Harvey Oswald and his assassin Jack Ruby were once incarcerated in the Criminal Courts Building, which earlier also held the bank robber Clyde Barrow.

The triple underpass is behind you, or to the west. **Morton's** steakhouse is diagonally from where you stand, and beyond it starts the **West End Historic District**.

Turn right and walk southward on North Houston Street. You will pass the length of **Dealey Plaza,** named for the founder of the *Dallas Morning News* whose statue you will also pass shortly on your right. The plaza is the most visited sight in Dallas because of the Kennedy assassination. The triple underpass, where Dallas sprouted its first settlements, is now on your right, and beyond it the **Lew Sterrett Justice Center**.

As you cross Main Street, there is the **"Old Red" Courthouse** (see entry), which was completed in 1892, on your left. The first log courthouse was built in 1846, when Dallas County was created, but it was burned down by drunks on Christmas Day two years later. A two-story brick building was erected in 1855, to be followed, in 1874, by a granite structure, which burned badly in 1880. The "Old Red" was renovated in 1998 and again in 2003.

Immediately ahead and to your right stands the former U.S. Post Office Terminal Annex, built in 1937, and now known simply as the **Federal Building**. Lee Harvey Oswald rented a post office box here and through it ordered the rifle believed to be used in the assassination. The five-story bulk mail facility was built with the help of the federal Works Project Administration (WPA) in 1937.

A block ahead of you is the **Hotel Lawrence,** and still another after that the original building of the *Dallas Morning News*, which began publication in 1885 and is the oldest daily in the state. In front of it is **Ferris Plaza** and across the street the **Union Station** rail depot, in 1916, when it was built, the costliest Dallas structure.

Beyond it rises the Reunion complex, consisting of the **Hyatt Regency Hotel, Reunion Tower,** and **Reunion Arena**.

Continue East on Commerce Street

Cross what is now South Houston Street—named for Gen. Sam Houston, first president of the Republic of Texas—and continue east on Commerce Street. On your right is the 20-story **George L. Allen**

County Courthouse that was under construction during the Kennedy assassination. Allen (d. 1991) was appointed the first African-American city councilman in 1968.

As soon as you pass the "Old Red," the two-square-block Dallas County Historic Plaza comes into view on your left. The **John F. Kennedy Memorial** (see listing) is the nearest sight to you on the spot where Wagner's grocery and liquor store stood for almost one hundred years, until 1967. Behind it is the **John Neely Bryan Cabin** (see entry), a replica of what the founder of Dallas is believed to have built after 1841. The cabin is usually closed to visitors.

Cross Market Street, and the first structure on your left is the historic **Katy Building** erected in 1912. It was purchased by the Missouri, Kansas and Texas Railway Co. of Texas and restored in 1978. The Katy operated a railroad business from the Gulf Coast to the lower Midwest. In addition to a passel of lawyers, the Katy also houses the **Conspiracy Museum** (see entry), which faces the plaza. On the next block, north of it, is the El Centro Community College.

Before crossing the next street, you will see the new Belo building and a few blocks to your right (or south) a part of the **Dallas Convention Center**. Cross now South Austin Street, and the corner building on your left is the Bank of America Plaza parking garage, diagonally across the 72-story **Bank of America,** with the **Texas Club,** a health facility atop it. You are passing on your right the Greyhound Bus Depot, not the safest area even during the day. If you look several blocks farther to your right and ahead before crossing South Lamar Street, you will also see part of the **Dallas City Hall** (see entry), a distinct cantilevered building drafted by architect I. M. Pei that was inaugurated in 1978.

The block after South Lamar contains parking lots on both sides and a McDonald's fast-food restaurant on your right that was refurbished several times. It once played classical music to drive away loiterers.

"The area surrounding the McDonald's, police say, has long had a reputation for being one of the toughest spots downtown," reports the *Dallas Morning News*. "The restaurant has been a hangout for truants, homeless people, drug users and 'riffraff'" for years. It was near here that a homeless man grabbed a police officer's gun in 1988 and shot him to death. In 1993, during a Dallas Cowboys parade, innocent bystanders were beaten here by gangs of African-American youths.

On the next block on your left (or north), you will see the 38-foot-high (or 11.5-meter) steel sculpture painted red in front of the Bank of America building by the Russian-American artist Alexander Liberman. Behind the bank is the **Doubletree Hotel** (see entry) and, farther off, the television antenna of the local Fox television affiliate station. That little pyramid east of Doubletree is nothing more impressive than the Renaissance Tower underground food court.

Just as you are about to cross South Griffin Street, you could turn right and go to the **Pioneer Plaza & Cemetery** (see entry), in front of the Convention Center, three blocks south of here. Its ensemble of Texas longhorn steers and horseback riders is touted as the world's largest. The bronzes are memorializing what was supposedly the historic Shawnee cattle trail that ran on what is today Preston Road, also known as State Highway 289. By 1870, the main cattle trails were located farther west, but Preston Road was still an important route for entry into north-central Texas. The Pioneer Cemetery, whose graves date back to 1853, is adjacent to the plaza and the convention center. A Confederate memorial here, unveiled in 1897 and transferred from the Old City Park, is the oldest public sculpture in the city.

As you cross South Griffin Street, there are two Federal buildings on your right, followed by the **Manor House** apartment building at the end of that block. Cross the next street, South Field, and most of this block is taken up by the venerable **Adolphus Hotel** (see entry), which was inaugurated in 1912. Before the Adolphus there stood on this spot the City Hall that was constructed in 1889. On the corner with South Akard Street, where the **Walt Garrison Rodeo Bar** is located, you can cross Commerce Street and check out the **Telephone Pioneer Museum,** on the second floor of One Bell Plaza. In 1892, an extravagant Orient Hotel was built here at the unheard of cost of $500,000 whose owner fell victim to the depression of the following year. On your left on the next block is **Jeroboam** brasserie (see entry).

If you cross South Akard Street, continuing east on Commerce Street, the first structure on your left is the historic **Magnolia Building** (see entry), now a hotel, with a Starbucks café on the ground floor. Completed in 1922, it housed the offices of Magnolia Petroleum Co., later Mobil Oil, and was the tallest Dallas building for more than 20 years. As you continue up the block, look up the Magnolia Building to see its flying red horse, weighing 15 tons, atop it. Behind Magnolia, farther to your left, on the corner of Main and South Akard, stands **Pegasus Plaza,** largely underwritten by the late Irish-born actress Greer Garson, who had lived in Dallas from 1949 until she died in 1996. About the middle of this block, you can again spy the Dallas City Hall, three blocks south, or on your right. The Main Mall, which follows on your left, is a miniature shopping area now largely empty and deserted. Across from it is the former Dallas Power & Light Building.

Following both, on your left, stands **Neiman Marcus** (see entry), the most famous Dallas luxury department store, which has a restaurant, the Zodiac, on the fifth floor, as well as a café on the ground floor overlooking Commerce Street. As you cross the next street, South Ervay, you will see on your right, two blocks south, part of the **Dallas Public**

Library and behind it, for the last time on this walking tour, the City Hall. On your left is a block-long **Mercantile National Bank** complex that has been vacant for years. It was constructed by Robert Lee Thornton, a candy salesman, banker, and four-term Dallas mayor who served in that capacity from 1953 to 1961.

The next street to cross is South St. Paul, and as soon as you do you will have the former Dallas Grand Hotel on your right and farther east on that same block the old Dallas Public Library, which in 1954 supplanted a handsome classical building that philanthropist Andrew Carnegie made possible with a $50,000 gift. Two years later, Picasso's artworks were removed from this library because of the artist's alleged communistic sympathies. On the next block to your left is the Universities Center at Dallas. This area was forlorn and deserted in 2003. An indirect victim of September 11, 2001, terrorist attacks, the Grand stood bleak and shuttered. There was talk that the building might be demolished and a public park created.

I brought you this far east, to the 2000 block of Commerce and South Harwood Streets, so you could see two more buildings: two blocks to your right (or south) stands the **First Presbyterian Church** (see listing), which was founded in 1856 but moved to this location in 1913. It was designed by architect C. D. Hill, who also drafted the **Municipal Courts Building,** known as the Old City Hall, across the street to your left. In 2003, many of the city employees and the police vacated this building for the **Jack Evans Police Headquarters** at 1400 South Lamar Street.

In the basement of the Old City Hall, the alleged Kennedy assassin, Lee Harvey Oswald, was shot by Jack Ruby on live television.

Go North on Harwood, West on Elm, to Bryan & Pearl Streets

Now turn left and walk north and across Main Street, which parallels Commerce, whose length you have walked so far. The corner building on your left is the **Aristocrat Hotel** (see listing), which was originally built by hotelier Conrad Hilton in 1925. Just west of it is the former Titche-Goettinger department store, built by the Louisianian Edward Titche and his partner Max Goettinger in 1929.

Go on to Elm Street, which you left at Dealey Plaza, at the beginning of this tour, and turn left, going west. Until the early 1960s, Elm Street was known as Dallas's Theater Row. On the corner in front of you stands the 3,000-square-foot (or 278-square-meter) restaurant and night club complex **Blue** (Internet www.bluevip.com), which opened in 2003. On your right stands the **Majestic Theatre,** which opened in 1921 as a vaudeville house and where Duke Ellington played and Ginger Rogers broke into show business. On your left is again the Titche-Goettinger building, now converted into loft apartments.

When you reach North St. Paul Street, check out on your left that imposing 60-story **Bank One Tower** (see Bank One Center entry), designed by architect Philip Johnson, who also created the John F. Kennedy Memorial. Its interiors are equally impressive. Inside is **Guthrie's,** a restaurant described in the DINING chapter. Directly across Elm Street from it, on your right, is the 50-story, red-granite 655-foot (or 200-meter) **1700 Pacific Tower,** built in 1983 and one of the ten largest office buildings in the city.

Continuing on Elm Street, by the time you get to North Ervay Street, you will see diagonally across the street the classic **Wilson Building** (see entry) inaugurated in 1903 by the Dallas businessman of Canadian birth, John Wilson. It was patterned after the Grand Opera House in Paris and designed by the Fort Worth architects Sanguinet & Staats. Post Properties of Atlanta converted it into one- and two-bedroom loft apartments. A couple of restaurants are located on the ground floor.

That tall building ahead of you is the Bank of America structure again. Turning right and going north on Ervay Street, you will pass several food shops hidden inside a food court on your right, including another Starbucks. As you reach Pacific Avenue, there is the **Thanksgiving Square** (see entry) across the street on your left. It was also designed by architect Philip Johnson and inaugurated in 1977 in observance of the 200th anniversary of the Thanksgiving holiday. The square, which is really a triangle, is bounded by the **Thanksgiving Tower** (see entry) on Pacific Avenue, the **Republic Towers** on North Ervay, and 1983 TXU Corporation Tower (an I. M. Pei & Partners building) on TXU Plaza. On the seventh floor of the Republic Towers, you will find the Dallas Convention Bureau.

As soon as you pass the length of the Republic Towers, on your right, you will find yourself at Bryan Street, named for the founder of Dallas, John Neely Bryan. Across the street on your right is the old U.S. Post Office and Courthouse, designed by James Wetmore and built in 1929, and reconstructed into lofts.

Turn right and continue in a northeasterly direction until crossing North St. Paul Street, where you will find the St. Paul light-rail station, from which you can take a train to the West End Historic District, if you are too tired to continue or need to get quickly back to Dealey Plaza, where you came from. Should you continue, you will pass, on your right, Henry Cobb's 30-story, rhomboid-shaped 1979 One Dallas

Centre tower, at 350 North St. Paul Street, which houses **Tolbert's Chili Parlor** (see listing), one of the few remaining chili joints in Dallas.

As you approach the intersection with Harwood Street, see a miniature maquette of downtown Dallas on the right-hand sidewalk. Even before crossing the street, you will not be able to ignore an 11-foot-high (or 3.35-meter) bronze, ***Pegasus and Man,*** by the Swedish-born Carl Milles, in front of the 2001 Bryan Tower. On your right is the newest addition to **Adam's Mark** (see listing), the largest Dallas hotel, which spills across Olive, the next street to the east.

Cross Olive Street, and you will find yourself on the **Cancer Survivors Plaza,** located on your left. On the corner of Pearl and Bryan Streets, the next block, you have one more chance to take a light-rail train to West End or to north Dallas at Pearl Station. North of it is the **Plaza of the Americas** (see entry) office complex and shopping mall. Turn left and continue northward on Pearl Street, and you will pass **Le Meridien Hotel** and its well-regarded **650** restaurant on your right (see listings).

As soon as you cross San Jacinto, the next street, which was named for the historic battle of Texas independence, you will spot **La Madeleine French Bakery & Café** (see listing) on the ground floor of the 33-story, 456-foot (or 139-meter) tall pink granite San Jacinto tower on your left. Read the plaque on the southeast corner of the building for an overview of this site since 1854, when early Dallas merchants paid $1 per acre (or 0.4 hectare) of its land.

As you continue in a northerly direction, you will soon stand on the corner of North Pearl Street and Ross Avenue, which, from 1880 to 1910, was one of the most fashionable Dallas streets. It was named after William and Andrew Ross, Dallas wine merchants. Dallas's Arts District starts here. If you continued on Ross to your right, going east, you would pass through a mile (or 1.6 kilometers) of used car dealerships until you reached the Lower Greenville entertainment district that comes alive at night. Diagonally across the street from you stands the Catholic **Cathedral Santuario de Guadalupe** (see entry), which can seat 1,100 and was dedicated in 1902. Behind it, going north, lies the **Meyerson Symphony Center** (see entry), designed by I. M. Pei, who also created the Dallas City Hall. Farther northwest, across Woodall Rodgers Freeway, you can see the new **Federal Reserve Bank** building, and still farther behind it the **Crescent Court** development, which includes a hotel under the same name, and several restaurants. Here also begins Uptown and the McKinney Avenue restaurant row, where **Hard Rock Café** and **The Old Warsaw** will be found (see listings).

Immediately across Ross Avenue, you will see the **A. H. Belo**

Mansion (see listing), the house that the Civil War colonel Belo bought in 1888. The sole early Dallas residence left standing in the central business district, it was a funeral home from 1926 on, and in 1934 the infamous bank robbers Clyde Barrow and Bonnie Parker were displayed here after having been ambushed and killed in Louisiana. Across Pearl Street stands the 55-story **J. P. Morgan Chase Bank** tower. Between 10 AM and 5 PM, you can go to the observation area on the 40th floor and enjoy a view of Dallas.

Continue the Length of Ross Avenue to the West End

Turn left and go southwest on Ross back toward the West End Historic District. Even before you cross Olive Street, you will not fail to notice Bourdelle's ***Horse for Alvear*** monument on the southeast corner of the **Trammell Crow Center** (see entry), where no fewer than 22 sculptures by Rodin, Bourdelle, Maillol, and others are displayed inside and out of the 49-story 2001 Ross Avenue tower. It is named after a billionaire Dallas family that has generously shared its cultural riches with the city not known for its arts. Read the plaque on the northwest side of the building for a brief history of the immediate area. Located on the mezzanine of this building is **Aija** restaurant with bar, which is open for lunch and dinner Mon-Fri 11:30 AM-7 PM.

On the north side of the building, you will find the **Trammell & Margaret Crow Collection of Asian Art,** and just behind it the new **Nasher Sculpture Center** (see entries).

Continuing in a westerly direction on Ross, you will cross North Harwood Street and notice on your left the **First United Methodist Church** (see entry), designed by architect Herbert M. Greene and built in 1924. On your right you will be greeted by Mark di Suvero's red-steel I-beam sculpture, titled ***Ave,*** located on the south lawn of the **Dallas Museum of Art,** which was completed in 1973, and whose architecture promises more than it delivers. Many Dallasites associate the museum with ***Stake Hitch,*** a huge aluminum and steel sculpture commissioned from Claes Oldenburg and his wife in 1984 and displayed until 2002 on the ground floor (see entry). It has since been dismantled. If hungry, enter from Ross Avenue and walk up the stairs, where an austere but civilized **Seventeen Seventeen** restaurant awaits you. A few steps farther on will get you to the entrance of the sculpture garden whose works are listed in the VISUAL ARTS chapter.

You are about to cross North St. Paul and North Akard Streets. On your right is the **Fairmont Hotel** with its **Pyramid Grill** restaurant (see listings). Just north of it is the Victorian-style former Cumberland Hill School built in 1888. On your left is the YMCA fitness center. Also on your left, but a block south, on Ervay Street, you can see a part of the **First Baptist Church** (see entry), with its original brick building, which was erected in 1890 and is now part of a complex that occupies several city blocks. As soon as you cross Freeman Street, behind the Fairmont, you will again see the tallest Dallas structure, the Bank of America tower, some distance to your left, and the Renaissance Tower still farther to the left.

On your immediate right is the **Fountain Place** (see entry), vying with the Bank One Center and J. P. Morgan Chase Tower for the honor of being one of the tallest buildings in Dallas. Designed by Henry Cobb, an associate of I. M. Pei, the huge beveled-glass prism was completed in 1986. Hundreds of tourists seek shade under its cypresses every summer. Short of the Gulf of Mexico, there are few places in Dallas where you will be surrounded by so much bubbling water. If you are tired, there are plenty of benches around the Fountain Place, if hungry, there is Italian-cuisine **Cafe Avanti,** "an oasis of ambience and culinary delight." It is located on the ground floor of the northwest corner of the building and open 11 AM-2 PM for lunch.

After you have caught your breath, continue westward, cross North Field, and go on to North Griffin Street. As you are crossing it, the Fox television studios and Doubletree Hotel will all be on your left. To your right is the **Dallas World Aquarium** (see entry), with more than 85,000 gallons (or 321,800 liters) of saltwater exhibits from around the world and a glass-enclosed tropical rain forest. Between you and the aquarium stands an apartment complex. Farther away on your right, you can see once more the Crescent Court. By the middle of the block, you will see on your left the 72-story Bank of America building in all its glory. You can again spot the familiar Reunion Tower farther ahead of you.

You are now crossing North Lamar Street and entering the West End Historic District. If you have been able to resist the temptation of food so far, your major test is yet to come because the West End means food and more food. By the time you reach the crossing of Ross Avenue and North Market Street, you will already have passed **The Palm** steakhouse (see listing) on your right, as well as **Y.O. Ranch,** which is named after a ranch near Kerrville, Texas, and serves Tex-Mex cowboy cuisine, and **Tony Roma's,** serving barbecue ribs in every conceivable configuration, both on your left. **Friday's** and **Lombardi's** are across the street. **West End MarketPlace** (see entry), where some 50 shops are located in one building, is a couple of blocks northwest, or to your right.

Turn left, going south, and you will pass **Lombardy's** seafood restaurant on your left and **Hoffbrau,** a casual Texas-style pub, on your right.

On the corner of Pacific Avenue and North Market Street is the West End light-rail station. Walk on to the next block, which is Elm Street, from which you started this tour, turn right, and continue in a westerly direction. The replica of the **John Neely Bryan Cabin** is now on your left.

EXCURSIONS

Marketers have spent years telling non-Texans that Dallas-Fort Worth is one easily-accessible area. "But as a quick getaway destination, the 13-city Metroplex is an unimaginable mess," declares the *Houston Chronicle*. "Coordinating visits to the Stockyards of Fort Worth, the theme parks of Arlington, the wineries of Grapevine and the museums of Dallas is counterproductive to a relaxing getaway." The *Chronicle* suggests focusing on just one city at a time.

There are several worthwhile options for excursions around Dallas. Some visitors head toward Granbury, others for Glen Rose.

Granbury and Glen Rose

Granbury, (800) 950-2212, Internet www.granbury.org, is a scenic town on Lake Granbury, located about 75 miles (or 120 kilometers) southwest of Dallas, almost half of it going on Interstate 20. It is named after Gen. Hiram B. Granbury (b. 1831), who came to Texas at age 20 and was killed in battle in 1864. The town's 1886 Opera House was restored and reopened in 1975 and offers plays and musicals on weekends. The downtown square is listed on the National Register of Historic Places and has a courthouse surrounded by shops.

Glen Rose, (888) 346-6282, Internet www.glenrosetexas.net or www.glenrose.net, is located about 93 miles (or 150 kilometers) from Big D. Of that, you will travel about 26 miles (or 42 kilometers) on Interstate 20, then exit to Interstate 35 West. The rock bottom of the Paluxy River that flows through Dinosaur Valley State Park, five miles (or eight kilometers) west of Glen Rose, contains dinosaur tracks that go back 100 million years. Fossil Rim Wildlife Center with more than a 1,000 animals roaming free is nearby. From June through October, *The Promise*, a long-running religious drama of the life of Jesus Christ, is staged on weekend nights in the open-air Texas Amphitheatre.

Those wishing to take their children to **Six Flags Over Texas** and **Hurricane Harbor** water parks, both in Arlington, will find the basic information in the SIGHTS & ATTRACTION chapter. If you plan to visit some outstanding museums in Fort Worth, while soaking in a bit of the genuine West, you may want to consult the *Marmac Guide to Fort Worth & Arlington.*

Then there is Crawford.

Crawford, the Texas White House (George W. Bush's Ranch)

Crawford is located in western McLennan County, about 120 miles (or 193 kilometers) southwest of Dallas, 90 miles (or 145 kilometers) south of Fort Worth, and 18 miles (or 29 kilometers) west of Waco. It takes about two hours by car to drive from Dallas to Crawford. An eight-mile (or 13-kilometer) Prairie Chapel Road leads from the town to the **Bush ranch**.

There are no hotels in Crawford, so most visitors have to stay in Waco, 20 miles (or 32 kilometers) away, where there is also the **Texas Ranger Hall of Fame & Museum,** located in Fort Fisher Park, Exit 335 B, off Interstate 35, (254) 750-8631. Inside, you will find details about the band of law enforcers that Stephen F. Austin founded in 1823. Waco also boasts the **Dr Pepper Museum,** housed in the 1906 bottling plant at 300 South Fifth St., (254) 757-1024.

The dusty, cotton-farming, one-flashing-light town of Crawford has about 730 residents, a police chief and a part-time police officer. It gained popularity in January 2001, when George W. Bush, who had bought a ranch here, became president of the United States.

None of the dramatic terrain of the 1,583-acre (or 641-hectare) Bush ranch, located halfway between Crawford and Valley Mills, can be seen from the road. The No Stopping, No Parking sign is all that tourists can see at the entrance to the Bush ranch. If you try to take photos near a concrete barricade, security men will probably ask you to move on.

There are no horses on the ranch that claims some 200 head of cattle and a few bulls and longhorns that belong to the foreman. Three miles (or 4.8 kilometers) of the middle fork of the Bosque River runs through the property, which also features seven limestone canyons replete with waterfalls. Deer, wild turkeys, wild hogs, coyotes, and rattlesnakes populate the ranch.

The ranch is situated about eight miles (or 13 kilometers) northwest of Crawford and is patrolled by the Secret Service with bloodhounds. No aircraft may come within a three-mile (or 4.8-kilometer) radius of Crawford at any time, or ten miles (or 16 kilometers) when the president is at the ranch.

Corn grower Kenneth Engelbrecht, the great-grandson of the

original German settler, sold Bush his ranch in 1999 and manages it when the president is away. It includes a 4,000-square-foot (or 372-square-meter) eight-room limestone ranch house with a swimming pool built in 2001 and designed by Austin architect David Heyman.

An artificial nine-acre (or 3.64-hectare) lake, 20 feet (or six meters) deep, allows Bush to fish just steps away from his home. Lined with rocky walls, it is stocked with various types of fish, including a hybrid bass that grows to a size perfect for trophy photographs. Trucks and all-terrain vehicles are the favored means of transportation on the property.

The real estate agent who owns a ranch next to the president's estimates that Bush paid about $1.5 million for the property. Ranch land prices have risen from $500 an acre (or 0.4 hectare) to as high as $4,000 an acre over the years. Rock guitarist Ted Nugent also lives in the area.

The newly air-conditioned Crawford Elementary School's 42-year-old gym is where some of the public events in the government take place. Russian president Vladimir Putin was, in 2001, the first foreign leader to be invited to Crawford. At the ranch, he and his wife got a chuck wagon on the lawn, cowboy cooks, beef tenderloin, a Western swing band, and, of course, pecan pie and Blue Bell ice cream. The Fort Worth pianist Van Cliburn, who owes much of his fame to his winning the first International Tchaikovsky Piano Competition in Moscow in 1958 at age 23, was among the guests.

Others to follow Putin to Crawford include British Prime Minister Tony Blair, Saudi Crown Prince Abdullah, who stayed only a few hours, and Chinese President Jiang Zemin. Mexican President Vincente Fox canceled his 2002 trip after Texas executed a Mexican citizen who had murdered an undercover Dallas police officer in 1988.

Security at the ranch is "as tight as Madonna's wedding" when Bush is in town. Since the September 11, 2001 terrorist attacks, military jets patrol the skies over Crawford when the president is there. Secret Service agents, dressed in Western garb, are regulars at the Coffee Station, the only restaurant in town that also doubles as a gas station, and a presidential souvenir emporium. A block away, the town's barber who had charged $5 for a haircut, closed shop after 42 years in business.

Crawford is a dry town where alcohol is not sold, and the sidewalks are crumbling. "But it has a certain authentic-Texas hardscrabble charm," claims the *Dallas Morning News*, while the British weekly *The Economist* notes: "The centre of America certainly contains many wonderful vacation spots, but Plains, Georgia, and Crawford, Texas, are not among them."

A Web site, www.crawfordtx.com, was created for the curious who also want T-shirts.

Crawford was first settled in the 1880s by German and Austrian farmers and ranchers, and incorporated in 1897. Henry Engelbrecht, a

German immigrant and Civil War veteran, lived in the original homestead on the Middle Bosque River, where Bush's ranch house now stands. He is buried in the cemetery at the Canaan Baptist Church, up the hill from the Bush ranch, which until 1940 had services in German.

"The earliest people who came to Crawford were from wealthy, well-educated families who wished to provide a good education for their children," observes one source. In the 1930s and 1940s—Crawford's heyday—the town had a movie theater, two or three grocery stores, a car dealership, even a bank.

Most of the businesses died out as local residents moved away from family-owned farms to Waco and Dallas. Now, souvenir and T-shirt stores are popping up—there already are eight—catering to an unending stream of tourists. Crawford County Style shop features brown ranch jackets like the one George Bush wears, and tote bags with the inscription, Western White House.

The town's citizens are philosophical about their newly discovered fame. "We're probably going to end up with nothing but T-shirt shops and antique stores if we're not careful," commented one.

Crawford Mayor Robert Campbell (b. 1942), one of the town's 31 African-Americans, is also pastor of Perry Chapel United Methodist Church which sits at the heart of Crawford's tiny black community, east of the railroad tracks. There are five churches in Crawford.

Campbell, who had earned bachelor's degrees in business administration and social work at Baylor University and a master's in divinity at Southern Methodist University in Dallas, retired from the U.S. Air Force in 1982. Once a Crawford maintenance man, he served for nine years on the city council and became mayor in 1999. The mayor looks to Plains, Georgia—former President Jimmy Carter's hometown—as a role model for how to adjust to Bush's presence.

The local post office advises that you write to Bush in care of the Bush Ranch, Crawford, Texas 77638.

THE INTERNATIONAL VISITOR

Although almost one-tenth of Dallasites are foreign-born and nearly 100 languages are spoken in the area, only a Texan would consider Dallas an international city. That does not mean that Dallasites will not greet you warmly, no matter how far you come from. They are attentive hosts, although men in particular like to impress you, be it with the size of a steak or their swimming pool.

Writes a reporter for the *London Financial Times*: "Dallas exceeded all my expectations and overturned many of my preconceptions; the heat was more intense, the terrain flatter and more arid than I had imagined; the size of the trucks, the freeways and the airport were overwhelming. Everywhere ruggedness was set alongside politesse."

Here are a few general observations about Dallas.

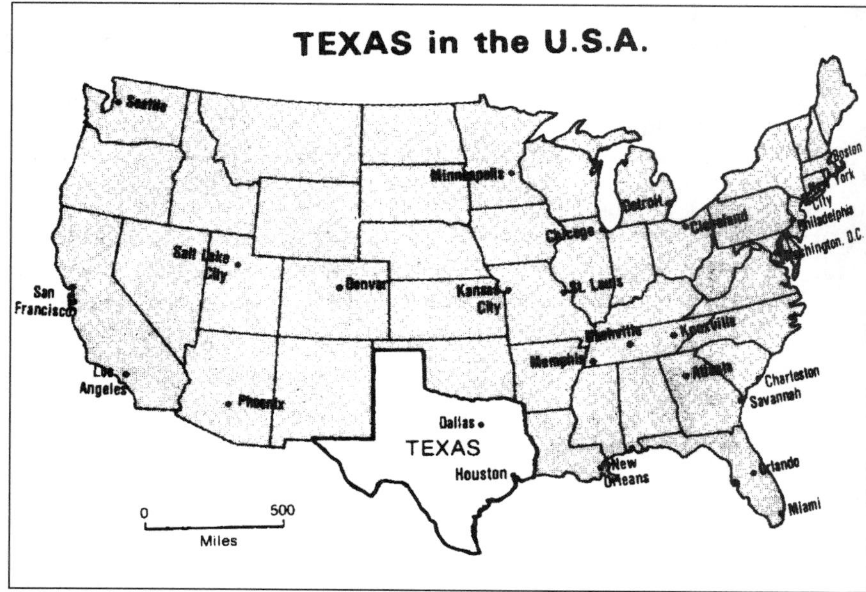

Your Safety

Gone seem to be the days when smug Europeans could routinely label the United States as being equal to the Wild West. If you come from France, where 4,244 crimes per 100,000 inhabitants annually were recorded recently, you may have a hard time believing that compared with 4,135 crimes in the United States.

The United States still leads France in the number of murders and rapes, but France leads in violent thefts. It follows that you should be as careful in Dallas as you are in Paris, Rome, or the British capital, where, "Your chances of being robbed in London are now six times greater than in New York," according to London's *Financial Times*.

Gun-related injuries are the second-leading cause of death among Americans aged 10 to 24 years. The police are sometimes unable to cope with the violent crime. While they will try their best to protect you, do not put all your faith in them and rely on yourself as much as you can. Only you can be responsible for your safety.

Violent crime in Texas declined for several years, taking its homicide rate to its lowest level in 20 years. The state prison population, however, soared from 49,600 in 1991 to 150,000 now.

Homicides in Dallas reached an all-time high of 500 in 1991 and decreased to a low of 185 in 1999. The number of homicides grew to 239 in 2001 and was 197 in 2002. There were 8,041 robberies in 2002, compared with 8,330 the previous year.

With 913 crimes per 10,000 residents, Dallas kept its title as the city with the highest crime rate in Texas recently. It was followed by Grand Prairie, with 531 crimes, Irving with 510, Garland with 433, Plano with 396, and Carrollton with 343 crimes per 10,000 residents.

FBI statistics in 2003 showed that "Dallas residents are more likely to experience crime than residents in many other cities," according to the *Dallas Morning News*, which also said that the city posted the highest per capita rate for robberies in the United States, with about 2.9 per every 1,000 residents.

Do not display cash, particularly since the various denominations of American currency are all of the same size and similar color so a potential thief can never tell for sure how much cash you carry. If you have an international credit card, you can probably charge most of your purchases. Never leave cash in your hotel room.

If you drive, never let a stranger inside your automobile. Be careful even when you stop at an intersection. You could be carjacked in broad daylight. If you become so victimized, you will be forced out, if you are lucky, and the thief will drive off to sell your car for its parts.

As a rule, do not wander alone at night. During the day, be on the lookout for one of the two dozen Dallas Ambassadors, men and women roaming downtown since 1994 to assist visitors with information. They work seven days a week and are also trained to serve as additional "eyes and ears" for the Dallas police department. The Ambassadors always wear uniforms, which consist of red shirts and jackets with a star emblem and blue slacks. For police, ambulance, and fire emergencies in the Metroplex, call 911.

Mostly for Women

Everything said above, *amplified*, applies to women. While it is an age-old fact that many women are irresistibly attracted to dangerous men, I suggest that you exercise your utmost discretion when your hormones take over and you want to forget yourself in the arms of a bad-apple cowboy. Many men, and by no means only American, will tell you whatever you want to hear so they can get whatever they want.

Select the most expensive hotel you can afford, even if you stay in the cheapest room. Generally, the better the class of a hotel, the less harassment you will likely endure if you travel alone. Many Dallas hotels have entire floors where only guests with their electronic keys can enter, and women will feel quite safe. Ask about safety before you arrive and again before you register.

When staying in a downtown Dallas hotel, you must be particularly cautious. You would be well advised not to walk alone downtown after 6 PM, when office workers leave for their suburban homes and dubious characters prey over empty streets.

It really is not a good idea for a single woman in Dallas to walk around alone downtown, in the West End, Deep Ellum, or Fair Park after dark. If you plan to have a dinner alone outside your hotel, decide on your restaurant, then take a taxi. Return the same way, unless you are absolutely convinced the risk of walking is worth taking.

OTHER MATTERS

Automobile Rentals

To rent an automobile, you must have a valid international driver's license and at least your passport. Unless you have made arrangements through your local travel agent abroad, you will need an internationally accepted credit card to pay for your rental. Cash payments are not welcome.

Driver's minimum age requirement may vary from one company to the next. You can never ask too many questions when renting a car. (For more details, please see the TRANSPORTATION chapter.)

Bank Hours

The banking hours in Dallas are generally from 9 AM to 3:30 PM, with some banks open until 5 or 6 PM on Fridays and until noon on Saturdays. Some also have drive-in branches that are also open weekdays and Saturdays.

For Currency Exchange and International Banking, see below.

Consulates

The U.S. Department of State has a visa waiver program, which allows citizens of 28 countries, including Argentina, Australia, Austria, Belgium, Denmark, Finland, France, Germany, Iceland, Ireland, Italy, Japan, Luxembourg, the Netherlands, New Zealand, Norway, Portugal, Slovenia, Spain, Sweden, Switzerland, and the United Kingdom, to stay up to 90 days without a visa. They need only a valid passport and a round-trip ticket upon their arrival.

Citizens of other countries need a valid passport that expires at least six months before their departure from the United States and a tourist visa they can obtain from an American consulate. These countries include South Korea, Venezuela, and Brazil.

The consulates in Dallas have one of the following designations: CG for Consulate General, C for Consulate, and HC for Honorary Consulate.

Belgium (HCG), 8350 North Central Expwy., Suite 2000, Dallas, (214) 987-4391.

Belize (HC), 1315 Nineteenth St., Suite 2-A, Plano, (972) 579-0070.

Bolivia (HC), 809 Singleton Blvd., Suite 315, Dallas, (214) 571-6131.

Canada (CG), 750 North St. Paul St., Suite 1700, Dallas, (214) 922-9806, Internet www.can-am.gc.ca/dallas.

Chile (HC), 3500 Oak Lawn Ave., Suite 110, Dallas, (214) 528-2731.

Costa Rica (C), 7777 Forest Lane, Suite B-445, Dallas, (972) 566-7020.

Czech Republic, Box 7306, Dallas 75209, (214) 351-2074, Internet www.mzv.cz/washington.

Denmark (HC), 2100 McKinney Ave., Suite 700, Dallas, (214) 661-8399.

Ecuador, 7510 Acorn Lane, Frisco, (972) 712-9106, Internet www.ecudarianconsulatedallas.com.

El Salvador (CG), 1555 West Mockingbird Ln. at Oakbrook Blvd., Suite 216, Dallas, (214) 637-1018.

Finland (HC), 3200 Trammell Crow Center, 2001 Ross Ave., Suite 3200, Dallas, (214) 855-4500, Internet www.finland.org.

France (HC), 6370 Lyndon B. Johnson Frwy., Suite 272, Dallas, (972) 789-9305, Internet www.consulfrance-houston.org.

Germany (HC), 4265 Kellway Circle, Addison, (972) 239-0788.

Iceland (HC), 1301 Commerce Dr., Plano, (972) 699-5417.

Italy (HVC), 6255 West Northwest Hwy., Suite 304, Dallas, (214) 368-4113.

Jamaica (HC), 3068 Forest Ln., Dallas, (972) 396-7969.

Japan (HCG), 7115 Fernmeadow Circle, Dallas, (972) 661-2346.

Korea (HC), 3828 Oak Lawn Ave., Dallas, (214) 525-3908.

Malta (HC), 2601 North Floyd Rd., Richardson, (214) 528-6245, Internet www.searchmalta.com.

Mexico (CG), 8855 North Stemmons Frwy. at Round Table Dr., Dallas, (214) 522-9740. Parking has been a problem since 1995, when the consulate moved here. Of the original 40 parking spaces on the consulate's property, about half are designated for staff. The remaining 20 spaces are supposed to accommodate more than 500 people who come to the consulate on an average day.

Ezequiel Padilla Couttolenc (b. 1943), previously Mexican ambassador to Canada, Switzerland, and the Netherlands was appointed Mexican consul general in 2001. The Mexico City native, who has a master's degree in public administration from Harvard University, represents more than one-and-a-half million Mexicans living in north Texas, Oklahoma, and Arkansas.

Monaco (HC), 4700 St. Johns Dr., Dallas, (214) 521-1058. Doris Canaan met Monaco's Prince Rainier III and his wife, actress Grace Kelly, at a party in the early 1970s at the downtown Neiman Marcus and was named an honorary consul. Her husband, Gershon Canaan, a German-American architect who died in 2002, served for 25 years as honorary consul of West Germany.

Norway (HC), 4605 Live Oak St., Dallas, (214) 826-5231.

Peru (HC), 3424 Spring Mountain Dr., Plano, (972) 712-3159.

Spain (HC), 5499 Glen Lakes Dr., Suite 209, Dallas, (214) 373-1200.

Sweden (HC), 1341 West Mockingbird Ln., Suite 500, Dallas, (214) 630-9112.

Switzerland (HC), 2651 North Harwood St., Fourth Floor, Dallas, (214) 871-0871, Internet www.swissemb.org. Developer Gabriel Barbier-Mueller, Harwood International chief executive, serves as Switzerland's honorary consul.

Taiwan, 1168 West Main St., Suite E, Lewisville, (972) 436-4242.

Thailand (HCG), 3232 McKinney Ave., Suite 1400, Dallas, (214) 740-1413.

United Kingdom (C), 2911 Turtle Creek Blvd., Suite 940, Dallas, (214) 521-4090, Internet www.britainusa.com/consular/dallas.

Credit Cards & Travelers Checks

Credit cards are accepted in most hotels, restaurants, and retail stores throughout the Metroplex. Some of these establishments may not accept them for charges under $2 or $3. Credit cards can also serve as a deposit for a rental car or as a cash card, enabling you to draw money from automated teller machines (ATMs). You may be charged up to $3 per each transaction. To eliminate some of these fees, ask for cash back at supermarkets and other stores when you buy something.

There are at least a dozen automatic teller machines at the Dallas/Fort Worth International Airport, operated by the Bank of America.

Guard your credit card as you do your cash because in the wrong hands your card becomes a potent criminal tool that can go through thousands of dollars in minutes.

To report lost or stolen credit cards, contact a number to be found on these Web sites:

American Express .... www.americanexpress.com
AT&T Universal Card .... www.att.com/ucs
Diners Club .... www.dinersclub.com
Discover Club .... www.discovercard.com
MasterCard (Eurocard, Access, Diamond) .... www.mastercard.com
VISA (BarclaysCard) .... www.usa.visa.com

While in one respect they are even better than cash, because when they get lost or stolen you can have them replaced, the travelers checks' drawback is that they cost you money when you purchase them. Some merchants in the Metroplex are just a bit reluctant to accept them because they are not widely used. They might ask for your passport or driver's license to verify your identity and your counter-signature. Never agree to pay any fee to cash travelers checks.

Currency Exchange & International Banking

The Metroplex is rather provincial when it comes to foreign currency exchange. Texans assume that the dollar should be used universally. You can exchange your foreign banknotes at the Dallas/Fort Worth International Airport and a few banks downtown, but the rate may not be as competitive as you might get at home. Consider exchanging at least some of your local currency before arriving in Texas.

Provided that the currency you want to exchange is a major one, such as the euro, Australian or Canadian dollar, British pound sterling, or Japanese yen, try one of these Dallas establishments:

American Express Travel, 8317 Preston Center Plaza mall, at the southeast corner of Preston Rd. and West Northwest Hwy., near the Park Cities Baptist Church, Dallas, (214) 363-0214. Open Mon-Fri 9 AM-6 PM, Thursdays until 8 PM, Saturdays 10 AM-4 PM.

Another Amexco location is above Tiffany's on the third level at the Galleria mall (see listing), 13350 Dallas Pkwy. at Lyndon B. Johnson Freeway in north Dallas, (972) 233-9291. Open Mon-Fri 9 AM-6 PM, Sat 10 AM-4 PM.

An Amexco office is also situated near Dillard's and Sears department stores, on the upper level, in Suite 2158 at Collin Creek Mall (see listing) at North Central Expwy. and West Plano Pkwy. in Plano, (972) 424-7554. Open Mon-Fri 9 AM-6 PM, Sat 10 AM-4 PM.

The services to exchange foreign currencies at local banks are decidedly pedestrian. Call ahead and ask most of your questions before you go to a bank in person.

Bank of America, 1401 Elm St. at Akard St., or 901 Main St. at Lamar, both downtown, (214) 508-6881. Open for foreign exchange transactions Mon-Fri 9 AM-3 PM.

J.P. Morgan Chase Bank, 2200 Ross Ave. at Pearl St., roughly between Meyerson Symphony Center and Plaza of the Americas, downtown, (214) 965-2925. Open Mon-Fri 9 AM-3 PM. Validated ticket entitles you to complementary underground parking.

Travelex/Thomas Cook (Internet www.travelex.com). (For D/FW International Airport locations, please see the TRANSPORTATION chapter.)

•2911 Turtle Creek Blvd. at Cedar Springs Rd., Suite 125, in the lobby of the Park Place office building, (214) 559-3564. Located across the street from the Mansion on Turtle Creek Hotel (see entry) in Oak Lawn. Open Mon-Fri 9 AM-5 PM.

•The Village on the Parkway mall, Addison, Suite 532, on the southeast corner of Belt Line Rd. and North Dallas Tollway, around the corner from Blue Mesa Grill, (800) 433-7300 or (972) 991-0191. It is open Mon-Fri 10 AM-6 PM, Sat 10 AM-5 PM.

For details about Travelex branches, currency quotes, travelers checks, or travel insurance, please call toll-free (800) 287-7362, or visit the Web site.

Customs Allowances

Foreign nationals over 21 years of age may bring into the United States duty free one liter of wine, beer, or hard liquor, 200 cigarettes, 50 cigars (not from Cuba), or two kilograms (or 4.4 pounds) of smoking tobacco, and gifts valued up to $100. You may claim these exemptions if you spend at least 72 hours in the United States and have not claimed them within the previous six months. An additional 100 cigars may be brought in under your gift exemption.

Bringing in certain foodstuffs, such as fruits, meats, and many canned goods, also vegetables, seeds, and tropical plants, is forbidden. Bakery items and all cured cheeses are admissible. Narcotics and dangerous drugs are prohibited.

Foreign visitors may bring in up to $10,000 in U.S. or foreign currency with no formalities. The United States does not have a value-added tax (VAT), and the federal government cannot refund the Texas state sales tax of 8.25 percent. You can get some of the tax refund through a service at NorthPark Center (see entry).

You may import your automobile for the transportation of yourself, your family, and your guests for up to one year, but it cannot be sold in the United States. Clothing, jewelry, toiletries, cameras, portable radios, and similar personal effects are exempt from duty if they are for personal use and you take them out upon your departure.

Check the U.S. Treasury Web site, www.customs.ustreas.gov, section Customs Regulation for Nonresidents, for more details.

Driving

Driving in the United States is in the right lane. You need a valid international driver's license, although some foreign driver's licenses, especially from the English-speaking countries, are accepted. Most gasoline stations are open 24 hours a day, and you have the option of pumping your own gas or paying a little extra to have an attendant do it for you.

By Texas law, the driver and front seat passengers must wear a safety belt or risk a $200 fine. In Dallas, you may turn right on a red light after you have stopped and looked in both directions. Red-light runners are responsible for 17,000 crashes a year in Texas, and cause about 82 traffic fatalities statewide.

In 1996, the speed limit in the Metroplex was raised to 60 miles (or 96.5 kilometers) per hour on many highways, except for short stretches of Interstates 30 and 35E and U.S. Highway 175 near downtown, which remain at 55 mph.

Most rural interstates and state highways have a 70 miles (or 113 kilometers) per hour limit. However, to improve the air quality in the nine-county north Texas area, some 900 miles (or 1,448 kilometers) of Metroplex roads with 70- or 65- miles-per-hour (or 112- or 104-kilometers-per-hour) limits had speeds lowered by five miles (or eight kilometers) in 2001.

Highway traffic has the right of way and is not required to yield to entering traffic; exiting traffic has the right of way on access roads. The speed limit on most residential streets is 30 miles (or 48 kilometers) per hour, and 20 miles (or 32 kilometers) per hour in school zones with flashing yellow lights.

Speeding is a major problem in the Metroplex and could quickly get you a $100-plus ticket.

Children under 18 years of age are prohibited from riding in the open backs of pickup trucks. Children under four years of age, or under 36 inches (or 58 centimeters) tall, must ride in car seats. Others under 17 must wear seat belts. Fines for failing to strap children into car seats and seat belts range from $100 to $200.

Open containers of alcohol in all cars and trucks are banned, regardless of whether the driver or passengers are involved, with violations subject to a fine of up to $500.

Texas leads the nation in deaths related to drunken driving, with more than 1,700 alcohol-related traffic fatalities annually compared with 1,600 in California, which has millions more residents. Texas automobile speeders cause another 1,300 fatalities a year. Forty-three percent of all fatal Texas automobile crashes involve someone who is legally intoxicated.

To deal with the problem, in 2001 the governor signed legislation authorizing police to confiscate a driver's license during a drunken-driving arrest if the driver refuses a breath test. License suspensions were increased from 90 to 180 days for those who refuse to take a breath test. Suspensions increased from 60 to 90 days for those with no alcohol or drug-related offenses in the past ten years who fail a breath test.

Electricity

The standard is 110 volts 60 cycles A.C. You will need a plug adapter and a voltage converter for foreign electrical appliances. You may find them at Rand McNally Map & Travel Store in NorthPark shopping center, at North Central Expwy. and West Northwest Hwy., (214) 987-9941. The store also sells travel guides and other travel accessories.

Health Insurance

Medical insurance should be secured prior to your arrival. Forty-two million Americans lack such insurance. There is no national health service system in the United States, although you will receive emergency medical care. Health care is perhaps the costliest in the world, and payment is usually required at the time of treatment.

One insurance plan that foreign visitors might consider is **Health Care America,** a short-term medical insurance and assistance for foreign nationals visiting the United States. For about $5 a day, if you are up to 55 years old, or $9 a day if aged 56 to 70, you will receive a $100,000 accident and sickness expense benefit. You will have to show your Health Care America identification card and your passport. Pre-existing medical conditions are not covered. The first $100 in expenses for each incident is your responsibility.

The Health Care America plan includes medical evacuation to your home, and dental expense benefit of up to $1,000 for dental work, which barely covers the equivalent of one crown. The coverage also includes $25,000 accidental death and dismemberment benefit. It must be purchased and in effect within the first 20 days of your arrival in the United States. You can only be covered by this plan for up to 90 days and extend it for an additional 90 days upon expiration of the original policy. The plan is available in the United States and Canada only.

For more information, contact Wallach & Company, 107 West Federal Street, Middleburg, Virginia 20118-0480, or by phone at (800) 237-6615 or (540) 687-3166, Fax (540) 687-3172, Internet www.wallach.com.

Hospital Emergencies

In a true emergency call 911 first. Most Metroplex hospitals have 24-hour emergency care. Among the best-known ones are:

Baylor University Medical Center, 3500 Gaston Ave. at Hall St., (214) 820-2501, Internet www.baylorhealth.com. Located about one mile (or 1.6 kilometers) northeast from the central business district.

Children's Medical Center, 1935 Motor St., (214) 456-2100, Internet www.childrens.com. Located five miles (or eight kilometers) north of downtown, southeast of the Parkland Hospital (see entry), roughly between Interstate 35 East and Harry Hines Blvd.

Medical City Dallas Hospital, 7777 Forest Ln. at North Central Expy., (972) 566-7200, Internet www.medicalcityhospital.com. Located about 12 miles (or 19 kilometers) north of downtown Dallas and south of Lyndon B. Johnson Freeway.

Methodist Medical Center, 1441 North Beckley Ave., (214) 947-8100, Internet www.mhd.com. Located less than two miles (or 3.2 kilometers) southwest of downtown Dallas.

Parkland Memorial Hospital, 5201 Harry Hines Blvd., (214) 590-8000, Internet www3.utsouthwestern.edu/parkland. Located about three miles (or 4.8 kilometers) northwest of downtown, northwest of the Childrens Medical Center, north of Interstate 35 East (or Stemmons Freeway).

Presbyterian Hospital of Dallas, 8200 Walnut Hill Ln., (214) 345-6789, Internet www.texashealth.org/presbydallas. Located about 7.5 miles (or 12 kilometers) northeast of downtown Dallas, just east of North Central Expressway (or U.S. Hwy. 75).

St. Paul University Hospital, 5909 Harry Hines Blvd. at Inwood Rd., (214) 879-2790. Located four miles (or 6.4 kilometers) northwest of downtown Dallas, north of University of Texas Southwestern Medical Center (see entry).

Money

The U.S. dollar is divided into 100 cents. The coins are the penny, worth 1 cent (copper-colored); nickel, worth 5 cents; dime, worth 10 cents; quarter, worth 25 cents; and half-dollar, worth 50 cents (all silver-colored); and occasionally a dollar coin. The bills or notes are, unlike in other countries, all of the same size and predominantly printed in green and black ink on white paper. Denominations are one dollar, five dollars, ten dollars, twenty dollars, fifty dollars, and one hundred dollars. American currency is printed in Washington, D.C., and Fort Worth, Texas, and distributed by the 12 Federal Reserve banks.

The Fort Worth plant prints about one-half of the nation's paper money. Coins are minted in Philadelphia. About 95 percent of the notes printed each year are used to replace notes already in circulation. Some 48 percent of all notes are $1 bills. Sixty-six percent of all U.S. currency is in circulation overseas.

The $20 bills, the most widely used denomination, are being redesigned and, since 2003, sport a purple tint. The redesign is an attempt to foil counterfeiters.

The U.S. Mint stopped printing bills larger than $100 in 1945. While such bills are still legal tender, the government has been quietly removing them from circulation since 1969. There are an estimated 400 $10,000 bills, bearing the likeness of President Abraham Lincoln, still in existence and could fetch up to $70,000 each.

The first currency authorized by the government of the Republic of Texas began circulating in the fall of 1837. It was called Star Money because of the star printed on the bills. It was replaced the following year with engraved notes. Hard economic times depreciated the 1838 dollar to 40 cents by January 1839, when the so-called "redback" notes were issued. They lost value even faster and were worth only about two cents on the dollar by the winter of 1842.

When Texas became part of the Union in 1845, the bills were replaced with U.S. currency.

Pharmacies

For details about any **Eckerd pharmacy,** call (800) 325-3737, or check the Web site www.eckerd.com. The nation's fourth-largest drugstore chain is part the Plano-based J.C. Penney Co. Among the most visible Dallas locations are:

- 10455 North Central Expwy. at Meadow Rd. in north Dallas, (214) 369-3872. Open 24 hours.
- 703 Preston Forest Shopping Center, Preston Rd. at Forest Ln. in north Dallas, (214) 363-1571. Open 24 hours.
- 901 Main St., (214) 742-1044, and 2939 Main, 747-0004, both located downtown and open Mon-Fri 7 AM-6 PM.
- 3012 West Mockingbird Ln. at North Central Expwy., (214) 363-5525. Open Mon-Fri 8 AM-9 PM, Sat 9 AM-7 PM, Sun 9 AM-6 PM.

U.S.Postal Service, Internet www.usps.gov

First-class letters inside the United States are usually delivered within two to five days, provided they contain the recipient's proper zip code.

Various other classes of mail are also available, including express and priority mail, at charges corresponding to how fast the letter or package arrives. Airmail envelopes, used elsewhere worldwide, are not in common usage in the United States because most first-class mail is automatically transported by air.

Global Priority Mail is an international service comparable to express mail, but at a lower price. It is available for delivery in Canada,

Western Europe, and the Pacific Rim in flat-rate envelopes or packages of up to four pounds (or 1.81 kilograms).

For general postal information, weekdays 8 AM-5 PM, call (214) 741-5508; for claims information, (972) 393-6684; for express or global priority mail pickup, (800) 222-1811 or (214) 760-4640; and for zip code information, weekdays 8:30 AM-5 PM, (972) 647-2996.

Two among the downtown post offices are located at 400 North Ervay St., across the street from Thanksgiving Square, and in the basement of the One Main Place building. Another one in northeast Dallas is on Upper Greenville Ave., (214) 739-3331, near Mockingbird light-rail station and across the street from the Central Market (see entry).

Public Holidays & Notable Dates in Texas History

Days marked in **bold** are recognized as Federal holidays, when most government offices, banks, and other institutions are closed.

The two most widely observed holidays are Thanksgiving and Christmas. Practically all businesses, even supermarkets and most restaurants, are closed on those two days, as are the stock and commodity exchanges, schools, city, county, state, and federal offices. Only the main post office at Interstate Highway 30 and Sylvan Avenue is open. If you are not staying at a hotel, the 7-Eleven convenience shops may be one of the few places to get beverages, food, and newspapers. Compared with how enthusiastically it is celebrated in Europe, New Year's Day is not a major holiday in the United States.

January 1:	**New Year's Day.**
January 7, 1905:	First large oil strike is made in Harris County, Texas.
Third Monday in January:	**Martin Luther King (1929-1968) Birthday** (assassinated African-American civil rights leader).
January 20, 1925:	Mrs. Miriam "Ma" Ferguson (1875-1961) is inaugurated first female governor of Texas, eight years after her husband Jim (1871-1944) was bounced from the same office fornumerous financial improprieties.
February 14:	Valentine's Day celebrates lovers.
Third Monday in February:	**Presidents Day** (originally celebrated Lincoln's birthday on February 12 and

	Washington's on February 22. In 1971, President Richard Nixon proclaimed it Presidents Day instead).
March 2, 1836:	Declaration of Independence of the Republic of Texas is signed at Washington-on-the-Brazos. This is now Texas Independence Day.
March 2, 1793:	Sam Houston, president of the Republic of Texas, is born in Rockbridge County, Virginia; died 1863.
March 6, 1836:	More than 180 defenders of the Alamo in San Antonio and at least 600 Mexican soldiers under Gen. Santa Anna are killed as the fort falls early this morning.
March 17:	St. Patrick's Day.
March 26, 1918:	Texas governor William P. Hobby gives women the right to vote.
March 30, 1846:	Dallas County is created.
First Sunday in April:	Daylight Savings Time begins (clocks should be set one hour forward at 2 AM Dallas time). Benjamin Franklin, one of America's founding fathers, came up with this idea in 1784 to save on lamp oil. The U.S. went on DST in 1918 to conserve energy for the war, but it was in 1966 that Congress mandated DST. Western Europe goes on DST on the last Sunday in March.
April 21, 1836:	Slaughter of 610 Mexicans at San Jacinto leads to Texas independence.
Second Sunday in May:	Mother's Day.
Last Monday in May:	**Memorial Day** (in remembrance of war dead).
June 6, 1849:	City of Fort Worth is established.
Third Sunday in June:	Father's Day.
June 19, 1865:	Texas Emancipation Day (Juneteenth), when Union general Gordon Granger arrives at Galveston, Texas, proclaiming U.S. authority over Texas two and a half years after President Abraham Lincoln's Emancipation Proclamation. There were

	an estimated 200,000 slaves in Texas at the ti'me.
July 4:	**Independence Day** (commemorates the adoption of the Declaration of Independence in 1776).
August 27, 1908:	President Lyndon Baines Johnson's birthday. The 36th president died in 1973.
First Monday in September:	**Labor Day** (recognizes American workers). The Dallas City Council in 2001 designated this as an official city holiday in honor of Cesar Chavez (1927-1993), the farm workers' leader. It is now one of nine city holidays.
Second Monday in October:	**Columbus Day** (originally commemorated landing of Columbus in the Bahamas in 1492, now an increasingly controversial holiday).
October 14, 1890:	President Dwight D. Eisenhower's birthday. The 34th president died in 1969.
October 16, 1836:	Soldier and politician Sam Houston (1793-1863) becomes president of the Republic of Texas.
Last Sunday in October:	Daylight Savings Time ends (clocks get set back one hour).
October 31:	Halloween.
November 3, 1793:	Birthday of Stephen F. Austin (d. 1836), "Father of Texas."
November 11:	**Veterans Day** (commemorates the end of wars in 1918 and 1945, and honors veterans of both, as well as of Vietnam War).
November 22, 1963:	President John F. Kennedy is assassinated in downtown Dallas. (For details see entry Sixth Floor Museum.)
November 24, 1963:`	Kennedy's alleged assassin Lee H. Oswald is shot.
Fourth Thursday in November:	**Thanksgiving Day** (since 1674, a day for giving thanks for Divine Goodness).
December 25:	**Christmas Day.**
December 29, 1845:	Texas becomes the 28th state of the Union.

Telephone & Telegrams

The resources you can tap into over the telephone are considerable. Consult the alphabetical **Greater Dallas Business White Pages** directory (with its blue pages of government listings at the beginning) if you know the exact name of the organization, but not its telephone number. The residential white-page directory is just as useful if you know an individual's exact surname.

The 2,300-page two-volume **Yellow Pages** directories, which are arranged alphabetically, according to subjects, will come in handy when you try to find listings in a variety of categories, such as hotels and restaurants. The alphabetical index is at the beginning of the second, M-Z volume. A full-page listing in yellow pages does not mean that an establishment is preferable to the one that only identifies itself with one line, it just means the first one can afford to pay for a full page.

Calling inside Dallas—within 214, 469, or 972 area codes, that is—is always a local call, which at some hotels may be free, while others may charge you 25 cents or more. If you call Fort Worth or Arlington from Dallas, for example, this is always a long distance call, unless a so-called "metro" number is available. Ask your hotel for details before you make such calls.

Public pay phones charges have increased to 50 cents a call, supposedly because more than 110 million Americans subscribe to cellular service and now have a lesser need for public telephones.

If you need to use a public phone, simply lift the receiver, listen for the dial tone, deposit the coin, and dial the number. Local calls have no time limit within reason. If the line is busy, the coin will be returned when you hang up. When calling long distance, at additional expense, of course, first dial 1, followed by the area code, then the telephone number.

Numbers preceded by (800)—and several other numerical prefixes, such as 888—are toll-free and can be made nationwide. Dial first 1, then (800), or whatever the three-digit prefix, followed by the seven-digit number. If there is a local equivalent, use the local number. You can dial toll-free (800) numbers anywhere in the United States or Canada.

Since 1996, the area code for central Dallas, south and west of Lyndon B. Johnson Freeway (also known as Interstate Highway 635), north and east of Loop 12, is mostly **214**. Outside that immediate area, in suburbs like Irving, Carrollton, Addison, Plano, Richardson, most of Garland and Mesquite, Lancaster, DeSoto, Duncanville, or Grand Prairie, the area code is **972**. The area code for Fort Worth and vicinity or Arlington is usually **817**.

Area codes for a few other Texas cities: **Abilene, El Paso,** and **San Angelo**—915; **Amarillo** and **Lubbock**—806; **Austin** and **Corpus**

Christi—512; **Beaumont** and **Galveston**—409; **Houston**—713 or 281; **San Antonio** and **McAllen**—210; **Midland** and **Odessa**—915; **Tyler**—903; **Fort Worth** and **Waco**—817.

All telephone numbers in this guide include the proper area code.

To place an international call directly, dial **011,** then the country code, followed by that city's code, and finally the telephone number.

Tipping

Dallasites generally tip 10-20 percent for good service; a few tip nothing to show their displeasure at unacceptable service. Some tip regardless of the quality of the service "because as Americans we're neurotic, guilt-prone, and we don't want to be thought of as cheap or ignorant," claims *Money* magazine.

Practically the minimum tip in a coffee shop is $1 and twice as much in a better class of restaurant. A man would tip about $2 for a haircut, a woman 15-20 percent. Hotel housekeepers get about $2 a night. Bellhops and porters receive $1 for each bag. A usual tip for a taxi driver would be 15 percent. You need not tip a gas attendant, unless he performs additional duties.

Tours

The largest tour operator in the Metroplex is **Gray Line,** which was bought by Greyhound in 2002 and offers at least one of the tours daily. Call (214) 698-5936 in Dallas, or (866) 767-9849 toll-free elsewhere, Internet www.grayline.com. Foreign languages guides are available at an additional cost and by prior arrangements.

Dallas Landmark Tour, 3 hours. Tour sights include Highland Park, SMU's Meadows Museum, the Wilson Block on Swiss Avenue, Pioneer Plaza, "Old Red" Courthouse, Neiman Marcus department store, Farmer's Market, Union Station, and the Historic West End.

Departs 1:30 PM Sundays, Wednesdays, and Saturdays. The cost is $26 for adults and $13 for children under 12 years of age.

J.F.K. Historical Tour, 3 hours. Includes Dealey Plaza walking tour, visit to the Sixth Floor Museum, presidential motorcade route, Lee Oswald rooming house, site of officer Tippit's killing at 214 Neely St., Texas Theater, where Oswald was arrested, and Old City Courthouse jail.

Departs 8:30 AM Mon-Wed, Fridays, and Saturdays. The cost is $30 for adults and $15 for children under 12 years of age. Admission to the Sixth Floor Museum is included.

Downtown Dallas & Southfork Ranch Tour, 3 hours. Begins with a tour of downtown Dallas, including Pioneer Plaza, "Old Red" Courthouse, and the original Neiman Marcus department store. Departs on Mondays and Thursdays at 1:30 PM. The cost is $30 for adults and half that for kids, including the admission at the ranch.

Rodeo Round-Up Tour, 4 hours. Attend the Mesquite championship rodeo for a taste of the Old West, including cowboys, bull riding, barrel racing, and calf roping.

Departs 6:30 PM Fridays and Saturdays between March and October. Pick-ups for tours are from many hotels uptown and downtown. Several combination tours, lasting up to nine hours, are also available.

The presentation and knowledge of the guides on these tours is satisfactory. The buses are comfortable, and there are enough breaks to stretch your legs and get a bite to eat. Our only concern is for those whose knowledge of English is limited. They may have a hard time following a heavily accented Texas English on some tours.

For more tours options, please see the Tours section in the TRANSPORTATION chapter. Also call the Dallas Convention & Visitors Bureau, 1201 Elm St., Suite 2000, (214) 571-1000; Visitor Information Center, (214) 571-1300; 24-Hour Events Hotline, (800) 232-5527, Internet in English, French, German, Japanese, Portuguese, and Spanish at www.dallasconventioncenter.com.

NEW RESIDENTS

If Dallas is your new home, welcome. You may be one of the 100,000 Metroplex newcomers every year. About half of you come from New York, California, and the adjacent states of Oklahoma, Louisiana, and Arkansas. The rest of you may be Mexicans, Vietnamese, Indians, Salvadorans, or Chinese, in that order.

Almost 31 percent of all Dallasites are under 20 years of age, more than 20 percent have bachelor's degrees, and the median household income in Dallas County is $43,324.

As in any other city, you will like some things about Big D and perhaps be frustrated with others. As you try to locate housing, place your children in school, and open a bank account, I will assist you with some basics that will make that transition easier. Please refer also to other parts of this guide that contains much information that will come in handy.

AN INTRODUCTION TO DALLAS LIVING

Dallas is not called Big D for nothing. It measures no less than 400 square miles (or 1,036 square kilometers). That makes it the seventh largest urban area, with the greatest sprawl in the country, ahead of San Antonio, but behind Houston, with 638 square miles (or 1,652 square kilometers). Dallas covers an area similar to that occupied by Moscow, Russia, which has almost ten times as many inhabitants.

So far it has been mostly a boom town, with an occasional bust, with the last two having passed through after the Texas banking crisis, in the 1980s, and the dot.com bust, starting in 2001. Having a city manager, Dallas is run somewhat like a business, and it is a popular destination for corporate relocations, the third largest in industrial company headquarters. Some feel that Dallas has been controlled by the real estate interests for generations, with several past mayors speculating in land.

Big D is obsessed with sports and not only football. The Texas Rangers baseball team, which, unfortunately, does not have much to show for its efforts, and the Dallas Mavericks basketball franchise, seem to draw almost as many fans as the Dallas Cowboys, the five-time Super

Bowl champions of the National Football League. Initiate a conversation about one of these teams, and white, Mexican-, and African-American citizens, who at times may despise each other, will chatter contentedly like children.

Dallas is also a favorite with those who cannot tolerate Minnesota's winters or Chicago's winds. Spring and fall, even stretches during the winter, are quite enjoyable. Summers, of course, are something else, unless you lock yourself inside and have good air-conditioning.

Geographical Profile

Dallas is situated at a latitude of about 32 degrees and 47 minutes north, and a longitude of 96 degrees and 48 minutes west. Located 500 feet (or 152 meters) above sea level, it seems as flat as a tabletop. Big D is less than an hour's driving time east of Fort Worth, and four hours north of Austin, the capital.

The U.S. Census Bureau resurrected the city's bragging rights in 2001, when it reinstated Dallas as the eighth largest in the country, with 1,188,000 residents, compared with San Antonio's 1,144,000.

"Dallas is ugly," claims an editor of *D Magazine*, usually a civic booster. "Not a little rough around the sprawling edges like Atlanta or Phoenix, but really, really unattractive." Saying so may be impolite, but it is true, she continues. Dallasites tend not to notice just how "drably bad the city looks, because they're used to it." It is not just nature that makes Dallas "ugly," insists the editor. People help. The Texas-sized monuments downtown make for a nice skyline, a substitute for mountains from a distance, but they do not do much for ground-level appeal. From the sidewalk or the road, the typical skyscraper is just another hostile facade, she claims. And even well-executed monuments supposedly cannot alter a city's look and feel.

Dallas is part of the Metroplex, a community of more than five million inhabitants scattered over at least four counties, including Fort Worth and such fast-growing cities as Arlington, Garland, Plano, Irving, Mesquite, Grand Prairie, Carrollton, and Richardson. Each of these has something unique to offer. Highland Park, University Park, and Plano, for example, have good schools. Richardson cultivates high-technology companies. Addison and Arlington love to entertain. Irving has football, Mesquite rodeo.

The time zone in Dallas is Central Daylight Standard Time. Noon in Dallas is 1 PM in Toronto and New York, 6 PM in London, 7 PM in Paris, Berlin, and Rome, 8 PM in Helsinki, 9 PM in Moscow, 3 AM in Adelaide, Australia, 4 AM in Sydney, and 6 AM in Auckland, New Zealand.

People Profile

Dallas proper has a population of about 1,200,000—an increase of more than 180,000 since 1990—of which 49 percent are males and 51 percent females, with a median age of 30.5 years.

Since 1990, the city's Caucasian population has dropped 13 percent to about 418,000, or 35 percent, continuing the white flight to the suburbs. Hispanics account for almost 36 percent of the population, or 423,000 residents; their population doubled between 1990 and 2000. The city's African-American populace stands at 310,000, or about 25 percent. Asians number about 32,000, and Native Americans 3,700 in the 2000 census.

You will find every conceivable nationality in Dallas, from Eritreans to Russians, from Brazilians to Slovenians, as well as the thousands of Britons who work and live here. The city has become a veritable melting pot, spiced with some of the most exotic races of the world, even if at the end of the day each one goes its separate way and to an area where other settlers of like cultural background congregate.

Dallasites, while among the friendliest people you will find anywhere in the nation, can also be clannish and reserved. While they will rub elbows with you at mega shopping centers, do not expect to find them crowding the sidewalks of downtown Dallas, except on workdays at lunchtime. If you should come from one of the great European cities, whether London, Paris, or Moscow, you will be startled at how empty the city seems. People just are not milling around, not even like in New York City's Manhattan. The oppressive heat in the hot summers may account for part of it. For another, Dallasites have lots of entertainment options in their large homes and see no pressing need to go out, except when going to work, to shop, to be entertained, or to eat. Particularly on weekends, they love to watch sports on television, surrounded by their favorite friends and snacks. Instead of walking outdoors to exercise, many are just as likely to do the same on equipment installed at home.

Only 5 percent of respondents to a poll by the *Dallas Morning News* said they lived in the Dallas area because "I find this region of the country attractive." And only 7 percent said they preferred Dallas to other cities.

While generous hosts and friendly when on foot, some Dallasites change colors faster than chameleons when behind the wheel. Beware particularly of those in pickups who will tailgate or cut ahead of you just as often as in any other American city.

Dallas Insight

Dallas: A major U.S. finance center with the largest exposition "in all of North America," having an airport larger than the island of Manhattan, the largest convention center in Texas, and the largest wholesale merchandise mart in the world.

Do you care that Dallas has "more shopping centers per capita than any other major U.S. city," that the McKinney Avenue Trolley is the "largest volunteer run system in the world," and that DFW "has more active runway space than all the major airports in Japan combined"?

The irrepressible Dallas also wants you to know that its Arboretum & Botanical Garden "features the largest public selection of azaleas in the U.S.," that its giraffe statue at the Dallas Zoo is "the tallest statue in Texas," and that the Dallas Parkland Hospital System is "the largest birthing center in the nation."

Dallas Cowboys are touted as "world" champions, even if it seems that only a couple of other countries in the entire world regularly play American-style football. Dallas Museum of Art is sometimes lauded as "world-class," even if few outside of Texas have even heard of it. Those are the kinds of statistics you will find bandied around every time you open a convention or visitors bureau flyer.

What they really suggest is that Dallas desperately wants to be a "world-class" city, even if few residents would ever agree on what "world-class" really means. In Dallas, it just might be the largest stadium, the tallest office building, or the world's largest bronze monument in the state of Texas, which loves to point out that it is "larger than the countries of France, Belgium, Holland, Switzerland, and Luxembourg combined."

One is tempted to dismiss this search for approval as just so much bragging brought about by insecurity. Dallas is such a young city that 50 years here implies history when 500 years is taken for granted elsewhere. Few would accuse Dallasites of being modest. Boosterism goes back to Dallas' youth when a number of its wealthy citizens gave selflessly of their time and expertise to advance the interests of their beloved Dallas, which had to struggle for every accomplishment since its founder John Neely Bryan set his foot here.

Dallas has 10,000 millionaires and 300,000 households with an annual income of at least $100,000 or a net worth of $500,000. It also has the sixth highest wealth concentration in the country. Dallasites, like so many Texans, dream of possessing the best of everything, whether a $2,000 fountain pen or a $5,000 watch. They love to impress you with their houses, cars, giant television screens, or cellular telephones that do everything but make coffee, and they cannot imagine that anybody could have a taller statue or a bigger State Fair.

But this boundless optimism does not work always to the city's liking. In 2001, Dallas lost Boeing for its corporate headquarters, although the city thought it had the company in its pockets. A few months later,

Big D was dropped from further consideration as a 2012 Olympic venue. "North Texas perceives itself as one of the world's leading regions," opines one *Dallas Morning News* columnist. "Others do not."

Neither is Dallas one of the racially more harmonious cities, although it has in the past escaped riots of the kinds that paralyzed Newark, New Jersey, or Los Angeles. White, black, and Hispanic citizens often accuse each other of racism, and it does not look like harmony will prevail any time soon. A few city council meetings are all you need to see on the evening news to draw your own conclusions about the Dallas political climate.

But there are also many, many defenders of Dallas, too.

DALLAS FACTS

Automobiles

More than 20,000 cars are stolen each year in Dallas County. Only Harris County, of which Houston is its seat, has more automobile thefts. About one-fifth of all the cars stolen in Texas are probably taken because the keys are left inside.

It is against the law in Texas to leave the keys in the ignition or the vehicle engine running. For more information visit the Texas Automobile Theft Prevention Authority's Web site, www.txwatchyourcar.com, or call (800) 227-9282.

Auto Insurance

The minimum liability insurance required in Texas is $20,000 for bodily injury per person, $40,000 per person for each accident, and $15,000 for property damage. You can be fined up to $1,000, have your driver's license suspended, and have your car impounded for up to 180 days if you cannot show a proof of insurance.

Your insurance company will issue a liability insurance card, which you must show in case of an accident or if a policeman asks for it. This card or a copy of your insurance policy must also be shown when you apply for or renew your car registration, your driver's license, and an inspection sticker.

Automobile Registration & Vehicle Inspection

Your vehicle must be registered within 30 days of your Texas residence and must pass inspection at a licensed station once a year. To register your car, you must submit a vehicle inspection certificate from an authorized car dealer, service station, or auto service center, along with your out-of-state title, and proof of liability insurance to the Dallas County tax office, at 500 Elm and Houston Streets downtown, (214) 653-7621/7811.

You can handle car registration, renewals, and property tax payments in person or, at additional cost, on the county's Web site, www.dallascounty.org, and can pay with a credit card. There is a charge for online car registration and renewal payments, while the fee for property taxes is about 3 percent of the total if paid by a credit card.

You can pay speeding tickets and other traffic violations on the county's Web site, www.tickets.dallascounty.org. Sheriff's deputies write about 7,000 tickets a month.

The emissions tests, part of a state vehicle inspection, are mandatory. Vehicles that are less than two years old and cars 24 years or older are exempt from smog testing. The tests are required of gasoline-powered vehicles registered in Collin, Dallas, Denton, and Tarrant Counties to remove some of the air pollution in the area.

The Dallas County offices are located at:

- 100 East Wheatland Rd. at Cockrell Hill Rd., in **Duncanville,** (972) 298-5885.
- 3443 St. Francis Ave. at R.L. Thornton Frwy., in **east Dallas,** (214) 321-2921.
- 10056 Marsh Ln. at Walnut Hill Ln., in **north Dallas,** (214) 904-3000.
- 2436 Valley View Ln. at Stemmons Frwy., in **Farmers Branch,** (972) 406-0427.
- 675 West Walnut St. at Glenbrook Dr., in **Garland,** (972) 494-0018.
- 525 West Hwy. 303, Suite 591, in **Grand Prairie,** (972) 264-2444.
- 530 North O'Connor Rd., in **Irving,** (972) 254-6102.
- 408 South Beckley Ave. at Jefferson Blvd., in **Oak Cliff,** (214) 943-7451.
- 516 Twilight Trail at Custer Rd. and Arapaho Rd. West, in **Richardson,** (972) 231-1459.

For more related information from the Texas Department of Transportation, please see also the Web site www.dot.state.tx.us.

To assist you with towing, battery charge, and other roadside emergencies, consider joining the **American Automobile Association,** (214) 526-7911 or (800) AAA-HELP. The AAA also provides tour books, maps, and discounts on car rentals and hotels. Established one hundred years ago and with more than 40 million members, it is the largest such organization. It now competes with other emergency road service providers, such as insurance companies, and extended car warranties.

AAA also offers banking, mortgages, and online travel services.

"Some wonder whether in trying to be all things to all its members, AAA has lost sight of what people sign up for in the first place—help when their car breaks down," observes the *Smart Money* financial monthly, noting that if it were a for-profit company, it would be ahead of Coca-Cola and Microsoft.

While AAA makes a lot of promises as to what it will do to help you in a roadside predicament, take such promises with a grain of skepticism, particularly if you need help at night. Having a cellular telephone is sometimes more important than being an AAA member.

In cities like Dallas, Fort Worth, and San Antonio, the Texas Department of Transportation maintains the **Freeway Courtesy Patrol,** a service paid for by taxpayers. The patrol will change a flat tire, help start your vehicle, call a tow truck for you, or help you get some gasoline. Call (214) 320-4444, or beeper at (214) 512-2726. The service hours in Dallas are Mon-Fri 4:30 AM-10 PM, Sat-Sun 9:30 AM-6 PM.

Oil @ Work, 11259 Goodnight Ln., Suite 1121, at Stemmons Frwy. North and Royal Ln. in northwest Dallas, (972) 481-1818, Internet www.oilatwork.com, is an on-site vehicle service company that has been favorably mentioned by *D Magazine*. It provides emergency services, such as a $40 spare tire mounting, as well as regular maintenance services, such as a $25 oil change, Monday through Friday 8 AM to 5:30 PM. Outside these hours there is a $25 surcharge.

Driver's Licenses

To obtain a Texas driver's license, you must either be 18 years old, or must be at least 16 years and have completed a certified driver's education program. You can take the driver's license test at one of these Dallas area locations of the Texas Department of Public Safety:

- 10233 East Northwest Hwy., between Plano and Jupiter Roads, (214) 553-0033.
- 721 Wynnewood Village, at West Illinois Ave. and Zang Blvd., (214) 948-7233.
- 2625 Old Denton Rd. and Trinity Mills Rd. in Carrollton, (972) 245-5800.

Other examination stations are located in Garland, Grand Prairie, Irving, and Plano.

A Texas driver's license must be renewed every four years. Renewals can only take place at the City Hall downtown, 1500 Marilla St., (214) 651-1859.

If you are a new Texas resident and hold a driver's license from another state, Texas law requires you to obtain a Texas license within 30 days of establishing your residency. When applying for your driver's license, take with you a certified copy of your birth certificate or a valid out-of-state driver's license or your passport, proof of insurance, and your Social Security card. You will have to pass both a visual test and a written examination. If you do not have a current driver's license, you will have to take a driving test.

For the first six months that teenagers are licensed, they are not allowed to drive between midnight and 5 AM, except to and from a job, for work on a family farm, or for school-related activities and medical emergencies. Minors can not carry passengers under 21 years of age, except for their brothers and sisters with their parents' permission.

Traffic Violations

The lowest fine in Dallas is $55 for jaywalking, one the highest $275 for speeding more than 20 miles (or 32 kilometers) over the limit in a school zone. Most other fines are $100 or more.

Fines of more than $200 can be issued for failure to surrender a drivers license to a police officer, possession of an altered or fake drivers license, lack of proof of car insurance, and speeding more than 20 miles over the limit in a non-school zone. Running a red light, improper lane change, improper turn, or failing to stop at a stop sign can cost $125 each.

You must contact the municipal court by mail or in person within 21 days calendar days from the date of your citation. If you fail to do so, a warrant will be issued for your arrest, and the original fine will be increased by $60. For more information call (214) 670-0109.

Payments of fines can be made in person at:

- **Old City Hall,** 2014 Main St., Ground Floor; Mon-Fri 7 AM-6 PM. You also appear at this location to plead not guilty, then you will be notified by mail of your hearing date.
- **Lew Sterrett Justice Center,** 111 Commerce St., Ground Floor, 24 hours a day.
- **Martin L. King Center,** Core Bldg., 2922 Martin L. King Blvd., Mon-Fri 8:30 AM-8 PM.

Banks & Savings Institutions

Dallas is a leading banking center in the Southwest, although the framers of the Texas Constitution did not even want the state to have banks. Branch banking was not allowed until 1986, and home equity lending was prohibited until 1998. The Constitution had to be amended to allow home equity lending.

The largest area banks and savings institutions are mostly out-of-state banks, which bought nine of Texas' ten largest institutions, starting in the late 1980s, when nearly 400 banks went belly up.

Bank of America (Home office Charlotte, NC), 901 Main St., 67th Floor, Dallas, (888) 279-3247 or (214) 209-0630, Internet www.bankofamerica.com. It has almost one-quarter of the D/FW market share, local deposits of about $14 billion, 140 local branches, and about 8,000 local employees.

Bank One (Chicago, IL), 1717 Main St., Dallas, (214) 290-2700, Internet www.bankone.com. It has a D/FW market share of 16 percent, local deposits of about $10 billion, 70 branches, and about 5,300 local employees.

J.P. Morgan Chase (New York, NY), 2200 Ross Ave., Dallas, (214) 965-2300 Internet www.chase.com. It has a D/FW market share of nearly 8 percent, local deposits of about $5 billion, 40 branches, and about 4,400 local employees.

Wells Fargo Bank Texas (San Francisco), 1445 Ross Ave., Suite 300, Dallas, (800) 869-3557, Internet www.wellsfargo.com. It has a D/FW market share of 6 percent, deposits of about $4 billion, 100 local branches, and 2,500 local employees.

Washington Mutual Bank (Seattle, WA), 6341 East Campus Circle, Irving, (972) 714-7477, Internet www.wamu.com. It has deposits of about $3 billion, 100 branches, and 1,200 local employees.

Compass Bank (Birmingham, AL), 8080 North Central Exwy., Dallas, (214) 706-8000, Internet www.compassweb.com. It has deposits of about $2 billion, 33 local branches, and 700 employees.

Comerica Bank-Texas (Detroit, MI), 1601 Elm St., Dallas 75265, (214) 589-1400, Internet www.comerica.com. It has deposits of $2 billion, 30 local branches, and about 950 local employees.

Guaranty Bank (Dallas), 8333 Douglas Ave., Dallas, (214) 360-3360, Internet www.guarantygroup.com. It has deposits of about $1.85 billion, 23 local branches, and 700 local employees.

Chambers of Commerce

Dallas Black Chamber of Commerce (1,500 member firms), 2838 Martin Luther King Jr. Blvd., (214) 421-5200, Internet www.dbcc.org.

Dallas Northeast Chamber of Commerce (500 member firms), 6260 East Mockingbird Ln., (214) 828-1400, Internet www.dallasnortheastchamber.net.

DeSoto Chamber of Commerce (690 member firms), 205 East Pleasant Run Rd., DeSoto, (972) 224-3565, Internet www.desotochamber.org.

Denton Chamber of Commerce (925 member firms), P.O. Drawer 1719, Denton, (940) 382-9693, Internet www.denton-chamber.org.

Flower Mound Chamber of Commerce (725 member firms), 700

Parker Square; (972) 539-0500, Internet www.flowermoundchamber.com.

French-American Chamber of Commerce (200 member firms), 2665 Villa Creek Dr., Dallas, (972) 241-0111.

Frisco Chamber of Commerce (1,200 member firms), 6843 Main St., Suite 1041, Frisco, (972) 335-9522, Internet www.friscochamber.com.

Garland Chamber of Commerce (600 member firms), 914 South Garland Ave., Garland, (972) 272-7551, Internet www.garlandchamber.com.

Grand Prairie Chamber of Commerce (555 member firms), 900 Conover Dr., (972) 264-1558, Internet www.grandprairiechamber.org.

Greater Dallas Asian American Chamber of Commerce (1,000 member firms), 11171 Harry Hines Blvd., Suite 115, (972) 241-8250, Internet www.gdaacc.com.

Greater Dallas Chamber of Commerce (3,800 member firms), Plaza of the Americas, North Building, 700 Pearl St., 12th Floor, (214) 746-6600, Internet www.dallaschamber.org. This is the largest Metroplex chamber, serving eight counties, with minimum annual dues of $350 and a yearly budget of about $7 million. The facility includes a 5,000-square-foot (or 464-square-meter) executive center. Albert Black (b. 1959) is its first African-American board chairman, and former Dallas city manager Jan Hart Black (no relation) is its president.

Greater Dallas Hispanic Chamber of Commerce (1,600 member firms), 4622 Maple Ave., (214) 521-6007, Internet www.gdhcc.com. This is one of the largest chambers in the area, serving Dallas and Fort Worth.

Greater Irving-Las Colinas Chamber of Commerce (1,200 member firms), 3333 North MacArthur Blvd., Irving, (972) 252-8484, Internet www.irvingchamber.com.

Lewisville Chamber of Commerce (850 member firms), 551 North Valley Pkwy., Lewisville, (972) 436-9571, Internet www.lewisvillechamber.org.

McKinney Chamber of Commerce (980 member firms), 1801 West Louisiana, McKinney, (972) 542-0163, Internet www.mckinneytx.org.

Mesquite Chamber of Commerce (700 member firms), 617 North Ebrite St., (972) 285-0211, Internet www.mesquitechamber.com.

Metrocrest Chamber of Commerce (730 member firms), 1204 Metrocrest Dr., Carrollton, (972) 416-6600, Internet www.metrocrestchamber.com.

North Dallas Chamber of Commerce (800 member firms), 10707 Preston Rd., (214) 368-6485, Internet www.ndcc.org.

Oak Cliff Chamber of Commerce (980 member firms), 660 South Zang Blvd., Dallas, (214) 943-4567, Internet www.oakcliffchamber.org.

Plano Chamber of Commerce (1,450 member firms), 1200 East 15th St., Plano, (972) 424-7547, Internet www.planocc.org.

Richardson Chamber of Commerce (1,600 member firms), 411 Belle Grove, Richardson, (972) 234-4141, Internet www.telecomcorridor.com.

Churches

There are 18 pages of churches, synagogues, temples, and mosques listed in the SBC Communications' Dallas Yellow Pages directory. The *Wall Street Journal*'s Dallas real estate Internet page claims there are 1,446 religious institutions of various denominations located within the city.

The church with the largest congregation in Dallas is the Catholic Cathedral Santuario de Guadalupe (see entry in the SIGHTS & ATTRACTIONS chapter), with 50,000 members.

The **Potter's House** (Internet www.thepottershouse.org), at 6777 West Kiest Blvd., which tops a hill in the Mountain Creek area of southwestern Dallas, seats 8,200 in the main sanctuary and is one of the largest church halls in Texas. By comparison, Notre Dame in Paris seats 9,000.

Established in 1996 with 50 families, it employs close to 300 and draws on help from 1,500 volunteers. The two-acre (or 0.8-hectare) sanctuary with 90,000 square feet (or 8,361 square meters) of space cost more than $32 million to build. The non-denominational church reports a multicultural membership of more than 28,000, although 77 percent are African-Americans and 13 percent Caucasians. It is the house of worship of Bishop T. D. Jakes (b. 1957), the larger-than-life television preacher who moved his headquarters from West Virginia, where he was born and raised, in 1996.

According to the church's Web site, the young Jakes was "called" to the ministry at age 17, "and first began preaching part-time while a student at West Virginia State [University], where he was enrolled as a psychology major."

Jakes' congregation watches him preach as his image is projected onto two 400-square-foot (or 37-square-meter) screens on opposite sides of a huge stage. The sanctuary is also a full-broadcast studio, with services airing on both the Trinity Broadcasting Network and Black Entertainment Television. According to the *Dallas Morning News*, Dakes "has initiated programs that feed the homeless, assist the families of imprisoned men and women, and help AIDS sufferers." The bishop was quoted as saying: "Our goal is not to be rich, but to mine the treasures that every individual has inside."

Governor George Bush, Vice President Al Gore, Coretta Scott King, former Dallas mayor Ron Kirk, and television evangelist Pat

Robertson have all attended ceremonies, dedications, or services at the nondenominational church.

Potter's House congregation is followed in size by four Catholic churches: St. Cecilia of Dallas and St. Elizabeth Ann Seton in Plano, both with 20,000 parishioners each, and St. Edward in Dallas, and St. Mark's Catholic in Plano with 19,000. Prestonwood Baptist Church in Plano has a sanctuary that seats 6,500 and has about 18,000 members.

Concealed Arms

Texas is one among more than 40 states that allow residents to carry concealed handguns.

Legal residents of Texas, at least 21 years old, not convicted of a felony, not addicted to drugs, of sound mind, and meeting ten other eligibility requirements, can apply for a license to carry a concealed handgun. They must undergo at least ten hours of classroom instruction on gun law and safety and pay a $140 fee. The total cost of a permit generally runs more than $300.

There are now more than 250,000 such permit holders in Texas, or a bit over 1 percent of the state residents, 90 percent white and mostly males. About 10 percent of them are Dallas County residents.

With more gun shows and licensed firearms retailers and manufacturers than any other state, Texans have perhaps the easiest access to guns. Almost one-half of all Texans claim to own a gun. The state passed a right-to-carry law in 1995. Since then, many cities and counties have posted signs saying firearms are prohibited on their property, including city hall, parks, and buses. Under the state's concealed weapons law, guns are not allowed in bars, prisons, amusement parks, or at high school, collegiate, or professional sporting events. In bars and prisons, carrying such a weapon is a felony; all other violations are a misdemeanor.

If you need training to obtain such a permit, try **D/FW Gun Range & Training Center,** 1601 West Mockingbird Lane, (214) 630-4866, Internet www.dfw-gun.com. This indoor facility has 14 shooting lanes. Formal instruction is available.

The catalyst for the concealed arms law in Texas might have been a lunatic who in October 1991 rammed a truck through the window of a Luby's cafeteria (see listing) in Killeen, southwest of Dallas, killing 23 diners and wounding another 21, until then the nation's deadliest mass shooting ever.

In 2002, the U.S. Justice Department asserted to the U.S. Supreme Court that the Constitution "broadly protects the rights of individuals" to own firearms, reversing decades of governmental policy on the meaning of the Second Amendment. One million hunters are also licensed in Texas.

Corporate Metroplex

The following are the largest publicly owned companies headquartered in the Metroplex, all with revenues exceeding $3 billion. Only the number of local employees is shown here. The symbol in parenthesis is the company's stock symbol.

The 100 largest companies in the Metroplex—a geographical area that usually includes Collin, Dallas, Denton, and Tarrant counties, sometimes also Ellis and Kaufman Counties—all have revenues of more than $175 million a year, and the top 150 area firms have sales of at least $50 million annually.

Mexico is the state's largest export market for goods totaling up to $45 billion a year, or almost one-half of all exports, followed by Canada, Taiwan and Japan, Singapore, and the United Kingdom. In 2002, Texas actually outsold California and New York, the nation's largest exporting states. Texas exports approach $90 billion and include electronic equipment, industrial machinery and computers, chemicals and transportation equipment. Exports to Europe are close to $9 billion. The Metroplex exports more than $11 billion worth of goods.

Exxon Mobil Corp. (XOM), 5959 Las Colinas Blvd., Irving, (972) 444-1000, Internet www.exxon.mobil.com. Revenues $205 billion, 1,300 local employees. An integrated oil company and by *Forbes* measure the nation's third largest corporation that is also one of the biggest in the world. ExxonMobil is in fact larger than the economies of Pakistan, Peru, or New Zealand.

After Triton Energy was bought out by New York-based Amerada Hess in 2001, only Exxon Mobil was left in Dallas, the city that for decades was associated with oil and gas and, in the minds of naive foreigners, with J. R. Ewing from the television soap opera *Dallas*. The industry has been consolidating in Houston since the collapse of oil prices in the 1980s, and Texas' largest city is now the energy capital of the United States.

Dallas prospered because it was a financial center and only 120 miles (or 193 kilometers) west of Kilgore. A 70-year-old wildcatter, Columbus Marion "Dad" Joiner, discovered oil on October 3, 1930, on a farm eight miles (or 12.9 kilometers) south of Kilgore that was owned by the widow Daisy Bradford. Seventeen dry holes had already been drilled there before him.

As the East Texas field became the largest in the world, Haroldson

Lafayette Hunt of Dallas stepped in, and the Dallas economy shifted from cotton to oil. Dallas, with about 12,000 oil-related jobs, is now in fourth place nationwide, behind Houston, New Orleans, and Oklahoma City. The closest oil pump in Dallas County is probably the one in front of the Hard Rock Café (see entry) on McKinney Avenue, but it is just a decorative piece.

After 107 years in New York, Exxon in 1989 announced it would relocate its corporate headquarters to Irving, Texas. That same year, the *Exxon Valdez* tanker ran aground and 11 million gallons of crude oil invaded Prince William Sound in Alaska, damaging wildlife, livelihoods, and the company's well-maintained public image. The court battles ended with a $5-billion punitive-damage award against the company in 1995, although it was later reduced. In 1997, Exxon and Mobil merged in what became the nation's largest publicly held oil company, which now has revenues below Wal-Mart Stores.

J.C. Penney Company Inc. (JCP), 6501 Legacy Dr., Plano, (972) 431-1000, Internet www.jcpenney.com. Revenues $33 billion, 10,850 local employees.

The one-time icon of Middle America, which was 100 years old in 2002, the department store chain also owns Eckerd drug stores, the fourth-largest drugstore chain in the United States. When measured by sales, it is one of the 50 largest companies in the country.

Electronic Data Systems Corp. (EDS), 5400 Legacy Dr., Plano, (972) 604-6000, Internet www.eds.com. Revenues $22 billion, 8,200 local employees. Provides information services. Controlled by General Motors, this is one of the country's 100 largest firms.

The EDS story is as familiar in Dallas as its creator: When H. Ross Perot (b. 1930) sold his yearly quota of IBM computers in 1962 by mid-January, he quit the Big Blue and started EDS on his 32nd birthday on an investment of $1,000 from his wife's savings. Within a few years he employed 300. EDS went public with stock priced at 118 times its earnings, and three dozen employees became instant millionaires. Perot owned 78 percent of the company worth $1.5 billion when EDS went public in 1968. The company's stock shot to $162 two years later.

In 1969, Perot gained notoriety by spending $4 million to personally deliver Christmas gifts to prisoners of war in North Vietnam and show how badly they were treated. Ten years later, the Texarkana, Texas-born Perot became even better known for his daring rescue of two of his EDS employees from Ayatollah Khomeini's Iran.

Ross Perot sold the company to General Motors for $2.55 billion in cash and stock, and a seat on the GM board in 1984. Two years later, the GM board paid Perot twice the stock's market value for his 11.3 million shares. He accepted and tooled around in his 1984 Oldsmobile. Perot's few extravagances included purchasing the John Neely Bryan deed for the land that became Dallas and William B. Travis's February 24, 1836, letter from the Alamo, asking for reinforcements and exclaiming, "I shall never surrender or retreat."

In 1988, Perot the elder started a new company, **Perot Systems** (Internet www.perotsystems.com), which provides information technology services and business solutions to the health care, financial and industrial services, hospitality and telecommunications industries. It grew to become one of the 40 largest corporations in the Metroplex, with revenues of $1.3 billion and 1,400 local employees. Its stock opened at $16 a share, zoomed to $43.50 on the first day, and reached an all-time high of $85.75 a share.

The elder Perot's wealth is valued at about $3.7 billion, according to *Forbes* magazine, which would make him one of the 100 richest people in the world and one of the top three Texans. His palatial 20-acre (or eight-hectare) walled estate on Strait Lane in Dallas was appraised at $19.7 million, but Perot appealed and "succeeded in knocking $2.7 million off the original appraisal," according to the *Dallas Observer*.

"He is adorable, like a little Brooks Brothers ventriloquist dummy," writes in *Forbes* the creative fashion director for Barneys New York in a feature story, titled "America's Best-Dressed Billionaires." Perot Sr. told the magazine that his tidy appearance helped him win the heart of his future wife, Margot.

In 2000, Ross Perot Jr. (b. 1959), the oldest of his five children and the only son, was installed as president and chief executive officer of Perot Systems. The younger Perot is a 1981 business administration graduate of Vanderbilt University. He and another man completed the first circumnavigation of the world by helicopter in 29 days the following year. In 1983, Perot joined the U.S. Air Force.

Ross Perot Jr. is, however, better known as developer of the Alliance Airport, which is surrounded by a 9,600-acre (or 3,885-hectare) industrial park in far Fort Worth. Some 100 companies now have their distribution and manufacturing operations there.

Hillwood, a company he founded in 1988, is developing Circle T Ranch in northeast Tarrant County, a 2,500-acre (or 1,011-hectare), mixed-use corporate campus and residential development, with homes starting at $450,000. A 2,300-acre (or 930-hectare) Heritage development is also nearby. Hillwood Development Corp. and its subsidiaries control 8,953 acres (or 3,623 hectares), "the largest chunk of Tarrant County's undeveloped land," according to the *Fort Worth Star-Telegram*. That is more than even the billionaire Bass family of Fort Worth, which owns 6,800 acres (or 2,752 hectares).

Perot Jr. was also instrumental in realizing the Victory mixed-use development adjacent to the American Airlines Center (see entry) in downtown Dallas.

AMR Corporation (AMR), 4333 Amon Carter Blvd., Fort Worth, (817) 963-1234, Internet www.amrcorp.com. Revenues $16 billion, 25,000 local employees, and 100,000 worldwide. The holding company for American Airlines and American Eagle Airlines. By its revenues, it is one among the 100 or so nation's largest companies. American serves more than 100 cities directly.

The airline lost a record $3.51 billion in 2002 alone and had to lay off thousands of employees, many as a result of the September 11, 2001, terrorist bombings. The airline's employees in 2003 agreed to a six-year contract that saved the company $1.6 billion in wage and benefits cuts. Thousands of jobs were eliminated, and the carrier was losing $5 million a day. AMR's stock, which stood at nearly $33 a share in 1998, dropped to $1.25 following a delisting from the Standard & Poor's 500 index in 2003. Meanwhile, AMR was paying the Dallas Mavericks and Dallas Stars $6.5 million a year for the right to name the American Airlines Arena (see entry), the most expensive such facility in the United States.

Kimberly-Clark Corp. (KMB), 351 Phelps Dr., Irving, (972) 281-1200, Internet www.kimberly-clark.com. Revenues $14 billion, 650 local employees. Manufactures household and personal care products. By *Forbes*' measure, this is one of nation's 100 largest corporations.

Kimberly-Clark—along with the Container Store (see below), TDIndustries, Beck Group, community-owned health care company VHA, Alcon Laboratories, and Texas Instruments—has been named one of *Fortune*'s "100 Best Companies to Work For."

Halliburton Co. (HAL), 3600 Lincoln Plaza, Dallas, (713) 759-2600, Internet www.halliburton.com. Revenues $13 billion, 1,400 local employees. An oilfield services, construction, and engineering company, one among the 150 largest in the United States, with operations in 100 countries.

Earle P. Halliburton founded Halliburton Oil Well Cementing Co. in 1919 in Duncan, Oklahoma. The company went public in 1948, and in 1961, after his death, moved its headquarters to Dallas. Halliburton, which has 14,000 employees in Houston, was in the process of moving its corporate headquarters there.

The stark wedge-shaped 1984, 45-story Lincoln Plaza building housing Halliburton may have borrowed its saw-tooth window bays style and granite skin from the Bank of America in San Francisco. With 1.1 million square feet (or 102,190 square meters) of space, it is one of the 15 largest office buildings in Dallas. It was bought by the California State Teachers Retirement System for $126 million in 1999.

AdvancePCS (ADVP), 750 West John Carpenter Fwy., Irving, (469) 524-4700, Internet www.advancepcs.com. Revenues 13 billion, 1,500 local employees. Provides pharmacy benefits management services for large employers and health plans. By sales, one of the 120 largest companies in the nation.

7-Eleven Inc. (SE), 2711 North Haskell Ave., Dallas, (214) 828-7011, Internet www.7-eleven.com. Revenues $10 billion, 3,370 local employees. Operates more than 6,000 7-Eleven convenience stores, 230 of them located in the Metroplex.

This is one of the nation's 220 largest companies. IYG Holding Co., a unit of Ito-Yokado Group. of Japan, and Seven-Eleven Japan hold 90 percent of 7-Eleven common shares.

(For more details about 7-Eleven, please see also entry Cityplace in the SIGHTS & ATTRACTIONS chapter.)

TXU Corporation/Oncor Group (TXU), Energy Plaza, 1601 Bryan St., Dallas, (214) 812-4600, Internet www.txu.com. Revenues $10 billion, 7,200 local employees. A utility holding company previously known as Texas Utilities and among the 65 or so largest American companies.

Aside from Texas, the company also had operations in the United Kingdom, where it was once the third largest utility. Its troubled British operations, acquired for $11 billion in 1998 and sold four years later for $2 billion, caused the stock to drop 70 percent in October 2002, when the dividend was slashed by 80 percent.

Oncor Group is the energy-delivery affiliate of TXU Corp. that maintains the company's transformers and power lines. TXU, which owns this building, is one of the 90 largest American companies. The 49-story, 1.1 million-square-foot (or 102,190-square-meter) 1983 building in which it is housed was designed by Henry Cobb, an I. M. Pei partner.

Dean Foods Co. (DF), 2515 McKinney Ave., Dallas, (214) 303-3400, Internet www.deanfoods.com. Revenues $9 billion, 1,600 local employees. Manufactures and distributes dairy products. The company merged with Suiza Foods, the nation's largest processor of dairy products, in 2002, but retained the Dean Foods name.

Burlington Northern Santa Fe Corp. (BNI), 2650 Lou Menk Dr., Fort Worth, (817) 867-6427, Internet www.bnsf.com. Revenues $9 billion, 3,400 local employees. A railroad and transportation company that is by sales also among the 200 largest corporations in the United States.

Fleming Companies Inc. (FLM), 1945 Lakepointe Dr., Lewisville, Internet www.fleming.com. Revenues $9 billion, 1,700 local employees. One of the nation's largest wholesale grocery distributors.

Founded in 1915, the company experienced turbulence with the 2002 bankruptcy of Kmart—with whom it had a ten-year, sole-supplier contract—after which its stock traded at a 30-year low. Fleming filed for bankruptcy protection in 2003, when its shares were priced at less than 50 cents.

Texas Instruments Inc. (TXN), 12500 TI Blvd., Dallas, (800) 336-5236, Internet www.ti.com. Revenues $8.5 billion, 10,200 local employees. Semiconductors manufacturer that contributes millions of dollars every year toward the arts and other charitable causes in the area. Texas Instruments is one of about 225 largest companies in the country.

On December 6, 1941, Cecil Howard Green, Eugene McDermott, J. Erik Jonsson, and H. Bates Peacock bought a Dallas company called Geophysical Service Inc. GSI was working on seismic exploration for oil, but moved into electronics during World War II, when it began making submarine detection devices and radars.

Ten years later, the company changed its name to Texas Instruments and retained the Geophysical Service name for one of its subsidiaries. The following year it entered the semiconductor business, and in 1954 it produced the first pocket-sized transistor radio. In 1958, TI developed the integrated circuit that made possible a new range of electrically controlled machines.

The company went public on October 1, 1953 at $5.25 per share, and by May 1960 its shares were trading at $210 a share. As a result of this windfall, the British-born Cecil Green (1900-2003) alone among the founders gave away more than $200 million to academic and medical institutions.

Another well-known TI employee is Jack St. Clair Kilby who, along with Fairchild Semiconductor's Robert Noyce, invented the integrated circuit in 1958. Noyce (d. 1990) co-founded Intel Corp. and became a billionaire. Kilby became TI's deputy director for semiconductor research, developed the company's well-known calculators, and lived comfortably on a six-figure salary. He received the Nobel Prize in 2000 for his integrated circuit invention. (For more about Kilby, please see the section 1960s in the chapter DALLAS PAST.)

The Metroplex claims about 90,000 high-technology jobs at 4,000 firms like TI, according to *Newsweek* magazine. The Telecom Corridor along Route 75 between Dallas and Richardson houses some 700 telecom companies.

Another Texas Instruments luminary is Sanjiv Sidhu (b. 1957). He took a job at Texas Instruments' artificial intelligence laboratory in 1984, but quit four years later and began writing software code in his small Dallas apartment.

He controls about one-half of the Farmers Branch-based software manufacturer, **i2 Technologies** (ITWO), a global provider of intelligent e-business solutions with almost 1,000 employees locally. Sidhu, the son of an Indian government chemist, competes with the likes of Oracle and the German company SAP.

While i2's shares traded as high as a stock split-adjusted $111.75 a share in the dot-com heyday, they sold below $1 a share in 2002-03. With an estimated net worth going into the billions before the 2002 stock market crash, Sidhu, was one among the wealthiest Dallasites during the late 1990s. By 2003, i2 slashed its workforce by almost one-half, and Sidhu fell off of *Forbes*' list of the 400 richest Americans.

Centex Corp. (CTX), 2728 North Harwood St., Dallas, (214) 981-5000, Internet www.centex.com. Revenues $8 billion, 2,950 local employees. Homebuilding, construction, and financial services.

Centex is one among half a dozen of the Metroplex's highest rated new homebuilders in an annual survey of 6,300 homebuyers in four counties conducted by J. D. Power and Associates. The top four builders, based on their customer service, home readiness, and quality workmanship were the Dallas-based independent Huntington, Fox & Jacobs, Pulte, and Highland, another local builder. Nineteen other local builders, including D. R. Horton (see entry below), received marks at or below the average ranking. Since homebuilding is unlicensed in Texas, the Power survey is one of the few yardsticks to measure the quality of local builders.

Built by Centex, the headquarters ten-story building that it leases from Harwood International real estate company (Internet www.harwoodinternational.com), is one of the nation's most energy-efficient office buildings. It was designed by architect Richard Keating of Los Angeles and completed in 1996. The four-building, one-million-square-foot (or 92,900-square-meter) office park here, known as Harwood International Center, is "one of the most finely conceived and executed pieces of architecture in the Metroplex," according to one local architect. The development is among the ten largest in the Metroplex.

There are interesting historical exhibits in the Harwood building next to Centex's. Marie Gabrielle restaurant, which is open for breakfast and lunch, is located in the Centex lobby.

D. R. Horton Inc. (DHI), 1901 Ascension Blvd. Suite 100, Arlington, (817) 856-8200, Internet www.drhorton.com. Revenues $7 billion, 5,700 local employees. The nation's largest builder of single-family homes starting at about $85,000 is considering moving to Fort Worth.

The company was founded by Don Horton in 1978 with a $3,000 loan and a starter home in south Fort Worth. It caters to the entry-level and first time move-up home buyers, building and selling homes under the names D. R. Horton, Arappco, Cambridge, Continental, Dietz-Crane, Dobson, Emerald, Melody, Milburn, Regency, Schuler, SGS Communities, Stafford, Torrey, Trimark, and Western Pacific in 20 states and 45 markets.

In 2002, Horton surpassed Wall-Mart's record of 99 consecutive quarters of increased earnings, but celebrations were minimal because "frivolity of any sort is a rare occurrence for the self-described lean operator, which has its national headquarters in an old strip-shopping center," according to the *Fort Worth Star-Telegram.* "We don't have company planes. We don't fly first-class. We don't have any company cars," says the firm's president. "If you need those kinds of things, you pay for them yourself."

Southwest Airlines Co. (LUV), 2702 Love Field Dr., Dallas, (214) 792-4000, Internet www.southwest.com or www.iflyswa.com. Revenues $5.5 billion, 6,000 local employees. The nation's third largest airline and one of the 300 largest companies.

Southwest was the only major airline to make money in 2001, when the industry, dealing with fear of terrorist bombings, lost billions of dollars. Until 2002, Southwest posted 29 consecutive years of profits and was in its 31-year history of never laying off employees because of economic reasons. That year, it was the only major American airline still making profits.

(For a history of Southwest Airlines, please see also Dallas Love Field Airport in the TRANSPORTATION chapter.)

Blockbuster Inc. (BBI), 1201 Elm St., Dallas, (214) 854-3000, Internet www.blockbuster.com. Revenues $5.5 billion. Occupying eight floors of the Renaissance Tower downtown, it has 4,000 local employees. Rents and sells videos, DVDs, and games.

Founded in Dallas as a one-store operation in 1985, Blockbuster now has 7,800 video rental stores worldwide, including about 5,200 in the United States. Blockbuster is controlled by Viacom Inc., one of the world's largest media companies.

RadioShack Corp. (RSH), West Belknap St. at North Henderson, Fort Worth, (817) 415-3700, Internet www.radioshack.com. Revenues $4.5 billion, 4,400 local employees. Operates the RadioShack nationwide retail chain.

RadioShack was slated to relocate to its 31-acre (or 12.5-hectare) headquarters with 900,000 square feet (or 83,610 square meters) of office space in three six-story buildings in late 2004. It was to include a flagship RadioShack store and a 2,700-car company parking garage. The property, formerly a public housing complex known as Ripley Arnold, situated on a 100-foot (or 30-meter) slope to the Trinity River, was purchased for $20 million. A man-made Town Lake was to be created where the Clear Fork and West Fork of the Trinity meet.

The company's beginnings go back to 1919, when David Tandy and Norton Hinckley founded a leather, belt, and shoe-repair business. The men split up in 1950, and the Tandys continued as American Hide & Leather Co., with Tandy Leather as a subsidiary. Having relocated to Fort Worth, the company changed its name to Tandy Corp. and listed its stock on the New York Stock Exchange in 1960.

Three years later, Tandy bought 62 percent of the struggling Radio Shack Corp. nine-store electronics retailer in Boston.

The company launched the first personal computer, the TRS-80, using BASIC software, written by a young programmer named Bill Gates of Seattle, in August 1977. Although it was priced at $600 for 4KB RAM, 4 KB ROM, with a black-and-white video display, the company sold 10,000 during the first month alone and more than 200,000 in the first four years. A TRS-80 is included in the American History Museum collection at the Smithsonian Institution.

In 2000, Tandy shed its founder's name and was renamed RadioShack Corp. in favor of its 7,100 electronics stores.

Neiman Marcus Group Inc. (NMG.A), 1618 Main St., Dallas, (214) 741-6911, Internet www.neimanmarcus.com. Revenues $3 billion, 3,800 Metroplex employees. High-end specialty retailer. (For more about Neiman Marcus, please see also the SHOPPING chapter.)

The Canadian telecommunications giant **Nortel Networks** (Internet www.nortelnetworks.com) with 4,700 local employees, the Finnish telecommunications firm **Nokia Americas** (Internet www.nokia.com) with 3,600 local employees, and the French voice and data networking equipment manufacturer **Alcatel** (Internet www.alcatel.com) with 2,600 local employees, are the largest Metroplex subsidiaries of foreign companies.

They are followed by the Swiss orthopedic pharmaceuticals manufacturer **Alcon Laboratories** (Internet www.alconlabs.com), the Mexico-based **Bimbo Bakeries USA** (Internet www.bimbobakeriesusa.com), and the Mexico-controlled computer retailer **CompUSA** (Internet www.compusa.com).

The Japanese telecommunications firm **Fujitsu** (Internet www.fnc.fujitsu.com), the Canadian-owned transportation firm **Greyhound Lines Inc.** (Internet www.greyhound.com), and the Swedish telecommunications giant **Ericsson** (Internet www.ericsson.com) round out the list. They all employ at least 1,600 in the Metroplex.

Smaller foreign-owned subsidiaries here include the Swiss semiconductors manufacturer **STMicroelectronics** (Internet www.st.com), the French **Accor Economy Lodging** (Internet www.accorhotels.com), the Japanese telecommunications giant **NEC America** (Internet www.necamerica.com), and the French optical lenses manufacturer **Essilor of America** (Internet www.essilor.com).

European direct investment in Texas exceeds $60 billion, out of $890 billion nationwide.

The largest privately owned firm in the Metroplex, according to *Forbes*, is **Sammons Enterprises Inc.** (Internet www.sammonsenterprises.com), an industrial equipment and insurance firm founded in 1962, with revenues of $3 billion and 3,100 local employees. Sammons is also one of the 50 largest private companies in the nation.

It is followed by **Kinko's Inc.,** (800) 2-KINKOS, Internet www.kinkos.com, which relocated from California to the Galleria complex in far-north Dallas in 2001.

Founded in 1970 by a college graduate, who named it after his nickname, Kinko now has revenues of $2 billion, 1,165 locations in nine countries, and about 750 in the Metroplex. The company offers 24-hour services, including printing, binding, computer rentals, and document management.

Texas native and an MBA holder from Harvard, David Kusin, the older brother of Kinko's president Gary Kusin, created and patented the Kusin Classification Code, a Dewey Decimal-like system for fine artwork. His company can provide the going rate for most of the best-known artists during the last 15 years so auction houses can determine reasonable estimates for their bidding catalogs.

Kinko's is followed by independent bottler, **Dr Pepper/Seven Up Bottling Group,** (214) 530-5000, a firm with sales close to $2 billion and 950 local employees. The Addison-based **Glazer's Wholesale Distributors** (Internet www.glazers.com) follows with slightly smaller revenues and 3,900 local employees.

Next is **Hunt Oil** (Internet www.huntoil.com) and affiliated companies, with oil and gas interests managed through the Hunt Consolidated holding company. Hyatt hotels are also controlled by the scion of the oil family.

Mary Kay Cosmetics, (972) 687-6300, Internet www.marykay.com—with cosmetics sales of close to $2 billion in 33 countries and 2,000 local employees—is run by her son Richard Rogers. The great majority of the employees are women. (For more about Mary Kay, please see entry in the SIGHTS & ATTRACTIONS chapter.)

These are followed by **Dresser Inc.** (Internet www.dresser.com), which manufactures engineered equipment for the energy industry, **Builders FirstSource Inc.** (Internet www.buildersfirstsource.com), supplier of structural materials to home builders, and **VarTec Telecom** (Internet www.vartec.com), a local and long-distance telephone services company.

Next is **Minyard Food Stores Inc.** (Internet www.minyards.com), a privately held Coppell grocer, having more than 70 stores with sales of $1 billion and 5,800 employees. It is run by Liz Minyard and Gretchen Minyard Williams, making it the largest Metroplex company run by women. Each of the two women owns one-third of the supermarket chain, with Bob Minyard owning the remainder.

One local company that is consistently at the top of the *Fortune* magazine list of the best companies to work for is the Dallas-based **Container Store** (Internet www.containerstore.com), with 27 stores and $300 million in sales. A retailer of boxes and organizational products, it has about 1,680 employees, more than 60 percent of them women and 25 percent minorities. The privately held company was founded in 1978 by two men and has a friendly sales staff.

Simeus Foods International (Internet www.simeusfoods.com), owned by Dumas M. Simeus, is the largest African-American business in the area. Headquartered in Mansfield, it has revenues of $175 million and 325 employees.

Thos. S. Byrne Inc. (Internet www.tsbyrne.com), owned by John Avilla, is the largest Hispanic business in the Metroplex. The commercial general contracting and management business company has sales of $170 million and employs 150.

EDUCATION

As Texas governor Bill Clements (b. 1917) was about to leave office in 1983, he asked billionaire H. Ross Perot Sr. to head a committee on public education, set up to examine why Texas ranked 44th among the 50 states in the percentage of its students graduating from high school. The hearings ended the following year, and the committee issued 44 pages of proposals.

The committee recommended that every teacher pass a test of basic academic skills and that statewide testing of students take place. "But the reforms that created the most controversy were those that attacked Texas' most sacred institution next to the Alamo: high school football," writes one Perot biographer, noting that the proposal barred all students from participating in sports who did not maintain a grade of 70 or higher in all subjects.

The "No pass, no play" rule also demanded that practice be held after school, not during the academic day as was customary until then. Yet, the most resistance came from the parents, "the very people who should have been most outraged that their children were receiving second- and third-rate education." Fortunately, most reforms were adopted, although some have since been watered down.

"Most of all," claims the *Texas Monthly*, "Perot reforms changed the culture of education in Texas by putting the focus on measurable classroom achievement."

Be that as it may, Texas now ranks 48th in the nation in high school graduation rates. Only Arizona, with about 74 of every 100 students graduating, and Nevada with 78, rank lower.

Child Care Facilities

Although there are multiple pages of child care facilities for preschoolers and other schools listed in the Dallas Yellow Pages telephone directory, not many are what most parents desire. Visit as many as you can before you decide which one is best suited for your child.

In Dallas, day care expenses average $400 a month. Minneapolis, in contrast, averages $650 a month for a three-year-old placed in a private, for-profit day care center five days a week, eight hours a day.

Child Care Answers, (214) 631-2273, which is part of the 90-plus-year-old non-profit United Way-sponsored Child Care Group, can assist you in finding a day care facility for your tyke.

A church-affiliated day care facility that is uniformly praised for the quality of its child development program is the **Highland Park United Methodist Church Child Development Program,** 3300 Mockingbird Ln. at Hillcrest Ave., (214) 521-2600. It accepts all ages through kindergarten, but the cost is relatively high, and even after you join the church, it may take divine intervention to get your child into the program that has more applicants than the 250 it can accept. With more than 14,000 members, HPUMC is one of the largest United Methodist churches in the country This is one of only about 40 Dallas day care facilities accredited by the National Association for the Education of Young Children (NAEYC), Internet www.naeyc.org. Please see the Web site for more valuable details.

A high-priced alternative is available through **Creme de la Creme,** a chain of Colorado-based day care centers whose fees start at $1,000 a month. They boast computer labs, libraries, music and dance studios, gymnasiums, and interactive KREM-TV studios. The Plano Creme de la Creme is located at 5516 West Plano Pkwy., (972) 818-5736, Internet www.cremedelacreme.com, e-mail plano@cremedelacreme.com.

Among the day care facilities located in downtown Dallas is **Children's Courtyard,** 1200 Ross Ave. at North Field St., (214) 969-9424, located a block from the Fountain Place building (see entry), which accepts infants and children through preschool age.

First United Methodist Church, 1928 Ross Avenue at Harwood St., (214) 220-0453, situated across the street from the Dallas Museum of Art, accepts infants and children through age four.

Kareer Kids, 700 North Pearl, Suite 101, (214) 720-0168, situated inside Plaza of the Americas complex (see entry), accepts kids from infants through preschoolers.

Primary & Secondary Schools

With about 165,000 largely ethnic-minority students in some 218 schools, the **Dallas Independent School District** (DISD) is believed to be the tenth largest school district in the nation. It employs 10,500 teachers and 8,500 other workers, and has a budget of $1 billion.

About 58 percent of DISD students are Hispanic, 34 percent African-American, 6 percent Caucasian, and about 2 percent are Asian and American Indian. Some 170 schools are 90 percent or more black and Hispanic. "Most of the district's 11,000 white students are concentrated in a few racially balanced schools in North Dallas, East Dallas and Seagoville," reports the *Dallas Morning News*. In contrast, more than 83 percent of all students in Dallas public schools were Caucasian in 1955, more than 58 percent in 1970, almost 42 percent in 1976, 28 percent in 1982, and more than 20 percent in 1988.

The district spends about $6,000 per student for one school year, a few dollars less than nearby Fort Worth, which is slightly below the state average. The national average is about $6,835 a year. New Jersey and New York spend more than $10,000 per student. DISD teachers earn up to $60,000 a year for those with doctorate degrees.

Federal supervision of Dallas schools goes back to the Supreme Court's 1954 *Brown v. Board of Education* decision, which overturned the "separate but equal" doctrine upholding segregated schools. Integration of Dallas schools began in 1970, when an African-American construction worker and cab driver sued the Dallas school system to force it to let his black sons attend a nearby white school.

The initial resistance to desegregation, particularly the busing of African-American and Hispanic students into white neighborhoods, followed by an overwhelming dissatisfaction with the quality of education inside the DISD, led to an exodus of white families to the superior suburban schools that has yet to stop. Only 6 percent of DISD students are white.

The *Dallas Morning News* was of the opinion in 2002 that the district does not require federal supervision any longer. "With the minority student population in the Dallas schools now topping 93 percent," it said, "some assume the federal desegregation suit has long outlived its usefulness."

The U.S. District Judge overseeing the case agreed and ruled in June 2003 that segregation "no longer exists in the DISD."

Performance of Area Schools

The number of Dallas schools rated by the state as "low performing" (where more than 50 percent of students fail any portion of the Texas Assessment of Academic Skills test) fell from 28 in 2000 to 10 in 2001, and increased to 15 in 2002, still the most among Texas schools.

One hundred and twenty-nine Dallas schools were in the "acceptable" category (where at least 50 percent of students passed each section of the TAAS) in 2002, down from 154 in 2001.

The "recognized" category (in which at least 80 percent of the students passed the TAAS) numbered 40 schools, up from 32 in 2001, while the highest-rated "exemplary" category (in which at least 90 percent of the students and 90 percent of each student group—black, white, Hispanic, and economically disadvantaged—passed each section—reading, writing, and mathematics—on the TAAS test) rose to 27 in 2002, from 16 in 2001.

All of Carroll ISD's 11 schools and Highland Park ISD's seven schools earned the highest "exemplary" rating in 2002. Allen, Coppell, and Grapevine-Colleyville are also among the select few school districts in the area that have no schools in the bottom two of the four categories. For more about the Plano and Richardson schools, also among the best, please see below.

While federal supervision of Dallas schools continues, social promotions are rampant. "Social promotion," the *News* as so aptly put it, "is the practice of automatically passing students regardless of achievement." It is widespread, claim the critics, because the test requirement would supposedly "affect a large number of minority students, who tend to score lower on standardized tests than white students." A movement to end social promotions in Texas resulted in a law requiring students, beginning in 2003, to successfully complete a standardized test before advancing to the next grade. "In my experience as a parent," says a senior *Texas Monthly* editor, "there are two things wrong with Texas public schools. They need better principals—and they need better principles."

Texas public schools were not rated in the 2002-2003 school year so the state could adjust to a new, more stringent accountability system—known as Texas Assessment of Knowledge and Skills tests (or TAKS)-which includes a tougher standardized exam. "While Dallas students overall exceeded last year's performance on the old TAAS, DISD's passing rates [on the new TAKS tests] continued to lag behind the state's by 10 to 15 percentage points," the *News* reported in mid-2003. The Highland Park school district's passing rates on sections of the TAKS ranged from 92 percent to 100 percent.

The quality of education in Dallas has been one of the most contentious community issues in years, often pitting African-Americans against Hispanics, who are now the largest ethnic minority, but believe they are under-represented.

The National Center for Education Statistics, a research arm of the U.S. Department of Education, calculates the overall annual dropout rates for Dallas at 6.3 percent, while state officials claim it is 1.2 percent.

"Poorly negotiated contracts, overstocked warehouses, bloated management ranks and board micromanagement have contributed to the poor state of academics and finances in the Dallas school district," is how the *News* paraphrased a 494-page performance review of the DISD by the state, quoting the comptroller as saying: "You had bad management and bad leadership."

DISD Magnet High Schools

DISD maintains ten relatively respectable magnet high schools—where curriculum ranges from arts to business—seven middle school academies, six elementary schools for the gifted and talented, and the Skyline Center with 25 advanced academic and career clusters.

The magnet program started in 1976 because of a court desegregation order and remains in spite of the federal ruling declaring DISD desegregated in 2003. The court-ordered racial balance calls for a 32-percent Hispanic, 32-percent African-American, 32-percent Caucasian, 2-percent Asian, and 2-percent "other" racial composition.

Some magnet programs are freestanding schools, others function within a regular elementary, middle, or high school. Up to 5,000 students apply each year to magnet programs, but only half of them are accepted.

Among the most competitive magnet schools are Booker T. Washington High School for the Performing & Visual Arts, and the School for the Talented & Gifted at Townview Magnet Center.

Best Area Schools

All four elementary schools in the Highland Park Independent School District, which serves the towns of Highland Park and University Park, made the top-30 *D Magazine* list of the best among the 565 elementary schools in the Metroplex, with Armstrong Elementary being in first place.

"The secret of Highland Park's success is parental: mothers run the elementary school cafeteria programs; dads manage the sports support programs; fund-raising for school programs is nonstop," observes the monthly.

Not surprisingly, only one Dallas ISD elementary school, Everett DeGolyer, rated in the top 50.

Among the best public high schools in the area are Highland Park High School and Dallas' Booker T. Washington High. Irving's MacArthur and Nimitz High Schools are also above average. Highland Park was voted 14th among "the 100 best high schools in America" by *Newsweek* magazine in 2003.

Highland Park High is also known as the school from which "Hollywood sex symbol," Jayne Mansfield (1933-1967), who had moved to Dallas in 1939, graduated in 1950. "Dramatic art, in her opinion, is knowing how to fill a sweater," actress Bette Davis sniffed about the woman famous for her 40-inch bust. Mansfield died at age 34, when the car she was riding in slammed under an 18-wheeler near New Orleans, but her three children survived.

Robin Hood Law

Plano, Richardson, and Carrollton-Farmers Branch are also desirable school districts. They, as well as Highland Park and another 110 districts statewide, are wrestling with Robin Hood, the state law signed in 1993 by Gov. Ann Richards. "An egregious bit of socialism that levels public education to the lowest common denominator," *D Magazine* calls it. Robin Hood has been taking tax money from "property wealthy" districts and giving it to "property poor" districts whose property taxes are said to be insufficient to educate their children.

Until now, about 46 percent of the $26 billion a year for Texas schools came from the state, 50 percent from local property taxes, with the rest being federal funds. Texas school districts were considered property-rich if the value of their tax rolls divided by the number of students enrolled exceeded $305,000 per student.

About 400 of the 1,041 Texas public school districts were at or near the state-imposed tax rate cap of $1.50 per $100 for operating budgets in 2003. Of the nearly $11 billion in the state pot to finance public education, wealthy school districts contributed about $650 million.

Highland Park alone had to give away $56.4 million, or 62.1 percent of the district's $90.8 million property tax revenue in 2002.

"The Robin Hood strategy is forcing the Highland Park school district to send nearly half of its revenue to the state for distribution to other districts, a staggering drain that threatens to cripple exemplary programs," observed a *Dallas Morning News* editorial.

The Highland Park district pleaded with parents in 2001 to "raise $900,000 in individual contributions to pay for a three percent teacher raise" and again in 2002 to raise $400,000. The district began selling permanent naming rights to stadiums, auditoriums, tennis courts, and softball fields to bridge the financial gap.

Plano lost almost one-quarter of its school funds for the same reasons. Richardson ISD paid about $55 million in 2002, more than 20 percent of the district's operating budget. Eighty-four well-to-do Texas school districts had more than half a billion dollars of their property taxes taken away for the benefit of the remaining public schools.

The state Senate voted to pay for public education by increasing the state sales tax and establishing a new state property tax at 75 cents per $100 of assessed valuation. A provision would guarantee that districts not receive less money under the plan than they were previously getting from the state. Under the proposal, the state sales tax would increase from 6.25 percent to 7.25 percent, while local school property taxes would be sharply reduced. The Texas House rejected the plan in 2003.

Plano Independent School District (PISD); Enrollment hotline, (972) 519-8295, Internet www.pisd.edu, e-mail askpisd@pisd.edu.

For years, one of the most desirable school districts in the area, PISD encompasses 100 square miles (or 259 square kilometers) in the southwest corner of Collin County, including Plano, northern Dallas and Richardson, Parker and parts of Allen, Carrollton, and Murphy.

The district has 64 schools, with a total enrollment of nearly 50,700 and a budget exceeding $450,000. The cost per student is more than $6,000. There are 43 elementary schools with about 25,000 students and 11 middle schools with 7,000 students. PISD claims a total of 6,000 employees, among them 3,650 teachers and 120 principals.

Plano ISD, a small school district in comparison with the Dallas ISD, had 39 "exemplary" schools in 2002, up from 37 in 2001, and no "low-performing" schools in 2000, 2001, or 2002.

Plano's Bettye Haun, Matthews, Sigler, and Skaggs elementary schools are among the best in the area and the state, according to the nonprofit organization Just for Kids, as reported by the *Texas Monthly*. Plano East and Plano Senior have been named National Blue Ribbon Schools twice by the U.S. Department of Education.

The $19-million, 170-acre (or 69-hectare) Murphy Complex, a 9,800-seat athletic facility with an all-purpose track and football field in Murphy, a community just east of Plano, was completed in 2002.

The district provides bus transportation at no charge to students who live more than two miles (or 3.2 kilometers) from their assigned schools. District security guidelines require that all exterior doors of the school remain locked during the school day.

Your child's birth certificate, current immunization record signed by a physician, proof of Plano ISD residency, and social security card are required for enrollment. Children must be five years old on or before September 1 to be admitted to kindergarten, or six years old to attend first grade.

Richardson Independent School District (RISD), (469) 593-0000, Internet www.richardson.k12.tx.us. The district is located north of downtown Dallas and includes 38.5 square miles (or 100 square kilometers). Most of the city of Richardson and portions of Dallas and Garland are included in the district. Students attend schools in the areas where they reside. Some schools require uniforms.

Another highly rated Metroplex school district, although it has slipped in ratings over the years. RISD has an enrollment of 34,100 and a staff of 3,940 employees. It is composed of 35 elementary schools, nine junior high schools for grades 7-9, four high schools, and four magnet schools.

Richardson ISD had 13 "exemplary" schools in 2002, up from 12 in

2001, and, for a district that served for years as a yardstick in public education, a surprising two "low-performing" ones among its 52 schools, up from none in 2001.

Richardson's Brentfield, Lake Highlands, and Mohawk are considered among the best elementary schools in the state. James Bowie Elementary in Richardson was named a National Blue Ribbon School by the U.S. Department of Education in 2001, one of 13 schools so honored in the district.

Enrollment requirements at RISD are similar to Plano's, above.

A Special School

The Rise School of Dallas, St. Luke's Episcopal Church, 5923 Royal Lane near Preston Rd., (214) 373-4666, Internet www.riseschool.com. Located in north Dallas, just east of Dallas North Tollway, and behind the church.

The private, nonprofit preschool was established in 1997 to prepare children with disabilities, such as Down syndrome, for a normal kindergarten setting. The school accepts up to 50 children, some as young as 18 months, who are placed in one of the five classes. Music and speech therapy, as well as occupational and physical skills are provided.

The program is modeled after the Rise School of Tuscaloosa, in Alabama, and groups disabled children with other students. The Dallas school charges about $750 a month, about one-third of the real cost, with the difference made up through fund raising. More than 200 are said to be on the waiting list to be admitted to the school that utilizes five classrooms from St. Luke's Episcopal Church.

The first Rise School opened in 1974 at the University of Alabama. While the public schools are required to provide special-education services, Rise is the only private school in Dallas that serves toddlers.

Metroplex Private Prep Schools

A 1997 state law awards high school seniors in the top 10 percent of their class nearly automatic admission to the state's public colleges, including the University of Texas and Texas A&M. While the top-10-percent law accounts for less than half of the freshman class, in majors like business, most slots in the freshman class are filled by top-10-ranked students.

"The idea that every Texan has a birthright to become a Longhorn or an Aggie has vanished," observes the *Texas Monthly*, adding that, "Now, with the ten percent law, even really smart kids can't get in." For many, the preparatory schools are a way to gain such an admission.

The Dallas area private prep schools cost from $5,000 to $20,000 a year, often require a uniform, accept about half of applicants, and prepare their graduates for schools as lofty as Columbia, Cornell, Harvard, MIT, Princeton, Stanford, and Yale.

Bishop Dunne Catholic School (Est 1961), 3900 Rugged Dr. at Kiest Park, (214) 339-6561, Internet www.bdhs.org. Located on 22 wooded acres (or 8.9 hectares) in Oak Cliff, southwest of downtown Dallas.

A co-educational Catholic school with an enrollment of about 300, grades seven through 12. Tuition starts at $5,000, but more than a third of students qualify for loans and grants. There are annual registration, activity, facilities, books, and application fees. "Tuition must be paid up front by July 1." A payment plan is available at a finance charge of nearly 7 percent.

The student/teacher ratio is 20:1, and about one-half of the faculty has master's or doctorate degrees. They are among the lowest paid teachers in Dallas, yet feel rewarded by the success of their pupils. Uniforms are required.

Bishop Dunne has a good mix of ethnic diversity and intellectual ability, with 40 percent of the students being Hispanic and almost a third African-American. *D Magazine* calls it "an inner-city school," but "100 percent of all graduates go to college," and notes that it is "one of the most diverse and affordable private schools in the area." It has a good athletic program. Computers are widely available.

The school is named after Edward Joseph Dunne (1848-1910), the second Catholic bishop of Dallas, where he was installed in 1894. He invited the Sisters of Charity of St. Vincent de Paul to come to Dallas and establish a hospital that was completed in 1898.

Bishop Lynch Catholic High School (Est. 1963), 9750 Ferguson Rd. at Peavy Rd., (214) 324-3607, Internet www.bishoplynch.org. Located on 22 acres (or 8.9 hectares) east of White Rock Lake in northeast Dallas.

A private, co-educational Catholic school, with a good representation of African-Americans and Hispanics, the school was founded in the Dominican tradition and is sponsored by the Diocese of Dallas. It has an enrollment of about 1,130 in grades nine through 12.

Tuition starts at $7,300 for Dallas Diocese parishioners, or $9,500 for all other applicants, although a fifth of the students receive financial aid. It must be prepaid in full by the end of May. Monthly payments are possible by a pre-approved bank loan. The non-refundable registration fee is $300, and the matriculation fee is $325. Books cost up to $500 a year. Bus transportation is available at a fee, as is a summer enrichment program.

The student/teacher ratio is 14:1, and almost one-half of the 75 or so on the faculty have master's or doctorate degrees.

Placement tests, recommendations, transcripts, and family interviews are required. Almost three-quarters of graduating students go on to a four-year college. Discipline is enforced, and drinking and fighting off-campus can be grounds for dismissal. Uniforms are required.

There is lots of theological instruction. Community service is a high priority. "At Bishop Lynch," notes *D Magazine*, "every kid gets a chance." The school has twice been named a Blue Ribbon School by the U.S. Department of Education, in 1998 and 1991.

In 2003, the school opened a $7-million performing arts center featuring a 400-seat theater.

A well-respected **East Dallas Community School,** 924 Wayne St. at Gurley; is also located in East Dallas, and has about 90 mostly low-income students, pre-kindergarten through third grade. Although it costs $7,200 to educate a child here, the average tuition is below $4,000 and is based on the parents' volunteer involvement. Some 400 children are on the waiting list of this Montessori-style school.

Brighter Horizons Academy (Est. 1989), 3145 Medical Plaza Dr. at Belt Line Rd., Garland, (972) 675-2062, Internet www.brighterhorizons.org. Located northeast of downtown Dallas, north of Belt Line Rd., and east of Jupiter Road North. The Richardson campus at 329 East Polk Street and Abrams, located east of North Central Expressway and south of East Main Street, serves kindergarten and pre-kindergarten classes.

A private co-educational school that offers Arabic and Islamic classes to students in preschool through 12th grade. The academy, which started with about 40 students, now has 440. Any student failing two core classes, such as English, Arabic, math, or Islamic studies, must repeat the year.

Uniforms are required. The girls in fifth grade and higher must wear headscarves. They cannot, regardless of their age, wear make-up or nail polish. The boys and girls do not date or interact socially in a Western sense of the word because Islam forbids such practices.

The annual tuition starts at $4,000 in pre-kindergarten, also payable in nine monthly installments, and goes past $5,000. There are registration and new student testing fees, and a first-year enrollment fee of $1,000. Book fees go up to $200 a year for students in seventh grade or higher. Lunches are provided at an additional cost.

School newspaper and boys basketball team are some among the extracurricular activities available. The first graduates in 2002 continued their education at Southern Methodist University and Richland College in Richardson.

More than 100,000 Muslims are said to live in the Metroplex, mostly in Richardson and Garland. Many of the Muslims work with such well-known telecommunications companies as MCI, Ericsson, Texas Instruments, and Nortel.

The Islamic Association of North Texas (IANT) Quranic Academy is located at the Dallas Central Mosque, 840 Abrams Rd., (972) 231-5698, Internet www.iant.com, in Richardson. IANT is a non-profit Muslim organization "dedicated to worship, education and services" in north Texas.

The Young Muslim Program started with 40 boys and girls, ages seven to nine, in 2002. The school day is 9:30 AM-2 PM. Expenses include a $175 monthly tuition, a $250 registration fee, $200 for books and other materials.

Cistercian Preparatory School (Est. 1962), One Cistercian Rd., off Highway 114 (or John W. Carpenter Freeway), Irving, (469) 499-5400, Internet www.cistercian.org, e-mail admissions@cistercian.org. Located northwest of downtown Dallas, near Texas Stadium, Las Colinas, and the University of Dallas.

One of the most demanding and respected private schools in the Metroplex, it is situated on a 62-acre (or 25-hectare) campus along the Elm Fork of the Trinity River. The Cistercian was founded as a boys-only, Roman Catholic-affiliated school in 1962, although the Cistercian Fathers have lived and taught in the Dallas area since 1956.

Enrollment is about 330, four-fifths Caucasians, in grades 5-12. Tuition ranges from $10,000 to $11,100, including all required fees. Round-trip bus transportation costs an additional $450 each semester.

The Cistercian's annual budget is $4 million. The student/teacher ratio is 9:1, and about three-quarters of the faculty has master's and one-quarter doctorate degrees.

Middle school students stand when their teacher enters and sit when they are told to be seated. About 30 percent of applicants are admitted, and of those some 12 percent receive financial aid. Nearly every graduate goes to a four-year college.

Cistercian monks and lay teachers provide a classical European-based education that includes foreign languages, such as French and Spanish. The curriculum "reflects the Cistercian Order's deep roots in the history of Western Civilization," according to its Web site. Latin is the required foreign language throughout the middle school.

The school has tough admission requirements and a demanding curriculum, and it encourages community service. Each grade is assigned a "form master," usually a Cistercian priest, who moves with the class from one year to the next. Uniforms are required.

The Cistercian Catholic order was founded as a reform branch of the

Benedictine order in 1098 and has been involved in education since the Middle Ages. The Cistercians in Irving came from western Hungary, where the Cistercian Order has conducted secondary schools since 1776, and fled the Communist oppression after World War II. Their Irving abbey was built in 1958 on the campus of the University of Dallas, where the Cistercians also teach.

Father Damian Szodenyi (d. 1998), co-founder of the Cistercian, escaped from persecution in his native Hungary in the 1940s and came to Dallas in 1954. He helped found the University of Dallas before moving on to Cistercian. Father Damian was a "highly regarded" sculptor, painter, and teacher. His works in stone, wood, and metal, which are scattered throughout the campus, depict religious subjects with a modernist flair.

Dallas International School (Est. 1991), 6039 Churchill Way at Preston Rd., (972) 991-6379, Internet www.dallasinternationalschool.org. Located in a series of somewhat austere inward-facing buildings north of downtown Dallas, south of Lyndon B. Johnson Freeway (or Interstate 635), and across the street from St. Alcuin Montessori School and Cooper Fitness Center (see listings). Parking is hard to come by, and car pool pickups can be time consuming.

The only French-style preparatory school in the Metroplex and a godsend for residents who want to educate their children in French, English, and Spanish from an early age. A co-educational and non-denominational school, DIS has an enrollment of almost 400 students in preschool through 12th grade and a student/teacher ratio from 6:1 to 20:1. Uniforms are mandatory.

Students represent some 15 nationalities, including 40 percent American and 35 percent French. Tuition starts at $7,000 a school year and goes up to $12,000 in high school (lycée) grades 10 through 12. A non-refundable deposit of $1,000, which is applied to the tuition, is due by the end of the previous March. Financial aid is available to French citizens only through the French government, but DIS may graciously let you pay your child's tuition in monthly installments to ease the pain. Hot lunches are provided at an additional $700 to $900 a year. Before- and after-school care cost, between 7:30 AM and 6 PM, depends on how many hours your child remains at school.

DIS's objective is to provide a bilingual curriculum in a multicultural environment. Subjects are taught in both French and English, enabling children to achieve fluency in both languages. The French curriculum follows the guidelines set by the French Ministry of Education, and the school is accredited by the Ministry. The faculty consists of 40-plus teachers, about 40 percent of whom have master's or higher degrees.

The diploma your child receives is a French baccalaureate, which assures admission to virtually any university in the world, and "is at least the equivalent of an American High School diploma (perhaps better)," according to *D Magazine*, which claims that the catered lunches are "tres bien."

There is a 50 percent French-language instruction and 50 percent in English through kindergarten. In primary grades, the French-language instruction increases to 80 percent. Spanish is taught as the third language. Average class size in preschool is 12 students, 15 in elementary grades, and six or more thereafter. About 70 percent of applicants are accepted.

The campus features 30 classrooms, two libraries, a science lab, a computer center, and a gymnasium. The newest addition to the campus was constructed in 2001, drafted by Cunningham Architects, and cited for a design award by the Dallas Chapter of the American Institute of Architects.

Fencing, piano, guitar, flute, and gymnastics lessons are available after school hours.

DIS also offers up to six weeks of half-day and full-day summer language instruction for children ages three to ten, as well as adults, in French and Spanish. The language classes run from the middle of June through August. Full-day tuition with lunch costs about $200 a week. Before- and after-school care, again from 7:30 AM to 6 PM, is an additional expense.

DIS goes back to 1987, when Jeanne Jeannin established the French School of Dallas, mostly for adults. In 1991, La Mission Laique Francaise acquired the school and renamed it the Dallas International School. DIS became part of 75 schools with 25,000 students in 35 countries owned and operated by the non-profit Mission Laique, which was founded in 1902 and is headquartered in Paris. Other schools are located in Croatia, Lebanon, Morocco, Spain, Syria, and Turkey.

A couple of blocks from DIS, at 6210 Churchill Way, is **Akiba Academy,** a Jewish school established in 1962 that serves pre-kindergarten through eighth-grade students.

The Episcopal School of Dallas (Est. 1974), 4100 Merrell Rd. at Midway, (972) 358-4368, Internet www.esdallas.org/esd. Located north of downtown Dallas and west of Marsh Lane alongside a natural lake quarry.

A co-educational Episcopal school located on a 36-acre (or 14.5-hectare) campus with five buildings. Enrollment is more than 1,100, grades pre-kindergarten-12, about 90 percent Caucasians from the affluent North Dallas, and 3 percent African-Americans.

ESD has a unique advisory system in which each teacher guides eight students for two years, even eating lunch with them every day. Chapel attendance is mandatory each morning.

Tuition starts at $6,000 and goes beyond $16,000, making it one of the costliest private schools in the Metroplex. With up to $700 for textbooks, a variety of other fees, and from $700 to $850 for hot lunches, it all adds up to a yearly salary. The tuition deposit is from $500 to $1,000. Tuition is payable up front or through bank loan payments. ESD's annual budget is about $16 million.

The student/teacher ratio is from 10:1 to 18:1, and more than one-half of the faculty of 120-plus has master's or doctorate degrees. The average length of faculty tenure is ten years. All applicants in grades five through 12 must take the Independent School Entrance Examination (ISEE). ESD "gives preference in the admission process to children of alumni, communicants of St. Michael and All Angels Church, and Episcopalians," according to its Web page.

Fewer than 25 percent of applicants are accepted, and barely 10 percent of them receive financial aid. Practically every graduate goes on to college, including Yale, Brown, and Rice. There is a waiting list, and uniforms are required.

Wilderness program, which starts in the fifth grade, is an integral part of education at ESD. Sports activities include baseball, basketball, cheerleading, football, golf, hockey, soccer, and tennis.

The school's Gill Library, for grades five through 12, boasts more than 15,000 books.

The Episcopal School became one of the largest private schools when it merged with St. Michael's School in 1995 and kept its campus at Colgate and Douglas Avenues in University Park.

Fairhill School (Est. 1971), 16150 Preston Rd. at Arapaho, Dallas, (972) 233-1026, Internet www.fairhill.org. Located on a 16-acre (or 6.4-hectare) wooded campus in far-north Dallas and north of Lyndon B. Johnson Freeway. Shelton School (see entry) is located nearby.

A co-educational, non-denominational school that accepts children from first through 12th grades with learning disabilities, such as dyslexia, dysgraphia, auditory processing disorder, or attention deficit/hyperactivity disorder.

An upper school was added in 1977, and the first class of seniors was graduated in 1981. During its first 19 years, the school was located on Churchill Way, south of the LBJ Freeway.

"Fairhill places great importance on the basic skill areas of reading, math and language arts," according to its Web page. A diagnostic assessment center is also on the premises.

Enrollment is about 230, and the student/teacher ratio varies from 7:1 to 10:1. Some 98 percent of students are Caucasian. Some 85 percent of applicants are accepted. No before- or after-school care is available.

Tuition goes up to $11,000 a year. Catered lunches are available.

The school's annual budget is about $2.5 million. Fewer than 5 percent of students receive financial aid. Some 45 percent of the teachers have master's degrees. There is usually a waiting list, and uniforms are required. Summer classes are held every year.

Fairhill students can participate in art, choral groups, drama, and vocal music. Baseball, basketball, cheerleading, golf, soccer, softball, swimming, tennis, track and field, and volleyball instruction is also available.

Almost 30 percent of Fairhill students live in Plano and Richardson, and 80 percent live within eight miles (or 12.9 kilometers) of the school.

First Baptist Academy (Est. 1972), Ervay Street at Patterson, Dallas, (214) 969-7861/2479, Internet www.fbacademy.com. Located downtown, a couple of blocks south of the Dallas Museum of Art and the Nasher Sculpture Garden (see individual entries). East Campus, (214) 327-8244, for pre-kindergarten through grade six, was added in 1985 and is located northeast of downtown Dallas, at 2380 Dunloe Dr., one block north of Gus Thomasson Rd., in the Casa View area.

A co-educational, Baptist-affiliated, pre-kindergarten-through-12th-grade school with about 900 students. Tuition starts at about $5,500 and goes up to $9,500 a year, not including the application fee, $300 entrance fee, and $350 enrollment fee for the first child. "All monies paid are non-refundable."

First Baptist's annual budget is more than $5 million, and one in five applicants receives financial aid. Parking for 10th, 11th, and 12th graders is available at an additional cost. The student-teacher ratio is 18:1. Uniforms are required apparel.

Hot lunches and school care, after 4 PM, are additional expenses. The academy offers opportunities in art, band, choir, debate, drama, journalism, and speech. Weekly classes in Spanish are also available. FBA students can also participate in baseball, cross-country, football, golf, softball, swimming, tennis, track, and wrestling.

Good Shepherd Episcopal School (Est. 1959), 11110 Midway Rd. at Royal Ln., (214) 357-2968 or 357-1610, Internet www.gseschooldallas.org, e-mail admissions@gsesdallas.org. Located northwest of downtown Dallas, roughly between Stemmons Freeway (or Interstate 35 East) and Dallas North Tollway.

Good Shepherd has an enrollment of about 600 boys and girls, pre-kindergarten through eighth grade. Caucasian pupils form a majority just shy of 90 percent, followed by 6 percent Hispanic, and 4 percent Asian-American.

Tuition starts at $6,500, goes to $9,000, and is payable annually, by semester, or monthly. There is an application and enrollment fee of $500 to $750. After-school care is available from 3 PM to 6 PM at $2,200 annually. Hot lunches are an additional expense.

Only one in four applicants is admitted, and fewer than 5 percent of students receive financial aid. More than 40 percent of the faculty hold advanced degrees in their fields. The student-teacher ratio is from 6:1 to 11:1.

Good Shepherd's annual budget is about $5 million. There is a waiting list to get a child into this school, and uniforms are required.

An admission test and a classroom visit are required to enroll. A typical day may include chapel services, music and art, as well as nature walks and hikes, and overnight camping. A great variety of sports activities is available.

Nearly all eighth-grade graduates go on to high schools of their choice. This school was recognized by the U.S. Department of Education as an early Blue Ribbon School of Excellence.

Greenhill School (Est. 1950), 4141 Spring Valley Rd. at Midway Rd., Addison, (972) 628-5400, admissions 628-5910, Internet www.greenhill.org. Located on a 78-acre (or 31.5-hectare) campus northwest of downtown Dallas, north of Lyndon B. Johnson Freeway (Interstate 635) and west of Dallas North Tollway.

One of the oldest, largest, and costliest private schools in the area. Enrollment is about 1,240, pre-kindergarten through 12th grade. Its founder, Bernard Fulton (b. 1910), who had come to Dallas in 1937, started it with 62 students on Walnut Hill Lane and was its headmaster until 1976.

Tuition starts at $12,000 and goes beyond $16,000, not counting a slew of charges, such as application and other fees. Unless you qualify for financial aid, there is also a $1,000 facility fee. A $1,000 tuition deposit is due within two weeks of enrollment contract. Lunches cost $750 a school year, after-school care up to $250 a month. Greenhill's annual budget is about $19 million.

The student/teacher ratio is from 8:1 in the preschool to 18:1 in the upper grades. More than one-half of the faculty of 150 have master's or doctorate degrees. The school's average SAT math/verbal scores are among the highest in the area. Less than one-quarter of applicants are admitted, and about 15 percent of them receive financial aid.

Many of those graduating attend colleges such as Princeton, Stanford, Duke, and the University of Texas. According to *Worth* financial magazine, Greenhill is one of the nation's 40 best "feeder schools" to Yale, Harvard, and Princeton. That is better than the ranking of such well-known Northeast prep schools as New Jersey's Lawrenceville.

Among the subjects offered are algebra, art and art history, biology, calculus, computer math, creative writing, dance, drama, ecology, economics, European history, fine arts, French, journalism, Latin, Mandarin, music oceanography, philosophy, Spanish, theater, and world literature.

In 1950 this was the first co-educational, non-denominational private school in the city. Greenhill is known for encouraging individuality in its students, sometimes at the expense of scholastics, claim some. Uniforms are not required, but there is a dress code.

Your child will learn in a good ethnic mix, but will have only an uphill chance of snagging a scholarship. More than three-quarters of the student body are Caucasian, more than 10 percent Asian-American, and about 7 percent African-American.

The campus with 11 buildings includes a football stadium and a dozen tennis courts. Baseball, golf, and lacrosse are also available. The school has a large summer program that includes sports camps.

"Greenhill is the flower child of Dallas' top private schools," observes *D Magazine*. "But these hippies are learning Spanish as toddlers and getting into Ivy League schools when they graduate."

The Hillcrest Academy (Est. 1976), 12302 Park Central Dr. at Coit Rd., (972) 788-0292, Internet www.hillcrestacademy.org. Located south of Lyndon B. Johnson Freeway (or Interstate 635) and west of North Central Expressway (or U.S. Highway 75), just north of Medical City Dallas Hospital (see entry).

A non-profit, non-denominational, co-educational school with an enrollment of about 250, from pre-kindergarten through eighth grade. About half of applicants are admitted. The student-teacher ratio ranges from 8:1 to 15:1.

The school's tuition starts at $7,000 and goes beyond $9,000 a year. That does not include an application fee, a $200 testing fee, textbooks, and before- and after-school care. School lunches are another expense. There are also parent association dues. Uniforms are required.

Summer camps are provided at an additional expense, and a separate registration fee is charged. Baseball, softball, basketball, soccer, swimming, track and field, and volleyball programs are available.

The Hillcrest Academy began as the Willows Academy on Willow Lane in north Dallas. It has an annual budget of about $2.5 million.

The Hockaday School (Est. 1913), 11600 Welch Rd. at Forest Ln., (214) 363-6311, Internet www.hockaday.org. Located northeast of downtown Dallas and east of Dallas North Tollway and Inwood Road.

The nation's largest nonsectarian girls' school, it is also one of the most expensive such private schools in the Metroplex. Hockaday has an enrollment of about 1,000, pre-kindergarten to 12th grade. Four girls apply for each vacancy.

Tuition starts at about $11,000 and goes to $16,000, including lunches, although one in ten students receives financial aid. A non-refundable $1,000 deposit is applied toward tuition. After-school care for girls up to fourth grade costs as much as $1,300 a school year. Private music lessons run up to $700 a semester. Textbooks, uniforms, and lunches are still additional expenses.

The student/teacher ratio is 9:1 or higher. More than 40 percent of the faculty's more than 100 teachers have master's degrees, and several also have doctorate degrees. The school's endowment is $75 million. Many Hockaday graduates go on to the University of Texas, Rice, Stanford, and the University of Pennsylvania.

Some of the wealthiest and most influential Texas families educated their daughters here, including the Bushes, Crows, Perots, and Murchisons. Foreign students come from all corners of the world, from Belgium to Yemen, but pay up to an additional $15,000 a year to board at the school. Seventy-five percent of the pupils are Caucasian, more than 10 percent Asian-American, and about 5 percent each African-American and Hispanic. French and Spanish are taught from the second grade on. The Hockaday cooperates closely with St. Mark's School (see below).

This is one of the region's best private girls' prep schools, established in 1913 by Ella Hockaday (1875-1956) of Ladonia, Texas. Her father was a farmer and fluent in Latin, Hebrew, and Greek. She donated the school to Dallas in 1942, and it is now a nonprofit corporation.

The 100-acre (or 40-hectare), $33-million complex includes 12 buildings, with a 600-seat auditorium, a computer center, a 50,000-volume library, two theaters, piano and voice studios, a greenhouse, ten tennis courts, three basketball courts, and two swimming pools.

And speaking of swimming, Jerry Heidenreich—who won four medals, including two golds, for the U.S. swim team at the 1972 Olympics in Munich, Germany—was a coach at Hockaday. A former Southern Methodist University swimming star, Heidenreich (1950-2002) competed at the Munich Games against legendary swimmer Mark Spitz, winner of seven gold medals that summer. "Heidenreich was such a strong swimmer that his mere presence in the 100-meter freestyle almost prompted Spitz to withdraw from the event," observes the *Dallas Morning News*.

The Hockaday was designed by the Chicago-born architect Harwood K. Smith (1913-2002), who also drafted the Plaza of the Americas, Reunion Arena, and Thanksgiving Tower (see individual entries).

In 2002, Hockaday opened a 46,000-square-foot (or 4,273-square-meter) Academic Research Center, the largest building project undertaken so far at the school. It houses a library, a science exploration lab, and computer labs.

The Hockaday School was originally located on the corner of Belmont Avenue and Lower Greenville Avenue in near-east Dallas. Today, these buildings are occupied by the Vickery Towers retirement community.

Jesuit College Preparatory School (Est. 1944), 12345 Inwood Rd. at Dallas North Tollway and LBJ Frwy., (972) 387-8700, Internet www.jesuitcp.org. Located in far-north Dallas, south of the Galleria mall.

A Catholic boys' high school managed by the Society of Jesus, it requires four years of theology study. Enrollment is about 990, grades 9-12, 75 percent are Caucasians and 70 percent Catholic. The tuition goes up to $8,500, not counting an application entrance examination and other fees. Lunches are à la carte.

"Each applicant is asked to come to Jesuit for an interview," informs the school's Web site. Two students apply for each vacancy, and about a fifth of those accepted receive financial aid. The student/teacher ratio is 20:1, and about 60 percent of the faculty have master's or doctorate degrees.

Harvard, Cornell, Princeton, and Yale are among the universities that the prep school's students attend after graduating here. A high honor code and demanding community service are among the requirements. The Jesuit College gives chances to marginal kids and is competitive in various sports.

The school has its own museum, featuring some 400 works of contemporary Southwestern paintings and sculpture by artists such as Dali, Gorman, Moroles, Lara, Pena, Zapata, and Zuniga.

Except in Maryland, Virginia, and Texas, in all other states public and private schools compete in the same championships in high school athletics. To gain admission to the University Interscholastic League, the governing body for public school sports in Texas, the private Jesuit College filed a lawsuit in 2000. A federal judge dismissed the suit in 2002, but the school appealed to the 5th U.S. Circuit Court of Appeals.

John Paul II High School, 7823 Preston Meadow Dr. at Hedgecoxe Rd., Plano, (972) 208-4242, Internet www.johnpaulIIhs.org. Located north of President George Bush Turnpike, southeast of Stonebriar Centre shopping mall (see listing), and southwest from the Russell Creek Park.

John Paul II High was to be inaugurated in the fall of 2003 by the Catholic Diocese of Dallas. This is the first Catholic high school designed for students in Dallas and Collin counties, and the first north of the LBJ Freeway (or Interstate 635).

John Paul High anticipates a $17-million campus for up to 500 ninth- through-12th-grade students to serve parishes between Farmers Branch and Wylie. Twenty classrooms, a chapel, and an indoor athletic complex were planned for.

The Catholic church officials have been planning this high school since 1990, but continued fund-raising problems have stopped the project several times. Before the fund-raising campaign flopped, a 1,200-student high school was to cost as much as $35 million.

Lakehill Preparatory School (Est. 1971), 2720 Hillside Dr., between Vickery Blvd. and Llano Ave., Dallas, (214) 826-2931, Internet www.lakehillprep.org. Located on a six-acre (or 2.42-hectare) campus with two buildings northeast of downtown Dallas, west of White Rock Lake, and just east of Abrams Road.

Lakehill was founded by Greenhill School (see entry) educators, including its former headmaster Bernard Fulton. Its enrollment is about 400, kindergarten through 12th grade, half day or full day. Caucasians make up about 80 percent of the student body, while Hispanics claim about 5 percent, and African-Americans and Asian-Americans some 3 percent each.

Tuition starts at $8,000 and goes beyond $11,000 a year, also payable "in monthly installments at 15.9 percent interest." Add to that a $500 enrollment fee, a non-refundable application fee, books and materials, and an activity fee. Lunches are also a separate expense. Only after-school care is available, but at an additional charge. The school's annual budget is about $3 million.

The student/teacher ratio is 14:1, and about one-half of the faculty has master's or doctorate degrees. About one-third of applicants gain admission, and just one in ten receives financial aid.

Entrance testing is mandatory. Students in grades five through 12 must complete a questionnaire and write an essay. Uniforms are not required, but there will likely be a waiting list for your child's spot. Baseball, basketball, football, soccer, tennis, and volleyball are among the sports activities available.

Lakehill's facilities are simple, and the school is located in an old church, but it has a good drama department and requires community service toward graduation. "We are equally committed to both academic success and character development," claims the school's Web site. Practically all of its graduates attend four-year colleges.

The Lamplighter School (Est. 1953), 11611 Inwood Rd., just south of Forest Ln., (214) 369-9201, Internet www.thelamplighterschool.org. Located north of downtown Dallas, west of Dallas North Tollway, and south of the LBJ Freeway (or Interstate 635).

Lamplighter was founded with 23 students and two teachers in a north Dallas farmhouse on Churchill Way. The current facilities, designed by architects Frank Welch and O'Neil Ford, were inaugurated on a 12-acre (or 4.85-hectare) campus in mid-1969. The school was expanded to 30 classrooms in 1987. The co-educational enrollment now is about 460, pre-kindergarten through fourth grade. Some 90 percent of the pupils are Caucasians. The student/teacher ratio is from 9:1 to 31:1. The faculty numbers 45.

The annual tuition starts at $6,000 and goes up to $12,000, excluding the $525 to $1,000 deposit. There is a $175 non-refundable application fee. No before- and after-school care is available. "No refunds or transfers of enrollment fees or tuition shall be made," advises the school's Web site.

Application deadline is October 1 of the previous year. Only one-third of applicants are accepted, and barely 2 percent of students receive financial aid. About a quarter of the faculty claims master's degrees.

Music, theater, and art diversions are available, as is a health and fitness facility. Spanish is introduced in first grade. The school has a greenhouse and a barn with farm animals. Uniforms are not required, but there is a waiting list for enrollment. The Lamplighter graduates go on to St. Mark's, Hockaday, and Greenhill (see listings).

The Lamplighter is located in the zip code area 75229, where several other private schools are located.

Mesorah High School for Girls, 11315 North Central Expwy. at Northhaven Rd., (214) 691-4949, Internet www.mesorahschool.org, e-mail info@mesorahschool.org. Located northeast of downtown Dallas and University Park, just south of Forest Lane, and near Medical City Dallas Hospital.

The first Jewish high school for girls, and the only such institution in the Southwest, it opened in 2000 with seven students in four grades. Mesorah is Orthodox, meaning it is affiliated with the most traditional of the major Jewish movements; fewer than 10 percent of Jews in America are Orthodox. Keeping boys and girls apart is a long-standing Jewish tradition.

Part of the day at Mesorah is spent learning and speaking Hebrew and studying Jewish laws and customs. Its curriculum is designed to prepare students for college, as well as for a Jewish lifestyle. It also includes algebra, biology, world civilizations, computer applications, music appreciation, and physical education.

Tuition is nearly $9,000 a year and does not include lunches, transportation, or uniforms. There are also registration, extra curricular activities, book, laboratory, and supply fees. "No eligible student will be turned away for financial reasons," promises the school's Web site, adding that "excellent housing accommodations are available for out-of-town students."

Mesorah brings the total of Jewish day schools in Dallas to five. Isaac Mayer Wise Academy, at 6930 Alpha Road, which opened in 1998, is a Reform elementary school.

For more assistance in locating another Jewish school or day care center, call the Jewish Community Center, 7900 Northhaven Rd., (214) 739-2737, e-mail info@jccdallas.com

The Parish Episcopal School (Est. 1972), 14115 Hillcrest Rd. at Spring Valley, (800) 909-9081 or (972) 239-8011; admissions, (972) 852-8737, Internet www.parishepiscopal.org. Located in far-north Dallas, north of the Lyndon B. Johnson Freeway, and northeast of Valley View Mall and Galleria shopping center (see entries).

When architect I. M. Pei designed this building for Mobil Oil, he could not have known it would one day house a private school. The Parish Day School moved into the 337,000-square-foot (or 31,307-square-meter) building when established by the Episcopal Church of the Transfiguration in 1972. The Midway campus, for grades three through eight, is situated at 4101 Sigma Rd. and Alpha Rd. in Farmers Branch, a couple of miles (or 3.2 kilometers) west of the Hillcrest campus.

An Episcopal, coeducational school with about 480 students, pre-kindergarten through eighth grade, almost 90 percent Caucasians, and 3 percent each Asian- and African-American. The school is adding one grade a year through the twelfth grade, and the first class of seniors is to graduate in 2007. About one-third of applicants are accepted.

The school "provides a learning environment within a Christian framework in which each student is encouraged to excel academically, spiritually, emotionally, and physically. Corporate worship, religious education, and classroom application of Bible lessons are a key part of the curriculum," according to the school's Web site. "Community outreach instills lifelong lessons of service to others." One of the three daily chapel services is mandatory.

The expenses start with a $100 application fee, $500 new-student fee, $700 enrollment fee, and annual tuition from $5,000 to $10,500 for seventh and eighth graders. Hot lunches are available at an additional cost. About 7 percent of the students receive financial aid.

The student/teacher ratio is from 7:1 to 20:1. Some 13 percent of the teachers have master's degrees. Some of the selection criteria for admission include academic readiness or qualifications, maturity, and Episcopal church affiliation.

Uniforms are required. Programs include religion, art, music, Spanish, computers, and physical education. Before- and after-school care is available at an additional charge. Sports, such as baseball and softball, are encouraged.

St. Alcuin Montessori School (Est. 1963), 6144 Churchill Way at Preston Rd., (972) 239-1745, Internet www.saintalcuin.org, e-mail admission@saintalcuin.org. Located north of downtown Dallas and a few blocks south of the Lyndon B. Johnson Freeway, across the street from the Dallas International School (see listing).

This is the oldest Montessori-style school in Dallas offering education based on the philosophy and methods of Dr. Maria Montessori (1870-1952). It has no religious affiliation and accepts children regardless of race, color, creed, or national origin. There are at least two dozen Montessori schools located in Dallas, including two public schools.

The co-educational enrollment is more than 500, pre-kindergarten through eighth grade. The student/teacher ratio is from 6:1 to 13:1.

Tuition starts at about $6,500 for toddlers and rises to more than $12,500 in eighth grade, payable in a lump sum or nine monthly payments "with an interest charge of 10 percent." The non-refundable tuition fee is from $500 to $1,000, and the application fee is $100.

Only about one-half of applicants are accepted, and just 5 percent of students receive financial aid. Before- and after-school care, from 7 AM to 6 PM, is available for children three years old and older.

More than 80 percent of enrollees are Caucasian, 12 percent Asian, and 4 percent Hispanic. There is usually a waiting list. St. Alcuin has no athletic program, and uniforms are not required.

After-school activities include ballet, ceramics, drama, basic Spanish, choir, sports, Suzuki violin and private piano lessons. Summer camp is also available.

The staff consists of 70 teachers, one-fifth of them holding master's degrees. St. Alcuin's annual budget is about $4.5 million.

Wilderness program and orchestra are among the unique features of this Montessori school, which was designed by the Paris, Texas-born architect Frank Welch, who also drafted several homes across from the Mansion on Turtle Creek hotel. The school owns 80 acres (or 32 hectares) of blackland prairie in Melissa, north of Dallas.

St. Alcuin, named after Alcuin of York, an eighth-century scholar and tutor of Charlemagne's children, suggests that parents not familiar with the Montessori method first read one of the several books by Dr. Montessori or another author versed in the method.

Adjoining St. Alcuin is **Akiba Academy,** Internet www.akiba.dallas.tx.us, in 1962 the first Jewish school in Dallas serving students from pre-kindergarten through eighth-grade.

St. John's Episcopal School (Est. 1953), 848 Harter Rd. at Northcliff, (214) 328-9131 or (214) 321-6451, Internet www.stjohnsepiscopal.org, e-mail info@stjohnsepiscopal.org. Located northeast of downtown

Dallas, west of White Rock Lake, and a good mile (or 1.6 kilometers) northeast of the Dallas Arboretum (see entry).

The school is "dedicated to a program of academic excellence designed to train the mind, strengthen the character, and enrich the spirit of each student in a Christian environment," according to its Web site. It is an independent, co-educational day school for children in pre-kindergarten through grade eight. Close to 500 pupils are enrolled, more than 90 percent of them Caucasian and about 3 percent Hispanic. Only about one-third of applicants are accepted. The student/teacher ratio is about 14:1, and close to one-third of the faculty has a master's degree.

The annual tuition starts at about $5,000 and goes to almost $8,000 and includes all books and materials. New students pay a fee of $750, while uniforms and lunches are still additional expenses. There is usually a waiting list, and uniforms are the required attire. Only about 6 percent of students receive financial aid. St. John's graduates often go on to Bishop Lynch, Ursuline Academy, and Jesuit College preparatory schools (see listings).

An after-school program is available until 6 PM, but at an additional cost of $250 a month, and a separate application is required.

The parish of St. John's was established in 1946, when residents from the White Rock area petitioned the diocese for status as a mission of the Episcopal Church. The current building was designed by Texas architect O'Neil Ford and constructed in 1961.

St. Mark's School of Texas, 10600 Preston Rd. at Royal Ln., (214) 346-8000, Internet www.smtexas.org. Located north of downtown Dallas, just east of Dallas North Tollway, and a few blocks south of Preston Royal shopping center.

The first local all-boys school that imitated the exclusive Eastern schools, although it only goes back to the 1930s, when it was called Texas Country Day School. Some of the wealthiest and most powerful Texas socialites graduated as Marksmen. Among its graduates are developer Ross Perot Jr. and A. H. Belo Corp. chairman Robert W. Decherd, who controls the *Dallas Morning News*.

"This school's reputation precedes it," notes *D Magazine*. "Whether that reputation is accurate, though, is the question." While some parents claim that St. Mark's provides the best education in the area, quite a few place it academically behind Cistercian Preparatory School (see entry).

This is the most expensive boys-only private school in Dallas. Enrollment is about 800, grades one through 12, and the yearly tuition is upward of $14,000 for lower grades and beyond $18,000 for older students. It does, however, include lunches and textbooks. There is an enrollment deposit of $1,000 that is applied to tuition. Uniforms are mandatory.

The student/teacher ratio is 8:1, and some 80 percent of the faculty have master's or doctorate degrees. St. Mark's annual budget is more than $15 million.

Less than one-quarter of applicants gain admission, and even fewer receive financial aid. About one-quarter of its students and more than 15 percent of the faculty are minorities. The Marksmen often go on to Harvard, Princeton, New York University, and the University of Texas.

Spanish is a required language in the third grade, and Japanese is taught in the fifth. The 40-acre (or 16-hectare) campus includes fine arts and music buildings, tennis courts, a stadium, an Olympic-size swimming pool, a planetarium, and an observatory.

The original Texas Country Day School opened in 1933 and had one student graduating in 1935. St. Mark's moved to its present location in 1941, relocated to the Fondren Library at Southern Methodist University, and returned to Preston Road three years later.

St. Mark's is located in the zip code area of 75230, along with several other such private schools.

Shelton School (Est. 1976), Ward Campus, 15720 Hillcrest Rd. at Arapaho, Richardson, (972) 774-1772, Internet www.shelton.org. Located north of downtown Dallas and north of the LBJ Freeway (or Interstate 635). Pre-kindergarten through third grade, about 200 students, are situated on the Swift Campus, 9407 Midway Rd., north of Loop 12, in Dallas, (214) 353-9030.

A private, co-educational, non-denominational school specializing in children with learning disabilities, it has an enrollment of about 800, pre-kindergarten through 12th grade.

Tuition starts at $9,500 and goes beyond $14,500 a year. But, as with most other private schools, there is a slew of other fees that quickly add up to several hundred dollars, including the activities fee. Lunches are an additional expense, as is after-school care. The Shelton's annual budget is about $11 million.

Some 60 percent of applicants are admitted, but a mere 8 percent of students receive financial aid. The student/teacher ratio is between 6:1 and 8:1, depending on the grade. About 40 percent of the 150-plus teachers have master's degrees. Uniforms are required.

Some 97 percent of students are Caucasian, and 1 percent are African-American. There is usually a waiting list to enroll. Latin and Spanish are taught as foreign languages. Shelton's athletic programs include basketball, football, soccer, and volleyball. A summer school program is also available.

The Shelton Language, Speech, and Hearing Clinic serves adults and children in need of evaluation and therapy for difficulties with articulation, fluency, voice, language, auditory processing, and early reading problems.

Solomon Schechter Academy (Est. 1979), 18011 Hillcrest Rd. at Frankford Rd., Dallas, (972) 248-3032, Internet www.ssadallas.com. Located on a 10.5-acre (or 4.24-hectare) campus in far-north Dallas and west of the University of Texas at Dallas. The Montessori School of North Dallas is situated northwest of here.

A co-educational Jewish nursery-through-eighth-grade day school with an enrollment of more than 550 students. More than 90 percent of applicants are accepted. Tuition goes up to $13,000 a year, and up to 15 percent of students receive financial aid.

There is usually a waiting list, but the attrition rate is more than 10 percent a year. Schechter's pupils often continue their study at Greenhill and Hockaday schools (see listings). The academy's annual budget is more than $4 million.

The student/teacher ratio is 15:1, and more than one-third of the faculty have master's degrees. Uniforms are required. Before- and after-school care is available for preschool children at an additional fee. The school completed a $9-million expansion in 2002.

A nine-foot (or 2.74-meter) bronze sculpture, titled *Etz Chaim*, or *Tree of Life*, stands outside the entrance to the new middle school building. It was created by Veronique Jonas (b. 1952), who came from South Africa in 1982 and has taught art here for more than 19 years.

Trinity Christian Academy (Est. 1970), 17001 Addison Rd. at Sojourn, Addison, (972) 931-8325, Internet www.trinitychristian.com. Located on a 40-acre (or 16-hectare) campus with five buildings, north of downtown Dallas, north of Addison Airport, and just west of the Dallas North Tollway.

"Trinity Christian Academy remains unabashedly committed to being Christ-centered and Bible-bound," observes the school's Web site. "The best first-grade classroom makes Congress, IBM, and Wall Street seem provincial by comparison."

Enrollment is about 1,500, kindergarten-12th grade, and coeducational, with less than one-half of applicants being admitted. Tuition starts at $5,000 and goes to $11,000 a year, not counting a $1,500 admission and application fee.

Trinity Christian's annual budget is close to $12 million. About 15 percent of students receive financial aid. The student/teacher ratio is 11:1, and more than half of the faculty of some 130 have master's or doctorate degrees.

"We're conservative because we hold to an historical Christian orthodoxy that focuses on the truth of the gospel and the Bible," the headmaster told *D Magazine*. "We are liberal in that we teach a Christian liberal arts curriculum that enables our students to be free to think through all aspects of God's creation."

Trinity Christian teaches scientific and religious theory of evolution. One parent must be of the Christian faith for a child to be accepted. Not quite as tough on admissions as some other prep schools. Not elitist, but there are no dances on the campus. Baseball, basketball, cross country, golf, football, swimming, tennis, track, volleyball, and wrestling are available.

Ursuline Academy (Est. 1874), 4900 Walnut Hill Ln. at Inwood Rd., (469) 232-1800, Internet www.ursuline.pvt.k12.tx.us. Located on 25 acres (or ten hectares) at Preston Hollow, northwest of downtown Dallas.

A private girls' Roman Catholic preparatory school that was established by six nuns from Galveston's community of Ursuline Sisters in downtown Dallas. By 1878, the academy had 200 day students and 40 borders.

It is the oldest school in Dallas and has been at this location since 1950. Some of its campus was designed by the Chicago-born architect Harwood K. Smith (1913-2002), who came to Dallas in 1936 and also drafted such well-known structures as the Hockaday School, Plaza of the Americas, and Reunion Arena (see individual entries).

The academy, an order founded in Italy in 1535, was the first group of Catholic teachers to come to North America in 1639.

Enrollment is 800 in grades nine through 12; the elementary school closed in 1976. About 72 percent of the students are of Catholic persuasion. A little more than one-half of those applying are accepted, but fewer than 15 percent of students receive financial aid. Scholarships of up to $3,000 are awarded to outstanding students, regardless of their financial status.

Tuition is almost $9,000 a year, but does not include a $500 registration fee, books, parking, and athletic team fees. Every Ursuline girl is said to have a laptop computer and can study Russian literature.

The student/teacher ratio is 12:1. More than one-half of the faculty's 84 members have master's or doctoral degrees. The Ursuline's annual budget is about $8 million.

Uniforms, an additional expense, are required, although "shorts are no longer an option. Tatoos, facial jewelry and body piercing are not allowed," according to the school's Web site. At least 90 hours of community service is required for graduation.

Honor code is taken seriously at Ursuline: "A cheating offense requires a written apology from the student to the teacher in whose class she cheated." Penalties for lying, stealing, and vandalizing include a written apology to the parties involved, as well as parental notification.

An art club, jazz choir, dance company, drama club, and orchestra are some among the school's artistic endeavors. The academy's Beatrice M. Haggerty Library is equipped with 20 computers and holds more than 15,000 volumes. Ursuline's soccer team has won 11 state championships.

White Rock North Private School (Est. 1964), 9727 White Rock Trail at Kingsley Rd., (214) 348-7410, Internet www.whiterocknorthschool.com, e-mail msaaawrns@aol.com. Located northeast of downtown Dallas, north of White Rock Lake, and east of the North Central Expressway (or U.S. Highway 75).

A non-denominational, co-educational private school, located on a three-acre (or 1.21-hectare) campus, it claims about 250 pupils, prekindergarten through sixth grade, which was added in the 2002-2003 school year. About 80 percent of applicants are accepted, but there is no financial aid available.

The student/teacher ratio ranges from 8:1 to 12:1, and about 5 percent of the teachers claim a master's degree. Ninety-five percent of its pupils are Caucasian, with another 2 percent each African-American and Hispanic. An essay and completed questionnaire are required for acceptance in grades three to six.

White Rock North boasts a library, computer lab, gymnasium, swimming pool, three-acre (or 1.21-hectare) playground, 5,200-square-foot (or 483-square-meter) hardwood floor skating rink, and horse stable. Summer camps, dance and gymnastics, piano and swimming lessons are available.

The annual full-day tuition starts at about $5,500 and goes to $6,500. That does not include the testing, application, and new student enrollment fees. Before- and after-school care—from 7 AM to 6 PM—is included for full-day pupils. Uniforms are also required.

The Winston School (Est. 1975), 5707 Royal Lane at Dallas North Tollway, (214) 691-6950, Internet www.winston-school.org. Located on a five-acre (or two-hectare) campus with four buildings north of downtown Dallas, a few blocks from St. Mark's School of Texas (see entry).

One of the costliest private schools in the Metroplex, with tuition starting at about $12,000 and going up to $15,500, including a nonrefundable $750 deposit. Due prior to the first day of school, the tuition can also be paid by semester at an 8 percent "handling fee."

This does not include a $150 application fee, an $850 charge to new students to process and interpret records from any previous school, as well as hearing and vision screening, and a $250 graduation fee. There is a charge for class trips. Before- and after-school care is an additional expense. Breakfast and lunch (mandatory for lower school students) are available.

Enrollment is about 220 students, grades 1-12, with a student/teacher ratio of 8:1. There are two teachers in an average class of 16. Some 35 percent of teachers hold master's degrees. More than 90 percent of the students are Caucasian, and 7 percent African-American. The Winston's annual budget exceeds $4 million.

The co-educational school, which concentrates on children with learning disabilities, has programs in art, music, and drama, computer programming, journalism, Latin, and Spanish.

About one-third of applicants are admitted, and about 20 percent receive financial aid. A battery of tests, including IQ, diagnostic achievement, and language, are required for admission.

"Rather than make the kid fit the curriculum, we make the curriculum fit the student," says a school's manager. Cheerleading, football, and volleyball programs are also available to students.

Uniforms are not required, but "revealing, sagging, or tight clothing is unacceptable," according to the school's Web site. "No sweats, fleece, warm-ups, or wind pants are to be worn."

Metroplex Public Colleges & Universities

By some accounts, at least one-half of the best universities in the world are located in the United States. Perhaps as many as 40 American universities attain the world-level of excellence, a number that roughly corresponds with the *U.S. News & World Report*'s annual list of the so-called "tier one" national universities.

Dallas-Fort Worth, unfortunately, is the largest metropolitan area in the United States without one of those "tier one" institutions. The Metroplex universities, even by *U.S. News & World Report*'s standards, fall into the second, third, and fourth (the lowest) tiers of academic excellence.

When George W. Bush was governor of Texas, the state passed legislation guaranteeing all high school seniors graduating in the top 10 percent of their class admission into any state school. There are about 100,000 students enrolled at private and public universities in the Dallas-Fort Worth region, but there is no publicly funded university located within the city limits of Dallas. The campus of the University of Texas at Dallas is actually in Richardson.

The creation of the sixth public university in North Texas began in

2000. It will be located north of Interstate 20, between Houston School Road and Lancaster Road South, near Runyon Springs, a large residential development. The four-year University of North Texas at Dallas offshoot will attain university status once enrollment reaches 2,500 full-time students. The supporters envisioned up to 5,000 students by 2007, but only about 300 full-time students were enrolled in 2003. Its south Dallas campus would be a short drive from the University of Texas at Arlington, but 50 miles (or 80 kilometers) from the main campus in Denton.

Starting in 2004, public universities in Texas can, within certain limits, set their own tuition, a responsibility historically reserved for the state legislature. "Twenty years ago, four years of college in Texas cost less than a new Betamax [video player]," observed the *Dallas Morning News* in 2002. "Now, the price tag is more like that of a new car."

About 27 percent of Dallas County residents have at least a bachelor's degree. University Park and Highland Park lead Texas cities with the highest percentages of those with at least a bachelor's degree, 80 and 75 percent respectively. Some 25 percent of county residents, aged 25 or older, do not even have a high school diploma.

To search for information about individual colleges, please see their Web addresses below, or go to www.dallas.com/govt/college.html. The Education Department's campus security statistics can be accessed on the Web site www.ope.ed.gov/security.

Collin County Community College District (Est. 1985), 4800 Preston Park Blvd., Plano, (972) 985-3790, Internet www.ccccd.edu/ce. The total enrollment is about 16,000, almost one-fifth receiving financial aid. The student/teacher ratio is 10:1, and the median student age is about 26 years. Only associate degrees can be earned.

CCCCD's campuses include Preston Ridge in Frisco, CCCCD at Allen, Central Park in McKinney, College Center in Rockwall, Courtyard Center and Spring Creek, both in Plano.

Dallas County Community College District, 701 Elm Street, (214) 860-2135, Internet www.dcccd.edu, is the largest public community college in the county. Established in 1965, it consists of seven colleges enrolling 55,000 credit and 45,000 non-credit students each semester and is located throughout the county. The district receives about $100 million from the state and employs 2,000 full-time faculty and staff members.

Dr. William Wenrich (b. 1938), an educator for 30 years after he served as a foreign service officer in Bolivia, oversaw the district for 12 years and retired in 2003. He was replaced by Jesus Carreon (b. 1949) who had previously held a similar job in Portland, Oregon.

Tuition, starting at $550 per school year, is charged on a sliding scale, according to the number of credit hours a student is enrolled, and depending on residency in the county. However, in 2001, the state legislature allowed illegal aliens to pay in-state tuition. The seven colleges, which offer associate degrees only, are:

Brookhaven College (Est. 1978), 3939 Valley View Ln., Farmers Branch, (972) 860-4803. Enrollment is more than 9,000 students.

Cedar Valley College (Est. 1977), 3030 North Dallas Ave., Lancaster, (972) 860-8201. Enrollment is about 3,600. Median student age is 22 years, and student/teacher ratio 16:1.

Eastfield College (Est. 1970), 3737 Motley Dr., Mesquite, (972) 860-7100. Enrollment is almost 9,000 students whose median age is 27 years. Student to teacher ratio is 23:1.

El Centro College (Est. 1966), Main and Lamar Streets, downtown Dallas, (214) 860-2331. The three-building campus is located in the former Sanger-Harris department store, whose original lot cost $50 in the late 1860s, but sold for $100,000 in 1907.

Enrollment is about 4,700 students, a quarter of them Hispanics. Median student age is 26 years, and student/teacher ratio 14:1. Its full-time faculty includes about 80 members.

A two-story, 26,800-square-foot (or 2,490-square-meter), $6.9-million student and technology center, with classrooms, labs, dining hall, and an art gallery, between Lamar and Market streets, opened in 2003.

Mountain View College (Est. 1970), 4849 West Illinois Ave., (214) 860-8680. Enrollment is about 6,000 students, whose median age is 22 years, and student/teacher ratio 18:1.

North Lake College (Est. 1977), 5001 North MacArthur Blvd., Irving, (972) 273-3000. Enrollment is more than 8,000 students, having a median age of 24 years. Student to teacher ratio is 17:1.

Richland College (Est. 1972), 12800 Abrams Rd., (972) 238-6100. Enrollment is about 13,000 students, with a median age 25 years. Student/teacher ratio is 18:1.

Texas Woman's University, 304 Administration Dr., Denton, (888) 948-9984 or (940) TWU-2000; 24-hour information line, (940) 898-3469, Internet www.twu.edu. Located off Highway 380, one mile (or 1.6 kilometers) from downtown Denton and about 40 miles (or 64 kilometers) northwest of downtown Dallas.

A teaching and research institution, the university is "primarily for women" and emphasizes the liberal arts and professional studies. It claims to graduate the largest number of health care providers in Texas, including 13 percent of the state's new nurses.

Founded in 1901 as the Girls Industrial College, it was renamed College of Industrial Arts in 1905, Texas State College for Women in 1934, and assumed its current name in 1957. Male students were admitted for the first time in 1972.

The university has an enrollment of close to 8,000, with about 2 percent of international students that come from up to 75 countries, including India, South Vietnam, Mexico, Nigeria, China, and Korea. The median student age is 27 years, and the student/teacher ratio 13:1. TWU offers bachelor's, master's, and doctoral degrees in more than 100 fields of study, and it is one of the nation's largest universities primarily for women. Almost 60 percent of students receive financial aid.

The 100-year-old abstract artist Dorothy Antoinette "Toni" LaSelle (d. 2002), a native of Nebraska, started her teaching career here in the summer of 1928 and stayed for more than four decades. In 2001 *Texas Monthly* magazine called her "a towering eminence in our cultural landscape: Texas' first true modern, the oldest living veteran of the artistic revolution that reshaped our world."

Its Institute of Health Sciences has centers in Dallas and Houston.

Universities Center at Dallas, 1901 Main St., between St. Paul and Harwood, (214) 915-1900, Internet www.ucddowntown.org. Located in downtown Dallas, across the street from the Bank One Tower, as well as the Majestic Theatre (see individual entries).

The UCD was established in 1994 as the Dallas Education Center and is located in the former Joske's department store. It now claims more than 2,200 students. It was the first multi-institutional teaching center for higher education in Texas to provide access to higher education at the upper division and graduate level in downtown Dallas. Bachelor of science degree, bachelor and master's in business administration, bachelor of fine arts, and bachelor of applied arts degrees can be earned. Classes can be taken after work and during weekends.

The center consists of the following participating universities:

- Midwestern State University, (940) 397-4400
- Texas A&M University-Commerce, (888) 868-2682
- Texas Woman's University, (940) 898-3000
- University of North Texas, (817) 267-3731
- University of Texas at Arlington, (817) 272-6287
- University of Texas at Dallas, (972) 883-6379

University of North Texas, 801 North Texas Blvd., Denton, (800) UNT-8211 or (940) 565-2000, Internet www.unt.edu. The admissions office is located at 1401 West Prairie St. Located 40 miles (or 64 kilometers) northwest of downtown Dallas in a town with a population of 81,000. The campus is situated on 500 acres (or 202 hectares) and includes 134 buildings.

With 30,000 students from the United States and up to 100 foreign countries, and a faculty of 1,000, UNT is the fourth largest university in Texas. It has nine schools and colleges with 97 bachelor's, 126 master's, and 46 doctoral degree programs.

Its student/faculty ratio is 17:1. The median student age is just under 25 years. UNT claims to have more computers per student, more library resources, and more graduate students than any other university in the Metroplex.

Established in 1890 as a teacher education facility, the university has gone through six name changes. Texas novelist Larry McMurtry, who has written more than 30 books, attended it as an undergraduate when it was known as North Texas State College.

The Jazz studies graduate program at this university is one of the best in the United States; its journalism alumni have earned seven Pulitzer Prizes, perhaps the profession's top award. The university library includes the private jazz collection of big band leader Stan Kenton.

Faculty member Cindi McTee is also a composer whose First Symphony was premiered by the National Symphony Orchestra at the Kennedy Center in Washington, D.C., and whose composition "Timepieces" was introduced by the Dallas Symphony Orchestra at Carnegie Hall. Dr. McTee (b. 1953) studied under the renowned Polish composer Krzysztop Penderecki

There is no publicly funded university located within the Dallas city limits. The campus of the University of Texas at Dallas (see below) is located in Richardson. The University of North Texas Health Science Center at Fort Worth is also part of the UNT System. A UNT offshoot in an office park on Hampton Road, south of Interstate 20, is the beginning of the first full-fledged four-year university in southern Dallas County, which has never had a public university. The UNT System Center at Dallas began offering classes in 2000 and had about 300 full-time students. When enrollment at the campus reaches 2,500 full-time students, the new school can become a four-year university offering degrees.

At the helm since 1982, Dr. Alfred Hurley (b. 1929) stepped down in 2002 as the university's longest-serving president. Before joining UNT, the Brooklyn, New York, native spent 19 years as a professor of military history at the Air Force Academy in Colorado. He was replaced in 2002 by the former Dallas County judge Lee Jackson (b. 1950), who has a master's degree in public administration from Southern Methodist University. In 1976, he was elected to the Texas House of Representatives, where he served five terms. Jackson was elected Dallas County judge in 1986. Only Lew Sterrett, who served from 1949 to 1974, had a longer tenure as a county judge. Sterrett was instrumental in the creation of the John F. Kennedy Memorial (see entry).

The University of Texas at Dallas, 2601 North Floyd Rd., Richardson, (972) 883-2111; admissions & registration, (972) 883-2341,

Internet www.utdallas.edu. Located in the heart of the Silicon Prairie—the home to more than 600 telecommunications and other technology firms—18 miles (or 29 kilometers) north of downtown Dallas.

In spite of its name, the university is located in Richardson, not Dallas. A public university, established in 1969 by John Erik Jonsson, Eugene McDermott, and Cecil Green, the founders of what is today Texas Instruments, to attract local engineering talent.

Cecil Howard Green, who was TI president from 1951 to 1955, donated more than $200 million to medical and educational causes. In 1991, he was declared an honorary Knight of the Most Excellent Order of the British Empire in recognition of his life's work. Born in 1900 near Manchester, England, Green received his master's degree in electrical engineering from the Massachusetts Institute of Technology in 1924 and became an American citizen in Dallas in 1936. Married for 60 years to a woman he met while at General Electric in Schenectady, New York, he died at age 102 in 2003 in LaJolla, California. He outlived his wife by 17 years.

In the 1960s, the three men donated land, equipment, and cash valued at more than $17 million to establish the university predecessor, the Graduate Research Center of the Southwest, on 1,200 acres (or 485 hectares) in northern Dallas and southern Collin counties.

The bust of Cecil Green on the wall outside the university has become a good-luck charm for many students who rub the head before taking a test.

The university has an enrollment of about 13,000—some 55 percent Caucasian, 13 percent international—and a faculty of 500 on a 500-acre (or 202-hectare) campus. The student to teacher ratio is 19:1. It consists of seven schools that include arts, engineering, general studies, management, natural sciences, and social sciences. UTD's budget is about $186 million, its endowment less than $200 million.

The School of Management, UTD's largest, has 4,300 students. A new four-story, 180,000-square-foot (or 16,722-square-meter) School of Management facility opened in 2003. The $38-million facility is located at the southeast corner of University Parkway and Drive A.

A typical UTD student is said to be less than 27 years old, married, and has children. Most students work and take at least one evening class. The highest degree conferred is the doctorate, and about one-half of students receive financial aid. There are no social fraternities and no intercollegiate sports at UTD.

The university has a well-regarded **History of Aviation Collection,** (972) 883-2570, Internet www.utdallas.edu/library/special/index.html, open, free of charge, Mon-Thu 9 AM-6 PM and Fridays 9 AM-5 PM, and located at 2901 North Floyd Road. It is composed of 200 collections and consists of more than 30,000 volumes, several hundred thousand periodicals, and hundreds of thousands of photographs covering the entire spectrum of flight.

In 2000, Margaret McDermott, a founder's widow, donated $32 million toward paying for four years all of the academic and living expenses for 20 of the nation's brightest students in the annual Eugene McDermott Scholars Program.

A three-story, $40-million, 152,000-square-foot (or 14,121-square-meter) addition to the Erik Jonsson School of Engineering was completed in 2002 and brought the capacity from 3,000 to 5,000 students.

Dr. Alan G. MacDiarmid, a Nobel Prize-winning researcher in the field of nanoscience, joined the university as a scholar in residence in 2001. He likened UTD to the Stanford University of decades ago, "a good university not yet acclaimed worldwide."

A native of New Zealand and the youngest of five children, Dr. MacDiarmid (b. 1927) shared the 2000 Nobel Prize in chemistry for his work in the 1970s on how plastics can be modified to conduct electricity. To earn money to buy chemicals for his experiments, he took a milk-delivery job and a newspaper route during high school. Dr. MacDiarmid earned one doctorate at the University of Wisconsin, the second at Cambridge University in England.

The university's other Nobel laureate was **Polykarp Kusch** (d. 1993), who shared the physics prize in 1955 and was on the school's faculty from 1972 to 1992.

University of Texas Southwestern Medical Center at Dallas, 5323 Harry Hines Blvd., (214) 648-3111 or 648-7500. Visitors Information Center is open Mon-Fri 7:30 AM-5 PM. Located northwest of downtown and south of Love Field Airport, between Motor Street and Mockingbird Lane.

A public university whose roots under a similar name go back to 1943, when a small wartime medical school was housed in a few abandoned barracks, UT Southwestern is one of eight medical schools in Texas, but the only one in Dallas. Its predecessor has been part of the University of Texas since 1949.

UT Southwestern's 60-acre (or 24-hectare) campus has 16 buildings, about 810 medical and 450 graduate students. About one-third of the 1,100 full-time faculty members are women, including the dean of the graduate school of biomedical sciences.

A 90-acre (or 36-hectare) North Campus across the street from the original campus is the site of another four structures: the Rogers Magnetic Resonance Center, the Simmons Biomedical Research Building, the Hamon Biomedical Research Building, and the Seay Biomedical Building, which are located on Prothro Plaza. Another research tower is in the planning stages.

By 1968, Southwestern surgeons had performed the 21st heart transplant in the world. The health science center personnel treated victims of the crash of Delta Air Lines Flight 191 at D/FW Airport in 1985.

The medical center includes three degree-granting institutions: Southwestern Medical School, Southwestern Graduate School of Biomedical Sciences, and Southwestern Allied Health Sciences School. They employ almost 5,000 and train more than 3,000 students each year. The center's budget is more than $700 million, 65 percent of it in private grants and gifts.

More than 2,000 research projects in cancer, neuroscience, heart disease and stroke, arthritis, and diabetes, totaling $200 million annually, are conducted at UT Southwestern. The center now ranks fourth among some 7,000 institutions in the world in the number of investigators conducting clinical trials on new drugs.

Among medical schools, Southwestern ranks third with more than 130 investigators, while the Mayo Clinic in Rochester, Minnesota, is believed to be first.

Faculty physicians and residents provide care for about 75,000 hospitalized patients and oversee some 1.6 million outpatients a year. UT Southwestern's full-time and volunteer faculty members provide millions of dollars in free professional services each year.

Dallas financier Harold Clark Simmons alone gave $41 million to the Southwestern Medical Center, and Nancy T. Hamon, the wife of oilman Jake Hamon (d. 1985), $25 million.

In 2001, the university initiated construction of a $240-million, 16-story, 760,000-square-foot (or 70,604-square-meter) research facility, using state and federal money, to create the Institute for Innovations in Medical Technology.

Four of its researchers are Nobel Prize winners. **Dr. Michael Brown** (b. 1941) and **Dr. Joseph Goldstein** (b. 1940), professors of molecular genetics, shared the 1985 Nobel Prize in medicine for their research on the basic mechanism of cholesterol metabolism. The two have worked together for 30 years. For the work they have done since the Nobel, they shared the $500,000 Albany Medical Center Prize in 2003.

Dr. Johann Deisenhofer (b. 1943), professor of biochemistry, shared the Nobel Prize in chemistry in 1988 for detailing the structure of protein in the membranes of cells with German scientists Dr. Robert Huber and Dr. Hartmut Michel. Deisenhofer, who in 1997 became a member of the National Academy of Sciences and an American citizen in 2001, says he has a small problem: he has difficulty finding good, German-style rye bread, he confided in the *Dallas Morning News*.

Dallasite **Dr. Alfred Gilman,** chairman of pharmacology at UT Southwestern, shared the prize in medicine in 1994 for his discovery of how cells communicate, together with the late Dr. Martin Rodbell of the National Institute of Environmental Health Sciences.

Twelve UT Southwestern faculty staffers are members of the National Academy of Sciences, and another 12 have been elected to the Institute of Medicine.

The medical school and Parkland Hospital staff treated President Kennedy and Gov. John Connally after they were shot in 1963 in downtown Dallas.

Dr. C. James Carrico, a first-year surgical resident in 1963 and the first physician who tended President Kennedy after his assassination, was the top graduate in the 1961 class of UT Southwestern Medical College. He inserted a tube into the barely breathing president's trachea and then stayed at his side for 25 minutes until a colleague pronounced Kennedy dead.

Dr. Carrico, who died in 2002 at age 67, moved to Seattle in 1974 and became chief of surgery at Harborview Medical Center, a county teaching hospital. In 1983, he was named chairman of the University of Washington Medical School's surgery department, a job he left to take over UT Southwestern medical center in 1990 as chairman of the surgery department.

Parkland, Zale-Lipshy University Hospital, and Children's Medical Center, all located nearby, are three among its primary teaching hospitals.

In 2000, Southwestern Medical purchased for $30 million the physical assets of St. Paul Medical Center, which is operated as a Southwestern's subsidiary under the name St. Paul University Hospital (see entry).

Metroplex Private Colleges & Universities

Amberton University, 1700 Eastgate Dr., Garland, (972) 279-6511, Internet www.amberton.edu. Located at the intersection of Interstate 635 (popularly known as the LBJ Freeway) and Northwest Highway.

The independent, private, non-denominational Christian college, once part of Abilene Christian University at Dallas, was established in 1971. The name Amberton University was chosen by a group of students and staff "because they liked the sound of the name." Having an enrollment of about 1,500, the average age of its student population is in the mid-30s.

Amberton offers undergraduate and graduate degrees in business, management, and professional development. It claims to have the lowest tuition of any private university in the Metroplex.

Art Institute of Dallas, Two NorthPark, 8080 Park Ln. #100, (800)

275-4243 or (214) 692-8080, Internet www.aii.edu, e-mail crispmaii.edu. Located north of downtown Dallas, east of North Central Expressway (or U.S. Hwy. 75) and across it from the NorthPark mall (see entry).

A private commercial art institute, established in 1987, with an enrollment of about 1,100. It charges tuition and fees of up to $55,000 per school year, although several scholarships are offered. The school's programs include interior design, culinary arts, fashion design, video production, graphic design, multimedia and Web development, and animation art and design. The student body includes up to 60 international students, who might come from countries as varied as Brazil, Switzerland, Iraq, Colombia, Russia, Germany, Canada, India, Venezuela, and England.

AIA is a wholly owned subsidiary of the Art Institute International. It awards associate and bachelor of fine arts degrees. AIA was founded in 1964 as Dallas Fashion Merchandising College. It changed its name and location in 1984.

Baylor College of Dentistry, 3302 Gaston Ave. and Hall St., (214) 828-8100, general clinic inquiries 828-8440 or 828-8441, Internet www.tambcd.edu, e-mail admissions@tambcd.edu. Located a mile (or 1.6 kilometers) northeast of the downtown business district and just north of Deep Ellum historic and entertainment district, it is adjacent to the Baylor University Medical Center.

Established in 1905, it was affiliated with Baylor University from 1918 to 1971, and an independent, private institution until 1996, when it became a member of the Texas A & M University System Health Science Center. The college claims to be "the largest single provider of oral health care in Dallas. Almost two-thirds of all the dentists in the Dallas area received their education at BCD," notes its Web page.

BCD offers a four-year program leading to a doctor of dental surgery degree, as well as master's and doctoral degrees. Enrollment is about 500 students. Each year, the college completes more than 100,000 patient visits, almost half of them benefiting the poor. An initial screening appointment takes up to two hours.

However, if you can afford to pay the going rate of a well-to-do Richardson orthodontist, located at 1920 North Coit and Campbell Roads, (972) 680-9882, consider Dr. Douglas Crosby. With a carpet depicting a baseball diamond and countless other sports-related touches, it is one of the most unique dental offices in Dallas. There are carpeted "bleachers" for waiting parents. The big-screen television is usually tuned to the ESPN channel. Dr. Crosby, who teaches part time in the orthodontic department at this college, also has an office in Plano.

Baylor School of Nursing, 3700 Worth St., (214) 820-3361.

Located northeast of downtown Dallas, between Hall and Washington Streets.

The nursing school has an enrollment of about 250. Upon receiving a $13-million gift from a Tyler businesswoman, the school was renamed Louise Herrington School of Nursing. The school was established in 1909 as a diploma program within Baylor Hospital, which is now Baylor Medical Center, and in 1950 became one of the six degree-granting schools of the university. It is one of the oldest baccalaureate nursing programs in the nation.

Dallas Baptist University, 3000 Mountain Creek Pkwy. at West Kiest Blvd., (800) 460-1DBU or (214) 333-5360, Internet www.dbu.edu. Located southwest of downtown Dallas, on the eastern shore of Mountain Creek Lake, a 2,710-acre (or 1,097-hectare) man-made body of water created in the 1930s to cool a nearby electric plant.

A private Southern Baptist college situated on 293 acres (or 118.5 hectares) and having an enrollment of about 4,000. This is the successor to Decatur Baptist College, which was founded in 1891, and which moved to its present location in 1965. The student to teacher ratio is 19:1, and the median student age is 23-28 years. It offers bachelor's and master's degrees in education, religion, and business administration. Its north Dallas center is located at 4120 International Pkwy. in Carrollton.

Dallas Naval Air Station is located across the lake from DBU. Once a major naval-reserve installation, it was established in 1929 by the city of Dallas as a training field for reserve pilots and leased to the U.S. Navy for 70 years at a symbolic $3.

The 750-acre (or 303-hectare) station was decommissioned in 1999 because of federal budget cuts. Two years later, the city filed a suit against the Navy, claiming it would take $1 billion to clean up the solvents, fuel, and paint that have "seeped into the ground and have poisoned nearby Mountain Creek Lake." In 2002, the Navy and the city settled on $53.5 million to clean up the contaminated site.

Dallas Theological Seminary, 3909 Swiss Ave., (800) 992-0998 or (214) 824-3094. Located in east Dallas, northeast of the downtown business district.

A private non-denominational Protestant college, established in 1924 with 12 students. By 1976, the student body had increased to 1,000 and now has an enrollment of about 1,600 students, with about half of them receiving financial aid. The theologically conservative seminary describes itself as the second-largest interdenominational seminary in the world.

DeVry Institute of Technology, 4800 Regent Blvd., Irving, (972)

929-6777, Internet www.dal.devry.edu. Located in a 95,000-square-foot (or 8,825-square-meter) facility in Freeport Business Park.

DeVry was established in 1969 and offers bachelor's degrees in accounting, business information systems, computer and e-commerce in 23 cities and 13 states, as well as in Canada. Enrollment on the Irving campus is more than 3,500 students with a median age of 27. The student/teacher ratio is 23:1.

Keller Graduate School of Management, which offers master's degrees, is also located on the DeVry campus. It was founded in 1973 and now has 45 graduate centers.

LeTourneau University, 5710 Lyndon B. Johnson Frwy., Suite 150, (800) 688-5327 or (972) 387-9835, Internet www.letu.edu. Located in north Dallas, between Montfort Drive and Preston Road, across LBJ from Valley View Mall (see entry).

A private non-denominational Christian college, established in 1946, with an enrollment of almost 3,000 from the United States and several other nations. You can get your business administration, business management, and business administration degree here evenings or weekends. The school brags in its advertisements that it offers a "world-class education with a Christian worldview." Other LeTourneau campuses are located in Bedford and Sherman, Texas.

Paul Quinn College, 3837 Simpson Stuart Rd. at Bonnie View, (214) 376-1000 or (800) 237-2648, Internet www.pqc.edu. Located about eight miles (or 12.9 kilometers) southwest of downtown Dallas, west of Julius Schepps Freeway South (also known as Interstate 45).

Paul Quinn was founded by African Methodist Episcopal circuit-riding preachers in Austin, Texas, in 1872. The collage, named for Bishop William Paul Quinn, was relocated to Waco, Texas, in 1877 and to Dallas, where it took over the facilities of the defunct Bishop College, another historically black school, in 1990.

It is the oldest liberal arts college for African-Americans in the state.

Paul Quinn moved to a 138-acre (or 55.8-hectare), 24-building campus site in southeast Oak Cliff, in Dallas, in 1990. In that year, Comer J. Cottrell, the African-American owner of Pro-Line cosmetics company, purchased the campus of the former Bishop College for $1.5 million and leased it to Paul Quinn until 1994, when Paul Quinn agreed to buy it back for $3.5 million.

When Alberto Culver purchased Pro-Line for a reported $75 million in 2000, it forgave the school's remaining $1.7 million in land debt. Cottrell started Pro-Line in Dallas in 1970 with $600 and a borrowed typewriter.

Bachelor degrees in arts, sciences, and applied sciences are offered.

The student/teacher ratio is 17:1. Almost one-half of the faculty of 100 has doctoral degrees. Enrollment is below 800, more than 90 percent African-American and 60 percent female.

Southern Methodist University, Hillcrest Ave., at Mockingbird Lane and North Central Expwy., (214) 768-2000; arts events, SMU-ARTS; Meadows Museum, 768-2516; calendar listings 768-7650, Internet www.smu.edu. The campus has 5,735 parking spaces. Located north of downtown Dallas, on the southeastern edge of University Park. It also has a satellite campus in north Plano.

The original gift of land to SMU was by Alice Armstrong, the widow of grocer John Armstrong, who founded the town of Highland Park and died in 1908. The 100 acres (or 40 hectares) she gave in 1911 were enlarged by the generous Caruth family, who came from Kentucky in 1848 and contributed additional land to make today's university possible. When William Caruth died in 1885, he owned an estimated 20,000 acres (or 8,094 hectares) of prime agricultural land north of Dallas. In 1927, the now-popular Snider Plaza opened nearby.

The university began with 706 students and 35 faculty in September 1915 at Dallas Hall. Dallas Hall architecture was inspired by the Roman Pantheon and influenced by Jefferson's library at the University of Virginia. It was then surrounded by open fields and farms, more than a couple of miles (or 3.2 kilometers) north of the Dallas city limits. The Classical Revival building was designed by Shepley, Rutan & Coolidge of Boston.

Dr. Umphrey Lee (d. 1958), a native Texan who was one of the 1915 original students, took SMU's reins in 1939. He resigned in 1954.

One of its best known and longest serving presidents, Willis McDonald Tate (1911-1989), graduated from SMU with a B.A. in 1932 and an M.A. in 1935. He became SMU's assistant dean of students in 1945, president of the university in 1954, and chancellor in 1971. Five years later he was made president emeritus. Tate is known for his defense of academic freedom: he refused to ban books about communism in SMU libraries in the 1950s and stood behind Dr. Martin Luther King, who spoke on the campus in the 1960s.

A. Kenneth Pye was in charge from 1978 to 1994. "Tough, gruff, often skeptical, Pye was a warm, kind humorous person," according to historian Terry. Suffering from health problems, he resigned from office in June 1994 and died of cancer the following month. He was followed the next year by Dr. R. Gerald Turner, Chancellor of the University of Mississippi, as SMU's 10th president.

SMU is one of the larger private universities in the Southwest, with an enrollment of more than 10,000 students, and a median age of 21. SMU is a coeducational school numbering 70 buildings on a 1,634-acre (or 661-hectare) campus that employs 1,400, including about 530 as full-time faculty. The student to teacher ratio is about 12:1. SMU offers degrees in four undergraduate and two graduate schools.

Its $20-million law school was renamed after the late Dallas billionaire Robert H. Dedman and his wife of 49 years, both SMU graduates, who gave more than $77 million to the university. The Dedman College of Humanities and Sciences, the largest and most diverse school on the campus, was named for the Dedmans after they gave it $25 million in 1981. The Dedmans also gave $12 million for the Dedman Life Sciences Building, which was completed in 2002, and the 43,000-square-foot (or 3,995-square-meter) Dedman Center for Lifetime Sports, which opened in 1976.

Robert Dedman (1926-2002) a dirt-poor south Arkansas native, was, in his own words "too poor to paint and too proud to whitewash." He sold insurance and real estate while earning degrees in engineering, economics, and law, but soon realized he would not reach his goal of earning $50 million before he turned 50 by working for other people. In 1957, when 31 years old, he founded ClubCorp, which now has a stake in 200 resorts and golf clubs worldwide and publishes a monthly magazine with a circulation of 225,000.

Dedman graduated from North Dallas High School, just north of West Village shopping center, in 1944. Fifty years later, he established a scholarship fund that sends four top graduates from North Dallas High to Southern Methodist University each year. At the time of his death in 2002, he was one of the 220 richest Americans and among the ten wealthiest Dallasites, according to *Forbes* magazine. "They don't put luggage racks on hearses," he once told *Texas Monthly*, explaining the reasons for his philanthropic endeavors, "You can't take it with you." His son, also an SMU graduate, has been running the company's daily operations since 1998. ClubCorp Inc. (Internet www.clubcorp.com), located at LBJ Freeway and Webb Chapel Road, is the tenth largest privately owned company in the Metroplex, with revenues of $1 billion a year and about 2,560 local employees.

The Meadows School of the Arts, Cox School of Business, and Perkins School of Theology are all named after other prominent businessmen.

Dr. Marion Sobol, a former New Yorker who has been teaching at SMU for 30 years, saved the royalties from her statistics textbook to buy for the university a free-form abstraction by the Dallas-based architect-turned-sculptor, Tom Woodward. The six-foot-high (or 1.82-meter) bronze, titled *Curl*, "a curving, organic, feminine form" is located in the Cox courtyard, on Bishop Drive.

The 50,000-square-foot (or 4,645-square-meter), three-story electrical engineering school is named after Jerry R. Junkins, a former Texas Instruments chief executive officer, who gave SMU $15 million. The school has about 600 undergraduate and 500 graduate students. Its basement houses a "clean room," where researchers work on semiconductors and high-tech manufacturing experiments in an ultra-clean environment.

Hughes-Trigg Student Center, located at 3140 Dyer St. and opened in 1988, is the busiest building on the campus. The *Daily Campus* editorial office, an art gallery, auditoriums, the Student Activities Center, and fast-food restaurants are located here. The center was made possible with a $10-million donation from Charles H. Trigg (d. 1996) and Mary Katherine Hughes (d. 1997), who "had their first kiss under a tree that stood where the building is today."

The $13-million, 60,000-square-foot (or 5,574-square-meter) Laura Lee Blanton Student Service Building, located on the west side of Airline Road near SMU Boulevard, was completed in 2003. The Blanton's contributed $5 million toward its completion. The Blanton building will house a welcoming center, the registrar's office, the enrollment services division, information technology services, and the international student services center.

The $5-million Belo Digital Television Studio and Newsroom, donated by the parent company of the *Dallas Morning News*, is located in the Umphrey-Lee Center.

The third permanent building on the campus, following Dallas and Clements Halls, was the 2,400-seat McFarlin Auditorium, secured by a donation from a devout Methodist and San Antonio businessman, Robert M. McFarlin, and built in 1926. Concerts and other events are held in the auditorium, where the Dallas Symphony performed from the 1930s until 1989.

Poet W. H. Auden, ballet dancer Mikhail Baryshnikov, Nobel Prize novelist Sinclair Lewis, civil rights leader Martin Luther King Jr., and actors Cary Grant, Sidney Poitier, and Orson Wells all participated at events here. Poitier's daughter Beverly earned a fine arts degree in theater at SMU.

In 1958, Lon Tinkle, SMU's professor of French and a former *Dallas Morning News* book critic, brought T. S. Eliot to Moody Coliseum, where more than 9,000 listened to the "world's most famous poet" reading "The Fire Sermon," "Death by Water," and "What the Thunder Said," during the "blackest, rainiest, blowiest night" some had ever seen.

About 600, or 6 percent of SMU's students, hail from up to 90 countries, with the largest contingents coming from China, India, Mexico, South Korea, Canada, Japan, and Russia. The son of Count Anton von Faber-Castell, president of a well-known German manufacturer of the same name, is just one among them.

Although having an endowment of about $800 million, the university is not embarrassed to look for funding even among those who traditionally were not expected to give. "A German count, a Chilean golf-resort owner and a Guatemalan bank president recently joined SMU president Gerald Turner for lunch," reported the *Dallas Morning News*. "After dessert, Dr. Turner asked them and his other international guests to donate money for a future building."

In 2002, SMU celebrated a five-year capital campaign that brought in $532,668,000 from 40,000 donors, almost 65 percent of them alumni. "This shows that SMU has broad-based support to aspire to be in the top 50 [universities]," noted Turner.

University of Dallas, 1845 East Northgate Dr., Irving, (972) 721-5000 or (800) 721-5235; admissions, (972) 721-5266, Internet www.udallas.edu. Located northwest of downtown Dallas, four blocks northwest of Texas Stadium, off State Highway 114 (also known as John W. Carpenter Freeway).

A private Roman Catholic university, founded in 1956, with an enrollment of about 3,500 students with a median age of 18 years. The student/teacher ratio is 11:1. There are 28 buildings on a 225-acre (or 91-hectare) campus. It also has campuses in Richardson and Plano.

The University of Dallas has the largest master of business administration enrollment of any Metroplex college, followed by Southern Methodist University, and the University of Texas at Dallas. The university boasts the Margaret Jonsson Theater, (972) 721-5314, where plays, such as *The Beggar's Opera*, are staged.

Holy Trinity Seminary here, founded in 1967 and sponsored by the Diocese of Dallas, is the only four-year college-level seminary in Texas, the first stop in a seminarian's training before going to a graduate-level theological seminary.

In 2000, the university inaugurated three new buildings at Haggerty Art Center, named for a Texas Instruments founder and designed by architect Gary Cunningham. The original art center was drafted by the well-known Texas architect O'Neil Ford in 1960.

The university dedicated its 12-acre (or 4.85-hectare) Italian campus (e-mail udtravel@acad.udallas.edu), located among vineyards 15 kilometers (or 9.3 miles) from Rome. The estate's three-story winery barn, thought to have once belonged to Julius Caesar, was converted into classrooms, a dining room, and a kitchen.

The German-born sculptor Heri Bartscht founded the sculpture department and taught here until the early 1990s. After a brief career in Munich, Bartscht moved to the area in 1953 and gained critical acclaim. A devout Roman Catholic, the sculptor completed some 50 commissions for churches in Texas. He died in 1996 at age 77.

GOVERNMENT

For an abundance of information about the city, county, and state governments and their elected officials, please check also the state's Internet site www.texas.gov.

City Government

Dallas has a council-city manager form of municipal government. The mayor heads a 14-member elected city council, which functions like a corporate board of directors, deciding policy and charting the city's future, with the city manager acting as the chief executive officer. The council had eight Anglo members and seven minorities in 2003. Only two of the council members were Hispanic, although the 2000 Census claimed that Hispanics then accounted for 35.6 percent of Dallas residents, outnumbering both Caucasians and African-Americans.

Since 1931, the council has employed a professional city manager who is responsible for the daily operations of all city departments, with the help of seven assistant city managers. If the council members want to get something done, they go to the city manager or one of his assistants. Until the federal courts ordered Dallas to start electing its council members from individual districts, the city manager was insulated from political pressure.

"Council members, who feel heat from constituents to hold the line on taxes while meeting expanding service needs, put ample political pressure on the city manager," observes the *Dallas Morning News*. The mayorship is largely a ceremonial position, although the majority of Dallas residents believe that an elected mayor rather than a hired city manager is best suited to implement day-to-day city policies.

"The voters of Dallas never approved the current 14-1 city council system," reminds *D Magazine*, adding that the voters actually rejected it, and the system was imposed by a federal judge. The monthly alleges that council districts have turned into little fiefdoms, with council members working them "like ward-heelers. Dallas, in effect, has 14 little mayors ordering around the city staff and trading favors to get their pet projects approved."

Only a handful of the nation's largest cities besides Dallas have council-manager governments. They include San Antonio in Texas, Phoenix in Arizona, and San Diego and San Jose in California.

The city charter limits council members to four consecutive two-year terms, and the mayor to two consecutive four-year terms. The city has some 13,000 employees and a budget of about $1.5 billion.

The president of the Dallas Area Rapid Transit earns $215,00, the Dallas city manager $263,000, and the Dallas Independent School District superintendent $280,000 annually.

Unlike Austin, where the city council members receive an annual salary of $35,000 and the mayor $45,000, the Dallas city council members and the mayor were paid a flat fee of $50 for each meeting. Seven times after 1968, the council asked voters for a raise, and seven times the voters said, "No." In 2001, the council members asked voters for an annual salary of $37,500, which was slightly above the median household income in the city, and the mayor for $60,000. The proposal squeaked through by a 3,413-vote margin.

The city council meets every second and fourth Wednesday at 9 AM. To make public comments, you must register with the city secretary in Room 5-D South, Dallas City Hall, 1500 Marilla, or call (214) 670-3738. You must provide your name, address, daytime telephone number, and the subject of your comments. The deadline for registering is 9 AM on the day of the council meeting, which is broadcast on the city-owned classical music station, WRR-FM 101.1 FM. The first five citizens who register can speak at the beginning of the council meeting, others must wait until the council finishes its business, usually in the afternoon. Speakers are limited to three minutes, and Dallas residents can speak before nonresidents.

County Government

On the Dallas County Web site, www.dallascounty.org, you can pay property taxes, handle vehicle registration renewals, pay court fees for protective orders, traffic fines, civil court fines and fees, and download applications for several permits. There is a "convenience fee" for some of these transactions.

The county comprises 902 square miles (or 2,336 square kilometers) of mostly flat Blackland Prairie. The highest elevation is only 584 feet (or 178 meters) above sea level.

Dallas County was officially formed on March 30, 1846, from portions of Nacogdoches and Robertson Counties. In 1850, when the county had a population of 2,743—8 percent of them slaves—an election was held to determine a permanent county seat, which went to Dallas.

The county is divided into four precincts with two justices of the peace, who serve four-year terms and handle disputes in matters such as evictions, hot checks, truancy, and towing, and earn more than $85,000 a year. They also keep the money they make performing weddings, which can add thousands of dollars to their income.

Each precinct has a constable, who serves civil papers and criminal warrants, makes arrests, and has some traffic enforcement responsibilities.

Dallas County is governed by a county judge, who earns about $125,000 a year, and four commissioners elected by the citizens every four years. The county judge is not really a judge, he does not preside over a courtroom, and he usually is not even a lawyer. The commissioners are members of the County Commissioners Court that runs county government. They set the county tax rate and supervise the jail system, the Sheriff's Department, the district attorney's office, Parkland Health & Hospital System, and other county operations.

The *Dallas Morning News* calls the county government an "enigma," continuing: "The Commissioners Court is not a court, and the county judge has no judicial responsibilities."

While the county grew in population by 20 percent from 1990 to 2000, it lost more than 131,000 Anglos, or non-Hispanic whites, during the same time period. That was the sixth largest loss of any large county in the United States, according to the 2000 U.S. Census figures. Having a high per capita murder rate and one of the worst school ratings in the state are probably only two reasons why.

The county has about 5,000 employees and a budget of $330 million.

State Government

Texas is called the Lone Star State for its red, white, and blue flag containing a single white star.

Texans love to remind visitors from abroad that their state is larger than France, Belgium, Holland, Switzerland, and Luxembourg combined. Texas measures 267,277 square miles (or 692,247 square kilometers), has more than 2,000 cities in 254 counties, and boasts a population of about 21 million. It also has more than 300,000 miles (or 482,000 kilometers) of roads.

Fifty-three percent of the residents are Caucasians, 32 percent Hispanics, and more than 11 percent African-Americans. On an average day in Texas there are about 1,000 births (more than 100 of them in Dallas), more than 400 deaths, 500 marriages, and 200 divorces.

The state's median household income is nearly $40,000, according to the U.S. Census Bureau, while the national figure is about $42,000. More than 15 percent of Texans live in poverty.

Twenty-three percent of Texas residents have at least a bachelor's degree, ranking the state as 26th in the nation, as opposed to one-quarter of all Americans. The statewide median age is 32.3 years, up from 28 in 1980.

Nearly 14 percent of all Texas residents are foreign-born, almost 69 percent speak only English at home, but there are no fewer than 27 percent who speak only Spanish at home, according to the Census Bureau. Excluding Mexico and Canada, Texas has more than 800,000 foreign visitors.

Texas, where 97 percent of the land is privately owned, has 226,000 farms, averaging 575 acres (or 232 hectares) each, and 83,000 full-time farmers. Agriculture is the state's second largest industry and accounts for 15 percent of jobs statewide. The Lone Star State is second in the nation in farm receipts, behind California, with $13 billion.

The Texas Senate is made up of 31 members, and the House of Representatives of 150 members. Senators serve four-year terms, while representatives serve for two years. The Texas Legislature meets in regular sessions every odd-numbered year for 140 days and for special sessions as called by the governor.

The judicial system in Texas is headed by the Supreme Court and the State Court of Criminal Appeals.

The Texas Legislature approved a $118-billion budget for the two-year fiscal period 2004-2005, with the largest portion of it going for public education. By 2003, the budget was headed toward a $10-billion shortfall.

Texas has more than 2,100 special-interest groups registered to lobby the 181-member Legislature and other branches of the state government. The insurance industry, with more than 200 companies and associations, leads the lobbying activity. Only California has more lobbyists.

(For more information about Texas, go to the Web site www.state.tx.us.)

U.S. Senators from Texas

Senator Kay Bailey Hutchison, Republican, has a Dallas office at 10440 North Central Expwy. #1160, (214) 361-3500, and in Washington, D.C., (202) 224-5922, Fax (202) 224-0776, Internet www.hutchison.senate.gov, e-mail senator@hutchison.senate.gov.

"In terms of votes received, she is by far the most popular politician in Texas history," notes the *Texas Monthly* about Hutchison (b. 1944), whose husband Ray is a prominent bond attorney in Dallas. In 1973, she became the first Republican woman to serve in the Texas House and has been in the public spotlight for more than 30 years. Her great-great-grandfather was a signer of the Texas Declaration of Independence, and her Washington office displays an oil painting of William Barret Travis.

Senator John Cornyn, Republican, has his Dallas office at 5005 Lyndon B. Johnson Frwy., Suite 1150, (972) 239-1310, Fax (972) 239-2110, and in Washington, D.C., (202) 224-2934, Fax (202) 228-2856, Internet www.cornyn.senate.gov, e-mail senator@cornyn.senate.gov.

HEALTH & DENTAL CARE

"We have world-class medical minds in Dallas—four Nobel laureates work at University of Texas Southwestern Medical Center, just to name a few—which means patients here receive some of the best medical care in the world," claims the city's *D Magazine*, quoting a physician recruiter as saying, "It's really one of the last places left where there is a common bond of excellence in medicine."

Dallas County has 8,000 hospital beds, nearly 5,000 doctors (1,300 among them women), and 17,600 registered nurses. There are more than 40 hospitals in the city. It also has one of the largest concentrations of research hospitals in the nation and perhaps boasts more award-winning researchers than most other cities in the country.

Web sites, such as www.healthgrades.com and www.hospitalprofiles.org, post volume, death-rate, and cost information about some hospitals. The data typically come from government reports and private surveys.

Parkland Hospital (see entry), where President Kennedy, his alleged assassin, and Oswald's killer were all taken and died, is usually rated one of the two dozen best hospitals in the United States. The emergency rooms, where Kennedy and Oswald were rushed to, have both been dismantled. Parkland's trauma and burn centers are internationally recognized. However, being a public hospital, you can spend an entire day there waiting your turn; you should consider it only in an emergency, such as a heart attack.

For the usual medical needs, consider one of the hospitals below, where most of your minor ailments can be taken care of at the outpatient or emergency clinic. The cost, however, will be higher than if you sought one among some 150 doctors at the Woodhill Medical Park, (214) 696-8883, on Walnut Hill Lane, across from the Presbyterian Hospital.

Unless a resident, you will most likely have to pay cash or with a universally recognized credit card, such as American Express, MasterCard, or VISA.

Baylor University Medical Center, 3500 Gaston Ave. at Hall St., (214) 820-0111; 24-hour emergency, 820-2501, Internet www.baylorhealth.com. Located about one mile (or 1.6 kilometers) northeast of the central business district and north of the Deep Ellum entertainment district.

This medical center began in 1903 as a 25-bed Good Samaritan Hospital in a two-story, 14-room brick house converted into a private hospital. In 1909, the five-story, 114-room Texas Baptist Sanitarium—later renamed Baylor Hospital—was built, largely thanks to the largess of the devout Baptist and wealthy cattleman, Col. Christopher Columbus Slaughter, who contributed $200,000.

Its College of Medicine moved to Houston in 1943. Comprising five connecting patient hospitals and a cancer center, Baylor is the second largest nonprofit private hospital in the nation. Serving as the flagship hospital of the Baylor Health Care System, the center cares for more than 500,000 people each year. The largest private hospital in the Metroplex, it has 1,200 physicians, 1,900 nurses, 950 beds, and a staff of about 5,300. Baylor University has Level I trauma services and 24-hour emergency services. Top specialties are oncology, cardiovascular services, organ and bone marrow transplants. It was here that the beloved former Dallas Cowboys coach Tom Landry battled acute myelogenous leukemia, unable to receive visitors or flowers, before he died on February 12, 2000.

The *U.S. News & World Report* weekly ranks Baylor as one of the top 40 hospitals in the nation in digestive disorders, and one among the 50 most successful in treating cancer.

The Baylor Health Care System, which has revenues in excess of $1 billion, consists of nine hospitals: Baylor University Medical Center, which includes the 92-bed Baylor Institute for Rehabilitation, Baylor Specialty Hospital, Our Children's House at Baylor, Tom Landry Center, and Baylor Geriatric Center.

Also part of Baylor are:

Baylor Medical Center at Garland, 2300 Marie Curie Dr., (972) 487-5000; Physician referral line, (800) 4BAYLOR, Internet www.baylorhealth.com. It has 24-hour emergency services.

A general hospital with 220 beds, 500 physicians, and 400 nurses, it provides family practice, cardiac rehabilitation, gynecology, neonatal care, obstetrics, pediatrics, inpatient and outpatient surgical services.

Baylor Medical Center at Irving, 1901 North MacArthur Blvd., (972) 579-8100. A general hospital with 300 beds and almost as many doctors that provides primary care, oncology, neurosurgery, neurology, cardiology, and gastroenterology services.

Its Women's Pavilion of Health is equipped to handle high-risk pregnancies and deliveries. Baylor's diabetes center is recognized by the American Diabetes Association.

Baylor/Richardson Medical Center, 401 West Campbell Rd., (972) 498-4000. A general hospital with 174 beds, 250 physicians, and 200 nurses, it provides services including oncology, cardiology, gynecology, obstetrics, orthopedics, pediatrics, and outpatient surgery.

The nonprofit Baylor also maintains primary care centers at Colleyville, Coppell, Flower Mound, Garland, Irving, Mesquite, Park Cities, Rockwall, Rowlett, Southlake, and Terrell, more than a dozen rehabilitation facilities, and several senior health centers.

In a survey conducted by the *Fort Worth Star-Telegram*, this hospital had one of the lowest heart attack death rates—6.98 percent of 112 patients—among Dallas and Tarrant county hospitals between 1999 and 2000.

Children's Medical Center of Dallas, 1935 Motor St. at Harry Hines Blvd., (214) 456-2000 or (817) 332-3116 from Fort Worth; 24-hour emergency, (214) 640-2100, Internet www.childrens.com. Located about three miles (or 4.8 kilometers) north of downtown Dallas near Interstate 35 East (or Stemmons Freeway), and south of Love Field Airport.

A private, not-for-profit hospital specializing in diseases and disorders among children from birth to age 18. It has 320 beds, 700 physicians, 800 nurses, and a total staff of 3,400. Children's admits nearly 14,000 patients a year, claims 250,000 outpatient visits, and performs more than 8,000 day surgeries.

Top specialties are pediatric hematology and oncology, pediatric cardiology, and gastroenterology. More than 90 percent of the staff is board-certified in pediatrics.

The hospital features a 26-bed pediatric intensive care unit, an 11-bed pediatric cardiac intensive care unit, a 10-bed pediatric trauma intensive care unit, a 12-bed psychiatric unit, and these specialty clinics for children:

•400 West Interstate 635, Plaza One, Suite 145, (972) 501-0000, Irving.

•6124 West Parker Rd., Medical Office Bldg. III, Suite 336, Plano.

Children's Medical is home of the only emergency transport service certified for ground ambulance, helicopter, and fixed-wing aircraft. It has been chosen as a Starbright World link site enabling patients to communicate with other ill children on computers.

Children's was established in 1958 as an umbrella organization for several existing facilities located in Oak Lawn. During the 1950s, they merged and in 1967 moved into a new complex adjacent to Parkland Hospital (see entry) and the University of Texas Southwestern Medical Center (see entry), with which the center retains a close relationship.

Children's signed a $30-million lease for 152,000 square feet (or 14,120 square meters) of space at the nearby Market Center (see entry) on Stemmons Freeway at Motor Street. It turned the former Menswear Mart into a surgery center renamed the Children's Pavilion. Its ground floor houses an ambulatory surgery center that can support more than 5,000 day surgeries annually. A new $100-million tower with six floors and 132 beds at its Motor Street location was slated for completion in 2004.

Child magazine selected it as one of the eight "best" children's hospitals nationwide, tying its ranking with Children's Hospital of San Diego, California. The monthly singles out as a "remarkable" accomplishment of its surgical team a 39-hour operation to save a two-year-old boy whose face was severely disfigured by the family dog.

The Motor Street Children's Medical runs eight model trains around 1,300 feet (or 396 meters) of track in a $200,000 lobby trainscape, one of the largest such indoor attractions in the country.

Medical City Dallas Hospital, 7777 Forest Ln., (972) 566-7000, Internet www.medicalcityhospital.com, e-mail medcity.main@lonestarhealth.com. Has 24-hour emergency services. Located north of downtown Dallas and south of Lyndon B. Johnson Freeway, just west of North Central Expressway (also known as U.S. Highway 75).

The fourth busiest hospital in the Metroplex, with 588 beds, 1,300 physicians, and 1,000 nurses. This for-profit hospital has been serving the city since 1974, when 100 physicians banded together.

Top specialties at Medical City are heart and lung transplants, women's and pediatric services, and oncology. Other services available include heart, lung, pancreas, kidney, and bone marrow transplants, cardiovascular and cardiopulmonary services, surgical care, hematology and oncology, pediatric services, radiation therapy, and sports medicine.

Medical City is owned by HCA-The Healthcare Co., the nation's largest hospital chain, which includes some 200 hospitals and 70 outpatient surgery centers in 24 states and abroad.

Also part of this facility is the **North Texas Hospital for Children,** (972) 661-0595. Medical City and **Children's Choice Learning Center** (Internet www.childrenschoice.com) of Dallas maintain a 24-hour-a-day, seven-day-a-week child care center on the hospital campus. The $4-million, 21,000-square-foot (or 1,951-square-meter) facility, intended for Medical City employees and outsiders, is open 365 days a year and can accept up to 330 children ages six weeks to 12 years.

Methodist Medical Center, 1441 North Beckley Ave. at Colorado Blvd., (214) 947-8181; Methodist referral service, 947-000; emergency, 947-8100, Internet www.mhd.com. Located about two miles (or 3.2 kilometers) southwest of the downtown business district and south of Interstate 30.

It has 430 physicians, 630 nurses, and 478 beds, with a total staff of almost 2,000 and 24-hour emergency services. The private non-profit hospital was established in 1927. In 2003 its liver transplant center became the second such north Texas facility, joining Baylor Regional Transplant Institute.

Top specialties include multi-organ transplantation, cardiology, oncology and physical rehabilitation services, maternity, and neonatology. *U.S. News & World Report* ranks it one of the best in the nation in hormonal disorders. Methodist also has one of the highest-rated neonatal intensive care units in the country. Also part of the Methodist Hospitals chain is:

Charlton Methodist Hospital, 3500 West Wheatland Rd. at Bolton Boone and Hwy. 67, (214) 947-7777; information desk, 947-7680. Located south of Interstate 20 and west of Hampton Road.

A general hospital with 191 private-room beds, 440 physicians, and 220 nurses that provides general medical, surgical, obstetrical treatment, it also has 24-hour emergency services. A cancer center opened in 1998. A cafeteria is located on the ground floor.

Parkland Memorial Hospital, 5201 Harry Hines Blvd., (214) 590-8000; 24-hour emergencies, same number; administration, 590-8006, Internet www.pmh.org. Located about three miles (or 4.8 kilometers) northwest of downtown Dallas, roughly between the University of Texas Southwest Medical Center and Children's Medical Center (see entries).

By some measures the busiest hospital in the Metroplex, it has 700 beds, almost 900 physicians, 2,000 nurses, and employs 7,350. Its annual budget is about $810 million. Top specialties are trauma center, high-risk pregnancy, and the only burn unit in the region.

Dallas County's only public hospital, Parkland is the primary teaching institution of the University of Texas Southwestern Medical School (see entry). Accessible to rich and poor alike, but be ready for waits as long as ten hours, whether at the main hospital or its seven neighborhood-based health centers.

Parkland treats about 800,000 patients a year, 115,000 among them emergency cases, admits 40,000 patients, and delivers more than 16,300 babies a year, perhaps the most in the nation. Dallas' Presbyterian Hospital, in comparison, delivers about 5,400 a year, and Methodist Hospital 5,100.

The *U.S. News & World Report* weekly magazine ranks Parkland as one of the top ten hospitals in the nation in gynecological treatments; one of the 20 best in treating digestive and hormonal disorders, kidney disease, as well as heart and heart surgery treatment; one of the 30 best for ear, nose, and throat treatments, as well as orthopedics, and rheumatology; one of the 40 best in geriatrics; and one of the top 50 hospitals in the country in urology, neurology, and neurosurgery.

A much-needed $300-million, 670,000-square-foot (or 62,243-square-meter) maternity hospital and a 75,000-square-foot (or 6,967-square-meter) ambulatory outpatient surgery center are planned for.

The modern Parkland opened in 1954. It was the first Texas hospital to be licensed as an HMO and has the state's largest public-hospital-based managed care program.

North Texas Poison Center, (800) 764-7661, located inside Parkland and open 24 hours a day, is the area's only certified regional poison center. It has access to information on 750,000 toxic substances and drugs and responds to 200 emergency calls daily.

Dr. Ron Anderson has been president of Parkland Health & Hospital System since 1982.

The Old Parkland Hospital, now called Woodlawn Hospital, was originally constructed in 1894 on land the city bought for $40,000 to build a park. Thus the name Parkland. It stands on 17 acres (or 6.87 hectares) north of downtown, at the northwest corner of Maple and Oak Lawn Avenues, where an amusement park and picnic grounds were once located.

The *Dallas Daily Times Herald* noted in 1903 that the hospital had "accommodations for 65 patients," and that "the requisites for admission are that patients must be citizens of Dallas; strangers, however, who are victims of accidents or suffering from acute illness, if in indigent circumstances, will be temporarily cared for." The article claimed that "the house staff of physicians are very diligent and zealous in their work."

Over the years, Woodlawn Hospital has served variously as a general hospital, a psychiatric institution, a jail, and a makeshift homeless shelter. In 1913, the wooden, 188,000-square-foot (or 17,465-square-meter) structure was replaced with a brick building which, after Parkland moved to its current facility in 1954, served as a detention center.

Texas Scottish Rite Hospital for Children is located a block south of here.

Presbyterian Hospital of Dallas, 8200 Walnut Hill Ln. at Upper Greenville Ave., (214) 345-6789; Physician referral, (800) 477-3729, Internet www.presbydallas.org. Located about 7.5 miles (or 12 kilometers) north of downtown Dallas, roughly between North Central Expressway (or U.S. Highway 75) and Greenville Avenue.

Opened in 1966, this is the third busiest facility in Dallas, a hospital with 900 beds, 1,200 physicians, 1,100 nurses, and a total staff of 3,800. The average daily private room rate is more than $625. Top specialties are women's and infant services, cardiovascular services, and oncology. *Dallas Child* magazine claims it is the best place to have a baby.

Presbyterian also offers an arthritis consultation center, obstetrics, ophthalmology, Parkinson's center, senior care, urology, women's diagnostic and breast cancer services, and wound care. The Margot Perot Center here is the only local hospital with a separate facility dedicated exclusively to women.

Presbyterian Hospital's parent company is **Texas Health Resources,** 611 Ryan Plaza Dr., Suite 900, Arlington, (817) 462-7900. It has 4,200 hospital beds, 4,500 physicians, and 16,000 employees. Other Texas Health facilities include:

Presbyterian Hospital of Plano, 6200 West Parker Rd. at Dallas North Tollway, Plano, (972) 981-8000. An acute-care hospital with 183 beds, 350 physicians, and 200 nurses, it provides emergency services, women's and newborn services, pediatrics, and surgical services. A $120-million expansion of this facility was to begin in 2004.

The land where the Presbyterian Hospital of Plano sits was given to the hospital by Louisiana-born John A. "Jack" Jackson, who grew up in Dallas, and received his degree in petroleum engineering from the University of Texas at Austin in 1940. In 2002, the 88-year-old co-founder of Katie Petroleum pledged more than $150 million to improve UT's program in earth and environmental sciences, in addition to the $34 million he gave to the university system previously. He also gave more than $14 million to the Presbyterian Healthcare System.

"Money is not important," Jackson once said. "People try too hard to earn it to become somebody. But money is only good for helping build things for others."

St. Paul University Hospital, 5909 Harry Hines Blvd. at Inwood Rd., (214) 879-1000, Internet www.stpauldallas.com. Located on 26 acres (or 10.5 hectares) about four miles (or 6.4 kilometers) northwest of downtown Dallas and north of the University of Texas Southwestern Medical Center (see entry).

What was previously known as St. Paul Medical Center was purchased in 2000 by the University of Texas Southwestern Medical Center at Dallas (see entry) for almost $30 million and is operated as a Southwestern subsidiary. A full-service, acute-care hospital, it has 600 beds, 500 physicians, 300 nurses, and a total staff of more than 1,700. The average daily private room rate is more than $500. Top specialties are bone and joint outpatient services, radiation and oncology, and cardiovascular services. St. Paul delivers 2,600 newborns annually. Originally a Roman Catholic hospital, St. Paul is now a UT Southwestern teaching hospital.

In 1896 Edward Joseph Dunne (1848-1910), the second Catholic bishop of Dallas, invited the Sisters of Charity of St. Vincent de Paul to establish a hospital, which was completed four years later. The hospital established the first school of nursing in Dallas in 1900 and the first clinic dedicated to helping the indigent in 1906. It remains the only Catholic health care facility in the Metroplex, a geographic area that usually includes Collin, Dallas, Denton, and Tarrant Counties, sometimes also Ellis and Kaufman Counties.

The first open-heart surgery ever performed in Dallas—a triple valve replacement—took place at St. Paul in 1966, and the following year the hospital was the first in the area to open intensive care and coronary care units. The first heart transplant in Dallas took place at St. Paul in 1985.

Zale-Lipshy University Hospital, 5151 Harry Hines Blvd., Dallas, (214) 590-3000; guest & patient service desk, 590-3101, Internet www.zluh.org. Located near Parkland Hospital (see entry).

This crowded, private, not-for-profit hospital is part of and located on the campus of the University of Texas Southwestern Medical Center at Dallas (see entry). It became a UT Southwestern private referral hospital in 1989. The facility is named after the Zale family, founders of the world's largest chain of jewelry stores.

Zale-Lipshy has 151 beds, 480 physicians from among the faculty members at Southwestern Medical Center, 160 nurses, and a total staff of more than 800. The average daily private room rate is more than $500. Top specialties include neurosurgery, urology, and orthopedic surgery, but Zale-Lipshy also provides ophthalmology, cardiology, and cancer treatment. Hospital admittance is through a primary care doctor at UT Southwestern.

It was here that Stanley Marcus, the "Merchant Prince of Texas" and one of the founders of the Neiman Marcus luxury-goods empire, died of cardiac arrest in 2002 at age 96.

JURY DUTY

Selection for jury duty is made from voter registration and driver's license lists. If an American citizen, you could be called for jury duty on weekdays, Monday through Thursday, for civil and criminal cases in city, county, and federal cases once every six months.

Not many are exempt from jury duty, but they include parents who have children under ten years of age or those who are incapacitated due to illness. "Willful disobedience of your summons is subject to contempt action punishable by a fine of $100 to $1,000."

A proposal is in the works to increase minimum juror pay statewide from the current $6 a day, the lowest in the nation, to a maximum of $50, the first boost since 1955, when it was raised from $2 a day.

For more details, call the Dallas County Jury Services Department, 8 AM-4 PM, at (214) 653-3595, and follow the prompts.

LIBRARIES

Dallas Public Library, 1515 Young St. at South Ervay, (214) 670-1400/1700; English/Spanish storyline hotline, (972) 293-5550, Internet www.dallaslibrary.org. Open Mon-Thu 9 AM-9 PM, Fri-Sat 9 AM-5 PM, Sun, 1 PM-5 PM. Located across Young Street from the Dallas City Hall and two blocks south from the Neiman Marcus luxury department store. (See individual entries for more details.)

The eight-story, $44-million Central Library was designed by Dallas architects Fisher & Spillman and opened in the spring of 1982. Twelve million dollars of it came from private contributions. The library "occupies its prominent corner location with as much dignity as can be mustered in the face of City Hall across the street," observes the Dallas chapter of the American Institute of Architecture.

Since 1986, the library has been named for J. Erik Jonsson (1901-1995), a Brooklyn, New York, native and former Dallas mayor, from 1964 to1971, who also co-founded the highly successful high-technology company, Texas Instruments. Jonsson, whose parents emigrated from Sweden, first came to Dallas in 1930 and many years later recalled a city of "fresh, clean air, white buildings, and clean, neatly dressed people who were unfailingly courteous and kind." He served as mayor following the Kennedy assassination and was instrumental in the development of the Dallas/Fort Worth International Airport.

May Dickson Exall (b. 1859), the wife of Henry Exall and president of the Shakespeare Club of Dallas in the 1890s, began campaigning for a library in 1899 and raised about $11,000, only enough either to construct a building or to buy the books. She appealed to the steel baron Andrew Carnegie:

"I do not believe there is another place in the U.S. where a public library is so much needed as in Dallas," she wrote. "Our citizenry are characterized by industry and sobriety and there is nothing in Dallas of the wild frontier town.

"We have never had any race trouble here," she continued. "Our colored population numbers about 8,000, and are given exactly the same rights as to voting, justice in the courts, etc., that our white citizens have."

The fact of the matter, as noted by Michael V. Hazel in his 2001 history of the library, was that Dallas was rigidly segregated. "The African American citizens of Dallas, therefore, were barred from using the public library their tax dollars were helping to support."

Carnegie responded within three weeks and agreed to provide $50,000 for construction of the library, if the city would donate a lot and commit $4,000 a year for upkeep. The classical library building of Bedford stone and Ionic columns was designed by Fort Worth architect

Marshall R. Sanguinet, whose identity was kept secret for a while because of the rivalry between Dallas and Fort Worth.

The cornerstone of the first central library on Commerce and Harwood Streets was laid in January 1901. Mrs. Exall presented the new library with 9,852 volumes to Mayor Ben E. Cabell (d. 1975) in October of that year. Among the patrons who donated books to the new library was botanist Julian Reverchon who gave 167 volumes of French literature that his father had brought from France in the 1850s and carried to the Utopian La Reunion (see entry) settlement near Dallas.

There was even a one-room Public Art Gallery on the second floor, as suggested by artist Frank Reaugh, who donated his 1883 pastel on paper to the library. In 1907, Mrs. Exall asked for another $35,000 to build an extension to the original library, but Carnegie said no. However, when the president of the library board wrote to Carnegie in 1911, asking for help to build a branch library in Oak Cliff, the magnate responded, "I would be pleased beyond measure to get rid of $25,000, thereby coming a little nearer to the dream of my life—to die poor."

Mrs. Exall's husband, Henry Exall (b. 1848), who came from Virginia and served in the Confederate forces, was a cattleman and banker who had arrived in Fort Worth in 1876. He moved to Dallas in 1888, the year he married May Dickson, and established the North Texas National Bank. He built the Exall Dam across Turtle Creek.

By 1938, the city had added five other libraries to the segregated system. Four were for whites in Oak Cliff, South Dallas, Oak Lawn, and Lakewood. The fifth, meant for African-American residents, opened in the State-Thomas neighborhood, now Uptown, in 1931.

The Carnegie building, measuring 21,200 square feet (or 1,969 square meters)—about one-thirtieth the size of the current Jonsson library—was so crowded "that a room formerly used to store coal became another book closet," according to the *Dallas Morning News*.

The main downtown library was almost 50 years old by 1950 and worn out. That year, a vice president and editor at E. P. Dutton called the library "shocking, absolutely shocking." To deal with the crisis, the Friends of the Dallas Public Library was organized.

Without much fuss, the handsome classic building, which today would be considered an architectural jewel, was torn down in 1954. It was replaced by an austere "sleek, modernistic" building on the same location, next door to what was once the Dallas Grand Hotel. The library was designed by architect George L. Dahl, who figured prominently in the creation of the Fair Park complex for the centennial celebration of Texas' independence from Mexico. Both, the library and the hotel, were being considered for demolition in 2003 to make space for a new downtown park.

Cleora Clanton (d. 1968) was chief librarian for 32 years until she retired with the old library. When libraries across the nation were asked to remove books on Communism in the fifties, Clanton refused, maintaining that knowledge of Communism was not harmful.

Before the new director—a 34-year-old male, James Meeks—could assume his duties, a controversy arose. A ten-by-20-four-foot (or three-by-7.3-meter) three-dimensional metal screen was commissioned by the new library's architect to hang over the circulation desk. It was created by artist Henry Bertoia (1915-1978) of Barto, Pennsylvania, at a cost of $8,500.

Then-mayor R. L. Thornton called it "a piece of junk," although, he allowed sarcastically, "It has good advertising possibilities." He said that spending $8,500 on new books "would be a much wiser investment for the taxpayers than a mural which only a limited number would understand and enjoy." A *Dallas Morning News* columnist called it "Big D Droodle." Architect Dahl paid for the screen and took it home.

"Embarrassed by the controversy, which seemed to depict Dallas as a cultural backwater," writes the library historian Michael Hazel, several prominent citizens offered to buy the screen and return it to its intended location in the library." The library board agreed, and the screen was restored to a permanent place on the ground floor. It can still be seen in the foyer of the current central library.

A six-level air-conditioned library with a capacity for 800,000 volumes and a roof garden was inaugurated by Mayor Thornton in September 1955. About the metal screen, the mayor now said, "I like it." Quietly, the new library became accessible to all, regardless of their skin color.

The following year, another piece of art, a 20-foot (or six-meter) sculpture was about to be hung against the black granite facade of the library and ignite controversy anew. The model shown to the library board depicted a nude boy and "they almost died. They immediately voted to put pants on that sculpture," according to an eyewitness. It did not seem to make any difference to the board that sculptor Marshall Fredericks had already fulfilled commissions for the Detroit Civic Center, the University of Michigan, and the Cleveland War Museum. So the 880-pound (or 399-kilogram) aluminum sculpture of a boy, cradled in a giant pair of hands and holding up an open book—representing the hands of God lifting youth in its quest for knowledge through literature, explained the sculptor—was clad in trousers.

Just a few months later, still another controversy erupted, when the library mounted an exhibit of paintings and hand-woven rugs by 13 contemporary French artists. Included among the works were a painting by Pablo Picasso of a woman's head and a rug designed by Picasso, titled *Keyhole*. In a matter of days complaints started coming in from conservatives that the library was displaying works by a Communist sympathizer, which Picasso was at the time. The library director consulted the arts critic of the *Dallas Morning News* and on his suggestion took the Picasso picture and rug down.

In 1958, the library hosted the first of three Composers Conferences. The second in 1960 featured the premiere of Symphony No. 11 in C Major by French composer Darius Milhaud (1892-1974), commissioned for $1,500, with Milhaud serving as conference moderator.

The third, held in 1965, attracted 250 submissions. The commissioned work was the First Symphony of Gunther Schuller (b. 1925), a jazz and classical composer and conductor from New Jersey.

By 1962, when Lillian Moore Bradshaw was named director—at a salary $1,500 less than her male predecessor—the library had two million books and had issued 193,000 library cards. Ten years later, the central library was so overcrowded the city agreed to a seven-year lease for space at 912 Commerce Street downtown. The old Commerce Street library closed in the spring of 1982.

Less than two years after the sixth library director took over, declining petroleum prices, real estate foreclosures, and bank failures stopped the library's growth and cut deeply into its budget of $16 million, which was reduced 25 percent. It took the city's first elected woman mayor, Annette Strauss, in 1987, to declare: "No longer will this library be dark at night."

Encompassing 650,000 square feet (or 60,385 square meters), the library now contains almost 2.5 million books, records, and other learning tools. It also has an 8,000-square-foot (or 743-square-meter) children's library and a 200-seat auditorium. About 2.4 million people visit the library annually, checking out 3.7 million items.

Free concerts, live dance and theater performances, art exhibits, films, lectures, and children's shows are held on its premises. However, a city audit claims that 12 percent of all books are missing and nearly $3.5 million in fines is delinquent.

"The downtown library, the country's second-largest central library, has never become the popular locale it was intended to be," observes the *Dallas Morning News*. One of the reasons may be the throngs of homeless encircling the building for much of the year, harassing patrons for money, sleeping and relieving themselves inside the library, and scaring away visitors with unpredictable behavior.

In 2002, one of them "attacked a guard who woke him up and tried to remove him from the building. The guard was beaten so badly that he lost consciousness, according to a police report," noted the *News* at another time. Panhandling was outlawed in 2003.

When the well-known Italian architect and urban planner Antonio di Mambro, with offices in Boston, proposed a renaissance of the Dallas libraries, the first step, he said, "is to provide other places for the homeless to gather. Other people will shy away from the library as long as the city uses it as a de facto homeless shelter."

Southern Methodist University Libraries, University Park; (214) SMU-BOOK.

The combined holdings of all SMU libraries amount to millions of volumes, including books, bound journals, and microforms. Visitors can use the materials in the libraries free of charge. You can check out items with a visitor's card. These are some among the SMU libraries:

The general collection **Fondren Library,** (214) 768-7378, is the largest on the campus and open daily. It includes 560,000 books, 4,000 journals, 65,800 volumes of bound periodicals, 205,000 U.S., U.N., and Texas government documents, and 172,000 microfilms. This was SMU's first air-conditioned building in 1941.

Fondren, named after W. W. Fondren, an oilman and a founder of Humble Oil Company who gave $400,000 for its construction, was SMU's first library in 1939. Its capacity, according to one SMU historian, "was 300,000 books but only 80,000 were on the shelves." It took the university more than a dozen years after building its $190,000 Ownby football stadium before it constructed a "desperately needed library" on the campus.

The Fondren Science Building, Perkins Chapel, and Bridwell Library are three among the 18 Georgian-style buildings on the campus that were designed between 1948 and 1959 by the Gainesville, Texas-born architect Mark Lemmon (1889-1975). He also assisted in the drafting of the Cotton Bowl stadium in Fair Park, the Museum of Natural History, and the Hall of State.

Hamon Arts Library, in Owen Arts Center, (214) 768-2894, contains 87,000 books, scores, and audio and video recordings. Hundreds of periodicals are available.

It is named after the Dallas philanthropist and arts patron who also gave $50 million to the University of Texas Southwestern Medical Center at Dallas, the Dallas Museum of Art, and the Dallas Public Library.

Jake Hamon amassed a $200-million fortune in the east Texas and Oklahoma oil fields and died suddenly in his sleep in Amsterdam during a trip with the Dallas Museum of Art in 1985. His wife Nancy gave another $25 million to the Southwestern Medical Center (see entry) in 1992.

The **DeGolyer Library** (Fondren Library West), (214) 768-3231, Internet www2.smu.edu/cul/degolyer/collections.html, was a gift to SMU in 1974 from the DeGolyer Foundation.

It contains 90,000 books and 350,000 photographs devoted to Western Americana, Texana, and Mexico. The library also includes a 1493 manuscript by Christopher Columbus.

(See Dallas Arboretum & Botanical Gardens listing in the SIGHTS & ATTRACTIONS chapter for more details about Everette Lee DeGolyer.)

The **Bridwell Library,** (214) 768-2481, is located in the Perkins School of Theology—funded by Brookston, Texas, businessman Joe J. Perkins (1874-1960)—and houses 370,000 volumes. Perkins gave the university more than $7 million for a new theology school and several other buildings.

The library itself was underwritten by Wichita Falls, Texas, oilman, rancher, and businessman Joseph Sterling Bridwell (d. 1966) in 1950. It claims 900 books that date to the origins of printing, before 1501, and are believed to be the largest such collection in the Southwest. They include a 31-leaf fragment of the Gutenberg Bible, one of the first books printed with moveable metal type, which was acquired in 1970 and is now kept in a climate-controlled vault. Bridwell is also one of only five libraries in the world to own all 17 versions of St. Augustine's classic work, titled *City of God,* and printed in Rome from 1467 to 1500.

As part of a long-term loan agreement with Baylor Medical Center, Bridwell also contains 250 rare books collected by Dr. Lyle M. Sellers (d. 1964), a Baylor chief of otolaryngology from 1946 to 1963. Over the years, he collected such rarities as a fragment of a 1,900-year-old Greek papyrus scroll, a European treatise on the rules of marriages from 1348, a 14th-century "book of hours" prayer book, the *Nurenberg Chronicles*, printed in 1493, and a first edition, second printing of Mark Twain's *Adventures of Tom Sawyer.*

Science & Engineering Library, (214) 768-2444, houses 400,000 books, 91,000 bound periodical volumes on biology, chemistry, physics, computer science, mathematics, civil, mechanical, and electrical engineering. It also contains 200,000 maps and aerial photographs.

Underwood Law Library, (214) 768-3216, has 500,000 books on law.

PETS

Had you thought that Dallas hates pets, you would be mistaken. To some residents they matter more than humans.

When Karen Bennett and Ed Guice divorced in 2000, they spent $16,000 in attorney's fees and a better part of the year fighting over the custody of their six-pound (or 2.7-kilogram) pet Chihuahua. Otherwise, they had no argument over division of money, cars, or furniture, even their Garland house. Guice, a 48-year-old AT&T technician, wept on the stand. She got custody, he got visitation rights every other weekend. "These people love that dog more than some of my clients love their children," said Guice's attorney.

Pets must be licensed and vaccinated against rabies. To register your pet, call **PetData,** which acts on behalf of the city, at (214) 821-3400. Dallas laws require that all dogs be on leash.

The city's **animal control shelters,** which pick up stray and injured animals, are located at:

•525 Shelter Place Dr. at R. L. Thornton Fwy. (or Interstate 35 East), next to the Dallas Zoo, in Oak Cliff, (214) 670-7430, open Mon-Sat 8 AM-4 PM. Lost pet hot line is (214) 670-1965.

•8414 Forney Rd. in Pleasant Grove, (214) 670-8216, open Mon-Sat 10 AM-4 PM, Sun 1 PM-4 PM. Lost pet hot line is (214) 670-8389.

By state law, the city must keep stray dogs and cats for at least 72 hours. Up to 35,000 animals are impounded in Dallas annually. Of those, perhaps 3,600 are returned to their owners or rescued by animal groups. Just 1,800 are adopted. The rest are destroyed.

The nonprofit Texas **Society for the Prevention of Cruelty to Animals** was organized in 1938. Its Dallas chapter is located at 362 South Industrial Blvd., (214) 651-9611, Internet www.spca.org. It is open Mon-Fri 9 AM-6 PM.

Humane Society of Greater Dallas, 7203 Skillman St., (214) 343-3666. There is also **Operation Kindness,** 3201 Earhart Dr., Carrollton, (972) 418-7297.

Dog Parks . . .

Several off-leash dog parks, open 5 AM-midnight, have been established in the city:

•1400 California Crossing Rd., east of Rochelle Boulevard, and at California Crossing Park. L. B. Houston Golf Course is located north of here.

•Harry S. Moss Park, intersection of Greenville Ave. and Royal Ln., in northeast Dallas.

•Kiest Park, at 3080 South Hampton Road, in south Dallas.

•8000 Mockingbird Ln. at West Lawther, at the northern edge of White Rock Lake Park.

Mockingbird Point Park, (214) 670-4100, located at the intersection of Mockingbird Lane and West Lawther Drive, has a 2.25-acre (or 0.9-hectare) area for large dogs and a one-acre (or 0.4-hectare) site for small dogs. This dog park, notes the *Dallas Observer* weekly, "is the place to go to see how dogs would behave if all human beings suddenly left the planet." *D Magazine* recommends it as the best spot to people-watch. Three hundred dogs use it every week.

A two-acre (or 0.8-hectare), double-gated, fenced dog park is located at **Jack Carter Park,** 2800 Maumelle Dr., along Bluebonnet Trail, near its intersection with the Chisholm Trail in central Plano. For details, visit Plano's Web site, www.planoparks.org.

Dogs must be inoculated and wear rabies and city registration tags. Owners must dispose of their pets' fecal material and be within sight of their dogs. Children under 12 years of age must be supervised.

PRESS, RADIO, & TV IN THE METROPLEX

The city's first newspaper, the *Cedar Snag,* was founded in 1849, renamed *Dallas Weekly Herald* in 1873, and began daily publication the following year. It was absorbed by the *Dallas Morning News* in 1885.

In the Metroplex—the term coined by an advertising copywriter in 1971—the most important newspaper is the ***Dallas Morning News*** (Internet www.dallasnews.com), even if it does have three pages of comics every day. Circulation-wise, it is one of the top ten dailies in the country, printing daily more than 530,000 copies and about 780,000 on Sundays. It is sold at 1,000 news racks citywide.

"Newest major-league player," *Time* magazine called it, adding, "After killing off the *Times Herald,* its afternoon competitor, the *Morning News* didn't get complacent; it got better." It has a good sports section and Friday's tabloid insert, **"Guide,"** which covers Metroplex events and restaurants.

No other media outlet in Texas has so many reporters covering state politics in Austin, and two dozen cover education. After being redesigned in 2001, the *News* looks a little like a busy CNN television screen.

Established in 1885 by Col. Alfred Horatio Belo and George Bannerman Dealey, the *News* is the oldest daily in the state. It was developed as a sister daily to the *Galveston News*, which was founded in 1842 by an itinerant printer from Boston, Massachusetts. The two papers linked across 315 miles (or 507 kilometers) by telegraph and a network of correspondents. They were the first two newspapers in the country to publish simultaneous editions.

Colonel Belo came to Texas from North Carolina in 1865 and joined the *Galveston News* as a bookkeeper. That was the year when General Order No. 3 was issued on June 19 in Galveston informing Texans that, in accordance with the Emancipation Proclamation of 1863, all of the estimated 200,000 slaves in the state were free. The date is now celebrated as Juneteenth, and it became a state holiday in 1980.

Belo advanced to a partner in the company and in 1876 became sole owner, renaming the firm after himself five years later. By 1895, its circulation had reached 15,000 copies. Since 1926, the Dallas establishment paper has been run by Dealey, his widow, his children, grandchildren, and other relatives.

Until 1991, there was a semblance of competition with the 112-year-old ***Dallas Times Herald,*** which went out of business on December 9, and was bought lock, stock, and barrel for $55 million by a more conservative *News*. By then the *News* had a two-to-one lead in circulation and 65 percent of the advertisers.

In 1963, then 29-year-old *Times Herald* photographer Robert H. "Bob" Jackson won a Pulitzer Prize for his photograph of Jack Ruby shooting Lee Harvey Oswald, the alleged assassin of President Kennedy. In the ensuing confusion, he had no idea what exactly he had shot with his Nikon S3 camera.

Six-tenths of a second earlier, before the actual murder of Oswald, Ira Jefferson "Jack" Beers took a similar photo with a Mamiyaflex for the *Dallas Morning News*. It won him nothing but the bitterness of losing out to a rival until he died in 1975 of a heart attack at age 51. Ironically, Jack Beers had worked for the *Times Herald* for two years upon his discharge from the military.

Jackson (b. 1934), who grew up in University Park, joined the *Times Herald* in 1960. "Bob was a rich kid who had never worked," says a fellow photographer. On November 22, Jackson rode in the motorcade, eight cars behind JFK. Upon hearing shots, he looked up and supposedly saw a rifle protruding from a sixth-floor window of the Texas School Depository, but he ran out of film and had no time to reload his camera.

(For more about the Kennedy assassination, please see entry Sixth Floor Museum in the VISUAL ARTS chapter.)

Jackson left the *Times Herald* for the *Denver Post* in 1968 and since 1980 has worked part-time for the *Colorado Springs Gazette* in Colorado. He estimates having made "tens of thousands of dollars" off the photo's reprint rights.

The *News* received six Pulitzer prizes between 1986 and 1994, two of them for photography, but of the 12 writers and photographers making the prizes possible only two remain on staff today. The *Columbia Journalism Review* named it one of the five best newspapers in America.

"Today it's a very good paper, the best in Texas," opines the *Texas Monthly* about the *News*. "But in spite of what [the retiring editor Burl] Osborne has done, no one is confusing the *Morning News* with the *Washington Post* or the *Los Angeles Times*."

In 2002, 117 years after it began publishing, the *News* acknowledged in a letter to its readers, "You should also know that we are not yet the paper we want to be."

In addition to the *Dallas Morning News*, A. H. Belo Corp. (Internet www.belo.com), also owns Channel 8, an ABC affiliate in Dallas, and more than a dozen other media properties nationwide. With $1.4 billion in revenues, Belo is among the 35 largest Metroplex companies.

Texas Cable News, TXCN, which Belo is pushing as a statewide cable choice, can be seen in the Metroplex on Channel 38, but is an uninspiring, "bland" copy of CNN's *Headline News*. "The investments may pay off eventually, but TXCN has been a commercial flop since it began three years ago," reported the *Fort Worth Star-Telegram*.

In 2001, Belo launched *The Dallas Morning News Express*, an abbreviated Monday-to-Friday English-language tabloid-size newspaper published in Mexico for business travelers, diplomats, and tourists. The Cuban government had authorized the *News* to establish a permanent news bureau in Havana, the fifth such international bureau for the daily, the year earlier.

Denton Record-Chronicle (Internet www.dentonrc.com), also owned by Belo, sells about 17,000 papers daily in Denton County.

In 2001, Belo's CEO Robert W. Decherd left a lot of Dallasites scratching their heads, when the chief executive officer called 2000 an "outstanding year," in his annual letter to shareholders, while earnings per share fell 14 percent and the stock price 16 percent. While the Standard & Poor's index rose 92 percent over the previous five years, Belo shares dropped 11 percent. By the end of 2001, "several hundred" among the company's 8,000 jobs were abolished to reduce costs.

Also available at Dallas newsstands and some vending machines is the ***Fort Worth Star-Telegram*** (Internet www.star-telegram.com), the fourth largest daily in Texas, with a daily circulation of about 240,000 copies and 336,000 on Sunday.

The national editions of the ***New York Times,*** as well as the ***Wall Street Journal,*** are also available on newsstands and a welcome relief from the somewhat provincial outlook of some state dailies. On some newsstands you will find the American edition of London's ***Financial Times*** and the ***Economist*** news weekly. French, German, and Italian magazines are available at Borders bookstore in the southeast corner of Preston Road and Royal Lane.

Among the weeklies, one would have to single out the ***Dallas Business Journal*** (Internet www.dallas.bizjournals.com), which covers the entire Metroplex and brings out useful information overlooked by other publications. A tabloid by format, it has editorial offices in Dallas and a Tarrant County bureau in Fort Worth. Its circulation is about 28,000 copies.

In 2002, the *Business Journal* was named the best medium-market special-interest newspaper for the second time in three years and received a Katie Award from the Press Club of Dallas which recognizes regional excellence in journalism.

The ***Dallas Observer*** (Internet www.dallasobserver.com), with a circulation of 110,000, is an alternative weekly that you can pick up free of charge all over town. Begun in 1980, it has an occasional biting cover story, good dining and entertainment reviews, and even better coverage of pop culture.

Three Dallas Spanish-language weeklies have a circulation of at least 28,000 copies each: ***El Heraldo News*** (Internet www.elheraldonews.com), ***El Hispano News*** (Internet www.elhispanonews.com), and ***El Extra***.

The monthly ***D Magazine*** (Internet www.dmagazine.com) was founded by two University of Texas graduates in 1974. Editor and publisher Wick Ellison recalls that at age 25 he met with merchant Stanley Marcus, who, without seeing a single draft or any advertising sales agreed to write a letter to Neiman Marcus customers about the forthcoming magazine.

"An astonishing 20,000 people responded by signing up." And *D Magazine* was launched.

Sixteen years later, *D Magazine* was sold to American Express, "which turned out to be an unsuccessful experience," the magazine's history notes politely, adding that "after suffering financial losses, American Express closed the publication in 1993." The monthly was resurrected in 1995 and now has a circulation of about 75,000. It is owned by Crow Holdings, the group of investment holding companies controlled by the Trammell Crow family of Dallas.

D Magazine has interesting, even provocative, feature articles and extensive coverage of local events, in addition to listings of Metroplex restaurants and entertainment venues.

The monthly makes a valiant effort, for example, with four pages of names of some 380 "best doctors in Dallas," but strains its credibility when they are followed by 26 pages of advertising titled "best doctors," four to a page. Three pages of 180 Dallas' "best lawyers" are followed by 51 pages of paid advertising, titled "The best lawyers in Dallas."

While the colorful magazine, which carries enough ads for plastic and laser surgeons to remove every wrinkle in the state, has the word Fort Worth on its masthead, it is struggling for recognition and respect outside of Dallas.

In 2000, publisher Wick Allison ordered all copies of the September issue destroyed after discovering two fashion advertisements that "were, to my mind, obscene."

D Home (Internet www.dhomeandgarden.com) is a *D Magazine* offshoot that caters to Dallas homeowners who do not wince at paying $12,000 for a six-foot (or 1.82-meter) tall vertical Vitra birch plywood couch for four. In 2002, it was named "the best city magazine in the country in its class," following in the footsteps of its parent which was honored as the best city magazine five times in seven years.

Parents of young children might find useful the complimentary monthly magazine ***Dallas Child*** (Internet www.dallaschild.com), which has a circulation of 80,000. It lists resources and entertainment venues, as well as offering lots of advertising to make it possible for you to spend even more than you already do on your kids.

And, finally, look for ***Texas Monthly*** (Internet www.texasmonthly.com), headquartered in Austin and published since 1973. Known for its excellence in writing, art, and design, it has won several National Magazine Awards, the highest honor for that medium. New York native Evan Andrew Smith (b. 1966), with the magazine since he was 24, became its editor in 2000. It covers Texas events and personalities and carries restaurant and cultural reviews from the entire state, although mostly from the largest Texas cities.

Out-of-state visitors will not want to ignore ***Texas Highways*** (Internet www.texashighways.com, www.traveltex.com, www.dot.state.tx.us), a 45-year-old monthly travel magazine of Texas. Published by the Texas Department of Transportation and until 2002 free of advertising, it often features photos that make Texas look better than it actually does, accompanied by informative articles on sights well known and not.

There is also the ad-free monthly ***Texas Parks & Wildlife*** (Internet www.tpwl.state.tx.us).

There is a radio station for every lifestyle, either on AM or FM band. The top five each have about 5 percent of the market. Among the most popular ones are:

KKDA-FM, 104.5 (Internet www.k104fm.com), which was established in 1970 and plays urban contemporary music.

Dallas' first African-American female news anchor, Iola Johnson, worked at this station for 12 years after she left WFAA-TV station in a contract dispute in 1985. She is now at Channel 11, a CBS affiliate.

KPLX-FM, 99.5 (Internet www.thewolf.com), established in 1980 and playing mostly Texas country music, it claims 200 employees. The Academy of Country Music and *Billboard* magazine named it the Station of the Year in 2002.

It, along with KLIF-AM, KTCK-AM (see entries), and **KDBN-FM,** 93.3 (Internet www.933thebone.com), known as the Bone, a "Classic Texas rock" station, are all owned by the Pennsylvania-based Susquehanna Radio Corp.

KSCS-FM, 96.3 (Internet www.kscs.com), which is based in Arlington, was established in 1948 and plays country-style music.

KLNO-FM, 94.1 (Internet www.netmio.com), is perhaps the most popular Spanish-speaking station in the Metroplex. Since its Dallas-based owner paid $65 million to improve reception in 2000, Estereo Latino, as the station is known, broke into the top ten. **KTCY-FM,** 104.9, also playing regional Mexican format, is the next most popular

Hispanic station in the area. **KAHZ-AM,** 1360, is a news and talk Spanish-language station.

KHKS-FM, 106.1 (Internet www1061kissfm.com), also known as Kiss FM, which plays Top Forty contemporary hits, was established in 1993.

Its talk host "Kidd Kraddick rules the morning airwaves" in Dallas-Fort Worth, declares *D Magazine*. The former native of the Tampa Bay area of Florida who came to Dallas in 1984 is number one with kids ages 12 and up, with women ages 18-49, and with women ages 25-54.

KLUV-FM, 98.7 (Internet www.kluv.com), an Infinity Broadcasting station, was established in 1983 and plays mostly pop and rock oldies.

WBAP-AM, 820 (Internet www.wbap.com)—which now broadcasts out of Arlington and is the most popular news-and-talk station in the Metroplex—in 1922 became the first radio station in the country to transmit cotton and grain exchange reports. The following year, it was the first station to broadcast rodeo from the Fort Worth Stock Show.

The "powerhouse" station, part of the Disney network, shares news and weather information with WFAA-TV (Channel 8). WBAP "has shifted its emphasis from sports-related programming to conservative political programming during the past several years," claims the *Fort Worth Star-Telegram*. It offers traffic reports every six minutes during the morning and afternoon rush hours.

KZPS-FM, 92.5 (Internet www.kzps.com), is an alternative rock station that goes back to 1993. It, along with **KDGE-FM,** 102.1 (Internet www.kdge.com), playing similar music, and **KEGL-FM,** 97.1 (Internet www.kegl.com), are among the half a dozen stations owned by the San Antonio broadcasting behemoth Clear Channel.

KVIL-FM 103.7 (Internet www.kvil.com), appeals to adults between the ages of 25 and 54 with light rock and soft pop, and "remains a veritable money-making machine."

Ron Chapman, a morning host for much of his 31 years with KVIL, retired in 2000. On September 18, 1964, he introduced the Beatles at the Dallas Memorial Auditorium, which was the first building of the Dallas Convention Center.

KOAI-FM, 107.5 (Internet www.smoothjazz1075.com), was established in 1987 and plays Top Forty tunes, seldom jazz, as the station's nickname would imply.

KEGL-FM, 97.1 (Internet www.kegl.com), was established in 1981 and plays so-called active rock.

KBFB-FM, 97.9 (Internet www.979thebeat.net), goes back only to 2000 and plays primarily urban contemporary music.

KRLD-AM, 1080 (Internet www.krldwebsite@cbs.com), is an all-news

Arlington-based CBS affiliate station that has been on the air since 1925. KRLD has a news staff of 30 and produces 15 hours of news daily—between 4 AM and 5 PM—more than any other station.

"Its news reporting is refreshingly straightforward and gimmick-free, telling you things you need to know as quickly as it can," claims the *Fort Worth Star-Telegram.*

In 1954, KRLD's nightly show, *Music 'Til Dawn*, hosted by Hugh Lampman (d. 2002), was so popular that singer Sammy Davis Jr. rode a bicycle from Oak Cliff to KRLD's downtown Dallas studio to be Lampman's guest.

If you want even more gabbing, try **KLLI-FM,** 105.3 (Internet www.kyng.com), an all-talk station broadcasting from 7901 John Carpenter Freeway in Dallas.

WRR-FM, 101.1 (Internet www.wrr101.com), is the city's oldest radio station and the only municipal radio station in the United States. It is also the only full-time classical music station in north Texas.

Founded in 1920 as a police and fire dispatch system, it started accepting advertising in 1926 and in 1948 branched out to FM broadcasting at 101.1 megahertz.

WRR-AM (now the sports-talk station KTCK) was sold in 1978, and its FM signal was boosted to 100,000 watts ten years later. Its broadcasting radius now reaches 100 miles (or 161 kilometers). WRR has been nominated for the Marconi Award for classical station of the year three times since 1996.

WRR, which the *Fort Worth Star-Telegram* calls "a priceless little gem," accepts no tax money, and its sales representatives work on commission. For years, the city has been considering selling or privatizing the station, prompting one *Dallas Morning News* columnist to note in 2002:

"We have eagerly labored to demonstrate that we have the same artistic sensibilities as those snobs up in Yankee Land. But if this city were to let WRR slip away, it would be dismal evidence that we're the very pack of barbarians we're afraid they think we are."

KLIF-AM, 570 (Internet www.klif.com), is an ABC affiliate and local talk station established in 1986. Located in Oak Cliff, KLIF was established by Gordon Barton McLendon (1921-1986), a nationally known radio programming innovator and sportscaster, who was born in Paris, Texas.

He attended Yale and Harvard, but gained fame for his live baseball broadcasts by paying men to sit in stadiums nationwide and feed him play-by-play information on games via Western Union. With 458 radio stations in 1952, he and his father had the second largest radio network in the United States. He is credited with the first traffic reports, the first jingles, and the first all-news radio station. He sold KLIF in 1971 for $10.5 million, then a record price for a radio station.

KERA, 90.1 FM, is the non-commercial National Public Radio station, broadcasting classical and jazz music and featuring news. **KNTU,** 88.1 FM, and **KTCU,** 88.7 FM, both feature lots of jazz. KNTU-FM, which opened in 1969, simulcasts WFAA-TV's 6 PM weekday newscast.

You might particularly enjoy the non-profit KNTU (Internet www.kntu.fm, listener line 940/565-3688), which is licensed to the University of North Texas in Denton. From 6 AM to midnight between Monday and Saturday, you will hear several hours of jazz daily. Classical music can be heard on Sundays, and Tejano on Saturdays.

For the 150,000-strong southern Asian community in the Metroplex, there is **KXEB 910-AM,** the Voice of Asia, which also broadcasts live on the Web, at www.voiceofasiaonline.com. Most of the station's music comes from Indian films, and several languages, from Hindi to Urdu, are used to communicate with listeners.

KTCK-AM, 1310 (Internet www.theticket.com), was established in 1994 and promotes itself as the king of sports radio that is popularly known as the Ticket. It features Dunham & Miller, two thirtysomething guys who "were thrown together at North Texas State University" and now host one of the most popular morning shows in the Metroplex.

In 2001, KTCK was joined by **KTRA-AM,** 1190 AM, which promotes itself as Xtra Sports and airs Fox Sports Radio.

There are Dallas/Fort Worth ABC, CBS, and NBC affiliates of the television networks based in New York. **WFAA-TV** (Internet www.wfaa.com), Channel 8, seems to have the most credibility with viewers. Local media giant A. H. Belo acquired WFAA in 1950.

Belo first launched radio station WFAA in 1922. By the next decade WFAA, whose call letters stood for Working For All Alike, reached four million listeners. In 1949, Belo purchased KBTV-Channel 8, the first television station in Dallas, which began broadcasting only three months earlier. In 1950, the call letters were changed to WFAA.

This ABC affiliate received the Peabody Award, the highest honor for television news, in 1987, 1996, and 2003, and a similar DuPont-Columbia Award five times between 1976 and 1997.

WBAP-TV is now known as **KXAS-TV,** Channel 5, which, like the radio station, was founded by the Fort Worth publisher Amon Carter. WBAP-TV was, in September 1947, the first television station in Texas. Its call letters stood for We Bring A Program.

This was the station, while still known as WBAP, that broadcast the shooting of the accused assassin Lee Harvey Oswald by Jack Ruby in the basement of the Old City Hall, at 106 South Harwood Street, in downtown Dallas.

Now an NBC affiliate owned by General Electric Co., KXAS-TV

(Internet www.kxas.com or www.nbc5i.com), has the most respected weather broadcasters. KXAS's forecasting reputation was built by the legendary weathercaster Harold Taft, who joined the station in 1948 and stuck with it until 1991 when he died of cancer.

Karen Hughes, one of the most powerful women ever in the White House and possibly one of President Bush's closest confidantes, worked for KXAS for seven years, until 1994, when she joined the future president during his first campaign for Texas governor.

The daughter of Maj. Gen. Harold Parfitt, the last governor of the Panama Canal zone, Hughes was born in Paris, France, in 1957 and graduated from Southern Methodist University. "We're a little homesick," she claimed to Texas reporters in the spring of 2002, when she decided to return to the Lone Star State to campaign for Republican candidates.

"I value her advice, and I value her friendship," noted President Bush about his departing communications director, who had an office just down the hall from the Oval Office.

Following the NBC purchase, claims a local print reporter and University of Texas at Arlington journalism teacher, whose father "had helped build Channel 5's news reputation" since the station's founding in 1948, "KXAS seemed to have tried every trick that the news doctors could summon, but it continued to lag in the ratings. Finally, after years of such nonsense, it dawned on me that you could watch an entire NBC/5 newscast and not have a clue about what the day's news really was."

The "gimmicks" he is talking about, not unique to Channel 5, are "'live shots' of a reporter standing in the dark at the scene of a news story that had been over for hours" or "'breaking news' about police investigating a minor accident, with overhead helicopter shots."

KTVT-TV (Internet www.cbs11tv.com), Channel 11, is a CBS affiliate that has about 225 employees, with offices in east Fort Worth, and is owned and operated by the CBS television network, which is part of the Viacom Inc. conglomerate. Until 1960, the station went by the call letters KFJZ.

KTVT is the only station in this market that earns a quality grade of A, according to a three-year survey by the Project for Excellence in Journalism, a journalists' group in Washington, D.C., affiliated with the Columbia Graduate School of Journalism (Internet www.journalism.org). WFAA and Fox affiliate were rated C, and KXAS was downgraded to D.

In 2000, Channel 11, much to the dismay of the ABC affiliate WFAA, snagged long-time Channel 8 anchor Tracy Rowlett at a reported cost of one million dollars a year. "Since then, Channel 11 has steadily made progress in its attempt to give viewers a meaningful newscast," claims the *Dallas Observer*, which proclaims Rowlett as the area's "best TV news anchor."

Also that year, the Metroplex's first African-American anchorwoman, Iola Johnson, joined Rowlett at KTVT. The pair read news at Channel 8 and dominated the ratings for more than a decade until she left in 1985 in a contract dispute. She joined the morning news operation at radio station KKDA in 1987 and stayed there for 12 years.

There is also the Fox group, locally known as **KDFW-TV** (Internet www.kdfwfox4.com), Channel 4, which is a Rupert Murdock News Corp. All four have nightly news reports at 10 o'clock, although Channel 4's starts at 9 PM.

The one problem with Channel 4 news, according to the *Fort Worth Star-Telegram*, "It's hard to tell whether you're watching news or entertainment. Channel 4 will never capture the top spot in total households in the news wars because it doesn't want to; it's just after a specific group of young, mostly male viewers."

Channel 4 is still remembered for a 30-minute travel program, *Texas Country Reporter*, which got its start in 1972, when Bob Phillips, a student at Southern Methodist University landed a $2-an-hour job at KDFW. At 21, he began crisscrossing the state searching for down-home stories that endeared him to Texans and visitors alike.

In 1986, KDFW unceremoniously canceled the show, and rival WFAA-TV, Channel 8, signed him up. *Eight Country Reporter*, (214) 741-1300, Internet www.texascountryreporter.com, can now be seen Saturday afternoons. It airs on 22 stations and reaches more than 500,000 viewers.

Local educational and commercial-free channels are **KERA**'s Channel 13 (Internet www.kera.org) and **KERA 2,** formerly KDTN, Channel 2, both part of the Public Broadcasting System. Watch for BBC and Canadian Broadcasting Corporation news programs on Channel 2.

KERA has consistently been one of the top-rated public television stations in the nation. Channel 13 also has my vote for what is by far the best children's programming. The three entities employ 120 and are budgeted at about $18 million annually.

KDFI, Channel 27, (Internet www.kdfi27.com) belongs to Murdock's News Corp., while **KXTX** (Internet www.kxtx.com), Channel 39, is an affiliate of Telemundo Communications Group, the nation's second largest Spanish-language television network. In 2001, NBC bought Telemundo for $1.98 billion.

The largest Spanish-language network nationwide is Univision, which in Dallas broadcasts on **KUVN-TV,** Channel 23. Univision launched its second network, called Telefutura, with its Dallas affiliate **KSTR-TV,** Channel 49.

KTXA, Channel 21, is a United Paramount Network affiliate, which in turn answers to Viacom, while **KDAF** (Internet www.wb33.com) belongs to the Tribune Co.

To find out what is on television, buy Sunday's *Dallas Morning News*, which carries a weekly TV magazine, or look up the programs in the daily *News*.

PUBLIC SERVICES

Electricity and gas are usually supplied by **TXU Electric & Gas,** (214) 741-3750 or (800) 460-3030, e-mail custinfo@txu.com. For outage report, call (800) 233-2133; for emergencies, (800) 817-8090. Oncor Group maintains the transformers and power lines carrying TXU electricity. Texas electricity rates were deregulated in 2002.

There are now several other companies competing for residential business, including ACN Energy, (877) 226-7441; Cirro Corp., (800) 645-0143; Energy America, (888) 305-3828; First Choice Power, (866) 469-2464; Gexa Energy Corp., (866) 961-9399; Green Mountain, (866) 473-3689; Reliant Energy, (866) 735-4268; and Utility Choice Electric, (866) 839-2782.

Ask about hidden fees, whether the rate is fixed or variable, and about terms of service and cancellation charges before you select your electricity provider. For more details, call (866) 797-4839 toll-free or check the Web site of the Texas Electric Choice, www.powertochoose.com, an educational campaign created by the Public Utility Commission of Texas.

If you need residential telephone service, one choice is **SBC Communications** (Internet www.swbell.com), call (800) 464-7928 or (214) 948-4811; (800) 585-7928 for billing inquiries; and (800) 246-8464 for 24-hour service.

AT&T and other nationwide companies also provide local and/or long-distance services. SBC's Internet service can be ordered by calling (800) 458-3341.

Local calls from public telephones cost 50 cents each.

Water Department can be reached at (214) 651-1441, 311, or 670-5111 for 24-hour emergency service. Dallasites use an average of 235 gallons of water a day per person, compared with 273 gallons per person in Plano, and 265 in Richardson.

Lakes Ray Hubbard, Tawakoni, Lewisville, Ray Roberts, and Grapevine provide the Dallas water supply, while Lake Palestine and Lake Fork are held in reserve for future needs.

Water is a precious commodity in Texas, but Dallas residents use almost twice the national average. They only pay one-half to one-third on average what their counterparts in Vienna, Osaka, and Paris spend on water.

During the summer, outdoor watering accounts for about half of all water use. There are watering restrictions in force during the summer, and violators face fines of $250 and up.

For newcomers, deposits are usually required on electricity, gas, telephone, and water. Give as much advance notice as possible.

Trash collections, (214) 747-2600, take place twice a week, Mondays and Thursdays or Tuesdays and Fridays. The service becomes effective with your water bill. While plastic bags are still accepted, the city will eventually give you a free gray hard-plastic container.

For questions or complaints about any city service, call **Dallas City Services,** 311 or (214) 670-5111.

TAXES

Texas is one of the nine remaining American states that have no personal income tax. It is also one of the half a dozen most tax-friendly states, according to the overall state and local tax burden borne by residents. Just over one-half of Texas' state-level revenue comes from state sales taxes. Fifty-three Texas towns have no property tax.

To pay for the American Airlines Center (see entry), the sports arena downtown, the hotel and motel room tax was increased to 15 percent in 1998. Car rentals are also taxed at 15 percent to pay for the sports arena. The car rental tax at D/FW Airport is 18 percent.

To finance the construction of a new $1-billion Dallas Cowboys stadium, the state legislature authorized what could add another percentage point to hotel room and rental car taxes. The fees and financing plan were to be approved in a 2004 referendum.

There is an 8.25 percent state sales tax on most purchases, such as clothes, electronics, and restaurant meals, except for non-restaurant food and prescription medications. Irving, Plano, Grand Prairie, and Fort Worth also charge the maximum 8.25 percent allowed by the state.

One percent of the sales tax goes to DART, the city's transit authority, 1 percent to the city, and the remaining 6.25 percent to the state.

More than three-quarters of state taxes come from property and sales taxes. The bulk of state taxes goes to pay for public and higher education, as well as health and human services. Schools receive about equal amounts of funding from state and local taxes.

For additional details, call the **Dallas Tax Office,** (214) 653-7711, or the **Dallas Central Appraisal District,** (214) 631-0910, Internet www.dallascad.org.

INDEX